'Casts light on the mentalities and political structures that shaped British foreign policy during the 1930s . . . Kershaw's account of all this is scholarly and meticulous. It is based on a wealth of original sources and a comprehensive understanding of the period' Piers Brendon, *Guardian*

'A timely book . . . Beautifully written' John Keegan, *Spectator*

'Compelling . . . A fascinating book, an important contribution to our understanding of the 1930s and a clever piece of storytelling' Patrick Higgins, *History Today*

'Refreshing and insightful . . . Few historians can equal the depth of Kershaw's research, and fewer still are capable of delivering profound insights with such seemingly effortless simplicity . . . a revelation' Gerard DeGroot, *Scotland on Sunday*

'Fascinating . . . Kershaw's brilliantly told story of Lord Londonderry's infatuation with the Nazis is another triumph for the acclaimed biographer of Hitler' Richard Aldous, *Irish Times*

'A complex, lucid and intelligent book . . . Kershaw uses the story of Charlie Londonderry, the saddest of protagonists, to tease out many fascinating questions about the British response, or lack of it, to the rise of the Nazis' Harry Reid, *Herald*

'The sprightly prose bowls the reader along effortlessly . . . neither Kershaw's subject nor his readers could have been better served'
Andrew Roberts, *Literary Review*

'Highly original in its approach, and exceptionally fair-minded'
Simon Heffer, *Country Life*

'Meticulously researched . . . a skilful miniature' Alex Danchev,
The Times Literary Supplement

'Sheds new light on the difficulty the British establishment had in coming to grips with the new European dictators' Steven King, *Irish Independent*

ABOUT THE AUTHOR

Ian Kershaw is Professor of Modern History at the University of Sheffield and one of the world's leading authorities on Hitler. For services to history he was given the German award of the Federal Cross of Merit in 1994 and knighted in 2002, and was awarded the Norton Medlicott Medal by the Historical Association in 2004. He was the historical adviser to two BBC series, the prizewinning *The Nazis: A Warning from History* and *War of the Century*. He is the author of *'The Hitler Myth': Image and Reality in the Third Reich*, *Popular Opinion and Political Dissent in the Third Reich: Bavaria 1933–45* and *The Nazi Dictatorship: Problems and Perspectives of Interpretation*.

Hitler 1889–1936: Hubris was shortlisted for the 1998 Whitbread Biography Award and the first Samuel Johnson Prize for Non-Fiction. *Hitler 1936–1945: Nemesis* received the Wolfson Literary Award for History, the Bruno Kreisky Prize in Austria for the Political Book of the Year, was jointly awarded the inaugural British Academy Book Prize, and was shortlisted for the 2000 Whitbread Biography Award.

Kershaw, Ian - Making Friends with Hitler, Lord Londonderry
and Britain's Road to War

Penguin Group (USA), Inc., New York (2005)

Trade Paperback Edition

IAN KERSHAW

Making Friends with Hitler

*Lord Londonderry and
Britain's Road to War*

PENGUIN BOOKS

PENGUIN BOOKS

Published by the Penguin Group
Penguin Books Ltd, 80 Strand, London WC2R 0RL, England
Penguin Group (USA), Inc., 375 Hudson Street, New York, New York 10014, USA
Penguin Group (Canada), 90 Eglinton Avenue East, Suite 700, Toronto, Ontario, Canada M4P 2Y3
(a division of Pearson Penguin Canada Inc.)
Penguin Ireland, 25 St Stephen's Green, Dublin 2, Ireland
(a division of Penguin Books Ltd)
Penguin Group (Australia), 250 Camberwell Road,
Camberwell, Victoria 3124, Australia (a division of Pearson Australia Group Pty Ltd)
Penguin Books India Pvt Ltd, 11 Community Centre,
Panchsheel Park, New Delhi – 110 017, India
Penguin Group (NZ), cnr Airborne and Rosedale Roads, Albany,
Auckland 1310, New Zealand (a division of Pearson New Zealand Ltd)
Penguin Books (South Africa) (Pty) Ltd, 24 Sturdee Avenue,
Rosebank 2196, Johannesburg, South Africa

Penguin Books Ltd, Registered Offices: 80 Strand, London WC2R 0RL, England

www.penguin.com

Published by Allen Lane 2004
Published in Penguin Books 2005
1

Copyright © Ian Kershaw, 2004

Printed in England by Clays Ltd, St Ives plc

Contents

List of Illustrations

Images courtesy of Lady Mairi Bury and from PRONI were taken by Esler Crawford.

Acknowledgements

It is an especial pleasure to express my thanks to those who have helped in the making of this book.

I am singularly grateful to Lady Mairi Bury, youngest daughter and sole surviving child of Lord and Lady Londonderry, for her enthusiastic support and encouragement. Lady Mairi invited me on two occasions to Mount Stewart for lengthy and frank discussions about her parents, particularly their relations with Nazi leaders, amplifying points and answering a number of further queries in several telephone conversations. She also provided me with a number of photographs of interest and relevance. Beyond that, she did me the inestimable service of waiving all restrictions she had placed upon the use of the Londonderry Papers in the Public Record Office of Northern Ireland, thereby giving me access to material which is otherwise closed for decades to come. I cannot expect her to be pleased by all that I have written about her parents. But I hope she will see my book as a fair attempt to understand her father's position and to provide a balanced appraisal of his political career.

Another exceptional debt of gratitude is to the Leverhulme Trust, an institution indispensable to the promotion of research in the humanities, whose award of a research professorship was a godsend, giving me the time and space – so difficult to find in the modern university environment – which I needed to complete this work.

I would also like to offer my warmest thanks to the archivists and librarians who have shown unfailing helpfulness, courtesy and efficiency in supplying me with materials and providing me access to their repositories. Pride of place goes here to the Public Record Office of Northern Ireland, to Mrs Aileen McClintock, Head of Access Section, and especially to Mrs Emer Wilson and the splendid staff of the Reading Room, whose kind and good-humoured assistance I enjoyed during a number of fruitful visits to Belfast. My sincere thanks are no less owing to directors and staff of the following archival repositories and libraries: the British Library (at St Pancras, at the lending library in Boston Spa and at the Newspaper Library, Colindale); the Borthwick Institute, University of York; the Bundesarchiv, Berlin-Lichterfelde; Cambridge University Library, Department of Manuscripts; Central Library, Belfast; the Churchill Archives Centre, Churchill College, Cambridge (where the Director, Dr Allen Packwood, was particularly helpful); Durham County Record Office; Durham University Library, Dean and Chapter Archives (and, for his assistance on the 1937 Mayoral Service attended by Lord Londonderry and the German Ambassador, Joachim von Ribbentrop, particularly Mr Brian Crosby); Hertfordshire County Record Office (notably Dr Katrina Legg for help and advice on the Desborough Papers); the Hoover Institution, Stanford, California (especially Ronald M. Bulatoff, for sending me copies of relevant de Courcy Papers); the Imperial War Museum; the Institut für Zeitgeschichte, Munich; the John Rylands University Library, Manchester; the Liddell Hart Centre for Military Archives, King's College, London; the London School of Economics Library; the Newcastle Chronicle and Journal library department; the Politisches Archiv des Auswärtigen Amtes, Berlin (where Dr Gerhard Keiper gave me good guidance); the Public Record Office, London; Queen's University Library, Belfast; the University of Birmingham Library; and the Wiener Library and Institute of Contemporary Research, London. I am most grateful, not least, to the staff of the University of Sheffield Library, particularly in the Inter-Library Loan Section, for invariably cheerful as well as prompt and proficient attention to my many requests.

Working for the first time systematically on the history of my own country during the 1930s made me realize how unfamiliar (compared with the history of Germany in that period) much of it was to me, and how exposed I was, therefore, to elementary pitfalls. If I have managed to avoid at least most of them, it is in no small measure owing to the kindness, as well as deep knowledge, of Professor Peter Clarke (University of Cambridge). I am extremely grateful to him for reading through the typescript for me to pick up glaring errors. It goes without saying, of course, that any which might have escaped his eagle eye are entirely my own responsibility.

Other individuals have also helped at various points with advice, encouragement, or references to useful material. I would like to thank in this regard: Ms Chloe Campbell, Professor David Cannadine, His Grace the Duke of Devonshire, Professor Niall Ferguson, Dr Neil Fleming, Professor M. R. D. Foot, Professor Peter Hennessy, Professor Peter Jupp, Dr Anthony Malcomson, Dr David Martin, Mrs Gloria McBean, Mr Laurence Rees, Professor David Reynolds, Mr Andrew Roberts (whose help at an early stage of the project I greatly appreciated), Professor David Smith and Mr Richard Thurlow. My friends and colleagues in the Department of History at the University of Sheffield have, as always, been most supportive.

My secretary and personal assistant of long standing (and long suffering), Beverley Eaton, warrants a special word of thanks. She helped immeasurably in locating some of the more obscure information and references I needed. She prepared the 'List of Works Cited'. Above all, she catalogued the scattered documentary sources which I had collected, constructing an indispensable guide to the materials as I worked through them.

Simon Winder has, as on previous occasions, been a superb editor. I have been enormously grateful for his cheery support and his invariably astute advice, drawing upon a winning combination of intellectual sharpness and unquenchable enthusiasm. All this can be repeated at the American end, where it has been a pleasure to work with Scott Moyers, a highly skilful and knowledgeable editor who has been both extremely helpful and immensely encouraging. For his part in placing the book with excellent publishing houses and thereby ensuring that it is dealt with by such outstanding editors, I am greatly indebted to Andrew Wylie, a marvellous agent and adviser.

In last place, though first in importance, come as always my thanks to my family. The idea of writing the book was Betty's. She took a keen interest in it throughout, read through the typescript, and made some good suggestions for amendments. To remind me yet again, if I need reminding, that there are many things more important than writing books about history, David, Katie and Joe on the one hand, Stephen, Becky and Sophie on the other, make it all seem worthwhile.

I. K., January 2004

European Territorial Issues Between the Wars

Preface

Lord Londonderry first struck my attention in 1991. While in Belfast to deliver a series of lectures, I was part of a private guided tour of Mount Stewart, the Londonderry family home in Northern Ireland. I became intrigued when we entered what had been Lord Londonderry's study and had pointed out to us a statuette in white Allach porcelain, about eighteen inches high, standing on the mantelpiece. It was a beautifully carved depiction of a helmeted SS man, carrying a Nazi flag.[1] It caught my imagination immediately. What was it doing there? It appeared so incongruous amid the elegant period furniture. The graceful stately home – a neo-classical building largely constructed in the first half of the nineteenth century (though with its origins in the late eighteenth), on the tranquil shores of Strangford Lough, overlooking the Mourne mountains and surrounded by glorious gardens (the creation of Lady Londonderry)[2] – seemed a million miles from the brutality, repression, war and genocide associated with Nazi Germany. Yet the guide told us that the statue had been presented to Lord Londonderry by Joachim von Ribbentrop, one of Hitler's chief henchmen, during a weekend stay at Mount Stewart in 1936. Ribbentrop was later convicted of war crimes at the International Military Tribunal at Nuremberg in 1946 and hanged. Why had Lord Londonderry, a prominent British aristocrat, been providing hospitality to a leading Nazi? Back in Belfast a couple of years later, I started to find some answers when I delved into the fascinating letters which Lord Londonderry and his wife exchanged with Ribbentrop, Göring and other prominent representatives of the Nazi regime. I collected a batch of material, thinking that at some point I would try to write perhaps a short piece exploring the background to the correspondence. In the meantime, however, I was fully preoccupied with work on my biography of Hitler.

The years passed by. My file gathered dust. By the time I could turn to it again – as a kind of intellectual convalescence after finishing my books on Hitler – the millennium had turned. And now, the more I researched it, the more complicated the story became. It also seemed – to me at least – to give new colour to the often somewhat arid politics of appeasement, the attempt to seek an accommodation with Hitler. That is, in the light of my deepening research on Londonderry's own involvement with Nazi Germany I thought I began to see more clearly than before why British politics in the 1930s embarked upon such a thorny road. Not only that: the options open to the leaders of British government for dealing with the menace of Hitler appeared to me to be more closed off than I had thought – and long before Neville Chamberlain's notorious attempt to buy peace by placating the Nazi dictator in 1938. So the intended short piece on Londonderry grew in size. The present book is the result.

It is often said that the past is a foreign country.[3] But a foreign country can be visited. We can, given time, absorb and begin to understand its culture. The past is different. It can only be visited through its remnants. The mentalities of bygone ages have to be grasped through what the past has bequeathed to us. Recapturing a lost mentality is not easy. And this does not just apply to the distant past. The 1930s are still within living memory for a by now elderly part of our society. But despite oral testimony, newspapers, mountains of documentary evidence and the graphic images on film, the decade seems far away. It has the feel of a remote epoch. Attitudes towards Empire, race, state and nation all have a distant ring. Not least, it seems strange today that anyone in Britain would actively have wanted to make friends with Hitler – the most recognizable face of evil in the twentieth century, the epitome of race hatred and war, the abnegation of all values held to be positive in civilized society. But in the 1930s such a mentality was anything but strange. Many looked to Hitler with admiration and pressed for a policy of friendship with Nazi Germany. This book explores that mentality.

Pro-German views were not identical with those that came to accept the need, arising from Britain's military weakness, to comply with German demands. But they were related. Some who favoured appeasement did so reluctantly. Others – like Londonderry – rejoiced when active steps to appease Hitler were eventually taken. Here, too, past mentalities cause difficulties. Appeasement – avoiding war through concessions to Hitler – became, once its failure was evident, a dirty word. But it was not like that for much of the 1930s. For a variety of reasons it enjoyed wide support. Through the focus on a single individual, the book tries to recapture the attitudes that underpinned and made possible policies of appeasement.

Lord Londonderry is a marginal figure at best in most accounts of British history in the 1930s. Having attracted much obloquy in his lifetime, he has passed into near historical oblivion. Yet Charles Stewart Henry Vane-Tempest-Stewart, the 7th Marquess of Londonderry, a scion of one of Britain's grandest and wealthiest aristocratic families,[4] held for some years high and important office as Secretary of State for Air – and at precisely the time, corresponding to Hitler's advent to power in Germany, that the question of Britain's military strength in the air was becoming critical. A pillar of the Conservative Party, Londonderry, socially and politically, could scarcely have been better connected. The King called him 'Charley'. Members of the royal family were frequently guests in his London mansion. The political establishment dined regularly at his table. Prime Ministers stood at the head of the magnificent staircase in Londonderry House to greet the hundreds of guests at sumptuous receptions. Londonderry was on first-name terms with all the major political figures of the day. Winston Churchill was a cousin. Londonderry's ascent to high office was crowned with his appointment as Air Minister in 1931. Instinctively pro-German, he visited Germany on a number of occasions after leaving the government in 1935, met Hitler several times, enjoyed staying with Göring at his hunting-lodge and wined and dined with Ribbentrop and other Nazi bigwigs. Ultimately, this meant for Londonderry political disaster, and personal misery. He spent his later years in a relentless, but fruitless, campaign to vindicate his heavily criticized record as Air Minister and his acquired reputation as a friend of the Nazis.

How did Lord Londonderry come to be mixed up with the Nazis, and to be regarded as Hitler's leading apologist in Great Britain? Was he, as his detractors claimed, a genuine Nazi sympathizer – 'a Nazi Englishman' as he was dubbed?[5] Or was he merely a gullible, naive and misguided 'fellow-traveller of the Right'? Why, in either case, did so many, inside and outside his circle, share his enthusiasm for Germany at the time? For Londonderry was far from alone in Britain in his search for closer, more friendly relations with Nazi Germany. Among the peerage alone those in the vanguard of the search for close friendship with Germany included the Duke of Buccleuch, the Marquess of Lothian, Viscount Rothermere, the Duke of Westminster, the Duke of Bedford, the Labour peer Baron Allen of Hurtwood, Baron Mount Temple, Baron Brocket, Baron McGowan, Baron Mottistone, Baron Redesdale, Baron Sempill and the Earl of Glasgow.[6] Many other influential individuals sympathized with Londonderry's aims, even if they were often less outspoken than he was in stating them. Were such views, seen from a contemporary perspective, as outlandish as they subsequently appeared in the light of later cataclysmic events? And was it as good as axiomatic that they would be ignored or discarded by the government? Did they even offer a viable option to British leaders – an option that would have led down a different path from that of the government and, as Lord Londonderry repeatedly claimed, a path that could have avoided war?

Of course, the scholarly literature on the path to appeasement is legion – much of it high in quality. Frequently, the focus is on the developments and events which led to the Munich Agreement and the carving-up of Czechoslovakia at the end of September 1938. Studies of the Prime Minister, Neville Chamberlain, and the Foreign Secretary, Lord Halifax, the chief architects of appeasement policy, naturally figure prominently. Some fine works explore the attitudes and mentalities that lay at the root of such policies, though general surveys mean inevitably that there is little space available for the detailed assessment of the views and attitudes of specific individuals.[7] The same applies to an existing excellent overview of Nazi sympathizers which, in examining the entire gamut of pro-Nazi attitudes, paints a fascinating panorama of British 'fellow-travellers of the Right'.[8] But, naturally, in such a broad survey, little detailed attention can be devoted to how the pro-German ideas of particular individuals were shaped, and changed, under the impact of Hitler.

This book aims to do precisely that. It is concerned with only one part of Londonderry's life and career: his involvement in the appeasement of Germany – not that he liked to be described as an 'appeaser'.[9] It is not an attempt to write his biography. Quite independently of the research and writing of this book, in fact, such a biography has recently been successfully undertaken, necessarily embracing numerous facets of Londonderry's life and career, such as his role in the early politics of Northern Ireland, which are of no direct relevance to his involvement with Nazi Germany.[10] Even so, within the context of Britain's relations with Nazi Germany during the 1930s, my book does, of course, adopt a biographical approach, if with the aim of casting light on more wide-ranging issues.

Biographically, the book describes a personal tragedy: how Londonderry's reputation was ruined by pursuit of the phantasm of friendship with Hitler's Germany. I make clear also, however, that Londonderry had no truck with the fanatical Fascists, or the wide-eyed cranks and mystics who fell for Hitler lock, stock and barrel. His views on Germany were part of an alternative political approach to the problem of Nazism. He thought this approach alone could produce peace in Europe and avoid another conflagration which, having experienced the devastation of the First World War, he felt would bring the end of civilization. His own pro-German stance was linked, therefore, to another important strand in his thinking: the need for Britain to rearm and, especially, to build up its air force. He later claimed, indicting the British government: 'There were really only two things I could do. Build an Air Force, or try to make friends with the Germans. They wouldn't let me do either.'[11]

In practice, a pact with Germany came to take primacy over his demands for rearmament – leading ultimately to an estrangement from Churchill. In pressing for rearmament while at the Air Ministry, he proved ineffective, though the obstacles he faced were great. Thereafter, the obstinate and persistent attempt to defend his own record became subsumed in his push for friendship with Germany. Both earned him little other than brickbats at a time when rearmament in the air was finally under way and the German menace all too obvious.

To understand why, and before taking up Londonderry's own story, the book looks first at British images of Hitler as Nazi rule was beginning, indicating the range of illusions and delusions that framed attitudes towards Germany. It then examines the critical period of Londonderry's failure as Air Minister, in the context of British policies on disarmament and rearmament in the early 1930s – the period that inexorably shaped the later policies of appeasement. Londonderry's dismissal from government office in 1935 – the crucial episode in his political career – is shown to open the door to his overt advocacy of friendship with Germany. His disillusionment, the short-lived resurrection of his hopes following the Munich Agreement, his belated realization that Hitler could not be trusted, and his stance once the war he had fought to avoid had broken out, are all explored in later chapters.

Lord Londonderry was not only seen as the leading exponent of pro-German views during the 1930s; politically, as a recent member of the Cabinet, he was the most prominent individual among those who could be described as 'fellow-travellers of the Right'. He was also an inveterate letter-writer – nowadays a lost art. He and his wife, the redoubtable Edith, Marchioness of Londonderry, one of the leading society hostesses of her day, left behind a vast correspondence – some 10,000 or so letters in all, many related to the political issues of the day, and hundreds dealing specifically with the problem of relations with Germany. The Londonderry letters not only tell the story of an individual's self-confessed political failure. They are, in addition, a contribution to understanding a wider question of *general* political failure in the search for appeasement. They illustrate the changing complexities of British attitudes towards Nazi Germany. Beyond that, they offer a prism which reflects in vivid colours the mentalities, fluctuating attitudes and political quandaries of a society beset with the mounting problem of the Nazi threat. They provide insight into the reasons, so alien to us today in full awareness of what Hitler would eventually inflict upon the world, why so many in Great Britain at the time – and in well-informed and well-connected sections of society – were attracted to Nazi Germany, or at least saw the need to come to a political arrangement with Hitler's regime.

Such views frequently had their own brand of idealism. That was certainly the case with Londonderry, as the following pages indicate. This idealism needs to be acknowledged, if the misjudgements and miscalculations that flowed from it are to be understood.

Lord Londonderry's story has wider ramifications, as a mirror of Britain's struggle to come to grips with the problem of Hitler. In a way, too, as the social world inhabited by the Londonderrys, and the values that underpinned it, have vanished, his rise to political prominence then his slide into disrepute have claim to be seen as an elegy on the decline and fall of the British aristocracy.

Ian Kershaw
Sheffield/Manchester, September 2003

Prologue: A Patrician's Progress

'One can't use a man's hospitality and not give him a job if he wants it.'

> Sir Cuthbert Headlam, on Londonderry's
> appointment to a Cabinet post, 1928

I

No country could endure anything like the four long years of suffering and slaughter in the Great War between 1914 and 1918 and emerge with its social fabric and mentalities unaltered.

Before the descent into the unimaginable carnage in the muds of Flanders and northern France, Great Britain's social order, resting upon age-old hierarchies and status divisions, had appeared resilient to change, its structures immutable. The backbone of the social order, and of Britain's ruling caste, headed by a monarchy enjoying a peak of popularity, was the landed aristocracy.[1] Its dominance still seemed assured. Those with wealth and titles rooted in ownership of vast landed property, their immense income now often augmented by revenue derived from commercial or industrial capital, remained at the top of society's hierarchy. A sense of public duty rested upon social power. It translated often into a hand in running the affairs of state, or, at a more parochial level, presiding paternalistically over matters of local government. Beyond British shores, the high-tide of imperial grandeur offered further opportunities of public service – with added rank, status and power – in the world Empire, quite especially in the prized possession of India. Land, Crown and country, Empire – and

Church (meaning the established Church of England) – formed the ideological props of an aristocracy conscious of its inherited right to rule, underpinned by traditional liberties – themselves seen as upheld only by the preservation of hierarchy and social inequality.

Appearances were in some ways deceptive. Many members of the privileged landed aristocracy were less self-assured than they seemed. Some looked gloomily to a future in which land and birthright would be threatened. Britain's industrial strength, from which they profited hugely, already posed perceptible and growing challenges to social power resting upon traditional hierarchy. Britain was by the eve of the First World War the most industrialized and urbanized country in the world. More than three-quarters of its population lived in densely populated towns and cities. The vast majority of urban dwellers were manual workers, often housed in slums and eking out a bare existence through back-breaking labour in workshops, factories and mines. Women, mainly, also provided an unceasing supply of domestic servants for the better-off from the burgeoning commercial and professional classes as well as the grander echelons of society, the 'men of property', whose fine houses in the more salubrious parts of the cities marked the symbols of their acquired opulence.

By the end of the nineteenth century, the political changes which reflected the longer-term social and economic transformation in an industrialized nation were making themselves felt. The politics of mass democracy had begun – and once begun could not be halted. Most men had been given the vote in the 1884 Reform Act. The remainder would acquire it just before the first post-war election in December 1918, when most (though still not all) women were allowed to vote, the last barriers to women's franchise on equal terms with men falling only in 1928. Though there could be no return to the narrow politics of deference and patronage, rigidly controlled by local landholders and lacking any genuine form of mass representation, the running of the two main political parties before 1914 – those of the Conservatives and the Liberals – remained largely in the hands of the traditional oligarchies, the landowners and, increasingly, businessmen who formed Britain's political establishment. But the House of Lords, the unelected second chamber of Parliament and bastion of landed privilege, saw its powers seriously curtailed in the Parliament

Act of 1911, when the rights of the Lords to veto legislation emanating from the elected House of Commons were removed at one blow. And with the loss of these rights, the political power of the aristocracy was significantly undermined.

A sign of a possible future challenge to the Conservative and Liberal duopoly of political power was the growth – still modest before the war – of the Labour Party, which by 1910 had forty-two Members of Parliament. The growth of trade unionism seemed a further indicator that organized labour could pose a political threat to the traditional political order. Only a quarter of the work force belonged to a union as Britain approached war. But this was a major advance on the 1870s, when only 4 per cent had done so, and there had been over a five-fold increase in union membership since the beginning of the 1890s. Twenty million working days a year lost in strikes between 1911 and 1913 conjured up a spectre for those in power of a growing threat from labour militancy.[2] The existing social order, then, was intact but the days when its existing hierarchies were taken for granted were passing. R. H. Tawney, later a leading socialist intellectual and eminent historian, sensed the mood when he wrote in 1912: 'there has rarely been a period when the existing social order was regarded with so much dissatisfaction by so many intelligent and respectable citizens as it is at the present day'.[3]

This was the social order with which Britain had entered the First World War in 1914. When the Armistice of November 1918 signalled an end to the bloodshed and devastation, the same social order had survived. Given victory, even at colossal human cost, there was no revolution, such as swept through many parts of Europe. British institutions had come through unscathed. The social pyramid on which they rested was still in place. One-third of national wealth was owned by 0.1 per cent of the population.[4] Much of it remained in the hands of the hereditary caste of great landowning families, which retained both social power and political influence. The old aristocracy was replenished by newly created peerages – some sold for handsome contributions to party funds. Of the 700 or so members of the aristocracy in the 1920s, around a fifth were recent creations.[5] Immense landed estates, imposing stately homes staffed by armies of servants and grand town houses close to the seat of power were the outward trappings of social standing. So were the traditions of lavish hospitality and visible extravagance. Photos of the aristocracy at weekend shooting parties, hunt meets or points on the sporting calendar like Ascot horse-racing (in the presence of the monarch) or the traditional cricket match at Lords between the top public schools, Eton and Harrow, were still regularly to be found in newspapers and magazines. Nor was aristocratic influence at the heart of national government a thing of the past. Seven peers occupied high offices of state in the early 1920s in the first Conservative government after the war.[6]

Beneath the façade of continuity, nevertheless, the social and political landscape was changing. The decline of the aristocracy, largely masked before the war, was more in evidence. Some great estates were broken up, a number of country houses sold off. There was less of the glitter and glamour of the pre-war high society. And there was more defensiveness about title and privilege in the face of a Labour Party whose rapid rise reflected the appeal of doctrines of social equality. Over 4 million people had voted for the Labour Party in 1922 – almost double the figure in 1918 – and by 1924 this had risen to 5.5 million.[7] Though it lasted only a few months in office, in 1924 a Labour government took power for the first time. The members of this government, headed by James Ramsay MacDonald, born in poverty in Scotland and a pacifist during the war, were scarcely revolutionaries. MacDonald himself, as we shall have cause to see, was deferential towards the high and mighty. There was little in practice to fear on the part of the aristocracy. But fears, even if not well founded, have their own form of reality. In upper-class eyes, a socialist government in power in Britain, even if for a short time, could only bode ill for the future. It seemed a harbinger of worse to come. And left-wing militancy outside Parliament was more noticeable. Forty million working days a year had been lost in strikes between 1919 and 1921 – double the already high level of the years of industrial unrest just prior to the war.[8]

Little of this had to do with Britain's Communists, who were few in number, organized in a tiny party established in the wake of Lenin's success in Russia and almost wholly ineffectual. But that was not the entire picture from the perspective of British aristocrats. Though the Russian Revolution had happened far away, in a country with a long tradition of violence and none of democracy, the ferocious blood-letting accompanying the Bolshevik triumph in 1917 had sent shock waves of horror reverberating through Europe, reaching even the British Isles. With the shock waves had come, in much of Europe, an upsurge in anti-Semitism, as Jews were portrayed in many countries in the violent fabrications of scurrilous publications and radical racist newspapers as the carriers of revolution and social upheaval. Such noxious publications had little circulation or influence in Britain.[9] But in some grand houses of the British aristocracy, a residual feeling was indirectly fostered through the new wave of anti-Semitism that Jews were somehow an alien body, not quite fully British, and possessing links to dangerous international forces which threatened the social order. It was never a powerful or mainstream political force. Magnates, such as the 8th Duke of Northumberland, giving voice to notions of a 'Jewish-Bolshevik' conspiracy, were not representative.[10] But the imagined threat of Communism helped to sustain prejudice, more latent than outward, towards Jews within the British upper class.

The image of what was in store if Bolshevism spread and triumphed was certainly real enough, and the leaders of the British Left, moderate as they were and not remotely to be associated with such barbarity, seemed to offer a possible doorway – or at best were unlikely to pose in the long run a sufficient bulwark – to Communism's progress. A stronger force seemed necessary to counter and destroy the threat from the Left, should it become acute, at home as well as abroad. This was one reason why, though distinctly 'un-British' in character, a new style of political party and a new type of political leader in Italy could gain much approval among Britain's social elite once Benito Mussolini's Fascists had destroyed the Left in establishing power.[11] Similar plaudits would later be won by another dictator, Adolf Hitler, in Germany.

Apart from the gnawing worries about the possible spread of Bolshevism, the aristocracy also saw much to make them apprehensive in the changing position of Britain in the post-war world. The war had massively increased Britain's indebtedness. She still ruled a world empire – one even extended by the addition of territories in Africa and the Middle East, confiscated from the defeated Germans and Turks and 'mandated' by the League of Nations to be administered by the British. But once more appearances were deceptive. The white-settler, largely

English-speaking Dominions – South Africa, Canada, Australia and New Zealand – were increasingly going their own way. By the early 1920s it was plain that they were no longer ready to give British overseas policy their automatic backing and to acquiesce automatically in any line determined from London. And Britain was visibly starting to lose its grip on India, the key to the Empire. Economically, India was ceasing to provide vast markets for British cotton goods, and instead was starting to manufacture them herself. Politically, British high-handedness and inept administration had helped foster an independence movement, inspired by the unlikely figure of Mahatma Gandhi, which a combination of autocratic rule and repression could not contain. Closer to home, too, there were serious problems in upholding British rule. Ireland, whose future had long been a source of bitter contention in British politics, had erupted in rebellion in the middle of the war then split in two, with the larger southern part breaking away from Britain in 1922 after six years punctuated by violent conflict and a form of guerilla warfare which armed might had been unable to eradicate. It was another manifestation of the nationalist politics which were starting to threaten Britain's power.

Nor did the post-war international order, framed by the treaty forced by the victors on the vanquished Germany at Versailles in June 1919, hold the promise of long-term stability. Many at the time and afterwards thought the Versailles Treaty unjust, simply storing up trouble for the future. Germany was blamed for the war and ordered to pay huge reparations – a source of lasting bitterness. She lost her colonies and her boundaries were redrawn, to the benefit of France and Belgium in the west, and, quite especially, Poland in the east. Her once-mighty army was reduced to only 100,000 men, the navy to 15,000. No tanks, submarines or air force were permitted. A strip of some thirty miles on German soil on the east bank of the Rhine was demilitarized, and the Rhineland designated to be occupied by allied troops for fifteen years. Under the principle of national self-determination, the map of central and eastern Europe took on new shape. The former Austro-Hungarian and Ottoman Empires were broken up. A new array of smaller states, such as Czechoslovakia and Yugoslavia, emerged – countries whose future stability seemed even at their foundation less than self-apparent, given the ample scope for future destabilization through nationalist demands, based upon the possibly conflicting interests of differing ethnic groups. Sandwiched between the fallen giants of Germany and Russia, Poland, re-established as a nation state after a century and a quarter of partition, was resurgent but, as time would tell, also insecure, exposed geographically should there be a revival of power on either side of her.

To keep in check the inevitable tensions of the new international order was the task of the League of Nations, incorporated in the Versailles settlement as the inspiration of the American President, Woodrow Wilson – though the Americans, favouring isolation over continued participation in Europe's travails, refrained from joining it. The League was idealistically viewed by the Americans and British as a vehicle of conciliation, aimed at defusing international problems and preventing them boiling over into armed conflict. The French saw it primarily as the guarantor of their own security, and as preventing any future threat from Germany. As long as the defeated enemy remained weak, the potential trouble in reconciling these two positions was not at first obvious, and much hope was invested in the League. The feeling was profound and widespread, the inevitable imprint of such recent and painful experience, that there could be no return to war. Preventing all possibility of a new conflagration was the outright priority. But the contrasting emphasis on the League's role – by the British on conciliation, by the French on security – would prove the source of much later difficulty, once Germany regathered strength. In any case, the League was given few coercive powers, other than the imposition of economic sanctions, either to conciliate or to provide security. Critics of the post-war settlement – and they were not few in number – already feared that German demands for a territorial revision of the Versailles Treaty and deep resentment over reparations could only fuel the shrill nationalism of the extreme Right and foster dangerous hatreds.

Abroad and at home, then, there were ample grounds for pessimism within the post-war British aristocracy. They were now forced to respond to a world where landed wealth was no longer the sole, or even main, route to power, and where democratic politics demanded major adjustment to the patrician expectations of deference and domination. Nor was their traditional political home, the Conservative Party, that which it had once been in what were coming, increasingly through rose-tinted spectacles, to be viewed as the heady days of Victorian and Edwardian grandeur.[12] Where the Prime Minister and leader of the Conservative Party at the turn of the century had been the Marquess of Salisbury, head of one of the grandest of England's aristocratic houses, by the mid-1920s it was Stanley Baldwin, son of a Worcestershire ironmaster. Power, in the country and even in the Conservative Party, had passed, it seemed, from the grandees to the provincials, from the great landowners to small-scale industrialists.

Moreover, the Party was not a united force. There were deep fissures on how to resolve 'the Troubles' in Ireland; on whether, in contradiction of the long-cherished idea of free trade, which had brought the country such prosperity, British manufacturing should be protected in a more challenging economic climate by imposition of a tariff against imported goods from abroad; and whether there should be concessions towards a limited sphere of self-government in India. To some, all change and reform seemed threatening – portents of Britain's decline. Signs of weakness in India, quite especially, appeared to foreshadow waning imperial might. The feeling was far from confined to members of the aristocracy. But it ran through the aristocracy, as it did through the rest of the Party.

All in all, the world in the 1920s was changing in ways that many in the British upper class neither liked, nor fully understood. The old certainties seemed to be eroded. New dangers threatened. The preservation of the old order in Britain and the maintenance of British power abroad seemed at stake. This was the world in which Lord Londonderry's political career took shape.

II

Lord Londonderry was brought up to regard wealth, privilege and power as a birthright. And so, throughout his life, he did. Carrying the weight of family expectations, he wanted to achieve great things. For long he expected to do so.

Instead, his career unfolded in unspectacular fashion, bringing advancement which to others might have seemed the mark of success without ever matching his own high ambitions, and punctuated with disappointments and setbacks which were already instilling in him a lingering sense that he was a failure.

Anxious to play a role of some importance in politics and with a strong, if paternalistic, sense of public service, Londonderry owed much of his career advancement to his patrician connections. His position as a major landowner in Northern Ireland opened a path for him in the newly formed government of turbulent Ulster in the early 1920s, until the complexities and limitations of Northern Irish political life frustrated him. Though his ambitions made him look to the larger political stage of government in Whitehall, the Ulster connection continued to provide Londonderry with a hinterland detached in some ways from his involvement in London politics and society. Another regional base of social power, also of no more than tangential concern to our inquiry into Londonderry's later dealings with Nazi Germany, lay in north-eastern England, where his extensive ownership of coal-fields, a source of vast wealth, took him into the centre of the most acrimonious labour dispute of the inter-war years, the General Strike of 1926. The aristocratic grandee and major industrialist was naturally antagonistic to the militancy of the miners' leaders. It confirmed his fears (already to be glimpsed in 1918)[13] of the threat from the Left at home, as well as abroad.

Two years later Londonderry was offered an opening in Westminister politics. Winston Churchill's friendship and backing helped him gain a seat in the Cabinet, if at first still in minor office. It lasted only briefly, since the Conservatives were forced out of office in 1929. But, in 1931, in the political crisis that led to the formation of the National Government, personal connections again ensured, somewhat contentiously, his appointment as Minister for Air in the National Government led by the former Labour Prime Minister, Ramsay MacDonald. It would prove the pinnacle of Londonderry's political career.

Londonderry's ancestors, Scottish Presbyterians, had initially gone to Ireland as plantationers in the 1620s, acquiring lands at Mount Stewart during the eighteenth century.[14] Political influence had brought the title of Marquess of Londonderry into the family by 1807. The 2nd Marquess, better known as Lord Castlereagh, the British Foreign Secretary who had helped engineer the European post-Napoleonic settlement at the Congress of Vienna in 1815, was the most famous of Londonderry's forebears. He had attempted, he said, 'to bring the world to peaceful habits' – a phrase which would last serve as Londonderry's inspiration in the 1930s as he sought to emulate his great ancestor.[15] Through marriage to Lady Frances Anne Vane-Tempest, the 3rd Marquess, Castlereagh's half-brother, came into possession of extensive estates and collieries in north-eastern England, significantly augmenting the Londonderrys' already huge and accumulating wealth. Further estates were added, again through marriage, at Plâs Machynlleth in Merionethshire, Wales, in the mid-nineteenth century. The Londonderrys continued to be active as soldiers and politicians (at home and in the Empire), aristocratic grandees, major landholders and mine-owners. By the 1870s, they owned 27,000 acres of land in Ireland and another 23,000 acres in England; their income from rents was in the region of £100,000 a year – vast millions in today's money; on top of this came the massive earnings from the Durham coal-field.[16] With their five country houses and magnificent London residence – Londonderry House in Park Lane, only a few hundred yards from Buckingham Palace – the Londonderrys could be reckoned among the highest nobility of the land.[17] The British Empire was in its heyday, and the aristocracy – among them the Londonderrys – seemed destined to continue their rule indefinitely. It was into this family, self-confidently wealthy and powerful, that Charles (known to family and friends as 'Charley'), later to become the 7th Marquess, was born on 13 May 1878.

His upbringing and education were traditional for scions of the British nobility. After preparatory school, he went to Eton (where the future British Foreign Secretary, Lord Halifax, was his 'fag' – a school-boy servant, whose duty it was to wait on a senior pupil at the school),[18] then on to the officers' training academy at the Royal Military College, Sandhurst, passing with very moderate grades before joining the Royal Horse Guards ('The Blues'), where he gained his commission in 1897. Soon afterwards, at one of the Court balls and dances, he met Edith Helen Chaplin, the strikingly attractive daughter of Henry, 1st Viscount 'Squire' Chaplin (a larger-than-life landholder, Conservative MP and racehorse owner, with a sizeable income which he got through with no difficulty) and granddaughter (on her mother's side) of the

Duke of Sutherland, then the greatest landowner in Britain.[19] Two years later, they were married. A strong, extrovert, vivacious personality, Edie (as she was known in the family) was the central prop in Charley's career from this time onwards. Aristocratic lifestyle in those days meant frequent separations, often in the interests of hunting, shooting, fishing and the other pastimes of the nobility. Towards the end of his life, Charley would remark that he had 'never stayed in the same place for 10 days'.[20] He and his wife were, sometimes together but often separately, indeed continually on the road or – increasingly – in the air, moving between their main homes, Wynyard in County Durham (which they did not much like), Londonderry House (at the hub of London's political and social life) and Mount Stewart (Edie's favourite). But, as her hundreds of personal letters to him over the next decades show, Edie remained, in spite of the constant separations, some bouts of moodiness and high-handedness on his part, his dalliances and the fathering of a child out of wedlock, utterly devoted to him.[21]

In 1906, her husband left the army and became Conservative Member of Parliament for Maidstone in Kent, which he continued to represent, without much enthusiasm, until he succeeded his father as 7th Marquess of Londonderry in 1915. By then, he was serving in northern France, with the rank of captain, as aide-de-camp to General William Pulteney in the latter's comfortable staff headquarters, frustrated at seeing so little action. 'The French', he wrote in a letter to his wife of 5 September 1914, 'I fancy are useless. I do not believe they ever put up a fight'[22] – an early indication of prejudices about the French which would stay with him throughout the 1930s. Early in 1916 he finally gained a posting as second in command of his old regiment, 'The Blues', and was twice mentioned in dispatches but still remained irritated that he was 'just an understudy with no duties' and 'bored at not having my own show'.[23] Again, this was a feature of his character that would remain with him: impatience and annoyance when he was not in charge and able to run matters to his own liking. He served at the front during the battle of the Somme in July 1916, witnessing at first hand the carnage that left almost half a million British dead and wounded (still more on the enemy side) and losing his best friend in action – experiences which, as for so many others, would leave an indelible mark on him.

In April 1917, Londonderry was involved with his regiment, 'The Blues', in the battle of Arras, and temporarily took charge when the regimental commander was shot dead. But his wife, Edith, and mother, Theresa Lady Londonderry, were doing their best to have him brought home. Shortly afterwards, following indications that he was anxious to enter Irish politics to help find a settlement to the problems of the troubled country, he arrived back on indefinite leave.[24]

Ireland had been in turmoil since the Easter Rising in Dublin the previous year. The British Prime Minister, David Lloyd George, now set up a hundred-strong 'Irish Convention' – unelected, unrepresentative and to prove utterly ineffectual – which came together for the first time in July 1917 and lasted until April 1918. It was as an Ulster Unionist Party delegate to the Convention, created with the futile hope of establishing the future constitutional arrangements of Ireland, that Londonderry joined the maelstrom of Irish politics that July. The change in his circumstances had been accompanied by an early indication of a sense of failed ambition – at this point his hopes of a military career at the top. Though 'a peace time job' held little appeal, he saw his political involvement in Ireland as a chance to 'satisfy a desire to be someone'. He was anxious for 'a place somewhere which carries responsibility with it'.[25] He enjoyed his time in Ireland, he said, but soon enough realized that the Convention was leading nowhere. He made known his own preference for a federal, all-Ireland, solution, emphasizing his keenness to preserve Ireland as part of the British Empire. Some were impressed. But far more Unionists vehemently opposed his suggestions of federalism. The Ulster delegation agreed not to present Londonderry's proposals to the Convention. By March 1918, Londonderry was convinced that the Convention had no future. A few weeks later it adjourned indefinitely.[26] Far from framing a possible constitutional settlement, it had simply pointed up the unbridgeable gaps in Irish politics.

By the end of the year, soon after the end of the war, Londonderry had his first opportunity of government office, if at a somewhat lowly level, in England, thanks to his kinsman, Winston Churchill. In Lloyd George's coalition government, Churchill was made Secretary of State for War and Air and saw to it that Londonderry was appointed Finance Member of the Air Council, an unpaid post, but carrying responsibility for demobilization and disposal of surplus equipment. Londonderry recognized that 'friend Winston has come to the rescue just when I was going to turn into a "Local Magnate"'.[27] Not only did the post give Londonderry a toe-hold in central government in Whitehall; it awakened his interest – which would become a lasting passion – in the novel field of aviation.

When Churchill's Under-Secretary for Air, Colonel J. E. B. Seeley (later Lord Mottistone), resigned in 1919, Londonderry confidently expected to succeed him. He had, however, offended Lord Curzon, the Foreign Secretary and a powerful figure, when he had refused to intervene to have the noble lord's footman prematurely demobilized. Curzon took petty revenge in helping to block Londonderry's appointment. The exaggerated sense of 'deliberate slight' which Londonderry felt was an early foretaste of his propensity to brood resentfully over setbacks. Even becoming a Knight of the Garter at this time, the highest honour in the gift of the Crown, seemed insufficient compensation. In this case, Londonderry's disappointment was shortlived. A few months later, in April 1920, Seely's successor, Major G. C. Tryon, was moved to another government post, and Londonderry was this time elevated without any hitches to the post of Under-Secretary of State for Air.[28]

It was a vital time in the early development of an air force. Londonderry vigorously supported the efforts of Sir Hugh (later Lord) Trenchard, the dynamic if querulous Chief of the Air Staff, whose aim to build a new air force encountered serious obstacles from the army and navy, unwilling to concede any of their traditional and entrenched powers.[29] With his own considerable energies largely directed elsewhere, Churchill left Londonderry a good deal of scope in matters relating to aviation, and seemed well enough satisfied with the work of his protégé.[30] Londonderry enthusiastically warmed to the demands of his new post.

Just a few months into his tenure of the post of Under-Secretary of State for Air, Londonderry had to face another sore disappointment. Since as early as 1905, when he and his wife had visited the country and been thrilled by the might and splendour of the British Raj, he had hoped one day to become Viceroy of India, the most prestigious post in Britain's world Empire. Towards the end of 1920, with the retirement of the current Viceroy, Lord Chelmsford, imminent, Londonderry thought he had a good chance of fulfilling his ambition. But his hopes were soon dashed.[31] The appointment went instead to Lloyd George's friend, Lord Reading. Londonderry would be yet again frustrated when the Viceroyalty once more fell vacant in 1925 and was this time offered to his one-time junior at Eton, Edward Wood (Lord Irwin, when he went to India, though better known by his later title, Lord Halifax).[32] Many years after these disappointments, Londonderry would still return with a tinge of bitterness to his regrets at being passed over twice for the cherished office of Viceroy of India, while his wife dropped hints in high places even in the mid-1930s that India would be the ideal post for him to round off his career.[33] The offer by King George V of the post of Governor General of Canada in 1931 provided in Londonderry's eyes no substitute for the coveted but unobtainable Viceroyalty of India. He had little hesitation in declining the position since, in his view, it amounted to that of no more than a figurehead.[34]

Already in the early 1920s, Londonderry's failure to attain a government position which he imagined would befit his status was starting to irk him. The feeling that he was destined to miss high office, and the chagrin that accompanied such a sentiment, had been enhanced by being overlooked for the Viceroyalty. Whether this played any part in his somewhat surprising decision, in 1921, to resign from the Air Ministry to return to Irish politics, now accepting the position as Leader of the Senate and Minister of Education in the newly created Parliament of Northern Ireland, cannot be ascertained. He depicted the move as a call of duty, to helping to shape the affairs of the province where his family had for so long had deep roots. Winston Churchill suspected, however, that there was also an element of pique that, with his own move to the Colonial Office, Londonderry had not been appointed Air Minister in his place.[35]

Whatever the reasons for his retreat from the London political scene, Londonderry now plunged into his work in the government of Northern Ireland. The division of Ireland that year determined that the predominantly Protestant northern part would remain part of the United Kingdom while the larger, overwhelmingly Catholic, southern part took the route to independence in an uneasy beginning of what would turn out to be a continually troubled future. Londonderry's Anglo-Irish brand of Unionism – looking to a federal solution embracing regional governments in north and south, both remaining within the framework of British rule – had from his time in the Irish Convention sat uneasily with the 'little-Ulster' exclusionist Unionism, anxious to reject all connection with the Catholic south and insist upon Protestant dominance in Northern Ireland, which eventually prevailed. He was sure that the division of the country, finalized in December 1921, which he deeply regretted, could not bring peace. But he committed himself – for the time being – to Northern Ireland when in October 1922 he declined the offer by the new Conservative Prime Minister, Bonar Law, of the Air Ministry and a return to central government. It was a tortured decision. He spoke of his 'sacrifice' and giving up 'the summit of many ambitions'.[36] He was certainly under pressure from his colleagues in Northern Ireland, dismayed at the prospect of his departure, to stay. Whether, in addition, he sensed, given his own difficult relationship with Bonar Law (who was critical of the so-called largely aristocratic 'Diehard' right-wing faction of the Conservative Party, with which Londonderry was associated), that the time was not ripe for a return to London, cannot be ascertained.[37]

He continued as Leader of the Ulster Senate to play a significant part in the affairs of Northern Ireland during the early 1920s. And as its Minister of Education he introduced in 1923 a piece of progressive legislation – known as the 'Londonderry Act' – which, had it not eventually been destroyed by the implacable opposition of the Churches, would have ended the segregation of Protestant and Catholic children in denominational schooling in Northern Ireland. The attritional struggle over his education act and his problems with the more populist and intransigent strains of Ulster Unionism frustrated him and encouraged him to think of moving back to mainstream British politics.[38] When he resigned his offices early in 1926 it was again following a disappointment and sense that he had been slighted: he was disgruntled at his exclusion from the talks to resolve the still-disputed boundary question between the divided parts of Ireland.[39] But Ireland had never in any case been sufficient to fulfil his ambitions. He was drawn to a wider arena of politics, still hoping that he would be called upon to play a significant role in shaping the affairs of the nation – perhaps one day, like the great Castlereagh, as Foreign Secretary.[40]

Meanwhile, however, he had to attend to his own affairs. As a major coal owner, he was inevitably drawn into the escalating coal dispute of 1926, which culminated in the General Strike. Londonderry was far from the most militant of the mine-owners, and indeed kept one of his unprofitable pits open at considerable personal cost for two years at the request of the Miners' Federation.[41] He was, of course, fervently opposed to nationalization of the mines. But his reputation was better than that of many mine-owners.[42] Early in the dispute, at least, he portrayed himself as conciliatory, looking for a compromise. He claimed he and others did not want to reduce wages. He advocated better facilities for miners, the establishment of pit committees, and improved arrangements for cooperation between owners and miners at the local level.[43] None of this went to the heart of the dispute, however, and his own strong backing for local agreements on wages, hours and conditions of work flew in the face of the demands of the Miners' Federation for a national agreement. As the dispute dragged on, Londonderry increasingly backed the mine-owners and blamed the intransigence of the Federation leaders.[44] His strong opposition to the Left was unmistakable in his rhetoric, deploying military imagery to portray the owners as engaged in a fight against Socialism – remarks which brought him a rebuke from Churchill for turning an industrial dispute into a political battleground.[45]

The defeated miners eventually called off their strike in November 1926. Londonderry had no sympathy for their plight, which he regarded as self-inflicted, and continued his public criticism of their leaders, accusing them in January 1927 of being revolutionaries, with allies in Moscow.[46] Later that year he was an advocate of the Trades Disputes and Trade Union Act, which declared as illegal strikes 'designed or calculated to coerce the government'.[47] If, previously, Londonderry's political standing had largely been established only within Northern Ireland, his stance on the General Strike had now helped to bring him to some national prominence.

Despite their brushes during the General Strike, it was at Churchill's instigation that in 1928 Londonderry was called into the Cabinet during Stanley Baldwin's second Conservative administration as First Commissioner of Works, responsible for the upkeep of public buildings. With Labour returning to government in the 1929 elections, his term of office was limited to only eight months. But the post had been a good one for Londonderry. While politically it was scarcely in the limelight, equally it attracted little criticism or acrimony.[48] And meanwhile Londonderry was able to use his wealth and social status to good advantage.

Buffeted by the 'economic blizzard'[49] that was beginning to afflict Britain, along with much of Europe, the second Labour administration of Ramsay MacDonald was unable to ride the storm and was replaced in the summer of 1931 by a National Government, largely Conservative in complexion – although MacDonald (now seen as a class renegade, or worse, by most Labour supporters) remained Prime Minister and the Cabinet included a number of other National Labour representatives who had broken with the main Labour Party and Liberals. After a brief second spell at the Office of Works, it was on 5 November 1931, on his appointment as Secretary of State for Air in Ramsay MacDonald's government, with a seat in the Cabinet, that the most important and fateful years of Londonderry's public life began.

III

Londonderry was not without qualifications for his new post. He had after all previously held two positions in the Air Ministry, had indeed already declined the post of Minister in 1922, and was a passionate aviation enthusiast (who would, in 1934 at the age of fifty-six, go on to qualify for a pilot's licence). However, it was generally reckoned – and Lord Londonderry himself came close to admitting it – that he owed his elevation to the post as Secretary of State for Air to his wife's close friendship with the Prime Minister, Ramsay MacDonald.[50] Indeed, David Lloyd George, Welsh firebrand politician and Prime Minister of Britain during the First World War, went so far as to claim that Lady Londonderry's influence lay behind the very formation of the National Government, while his lover, Frances Stevenson, described Ramsay MacDonald as the Marchioness's 'tame lion'.[51]

The relationship between the former Labour Prime Minister, now in his sixties, the illegitimate son of a poor Highlands crofter, and the Marchioness of Londonderry, the grandest and most glamorous of Tory society hostesses, had long since started tongues wagging. They had first met when fortuitously seated next to each other at a dinner at Buckingham Palace back in 1924. MacDonald lost no time in inviting her to Chequers, the Prime Minister's residence. The Londonderrys were among the first names in his guest book – to the chagrin of those in his own party who objected to a Labour Prime Minister inviting 'society *"grandes dames"*'.[52] Lady Londonderry was evidently keen to retain the contact. In January 1926 she wrote to MacDonald, then in opposition as Labour leader, chiding him gently for not giving her his private address and asking him to 'come and see me sometime, if you are not too busy', adding, 'I should so much like to see you'.[53]

Drawn by a common passion for the Scottish Highlands and Gaelic customs, they formed an increasingly close mutual affection. A large number of their semi-flirtatious letters survive – the florid outpourings of MacDonald's particularly grating in style and embarrassing in expression. 'My Dear, You were very beautiful, and I loved you,' ran one of his missives in 1932. 'The dress dazzling in brilliance and glorious in colour and line, was you, and my dear, you were the dress. I just touch its hem, and pray for your eternal happiness.' A few months later, he wrote: 'My Dear One, . . . The only thing I lack is you to come blowing in to lift me away from everything but serenity and the things which pertain to beauty and happiness. You dear thing, how do you do it? What is your secret?'[54] He certainly placed great store in her friendship and emotional support at a difficult time for him, both politically and personally. And – to the derision of his former Labour supporters – there was nothing he enjoyed more than to stand by her side at the top of the grand staircase in Londonderry House to greet the guests at her glittering receptions.[55] 'Amusing sight to see Ramsay [MacDonald] and Lady Londonderry, all glorious in salmon pink,' remarked the young Liberal MP Robert Bernays. 'No less amusing, when one remembers the Londonderry fortune has been built up on coal mining royalties, against which Ramsay has spent a lifetime of protest.'[56]

Lady Londonderry, for her part, evidently encouraged the elderly and increasingly ailing Prime Minister in his affection. Her effusively gushing style played upon his emotional vulnerability. When he reported in summer 1933 the progress he had apparently made at Geneva with his plan to reduce armaments, she wrote, admiringly: 'Your telephone message gave me *such* joy – not only for the greatest event, but on account of the success of your very dear self . . . My whole heart goes out to you in joy and admiration at the manner in which you have pulled it off. Bless you – all my love is yours.'[57] And when he was ill and depressed, a year later, her letter ran: 'I feel so distressed about you and so is [sic] Charley . . . My heart is with you. We can't get on without you. You do realize that, don't you? . . . all our prayers and thoughts – and lots and lots of love and all good wishes, you dearest dear brave creature.'[58]

The relationship provoked much scurrilous gossip. Lady Astor spread the story around the Westminster lobbies of MacDonald and Lady Londonderry retreating after a dinner-party to a darkened room while 'the common herd' was led into a different, more brightly lit salon.[59] Robert Bruce Lockhart, a diplomat and socialite with a distinct penchant for the scurrilous, recounted in his diary that at Geneva, during the Disarmament Conference, Ramsay MacDonald would go to Lady Londonderry's bedroom every night from 11.30 p.m. until 2.00 a.m. to talk to her – 'visits, of course, quite innocent'.[60] Lady Londonderry herself reminded Ramsay MacDonald of the nocturnal visits when she wrote, while staying at Windsor Castle for a royal gathering: 'I am writing in the sitting room of Victoria Tower in my pyjamas – as I did at Geneva and picturing you back there in those nice rooms. I should like to be with you so much.'[61] Since her friendship with MacDonald had brought advantages for Lord Londonderry's career, it bordered on the politically as well as socially scandalous. But whether it went beyond middle-aged flirtatiousness on both sides is of no consequence other than as a source of idle speculation. Oswald Mosley, the British Fascist leader, later attributed MacDonald's delight at 'sitting up all night talking to Lady Londonderry' not to any amorous designs, but to the fact that 'he was a snob and liked idle talk'.[62] In this, if in little else, Mosley might well have been right. Lady Londonderry seems genuinely to have been fond of MacDonald, as, indeed, was her husband. But privately she is said to have referred to him as 'that old fool'.[63]

Both Lord and Lady Londonderry were in appearance, bearing and demeanour archetypal representatives of the British aristocracy of their age. About six feet tall, Lord Londonderry had what was seen as a 'distinguished-looking presence', a 'quiet and gentle manner of speech', and – it goes almost without saying – impeccable manners.[64]

With 'the reputation of being a rather soft, Regency-beau type of man', there was something of a bygone age about his appearance.[65] He looked, commented one contemporary, '1760 in 1936'.[66] Another described him as 'a grand seigneur of the old school; even his appearance was almost theatrically 18th century. Slim, with an elegant figure and pointed features he was red in the face and dressed with distinction.'[67] The last point presumably alluded to such affectations as the brown cane with an 'L' embossed in gold on its top, and the frequent wearing of a cravat instead of a tie.[68] His perceived haughtiness was in many ways merely the product of his natural nose-in-the-air posture. He was viewed as 'always gay and amiable and completely sure of himself', but was in many ways somewhat shy, highly sensitive, even introverted, aloof, reserved and tending towards pessimism.[69] He was well liked by those who knew him or came directly into contact with him, though not seen as acutely intelligent. One casual acquaintance noted that Londonderry was 'extraordinarily pleasant', but was 'too rambly to be impressive in what he says' and 'flits lightly from point to point . . . Really slow in the uptake sometimes.'[70] A longstanding political associate, though a strong critic of his role in the politics of north-eastern England, saw him as 'very affable', but added: 'how I wish that he could even for a few moments forget that he is Lord Londonderry. He really is at heart such a good fellow that it is a pity he can never relax – a greater pity still that he should imagine that just because he happens to be a very rich nobleman he is more important and intelligent than he really is!'[71] The same contemporary, the rather sour Sir Cuthbert Headlam, remarked on other occasions that Londonderry was vain, weak, self-centred, naive in his views, even 'stupid' and 'simple-minded'. No great intellect himself, Headlam's judgement was influenced by his constant irritation at the Londonderrys' interference (as he saw it) in the running of the Conservative Party in the north-east. He tempered such criticisms, however, by adding that 'Charley' was 'extraordinarily conscientious', 'a good citizen', 'modest and unassuming' – adjectives appearing to contradict suggestions of vanity and arrogance – 'kindly', having 'a heart of gold', 'a real friend' – someone to turn to in difficulties.[72] Such sentiments were later endorsed by Harold Macmillan, who would rise to become Prime Minister long after the war but in the 1920s and 1930s was the Member of Parliament for

Stockton-on-Tees, at the heart of the Londonderry political fiefdom in the north-east. Sharply critical of some aspects of government policy, Macmillan was for a lengthy period out of favour with his party's leadership, during which he was particularly grateful for the 'special kindness' and staunch friendship of both Lord and Lady Londonderry.[73]

A description of Lady Londonderry from a hostile source, dating from 1933, conveys a vivid image of her appearance and personality:

I saw her Ladyship in Park Lane. The butler took me up in a narrow lift to a study or boudoir in the roof of the house and I had half an hour or 40 minutes with her Ladyship who talked at me about starving and dying children, ordered cocktails, 'phoned to a servant to take the dogs out for their exercise . . . all with a ceaseless volubility and an attempt to charm and hypnotise which entirely failed in its object. She is 54 and still handsome and a few years ago must have been extremely so. She is perfectly dressed . . . agitated and over-wrought . . . 'scrambling eggs' with a pair of gloves, hiding and revealing fingers blazing with diamonds.[74]

A more sympathetic contemporary highlighted her sense of fun, youthful looks for her age, 'fascinating' personality, but also her ostentatious display of wealth, noting that at one reception, as the room 'glittered with jewels', she 'looked like a Christmas tree', on another, later, occasion that 'she was literally dressed in diamonds'.[75]

Lady Londonderry's personality contrasted sharply with that of her husband. She was flamboyant, assertive, outgoing, warmly gregarious and by nature optimistic. Certainly, to those outside her social ambit, she could appear arrogant, insensitive and unduly status-conscious – 'the silliest and most conceited donkey that ever lived', in one uncharitable description.[76] In a later, contrite self-portrait provided for her husband, following a marital altercation, she admitted that she was 'a nasty, selfish, self-engrossed and self-opinionated female'.[77] But even if to her political enemies she seemed the embodiment of all that was repellent in the British class system, to those who moved in her circles her beauty and grace were striking, her glamour and vivacious charm infectious. It was hardly surprising that she had an unending array of male admirers as well as many female friends. There was from early times a streak of independence in her. She had caused consternation as a child by riding Highland ponies bareback and astride, instead of in the expected, demure side-saddle fashion; on a trip to Japan in 1903, distinctly avant garde, she had had the figure of a large snake tattooed on one of her legs, which meant eyebrows were raised as skirts were shortened; and, politically, her establishment conservatism had been aligned to at least one tinge of radicalism, as she had supported the suffragettes and campaigned to allow women the vote.[78] Both as a young woman and later in life, she was extraordinarily active, following with great vitality the whole range of pursuits expected of the aristocracy: voluntary work in support of good causes, country sports, foreign travel, designing the wonderful gardens of Mount Stewart, and entertaining on the grand scale. Into this non-stop lifestyle she accommodated the upbringing of five children: Maureen (born in 1900), Robin (1902), Margaret (1910), Helen (1911), and – the baby of the family, born much later – Mairi (1921).

Her social attributes, as well as her purposeful encouragement and ambitious drive on his behalf, were of great help to her husband as she continued and even extended the legendary hospitality that had been associated with her mother-in-law, Theresa, the colourful wife of the 6th Marquess, embracing a huge network of friends and contacts in the political establishment and ruling caste of Great Britain. During the First World War – a time when she had founded and run the Women's Volunteer Reserve (subsequently the Women's Legion), which organized the varied work of tens of thousands of women in the war effort – she had established her own political, literary and artistic circle, an exclusive dining-club of the rich and famous. Its name, 'The Ark', was intended to suggest a place of refuge from the storms blowing outside. 'The Ark' continued in existence to the end of her life and numbered among its company some members of the royal family (among them the future King Edward VIII and King George VI) and many leading politicians (including, in the 1930s, every Prime Minister). All members were given names of an animal, mythical beast or figure of fable – Winston Churchill was 'Winston the Warlock', Ramsay MacDonald 'Hamish the Hart', Stanley Baldwin 'Bruin the Bear', Neville Chamberlain an unlikely 'Neville the Devil', and Lady Londonderry herself 'Circe the Sorceress'. Her husband, 'Charley the Cheetah', was so called, noted Lady Londonderry, because the animal, though swift in action, could be caught and tamed though was 'always in pursuit of game'. Lady

Londonderry later described 'The Ark' as a 'a salon where stage and star met statesmen, Liberals and Conservatives, writers and charmers, University dons, artists and playwrights', who 'all scratched, pinched or bit each other jocularly or argued fiercely together but all answered to their names'. 'Recreations' in 'The Ark' laid down that 'Frisking is permitted, coaxing and coquetting, and "Gambolling" within limits. Games of chance, such as "Hunt the Slipper", are encouraged if not played too high. "Beg of my Neighbour", Animal Grab, Rabbits, Puss in the Corner, Gathering Nuts in May, Kissing the Ring, and Bumps.'[79] Such were the leisure pursuits of the great and the good, the rich and the famous, in England in the 1930s.

The shenanigans were, however, not merely frivolous entertainment, the decadent playtime of the upper class in a world that was passing. Indirectly, they had a political as well as social purpose. 'The Ark' was the British Establishment – at least a notable part of it – at play. Amid the harmless amusement, contacts could be made, connections established, relationships built up, gossip exchanged and minor plots hatched. The high-society 'frisking' and 'gambolling' paid a dividend, not least, for Lady Londonderry herself. The friendships forged and promoted in the meetings of 'The Ark' were of value to Lord Londonderry's political career, particularly while Ramsay MacDonald was Prime Minister.[80]

The hospitality provided for the dinner-parties of 'Ark' members each week was extended periodically to the grandiose receptions given at Londonderry House, when, standing at the head of the magnificent staircase, its balustrades lined by 'powdered flunkeys in knee-breeches',[81] Lady Londonderry, extravagantly bedecked in a tiara and glittering jewellery and accompanied by the Prime Minister of the day, welcomed as many as 2,000 guests on the eve of the opening of Parliament each year, providing an important social outlet both for the Conservative Party and for furthering her husband's career.[82] This was not lost on contemporaries. 'One can't use a man's hospitality and not give him a job if he wants it,' the jaundiced Cuthbert Headlam had already cynically remarked at Londonderry's appointment to the Board of Works in 1928.[83] The Londonderrys had 'proceeded to entertain politically on a vast scale with, of course, the set purpose of political advancement', Stanley Baldwin later commented, and thought, though 'very magnificent and beautifully done', it was 'in dubious taste'. He recalled the acidic wit of F. E. Smith (later Lord Birkenhead), that Lord Londonderry had been 'catering his way to the Cabinet'.[84]

Whatever backbiting, sarcasm or petty jealousies accompanied his appointment as Secretary of State for Air in 1931, Londonderry could at last feel that he had arrived at a position of importance commensurate with his status and talent, as well as with family expectations. And his enthusiasm for aviation made the post particularly attractive to him. Lady Londonderry was equally thrilled at the appointment. For her husband, and for herself, friends of royalty, close to the seat of government and pillars of the British Conservative social and political Establishment, it seemed that even greater things beckoned.

Apart from his most recent advancement, Londonderry's rise to prominence had been largely unremarkable. But it had rested heavily upon patronage linked to his aristocratic status and connections – hallmarks of the British class system – and this dependency would leave Londonderry increasingly exposed as the tensions of the 1930s mounted. The world into which he had been born was rapidly changing. Though anxious to embrace the technological advances of a new era, particularly in air travel, his political outlook remained in essence that of a nineteenth-century nobleman. His political style and personal temperament could not easily adjust to the harsher and more populist politics of the inter-war years. At root, he was at best condescending, then subsequently disparaging, towards what he viewed as the limited horizons and abilities of the middle-class political leaders under whom he had to serve. But they now wielded far greater power and patronage than he himself did. Though it inwardly rankled, he was dependent upon them. And his ingrained authoritarian streak, prompting an insensitivity to the need to attune to public opinion, was a further reflection of the background and upbringing that had paved the way for his successful career, but which was now to prove a political weakness. He would soon enter troubled waters.

Before we take up Lord Londonderry's story again, however, we need to understand the widespread misconceptions of Hitler during his first years in power, and how they affected the constrained policy options of the British government in facing up to the new, potentially grave threat to peace in Europe.

I

Illusions and Delusions
about Hitler

'Are we still dealing with the Hitler of Mein Kampf, lulling his opponents to sleep with fair words in order to gain time to arm his people? . . . Or is it a new Hitler, who has discovered the burden of responsible office . . . ? That is the riddle that has to be solved.'

Sir Maurice Hankey, Secretary to the Cabinet,
24 October 1933

Hitler was a puzzle. This much can be deduced from the errors of judgement of so many observers of his meteoric rise then rapid grasp of an unshakeable hold on power.

Most of those, even within Germany, who thought they understood Hitler turned out not to understand him at all. Misjudging Hitler, underestimating him, misconstruing his aims, 'getting him wrong', was commonplace. Many on the political Left thought he was little more than a sham and a charlatan, the puppet of big business, the brutal weapon of capitalism in terminal crisis, whose rule would be shortlived and collapse as capitalism collapsed. The church-going public and their representatives veered in their views between seeing him as the incarnation of evil, the anti-Christ and exponent of a variant form of 'godless Bolshevism', to imagining in him a statesman who was God-fearing (in contrast to the radical anti-Christians in the Nazi movement) and the herald of national redemption and moral renewal in Germany. The conservative Right tended to presume that, though he had his uses in whipping up emotions in the national cause, he was not much more than a mouthpiece of the disaffected masses, the demagogic leader of a protest party without a clear political programme, who, if properly 'boxed in', could be contained and controlled until the 'traditional forces' of rule could re-establish themselves.[1] Many were to learn soon enough after 1933 the extent of such calamitous misjudgement.

If assessments of Hitler, just before and after he had gained power, could vary so widely and err so disastrously *within* Germany, it is little wonder that outsiders found difficulty in recognizing what he was striving for, and the full extent of the danger he posed to the peace of Europe. In Great Britain, the press, which played such a crucial role in shaping public opinion, reflected in good measure (if not completely) party-political divides and offered readers a wide spectrum of views on Hitler, not infrequently betraying profound ignorance or complete misunderstanding of what he and his party stood for. It was unsurprising, therefore, that opinion towards Nazism in the early phase of Hitler's rule varied massively in Britain, between the poles of those on the Left who shared the view that the German dictator was a capitalist lackey, and were above all appalled at the brutality and terroristic onslaught on human rights by the new regime, to supporters of Fascism, who were uncritical admirers of Hitler and would have liked to see a similar system of government replace 'decadent' democracy at home. Between these extremes, many of those who took an interest in Germany – a relatively small minority of the British public in the first years of Hitler's dictatorship – were uncertain, and at times contradictory, in their opinions. They were prepared to applaud some aspects, such as the restoration of order, the speed of economic recovery, the revitalization of national life, and the crushing of Communism, while deploring others, especially the extreme violence of the Nazi hordes in their treatment of Jews and political opponents. Such ambivalent attitudes often went hand in hand with a sense of unease at how a resurgent Germany might assert itself internationally, but at the same time a feeling that such assertiveness was both inevitable and not altogether unjustified given what many regarded as the unfair treatment meted out to Germany in the Versailles Treaty of 1919. In any case, it was widely felt that, however unpalatable the Hitler regime was in many respects, Britain had still somehow to work together with it – and that a strong

Germany could prove useful as a bulwark against the even less appealing, more brutal and more alien creed of Bolshevism, whose spectre was seen to loom as a future threat to western civilization.[2]

Those holding such views were for the most part neither fools nor knaves. It is easy in retrospect to see how misguided some of the opinion was. It was less easy at the time to grasp the enormity of what Hitler meant, or to arrive at clear, unambiguous policies for dealing with him. This was true not least, and most fatally, of officialdom in Whitehall, notably the Foreign Office, which was also hesitant, unsure and often divided in its views on how to tackle the problem of Hitler and Nazism. And this was in spite of receiving perceptive reports from the British Embassy in Berlin, which provided some of the clearest indications of the character of the Nazi Party and its enigmatic leader.[3] Those involved in shaping policy in the Foreign Office were, despite the lasting, negative views of posterity for the failures of appeasement, highly intelligent and able individuals. And the members of the Ramsay MacDonald Cabinet, in office in the period that Hitler consolidated his authority, were nothing if not well-intentioned, and in some respects even idealistic. But, nevertheless, almost all were in some degree baffled by Hitler, and the later weakness of the British government, which was to be fully laid bare in the humiliation of the failed attempt to 'appease' him, was prefigured in the uncertainty and miscalculation about how to handle him while he was still weak in the first years of his power. These were the years in which Hitler was able out of an initial position of international vulnerability and isolation to forge one of formidable strength. They were the years that provided the bully with the big stick he was more than willing to use – in the process gradually taking German foreign policy spiralling out of control and Europe into war.

I

Though Foreign Office representatives in Germany had charted his progress since he had first registered his political presence in Bavaria in the early 1920s, to the general public in Britain Hitler was largely unknown when he burst on the scene with his electoral breakthrough in 1930. After attracting some fleeting attention in British newspapers at the time of his Putsch fiasco in November 1923, he had sunk into near obscurity, apart from some reportage in the quality press (with fairly low readership figures) of Nazi gains in provincial elections from late 1929 onwards.[4] But from being a tiny movement on the fringes of German politics, which had gained only 2.6 per cent of the vote at the previous Reichstag election in May 1928, the Nazi Party leapt into the political limelight as a political force to be reckoned with two years later, as the world economic depression started to bite in Germany. In the September election of 1930, Hitler's movement won 18.3 per cent of the popular vote and 107 seats in the German Parliament, making it the second-biggest party in the country.[5] All at once, outside Germany as well as within the country, people had to take notice of Hitler.

How little the British public had known about Hitler before this date can be seen in stories in the press that he had fought in the Boer War – which had ended when he was thirteen years old.[6] This level of ignorance was soon dissipated. But it was replaced by largely distorted images presented in British newspapers. Remarkably, in fact, even now relatively little attention was paid to Hitler himself, who was, with typical underestimation, generally seen as dependent upon financial backing from German conservatives and in thrall to his own stormtrooper activists.[7] The most penetrating criticism of the Hitler regime after 1933 would regularly come from the *Manchester Guardian*, a liberal, provincial newspaper with a small circulation of some 25–50,000,[8] but possessing influence in liberal-Left circles that bore no relation to these figures, a reputation for 'preach[ing] enlightenment to the enlightened',[9] and outstanding European correspondents who were uncompromising in their hostility to Nazism. In 1930, however, even this newspaper dismissed Hitler as a mere braggart without genuine or sustainable principles, and thought those in his party, though more aggressive, violent and barbaric than in any other except the Communist Party, would behave as 'ordinary politicians when in office'.[10] Only a few weeks after the Nazi breakthrough in the election of September that year, the same newspaper was playing down the danger of the Nazi movement and its 'preposterous leader', asserting that this was 'not anything as fatal, sinister, and calamitous as fear, nervousness and sensational journalism made it appear'.[11] Not dissimilar was the verdict of the *Observer*, that Hitler was 'dramatic, violent, and shallow', a 'ranting fool' amounting to little more than a 'megaphone' of the widespread discontent.[12] *The Times* thought it was difficult to know what the Nazi Party wanted, apart from making Germany strong again, but was optimistic that Hitler would eventually guide its revolutionary spirit into 'useful channels'.[13] Oddly, the *Daily Mail*, a mass-circulation newspaper whose owner, Lord Rothermere, was sympathetic to Hitler (and, in the early 1930s, to Oswald Mosley's British Union of Fascists), was practically alone in at least acknowledging – from a position of admiration – that the Nazi leader was not just a talented demagogue but also ideologically driven, that there was 'intense conviction behind his words'.[14]

Hitler soon faded from view again, as far as most members of the British public were concerned, increasingly preoccupied as they were with the government's inability to cope with deepening economic depression in their own country. The newspapers for long paid only sporadic attention to the Nazi leader and his movement. Reference to Hitler, where it was made, was still often dismissive. The *New Statesman and Nation*, a weekly on the Left of the British political spectrum, went so far as to describe him, in April 1931, as 'a somewhat colourless personality', who had been 'found wanting' as Germany's equivalent to Mussolini.[15]

The following year, 1932, as the dramatic, terminal crisis of the Weimar Republic unfolded, Hitler, at the centre of five election campaigns that year, naturally came to occupy far more column inches in British newspapers. Even now, however, the images of him were often grossly misleading. The *Manchester Guardian* remained insistent that Hitler was not a revolutionary, but a reactionary, and not in control of his own party.[16] The *Observer*, playing down Hitler's anti-Semitism, still thought he was no more than a rabble-rousing demagogue when, in the spring, he chose to stand for the Reich Presidency, then changed its mind and depicted him as a moderate within his own movement. In any case, it saw power lying in the hands of the wealthy nationalist elites.[17] *The Times*, the most important newspaper for the British political class, agreed that Hitler was a 'moderate', compared with some of the more radical figures in the Nazi Party, and thought that he was gradually gaining a sense of responsibility. It even suggested that Hitler should constitutionally be made President of the German Reich, imagining that the Nazi movement might break apart if its leader were to be elevated 'above politics'.[18] For the *Daily Telegraph*, read by increasing numbers of the Conservative middle and upper classes, Hitler was, in any case, 'done for' by the end of 1932, and his only hope was to take his movement, with a 'chastened spirit', into coalition with the nationalist and the Catholic Centre Party, though he would then inevitably come under the control of the 'holders of real power' in Germany.[19]

There was neither surprise nor great excitement in the British press at Hitler's accession to the Chancellorship on 30 January 1933. Nazi participation in government had been widely expected, the appointment of Hitler as Reich Chancellor had legally and procedurally been no different to that of his predecessors, and, not least, his readiness to work within a mainly conservative Cabinet appeared to suggest that he had dropped his earlier insistence on absolute power. *The Times*, for instance, had already indicated on 29 January, the day following the fall of the government of General von Schleicher, that a government headed by Hitler commanding majority support in the Reichstag was 'held to be the least dangerous solution of a problem bristling with dangers'.[20] Following Hitler's appointment to the Chancellorship, the newspaper saw comfort for observers abroad in the continuation in office of the Foreign Minister, Baron von Neurath, and the Finance Minister, Count Schwerin von Krosigk, 'men of nationalist outlook and no close party association'.[21] The leading article of the liberal *News Chronicle* took a similar line, welcoming Hitler's appointment as 'a good and necessary thing', and assuming that, as head of a coalition government, his power 'cannot under any circumstances be anything like absolute'.[22] It was a British version of the view notoriously – and extremely briefly – held at the time by the conservatives in Hitler's Cabinet themselves that they were 'boxing him in'.[23] In its own leading article, *The Times* thought it had always been desirable that Hitler should be given 'the chance of showing that he is something more than an orator and an agitator'. Though the German attitude towards armaments would be watched abroad with some misgivings, 'in fairness to the Nazis' the newspaper suggested that they had 'said little more on the subject of German disabilities under the Treaty of Versailles than the most constitutional German parties', though they had said it much louder.²⁴ Of the mainstream, conservative press, only the *Economist*, the highbrow weekly, voiced 'bewilderment and concern', along with apprehension for the future once Germany had recovered its strength. Here, as in other press outlets, the main preoccupation was with German domestic politics, although the *Economist* indicated its pessimism about the prospects for the negotiations on disarmament in Europe that were taking place at Geneva.²⁵

In the liberal press and on the Left, there was some consternation about what a Hitler-led government would bring, though accompanied by much uncertainty, hesitation and misapprehension. Very rapidly, revulsion about the vicious assault on German Socialists and Communists, bestial attacks on Jews, and other early manifestations of the savage inhumanity of the regime, would come to characterize the reportage on Germany of the left-of-centre press, and be linked to increased worry about the prospects of avoiding war. But the immediate reaction of, for example, the *Daily Herald*, linked to the Labour Party and, with a circulation of over 2 million, the biggest-selling newspaper in Great Britain, was that Hitler was a 'clown' who would soon fail to master the economic difficulties and the powerful vested interests he faced. Describing him as 'a stubby little Austrian with a flabby handshake, shifty brown eyes, and a Charlie Chaplin moustache', the newspaper suggested that nothing 'in the public career of little Adolf Hitler, highly-strung as a girl and vain as a matinee idol, indicates that he can escape the fate of his immediate predecessors' whose terms of office as Chancellors of Germany had lasted only a matter of weeks.²⁶ On the extreme Left, the *Daily Worker*, organ of the tiny Communist Party of Great Britain (which, like the Communist International generally, was singularly ill-prepared for what was to come) toed the line laid down in Moscow and also took solace in the presumption that Hitler signified the last fling of capitalism in the 'extreme intensification of the class contradictions in Germany' and 'the dictatorship of the big capitalist exploiters', and would soon disappear, along with the evil it represented.²⁷ Most newspapers were prepared to 'give Hitler a chance' and hoped for the best, implying that he might settle down into a strong but conventional head of government, once the initial crisis had been overcome. This corresponded to the view still put forward by *The Times* that Hitler was essentially a moderate and decent person.[28]

Such illusions were swiftly dispelled for much of the press, and for the bulk of public opinion shaped by newspaper reports, during the dramatic months of the Nazi consolidation of power in Germany. The violence and intimidation, the shootings, beatings, arrest and torture of political opponents and Jews which accompanied the ruthless extension of Nazi control over the whole of German society during the first months of 1933 were fully reported in the British press. The *Manchester Guardian* was especially prominent in its well-informed reports and its vehement denunciation of Nazi brutality and repression. 'How can a great and civilized nation like the German tolerate these horrors?' the newspaper asked in March 1933, and published detailed accounts of 'facts about the Nazi terror', 'the beating and robbing of Jews', 'German workers under the Nazi terror' and 'examples of beatings and murder'.[29] 'Any German who dares say a true word about the Terror in his own country runs the risk of a fearful beating, or long imprisonment or even of death, and no one can reasonably be expected to run such a risk,' commented the *Manchester Guardian* on 8 April 1933, adding: 'all Germany is being converted into a huge prison'.[30] Violence directed at the Jews was repeatedly and prominently reported, in the *Manchester Guardian* and in other newspapers.[31] The nationwide boycott of Jewish stores in Germany on 1 April 1933, the widespread and vicious accompanying violence and the ruthless discriminatory legislation that followed it received massive coverage in Britain.[32] As the violence subsided during the summer and the Nazi political revolution reached the first stage of its completion with the law of 14 July 1933 forbidding the existence of parties other than the NSDAP (Nazi Party), attention to German internal affairs in the British press naturally ebbed away – though not to the point of disappearance. The next major surge of interest came with Hitler's murderous destruction of the leadership of his own stormtroopers in the infamous 'Night of the Long Knives' of 30 June 1934, readily seen as a type of political gangster-style massacre.[33]

ILLUSIONS AND DELUSIONS ABOUT HITLER

The Times used a different analogy and spoke of reversion to 'medieval methods' in a land which 'has ceased for the time being to be a modern European country'. The newspaper voiced the widely felt revulsion at 'the savagery, the disregard for all the forms of law which are the indispensable safeguards of justice and which are sacrosanct in every modern civilized State', and expressed incredulity 'that the head, even the despotic head, of a modern Government should order the arrest and the summary execution of a number of his principal lieutenants'. Strikingly, however, *The Times* drew the conclusion that probably 'during the next few years there is more reason to be afraid for Germany than to be afraid of Germany'.[34] 'There is no reason why opinion in England and the United States should be hoodwinked,' the *Manchester Guardian* had remarked as early as April 1933.[35] But the complacent view of *The Times* that there was no need to fear Germany for some years hints that misjudgement of Hitler was still current. No connection was made between Hitler's domestic brutality and disregard for legal constraints and his likely actions in the realm of foreign policy.

The view was sustained that, however regrettable and repulsive, German domestic affairs were no concern of Britain unless and until they affected the conduct of foreign policy.[36] There were also those, not just on the extreme Right, prepared to minimize the internal repression in acknowledging that power in much of Europe was in the hands of anti-democratic forces, meaning the need, like it or not, to cooperate with unpalatable bedfellows in formulating policy. The former Prime Minister, David Lloyd George, for instance, who thought Hitler 'a great man', said privately he had not shown half the ferocity in the persecution of the Jews that Cromwell had shown towards the Irish Catholics.[37] And some hope was still cherished that, beneath the propaganda bluster, Hitler was – at least in external affairs – a pragmatic realist, open to reasonable argument, and that once rid of the 'wild men' in his movement, he would 'settle down' into a more moderate mode. Hitler's most significant move in the foreign arena during his first two years in office, his withdrawal of Germany from the Disarmament Conference in Geneva and from the League of Nations on 14 October 1933, did not seem to challenge this expectation. Not only did the move come as no outright surprise;

it was even in part sympathetically received since there was much feeling in Britain that Germany was being unfairly treated in the question of disarmament, and that French intransigence, not German aggressive intent, had brought about the withdrawal. Returning to the issue in May 1934, in the context of attempts to persuade Germany to return to the Disarmament Conference, a leading article in *The Times*, entitled 'The German Case', acknowledged that Germany's 'impatience' had been understandable since the country was still waiting 'for that "general limitation of the armaments of all nations" that it had been told to expect at Versailles'.[38]

The continued unclarity in the press about Hitler's aims in foreign policy was influenced not only by his public avowals of his peaceable motives and striving for no more than equality with other powers in armaments for defensive purposes, but by soundings taken from supposedly well-informed politicians. A month before Germany's withdrawal from the Disarmament Conference and League of Nations, Arthur Henderson, former Foreign Secretary and leader of the Parliamentary Labour Party, currently President of the Disarmament Conference, spoke to W. P. Crozier, editor of the *Manchester Guardian*, about the importance of persuading Germany to enter freely into an armaments treaty. 'He had seen Hitler', Henderson said, 'and believed him to be sincerely pacific.' Norman Davies, chief US delegate to the Disarmament Conference, spoke to Crozier in identical terms the same day. 'His view', noted Crozier, 'was that Hitler was sincerely pacific. He had talked to Hitler and had said to him, "What do you want – rearmament or disarmament, peace or war?" Hitler had replied that they wanted disarmament and peace. But they were helpless, etc.; he talked about all the armed nations round Germany and said they must have equality.' Davies thought Hitler was 'a *good* man – stupid and uneducated but still a good man', though he went on to qualify this by claiming that Hitler 'had good in him', admitting that experienced American correspondents in Berlin disagreed with him and thought Hitler 'meant war in his own time'.[39] When, a few weeks later, the strongly anti-German head of the Foreign Office news department, Rex Leeper, spoke to Crozier, he made plain the ambivalence about Hitler in the Foreign Office. One view held 'that the Nazi system would eventually result in a quite new sort of Germany . . . which would be genuinely pacific; the other, which most people held, and which it appeared that he shared, that the Nazis were a dangerous and threatening force in Europe.' The British aim, he said, was to improve on the current disarmament proposals. When Crozier asked 'what we were to do with Germany if she were found undoubtedly to be rearming', Leeper stated that 'it would be very difficult for the British Government to commit itself to anything at all because "the country" would not like it'.[40]

Leeper's comment was a clear indication of the British government's sensitivity to public opinion in its policy towards Germany. Divided though this public opinion (as articulated by the newspapers) was on Hitler and Nazi Germany – more or less along Left–Right lines – it was united in its abhorrence at the prospect of another war. The legacy of the First World War in all its horror was the overwhelmingly most important influence upon the shaping of opinion in Britain on foreign affairs generally and, quite specifically, on the new problem posed by Hitler's Germany. This directly affected views on the question of rearmament. While newspapers on the Left voiced opposition to rearmament and pressed for multilateral disarmament progress in Geneva – seeking the ideal, but rejecting any notion of a big stick behind the kind words – the right-wing press advocated moderation and the attempt to construct cordial relations with Germany as with other nations.[41] Curiously, it was the *Daily* Mail, the newspaper most sympathetic to Nazi Germany, whose owner, Lord Rothermere, made a point of visiting Hitler in 1934, which was the strongest proponent of rapid rearmament as the best safeguard even against an over-firm clasp of friendship let alone an insurance should things turn out badly after all. It was not far from the line which Lord Londonderry would seek to press.

For the majority of the British public, however, the question of British rearmament only became a matter of urgency when, in March 1935, Hitler broke another stipulation of the Versailles Treaty, that limiting the German army to a size of no more than 100,000 men. He now announced that Germany was introducing conscription and an army of 550,000 men, and, even more stunningly, later in the month, he told the British Foreign Secretary, Sir John Simon, that Germany had already reached parity of air armaments with Britain. The prospect of British cities bombed to ruins by the Luftwaffe, whose existence Göring had recently announced (again in contravention of the Versailles Treaty), rapidly concentrated minds. As British opinion became more anxious, government policy towards Germany entered a new phase.

II

British newspapers were not alone in their uncertainty about Hitler, and how to handle him. At the heart of the British government, too, Hitler was a puzzle. Ten days after Hitler had withdrawn Germany from the League of Nations, on 24 October 1933, Sir Maurice Hankey, Secretary to the Cabinet, asked in a memorandum: 'Are we still dealing with the Hitler of *Mein Kampf*, lulling his opponents to sleep with fair words in order to gain time to arm his people? . . . Or is it a new Hitler, who has discovered the burden of responsible office, and wants to extricate himself, like many an earlier tyrant, from the commitments of his irresponsible days? That is the riddle that has to be solved.'[42]

This was in spite of the fact that reports reaching the British government from its official representatives in Germany provided a reasonably accurate and realistic appraisal of the Nazi leader, and of the potential dangers he and his regime might pose to British interests. The British Ambassador in Berlin during the rise of Hitler, Sir Horace Rumbold, proved a notably shrewd and acute critic of Nazism, and was well served by his consular officials. Before 1933, his own reports to the Foreign Office in London were a clear warning of troubled waters ahead, should Hitler gain power.[43] Since such reports, rather than newspaper accounts, offered the raw material that helped to shape attitudes within the Foreign Office towards Germany, it seems – at least at first sight – all the more remarkable that Hitler remained a 'riddle', and that government policy in the early years of the Nazi regime was so hapless, supine and vacillating – so unsure about Hitler and how to handle him.

British officialdom's first flurry of interest in Hitler had arisen during 1922–3 as the crisis in Germany, acutely reflected in the mounting political turbulence in Bavaria, reached its climax with the notorious Beer Hall Putsch attempt by the Nazi leader and his followers on 8–9 November 1923. Though their reports were not altogether free of ambiguities and uncertainties, successive British Consuls-General in Munich were clearly aware of the dangers which a Nazi advance posed and were far from dismissive of Hitler's own political abilities. They recognized that the Nazi movement was a different kind of force in German politics, something similar to the Fascist Party in Italy (which had by then taken power) and not easily to be located on the German political spectrum, combining as it did 'Socialist' elements commonly associated with the Left as well as evident 'reactionary' components of the Right. They acknowledged its appeal, not least to the forces of 'reaction', as a vehicle to mobilize the masses and a 'bulwark against Bolshevism', and guessed that it had powerful financial backing. They also saw the importance of anti-Semitism to the movement, and how Hitler was able to tap vicious hatred of the Jews in sections of the population. For Hitler himself, it was pointed out, 'anti-Semitism was an obsession'. Had his Putsch attempt succeeded, it was clear, 'the Jews would have had an exceedingly bad time'.[44]

The reports echoed the sentiment frequently expressed by Nazi supporters at the time that Hitler was 'Germany's Mussolini'. There was relatively little of the underestimation of Hitler which was later to be so frequently encountered, inside and outside Germany.[45] Already by autumn 1922, the British Consul-General was reporting that Hitler had 'developed into something much more than a scurrilous and rather comic agitator', and had formed 'an efficient and active organisation'.[46] It would, the British Embassy in Berlin added, be a great mistake to underrate Hitler and 'to treat him as if he were a mere clown'.[47] A consular report from the day before Hitler launched his ill-fated Putsch, describing him as 'a demagogue devoid of political intelligence',[48] seemed in danger of doing precisely that, and points to the contradictions which often underlay British approaches to the Nazi phenomenon. Nevertheless, the same Consul-General clearly saw the international, not just national, dangers which Hitler would have posed had his attempted *coup d'état* proved successful, remarking that a takeover of power by Hitler would without doubt have led to a French occupation.[49] A consular report earlier in the year had indicated that a resurrected Germany would be dangerous and could lead to moves for an Anglo-German understanding as a preliminary to a war of revenge against France.[50] Looking back on events, the Consul-General was plain that during 1923 Hitler had not only 'made himself into an international danger', but had stirred up 'more bad blood than far greater men than he have done in a lifetime'.[51]

During the years of relative stability in Germany, between 1924 and 1929, when the Nazi Party existed only on the outer fringes of politics, Hitler unsurprisingly dropped from the centre of attention of British officials. Their interest began to be reawakened in the light of the Nazi advances in regional elections in 1929. Sir Horace Rumbold, British Ambassador in Berlin since the summer of the previous year, acknowledged that Hitler had 'proved to be more than the leader of a spasmodic movement', and attributed to the Nazi Party 'the magnetic attraction of a jazz band' among the 'more sober party orchestras'.[52] Rumbold highlighted the 'youthfulness and vigour' of the Nazi movement, which appealed to the disaffected.[53]

The Foreign Office in London drew the main conclusion from the sensational advances of the Nazi Party in the election of September 1930 that Hitler's rise and the revival of nationalism in Germany would affect the political climate in Europe and threaten British interests.[54] Even so, it was presumed that, should the Nazi Party not fall apart (as many predicted) on account of its evident internal tensions, it would be drawn into cooperation with the government and play a more constructive role, which would then have a moderating effect on its more extreme elements. Hitler's 'oath of legality', sworn (for tactical reasons) in the Reich Supreme Court in Leipzig in September 1930 – at the same time that he was threatening that 'heads would roll' after a Nazi takeover of power – was taken to be an indication that his hot-headedness would yield to rational calculation, pragmatism and moderation as the possibility of power loomed larger. That Hitler was, beneath the rhetoric, ultimately a politician like others who, whatever the distaste for his actions in internal matters, could be dealt with as regards foreign affairs on rational grounds of balancing respective interests, that he would be a 'moderate' once in power, was an illusion which would last through the 1930s.[55] It was an illusion under which, not least, Lord Londonderry would labour in his endeavours, after 1936, to bring about a basis of friendship between Great Britain and Hitler's Germany.

Some ambiguities remained in the Foreign Office's understanding of Hitler as the Weimar Republic collapsed and he approached the threshold of power. In the months before Hitler was handed the Chancellorship, the Foreign Office was still unsure whether he was fully in control of the Nazi movement. Only in December 1932, when his most powerful henchman, Gregor Strasser, resigned his offices after a final breach with Hitler, did the latter's unassailable position within the party seem beyond dispute.[56] Rumbold himself fluctuated at times between a view that Hitler was so strong that he could command instant obedience within his movement and the sense that he was buffeted by the influence of competing factions.[57] Hitler plainly remained an enigmatic figure. One lengthy and informed report in late 1931, in many respects close to the mark and well received in the Foreign Office, portrayed Hitler as unstable, unreliable, with the temperament of an artist, more of a loud-mouth than a statesman, whose outbursts of rage could be attributed to an inferiority complex deriving from his lack of education. But whatever the view of his personal characteristics, the report went on to emphasize the need to treat him seriously as a dangerous politician, to see close parallels between Nazism and Italian Fascism, and to surmise that Hitler would 'try to govern Germany, at least for a time, very much after the Fascist system in Italy'. Here, too, however, it was presumed that foreign policy under Nazi aegis would be less aggressive than had been feared.[58]

When Hindenburg appointed Hitler Reich Chancellor around midday on 30 January 1933, it was, though unwelcome, scarely a surprise to the British Foreign Office and its representatives in Germany. Hitler was no closed book for them.[59] But what he signified was still indistinct. Though they had followed his path to power with interest, consternation and often notable insight, the variety of impressions and images of Hitler which had been accumulated still left big question-marks over his future behaviour as a partner in European diplomacy. Early indications were not unpromising. The German Ambassador in London, Leopold von Hoesch, told Sir John Simon, the British Foreign Secretary, that the 'domestic changes in

Germany did not betoken any change in the line of German foreign policy', and Simon was reassured by the continuation in office of the Foreign Minister, Konstantin Baron von Neurath.[60]

Rumbold, however, watched the first outpourings of state-sponsored violence and repression in Berlin and the rest of Prussia, directed in the main at the Nazis' left-wing opponents, with mounting disgust and foreboding. A lengthy report on 22 February left the Foreign Office in no doubt about the gravity of the assault on popular liberties and the abolition of representative government. 'Hitler may be no statesman,' wrote Rumbold, 'but he is an uncommonly clever and audacious demagogue and fully alive to every popular instinct.'[61] Rumbold was certain that Hitler's government would not allow itself to be swept from power. 'They have come to stay,' wrote Rumbold.[62] Whatever baleful effects on German internal politics this might have was not seen as the direct concern of the British government. But for one leading figure in the Foreign Office who would establish himself as the most vehement advocate of a tough anti-German policy, Sir Robert Vansittart, the Permanent Under-Secretary, the consequences for foreign affairs to be inferred from Rumbold's report were dire. If Hitler surmounted all opposition and internal challenge to the consolidation of his rule 'then another European war will be within measurable distance', he thought.[63] The Foreign Secretary, Sir John Simon, was scarcely more optimistic. Hitler's 'militant, very dangerous and incompetent administration will remain in charge of the centre of Europe in strict training for mischief', he noted. There were justified fears that his regime would bring about 'the reestablishment of Germany as an armed menace of Europe . . . We are now being confronted by a Germany more menacing than pre-war Germany.'[64]

Initially, still adhering to the notion that Hitler was a moderate who belonged to 'the more reasonable elements' of the regime, the Foreign Office, taking its lead from Rumbold, had made Göring responsible for the wild terroristic actions of spring 1933, commenting that 'Göring will have to go, if Hitler is to rid his Government of its present mad dog strain.'[65] However, the boycott against the Jews on 1 April 1933 opened Rumbold's eyes. In its aftermath, he read *Mein Kampf* (or at least, lengthy sections of it) and, following an audience with the Reich Chancellor on 11 May, concluded 'that Herr Hitler is himself responsible for the anti-Jewish policy of the German Government and that it would be a mistake to believe that it is the policy of his wilder men whom he has difficulty in controlling'. He saw it plainly as Hitler's intention, if possible, to 'expel the Jewish community from Germany ultimately'. Rumbold had recognized, and reported to London, that anti-Semitism was no propaganda ploy or superficial, passing phenomenon, but lay at the core of Hitler's policy.[66]

This, of course, though deplorable, could still be seen as an issue for German domestic politics and no direct concern of Britain. But Rumbold took his analysis of *Mein Kampf* much further in a special dispatch he sent to the Foreign Office on 26 April 1933 and drew from Hitler's tract prognoses for the likely dangers in store for Europe.[67] Rumbold's reports had invariably been characterized by cautious, balanced judgement and the absence of empty speculation. His assessment of Hitler's likely course in international affairs was, consequently, taken all the more seriously by the Foreign Office, read by the Prime Minister, Ramsay MacDonald, and circulated to the Cabinet.[68] The dispatch was remarkably perceptive. Rumbold suggested Hitler would resort periodically to protestations of peaceful intent to induce a sense of security abroad. But he was gloomy about the prospects of peace. Hitler's foreign policy, as expressed in his speeches as well as in his earlier book, was 'disquieting'. Rumbold emphasized Hitler's aim of expansion for territorial gain at the expense of Russia, and was adamant that Hitler could not 'abandon the cardinal points of his programme' and would meanwhile seek to lull adversaries 'into such a state of coma that they will allow themselves to be engaged one by one'. Germany needed a period of peace until her renewed strength made her difficult to challenge. He thought it misleading to expect 'a return to sanity or a serious modification of the views of the Chancellor and his entourage', and was sure that 'a deliberate policy is now being pursued', whose aim was to prepare Germany militarily before her adversaries could interfere.

Correspondingly, Rumbold felt 'that Germany's neighbours have reason to be vigilant, and that it may be necessary for them to determine their attitude towards coming developments in this country sooner than they may have contemplated'. He foresaw it with the passage of time becoming 'increasingly difficult to ascertain what is actually taking place in this country and to gauge the real intentions of the German Government'.

The Foreign Office was divided in its reactions to Rumbold's warning. One argument, forcefully advanced by Major-General A. C. Temperley, Britain's Military Representative at the Disarmament Conference in Geneva, was that it was too dangerous to wait for Germany's avowed peaceful intentions to be put to the test. Great Britain, France and the USA should give Germany a warning that revision of Versailles and military equality were dependent upon an immediate halt to Germany's militarization. This would provoke a crisis, and war would be closer. 'But Germany knows that she cannot fight at present and we must call her bluff.' The alternative was 'to allow things to drift for another five years, by which time, unless there is a change of heart in Germany, war seems inevitable'.[69] Vansittart, who had already established himself as the most prominent voice among the 'hardliners' on the German question, was among those who argued that goodwill towards Germany would not suffice, and agreed that Germany should be put under strong pressure to comply with international demands on armaments if a war, once the country was strong enough, was to be avoided.[70] The counter-position was adopted by Ralph Wigram, head of the Central European Section of the Foreign Office, who pressed for Hitler to be made fully aware of the solidarity of Britain, France and the USA and the joint concern over German militarism, but also their readiness to guarantee Germany's equality as a European great power through a four-power pact (with Italy, France and Great Britain), as proposed by Mussolini.[71] The problem with this approach was that the 'carrot' was not tempting and the 'stick' not threatening.

Sir John Simon, the Foreign Secretary, presented a digest of the Foreign Office's thoughts to the Cabinet on 17 May 1933 – just before Hitler gave the first of his major 'peace speeches' to the Reichstag in which he promised to 'respect the national rights of other peoples' and expressed his wish 'to live with them in peace and friendship'.[72] The language of Simon's memorandum was tough. He took over Temperley's description of Germany as a 'mad dog' in international affairs, said (as the Major-General had done) that

Britain must call her bluff, and was insistent that Hitler must give way.[73] But, characteristically, the careful and legalistic Simon then backed a more cautious approach than Temperley had wanted. The hard line towards Germany would only be taken if disarmament talks failed. It was crucial to prevent this happening since, without success in Geneva, Germany would rearm without constraint. All the Cabinet could agree was to express to Germany Britain's hopes that she would 'collaborate in the common task of establishing that confidence which is necessary to the success of the Disarmament Conference' and the aim of the four-power negotiations. Further discussion of German aims and possible counter-measures would await Hitler's speech.[74] Even though Hitler's promises that very day were treated with reserve and not taken at face value, his speech served to instil further uncertainty into British deliberations. Hope was not given up entirely that German foreign policy would take a more moderate direction once the internal revolution had run its course.[75]

Such illusions did not altogether fly in the face of the information provided by the Embassy in Berlin. Though Rumbold had been forthright in his analysis of *Mein Kampf* about the danger Hitler represented, he admitted in his final report, on 30 June 1933, before leaving Berlin for retirement, that he was unsure of the course of future German foreign policy. He was still uncertain whether Hitler was determining policy or was under the control of those around him, and hoped that he could rid himself of 'the undesirable leaders and elements in his party'.[76] A few weeks earlier, Vansittart had, in fact, specifically asked Rumbold to assess which was the most likely of three possible scenarios: collapse of Hitler's dictatorship through economic problems (resulting in either a military dictatorship or, less likely, Bolshevism and internal chaos); a complete consolidation of Hitler's hold on power, leading within four or five years to a new European war; or a preventive war against Germany before she became unassailable on account of rearmament.[77] A fourth, in his view unlikely but possible, development had been added at the time to Vansittart's trio, for presentation to the Cabinet, by Sir John Simon: a non-expansionist, peaceful foreign policy along the lines which, to this point, had been followed in Italy as the Fascist regime had settled down following the turbulent phase of the seizure and consolidation of power.[78] Significantly, if markedly at variance both with Simon's most likely scenario – successful establishment of power by Hitler, and a European war within four or five years – and with his own conclusions drawn from *Mein Kampf*, Rumbold chose the fourth prognosis as the most likely, envisaging, however, an eventual failure of the Nazi regime on account of economic problems and its replacement by a military dictatorship.[79] A Hitler aware of the dangers for Germany and for his regime of foreign intervention, and open to moderating influence from abroad, 'settling down' much as Mussolini had done in Italy, provided another straw for the Foreign Office experts on Germany to cling on to.

In a further misreading of the situation, these experts repeatedly expressed concern that Hitler was the 'front-man' for even more dangerous forces. In this case, there was less worry about the 'wild men' in the party, and more that Nazism was preparing the ground for a return to the militaristic and nationalistic 'Prussianism' – under the aegis of the army, the landowners, and the industrialists – that had led to the First World War. These traditional and powerful 'Nationalists', it was thought, would be even worse, even more dangerous, than the Nazis themselves. This bizarre notion that Hitler was not the worst outcome facing Britain persisted even down to the aftermath of the Röhm affair (in which the stormtroopers' leaders were massacred on Hitler's orders on 30 June 1934), when it was initally presumed that power had now shifted to the military.[80]

Some support for the notion that Hitler, if properly handled, could be utilized against the more dangerous forces in Germany that had once before plunged Europe into war, could be gleaned from the reports of the new Ambassador in Berlin, Sir Eric Phipps, a man of different calibre to Rumbold.[81] On his first encounter with the German dictator, Phipps had thought him 'unbalanced', and imagined that Britain would on any vital issue have to appeal to his emotions rather than to his reason.[82] In October 1933, Phipps was sceptical about Hitler's supposed pacific intentions. But he was prepared to qualify his scepticism by pointing to an idealism in National Socialism which, he thought, might 'prove of value to European politics'. He suggested that 'with skilful handling Herr Hitler and his movement may be brought to contribute some new impulse to European development', and that 'a sound disarmament convention with present-day Germany is, perhaps, not entirely a Utopian idea'.[83] A month later, Phipps again posed the fundamental question that puzzled British observers: was the 'true' Hitler the man who spoke of peace in his speeches, or the author of *Mein Kampf*, set on German expansion? Phipps gave an equivocal, but highly significant, answer. 'To revert to Hitler,' wrote Phipps. 'We cannot regard him solely as the author of "Mein Kampf", for in such [a] case we should logically be bound to adopt the policy of a "preventive" war.' In this strange way of thinking, the option of seeing Hitler as he actually was had to be ruled out because the consequences were unacceptable. But nor could Hitler be ignored. So, was not the best hope, Phipps asked, 'to bind him, that is, by an agreement bearing his signature freely and proudly given?' His sceptical response to his own question followed immediately: 'By some odd kink in his mental make-up he might even feel compelled to honour it.' Though any such agreement was unlikely to prove wholly satisfactory to Great Britain, France and Italy, it would buy time and could at least temporarily prevent 'any further German shots among the International ducks'.[84]

Peculiar though the argument was, Phipps was coming close to formulating what would be the guidelines of British policy towards Germany – guidelines which would eventually usher in appeasement: a preventive attack on Germany in 1933, it was widely agreed, had to be ruled out. Only fifteen years after the end of the war, public opinion in Great Britain, anxious above all to preserve peace, would, as the government knew, offer scant support for such a venture.[85] Disarmament, not the risk of a new conflagration, was the dominant theme – in government as well as in the public mood. Beyond that consideration, the state of British armaments made such an enterprise unthinkable. Moreover, no backing for such a move could be expected from the heavily isolationist USA. And in the light of the experience of 1923, when French troops had marched into the Ruhr, triggering political and economic crisis in Germany with wide international ramifications, France was also cool about a preventive strike.[86] In fact, the French Prime Minister, Edouard Daladier, categorically ruled out the possibility in a democratic country.[87] In any case, once Hitler had so rapidly consolidated power and won huge popular backing within Germany, such a move could scarcely be contemplated.

The only other possibilities, in Phipps' view, were the imposition of sanctions or the conclusion of an agreement with Germany which would grant her limited, but controlled, rearmament. Both courses depended upon 'a united front against undue German pretensions'. The Germans had to be made to fear that if they were unreasonable about an armaments convention, sanctions would follow. How illusory such musings were was evident to Phipps. The sense of fear was non-existent, 'for they bank on our all too palpable differences and inertia'.[88]

As Phipps had seen, British policy choices were severely constrained. The fabric of international security was already creaking dangerously. The League of Nations, however idealistic its principles, would soon prove its feebleness as a framework for ensuring collective security. Japanese aggression in Manchuria had already exposed the League's near paralysis in responding to armed might. Italy paid lip-service to the League's peaceable aims while hoping to profit from diplomatic disarray in making gains in the Mediterranean, largely at France's expense. The United States, still recoiling from its involvement in the First World War and anxious to remain aloof from Europe's own problems, had not joined the League. And the divisions between Britain and France, the two most important members, were plainly visible.

The insuperable difference between the British and the French on how to handle 'the German question', now that it had once again become acute, was indeed the crucial weakness in upholding the post-war order, as Hitler had quickly recognized. In the early post-war years, the French had sought far more punitive reparations than had the British – unsurprising given that the war had in part been fought on their soil. But with the ending of reparations in 1932, disarmament had become the dominant issue, and one that sharpened the divisions between the Allies, especially once Hitler introduced a new assertiveness into German foreign policy. The British government was anxious that Britain should disarm, and keen to press for international disarmament. In idealistic terms, it saw disarmament as the key to European peace and future prosperity. Materially, faced with deep economic depression at home, the government was keen to avoid further expensive commitments in Europe, particularly at a time when it had more than enough on its hands in upholding its interests in a worldwide empire and coping with the threat posed in the Far East by the prospect of Japanese expansionism. Disarmament was, therefore, vital. But the price was concession to German demands for equality of status. For the British, this was a sensible concession, as well as being fair. It would remove a serious grievance in Germany. And if it were not granted, it seemed likely that Germany would rearm anyway, ensuring in the medium if not short term both the dangers as well as the high cost of an expensive arms race. So the arguments for acceding to German demands for equality in armaments within the framework of general disarmament were, for the British government, compelling.

None of this assuaged the French. Equality of status in armaments for Germany meant, logically, either permitting Hitler's regime to rearm up to existing French and British levels, or reducing the armed capacity of the western powers to that of Germany. Neither could be contemplated by the French. Their country had been invaded twice in recent history by Germany, in 1870 and in 1914. The demilitarized strip along the Rhine, established at Versailles and confirmed in 1925 at the Treaty of Locarno, was insufficient safeguard against further aggression from a newly resurgent Germany. Not unnaturally, therefore, the French favoured security over disarmament. The British, on the other hand, thought that security could come about only *through* disarmament. Moreover, the French were prepared to make concessions on disarmament only if the British were ready to offer guarantees of intervention should Germany step out of line. The British were unwilling to give such guarantees. So the French continued adamantly to reject proposals directed towards equality of status for Germany since they saw in this a plain threat to their own security. But, however strong the rhetoric, the French position was much weaker than it seemed. Alliances with Poland and Czechoslovakia were, as time would show, to offer no genuine bolster to France's security in the face of a resurgent Germany. The League of Nations provided scant grounds for confidence. And though France still had the largest army on the Continent, it was unmodernized and structured heavily around defence.[89] The defensive mentality was most plainly evident in the building of the mighty fortifications, the Maginot Line, stretching along France's eastern frontier as a bulwark against German aggression. The reality was that France was in no position to take action against Germany without British backing – which, diplomatic niceties could barely conceal, would not be forthcoming. Despite apparent strength, therefore, France was in practice severely limited in its scope for action.

On her side, Britain was left with a threat, a bluff which before 1939 Hitler repeatedly and successfully called, that she would act to defend her interests; and the hope that the German dictator could be brought to the conference table to agree a general settlement of Europe's problems.[90] But real hopes of involving Hitler in multilateral arms talks and a European agreement were already dashed by the autumn of 1933. With the German withdrawal from the League of Nations on 14 October, the prospects of the four-power pact, initiated by Mussolini and signed on 15 July (though not ratified), were effectively killed stone dead.[91]

Britain did not give up hope, even then, that Germany could be persuaded to return to Geneva and reintegrated into a cooperative European security system. An immediate reaction to the German withdrawal from the League of Nations was the establishment in London of the Defence Requirements Committee, with a remit to explore the deficiencies of Britain's armed forces and to propose steps towards rearmament. The Committee, chaired by Sir Maurice Hankey, the longstanding Cabinet Secretary, defined 'Germany as the ultimate potential enemy against whom our long-range defensive policy must be directed'.[92] Another major and obvious threat was Japan, already ominously menacing British interests in the Far East. And a resurgent Italy could pose future problems in the Mediterranean, if not handled properly. Britain's international position plainly did not make the problem of Hitler's Germany any easier to deal with.

Ramsay MacDonald, the Prime Minister, was even now dissatisfied at the singling out of Germany and dispatched Anthony Eden, Parliamentary Under-Secretary in the Foreign Office, to European capitals to attempt to revitalize the negotiations for a European settlement. Eden returned reasonably optimistic about Hitler's peaceful intentions, and hope momentarily flickered that Germany could, after all, be brought back to the conference table. Any illusions were dissipated by the publication of the Reich budget on 26 March 1934, indicating substantial increases in military expenditure. On 17 April, the French government made it plain that, with Germany evidently rearming, further disarmament talks were pointless. At the end of April the Disarmament Conference adjourned indefinitely.[93] One strand of the British strategy to rein in Hitler had failed at the first hurdle.

The other was to make plain to Hitler that Britain would defend her interests. But, particularly to impress such a man as Hitler, and with German rearmament plainly making rapid progress,[94] this needed the backing of armed strength. And in this regard, the results of the Defence Requirements Committee's recommendations on rearmaments had been meagre. In the question of air defence in particular – Lord Londonderry's sphere of responsibility, to which we will return – only modest steps were taken.[95] Despite awareness that Germany was rearming, the shock was all the greater, therefore, when, in March 1935, Göring announced the existence of a German air force and Hitler the reintroduction of conscription and plans for a *Wehrmacht* of 550,000 men – both plain breaches of the Versailles Treaty. Vain British and French attempts a month earlier to prevent precisely such a unilateral flouting of the military stipulations of Versailles by incorporating Germany in a 'general agreement' on European security, particularly air armaments and border questions in central and eastern Europe, were at one fell swoop vitiated by Hitler's spectacular move.[96] The lame British response was restricted to a diplomatic protest and the postponement of a planned visit to Berlin by Simon and Eden. Even this visit was then shortly afterwards reinstated, to Berlin's delight.[97] Britain's weakness could scarcely have been more plainly advertised. And all that came from this latest attempt to persuade Hitler of the need for Germany's involvement in a general European settlement were an indication from the German dictator – which shocked the British public as well as the government – that Germany had already reached parity in air strength with Britain, and Britain's readiness to pursue bilateral talks aimed at a naval treaty (which would come to fruition, as a major triumph for Germany and to the chagrin of Britain's allies, the French, in June 1935).[98]

Britain was by now fully embarked upon her fateful course of foreign policy towards Germany. Ambivalent about Hitler, she had preferred to believe his peaceful intentions to the implications of a literal reading of *Mein Kampf*. Belief that he could be persuaded to negotiate around the conference table had simply led to Britain being outmanoeuvred by Germany. And now the chance for action while Germany remained weak had gone – if it had ever existed in the first place. All that was left was the ever more transparent fig-leaf of strength in a fading world power to confront the ever more obvious military might of a revitalized and powerful nation at the centre of Europe with plainly stated (and, it was widely thought, justifiable) revisionist intent. The road to a belated policy of appeasement – that is, offering concessions from a position of weakness – was open.

III

There were those in Britain, not in government but nevertheless possessing some standing, who favoured a different policy altogether towards Germany and a completely different way of handling Hitler – one aimed more directly and uncritically at courting the friendship of a country with, in their eyes, legitimate grievances and a leader who had repeatedly emphasized his desire for good relations with Britain. In their view, it was still not too late to make every effort to win German friendship – necessary, they believed, if the catastrophe of another war were to be avoided. Actively working to bring about the revision of central and eastern European borders in Germany's favour would, they thought, contribute towards achieving this worthwhile end, and would in any case be merely putting right what Britain had helped to put wrong through the Versailles Treaty. Beyond that, Germany was seen as the best hope of preventing the spread of Bolshevism. However objectionable it might be in some respects, Nazism, they claimed, was preferable to Communism.

It is impossible to know with any degree of precision how many people thought this way, how many German sympathizers or 'fellow-travellers' there were in Britain at this time. But the number was not small, and it included some influential figures (even if the Foreign

Office, with its detailed sources of information not generally accessible, remained immune to their arguments). Those from an aristocratic, gentry or military background, whose natural political home was the right wing of the Conservative Party, were prominent among them. Support for German revisionist demands fitted easily for many from such social strata not only with a pronounced anti-Communism and a belief that Britain's interests lay in protecting her Empire, not in 'interfering' in Europe, but also with a deep-seated cultural pessimism, a racist leaning towards the superior 'teutonic stock' binding Germany and England together and admiration for the 'revitalization' that Hitler had achieved in contrast to a perceived democratic decadence and decline. Generalizations, even about these sectors of British society, are hazardous. Many, from similar backgrounds, held quite different and conflicting views. And for the wider public, in the absence of modern forms of opinion survey, we must depend upon such crude measures as newspaper circulation figures as the roughest of guides to shadings of attitude.

In the early years of Hitler's rule, the most pro-German daily newspaper in Britain with a national readership was the *Daily Mail*, whose circulation each day was over 1.5 million.[99] Regular readers of a newspaper that repeatedly expressed its admiration for Hitler were at least potential supporters of a more active attempt to court German friendship. If readership can be estimated at three or four times the circulation figure, then 4.5 to 6 million people in Britain at the time were not adverse to a more pro-German policy than the government was pursuing. In addition, such views certainly had at least some following among readers of other newspapers on the political Right, including, from the quality press, *The Times* and the *Daily Telegraph*. In direct opposition were the attitudes of those broadly on the Left. Pro-German sentiment was, naturally, anathema to a larger swathe of opinion among readers of the *Daily Herald*, the Labour Party newspaper (circulation over 2 million per day), the *News Chronicle* (circulation around 1.3 million daily), with its longstanding links to the Liberal Party, and the liberal *Manchester Guardian*, small in circulation but important in influence. In between were those, from all classes of society and walks of life forming a substantial, if unquantifiable, body of opinion, who thought Hitler's rule in various ways repellent but that domestic affairs were the

Germans' own business. The threat of external aggression towards Britain and eventual war did not appear imminent in the early years of the Nazi regime, and the German nationalist clamour, if distasteful, was widely thought rather understandable and some adjustment to the unfair stipulations of the Versailles Treaty necessary. While not pro-German, and certainly not sympathetic to the Nazis, such opinion was not outrightly opposed to some concessions to Germany, perhaps in the colonial question, where the acquisition of Germany's colonies by the victors in 1918 was widely viewed as punitive and unfair.

With loathing at one extreme and admiration at the other, Hitler had done much to polarize opinion within Britain. If the admirers were in a distinct minority, it was a larger minority than is often imagined, and of the admirers, only a fraction were out-and-out Fascists and racial anti-Semites of the Nazi ilk. The British Union of Fascists, under the leadership of Oswald Mosley, was able at its peak in the early 1930s to gain a membership of, at most, some 50,000 persons and did not contest a single seat at the 1935 general election.[100] Moreover, the Mosleyites' model around this time was Italy, rather than Nazi Germany.[101] But 'fellow-travelling' stretched much further than outright Fascist supporters, and fanatics, eccentrics and crackpots. Among Conservative Party supporters, who in the early 1930s greatly outnumbered the adherents of the diminished Liberal Party and the defeated and broken Labour Party, backing for at least some facets of Nazi rule – authority, order, strong leadership, discipline, anti-Communism – was widespread.

The rise of German military strength and the threat to British interests that this posed was, of course, a mounting worry. But, since Hitler repeatedly claimed (in well-publicized statements and interviews for sections of the British press) that he had no wish to harm the Empire but wanted merely a fair hand for Germany in Europe, revision of the unfair provisions of Versailles, a united German people (prevented by the loss of territory populated by ethnic Germans) and British friendship – not least against the common enemy of Bolshevism – the feeling persisted in circles wider than those of fully fledged Fascist supporters that to reciprocate Germany's offer of an olive branch was more likely to head off future conflict than the weak but hostile posturing of the government.

An indication of the nuances of strongly pro-German feeling can be gleaned by glancing briefly at the quite differently motivated stance of three prominent individuals who enjoyed, in various ways, considerable influence and standing in British society around the time Hitler took power in Germany. None should be seen as necessarily representative of the views of a social class. In each case, the personal idiosyncrasies and ideological proclivities are plain to see. Yet, taken together, the distinguished elderly general, the aristocratic Conservative newspaper tycoon and the devout 'intellectual' Liberal peer do reflect attitudes that had wide currency in their social strata: belief in authority and military values; strident anti-Communism; a sense of British democracy in decline; and defence of a threatened empire.

General Sir Ian Standish Monteith Hamilton, aged eighty when Hitler came to power, former Chief of Staff to Lord Kitchener during the Boer War and subsequently Commander in Chief of the ill-fated British Mediterranean Expeditionary Force at Gallipoli in 1915, became after 1933 one notable advocate of friendship with Nazi Germany. Hamilton was Scottish President of the British Legion, the huge ex-servicemen's organization which already in the 1920s was prominent in its support for Germany (and would be so after 1933), based on the camaraderie among those who had fought, even on opposing sides, in the First World War.[102] Given these leanings, it was not surprising that Hamilton was a founder-member in 1928 of the Anglo-German Association, which long before the Nazis took power was cultivating and promoting pro-German feeling in Britain.

The foundation of the Association in 1928 owed a good deal to the initiative of Dr Margarete Gärtner, the director, inspiration and leading figure of an organization she had established in 1922, independent of the German government but financed predominantly by heavy industry, the Wirtschaftspolitische Gesellschaft (Political Economy Society). The Society's objective was to exploit contacts in Britain to build goodwill towards Germany, and particularly to capitalize upon the feeling that the Germans had been badly wronged in 1919, by garnering support for the German case aimed at revision of the territorial stipulations of the Versailles Treaty. Dr Gärtner was well situated to undertake such work – conducted through study tours, lectures and personal introductions – through her experience, from the beginning of the First World War onwards, in a variety of German propaganda activities.[103] By 1928, she had gathered sufficient backing to set up the Anglo-German Association, with branches both in England and in Germany, under the joint presidency of Lord Reading (a former Lord Chancellor and Viceroy of India) and Wilhelm Cuno (Reich Chancellor at the time of the great inflation of 1923 and chairman of the Hamburg-Amerika shipping line). The inaugural meeting of the London branch laid down the promotion of 'good understanding between Germany and Great Britain' as its purpose. Prominent names in political, economic and cultural life figured in the lists of those to be invited to join, both in Britain and in Germany. Among those included in a list of members in December 1929 was the Marquess of Londonderry.[104]

Sir Ian Hamilton was a Vice-President of the Association from its inception. At a dinner of the Association at the Café Royal in London in July 1929 in honour of a German guest, a member of the Reichstag, Hamilton gave an address in which he spoke of it being in Britain's interest to come 'to good terms with her German cousin. Seeing both countries had envious rivals who would try their level best to keep them apart, the sooner England came out into the open as the friend of Germany the better.'[105] In 1931 he thought it would be 'rather fun' to invite Hitler to an Association dinner, and was curious to see him, but thought better of the idea (especially when J. L. Garvin, the renowned editor of the *Observer*, whom he had consulted, told him it would be 'most unwise').[106] At the time, of course, Germany was still a democracy – if one in the throes of what would prove a terminal crisis. Hamilton did not change his tune on the need for Anglo-German friendship once the democracy gave way to dictatorship. What did alter, however, was his stance towards Jews in the Association.

In 1928 he had been happy to serve as Vice-President under the President, Lord Reading, a prominent British Jew. Even before the time Reading resigned from the Association, in April 1933 following the notorious Nazi boycott, Hamilton, while asserting that he had 'no anti-Jewish prejudice' (and had been favoured as a commander by Jewish soldiers during the war), was refusing to send a protest letter to the German Ambassador about the persecution of the Jews.[107] By May, Hamilton thought much of the press reportage about Germany was false but, worried about the prospect of further resignations, which '(unless they are Jews) would be a positive slap in the face for Germany and very much to be deprecated', took the view it might be better to put the Association 'into cold storage' for a while.[108] In June, he told the Association's secretary, he thought 'everyone will agree it would be unwise at present to offer our membership to any Jewish gentleman'.[109] To a German correspondent in November 1933, Hamilton acknowledged that he was 'an admirer of the great Adolph [sic] Hitler and have done my best to support him through some difficult times', while he excused *Mein Kampf* to a Dutch correspondent as no more than a product of Hitler's youth.[110] Hamilton's own negative opinion on Jews, which recurs in his correspondence during the 1930s, was certainly not Hitlerian. But it had a distinct racial edge to it, beyond the conventional anti-Jewish sentiment which was commonplace at the time in much of the British upper class, in that he was prepared to stipulate negative physical features and behavioural characteristics of Jews.[111] And it was coupled with a belief in the power of the Jews. 'It is extremely dangerous for anyone to displease the Jews,' he remarked in one of his letters, 'as they are so enormously powerful in the Press that they can usually manage to ruin their enemies in the long run.'[112]

The dissolution of the German branch of the Association in autumn 1934 (soon to be replaced by a thoroughly nazified version) – prompted by it still having some 'non-Aryan' members, and a natural corollary of the wider 'coordination' of organizational life in Germany under Hitler's regime – necessarily plunged the British branch into crisis and raised the question whether it could survive in its current form.[113] It evidently staggered on for some time, but by spring 1935 its dissolution was imminent. The issue of Jews as members of the society became a central one. Strong views on a dissolution were expressed in March at a meeting of the Executive Council in London, following which Hamilton consulted a British officer he knew, Andrew Thorne, who was attached to the Embassy in Berlin, on the 'ticklish affair'. 'I personally speak', he said, 'from the standpoint of one who is sympathetic with [sic] the Jews but does not feel it is patriotic or right of his countrymen to let the whole question of internationalism be clouded over by this one aspect of Germany's present condition.' The Jews and their sympathizers in the Association 'would prefer to smash up the whole concern', he added, rather than see it reconstituted with their exclusion. Thorne replied advising 'that only well-wishers of modern Germany should be invited to form the Committee or join the Association', thereby excluding 'the Jew with a grudge against modern Germany'. Since the Association only existed to encourage amicable relations between present-day states, he went on, those who insisted on living in the past 'whether Jews, Monarchists, Liberals or Republicans' had 'no right to a place in the reconstituted Association'. Hamilton relayed the gist of Thorne's letter to the treasurer of the Association, Dr J. G. Vance, who preferred dissolution to a discussion of the 'Jewish Question' at the next meeting. On 2 April 1935, the Anglo-German Association was duly dissolved. Already prior to this, Hamilton had been approached by a former member of the Association, Colonel Richard Meinertzhagen,[114] about joining a new organization currently being set up, the Anglo-German Fellowship, which, encouraged by the German Embassy, was to become far more assertive in its support of Nazi Germany (and would come to number Lord Londonderry among its members). Meinertzhagen, who had been a British intelligence officer during the First World War, was a distinguished ornithologist, later known for his exploits as a big-game hunter in Africa, and – curiously, given his pro-German stance at the time – for his pronounced support of Zionism. He had not agreed, he told Hamilton, with 'the negative policy pursued' by the Anglo-German Association and had been in touch with 'an influential body of business men and others' engaged in forming the new organization. Vance advised Hamilton to proffer a general expression of goodwill but no more. 'You know that the gentleman in question stands for the formation of a pro-Nazi group in England,' he wrote. 'I think that you and I stand for something utterly different. We do not wish particularly to support any Party, any Policy, any Constitution, nor any form of Government nor any scheme or plan. What we want is to work for some real understanding between two peoples who, apart from the barrier of speech, could so readily understand one another.'[115]

Vance was doubtless sincere in his own views, and in what he took to be Hamilton's. But it was naive to presume that working for understanding between Germany and Britain at this juncture could be possible without at least indirect sympathy and support for the Nazi regime – greatly welcome to the German government when it came from prominent individuals like Hamilton. On more than one occasion, Hamilton protested that he was taking no part in politics and that the British Legion was a non-political organization.[116] This was disingenuous. The British Legion, an organization with over 450,000 members by the mid-1930s,[117] was, despite its own protestations on non-political activity, dragged willy-nilly into the political arena with statements during official visits to Germany (where representatives met Hitler, Himmler, and other leading figures of the Nazi regime) that Britain's war against Germany had been an enormous mistake and must never be allowed to happen again.[118] Hamilton himself was given the red-carpet treatment when, aged eighty-one, he went to Berlin in January 1934 for the ceremonial reinstatement by Reich President Hindenburg, in the presence of General Werner von Blomberg, the Army Minister, of drums of the Gordon Highlanders which had been left in Belgium and brought to Germany during the First World War.[119] In later years, he was to host the visit of a German national delegation of ex-servicemen to Britain, lead an official British Legion visit to Germany (at which he spent a night, in August 1938, as Hitler's guest at his alpine retreat above Berchtesgaden), hold speeches and write letters to the British press in support of Germany, refuse on a number of occasions to intercede for Jews, and continue an extensive private exchange of letters (always impeccably courteous in tone, but repeatedly revealing his underlying anti-Semitism, apologias for Germany and admiration of Hitler) with German and British correspondents.[120] All this was 'non-political' only in his own interpretation of what amounted to politics, and that of those who shared his views.

Hamilton was a pillar of the British Establishment, certainly no Nazi despite his expressed approval of much that Hitler and his regime stood for, and undoubtedly well-meaning if guileless in his efforts to bring about friendship between Britain and Germany. He succeeded, however, only in making himself, and the organization he represented – the British Legion – vehicles of Nazi propaganda.

Lord Rothermere, a second example of figures of weight and importance who favoured a positive approach to the new Germany, took this still further by using his own mass-media outlets to publicize the case for support of Hitler's regime. The thick-set, heavy-jowled, pugnacious and dynamic owner of the *Daily Mail* was a living caricature of the archetypal press baron.[121] He had been born Harold Sydney Harmsworth in 1868 and was created Baron Rothermere in 1914, then 1st Viscount five years later (after he had served briefly in 1917–18 as Air Minister). He was the owner of the *Daily Mirror* between 1914 and 1931, and, after the death of his brother, Lord Northcliffe (with whom he had built up his newspaper empire), he had become the proprietor of the *Daily Mail* together with the *Evening News* and Associated Newspapers Ltd in 1922.[122] By the mid-1920s, when the circulation of the *Daily Mail* had reached the 2 million mark, Rothermere was reckoned to be among the richest men in England, and was moving politically ever farther to the Right. His wide-circulation newspapers gave him power and, potentially, significant influence. But he had few friends in government circles, where he was regarded as a maverick, unstable in his allegiances.[123] The trigger to his shortlived support for Mosley's British Union of Fascists and to his more protracted admiration for Hitler was his almost manic anti-Communism, which, somewhat bizarrely, had driven him to accumulate large estates in central Hungary as an insurance against a Communist invasion of Great Britain.[124] Rothermere believed fervently that offering Hitler friendship and a free hand in eastern Europe, where he could take on and destroy Bolshevism, was in Britain's national interest, and the only way to avoid a second disastrous war. But 'the salvation of Britain', as he put it, meant at the same time taking no chances. Disarmament had left Britain dangerously exposed. Rothermere was the earliest public voice – and initially isolated and disparaged in his views – clamouring for the speediest and most comprehensive British rearmament, most notably in the air.[125] In his combination of making friends with Hitler, but building a strong air force, he was advancing views close to those that Lord Londonderry would adopt.

Once Hitler became Chancellor, Rothermere lost little time in registering his approval. In July 1933, in a *Daily Mail* editorial, he voiced his confident expectation that Nazi rule would bring great benefits to Germany. Prior to Hitler, the German nation had been 'rapidly falling under the control of its alien elements', he asserted, with twenty times as many Jewish government officials as had existed before the war. Detractors of the Nazis in Britain were, he claimed, precisely those who were 'most vehement in their praise of the Soviet regime in Russia'. What they called 'Nazi atrocities' amounted to 'merely a few isolated acts of violence' which had been blown up out of all proportion.[126] Later in the year, he spoke of 'sturdy young Nazis' as 'Europe's guardians against the Communist danger' and saw no danger to western Europe in allowing 'the gigantic reservoir of German nationalist energy' to 'overflow' into 'the thinly populated areas of Western Russia'.[127] He saw Hitler as a 'creature of destiny', 'a great pacific regenerator and builder of his nation' (later claiming that he deliberately used flattering language to appeal to 'the better side of Herr Hitler' in working for good relations with Germany).[128]

Hitler, for his part, was keen to cultivate Rothermere's support. His Foreign Minister, Baron Konstantin von Neurath, had told him how important it would be to have Rothermere's backing.[129] Rothermere, Hitler later commented, had told him emphatically that it must never again come to war between England and Germany.[130] In December 1934, Rothermere, accompanied by his son, Esmond Harmsworth, and George Ward Price (the *Daily Mail*'s European correspondent, later a friend and frequent correspondent of Lord Londonderry), was a guest of honour in the Reich Chancellery at the first major dinner-party Hitler held for foreign visitors. Also present was the English merchant banker Ernest Tennant, an early apologist for Hitler's regime. Tennant had already proved useful in introducing Joachim von Ribbentrop, the one-time champagne salesman whose foreign contacts had enabled him to rise high in Hitler's favour, to influential figures in English society and in government.[131] Among the twenty-three guests on the German side were Hermann Göring and Emmy Sonnemann, the actress whom he was to marry, the Propaganda Minister Joseph Goebbels and his wife, Magda, the Foreign Minister, von Neurath, and his wife, and the Ribbentrops. Rothermere's delight at his reception was plain to see.[132] And the visit was predictably followed by yet a further effusive piece in the *Daily Mail* about the wonders Hitler had done for Germany.[133]

At the beginning of May 1935, Hitler, not for the first time, wrote to Rothermere. After the stir a few weeks earlier, at the reintroduction of conscription and announcement of a German air force, the dictator was keen to mend fences, and would later in the month hold another major 'peace-speech' in the Reichstag. Hitler stressed to Lord Rothermere his 'unalterable determination to render a historically great contribution to the restoration of a good and enduring understanding between both great Germanic peoples'. He rejected 'the so-called mutual assistance pacts which are being hatched today' as a recipe for discord, but claimed that 'an Anglo-German understanding would form in Europe a force for peace and reason of 120 million people of the highest type', and profusely thanked Rothermere again for his support.[134] Hitler plainly expected that Rothermere would circulate his letter among the high and mighty in the land. Rothermere did precisely that, assuming that his standing and his personal contact to Hitler would pave the way for a breakthrough in Anglo-German relations and forge the basis of friendship that he – and Hitler – wanted. It was far from the last time that a Briton bearing a noble title would make the same presumption. But, as in later instances, Rothermere would be disappointed. Hitler's letter, which reached even as far as King George V, was coolly received, not least since the notion of friendship with the Germans flew in the face of a central tenet of British foreign policy: maintenance of strong and friendly relations with the French.[135] This was the rock on which all subsequent attempts to pursue the same line would also founder.

Of quite different character to Lord Rothermere was Philip Henry Kerr, the 11th Marquess of Lothian, an 'insider' in political circles and a leading figure in the Liberal Party. But in his search for a way to avoid war and bring lasting peace to Europe, Lothian, too, was prepared to work for a policy of close friendship with Germany and ready to believe in Hitler's peaceful intentions.[136] Born in 1882, Kerr had in early 1905, together with others from his student generation at Oxford, gone to South Africa. There, where he remained for over four years, and then afterwards back in England, he came strongly under the influence of Alfred Lord Milner, the dominant figure in shaping British policy in the region prior to and immediately after the Boer War, and, following his resignation in 1905, the leading inspiration of imperialists and arch-protagonist of a strengthened and unified British Empire. Distinguished in appearance, somewhat aloof and austere, though not lacking personal charm, the strongly religious Kerr (a devout Catholic in early life who later became a Christian Scientist) had – in the less than flattering description of one of his friends – 'an oratorical temperament and delighted in communicating a profusion of opinions and ideals to any casual group of listeners, in elevated abstract diction', conveying 'a fallacious lucidity of one who had done the thinking and solved the difficulties'.[137] More bluntly, another contemporary labelled him an 'incurably superficial Johnny know-all'.[138] He fervently believed in the British Empire as a power for good in the world but, even before the First World War, saw looming crisis for the Empire as German antagonism to Britain's pre-eminence mounted.[139] From the middle of the First World War, Kerr served as Private Secretary to the British Prime Minister, David Lloyd George. In 1931–2 he briefly held positions in the National Government as Chancellor of the Duchy of Lancaster then Under-Secretary for India. By this time, after succeeding to the Lothian title in 1930, he was one of the Liberal Party's chief spokesmen in the House of Lords.

Once Hitler had taken power, Lothian rapidly recognized the new potential threat that a strengthened Germany would pose to the British Empire. It was an even more dangerous prospect than the one which had already concerned him so deeply before 1914. Given to slightly airy theorizing and leaning on his presumption that Nazism was a nationalist but not imperialist movement, Lothian argued that a less emollient approach to France and winning German cooperation through giving Germany 'a square deal in Central Europe' was the best way of preserving the Empire.[140] His lack of knowledge of the German language, the German people, or the character of the man who was now dictating the country's policy did not deter him from his nobly intentioned but short-sighted attempt to pursue this objective.[141] Like others who endeavoured to work together with the Nazis in the hope of peace, there was a certain gullibility about him. As late as July 1938 he was prepared to host, at his stately home, Blickling Hall in Norfolk, a weekend gathering of a number of German visitors, mostly Nazis, who engaged in cordial discussions with a number of British guests sympathetic to Germany, aimed at furthering good

Anglo-German relations.[142] His dealings with Hitler would tend to corroborate the view of one contemporary, who thought Lothian 'apt to be the victim of his most recent experience'.[143]

'Like most Liberals', Lothian wrote privately in November 1933, 'I loathe the Nazi regime, but I am sure that the first condition to reform it is that we should be willing to do justice to Germany.' Nazi excesses, he thought, were largely a product of their exploitation of a sense of injustice and inferiority (and were accompanied by 'much that is healthy and self-respecting' in the 'Nazi renaissance'). In any case, Germany had to be given equality by agreement, otherwise it would come about by illegal rearmament.[144] How the agreed equality in arms would be achieved, since France would not allow German rearmament and not disarm herself without the reassurance of cast-iron guarantees of immediate sanctions by other countries for breach of any agreement reached, was unclear. And since Lothian had scant confidence in the ability of the League of Nations to offer realistic safeguards, the question of how the universal disarmament he desired should be guaranteed by international agreement – even presuming Germany's willingness to be involved – and at the same time French fears of German strength allayed, was left in the air. He vaguely, optimistically and (given American isolationism) wholly unrealistically put his faith in the United States' readiness to cooperate with Great Britain in helping to put teeth into a guarantee of a disarmament agreement.[145] But, however utopian his thinking, the key to a future peaceful Europe for Lothian remained the removal of Germany's sense of grievance and injustice, which in his eyes was well warranted. However much he and others loathed the brutality of the Nazi regime, his view, and that of those who supported him, was that Britain had no choice but to work for a better understanding with Germany for the sake of European peace and the future of the Empire.

Like others who preceded him and were to follow him (including Lord Londonderry), Lothian deluded himself that, with official channels apparently stymied, he could achieve by way of personal contact what the Foreign Office was seemingly incapable of attaining through more conventional channels. The suggestion that he should seek a private audience with Hitler had apparently come in late 1934 from a great admirer of the new Germany, an Oxford graduate who had lectured on Anglo-German diplomatic history during the previous two years at Königsberg University in East Prussia, T. P. Conwell-Evans. Befriended by Ribbentrop, Conwell-Evans would more than once over the coming years serve as a go-between in establishing influential, or supposedly influential, links for the Nazi regime in England. Nazi leaders for their part, as would later be the case with Londonderry, were more than eager to believe that an Englishman with an aristo-cratic title and friends in high places could have his uses. Von Ribbentrop, then Reich Commissioner for Disarmament, and the German Ambassador in London, Leopold von Hoesch, duly engi-neered the meeting Lothian sought with Hitler, which was arranged for 29 January 1935. The Ambassador described Lothian as 'without doubt the most important non-official Englishman who has so far asked to be received by the Chancellor', and indicated that he was 'favourably inclined towards Germany and wishes to contribute to promoting better understanding between Germany and England'.[146]

Von Ribbentrop and Rudolf Hess, Deputy Leader of the Nazi Party, were also present, along with Conwell-Evans (who acted as interpreter), when Lothian and Hitler met. The audience lasted in all for some two and a half hours. Lothian began the proceedings by stat-ing the need for a political and armaments agreement, giving Germany fundamental equality. He was then treated to a classic – though skilfully couched and effective – Hitler monologue, surveying the diplomatic landscape, castigating Communism and emphasizing the threat it posed to British as well as German interests, indicating his distrust of the French and detestation of the Russians, and mak-ing plain that he saw no basis for any international agreement that was not preceded by an arms agreement worked out between Germany and Britain. He saw no reason why this should not be achieved, and welcomed the prospect of discussions between London and Berlin with the object of devising a plan to stabilize Europe for ten years. He explicitly ruled out the use of force towards Poland, France, the Low Countries and Austria, emphasized Germany's deter-mination not to have war, and ended by remarking that the 'greatest madness' had been the war of 1914 between the English and the Germans. Lothian said he would report back to London.[147] This he did, helping to pave the way for the visit to Berlin a few weeks later of Simon and Eden. He also advertised the outcome of his visit and his views about Germany in letters to *The Times* and actively involved himself over the coming months as an intermediary between the German government and Whitehall.[148] Among those to whom he expressed cautious optimism arising from his visit was Lord Londonderry. 'I had an interesting time with Hitler,' Lothian wrote. 'It is going to be a difficult job but I think it is possible to get a basis for assured peace in Europe for ten years if we go about it the right way.'[149] Within months, Londonderry would be following Lothian's path to the Reich Chancellery, with the same object in mind.

Rothermere and Lothian, with their entirely distinctive political outlooks, were among the first of a line of British visitors to beat a path to Hitler's door in the well-intentioned but deluded hope that their personal understanding of what the German dictator 'really' wanted and their publicizing of this, or use of personal contacts and influence at home (which, self-importantly, they invariably inflated), would succeed where officialdom was found wanting. As has been correctly noted, 'with the best intentions in the world they thus became the unpaid servants of German and Nazi Foreign Policy'.[150] Other than Londonderry himself, in early 1936, such visitors (invariably coming away enthused by their audience with the Führer and convinced of his sincerity and reasonableness) would include the Labour pacifists Lord Allen of Hurtwood[151] and the former party leader George Lansbury (the latter at least achieving something: the tightening up of the dress code in the Reich Chancellery after he had turned up in a woolly sweater and crumpled suit), and – notoriously – the former Liberal Prime Minister, David Lloyd George. In each case, as with Lord Lothian (who, indeed, went on to be appointed to the key position of British Ambassador to Washington in 1939–40), the contemporary reputation and standing of these individuals survived relatively little tarnished by their brush with the Nazi leader. With Londonderry, it was to prove a different story.

2

Downfall of the Air Minister

'There are three possible eventualities. The first is that we should be successful in converting the Germans into helpful partners in the scheme of the world; the second is that if the first fails we should be in a position, by knowing what the Germans are doing, to immobilize their hostile activities; and the third is that if the Germans are determined, as some think they are, to be wholly aggressive and unwilling to join in a peaceful comity of nations, then they will stand arraigned in their true colours before the world.'

Lord Londonderry, 22 November 1934

Lord Londonderry became notorious in the second half of the 1930s for his strong support of Nazi Germany. But in the first half of that dismal decade, only oblique signs of what was later so apparent could be glimpsed. During most of that time, between 1931 and 1935, he was Secretary of State for Air. As a great aviation enthusiast, and attracted by the power that went with high office, there was – with the possible exception of the post of Foreign Secretary, to which his aptitude and abilities (whatever his ambition and even a certain presumption of his suitability) did not qualify him – no position he coveted more.[1]

He was appointed to office on 5 November 1931, and showered with congratulatory letters and telegrams – including one from his kinsman, Winston Churchill.[2] A few days earlier, Lady Londonderry had visited Chequers, the Prime Minister's country seat in Buckinghamshire, and enjoyed a long Sunday walk with her friend

Ramsay MacDonald, who afterwards recalled in his characteristic overblown rhetoric the 'woods of gorgeous raiment', and 'a land of serene dignity and graciousness', telling her that she 'made me forget everything which did not belong to that order of things. I was your attendant gillie.'[3] That he owed his elevation to his wife's friendship with the Prime Minister would make difficulties for Londonderry throughout his term of office. But these difficulties would pale against the unforeseen problems which the new occupant of the Reich Chancellery in Berlin would cause Londonderry – and the whole British government.

Londonderry would rapidly become exposed to problems which neither he nor his colleagues in the British government were temperamentally equipped to handle. Having imbibed the aristocratic values of Victorian and Edwardian England, he was still idealistic enough to presume that politics (and most notably foreign affairs) were determined by goodwill, moral objectives, the gentleman's code of honour, the preservation of legal order – and of course the might of the British Empire. Grievous mistakes had been made before 1914 that had led to the carnage of the First World War and the destruction of old Europe. It was the supreme task of British politicians to prevent such a catastrophe ever recurring. With international cooperation this could be achieved. Londonderry thought the air force, as the newest of the armed forces and still in many ways a Cinderella, would gain its rightful place as part of the post-war order in ensuring the security of Great Britain and her imperial possessions, which was his overriding concern. He was wholly unprepared for the rough, tough world of the 1930s – for the world of the Mussolinis and the Hitlers, where the mailed fist and political thuggery were what counted. Londonderry's experience of trying to cope with the onset of Hitler in a ministry which, from relative unimportance, was catapulted into the very centre of the mounting political turmoil in Britain, as the country sought to respond to the challenge of massive and rapid German rearmament, would not turn him overnight into an outright supporter of the new Germany. But it would be a critical staging post on the way to his later German sympathies. It is important to see how, and to chart that path.

I

In 1932, Londonderry became a member of the British delegation to the Disarmament Conference in Geneva. Though only now called into existence, the roots of the Conference lay back in immediate post-war hopes and idealism. The insoluble problems which were to defeat it were equally a legacy of the war.

The Versailles Treaty did not just impose disarmament on the defeated Germany; it also envisaged this as a step to general arms limitation. It was widely believed that the build-up of arms had contributed signally to the calamity of 1914. To scale down levels of armaments in all nations would consequently, it was presumed, help to avoid the Continent once more plunging into disastrous war. It was a noble thought. Most people, certainly in the western democracies and also in the USA (which was to join the Disarmament Conference while staying out of the League of Nations), subscribed readily to it. Disarmament, many fervently hoped, was the prerequisite for future peace. But not all thought that way. And practice did not accord with such ideals. Some countries had no interest even in acceding to the principle, and strove to build up their armed power instead of aiming to reduce it. Japan was one, Soviet Russia (though consumed by internal problems) another. Italy's expansionist aims depended upon extending its armed strength. And in Germany's fragile and contested democracy, the military (and some other powerful groups), though compelled to accept disarmament, looked to a time in the future when such restrictions could be ended. The refusal of the western democracies, while preaching disarmament, actually to disarm themselves, could only fuel resentment.

By the mid-1920s, nothing had come of the aim of disarmament enunciated in 1919. To work for a general agreement on disarmament to the lowest limits compatible with national security was indeed now enshrined as an undertaking of the signatories to the Locarno Pact of 1925 and as a central objective of the League of Nations. By 1930, however, after four years of deliberation, a

Preparatory Disarmament Commission had failed to make any real headway on arms reduction and succeeded only in underlining the irreconcilable differences between Germany (anxious to abolish the detested one-sided military restrictions of Versailles, and to attain equality) and France (insistent for reasons of national security on retention of the military clauses of the Treaty). This unbridgeable gulf between German demands for equality and French insistence upon security would continue to bedevil the deliberations of the successor to the Commission, the Disarmament Conference, which was nevertheless eventually established and met, with delegates from sixty-one states (including the USA and USSR), for the first time at Geneva on 2 February 1932 under the Chairmanship of Arthur Henderson, the former Labour Foreign Secretary, by this time in his late sixties and in poor health. The British delegation to the Conference formally included the Prime Minister and a number of Cabinet ministers. In practice, not least since air armaments emerged as such a critical issue, Londonderry often found himself the most senior figure in the British delegation when (as was mostly the case) the Foreign Secretary, Sir John Simon, could not be present, and he became its most longstanding member.

Londonderry's own later accounts, though written as attempts to justify his own stance in Geneva, do not distort what he felt at the time, and make plain his mounting frustration and annoyance at the futility of the deliberations, his sympathy for Germany's arguments, his irritation with the French and his awareness of his growing isolation on the British side on the question of retention of bombers.[4] Nevertheless, he loyally represented his government and appears to have performed creditably during the difficult negotiations. At least one informed observer, the military strategist and writer Basil Liddell Hart, later praised Londonderry's work at Geneva, while criticizing Simon's ineffectiveness. 'Contrary to expectation', wrote Liddell Hart,

Londonderry succeeded wonderfully well in restoring Britain's shaken prestige. He achieved this by combining a maximum of 'presence' with a minimum of words, playing his role with such gracious dignity and apparent sincerity as to evoke from many foreign observers admiring comments about 'le grand seigneur' – and references to the guidance of his great ancestor, Castlereagh, in the peace settlement after Napoleon's overthrow.[5]

Londonderry was scarcely in a positive frame of mind when he arrived in Geneva in early February 1932. He had a bad cold, thought the city a 'most terrible place', complained about the bitter temperatures outside but hotels 'like furnaces', and was from the outset 'doubtful whether we shall see very much accomplished by the Disarmament Conference'.[6] He was convinced of the need for general disarmament if another war were to be avoided, and that this meant equality among the powers. But he was under no illusions about the difficulties facing the Conference. He was adamant, too, that the severity of the Versailles Treaty had produced the backing for Hitler's aims – already plain long before he attained power – to 'avenge the wrongs' against Germany, and that 'Hitlerism . . . derives much of its force from the argument that in disarming Germany and in failing to disarm themselves the victorious nations have broken faith with Germany'.[7]

By the end of 1932, Germany's hopes of removal of the constrictions of Versailles and equality of status with the other powers in disarmament were no closer to realization than they had been when the Conference had first met. A face-saving but empty formula was agreed on 11 December 1932, recognizing the German claim to equality as long as security for all nations were to be ensured. This persuaded Germany to return to the Conference which she had boycotted since September. But in practice things remained as they were, with the French in particular reluctant to make concessions which, they argued, would jeopardize their national security. It was at this point that Hitler became Chancellor of the German Reich.

Once the domestic turmoil of the establishment of Nazi power in Germany in the early months of 1933 had begun to settle down, it was a matter of time before the German claim to equality was reasserted with even greater vehemence – along with the certainty that rearmament would take place whatever the other powers at the Disarmament Conference wanted. Continued French intransigence and British unwillingness to expose a breach with their allies played into the hands of the hawks in the German Foreign Office and army who were pressing Hitler to act.[8] In reality, the German government had no intention of allowing concessions made by the Disarmament Conference to undermine the large-scale programme of rearmament (to be followed by territorial revision of Versailles) to which it was already committed. Fruitless concerns that some concessions, which would have been unwelcome, might follow British and American pressure on the French helped to confirm Hitler's view that Germany must make an early exit from Geneva.[9] In October, the German withdrawal from the Disarmament Conference condemned it to an inevitable, if lingering, death.

For Londonderry, irritation at the stalemate in Geneva and unease at the unwillingness to make the concessions to Germany which, in his view, were both just and necessary to break the deadlock, intermingled with the issue at the centre of his own concerns, and a highly contentious matter for the Disarmament Conference: aerial bombing. In this key issue, he found himself increasingly at loggerheads with his own Cabinet colleagues and members of the British delegation. By July 1932 he was writing that he had 'had a desperate time at Geneva' and that his mind was 'full of anxiety'. Though personal relations with his colleagues were friendly, he disagreed with them 'in their handling of international affairs'.[10] The disagreement revolved around the question of the abolition of bombing.

Fear of death and destruction raining down from the skies, should Europe once more be plunged into war, was palpable at the time, and felt in all sections of British society. The impact of the Japanese air attacks on the civilian population of Shanghai in January 1932, which had killed many women and children, had left a deep sense not just of revulsion but of shock at the apparent defencelessness of modern cities to aerial bombing. Some months later, in a spine-chilling, much-publicized few sentences during a speech to the House of Commons on 10 November 1932, Stanley Baldwin (Lord President of the Council and, given the weakness of the ailing Prime Minister, Ramsay MacDonald, and his own standing as a former Prime Minister, one the two most powerful members of the Cabinet beside Neville Chamberlain, the Chancellor of the Exchequer) was to declare: 'I think it is as well . . . for the man in the street to realise that there is no power on earth that can protect him from being bombed.

Whatever people may tell him, the bomber will always get through.'[11] Few forgot those words. Such a fate, many concluded, could only be avoided if bombing were altogether banned internationally – a vital development in which, it was widely felt, Britain must take the lead. But such sentiments were scarcely shared by the Secretary of State for Air, Lord Londonderry. In a climate shaped by fear of the bomber, he would come to be seen as 'the bomber's friend'. Meanwhile, the outlawing or retention of bombing became a focal point of disarmament deliberations and of differing views in the British government.

From the outset there was division within the Cabinet between ministers – including the Prime Minister and Foreign Secretary – who placed a high premium on disarmament, and the ministers representing the armed services (including, of course, Londonderry) who took the view that British disarmament had gone far enough and that to disarm further would put national safety at risk. Londonderry, backed by leading officials in the Air Ministry and briefed by the former Chief of the Air Staff, Lord Trenchard, was the most vehement in his determination not to lose the bomber arm of the service he represented. This was to take him down a collision course not just with the widespread leanings towards pacifism in the country, fearful of what bombing could inflict upon civilian populations, but with members of his own government.

Already by May 1932, Baldwin was describing attempts at prescribing limits to air warfare as pointless. Instead he advised the Cabinet to aim at realistic targets, one of which should be the banning of the building of new military aircraft altogether. He was supported by Sir John Simon, the Foreign Secretary. The Cabinet saw the proposal as an admirable position to take to Geneva. Anxiety about the risk to British cities in any future war helped drive the desire to work towards an ultimate complete elimination of aircraft capable of carrying bombs. However thorny the path to that desirable goal, practical and manageable steps, the Cabinet accepted, were necessary on the way.[12]

The Air Ministry was not slow to respond to what it saw as a highly damaging proposal – damaging to Britain's defences, and to the ministry's own interests. Londonderry lost little time in expressing his own 'grave misgivings' to the Prime Minister.[13] Quite apart from the deliberations in Geneva, the Ministry was already smarting from a 13 per cent reduction in the annual allocation for air expenditure by the Chancellor of the Exchequer, Neville Chamberlain, keen to balance the budget in a world economic crisis.[14] The Air Ministry's experts argued on technical grounds against Baldwin's proposal, which they saw as wholly impracticable. The banning of military aircraft capable of carrying bombs, they claimed, would have little point, since commercial aeroplanes could easily and speedily be adapted to carry bombs.[15] The Cabinet was unimpressed. Another argument was brought forward which would later come to haunt Londonderry, and even indirectly contribute to the train of events which would see him emerge as a 'friend of Germany': bombers were needed for policing purposes in some unruly outposts of the British Empire. When the Dominions had been consulted on Baldwin's proposal, the only opposition had come from Lord Willingdon, the Viceroy of India, who had resisted the abolition of bombing on the grounds that, without it, the control of the rebellious tribesmen on the North-west Frontier and in Iraq would be difficult. The argument would later be personally associated with Londonderry, and would see much opprobrium heaped upon him by pacifist and liberal opinion. But he neither raised the point in the first place; nor was he the only member of the Cabinet to accept it. Despite its willingness to incorporate the qualification, however, the government remained unmoved in its endorsement of Baldwin's proposal. The dangers to great cities and civilian populations remained at the forefront of ministers' minds; the Disarmament Conference needed new impetus if it were not to fail disastrously; and, in any case, reductions in spending on the air force were not unwelcome in a time of severe Depression.[16]

Londonderry was dismayed. He told the Prime Minister, Ramsay MacDonald, that his advisers at the Air Ministry saw in the direction of government policy 'the destruction of the Air Force', and held out for nothing to be done at Geneva unless – well aware of how illusory this was – unanimous international agreement to abolish all weapons of war could be achieved. He took the matter to the King himself and roused George V's indignation at 'any attempt to do away with the Air Force'.[17] By late June, the Americans had intervened with an initiative – advanced with at least one eye on the forthcoming presidential election – that came to be known as the Hoover Plan. It amounted to a recognizably utopian proposal to abolish tanks, large mobile guns, chemical weapons – and bombers.[18] Londonderry lost no time in restating the Air Ministry's case for more modest measures to regulate the use of bombing.[19] By 22 July 1932, the Conference had nevertheless adopted a resolution prohibiting attack from the air on civilian populations and abolishing all bombardment from the air – though (the saving feature from Londonderry's point of view) subject to agreement on the measures needed to make this effective.[20]

Privately, Londonderry did not restrain his anger at what he took to be the British government's weak stance. 'We have really surrendered all along the line,' he thundered to the Prime Minister, railing at the acquiescence of Sir John Simon and the Foreign Office in the total abolition of bombing. To the King's Private Secretary, Sir Clive Wigram, reminding him of George V's disturbance at the idea of the abolition of military aviation (something, in fact, far wider than what was now actually proposed), he poured out his bitterness that he had been fighting 'a lone hand' in his opposition to government policy, and berated the fact that 'we are doing the best we can to sacrifice the Air Force which, undoubtedly, whatever rules are made here, will play the leading part in any future war should we be faced with such a dreadful calamity'. Only the proviso to the resolution moderated Londonderry's apoplexy, since he immediately saw that any such agreement on the effective steps to accomplish the ban on bombers was a pipedream. Even so, he wished that Britain had not gone along with the formula of total abolition, as other countries would, whatever Britain did, plainly ignore it. He drew two conclusions: 'to preserve as strong an Air Force as possible for the British Empire', and 'that it was vitally important to bring the Germans back to Geneva'.[21] And he remained anxious. 'I feel we are playing with fire,' he told Ramsay MacDonald.[22]

The gulf between the government's increasing move in the direction of a defensive air policy and Londonderry's insistence on the retention of bombers (with its emphasis upon the aggressive capacity of the air arm) was gently pointed out by Ramsay MacDonald, trying to tread a soft line between the majority of his Cabinet and his friend, the Air Minister. 'Your weakness', MacDonald told Londonderry, 'is that you cannot secure us against bombardment though you can make a mess of the other fellow.'[23] Londonderry's stance was storing up future trouble for himself, and paving the way for his later vitriolic criticism of the government's defence policy and – interlinked with this – its policy towards Germany.

Two weeks before Hitler was appointed Reich Chancellor, Londonderry reasserted to the Prime Minister the need 'to be realists' in resisting 'the ideal of complete disarmament'. In view of the troubled situation in Europe and the Far East (where the Japanese occupation of Manchuria in 1931 had thrown the region into turmoil), and in the interests of the Empire and the League of Nations itself, Londonderry argued, 'we must allow the public gradually to grasp the truth, that no big measure of disarmament is possible under present conditions'.[24] Only a few days later the Prime Minister received a memorandum, prepared by his Cabinet Secretary, Sir Maurice Hankey, asking what course should be followed if the Disarmament Conference failed and Germany began to rearm.[25] This was just before Hitler took power in Germany. The question was soon to seek an ever more urgent answer, as both eventualities occurred. But however urgent the need for an answer, the British government, then as later, avoided providing one.

Londonderry was too busy enjoying an extensive tour of air force bases in the Middle East to be concerned by the political drama unfolding in Germany, and resulting in Hitler's takeover of power on 30 January 1933. On his return journey to England he took time to stop off in Rome, where he found himself greatly impressed by Mussolini and the Fascist regime, which he adjudged 'a great success' and 'making great progress in every direction' – a view fairly widespread at the time among British Conservatives, ready to contrast Fascist élan with the travails and weaknesses of liberal democracy.[26]

Hitler's advent to power made no immediate difference either to the government's position at Geneva, or to the views of Londonderry and the Air Ministry. Anthony Eden, Under-Secretary at the Foreign Office, critical of the Air Ministry's obstinacy in insisting that no satisfactory scheme could be drawn up to control civil aviation and that, consequently, attempts to ban bombers were doomed from the outset, pressed for a British initiative to break the stalemate at Geneva.

The outcome was the Draft Convention, proposing specific limitations in armaments, presented by the Prime Minister to the
Disarmament Conference on 16 March 1933 (and known, accordingly, as the MacDonald Plan) which, for the first time, mentioned
precise figures on reductions. In the deliberations that resulted in the
Draft Convention, Londonderry had forcefully reiterated on a number of occasions the Air Ministry's objections to undercutting the
country's defence capability by a policy of air disarmament certain to
find no reciprocation in some countries, and the readiness to accept
internationally agreed measures only if safeguards to guarantee their
effectiveness were introduced.[27] The familiar technical points about
civilian aircraft easily being convertible into bombers, and about the
need to retain bombers for policing purposes, were again advanced.
The retention of bombing for policing the North-west Frontier, later
blamed on Londonderry, was, as we have seen, not initially his suggestion, and was taken on board by the Cabinet, which, despite the
Air Minister's reservations, pressed ahead with the Draft Convention.
Londonderry himself felt 'the gravest apprehension' at proposals
which would still further weaken Britain's already parlous defences.
But he recognized his isolation in Cabinet, and, since his arguments
were by now so well known that he encountered gentle mocking from
the Foreign Secretary and others, he became increasingly silent on disarmament issues.[28]

Despite his dogged attempts to uphold the interests of the Air
Ministry, Londonderry's weakness and ineffectiveness as a Cabinet
minister were ever more apparent to those in the inner circles of power.
They were not affected by his attempt to use his capacity for lavish and
generous hospitality to advertise the importance of the Royal Air
Force to the Prime Minister and the Duke of York (the future King
George VI) in a splendiferous dinner-party at Londonderry House on
27 February 1933 attended by forty-four guests including the air force
top brass and leading officials from the Air Ministry.[29] When the Air
Estimates – the government's budgeted expenditure on the air force –
were presented four days later, they told their own story of Londonderry's inability to influence government policy. The emphasis
remained on savings and reductions. If expenditure fell only margin-
ally, from £19,702,700 to £19,683,600, this came on top of a cut of

£700,000 the previous year. And this was at a time when all the other leading powers were substantially increasing their spending. The air force was to be given no new additions to the current forty-two squadrons – still well below the target of fifty-two squadrons laid down ten years earlier, long before the international situation had deteriorated so drastically.[30] In response to the anxieties articulated by Londonderry and Lord Hailsham (Secretary of State for War), Neville Chamberlain cited a memorandum of the Treasury that 'today financial and economic risks are by far the most serious and urgent that the country has to face, and that other risks have to be run until the country has had time and opportunity to recuperate and our financial situation to improve'.[31] Apart from any other considerations, on economic grounds alone an arms race was the last thing the British government wanted – especially with the world-wide commitments of a global empire as well as its domestic problems to take into consideration.

At precisely the juncture when Hitler was consolidating his hold in Germany, with – as was plainly realized – the certainty of German rearmament if progress could not be made at Geneva, domestic constraints of an economy in the throes of unprecedentedly severe depression (as in much of Europe and in the USA, involving collapse of export industries, mass unemployment and severe financial retrenchment) were, then, a significant factor in shaping the British determination to press for international disarmament. But there was no evident mechanism in place for switching gears if the objective of disarmament, as seemed increasingly likely, should fail. Nor was there any pressure on the government to consider an alternative strategy.

One of the very few voices in the first phase of Hitler's rule loudly advocating a speedy and extensive programme of British rearmament was that of Lord Rothermere. But Rothermere's shrill criticism of the government in his newspapers, his strident – at times almost hysterical – anti-Communism, and his support for Mosley's Fascist Blackshirts, put him beyond the pale of those likely to have a serious influence on policy-making. Despite his position as a media mogul, he was ignored in government circles – and not just because he soon became, as we have seen, one of the most forthright supporters of Hitler in high places in Britain.

More weighty by far was the voice of Winston Churchill. Almost alone in the House of Commons, Churchill had warned against coming German might, even before Hitler took power, and had criticized the principled search for equality of status for Germany which had underpinned the work of the Disarmament Conference. He preferred to put his trust in the retention of armed superiority of the French and the British while German territorial grievances arising from the Versailles settlement were addressed. Churchill strongly criticized the economies of the Air Estimates, attacked Londonderry's Under-Secretary of State for Air, Sir Philip Sassoon, spokesman for the Ministry of Air in the House of Commons, for his equanimity in accepting the reductions, and warned that 'not to have an adequate air force in the present state of the world, is to compromise the foundations of national freedom and independence'.[32] But Churchill at this time had few political allies. His attack in the House of Commons on Ramsay MacDonald's disarmament plan, submitted to Geneva in mid-March, met with outraged rebukes on all sides of the chamber.[33] Churchill was isolated, without power, and lacking support for his views in the country at large.

Londonderry's own position, as we have noted, accorded with that of Rothermere and Churchill in deprecating cuts in the air force. But whereas Rothermere wanted immediate and massive rearmament, Londonderry's energies were wholly absorbed in trying to prevent further inroads into existing levels of armament. And whereas Churchill held out dire warnings of the consequences of German rearmament, opposed equality of status for Germany, and insisted upon retention of British and French armed superiority, Londonderry saw no danger from Germany within the coming five years and saw the granting of equality of armed status as a means of defusing German grievances and, therefore, of heading off the danger of a future return to war in Europe.[34]

Londonderry continued to be concerned – his ire largely directed at the Foreign Office – about what he termed a 'gesture at Geneva'[35] through a unilateral sacrifice of the air force and abolition of bombing. He also remained preoccupied – more so, it seems, since his visit to the Middle East at the beginning of the year – with the need to retain bombing for police purposes in unruly parts of the Empire, insisting on retention even when he was advised to drop the point, and even though he himself admitted it was a 'side issue', since it was said to pose an obstacle to an agreement on disarmament.[36] At the same time, he remained committed to the policy of arms limitation and avoidance of an arms race. Unlimited armaments would inevitably lead to war, as in 1914, he argued. The government's aim (which he shared) was 'such a careful limitation of forces of all kinds that no nation will be afraid of another and no nation will be tempted by a momentary superiority of forces to attack another'.[37] It was idealism wholly out of tune with the temper of the times.

Privately, nevertheless, Londonderry's frustration and irritation at the proceedings in Geneva were undiminished. And he placed the blame mainly at the door of the 'obdurate' French, who were 'not prepared to play'.[38] Whatever his personal sympathy for the German case for equality of status in armaments, as the British representative he was compelled to reject the formal demand put forward by Rudolf Nadolny, Germany's delegate to the Disarmament Conference, for air armaments to be granted to Germany, as to other countries, for means of defence.[39]

As regards the immediate position, Londonderry might have spared himself any worries about international agreement being reached on the basis of the British proposals. Predictably, the 'MacDonald Plan' rapidly withered on the vine. So did a proposal, put forward in March by Mussolini and swiftly adopted by the British government, for a four-power pact of Great Britain, France, Italy and Germany, aimed at securing peace in Europe for the next decade but rapidly running up against the vested interests of each of the countries and gradually petering out into a signed but not ratified statement of meaningless generalities.[40] By now, with disarmament talks stalled irredeemably and German rearmament – if still in secret – known to be underway, the withdrawal of Germany from the Disarmament Conference (and from the League of Nations), which the German leadership had in any case wanted all along, was simply a matter of timing. When it took place, on 14 October 1933, it marked not only the first of Hitler's 'weekend coups',[41] but also denoted the effective end of the futile attempts to produce a collective agreement on peace and security in Europe. Though disarmament talks in Geneva dragged on for some months, the last rites could not be long delayed. The patient finally expired gently in June 1934, even if some believers in a Lazarus-style recovery continued to try for long afterwards to breathe life into the corpse. European disarmament was dead.

II

Germany's official abandonment of the search for a common basis of disarmament – not that her pursuit of such a goal had ever been more than a cynical ploy – marked a turning-point. But the shift from disarmament to rearmament in Britain came only gradually, and painfully slowly. When it did come, the focus came to rest inexorably on power in the air. All experts agreed that air power would be decisive in any future war. And precisely in this crucial area, Britain had suffered significant decline, relative to the growing air strength of other countries, since ending the First World War as the world's leading air power.[42] Now, too, there was reliable intelligence that Germany was in the process of building a military air force.[43]

Londonderry recognized the opportunity to press for expansion of the Royal Air Force, not just to seek to prevent contraction. He saw the overriding priority (as he later expressed it) as ensuring security and strength, adding – hopefully, and illogically – that 'limitation of armaments would then follow automatically because everyone would see that their existing policies did not pay'.[44] But the government saw rearmament as a measure to be adopted only with extreme reluctance, when the prospect of collective disarmament had vanished. So it still clutched at the straw of disarmament as the priority – from a position of manifest increasing relative weakness, and confronting threatening new forces where goodwill and pious intentions were unlikely to prove effective. Londonderry's expressed hopes in the autumn of completing the 1923 programme to bring the air force up to fifty-two squadrons (from the current forty-two) were dashed when Baldwin told his Cabinet colleagues that it would send the wrong signals to Germany.[45] When the 1934 Air Estimates were presented, at the end of February 1934, they were based on the need to work towards the 1923 programme, but were still £1 million lower than the air budget of 1931. Londonderry expressed his 'grave perturbation', pointing out that 'other Powers' were far more actively building up their air forces. However, he agreed that 'with the fate of the Disarmament Convention still undecided, it would not be advisable to consider any more extensive measures in the coming year' (and was even prepared to countenance the sale of some engines to Germany which could be deployed in small fighters).[46] The Prime Minister commended Londonderry for his 'excellent example' in accepting containment of air expenditure for what he said would be the last time unless a satisfactory international agreement on disarmament were reached.[47] The outcome was an initial increase of four squadrons, which would remain compatible both with economic demands and with the pursuit of disarmament.[48] It meant a total of 888 instead of 850 aircraft – hardly a ringing commitment to strength in the air.[49]

Undoubtedly, Londonderry's position as Air Minister, anxious to build up the strength of the air arm and more aware than most of the dangers of slipping far behind other powers in offensive and defensive air weaponry, was a difficult one. For idealistic reasons, and also to balance the budget, the government was committed to pushing as hard as possible for disarmament. In addition, the government had to take public opinion into account (as well as an evident deep concern in the Dominions about the dangers of a new arms race). Beginning with the by-election at East Fulham in October 1933, where a pacifist campaign by the Labour Party candidate ended in sensational defeat for the government, a series of heavy by-election swings against the government over the following months (which in a general election with corresponding results would have converted the National Government's massive majority into a Labour majority of 100 seats) provided a significant discouragement to a policy of rapid and substantial rearmament.[50] The pacifist climate was tapped by Labour and Liberal leaders. George Lansbury, the pacifist Labour leader, proclaimed that he would 'disband the Army and disarm the Air Force', and would 'abolish the whole dreadful equipment of war'.[51] Other Labour leaders, including Clement Attlee and Stafford Cripps, joined in the denunciation of any increase in air armaments, as did the Liberal leader, Sir Archibald Sinclair.[52]

Londonderry was unfortunate to find such major obstacles as stringent budgetary controls and the force of public opinion in the way of the policy he favoured of rearming the air force while continuing to pursue the quest for the Holy Grail of European disarmament. But he did not play his poor hand well. The increases he sought were modest enough. Even so, he was not forceful or powerful enough to achieve them. Instead, he yielded to the pressure – considerable as it was – within the Cabinet (where he could usually depend for support only on Lord Hailsham, Secretary of State for War) to contain expenditure and to uphold the commitment to disarmament. Unlike Churchill, who from temperament and conviction, liberated also from the reponsibilities of government, could proclaim – if largely in vain – the need to build up Britain's air defences in speech after speech, Londonderry was too much the Cabinet loyalist to speak out against collective government decisions (whatever his private feelings), too weak within the Cabinet to carry the day with his arguments, and too committed – politically and personally – to Ramsay MacDonald to contemplate resignation.[53] Moreover, whatever the plain evidence to the contrary, Londonderry had himself – like the rest of the Cabinet – not given up hopes of Germany returning to Geneva.[54] Indeed, he saw that as the necessary prerequisite to establishing peace in Europe, worried as he was at the ominous signs of German rearmament and the reluctance of Britain to build up her defences.[55] He was, therefore, disappointed at the end of 1933 when 'the stubborn opposition of France and our failure to make any serious move in the direction of shaking that attitude' meant that 'peace proposals' of Hitler (cynically made, in reality, as always was to be the case following a German coup in foreign policy) were stillborn.[56] He was gullible enough – and not for the last time – to be taken in by Hitler's opportunistic but entirely empty rhetoric of peace.

In early 1934 British policy on Germany was approaching a crossroads. A Foreign Office memorandum the previous November had posed the stark alternative for Britain of vigorous rearmament or defencelessness if Germany could not be reintegrated into disarmament negotiations.[57] Well aware that Hitler was starting to rearm Germany, the government at this juncture still harboured faint hopes that a general disarmament agreement which included the Germans could, with some flexibility on all sides, still be achieved. However, Hitler's indication in December 1933 that he would be ready to conclude separate bilateral non-aggression pacts with France and Britain met with a stony response in December from both countries. Germany's insistence on an army of 300,000 men, while Britain would not budge from the 200,000 foreseen in the proposed Draft Convention, was one major stumbling-block. So was the German demand for an air force of 1,000 aeroplanes. In January 1934, Britain tried to engineer an opening by offering minor concessions to German rearmament (though still not the army of 300,000 men that Germany wanted, or the 1,000 planes),[58] and followed up this move by sending Eden on a diplomatic mission to Paris, Berlin and Rome. But Eden's momentarily inflated impression of the progress he had made with Hitler and Mussolini rapidly gave way, once he reported to the new French Prime Minister, Gaston Doumergue, and his Foreign Minister, Louis Barthou, to the realization that nothing whatsoever had been achieved.[59] The French would not move; and without the French, the British could not move. The Cabinet, with the Prime Minister most unwilling of all, began reluctantly to concede that only the slimmest of chances remained to reach any agreement on disarmament. The alternative – rearmament – had to be faced.

The mood among government leaders was one of depression and helplessness. There was talk of a possible war if Britain attempted to impose economic sanctions or a blockade on Germany. The Foreign Secretary correctly foresaw breaches of the Versailles Treaty by Germany, which Britain would be powerless to prevent, and prophesied unrestricted German rearmament leading to demands for British rearmament following from a failure to reach a disarmament agreement. The Prime Minister feared 'there was a grave risk of war unless we could devise something in a big way which, at present, he could not see'. He envisaged the prospect of a return to an arms race such as preceded the First World War and that 'after about 30 or 40 years history might repeat itself'.

Lord Londonderry was less pessimistic. His impatience with the French and readiness to concede more to the Germans was made apparent. He saw a way forward in persisting with figures for armaments limitations of the major powers, suggesting that the time had come to take a tougher line with French intransigence and that Germany should be allowed the same armaments ratio as Britain, France and Italy. In fact, he added, 'he would give them what we have got'. He thought Germany had no more than around 300 aircraft and would not pose any menace to Britain for at least four years.[60] As the gloom deepened a month later when the German budget indicated that substantial rearmament was taking place,[61] Londonderry favoured – a line he would pursue in the coming months – arraigning Germany's violations of the Versailles Treaty at the Disarmament Conference in Geneva. The flaw in such an apparently tough approach was, of course, that no action would follow. The French position – a more reasonable one than Londonderry would concede – continued to place the country's security above disarmament. But when, the previous year, the French government had sought a guarantee that sanctions would be imposed upon any power (meaning, naturally, Germany) breaching agreed armaments levels, they could win a commitment of support neither from Britain nor from the United States. Both countries were keener on disarmament, necessitating a conciliatory approach to German demands for equality of status, than they were on backing promises of sanctions to placate French security needs.[62] Moreover, Eden's recent visit to Paris had shown the French government to be fully preoccupied with its own survival at a time of serious domestic crisis and, seemingly paralysed, unable to reach any agreement with Britain on the way to deal with German rearmament.[63] As Londonderry knew only too well, therefore, threats towards Germany had no teeth. The retrospective musings of the Prime Minister were mere futile hand-wringing, as he wondered 'whether we had been firm enough with Germany. Could we, in any way, have brought Germany more to a sense of her sin than we had done?'[64]

At the end of February 1934, the Air Estimates, with (as we noted) their minimal increases for the expansion of the air force, had been accepted by the Cabinet. At precisely the same time, the Defence Requirements Committee, chaired by Sir Maurice Hankey, reported. The Committee had been created on account of the threat posed by Japan in the Far East. But it now concluded: 'we take Germany as the ultimate potential enemy against whom our "long-range" defensive policy must be directed'.[65] The Committee was nonetheless fairly sanguine about Britain's prospects of retaining an armaments advantage over Germany, particularly in the air. Germany would lag behind Britain for a few years in air strength, the Committee suggested. A programme to create twenty new squadrons would provide adequate defence.[66]

The Chairman of the Cabinet Committee that had to consider the implications of Hankey's report was Stanley Baldwin. With the Prime Minister, Ramsay MacDonald, still unwilling to face realities, Baldwin's conversion to the case for even modest levels of rearmament was crucial. On Eden's return from Paris a month earlier, France had sought to establish, before agreeing to the British Convention on Disarmament, what sanctions would be imposed on Germany if she broke the prescribed levels of rearmament. No answer had been forthcoming. Baldwin now argued that without the presence of the USA and Japan in the League of Nations, any notion of sanctions against Germany would be pointless. A move to appropriate and realistic levels of rearmament in the context of near-certain failure of disarmament talks was the logical conclusion. In early March, Baldwin announced in the House of Commons that the government would ensure that 'in air strength and air power this country shall no longer be in a position inferior to any country within striking distance of our shores'.[67]

During the next four months the government considered in great detail the need to expand Britain's air force. A remarkable feature of the deliberations was that Londonderry, far from grasping the opportunity presented by this shift in policy, was prepared to accept a relatively modest level of expansion in a programme aimed at completion over a period of ten years. He said 'the Air Ministry were not unduly alarmed for the next few years. The Chief of the Air Staff did not anticipate that we should find ourselves in a dangerous position for five years.' He believed that only then would Germany have an efficient air force, 'and if it was desired to produce the programme on a fairly comfortable and reasonable basis, the Air Ministry would like it spread out over ten years'.[68] Londonderry wanted an increase beyond the existing force of forty squadrons over the next five years (with a further twenty-five squadrons to follow over the subsequent quinquennium). But only ten of these would be allocated to home defence, bringing that force up to the fifty-two squadrons laid down in the 1923 programme. With some incredulity, Sir John Simon sought to clarify that, on the Air Ministry's recommendations, 'during the next 5 years we should be completing a programme which had been agreed upon in 1923 and never implemented'. He thought that 'a very remarkable state of affairs'.[69] At least as remarkable was the fact that, with Londonderry seeing little urgency in the air expansion programme, it was left to Neville Chamberlain, despite his concern with limiting expenditure, to press for a bigger expansion of home defence in the air, from ten to thirty-eight squadrons.[70] Somewhat ungraciously, Londonderry said 'he regarded the Chancellor's proposals as being better designed for public consumption than for real utility', argued for expenditure beyond that which Chamberlain had budgeted for, and repeated that 'the Air Ministry themselves were not in any great hurry'.[71] Somewhat begrudgingly, he accepted that Chamberlain's proposal was the best that could be achieved under current circumstances. Londonderry had obtained his expansion. But his own advocacy, and the case put forward by the Ministry he ran, had not impressed his government colleagues. 'When he disagrees he is cantankerous, when he acquiesces he surrenders his rights,' MacDonald later remarked of Londonderry. 'He has not developed the Cabinet mind or art of persuasion in getting on with others.'[72]

In July 1934, with the disarmament talks effectively dead and buried, Baldwin announced to the House of Commons a programme to increase the strength of the Royal Air Force by forty-one squadrons (including three to be provided for Singapore) over the next five years – what would turn out to be the first of a series of accelerating air rearmament programmes. Making a similar announcement in the House of Lords, in the face of much opposition, Londonderry reasserted Baldwin's promise of March in declaring that 'although we still ought not to abandon all hope of something materialising at Geneva, the idea of parity in the air with any Power within striking distance must be a cardinal principle of policy'.[73]

Londonderry could feel some satisfaction that, finally, his battle in an extremely unpropitious climate to strengthen the air arm had borne fruit, even if the tide had turned only when voices more powerful than his own had weighed in on the side of rearmament. But his stance was more complex than the mere advocacy of rearmament – and in the latter what was achieved was actually modest enough. Unlike Churchill, who, earlier than almost anyone, recognized unequivocally the inevitability of conflict with Germany in the foreseeable future and urged maximum rearmament so that Britain, in close alliance with France, would be ready to face the threat when it came, Londonderry did not see war with Germany as unavoidable at all, as long as the necessary steps were taken to accommodate what he saw as justifiable German grievances (which meant a harder line towards the 'obstructionist' French). He regarded rearmament largely as an insurance policy, to convince the Germans that Britain was arguing from a position of strength. And whereas Churchill was adamant that Germany was catching up fast in air armaments and would soon overtake Britain, Londonderry was convinced that Germany lagged behind and would remain for some years in a position of relative weakness. However, this made it all the more urgent, he concluded, that Britain act to establish the basis of a rapprochement with Germany while this superiority in armed strength existed. Should Britain do nothing towards this end and Germany, its grievances unaddressed, become powerful, then the chance would have been missed and disaster would loom.

He was irritated by the lack of action and the absence of a clear and consistent government policy on German rearmament. 'Germany was becoming increasingly stronger all the time, but at the present moment the only thing that happened was that people grumbled but did nothing at all,' he complained in April 1934. There were close parallels in his eyes with Bismarck's policy, which he saw as culminating in the Great War, and he foresaw that 'in the brief span of 10 to 15 years we might find a strong and determined Germany challenging everyone else'. Britain could simply not afford to stand back and wait for that to happen. But the only way he could envisage of stopping the German plans for expansion was that the League of Nations 'would get strong and would form some real concert of countries who would be in a position to move side by side with Germany and, perhaps, exercise a restraining influence'.[74] It was some hope. As expectations of any pressure on Germany emanating from Geneva waned to vanishing-point over the following weeks, Britain gradually replaced the League of Nations in Londonderry's thinking, as the only power that could exert influence on the course of German development. That, however, would need greater readiness to respond to and accommodate German interests than had hitherto been the case. This was, in broad terms, the position which would harden in Londonderry's mind over the next months, and subsequently turn him ever closer to a pro-German stance.

A first personal contact – if still indirect – between Londonderry and the Nazi leadership in Germany was established in October 1934. The background was of a private nature – though politics were never far away in the Londonderry household. The second daughter of Lord and Lady Londonderry, Margaret, had indicated that she wished to marry a divorced man, Alan Muntz, pilot, aviation entrepreneur and founder of Heston aerodrome, near London. Londonderry, when he was learning to fly, had met Muntz at Heston and taken a liking to him, inviting him on several occasions to stay at Mount Stewart. There Muntz and Margaret had formed a relationship. But Margaret's parents did not approve of their plans to marry. As an attempt to prevent the relationship developing further, it seems, it was decided to send Margaret on a trip to Germany along with her elder sister, Lady Maureen Stanley (the wife of the prominent Conservative politician Oliver Stanley). The plan backfired since Muntz ended up accompanying the sisters on the trip.[75] And soon after Margaret's return she announced that she and Muntz were engaged to be married. The nuptials took place at Kensington Register Office in late November with Margaret's younger sister, Helen, as the only family member present.[76]

While in Germany, Margaret and Maureen met Hermann Göring, the larger-than-life right-hand man of Hitler who, among his collection of titles, enjoyed those of Minister President of Prussia, Reich Master of Forestry and Hunting, and – most relevantly – Reich Minister for Air Transport. Though Londonderry's counterpart in Germany – and seldom can ministerial counterparts have been so different in appearance, personality and style of administration – the two had never met.[77] How the introduction of Londonderry's daughters to Göring was made is not apparent. But by this time, in his official capacity, Londonderry had met German visitors connected with aviation, and was of course known at the German Embassy.[78] Moreover, Londonderry's right-hand man in the Air Ministry, Philip Sassoon, the Under-Secretary for Air, had made Göring's acquaintance as early as February 1933.[79] Probably the Embassy set up the audience. It was plainly in the interests of both Göring and Londonderry that it should take place. Göring was keen to do what he could to further the chances of better relations with Great Britain, a main aim of German foreign policy, and in particular to use the opportunity to calm anxieties in the sensitive area of air rearmament. For Londonderry, it was a first tentative and indirect attempt, through personal contact, to gain greater insight into what German intention and policies were, particularly in his own domain of aviation.

The meeting took place in the palace of the Reichstag President – another of Göring's titles – in the evening of 4 October 1934. Lady Maureen mentioned that her father had said that she and her sister must on no account fail to visit his opposite number, the Minister for Air, during their stay in Berlin. Her father, she said, envied Göring's civilian air fleet. Göring replied that he would exchange it the next day in its entirety in return for permission to build a military air force (which, of course, was secretly in preparation). He went on to emphasize – a point he wanted repeating in flying circles in London – his distress at the growing belief in England that German air rearmament posed a threat. 'Never even in his wildest dreams (and here the General thumped the table vigorously)', ran the transcript of the interview, 'did he contemplate the building of a military air force directed against England' – though he did in saying as much unwittingly concede that he was building an air force that could be used elsewhere. The remainder of the meeting was taken up with Göring's lengthy eulogy of Germany's 'reawakening' and of his own popularity – the part, the translator noted, 'which the General clearly enjoyed the most' – and a disquisition on the virtues of dictatorship in Germany.[80]

In reality, it did not amount to much as far as the content went. But the important fact was that, with his daughters acting as intermediaries, Londonderry had forged an unofficial link with Göring, one of the most powerful men in the Nazi hierarchy. It was to be taken up again before long.

Londonderry was meanwhile increasingly preoccupied with the question of German rearmament in the air and anxious, on the diplomatic front, that the German question should not be allowed to drift. Publicly, he still held out hope for success in achieving agreed arms limitation at Geneva, and claimed that the expansion of the Royal Air Force, a necessary measure of ensuring security, was not inconsistent with that goal.[81] Privately, days later, he sounded a different tone. On 13 November 1934 he sent the Prime Minister, Ramsay MacDonald, a three-page draft memorandum setting out his position on German rearmament. In his covering letter, he explained why he had written the paper. He was very disturbed, he said, 'at having nothing to show after three years of strenuous work' at the Disarmament Conference. He wanted Britain to make 'a very bold representation in Geneva'. Britain should announce her awareness that Germany was breaking the Treaty of Versailles and rearming 'at a very rapid rate'. Under these circumstances, he added, 'it is quite impossible for the rest of the World to discuss disarmament'. At the same time, he wanted a British declaration 'that we were fully prepared to accept the equality of Germany' in the Draft Convention and press forward on that basis. If German cooperation could not be ensured, then Britain would at least have made it clear to the world that the danger of German rearmament was a real one and 'that it will be well for all of us to take some steps to meet the consequences which must ensue'. What those steps might be, he did not say.

The draft memorandum itself began by acknowledging that, with the shift to expand the Royal Air Force and repair deficiencies in defence, Britain was 'preparing for another outbreak of war in which we foresee that we shall be involved'. He asked whether nothing could be done to avoid such a catastrophe. The British, French and Italians agreed, he wrote, 'that Germany rearming in isolation would be infinitely more dangerous to the world's peace than Germany rearmed within the council of nations'. The justice of the German demand for equality of status had been accepted two years earlier. Only 'French intransigence' stood in the way of an international agreement that could give effect to that equality. Meanwhile, Germany was rearming rapidly and events were beginning to run out of control. The one way which still held out prospects of success was for Britain to 'take open cognizance of German rearmament at Geneva and ourselves bring forward the question of the revision of those Chapters of the Peace Treaty which deal with the disarmament of Germany and her allies'. The conclusion followed (and did not endear itself to the Foreign Office): French objections would have to be overridden. 'We must control German rearmament,' stated Londonderry, 'and to secure this we must be prepared to take a strong line with France and insist upon international measures being taken to allow to Germany that measure of justice which we acknowledged was hers two years ago.'[82]

Londonderry elucidated the position he had outlined to the Prime Minister in a private letter he wrote on 22 November 1934 to Lord Hailsham, one of his few allies in the Cabinet. It was the clearest statement he had made of the policy he favoured. He would return repeatedly to this letter in later years as vindication of his own stance and as evidence of the alternative policy he had proposed – one which held out promise, but was 'brushed on one side' with 'disastrous consequences'.

His object in suggesting that policy should be directed at bringing the Germans back to Geneva by drawing attention to their rearmament was, he said, quite simple. 'It appears to me', he went on, 'that there are three possible eventualities. The first is that we should be successful in converting the Germans into helpful partners in the scheme of the world; the second is that if the first fails we should be in a position, by knowing what the Germans are doing, to immobilize their hostile activities; and the third is that if the Germans are determined, as some think they are, to be wholly aggressive and unwilling to join in a peaceful comity of nations, then they will stand arraigned in their true colours before the world.'

He anticipated the objection that inviting the Germans to return to Geneva and granting them equality would be seen as 'a complete surrender to German policy', giving them 'domination over the rest of the world'. In his view, Germany was passing through a temporary phase, obsessed by fear married to a sense of inferiority, facing the arms of the French on the one border and those of the Poles on the other. Inviting Germany to return to Geneva would restore the lost prestige. A signed arms convention would then give the Germans the assurance of the fair deal they desired, while allowing Britain to know exactly the level of armaments necessary for defence requirements. Such a proposal, he thought, could not make matters worse. If the Germans were going to rearm anyway 'and to challenge the world at the moment they are in a position to formulate their demands and by reason of their strength make those demands effective', then there was nothing to be lost by 'calling upon Germany now to play their part as a member of the comity of nations envisaged in the constitution of the League of Nations'. His anxiety was, however, Londonderry concluded, that Germany's current inability to challenge the world would soon alter 'and we shall then find ourselves up against ultimatums from Germany and a power behind those ultimatums which will plunge the world once more into the catastrophe of war'.[83]

For all its apparent prescience in the light of later events, the seemingly clear alternative policy which Londonderry outlined was filled with flaws. His first 'eventuality', that the Germans could be converted into 'helpful partners in the scheme of the world', was the one which would become the focal point of his endeavours to engineer friendship with Germany. But it rested on the wholly false premiss that this is what the German leadership itself wanted (except in as much as Hitler wished for British acceptance of German expansion in Europe). Of course, Londonderry cannot be held wholly to blame for failing, as did so many, to realize how little German leaders wanted to be part of a Europe wedded to collective disarmament and respect for international agreements, and how intent Hitler was on a war of conquest in the foreseeable future. The full magnitude of German war aims only became clear after the end of the Third Reich. Yet, as we have noted, for all its failings in dealing with the emerging problem of Nazi Germany's threat to European peace, the British Foreign Office was not short of information on the potential menace of Hitler and had few grounds for optimism about his readiness to return to the framework of the League of Nations and an agreed regime of armaments limitation. Not surprisingly, therefore, the Foreign Office could see little in Londonderry's vain hope for German cooperation.

The second 'eventuality' produced an equally illusory deduction by Londonderry: that if the first aim failed, Britain would be in a position to 'immobilize' the 'hostile activities' of the Germans. Londonderry was well aware, from innumerable Cabinet discussions he had sat through, that this was a chimera. There had never been serious thought given to armed intervention against Germany, even when Hitler's regime was at its weakest. The international dangers from such precipitate action were grave and incalculable (as the French invasion of the Ruhr in 1923 had shown). Even economic sanctions were regarded as a hazardous proposition. Then there was domestic opinion, fearful of war, to be taken into account. The stance of the Dominions was a further difficulty. Here there was no unified approach. South Africa favoured neutrality (while sympathizing with Germany and voicing some anti-French sentiments), while Canada tended towards isolationism and Australia too wanted to avoid overseas commitments, leaving only New Zealand overtly ready to pledge support for Britain in war.[84] Beyond these considerations, in Londonderry's own view and that of many others some of Germany's grievances were justified. Action taken alongside the 'obdurate' French and against Germans widely perceived to be pursuing a fair cause was hardly likely to be popular. Here, too, Londonderry's proposition was scarcely designed to commend itself to the Foreign Office, or to the government in general.

Finally, Londonderry had held out the prospect, if all else failed, of arraigning the Germans 'in their true colours' before the eyes of the world. What this meant, and what consequences were meant to flow from a riven Europe with France and Britain themselves utterly divided on a course of action towards Germany, was anyone's guess. Reflecting at a later date, Londonderry stated: 'The line to have taken was quite simple. We should have drawn attention before the League of Nations, which had some power then, to every breach of the Treaty of Versailles.'[85] It was not a recipe to instil confidence. It was certainly unlikely to carry weight in informing government policy.

Though galling to Londonderry, it was, therefore, hardly surprising that what he saw as a proposal for an alternative policy was, as he plaintively put it, 'brushed on one side'. It was unrealistic to expect it to be taken up. For Londonderry, however, the fact that his suggestion was ignored amounted to contemptuous dismissal, tantamount to a smarting insult to his pride and position. It does not seem to be going too far to see in this episode, inconsequential as it was in real terms, a vital step in Londonderry's increasing alienation from the mainstream of government opinion and a turn to a more open pro-German stance.

III

In autumn 1934 questions about German rearmament in the air began to take on a new urgency. Just how fast were the Germans equipping an air force? And how powerful was that air force likely to be within the foreseeable future? How great was the threat to Britain? And what was the British government doing about it? Public anxieties had been stirred particularly by Lord Rothermere's alarmist, grossly exaggerated claims about the size of the German air force and Winston Churchill's more realistic, but deeply worrying, statements in speeches and newspaper articles about the weakness of Britain's air policy and Germany's growing air strength. As Air Minister, Lord Londonderry inevitably found his own department of state in the firing-line of much of the criticism, and was increasingly forced upon the defensive to justify the record of the ministry. This rankled intensely, not least since he had incessantly – and often alone it seemed – warned against the depletion of Britain's air defences which was now becoming precisely the criticism that was being levelled against him. Upholding the correctness of the ministry's own knowl-edge of German air armaments against the well-informed, withering criticism by Churchill, and justifying his own handling of affairs against the increasing doubters and critics within the government as well as the growing weight of public opinion that Britain was ill-served by its Air Minister, became a central theme of Londonderry's last months in office, before his dismissal in early June 1935. Closely intertwined with this was Londonderry's growing conviction that British foreign policy was feeble and misguided. This feeling, too, would intensify over the coming months.

Londonderry had implored the government as long ago as the end of April 1934, in the wake of the continuing discussions on the Defence Requirements Committee report, to be open with the public on the need to expand the air force, however unpopular this would be. He was supported by Hailsham's demands for increased expenditure of £70 million over five years for the armed forces – proposals which Neville Chamberlain, the Chancellor of the Exchequer, rejected as 'impossible to carry out' on economic grounds, though he recommended expenditure on the air force as a first priority. The Air Ministry's own plans indicated that the Royal Air Force would not provide a formidable weapon in the event of war before around 1942. Even that was contingent upon a further £10 million to the £20 million already requested, which the Treasury was unwilling to provide – thereby taking the risk of leaving the air force without reserves.[86] By July, pressure – including Londonderry's warnings about the weakness of the air force and those of the Chiefs of Staff about the deficiencies in defence forces owing to the preoccupation with disarmament since 1929 – had, as we noted earlier, brought the first programme for air rearmament. The sum of £20 million over five years was allocated to provide for forty new squadrons, aiming at a total first-line strength of eighty-four squadrons (960 aircraft) for home defence by 1939 and, including the Fleet Air Arm and overseas defence, 1,465 aeroplanes in all.[87]

Opinion in Parliament was still completely divided on the need for rearmament. Clement Attlee (who would become leader of the Labour Party the following year) questioned the need for rearmament at all since 'we can generally say today', as he put it, 'that his [Hitler's] dictatorship is gradually falling down', while both the Labour Party and the Liberals joined in a motion of censure of the government at the end of July for its announcement of increased air construction.[88] Churchill, on the other side, pressed for action without a moment's delay. Fed with intelligence figures on German rearmament in a series of leaks from Desmond Morton, head of the government's Industrial Intelligence Centre, he claimed that Britain, currently fifth or sixth strongest in the world in air power, would lag further behind by 1939, and would by then have been overtaken by Germany. On the basis of this information, which painted a more alarming picture than the Air Ministry's own estimates of the scale and speed of German air rearmament, he criticized the proposed increase in air strength as 'tiny, timid, tentative, tardy'. And he alerted the House of Commons to the scale of civil aviation in Germany, and the ease with which many pilots and planes could be converted to military use.[89] Shortly afterwards, Morton told Churchill that, from rumours he had heard, German air strength could be double that of Britain by 1939. Nourished with such information, Churchill prepared to attack the government's record on air defence in the House of Commons debate on the subject, scheduled for 28 November.[90]

It promised to be a difficult passage for the government. It was essential that their own intelligence should provide a sufficient basis to fend off the serious charge that they had greatly neglected Britain's air defences and at the same time allowed Germany to rearm in the air to a perilous level. Even in August, Hankey had told Baldwin that the Cabinet was overrating the danger from Germany in the air, and that this would take some years to materialize.[91] Precise estimates were not easy to arrive at and were dogged by difficulties in assessing exactly what counted as 'first-line' aircraft, apart from having of necessity to rely upon much guesswork from partial information. But the Air Staff's information that by October 1936 Germany would possess 1,296 first-line aircraft, with as many again in immediate reserve, and a grand total of 3,264 machines (including training planes and 540 bombers), which Londonderry passed to the Cabinet on 21 November, appeared to suggest that Hankey had been unduly optimistic.[92] On the day of the debate, several varying estimates of current air strength were available to the Cabinet.[93] The Air Ministry's own estimates – which Londonderry insisted should be accepted as reliable, given the wide range of intelligence sources on which they were based – indicated that the Germans at the time possessed about 1,000 military aircraft of all types (first line, reserve and training), but no more than 300 of these were first-line units.[94] However, the estimated rate of production was of 160 to 180 machines a month.[95] Germany would, on these figures, not catch up with Britain for some time – though by late 1936 or so, that point would be reached.[96] Churchill's figures, supplied by Morton, painted a more alarming picture. Morton put existing German first-line strength at between 800 and 900 planes and that, at current rates of industrial expansion, this could reach a total of 3,000 by 1937.[97] A few days before the debate on air defences, it was probably disagreements with his kinsman which led Churchill, in his criticism of the government, to speak of 'that half-wit Charlie Londonderry'.[98]

Two days before the debate, the Cabinet was faced with further disquieting information – that Germany's air budget for 1934–5 was as high as 210 million Reich Marks, practically five times the level of 1932–3.[99] Londonderry advanced the Air Staff's proposal that the recently agreed air programme should be accelerated, for completion by the end of 1936 instead of by March 1939. Chamberlain objected to the level of expenditure entailed. 'There was', he stated, 'nothing in our information in regard to German preparations to justify the proposed acceleration.' The Air Ministry's current programme, he added, 'was as much as could be accomplished efficiently and without waste of money and effort'. However, 'in view of the gravity of the position', the Cabinet agreed to a compromise: completion of twenty-two of the forty new squadrons by the end of 1936.[100]

The Cabinet discussion left Londonderry 'very anxious', as he made clear in a letter that same day to the Prime Minister. Churchill, he pointed out, would use the debate to claim that Germany would 'in a short time attain to such strength as will place her in an overwhelming position'. The government would reply that they were aware of German rearmament, but that the situation was less grave than Churchill was suggesting, and the defensive position much sounder. Lloyd George would then see the solution in granting the equality to Germany that should long ago have been accorded her and which was rightfully hers. He might justifiably ask why Britain had not raised the question at Geneva. Londonderry saw that an outcome of the debate would be 'that we have known all about the rearmament of Germany, that we have been helpless in face of it and that we are unable to propound any policy except that of preparing for another war'. This brought him to the need to link rearmament to foreign policy and to offer a positive inducement to Germany to return to the negotiating table in Geneva. What he wanted out of the debate was a statement 'that we are proposing to raise the whole question of German re-armament at Geneva and to link the practical realization of Germany's equality of status with the consideration of the continued applicability of Part V [the military restrictions] of the Treaty of Versailles'. His increasingly anti-French position (which was unwelcome to a Foreign Office anxious to avoid any rift with France) as the counterpoint to his readiness to accommodate German demands was apparent. France had been the 'stumbling-block to a Convention all along', so that 'we should be prepared to take the initiative and force the issue with France' in initiating what he was sure was 'the only Foreign Policy which holds any prospect of a real contribution to the cause of peace by securing a limitation of armaments . . . as a first step to reduction, and the sole hope of escape from the lunacy of a race in armaments'.[101]

In the House of Commons on 28 November 1934, Churchill, as expected, warned strongly against the dangers of one power gaining air mastery and stated that Germany's illegal air force was 'rapidly approaching equality with our own'. He urged the financial commitment by the government to a massive expansion of the air force which must at all costs be substantially stronger than that of Germany in the ten years to come.[102] Baldwin replied for the government. His aim was in the first instance to acknowledge awareness of German rearmament in the air but at the same time defuse criticism about British rearmament and to emphasize Britain's retention of air superiority over Germany. This is turn, he hoped, would have an impact beyond Britain's shores in pushing the French to negotiate on the basis that Germany had rearmed, and in persuading the Germans to return to Geneva on the understanding that their violations of the Versailles Treaty were to be condoned.[103] In response to Churchill's claim that Germany would approach equality in the air within a year, be 50 per cent stronger by the end of 1936, and almost twice as strong in 1937, Baldwin quoted figures supplied by the Air Staff, that Germany had a total of all types of aircraft of between 600 and 1,000, while Britain had a first-line strength of 560 planes, with 560 reserves, and 127 auxiliary forces, and by 1936, with the bulk of the air rearmament programme completed, would have a further 300 first-line machines. (Figures provided in December 1934, in fact, put the number of Germany's operational aircraft at 584.) Though Germany was rearming, added Baldwin, 'her real strength is not 50% of our strength in Europe today'. He stated categorically: 'It is not the case that Germany is rapidly approaching equality with us,' estimating that if there was no acceleration in the German air programme Britain would retain a margin in Europe alone of nearly 50 per cent. Though he could not, he said, look ahead beyond the next two years, Churchill's figures were exaggerated and Britain would still be 'able to maintain a position not inferior [to Germany's], whatever happened'.[104] These words would return to haunt Baldwin, and their repercussions would come to hurt Londonderry.

In the three months or so that followed the defence debate, the government's manoeuvres in foreign policy took it at least some of the way that Londonderry was keen it should go. He himself had written to the Foreign Secretary in mid-December urging immediate pressure on the French to accept an increased level of German air rearmament as the basis for German acceptance of a Convention.[105] In January 1935, the Cabinet agreed – taking cognisance of evident government unpopularity over rearmament (among other issues), as recent by-election results had testified – to attempt to persuade the French that the Germans had to be brought back to the League of Nations and to participate in an 'Eastern Locarno' to produce agreed security arrangements for central and eastern Europe. This meant some concessions to the French on their own pressing security worries. The French were meanwhile giving signals that they recognized the need to adjust to reality and accept the fact – though not, of course, the legality – of German rearmament. One proposition, coming from France, which Britain accepted, was an air pact between the two countries, offering mutual assistance in the event of attack from the air. On 3 February the British and French issued a joint communiqué proposing a general provision for European security on the basis of a series of pacts for eastern and central Europe, the dropping of the provisions of the Treaty of Versailles limiting the size of Germany's armed forces, and the resumption by Germany of her place in the League of Nations. As regards security against bombing attacks, the communiqué held out the prospect of an extension of the planned air pact between Britain and France to Italy, Germany and Belgium, thereby constructing a framework for collective security in the air over much of western Europe.[106]

Germany's response was encouraging, prompting Londonderry to summarize his own views on how to take advantage of what seemed a favourable juncture. He remained convinced that France would block any progress and that it was time for Britain to stand up to French opposition. He wanted the reversion to a foreign policy based upon Britain's 'historic part of "honest broker"' which had been the hallmark of an independent foreign policy in the nineteenth century. There was no reason, he argued, 'why French prepossessions should stand between our making direct contact with Germany'. He wished to 'treat the Germans in exactly the same way as we have treated the French, and invite them to a discussion in London' as a preliminary to wider negotiations. He ended with a rhetorical question: 'Can we honestly affirm that French foreign policy since the War has not been one long story of aggression against Germany?'[107] With this stance, Londonderry's distance from the government's position of avoidance at all costs of the split with the French which the Germans themselves were only too keen to promote was plain to see. It pointed towards the way he would move from 1936 onwards.

The Cabinet itself decided, encouraged by Germany's conciliatory response and despite some opposition from the Chiefs of Staff (worried about the automatic assistance guaranteed under the air pact and unwilling to be tied so inexorably to the French), to take up the German invitation to bilateral talks on the Anglo-French communiqué. How the talks should be framed, and where they should be held, were matters which ministers deliberated at length. There were concerns that a visit by British ministers to Berlin would amount to a further propaganda gift for Hitler, just after after the Saar plebiscite in January (when over 90 per cent of the population of the region, which had been under the control of the League of Nations for fifteen years, voted to belong to Germany) had given him a major triumph. The Prime Minister in particular was opposed to sending ministers to Berlin, which in his view would be 'a profound mistake'. Londonderry's line was surprising (except in his support for MacDonald) in its tone. He 'thought that from the proper psychological point of view the Germans ought to be made to come here and that it would be quite wrong for us to go after Germany'. This seemed, as Hailsham said, 'a point of etiquette' more than anything else. But Londonderry persisted, presumably seeing the position of Britain as 'honest broker' (as he had advocated in his memorandum the previous day) as open to doubt if British ministers could be seen as courting the Germans in their own capital city. Still on the issue of whether Germany should send representatives to London, he

thought that the Germans were the type of people who would take everything they could get. If you gave them one thing they promptly demanded everything. At the present time they were very overbearing and were rapidly achieving their aims. They had abrogated unilaterally Part V [the military constrictions] of the Treaty of Versailles. They had attained an air force with no formalities. He was against giving them anything else.

But having Hitler visit London was out of the question. Whatever Londonderry might have felt, the idea of inviting him to England would have appalled much of public opinion as well as most of his government colleagues, let alone the Labour and Liberal opposition. But a visit by his Foreign Minister, von Neurath, would be a poor substitute. As Baldwin put it, there 'was really very little use talking to anyone except Herr Hitler, and nothing would happen if his representatives just came to London'. And the prize of locking Germany into a European Air Convention as the prelude to a wider agreement on arms limitation was a tempting one. There was a difference of opinion on whether an Eastern Pact, which it was felt Germany was unlikely to accept, was vital from a British and French position. But Simon and Eden were both in favour of raising the matter of the Eastern Pact with the Germans. It was finally agreed that Simon should go to Berlin, and the Foreign Secretary asked that Eden, now Lord Privy Seal, should accompany him as 'the only member of the Government who had actually seen Herr Hitler face to face'.[108] The visit was eventually scheduled to take place on 7 March.

Three days earlier, the British government had issued a White Paper on defence, criticizing German rearmament, the bellicose atmosphere that had been stirred up in Germany and the insecurity that had resulted from it, necessitating the increases in expenditure to speed up the air force programme. The furious response in the German press was predictable. From Hitler's point of view, however, the furore was welcome. He had no intention of entering into the pacts which the British and French wanted, even if the propaganda value of a visit from leading British ministers was undeniable. And the visit was hardly opportune when the German government was about to announce the existence of a Luftwaffe. So Hitler developed a diplomatic cold and postponed it. Events now moved swiftly. On 10 March Göring publicly announced, in breach of the Versailles Treaty, that Germany possessed an air force. Just prior to this the French had renewed their military treaty with Belgium, dating from 1921. Then, on 15 March, the French National Assembly affirmed a decision reached some days earlier to extend the length of military service from one to two years. This was the trigger for Hitler to stage a major propaganda coup, on 16 March, when he proclaimed the dramatic news – again in breach of Versailles – that Germany was reintroducing conscription and building an army of 550,000 men. The western democracies confined their reaction to the most tepid of diplomatic protests. In fact, to Hitler's astonishment, the British asked in the same breath as they protested whether the postponed visit of Simon and Eden might nevertheless still take place. Hitler, in whose mentality upholding prestige played a vital role, could scarcely comprehend that the British ministers were still prepared to come to Berlin.[109] The propaganda gain was immense. And he knew now definitively that he had nothing to fear from the British, and that without their backing the French would not move. The way to even bolder action was opening up.

Predictably, from a British point of view nothing concrete came out of the visit by Simon and Eden on 25–6 March (except the prospect of a naval pact with Germany, which Hitler was keen to achieve and Britain ready to accept). The ministers returned home empty-handed. The talks had been cordial. But all British overtures towards a collective system of security in Europe had been deflected. In between his lengthy tirades against Bolshevism, Hitler proved himself a skilful negotiator as the talks ranged over questions of disarmament, the Eastern Pact, and the proposed air pact. Hitler's chief concern was recognition of Germany's claim to parity in the air with Britain and France. Simon asked him about the current strength of Germany's air force. After a moment's hesitation, he replied: 'We have already attained parity with Great Britain.'[110] The lapidary remark filled Eden with 'grim foreboding'.[111] How true the claim was depended upon how planes were counted and strength calculated. Germany had at the time around 800 operational aircraft, though not all these could, on British definitions, be counted as 'first-line'.[112] Britain's first-line strength for home defence had been put by Baldwin four months earlier at 880 aircraft. This was what Hitler had been told Britain possessed, when he responded that Germany had about the same number. As subsequent calculations were to show, the figure which Simon gave was too high (since it included auxiliary squadrons and the Fleet Air Arm), and Britain's actual existing first-line strength in the air of units stationed at home was no more than 453 aircraft.[113] But precise figures were scarcely the issue. The truth was unimportant to Hitler. As he knew only too well, it seldom mattered if the propaganda was bold enough. A few days later he was reported as telling Luftwaffe officers: 'I don't know how many aeroplanes Göring really has got, but that seemed about what there ought to be.'[114]

His ploy, along the lines that his War Minister, Werner von Blomberg, and the planning office of the newly formed Wehrmacht wanted, was to impress upon foreign governments the strength already acquired of German armed forces. It succeeded. Hitler's claim that Germany had caught up with Britain in air power struck Whitehall's corridors of power like a thunderbolt.[115] If it were true, Britain's defensive plight was far more grave than anyone had realized. The complacency reflected in Baldwin's statement in the defence debate the previous November – that Britain was substantially ahead of Germany in air armaments and fully expected to be in the same position within a year's time – was fully exposed. But who had given Baldwin the information on which he could make such misleading claims? The glare of criticism turned during the following weeks inexorably on the Air Ministry, and, in particular, on the Secretary of State for Air, Lord Londonderry.

IV

There was manifest alarm in Britain at Hitler's stunning assertion that Germany had attained parity in air strength. The British government, it was widely felt, had failed lamentably to recognize the growing danger and to take the measures necessary for the nation's defence. All at once, there was a new sense of urgency about the need to rearm

– though the Labour Party's leadership still continued to criticize all demands for arms made by the government down to 1939.[116] Visible signs of the change in tempo would only start to become apparent the following year. But the forced pace of rearmament, which would accelerate as the threat of war grew closer, dates back to the dawning recognition in spring 1935 that there was no time to lose. The Air Minister himself was strangely out of step with the shift in mood. Londonderry's failure to attune to the noticeably sharpened feeling of nervousness about the speed and scale of German rearmament contributed significantly to his political isolation and, within weeks, his removal from office.

Winston Churchill had for months, as we have noted, been strongly critical of the government's unwillingness to see the urgency of the menace of German rearmament, especially in the air. He had often seemed a lone voice in the House of Commons, but, greatly alarmed at the intelligence on the speed and scale of German rearmament that he was receiving from Desmond Morton, had been undeterred in pressing his case, inside and outside Parliament. Less than a week before Simon and Eden visited Berlin, in the House of Commons debate on the Air Estimates for 1935, he had attacked the Under-Secretary for Air, Sir Philip Sassoon, who, in announcing a further increase of 41½ squadrons in the next four years, had again insisted that Britain would retain a superiority over Germany in air armaments at the end of the year. Sassoon admitted that the margin might well not be the 50 per cent asserted by Baldwin the previous November, since the acceleration in German rearmament had been greater than anticipated. But superiority would not be lost. A further 151 aircraft, he stated, would be added to Britain's first-line strength over the coming year. Churchill pointed out that Germany was turning out at least 100, perhaps 150, a month, and that at the end of the year, when Britain had been promised 50 per cent superiority, air parity would have been lost and Germany would be three or four times as strong in the air as Britain.[117] Not surprisingly, Churchill felt vindicated by the sensational claim made by Hitler.

The Air Ministry's figures provided for a first-line strength in regular squadrons of some 1,330 aircraft by the end of 1938 and a further 130 aircraft in non-regular squadrons. Four of the 41½ squadrons had been formed in 1934 with a further twenty-five to be formed in 1935 and 1936.[118] But Foreign Office figures given to Churchill in early April told a worrying tale. They projected a German first-line strength of 1,296 planes by October 1936, compared with 710 planes in Britain.[119] On 10 April Simon drew the attention of the Prime Minister to the grave situation. The latest information he had suggested that German superiority over all first-line machines stationed at British aerodromes was about 30 per cent, and that the rate of growth of the Luftwaffe was far outstripping that of the Royal Air Force. He cast doubt on whether, having been overtaken by Germany, Britain 'would ever be able to obtain a level of parity with her again'. He sent a copy of his letter to Londonderry.[120] Londonderry later looked back on this as the letter that had 'destroyed' him.[121] The Prime Minister privately warned his friend 'that the [Air] Ministry will have to face rough days ahead owing to general lack of confidence which is being spread abroad'.[122]

Londonderry was now plainly on the defensive, faced with fighting a rearguard action to salvage his ministry's standing and his own reputation. He tried to draw some comfort from information coming from the Air Attaché in Berlin, Group Captain Don, that, in his interview with Simon, Hitler had not been making any precise comparison between the two air forces.[123] He pleaded on the telephone with Churchill on 13 April not to raise the question of air strength in the House of Commons a few days later, offering to provide him with 'the real figures' on the comparative positions of air armaments in Britain and Germany. These were the estimates which the Air Ministry had compiled, resting on their own military intelligence sources. Churchill said his figures (which were largely based upon Desmond Morton's information, taken from his private sources of industrial intelligence) were better.[124] Sharp words were exchanged. Churchill later told his cousin he was 'running a frightful risk with the life of the State' and that he might 'at any moment . . . become the political victim of national alarm'.[125]

Shortly afterwards, Londonderry circulated to his Cabinet colleagues, deploring the 'panic' over German air strength, a memorandum, prepared by Sir Edward Ellington, the somewhat complacent and undynamic Chief of the Air Staff, outlining proposals for a further expansion of the air force.[126] Since this new plan foresaw a German superiority of two to one over the home-based air force in 1937 and did not envisage achieving parity until 1942, the gloom was scarcely dissipated.[127] By now, there was strong press criticism of Britain's air defences. Lady Londonderry tried to bolster her husband's dented confidence against the 'constant belittling' by Rothermere and the anxiety that Churchill was causing him.[128] Londonderry was that same day writing to Churchill, hoping to arrange a discussion about air armament figures in the near future. 'The German policy', he commented, 'is becoming clearer every day. I have not had many doubts about it myself from the beginning but I had a faint hope that we might reach some measure of disarmament.'[129] Churchill in return sent Londonderry a copy of a lengthy memorandum he had prepared, laying out in detail his case against the government for its neglect of air armaments and criticizing the Air Ministry for supplying the figures on which Baldwin's misleading statement had been made to the House of Commons the previous November.[130] Londonderry's reply indicated, somewhat disarmingly (and incorrectly), that 'the only difference between us' related to the date when Germany would be powerful enough to challenge the rest of the world. Laconically, he stated: 'As you know we have been moving steadily forward and our paramount duty is to accelerate our rate of development.'[131]

There was more than a tinge of bitterness in the 'very private and confidential' letter Londonderry sent to the Prime Minister on 17 April, defending himself and his ministry against 'any suggestion that we have been supine or backward in anything which we have tried to do', and asserting 'that we have been hampered by my colleagues throughout'. He had 'fought an almost single-handed battle to save the Royal Air Force', he stated once more, criticizing the negative impression of the ministry's work left by statements of some Cabinet colleagues (and particularly singling out Baldwin). He ended: 'I hope you will forgive me for writing so strongly as I have done, but I resent the suggestions which I realise have been brought to you reflecting on the management of the Air Ministry.'[132] In a formal, accompanying letter, Londonderry spoke of 'these damnable attacks' which 'represent the annoyance of my political friends because of my independence of them and also because there are several who would like to take my place and reap the harvest which will be the result in two or three years time of the crop which I and my advisers have sown'.[133]

Londonderry was in difficulties – as was the government itself – when the Ministerial Committee on Defence Requirements (comprising members of the Cabinet and Chiefs of Staff) met on 30 April to discuss the effect of German expansion in air strength on the British position, prior to a further parliamentary defence debate. Ellington's memorandum was presented by Londonderry, who took a defensive stance from the outset in voicing objection to strong criticism of the Air Ministry's proposals in a paper prepared by Sir Robert Vansittart at the Foreign Office.[134] Though the Prime Minister promptly reminded the Committee that 'the situation was far too serious for interdepartmental friction', the Foreign Secretary went on, in a discussion of the likely current and intended air strength of Germany, to ask whether Ellington's memorandum, offering no change in the year 1935–6 and only four additional squadrons in 1936–7, was 'really a proper extent of new provision to meet the new German situation'. He drew the conclusion from the available figures 'that we were not keeping our pledge of parity with the German Air Force'. If couched in parliamentary language, it amounted nonetheless to a frontal attack on the Air Ministry's planning.

Londonderry's reply was weak. Once more he proved less than astute in responding to the drastic change of mood in government that had followed Hitler's startling claim to air parity. Whereas the government had earlier imposed severe financial constraints on air force expansion, it now wanted rapid expansion – and was prepared to fund it. But instead of openly endorsing the expansion he had long advocated, Londonderry remained fixated with defending the Air Ministry's earlier analysis of German air strength and current proposals for extending British air power, though these, in the new climate, could only seem far too modest. It was a serious misjudgement. He agreed generally, he said, with Sir John Simon's comments. But instead of taking them as an almost open invitation to press for maximum and most rapid expansion, he commented: 'From the technical point of view the Air Ministry did not wish to embark on a very rapid programme of expansion and be faced at the end of the period with a position in which they would have a large number of obsolescent aircraft on their hands.' Simon returned to the problem of the pledge that Baldwin had given the House of Commons (and the country) the previous November, implying that at no time would Britain have an air force inferior to that of any country within striking distance. The Air Ministry's proposals, he repeated, 'did not fulfil the pledge which had been given'. He pointed out that the Air Ministry's own figures revealed a slower rate of acceleration than the German plans; 'the longer the expansion went on, the farther ahead would Germany get'.

The question of how the government could defend its policy in the House of Commons, facing the certainty of a damaging attack based on what Baldwin had promised so recently, preoccupied the Committee. Londonderry tried to suggest that the actual meaning of first-line aircraft posed a definitional problem, and that confining comparison to the total number of aircraft in Britain and Germany might allow a claim to equality, if not superiority, at present. But this, the Prime Minister objected, would be to alter the whole basis on which Baldwin's statement had been made. Undeterred, Londonderry argued that Hitler's definition of first-line aircraft had differed from that used in Britain, and that the training of the German air force was inferior to that of the Royal Air Force. 'He could not agree, therefore, that Germany was stronger'. Simon asked whether, if need be, the Air Ministry could accelerate its current programme. Sir Edward Ellington, present as Chief of Staff of the air force, could provide no immediate answer. Further investigation would be necessary, he said. More rapid expansion would depend upon recruiting pilots and fitters, in both cases needing lengthy periods of training and qualification. On a voluntary basis – that is, short of emergency measures – it was not obvious that sufficient numbers would be forthcoming. Further expansion would necessitate obtaining large numbers of additional fitters from 'civil life'. The Air Ministry would have to compete with industry in the labour market. 'The programme he had put forward at present', he declared, 'was, in his opinion, the best that could be carried out in existing circumstances'. 'Ellington makes all of us despair,' Chamberlain privately remarked.[135]

On the thorny issue of how to defend government policy in the House of Commons in the light of the changed situation since Hitler's claim to parity, Chamberlain saved the day with a piece of sophistry. He thought 'that the Government were entitled to put their own construction on the Lord President's [Baldwin's] statement and decide what, in their opinion, constituted air power and air strength'. It was agreed to follow Chamberlain's recommendation 'that the Government intended to maintain the position as stated by the Lord President' – though in reality this position no longer existed – 'and were taking the necessary steps to this end'.[136]

The knives were by now out for Londonderry. He was fighting for his political life. The Rothermere press was particularly ferocious in its criticism. Lord Beaverbrook's *Daily Express* joined in with the implication that Londonderry was the weak link in the National Government and had let down his ministry. It mentioned the 'demand in some influential quarters for his replacement'.[137] Churchill had warned him in April of 'definite intrigues' to remove him from the Air Ministry.[138] He repeated the warning in early May. 'Look out, they are going to kick you out,' Churchill told his cousin. 'I should resign if I were you.'[139] Londonderry had no intention of doing so. He told his wife he was being 'squeezed out': he had several enemies; the Prime Minister was 'very sensitive' about his appointment; and Baldwin had always resented the relationship with MacDonald. 'If I survive I think it will be on your merits,' he added. But although he would be sorry to leave the Air Ministry, he said he was not taking the attacks lying down and intended to counter-attack strongly when he had the opportunity.[140] There was a certain amount of bravado in this. Inwardly, as his wife was aware, he felt a failure, and she tried to stir his waning morale and suggested – a vain hope – trying to get Rothermere and Chamberlain on his side.[141] It all smacked of desperation.

So did Londonderry's suggestion to Eden that the government should contact Hitler to seek 'a categorical statement' about the level of German air armaments. This was in response to Lord Rothermere's assertions that Germany already possessed around 11,000 planes (by any reasonable calculation a massively inflated figure).[142] The idea was that Hitler should either confirm 'what we believe to be his plan, which is to accept limitation and to work for peace', or to show by his evasiveness and insincerity 'that we must be prepared and make ourselves so formidable against attack that a plan of war against

England would not only be impossible but fantastic'. Eden gently dissuaded Londonderry, since 'if we approach Hitler again he will not give us a frank answer, and may possibly give us one which will embarrass us'.[143]

Behind Londonderry's suggestion, however, was a notion which serves as a pointer to his later actions, after he had left the government. He told Chamberlain he had been 'impressed by Hitler's saying that he wants to state his full case so that we shall be perfectly aware of his intentions'. He felt strongly that there was no time to lose in obtaining an arrangement with the Germans on aircraft numbers, and thought this was possible. He was well aware of the German mentality, and it needed firm handling, he went on, but Britain was doing no more than oscillate between Germany and France, and he had 'always thought that we have never been firm enough with the French and that we have the power to insist on their accepting whatever we do'. 'I should like to get hold of Goering myself,' he added, 'and would certainly consider any suggestion with that end in view.' Pointing to the forthcoming talks which would result in the Anglo-German Naval Treaty in June, he asked whether there could not be equivalent 'Air Conversations'.[144]

Meanwhile, with the big defence debate, scheduled for 22 May, fast approaching, Londonderry was becoming ever more edgy. He told Neville Chamberlain he was 'sick of the intriguing'.[145] This followed letters from Lady Londonderry asking Chamberlain to back her husband in his political difficulties – an attempt which backfired badly when she then came close to accusing Chamberlain himself of being behind the intrigues.[146] Ramsay MacDonald wrote privately to him, advising him on several points which he should address in presenting the case for the Air Ministry in the House of Lords. He encouraged him not to dwell on the Baldwin figures. 'Public opinion wants to know what we have now to do and how we are to do it, and will look for a determined and optimistic spirit in those who are to do the work,' he wrote. 'Be firm as regards the future,' he recommended, 'and do not try in any great measure to explain the past. The defence of the past can be made only by making it forgotten, and that can be done by demonstrating energy and will as regards the very immediate future.'[147]

Privately, the Prime Minister took the view that Londonderry and his Ministry had been 'caught napping' on the speed of German air rearmament. A meeting on 10 May of the Defence Requirements Committee had dealt with a 'very unsettling report', revealing that British heavy bombers were inferior to those of the Germans, and that no new designs had been tested. MacDonald admitted he had been taken aback by the position. It was difficult to combat 'the wildest rumours and figures', since reliable information was difficult to obtain. But, plainly, his confidence in his friend and the Ministry he was running had been severely dented. 'The Air Ministry', MacDonald noted in his diary, 'have had no imagination and have been slack and without foresight'.[148]

On 21 May, the day before the defence debate was due to begin, the Cabinet agreed to an extension of the air programme, which now aimed to produce a first-line strength of 1,512 planes by the end of March 1937. Even that would be insufficient if Germany were to continue the acceleration in the rate of aircraft production. Moreover, production in the new programme was, expert advice made clear, hampered by weaknesses in technical structures which had been allowed to develop.[149] It was another criticism of Londonderry's ministry. The driving force behind the new scheme was, in fact, not Londonderry but Sir Philip Cunliffe-Lister, still Secretary of State for the Colonies but, as Chairman of a newly established Air Parity Sub-Committee and a close ally of Baldwin's (and no political friend of Londonderry's), playing an increasingly important role in the crucial matter of rearmament of the air force.[150] It was another sign of how precarious Londonderry's hold on his office had become.

On the same day, Hitler held another big 'peace speech' in the Reichstag in Berlin. The background was Germany's isolation brought about through the Stresa Pact in mid-April agreed by Britain, Italy and France (to uphold Austrian independence), the League of Nations' denunciation of Germany's introduction of conscription, and the pact of mutual assistance between France and the USSR that had been concluded on 2 May, which, followed on 16 May by a Czech-Soviet Pact[151] and given France's existing treaty arrangements with Czechoslovakia, was seen to threaten Germany in the east. Hitler's speech, sounding reasonable and moderate, was largely directed at Britain, dismissing any threat to the country, seeking no more than air parity (along with a limit of 35 per cent of British naval tonnage), and ruling out demands for colonies.[152] It amounted to a bid for the alliance he so much wanted with Britain. And it was calculated to appeal to those who, like Londonderry, believed in Germany's good intentions.[153]

The parliamentary debate of 22 May 1935 on Britain's air defences was a disaster for Londonderry, whose speech in the House of Lords sounded the death-knell of his career as Minister of Air. The debate began that afternoon with Lord Lloyd, former Governor of Bombay and High Commissioner for Egypt and the Sudan, querying the state of national security in the light of Hitler's recent claim to air parity. Despite Ramsay MacDonald's advice to concentrate on future, not past, air policy, Londonderry launched into a defence of the Air Ministry's performance, insisting on the accuracy of its figures for German aircraft and current superiority of first-line strength over the Luftwaffe and criticizing the 'alarmist picture' presented by others, before going on to emphasize the substantial expansion envisaged for the Royal Air Force over the subsequent two years. He then returned to the past, and the difficult circumstances of economic depression in which air policy had been forced to develop. This was incontrovertible. But it was when he moved on to his own role, in a climate of disarmament, in defending the bomber – 'the weapon of the Air Force' – that he, quite unnecessarily, ventured on to extremely thin ice. 'I had the utmost difficulty at that time', he said, 'amid the public outcry, in preserving the use of the bombing aeroplane, even on the frontier of the Middle East and India, where it was only owing to the presence of the Air Force that we have controlled these territories without the old and heavy cost of blood and treasure.' This had little or nothing to do with the question at issue: whether or not Britain had sufficient air defence against Hitler's Luftwaffe. But it invited nemesis for Londonderry. And at a time when opinion had swung so swiftly to seeing a real and direct threat to Britain in the rapid expansion of Germany's air force, Londonderry again struck the wrong tone in indicating that he was gratified to find in Hitler's words 'a definite acceptance' of the doctrine of arms limitation in the air which had been the 'ultimate policy' of his Air Ministry.[154]

It was, however, his gratuitous reference (which had not been in his original text) to bombing on the frontiers of the Empire that brought him irreparable damage. In truth, as we have seen, he neither invented the policy, nor was he the first to advocate its retention. In fact, successive governments (including the Labour government of 1929–31) had long accepted it without demur. A practice which sounds today (and was) a brutal weapon of repression had its 'civilized' supporters beyond Londonderry who backed its efficiency, cost-effectiveness and (so, remarkably, it was claimed) its 'humanity' in maintaining peace and order with so little bloodshed, compared with 'the old-fashioned punitive expeditions ending in machine-gun fire and a round-up with the bayonet'.[155] The Left, and not just its pacifist wing, had long seen in Londonderry the chief defender of the bomber, whose threat from the air had come to symbolize the horrors of modern warfare.[156] His words now brought storms of protest from the Labour opposition and cemented his reputation as the champion of 'air bombing and all its attendant horrors'.[157]

The press outcry resembled the circling of vultures, scenting a wounded prey. But if the clamour came from the Left, it was on his own side, among his Conservative 'friends', that the real political danger lay. Londonderry had, as we have observed, become dangerously vulnerable in previous weeks. His main protector, the Prime Minister, was ill, wearied with office, and, as he now let it be known, ready to hand over. He let Londonderry know 'that knives are into the Air Ministry', which was 'in an awkward position' owing to 'the German revelations', but that, 'completely worn out', he was no longer able to provide support.[158] MacDonald's successor was not to be, as the Londonderrys had hoped, Neville Chamberlain, but Stanley Baldwin, whose bluff cordiality could not conceal the fact that he did not rank among Londonderry's political friends. In any case, a general election was looming and the Conservative Party (which by now provided almost the entire 'National' Government) could not afford to court unpopularity and likely loss of seats by holding on to a weak and damaged minister who was under intense fire from both sides – from the Left for his defence of bombing, and from the Right for his inability to provide for Britain's air defences.[159] Londonderry had become a political liability. As Baldwin later put it: 'I feel now that he should have offered his resignation at once,' that is, immediately after his speech. 'There was an outcry. The Opposition seized the opportunity and made it the spearhead of their election campaign, but a far bigger outcry came from the Conservative Party. Members were beginning to look to their seats and here was a Cabinet Minister giving the enemy ammunition free and for nothing. The Air Minister must go.'[160]

Though Londonderry had some justification for thinking that he had been made a scapegoat for the policies of an ineffective National Government, especially in defence, and that he had fought hard and often against the odds for the Air Ministry when there had been intense pressure to pare down or even abolish the Air Force, the truth was that he had not been a successful Air Minister and now, unfair as it seemed to him, he was being made to pay the price.

His period in office had not been devoid of achievements – though few were prepared to acknowledge them at the time, when he was widely seen as a failure, or even in years to come, when he had been stigmatized as pro-German. Londonderry did set in train the design and promotion of what would turn into the Hurricanes and Spitfires that were to play such a vital part in the Battle of Britain.[161] The beginnings of British radar development – and little could have been more important in the air war soon to come – also date back to his period of office.[162] It was under Londonderry as Air Minister, too, that the early British bombers (whose prototypes were revealed in 1936) – the Wellingtons, Hampdens and Blenheims – originated.[163] And though he was pilloried at the time for his defence of the bomber, an alternative policy would have done nothing to deflect the devastation of European cities by Stukas, Heinkels and Junkers which would follow within a few years. These achievements of British air policy under Londonderry need, in fairness, to be acknowledged and set against his limitations as a government minister.

His limitations, nevertheless, outweighed his attributes. His main fault was that he proved of insufficient standing (partly owing to his dependence upon MacDonald) to pull his weight against the Treasury during the contest for scarce resources in 1934. Politically, the Air Ministry was weak when in those times quite especially it needed to be strong. A less benign, less dependent and more ruthless individual than Londonderry would have been necessary to sustain and build up the position of the Air Ministry in such a difficult climate.[164] Though intensely loyal to his ministry (and well liked by those beneath him, who respected the fight he had put up when circumstances had been most adverse),[165] he was seen to have presided over the relative decline in Britain's air power which was then thrown into sharp relief by Hitler's parity claim in March 1935 and by Churchill's relentless, and well-informed, attack on the inadequacy of air defences. The editorial of the magazine *Flight* was not unfair in its assessment. In acknowledging that Londonderry held office during a difficult period, it continued: 'It was probably not entirely his fault that during his term of office Britain's Air Force fell far behind those of other nations in numerical strength. The blame for that must rest with the Cabinet as a whole, although a stronger personality might have succeeded in impressing the risks on the other members of the Cabinet.'[166]

The rise of German air strength had raised the Air Ministry from its status as the least important of the armed services to a position of crucial centrality. As Churchill was later to write: 'The Air Ministry did not realise that a new inheritance awaited them. The Treasury's fetters were broken. They had but to ask for more.'[167] But Londonderry's handling of the new pressure on his ministry after March – together with the new opportunities on offer – was anything but skilful. His pesistent attempts to prove the correctness of the Ministry's figures ended, repeatedly and predictably, in a statistical quagmire and amounted to a woeful misreading of the mood in the Cabinet and in the country. Perversely, just as this mood turned to favour the expansion of the Air Force which Londonderry had for so long advocated, he seemed uninterested in exploiting it and obsessed with justifying the ministry's past performance. It won him no favours, and made him look stubbornly inept at the same time.[168] And so, as Churchill pithily put it, 'after having gone through several years of asking for more', Londonderry was 'suddenly turned out for not asking enough'.[169]

Stanley Baldwin – son of a Worcestershire ironmaster, pipe-smoking, tweed-suited epitome of the solid country squire, provincial English to his roots, but the shrewdest of political operators – became Prime Minister for the third time on 7 June 1935 at the age of sixty-seven. His Cabinet had already been decided beforehand.[170]

Predictably, Londonderry was dropped as Air Minister. Baldwin took the view, which had been mooted in fact some weeks earlier during what Londonderry saw as 'intrigues' against him, that the importance of the Air Ministry now meant that the Secretary of State for Air should be on the front bench of the House of Commons, not in the Lords.[171] This was a kind way of indicating that someone tougher than Londonderry, more dynamic and energetic, and with wider experience of business and industry, should take over. Baldwin realized that he should have dismissed Londonderry altogether. But he recognized his 'inability to be a butcher'.[172] So he sugared the pill for Londonderry by offering him the position of Lord Privy Seal (an ancient office, now given to a minister without departmental responsibilities or specific portfolio), making him at the same time Leader of the House of Lords.[173] Though disappointed at having to leave the Air Ministry, the temptation to continue in high office was too great for Londonderry to refuse. In accepting, 'with certain misgivings', he did not forget to point out to Baldwin that, though the incoming Prime Minister had not mentioned it, he presumed that he would still be a member of the Cabinet.[174]

So Londonderry's eventful term of office as Secretary of State for Air ended. He had been discredited in the government position he held so dear. One reason put forward for his dismissal is, however, incorrect: that 'he had involved himself in a group whose sympathies were evidently pro-German'.[175] For this there is, during his period as Air Minister, no evidence at all. Before 1936, there is no indication that Lord Londonderry had any genuine sympathy with the Nazi regime.[176] He certainly lent towards Germany, as we have seen, in the policy he repeatedly urged the British government to adopt. But beyond this leaning, driven by what he saw as needs of British defence and security, there is little to suggest that he had any particular, or special, interest in Germany while he was Secretary of State for Air. Perhaps, even so, there were one or two straws in the wind. He had been an interested member of a small 'study-group', set up by Dr Margarete Gärtner (whom we encountered earlier, working to further Anglo-German friendship), to visit the German coal-fields in the Ruhr in 1929.[177] He was, as we noted – if only for a brief time, it seems, before becoming Air Minister – a member of the Anglo-German

Association, which, even before Hitler's advent, had looked to closer relations between the two countries. By late 1931, now as Minister for Air, Londonderry was prepared to introduce Dr Gärtner to influential members of the House of Lords.[178] And his enthusiasm for flying, all the more pronounced once he became responsible for government policy on air, brought him into increased contact with a world of aviation with marked pro-German (and some distinctly pro-Fascist) sympathies. Such sentiments were encouraged by interest in German civil aviation, a sense that Germany was being unfairly prevented from having an air force, and lingering notions of an earlier chivalric contest between the fliers of the First World War (of whom the spokesman for aviation in Germany, Hermann Göring, had been a great hero). Strong pro-German (and anti-French) feeling was propagated in the magazine *The Aeroplane*, which was widely read in aviation circles, and certainly by Londonderry himself. The magazine's idiosyncratic editor, C. G. Grey, made no secret of his admiration for Germany, while his vehement racism, anti-Semitism and anti-Bolshevism were a match for those of the Nazis themselves.[179] In the nature of things, it is impossible to prove that such views exerted any influence upon Londonderry. Perhaps they helped indirectly to reinforce Londonderry's latent anti-French prejudice, already perceptible (as we noted) during the First World War and enhanced by his experience of the frustrating deliberations taking place on international disarmament at Geneva, along with his strong hostility towards Bolshevism, both of which would affect his later stance towards Germany. But there is little to indicate that, while he was Air Minister, Londonderry was singularly pro-German, other than in his wish to come to an accommodation on arms limitation with Germany, at the cost if necessary of deteriorating relations with the French.

Yet within a few months of leaving the Air Ministry, Londonderry would emerge as one of Germany's most forthright champions in Britain. What brought about the transformation? Beyond the political inclinations we have followed, and the progressive sense that British foreign policy was hopelessly misguided, a psychological element probably came into play. For a sensitive as well as proud individual, his dismissal as Air Minister (and the circumstances which had prompted it) hurt deeply. His strong disapproval of the way the

Foreign Office had been conducting relations with Germany has been clearly apparent. This disapproval was now enhanced by the bitterness he felt at his treatment by his government colleagues, notably those in the Foreign Office. He felt that he himself could do better if he were listened to. With Samuel Hoare, a friend, as Foreign Secretary, he now, in fact, hoped for an improvement. And, indeed, the turn to Germany would only become transparent after another sacking – and the rancour which accompanied the embarrassment and humiliation – in November. This would prove the push which directed Londonderry into his open stance of approval for Nazi Germany shortly afterwards – and on to the road to public ignominy.

3

Nazi Friends

'To say that I was deeply impressed is not adequate. I am amazed. You and Germany remind me of the book of Genesis in the Bible. Nothing else describes the position accurately.'
Lady Londonderry, writing to Hitler in February 1936, on return from Germany

'I am a great friend of Lord Londonderry, and that is why I am here.'
Joachim von Ribbentrop, at the end of May 1936, on arriving in Northern Ireland to spend a weekend at Mount Stewart as the Londonderrys' guest

At the beginning of June 1935, Lord Londonderry still held the office of state he so cherished – that of Minister for Air. Though widely regarded as a failure in that position, nothing in his public image hinted that within a year he would become notorious as the most prominent member of the pro-German lobby in Britain. Yet by the beginning of June 1936, he had enjoyed every hospitality accorded by top-rank Nazis in Berlin, had spoken at length with Hitler, had been Göring's guest at his hunting-lodge, Carinhall, and was now himself entertaining a leading Nazi, Joachim von Ribbentrop, at his home in Northern Ireland in a visit that one newspaper described under the banner heading: 'Swastika over Ulster'.[1]

Within the space of those twelve months, Londonderry had experienced double political humiliation at home and, in stark contrast, had been warmly welcomed in Germany. His sacking in June 1935 as

Secretary of State for Air was followed, in November, by a second dismissal, this time from the Cabinet post he had been given as a consolation prize – that of Lord Privy Seal. As Lady Bracknell might have put it: to lose one Cabinet office might be seen as unfortunate; to lose a second within a matter of months smacked of carelessness. Londonderry's bitterness lasted to his dying day. Within weeks, now freed of government responsibilities, he was paying the first (since the Nazis took power) of a series of private visits to Germany, where he was given the red-carpet treatment and courted by the leading representatives of the Nazi regime, including Hitler himself.

It was no coincidence that Londonderry's turn to Germany followed so closely in the wake of his anger and depression at how his political friends had treated him. Humiliated at home, he felt esteemed abroad. His searing resentment at his treatment by Baldwin and flattery at his reception by Hitler fuelled the sense that, liberated from the shackles of Cabinet office, he could succeed where the Foreign Office professionals had failed. They had, he had long been preaching, followed the wrong path – one heading for disaster. Through getting to know and understand the German leaders, personal contact would offer another way forward. And if the British government, through his own connections and persuasion, could finally be brought to see the light, catastrophe could even now be averted. This was the basis of Londonderry's thinking. To see how this emerged, we must look more closely at the way he responded to his own fate, and to the increasing political tension during the last months of 1935 and the spring of 1936.

I

In the summer of 1935 the British public was as usual more preoccupied with domestic worries – housing, unemployment, how to make ends meet – than foreign affairs. Even so, there was a growing awareness (if, for many, still a dim one) that the dangers to peace and security were greater than they had been only a few years earlier, and were mounting not diminishing. The Abyssinian crisis, arising from Mussolini's ambitions to build a new Roman empire in east Africa, and running over the first months of Stanley Baldwin's new term of office as Prime Minister, was the latest manifestation of this. For a time this switched the focus of attention in Britain from Germany to Italy. But whether the dictator causing international turmoil was Mussolini or Hitler (both 'lunatics', in Baldwin's eyes),[2] it was increasingly obvious even to a layman that disarmament was dead – nothing more than a lingering illusion. Rearmament, like it or not, was now on the agenda in a way which, only a year earlier, had been scarcely imaginable. So, as it turned out, was the very purpose and future of the League of Nations, as the fabric of collective security began to unravel at alarming speed.

An insight into British attitudes towards collective security, and its mounting problems, was provided on 28 June 1935 when Viscount Cecil of Chelwood, a former Conservative minister who had long been the most prominent enthusiast for the League of Nations, announced the results of the 'Peace Ballot'. This was a type of unofficial opinion survey, carried out over the previous eight months by the League of Nations Union (in which Liberals were dominant) through a canvass of householders in Britain. In all, a remarkable 11½ million responses, from a sizeable majority of households, were gathered. The title was actually a misnomer, used by critics of the ballot to discredit it as pacifist. In fact, the ballot was not about pacifism, but international disarmament and collective security. Five questions were asked, couched in a way that suggested the desired answer. Over 10 million duly answered 'yes' to questions such as whether Britain should remain a member of the League of Nations; whether an all-round reduction in armaments should be achieved; military and naval aircraft abolished; and private manufacture and sale of arms prohibited; all through international agreement. The last question was in two parts. 'Do you consider that, if a nation insists on attacking another, the other nations should combine to compel it to stop by (a) Economic and non-military measures? (b) If necessary, military measures?' The second part drew a more differentiated response. And this was, by the time the results were announced, a question coming to acquire real meaning. Though almost all answers – still over 10 million – to (a) were affirmative, the number for (b) dropped to 6¾ million, while over 2 million said 'no' and another 2 million gave no answer. The answers suggested a strong commitment to collective security, and to the imposition of sanctions if necessary, but significant divisions if this commitment had to be backed by war.³ Though it was easy enough for the government to pour scorn on the over-simplified and tendentious nature of the questions posed, the Peace Ballot did provide (and was seen by the government to do so) a snapshot, even if the image was distorted, of public opinion on Britain's international responsibilities. These would soon be put to the test.

Mussolini's Abyssinian adventure provided an early opportunity. Thirsting for imperial glory and the chance to eradicate Italy's humiliating defeat by the Abyssinians at the battle of Adowa in 1896, the Italian dictator had exploited a minor border incident to stake a territorial claim to Abyssinia (now Ethiopia), a member of the League of Nations. Full-scale aggression loomed. The British government faced a dilemma. It desperately wanted to avoid conflict with Italy. Good relations with Italy would ensure sound lines of communication through the Mediterranean to the Far East, at a time when the Japanese were seen to pose a mounting threat to British interests in that region. Britain was also keen to see Italy as a counterweight to German expansionist aims, and to maintain the Italian antagonism towards Hitler's regime that had existed since the murder of the Austrian Chancellor, Engelbert Dollfuss, by the Nazis in July 1934 had prompted Mussolini to move troops to the Brenner Pass. At the same time the British government was anxious to uphold the authority of the League of Nations when faced with a crisis that threatened to undermine it completely. In June Britain put forward a compromise territorial solution to the Italians. It consisted of the offer of a small port by Britain to Abyssinia, thereby granting her access to the sea, in return for territorial concessions to Italy in the barren south of the country. Mussolini rejected the proposal out of hand, remaining implacable in his insistence on settling the Abyssinian question once and for all, through force if a negotiated settlement proved impossible. And Britain's proposal, advanced without prior discussions with France, further infuriated the French (concerned also about the protection of their own interests in the Abyssinian port of Djibouti), already embittered over Britain's bilateral agreement with the Germans in the Naval Treaty which had been concluded only a little while earlier that month. French distrust of the British Foreign Office's handling of the Abyssinian affair was now hard to dispel. This increased their interest in avoiding a breach with Italy and searching for a compromise solution to the conflict. For their part, the British were suspicious that Pierre Laval, the French Foreign Minister, had been over-ready to encourage Mussolini's designs on Abyssinia when he had visited Rome some months earlier.[4] The divisions between the British and their French allies hindered any firm stance towards Italy as the crisis dragged on over the summer months. Mussolini had staked Italian prestige on the outcome. As the diplomatic impasse continued, the threat, implied from the outset, that Mussolini might resort to armed force was a worrying prospect. In mid-September, at Geneva, Britain's new Foreign Secretary, Sir Samuel Hoare, appeared to make Britain's position, at least, crystal clear. He even obliquely referred to the Peace Ballot in stating Britain's commitment to its international responsibilities under the Covenant of the League of Nations and its readiness to provide 'steady and collective resistance to all acts of unprovoked aggression'.[5]

A new plan was put to Mussolini a few days later to settle the dispute, which once again he rejected outright. Then, on 3 October, Italy invaded Abyssinia. During the next weeks the creaky machinery of the League of Nations eventually moved into gear, imposing extensive sanctions on Italy. Italian credits were blocked, while, with few unimportant exceptions, League members stopped imports to and exports from Italy. The French had dragged their feet, but had nonetheless come into line. It seemed as if the League of Nations was finally fulfilling the purpose for which it had been established. And for the National Government in Britain the policy of sanctions was most timely. 'All sanctions short of war', as Baldwin put it, accorded entirely with the wishes of the British public as expressed in the Peace Ballot. This took the wind out of the sails of the Labour opposition in Britain, which had made sizeable gains in recent by-elections. When Baldwin went to the country in the general election on 14 November, in which a few months earlier the National Government had looked likely to suffer heavy losses, the result was victory for the Prime Minister.

The Labour Party certainly recovered some of the ground so disastrously lost in the débâcle of the previous election of 1931, when, split and demoralized, its vote had collapsed calamitously, returning only 52 Members of Parliament. Now, much of the traditional support had been regained, and Labour won 154 seats. The Liberals not aligned to the National Government continued their long-term decline, down now from 33 to 20 seats. The Conservative Party had won 473 seats in the unique circumstances of 1931, forming the National Government with the help of 35 National Liberals and 13 National Labour members – a total support of 521 MPs. Despite the worst slump ever experienced, the Conservatives under Baldwin still held on to as many as 387 seats, and the National Government continued to be backed by 429 MPs, providing it still with a huge majority over the combined Opposition.[6] Baldwin could feel pleased with himself. Rearmament had a mandate.[7] So had the policy of sanctions against Italy. Anxieties over Germany had faded temporarily into the background. And the economy was showing marked signs of recovery. It was business as usual.

Little tampering was needed with his Cabinet. There was minimal reshuffling. Only one minister was dropped. This was Londonderry – his second sacking within five months. He lost his position both as Lord Privy Seal and as Leader of the House of Lords (another title with more prestige than power), to be replaced in both posts by Lord Halifax. It meant the end of his governmental career. Hopes of continuing in high office, with the trappings of power and influence, were now dashed once and for all. The sense of humiliation ran deep. If anything, the second sacking hurt even more than his dismissal as Air Minister.

It could, even so, have come as little surprise to anyone but Londonderry himself, his wife and his immediate family. Lady Londonderry had, in fact, indicated that her husband might be making a mistake to accept Baldwin's offer of a continued position in the government when he was ousted from the Air Ministry. She interpreted it as 'merely another stage in the plot of squeezing me out altogether' and begged him to retire.[8] There was, of course, no plot – even if Ramsay MacDonald, in connection with Londonderry's dismissal, later spoke of 'disreputable wire-pullers' in the Conservative Party.[9] But she was not far wrong in presuming that Londonderry might be living on borrowed time. The reputation he carried with him from his days at the Air

Ministry did not bode well for the future, and there was some resentment among leading Conservatives at Londonderry holding on to office at all following his sacking as Air Minister. Leslie Hore-Belisha, for instance, Minister of Transport since June 1934, though resentful that he was not at this time in the Cabinet, commented privately that Lord Londonderry 'was a second-rate man, not capable at all and really ignorant, yet when they got him out of the Air Ministry he was made Lord Privy Seal'.[10] This was a harsh judgement, but politics is a rough trade, and it is an indicator of what others, too, were probably thinking, even if they were not so forthright in their expression. Londonderry had himself been aware that all was not well following the minor reshuffle in June at the start of Baldwin's new administration. 'In both the House of Lords and the House of Commons', he recalled, 'there was a general air of listlessness, for it was obvious there must be a dissolution and an appeal to the country.'[11]

Londonderry was now largely marginalized within the Cabinet. He made no significant contribution to Cabinet debate, not least on the mounting Abyssinian crisis which dominated the summer and autumn. Whereas he had for two years advocated a fairly consistent line of policy on Germany, he had little to say on Italian aggression towards Abyssinia. Probably this reflected in part his private distance from the official government position which, as a member of the Cabinet, he was obliged to support. When his wife passed on to him a letter sent to her expressing pro-Italian sentiments, with which, she said, she agreed, and strong criticism of the League of Nations he passed no comment.[12] Publicly, he placed his faith in finding a solution to the Abyssinian problem through the League, though showed sympathy for 'Italy's difficulties' and commented favourably on the country's 'progressive and satisfactory' development under Mussolini.[13] But by now his faith in the League had ebbed away, he did not want to make an enemy of Italy, whose leader he had long admired, and he was worried about the prospect of Britain becoming involved in a war between Italy and Abyssinia.[14]

He was, in reality, still too preoccupied with fending off the continued attacks on his record as Air Minister and his defence of bombing to give deep consideration to other concerns. Already, it seems, the depression which would grip him in the autumn was taking hold.

By September, encouraged by his wife, he was contemplating resignation. He told Ramsay MacDonald towards the end of the month: 'I am preparing for my exit and waiting for the moment of the announcement of a General Election . . . to tell Baldwin that I cannot with the minimum of self respect stay on in the ridiculous position in which I find myself'.[15] His chief ally in the Cabinet, Lord Hailsham, had already advised him to hold on until the election, which could not be too long delayed, since any resignation at that point would be taken as disagreement over policy towards Italy.[16] Despite this advice, a month later, in mid-October, Londonderry arranged a meeting with the Prime Minister, perhaps even intending to tender his resignation. If so, he changed his mind at the last minute, and instead followed up his audience with Baldwin by a letter. He had done no work, he wrote, since leaving the Air Ministry, did not serve on any committees, and felt that, as Leader of the House of Lords, 'my position is an impossible one unless I am able to be closely in touch with yourself and those who control policy'.[17]

As this indicates, Londonderry himself recognized that he was no more than a passenger in the government. And, though no longer Air Minister, his incautious remarks on bombing during the parliamentary debate in May meant that he remained an electoral liability for the Conservative Party once Baldwin had asked the King on 18 October for a dissolution of Parliament prior to elections on 14 November. The Labour Party made a personalized attack on Londonderry, still seen as the weakest link in the government, part of its electoral campaign. Clement Attlee, about to become leader of the Labour Party, who had resolutely opposed rearmament, launched the assault in a broadcast on 28 October, stating that 'at Geneva, Lord Londonderry worked hard on his own admission to prevent the abolition of air bombing', and implying that, but for him, the scourge of bombing would have been eliminated in the Disarmament talks.[18] It travestied Londonderry's actual position, but his blunder in May had left him a wounded political animal at bay, and his party-political enemies scented the kill. Londonderry vociferously defended himself in speeches and, later, in a lengthy letter to *The Times*. In fact, recognizing him as a liability, the Conservative Party Central Office kept him out of the election campaign and he remained for its duration in isolation at Mount Stewart.[19] Lady Londonderry lent her husband what support she could give, privately and in her own election speeches – though when she tried to hold a public address at Newcastle (close to the Durham coal-fields which Londonderry owned) 'she was greeted with a storm of cat calls and jeers', 'unable to speak a word', and the meeting had to be abandoned.[20]

As we noted, when the results were declared, the National Government had achieved a more than comfortable victory. But it is unlikely that Londonderry's extreme unpopularity on the Left contributed significantly to the Labour Party's improved performance at the polls. His fate had in reality almost certainly been settled long before the outcome of the election was known. Reading the incontrovertible runes, Lady Londonderry wrote to her husband just before his dismissal was made public, advising him to tell Baldwin that 'you feel you can do much better work outside the Gov[ernmen]t'.[21] But by now it was far too late for such gestures.

From Baldwin's point of view there was no purpose to be served by holding on to a minister who was playing no obvious part in government and was at the same time a magnet for the attacks of the Opposition. Even so, Chamberlain, who had urged the dismissal of Londonderry in the wake of his 'bombing' speech in May, was relieved to hear that he had been dropped since he had feared that Baldwin might not take the logical step.[22] Londonderry's replacement was Lord Halifax – tall, lugubrious, a deeply experienced Conservative patrician, former Viceroy of India, whose hunting interests and religiosity provided him with his punning nickname (invented by Churchill) of 'the Holy Fox', and in contrast to the dogmatic and maladroit Londonderry so tactically astute and skilled in diplomacy that he would go a long way to find a fence to sit on. The change made eminent political sense.[23] However, Baldwin took one step which made it difficult to justify the move to the sacked minister. He had told Londonderry in May – who for all his disappointment saw the force of the argument – that the post of Secretary of State for Air had become so important that it had to be held by a minister with a seat in the House of Commons. Londonderry, based in the Lords, had consequently made way for Sir Philip Cunliffe-Lister. But now, in his reshuffle five months later, Baldwin moved Cunliffe-Lister to the Lords, with the newly created title of Viscount

Swinton, thereby undermining in the plainest fashion his own argument for Londonderry's earlier removal from the Air Ministry. It compounded the pain of the second sacking. Londonderry, continuing to believe he had been a success in both his offices, never forgave Baldwin for what seemed to him a gratuitously humiliating form of dismissal.[24]

Cordialities were maintained in the exchange of letters – private, and not made public – which followed. Baldwin spoke of Londonderry as 'a loyal and trusted friend', said he held him 'in affection', and wrote that he was 'profoundly distressed' at being unable to offer him a place in the new government. Less ruthless than most Prime Ministers when the political axe had to fall, and doubtless wary, too, of the offence he was about to cause in the other half of the Londonderry household, he took the unusual step of adding a note of regret to Lady Londonderry.[25] In his reply, Lord Londonderry reciprocated kind words (which he scarcely felt) on maintaining personal friendship, but noted that he learnt of the decision 'with some surprise because I recollect that you very expressly said that if I joined your Government in June I might retain the Leadership of the House of Lords as long as I wished to do so'.[26] Baldwin later remonstrated to Londonderry's son, Lord Castlereagh, that no Prime Minister could have made such a promise and that there had evidently been some misunderstanding.[27] But nothing could assuage Londonderry. He was 'absolutely mortified' to be thrown out of office for a second time.[28] Lord Castlereagh, calling at Londonderry House on the morning after the dismissal with his sister, Lady Maureen Stanley, found his father 'a tragic sight'. He looked a broken man, 'sitting sideways in his chair with his legs dangling over the arm', holding Baldwin's letter in his hand and with tears running down his cheeks repeatedly muttering: '"I've been sacked – kicked out."'[29]

Unsurprisingly, in the circumstances, the Londonderrys did not feel up to offering Baldwin their Park Lane mansion for the usual lavish reception – with never fewer than 2,500 guests attending – on the opening of Parliament that November. Lady Londonderry issued a press statement – which Londonderry had suggested to Baldwin should be put out – saying that Londonderry House had been offered as usual to the Prime Minister 'but Mr. Baldwin considered that the present moment was not opportune'. Shortage of time to organize the reception and the continued deep depression in the coal-fields (with which Londonderry was associated) were offered as the (disingenuous) reasons. Baldwin did not comment. In fact, Londonderry himself had decided there should be no reception. A spokesman for him denied that there was any breach between the former Lord Privy Seal and the Prime Minister, and declared 'that their friendship is as ever'.[30] Though appearances were kept up (and though Baldwin stayed a member of Lady Londonderry's 'Ark')[31] this was hardly the case. Looking back, Londonderry, though claiming somewhat implausibly that he bore no grudge, acknowledged that he had 'never really got on with Baldwin' (or Chamberlain, for that matter), and 'that I feel irritated with Baldwin and those who brought about my downfall'. However, he did admit that, on reflection, he did not believe he was ever a good Cabinet minister or colleague 'because I like to lead and control and I detest supporting and playing a minor fiddle in the band'.[32]

Even as late as the end of 1938, Londonderry, saying 'you need not think that I have any vindictive feelings in my mind', was berating Baldwin, who had ceased to be Prime Minister nearly two years earlier, in a fourteen-page letter, for being 'callous', destroying 'whatever chance I had of doing useful public work', and injuring him in public estimation. He had, wrote Londonderry, with one stroke wiped him off the political map. He spoke of his 'impotent rage' at being 'discredited and my position destroyed by the manner in which you had treated me'.[33] For his part, Baldwin claimed he had always tried to be friends, but Londonderry was 'aloof and standoffish'. Baldwin went on to comment that Lady Londonderry, particularly through her friendship with Ramsay MacDonald, had been a damaging influence on her husband in politics.[34]

Among the two dozen or so letters of commiseration that Londonderry received after his second sacking were one from a former staff member of the Air Ministry, commending his 'single-handed' fight for the air force to save it; one from the Poet Laureate of English imperialism, Rudyard Kipling, applauding his 'courageous stand and speech on Re-Armament', which would not be forgotten; and one from his aristocratic friend, Lord Halifax, expressing his distaste at 'the events of these last days' and hating 'being asked to take over your job in the H[ouse] of L[ords]'.[35]

In his lengthy reply to Halifax, Londonderry did not hide his bitterness. 'Baldwin has not and never has had any knowledge whatsoever of me', he wrote, 'or he would have treated me quite differently from the beginning.' In removing him from the Air Ministry, 'he wounded my heart perhaps more than it has ever been wounded before,' the tone of pathos continued. He could take no objection to the reason given, he added, that the Air Ministry should be held by a member of the House of Commons, but when his successor, Cunliffe-Lister, had nevertheless been elevated to the House of Lords but retained the Air Ministry, he had been placed 'in an extremely difficult position'. He repeated Baldwin's offer (as he had undoubtedly misinterpreted it) that he could hold the office of Lord Privy Seal and Leadership of the House of Lords 'for as long as I wished'. After disregarding his own inclinations and advice from his wife and from friends to resign, since he did not want to 'appear to have gone off in a huff', he had thrown himself into the duties of his new office, only to find that he was kept isolated and out of all government work,[36] forced to lead 'a life of complete but strained idleness'. He went on to doubt the reason Baldwin had given him for having to leave him out of the Cabinet – that room had to be found for Halifax (who, he had heard at the time, was actually seeking to retire from active politics). In other words, the Prime Minister, in his view, had not been telling him the truth. He concluded that 'to have remained on as Lord Privy Seal and Leader of the House of Lords and to have been treated as I have been treated since last June was quite impossible', ending, somewhat disingenuously, by saying he had no complaints or recriminations.[37]

The next weeks saw Londonderry in a deeply depressed and embittered mood. Looking back in a private letter several years later, he wrote: 'When Baldwin removed me I instinctively knew that I had [sic] finished, that my active life was over and that I had to fall back on resources which it is difficult to cultivate when you have been in the middle of politics as I had been since the end of the last war.' He had, he commented, 'touched almost the lowest depths of despair'.[38] His wife, unwell herself at the time, tried to prop him up and bolster his severely dented self-esteem. He responded by recriminations that she had been no help to him in his public life.[39] The tension which flared up in these weeks was unquestionably a sign of the mental strain and distress that Londonderry felt after the abrupt and unhappy ending of his political career. He told Baldwin months after his sacking that he could not 'bear to feel that anybody should say that I failed at the Air Ministry which I loved or in leading the H[ouse] of L[ords] which I was proud to do'.[40] Yet in the last period of his life, looking back, Londonderry plaintively described himself as 'a miserable failure'. And he clearly dated the initial sense of failure to 1935, the year of his double dismissal from high office. Before then, he wrote, 'whatever I touched seem[ed] to turn to gold. I seemed to succeed in everything . . . and then suddenly it all came to an end'.[41]

But if the underlying psychological malaise stayed with him to the end of his days, the inertia did not last long. Something had to fill the vacuum. Londonderry needed activity, a sense of purpose and a feeling of commitment – even if his services were now unofficial – to public service. And he also had a private score to settle with Baldwin and his other detractors: to prove that he had been right all along, both about air armaments, and about the way to ensure peace for Europe. The prospect of attaining this goal through a personal visit to Germany, making use of his contacts in high places, took shape in his mind while, in a resentful and depressed mood, contemplating his future, he fished in the Brora, in the Scottish Highlands, in the late summer of 1935. In a letter to Ramsay MacDonald towards the end of September, he remarked, cryptically and hinting at the risks he would embrace, 'I feel I shall embark very soon on a different line of action so must guard the contacts I value.'[42] Londonderry's 'turn to Germany' was not born out of any love for that country, let alone for Nazism. It was quite plainly 'made in England' – a reaction to the way his views had been consistently ignored, and to the humiliation at the unjust way he felt he had been treated by Baldwin.

Londonderry had, as we have seen, long been at loggerheads with the Foreign Office, 'criticising all their telegrams and finding fault with the attitudes which they adopted on so many what seemed to me very important questions', primarily 'the whole German situation', which had been 'allowed to drift in the most deplorable way', allowing the Germans to gather strength and become 'masters of the situation'.[43] Londonderry's unfulfilled ambition had been to become

Foreign Secretary. That, it was clear, would for ever remain no more than a pipedream. But he thought that if his own proposals for a more accommodating position towards Germany, even now, were to be put into practice instead of being ignored, then war, otherwise inevitable, might still be averted. Possibly, he might even emulate his esteemed forebear, Lord Castlereagh, who had been instrumental in bringing about the settlement of Europe after the defeat of Napoleon, by restoring, at this late hour, the concert of Europe and putting an end to the catastrophe which he was sure he would befall the Continent, and with it western civilization, following another war.[44]

So he arrived at the decision, 'relieved of my official position', to 'pursue a more realistic policy'. This entailed visiting Germany, in a private capacity, to explore, in the first instance, the truth about the arms build-up, especially regarding the air force. Londonderry thought that, by going to Germany, he could see for himself 'the real state of affairs'. The alternative, in his view, to an arms race 'which could only have one end' was 'to try and arrive at some arrangement with Germany'. He hoped that, arising from a personal visit, a start could at last be made to bringing back Germany to the council chamber and persuading the French to desist in the opposition to German equality in arms – central points of his thinking for over two years.[45]

He had, he wrote later, wanted as Air Minister to visit Germany and to meet his opposite number, General Göring.[46] Though this had proved impossible, a feeler had been put out, as we noted, when two of his daughters had visited Göring on their trip to Berlin in October 1934. Now, out of office but still with influential connections, Londonderry was able to resurrect the idea of a meeting with Göring. Apart from his wish to learn what he could about the German air force (especially to vindicate his own much-criticized position on the strength of air armaments), he thought 'it would be useful to establish a contact, however humble I may be and private and independent though I am, with the German Government, so as to hear, at first hand, what their policy is now and what their policy is going to be'.[47] He travelled to Berlin, he told Göring, 'in the hope of making your acquaintance and that of the Reich Chancellor, so as to acquire for myself from your lips the opinions which are in your minds'.[48] That the leading representatives of the Nazi regime might not tell their visitor the unvarnished truth does not appear to have occurred to him.

The illness, then death of King George V, a friend of the Londonderry family, delayed matters.[49] But the visit, of Lord and Lady Londonderry and their daughter Lady Mairi Stewart, was finally arranged to begin at the end of January and last into the first two weeks of February 1936, in order to take in the Winter Olympics at Garmisch-Partenkirchen in southern Bavaria. How the trip was set up and organized is not clear. Almost certainly Ribbentrop, whom the Londonderrys had entertained at their Park Lane mansion as early as November 1934, was closely involved. Most likely, the London desk of his unofficial foreign-policy agency (the Dienststelle Ribbentrop) arranged it, as it did other German visits by prominent British representatives.[50] How far the German Embassy in London and the British Embassy in Berlin were incorporated in the arrangements is unclear. The Winter Olympics at Garmisch offered a pleasant diversion, from Londonderry's point of view. But the main purpose was to meet the Nazi leaders for the first time to see whether there was any prospect of an understanding with Germany which would avoid war.

Londonderry later remarked that he 'dabbled in diplomacy with an idea which I know was correct but I could not somehow work it with anyone who counted'.[51] The dabbling began in Berlin at the end of January 1936.

II

As the Londonderrys began to make their preparations for their German visit, international developments in Europe were starting to quicken again. Mussolini's decision to launch the Italian invasion of Abyssinia in early October had introduced a new, disturbing element into an already less than tranquil situation. The League of Nations had then imposed sanctions. But the continuing tensions between Britain and France were palpable. And now Italy, in search of new friends, was beginning to look across the Alps with different eyes, prepared to soften her stance on keeping Austria at arm's length from Germany. Treading cautiously, Hitler chose neutrality in the dispute over Abyssinia, though his Foreign Minister, von Neurath, had secretly favoured provision of substantial funding to help the Abyssinians fend off the Italian invasion, on the basis that a prolonged conflict would further weaken and divide the western democracies and work to Germany's advantage.[52]

The weaknesses were not long in surfacing. At Geneva there were demands for tightening the sanctions by cutting off supplies of oil to Italy. That might have brought Mussolini to reason. But the British government feared it would instead bring him to war against Britain which, without French support, would be left with its navy exposed to Italian air power in the Mediterranean. In any case, Britain wanted Mussolini on her side against Hitler, and the government was well aware that, in the Peace Ballot, the British people had fully backed sanctions short of war, but not war itself. Oil sanctions were accordingly blocked. Instead, an amended version (in Italy's favour) of the territorial offer to Mussolini that Eden had made the previous May was put together.

The British Foreign Secretary, Sir Samuel Hoare, and his French counterpart, Pierre Laval, devised a plan which gave Mussolini around two-thirds of Abyssinian territory – a precursor of what would again happen at Munich in 1938 as big powers disposed of parts of a sovereign state to reward an aggressor. Mussolini, warned by his army leaders that his war was not going well, was inclining towards accepting the offer. But news of what was afoot found its way into the French press. The outcry in Britain was enormous. Hoare was made the scapegoat and forced to resign, allegedly on grounds of ill health. Anglo-French relations reached a new low point.[53] The League of Nations was a broken reed. Oil sanctions were repeatedly rejected. By the spring, Mussolini had won an unexpectedly early victory in Abyssinia and could proclaim his new Roman empire. Meanwhile, smiling in the background were the Germans. Mussolini signalled to Germany that Italy's bonds with the western democracies through the Treaty of Locarno and, more recently, the Stresa Front (at which, on 11 April 1935, Britain, France and Italy had pledged to support Austria's integrity), were effectively terminated, and that he had nothing against Austria falling within Germany's orbit. From a German point of view, the implication was evident: Italy would not object to the remilitarization of the Rhineland.

Already in mid-December 1935, the British Ambassador in Germany, Sir Eric Phipps, following a lengthy audience with Hitler, had confided in his diary that the German Chancellor would probably remilitarize the Rhineland 'whenever a favourable opportunity presents itself'. He added, however, that he did not anticipate this happening before Hitler made 'a final attempt to "square" Great Britain'. The naval agreement of the previous summer had, from the German perspective, 'smoothed the path', he thought, and 'all eyes are now looking for a sign from the other side of the Channel'. Days before the Londonderrys set out on their visit to Germany, Phipps was emphasizing Hitler's keenness on 'a friendly understanding with England', which he would not abandon until it became clear that such a hope was illusory.[54]

Arrangements for the Londonderrys' trip to Germany had evidently been made in close connection with the German Air Ministry. A Junkers JU52 ferried them in comfort on 29 January from Croydon, across the North Sea, via stops in Amsterdam and Hanover, to Berlin. There they were met and escorted by Göring's representatives (who accompanied them throughout their visit)[55] to Berlin's best hotel, the Adlon, close to the Brandenburg Gate at the top of Unter den Linden, the broad boulevard which runs through the centre of the city.

Next day, 30 January, accompanied by the British Air Attaché in Berlin, Group-Captain Don, Londonderry was taken to view some Luftwaffe installations and fighter squadrons in the vicinity of Berlin.[56] That evening the Londonderrys were invited to view from the Reich Chancellery in the Wilhelmstrasse the huge torchlight procession of tens of thousands of stormtroopers brought from all over the Reich to celebrate the third anniversary of Hitler's takeover of power.[57] They were enthralled by the spectacle. It was for Lady Mairi, approaching her fifteenth birthday, 'the most impressive sight' she had ever seen. But she heard her mother say to Lord Londonderry: 'This means war, Charley.' Lord Londonderry was less pessimistic. A policy of friendship towards Germany, coupled with a position of British strength, would, he believed, see war averted.[58]

They spent the remainder of the evening as guests of Göring and his wife – formerly the actress Emmy Sonnemann – in the palace of the Reichstag President in Berlin's government district, dining in the grand style, listening to a Wagner recital, and watching a film illustrating Germany's military strength. The following day, they were driven out to Göring's hunting-lodge at Carinhall, named after his Swedish first wife, Carin, who had died in 1931, on an estate of several hundred acres in the picturesque Schorfheide north of Berlin.[59] Bluff, jovial and, in contrast to his more formally attired British guests, eccentrically dressed in a green hunting outfit with wide white sleeves, leather jacket and a feathered hat that reminded Lady Mairi of Robin Hood, Göring made an excellent impression upon his guests. They were taken out to hunt, Göring carrying a stick shaped like an ancient Germanic spear and a hunting horn, laughing with childlike pleasure as he shot dead a huge bison from his enclosure.[60] With much less panache, Londonderry shot a large red deer (and was presented by Göring with its teeth and antlers as a memento),[61] while his wife and daughter each shot a fallow deer that afternoon.

After tea, Lord Londonderry sat down with his host and the Foreign Ministry's leading interpreter, Dr Paul Schmidt, in huge wooden chairs at the large, plain table that dominated the long room at the centre of the lodge, to discuss politics. Schmidt had been used to formal diplomatic negotiations. What he now experienced was, for him, more like a 'pleasant table conversation' ranging generally over the issues rather than dealing with specifics. Londonderry sought a clear statement of German aims to allay European fears and win over British public opinion. Göring, strongly critical of France's opposition to 'Germany's legitimate aims and aspirations', and clearly wishing to drive apart the western democracies, emphasized the wish for a bilateral arrangement between Germany and Britain – presumably implying an Anglo-German air pact – along the lines of the recently concluded naval agreement. Schmidt was impressed by the skilful way in which Göring couched the case as he went on to stress the desire for good relations with Britain, and to underline Germany's need for expansion to the east and right to own colonies. Londonderry, far less forceful in manner, stated that if Germany's 'legitimate claims received no consideration and if France were to dominate the whole situation', then he would despair. But he refused to countenance such pessimism. He suggested that Germany make a gesture of goodwill to the French by accepting the demilitarized zone and that France might adopt a similar zone. Just how unrealistic this scenario was must have been abundantly plain to Londonderry at the time. But Göring registered the idea. As a tactical device it could prove useful. He passed the suggestion on to Hitler. And when the dictator came to make his 'peace offer', following the remilitarization of the Rhineland some weeks later, it contained the idea of a multilateral demilitarized zone, also stretching over territory of France and Belgium.[62]

The conversation drew to a close on the growing threat posed to Germany by the Soviet air force, and by Göring telling Londonderry as much (or little) as he thought he should know on German air expansion, speaking with an openness that surprised Schmidt but in reality still following the ploy of boasting of German achievements in rearmament to cajole the western powers into a policy of appeasement if not outright friendship. Londonderry for his part returned so insistently to the discussions between Hitler and Sir John Simon the previous March, and his doubts that Germany had attained air parity with Britain, that Schmidt realized this issue must have caused him serious difficulties as Air Minister. Londonderry ended by expressing the hope – one he himself now surely realized to be an utterly vain one – 'that Germany would take a leading part in the policy of [arms] limitation'.[63]

The talks were not publicized. But as word of a meeting between Göring and Londonderry trickled out, the rumour spread that they had been discussing the proposed air pact and the question of the demilitarized zone in the Rhineland, which, it was believed, Britain was now prepared to see ended.[64]

On 2 February the Londonderrys were again lavishly entertained – this time to lunch, along with twenty-five or so other guests, at the Ribbentrops' house in Dahlem. Rudolf Hess, Hitler's deputy in Party matters, was there. And, again, Schmidt was on hand to translate – especially necessary when Hess spoke, since his thick Bavarian brogue was beyond Londonderry's limited knowledge of German. After lunch, Ribbentrop, Hess and Londonderry discussed political issues, partly along the same lines as the conversation with Göring. Again, the desire for a bilateral agreement with Britain was expressed. The previous June, Ribbentrop had triumphantly negotiated a naval pact in which the British had been willing to concede, to widespread surprise and in contravention of the Versailles Treaty, that the Germans could rearm their navy to a strength of 35 per cent of the Royal Navy – a handsome concession given that Britain's fleet still had an empire to guard, and all the more generous since the ratio was not applied to the numbers of submarines, where the German navy was allowed to work towards eventual parity with the British submarine fleet.[65] A preference for agreed fixed ratios rather than uncontrolled, but certain, German naval rearmament as on land and in the air had prompted the British generosity.[66] The pact had fleetingly seemed to hold promise for a broader basis of agreement and cooperation between the two countries. Such a prospect was now trailed before Londonderry's eyes by his German hosts. But the main topics of discussion were the benefits to Britain by joining Germany's efforts to block the spread of Bolshevism, the hopes of a return of German colonies, and the need for Germany's eastern expansion – a part of the converation which Londonderry found 'somewhat disturbing, as if my worst fears of this development of German strength would be directed to this expansion in Europe and that no nation would be in a position to object'.[67]

An inspection of another aerodrome and of the Junkers factory at Dessau was followed, on the afternoon of 4 February, by the high point of the visit: a two-hour audience with Hitler himself. Looking back six or so years later, Londonderry reflected that he had found Hitler 'forthcoming and agreeable', but 'not quite sure of himself'. In fact, Londonderry continued, Hitler had been 'distinctly ill at ease', 'quite at a loss as to how to conduct an interview' and 'extremely embarrassed and awkward'. 'I even had to take the lead in sitting down – a lead which he followed with gratitude,' added Londonderry.[68] In reality, Hitler had no trace of an inferiority complex towards a British aristocrat. His feigned diffidence was aimed at encouraging confidence – perhaps even over-confidence – in his interlocutor, and at ensuring that his guest was not alienated by any hint of arrogance or implied German superiority when he was keen to impress a possible intermediary who could help secure Britain's friendship. The suggestive 'ordinariness' on Hitler's part was no more than an act to imply sincerity and humility. Londonderry's reaction reveals, for his part, a condescension towards Hitler and his shortcomings in etiquette which had been not uncommon among the German upper classes, too, in their grave underestimation of his political abilities.

Hess, Ribbentrop, and – once again – the necessary Schmidt, as interpreter, were also present in the Reich Chancellery when London-derry met Hitler.[69] As always in such audiences, Hitler did almost all the talking. And, as was invariably the case when he was aiming to impress, and to put across a message for foreign consumption, he spoke in measured terms, seemingly reasonable in tone, avoiding all ranting and histrionics. He concentrated heavily upon the mounting threat to the world from Bolshevism – an issue central to his ideology, and which was to play an increasingly prominent role in his thinking in 1936. Denying that Germany had any intention of attacking Russia, he portrayed Europe as a continent of weak and insecure governments which would soon be incapable of resisting the growing menace of the Soviet Union. When Londonderry, in a hesitant voice, searching (as it seemed to Schmidt) for the appropriate phrases to couch his argument persuasively, suggested that 'as a conception and theory the League of Nations was undoubtedly and indisputably the right solution of existing difficulties', Hitler was politely dismissive. 'The League of Nations', he declared, 'would finally become just a paper illusion, and would be represented by a few typewriters.' Admitting the Soviet Union to membership was like allowing 'germ carriers' into a society of healthy people: once established, she would go on to 'give the death-blow to the League of Nations itself'. Londonderry pointed out that less importance was attached to the 'the Bolshevist menace' in Britain, and the conversation switched to Anglo-German relations, anxieties in Britain about German rearmament, and the dangers of a clash over the colonial question. Londonderry repeated his remark to Göring that suspicions in Britain would be allayed by 'an exact statement of German aims'. This invited a further monologue from Hitler, of the kind he had given many times, indicating Germany's insistence on 'absolute equality with other nations', but her wish to avoid war over colonies, and desire for a 'close friendly alliance with England' to prevent a repeat of the 'absolute madness' of the Germans and British fighting each other, as happened in the First World War. Hitler none-theless made plain his expectation that the unjust removal of her former colonies would, as part of the basis of 'active friendship with Germany', have to be addressed and remedied at some point.

The audience drew to a close. It ended with a 'photo-opportunity' as Londonderry's gaunt figure was snapped alongside Hitler, in Party uniform, and a soberly dressed von Ribbentrop.[70] Hitler had been cordial, but formal, exuding none of the joviality and bonhomie that Göring had shown. The message, however, was the same: Germany's earnest desire for an 'understanding' with Great Britain, but need for expansion. 'It was almost like a wooing by Hitler of the coy Britannia,' was how Schmidt saw it. Londonderry was visibly impressed. For Schmidt, it was just another example of Hitler's ability to sway foreign visitors.

Londonderry's eventful day came to a close with a small dinner in his honour given by Hitler followed by a reception provided by the Foreign Minister, Baron von Neurath. Next lunchtime there was yet another reception, this time with the Londonderrys as guests of Ribbentrop and the German branch of the Anglo-German Fellowship. Lady Mairi still recalls meeting several of the Nazi grandees. Hitler, who gave her a signed photograph of himself, spent more than ten minutes, with the ubiquitous Schmidt interpreting, sitting on a sofa with her, talking about comedy films (especially *The Ghost Goes West*, starring Robert Donat, an American whimsy, which he particularly liked). He looked rather comical himself, she said, and left no positive impression. Himmler, the powerful head of the SS, reminded her of a 'shop-walker [department-store supervisor] at Harrod's in the old days'.[71]

With the round of receptions, discussions and inspections of air force installations over, the Londonderrys flew south on 6 February in Göring's private plane. They visited Göring's luxurious residence in the mountains above Berchtesgaden, close to Hitler's alpine retreat, before travelling on to Munich, then to the Winter Olympics at Garmisch-Partenkirchen. In the week they spent there, they met Hitler and Göring once more, and 'were again struck by the enthusiastic welcome which each received on every occasion when they appeared'.[72] Londonderry thought the ovation for Hitler at the end of the Games 'one of the most remarkable demonstrations I have ever seen', and was greatly impressed by Hitler's popularity.[73]

The Londonderrys returned to England by air at the end of the games. The Nazi courting of Lord Londonderry had paid dividends. He was dazzled by his experiences in Hitler's Germany. He remarked shortly afterwards to the British Ambassador in Berlin, Sir Eric Phipps, that

every minute seems to have been filled up with something or other, whether it was discussing politics with the Fuhrer [sic] or shooting stags at Karin-hall [sic], listening to the most wonderful music and seeing the most remarkable objets d'art, pictures, tapestries, or whether it was watching skiing, skating and ice-hockey at Garmisch . . . I feel that we have never spent so full, interesting and delightful a time as the last three weeks.[74]

Londonderry was now ready to sing the praises of the new Germany at every opportunity, and to work actively and with enormous enthusiasm for the 'understanding' with Britain that Hitler so much desired.

III

In a report of 22 February 1936, the German Ambassador, Leopold von Hoesch, told the Foreign Ministry 'it was unmistakable that Lord and Lady Londonderry were extraordinarily satisfied with their stay in Germany and took the most favourable impressions home with them'. Londonderry had told the Ambassador that he did not intend to do as Lord Lothian had done the previous March, in publicly presenting 'sensational declarations in favour of Germany' (when, following his audience with Hitler, he had advocated fair treatment and recognition of full equality for Germany as the only prospect of European peace), since this would only arouse animosity and would achieve nothing. Rather, said Londonderry, *he* would 'make full use of his impressions in quiet and suitable fashion in appropriate places and especially in the highest quarter'. The last phrase meant he would draw his experiences in Germany to the attention of the Prime Minister, Stanley Baldwin.[75]

Despite giving Hoesch the impression that he was going to avoid publicity, Londonderry had put out on 21 February a statement for the Press Association (largely based, it seems, on the interview he had given to the *Belfast News-Letter* two days earlier), which then appeared in some form in the newspapers the following morning, and was also extensively reported in Germany.[76] He stated that he had encountered everywhere 'a very friendly feeling towards this country, and a very strong desire for the friendship of Great Britain and France'. The development of an air force reflected Germany's desire 'to have a force of a size in keeping with her prestige as a great nation', and was necessary for her security. But he was equally certain, he said, 'that this development is not in any sense directed against Great Britain'. He had had a lengthy conversation with Hitler, he continued, whom he found 'very agreeable'. At many points in the conversation he had found himself in harmony with the German leader. He could not forecast how international politics would develop, 'but it must be realised that Hitler was doing his best to restore a great country with a population of sixty-five millions to a position which is fitted to its traditions, record, and rights'.[77]

In a speech at Durham shortly afterwards, Londonderry, reportedly referring to Hitler as a 'kindly man with a receding chin and an impressive face', said that 'there would be a lack of statesmanship in this country if in the event of war we should find ourselves engaged on different sides from Germany'. He spoke of the organizational capacity in Germany which enabled a rapid expansion of the air force, and indicated that the German armed forces, once their build-up was complete, would probably be the strongest in the world. 'What takes us weeks or months to do in Parliament', he stated, 'Germany can do by a stroke of the pen.' He also outlined Hitler's fears of the danger of Communism and his belief that he was building Germany as a bulwark against a Soviet drive to the west. But he added that he had left Germany 'with the strongest impression that the German nation as a whole, and the German Government, are actuated by a desire for friendliness towards this country', and that 'the last thing they want is an alignment of nations for war-like purposes and to find themselves opposed to Britain and France'.[78]

Londonderry's main aim in his Durham speech, as in the press interviews he gave following his trip to Germany, was to win support for a more pro-German policy (coupled with rearmament) by relaying the impressions he had taken away of German aims and rapid growth in military strength, but also of an earnest search for friendly relations with Britain. Despite his long experience in government, however,

Londonderry was politically anything other than astute. He failed to see that his speech, and the German visit which had preceded it, would be portrayed as carrying out the work of Nazi propaganda in Britain, and that he himself would be regarded as a gullible Nazi sympathizer.

In Liberal and Left circles, Londonderry was now derided. The *Manchester Guardian*, under the heading 'An Innocent's Return', made no attempt to conceal its scorn. 'After reading Lord Londonderry's speech at Durham on Saturday most people will be more than ever grateful to Mr Baldwin for having pushed him out of the National Government,' its article began. 'It is sad to think', it went on, 'that for four years he was head of an important Department and was permitted to interfere in the international effort at disarmament. For Lord Londonderry does not believe in disarmament or collective security through the League' – a distortion, of course, of the position which we have seen Londonderry advocating during the years when he was Air Minister. The article then criticized Londonderry's approval of a retreat from pacifism and move to rearmament. This was, in fact, a more realistic stance than the newspaper's own adherence to disarmament and pacifistic ideals despite the obvious looming menace across the North Sea. But when it moved to the impact of his German visit, the biting commentary was closer to the mark. It spoke of Londonderry being 'wonderfully impressed' after he had 'sat at the feet (for two hours) of Herr Hitler and Herr Göring'. It took his comments on the speed with which Germany's non-parliamentary system could manage rearmament as approval of the Nazi dictatorship and ridiculed the anti-Bolshevik fears he had picked up in Berlin which, 'because Herr Hitler has said it, Lord Londonderry believes'. The article ended in a highly sarcastic note which, whatever Londonderry's naivety, amounted to little more than a cheap jibe: 'Poor Lord Londonderry, what a world he must live in! But he might have told us, if it is so desperately imperative that we should rearm, why we are to do it. Is it to help our German friends in their great crusade of beating off this "disastrous and pernicious" Soviet menace, or is it just because a big Air Force is a pretty plaything to have?'[79]

As he had predicted, then, his public statements (which were fully reported in Germany)[80] stirred criticism and achieved nothing. 'From the first', he later wrote, 'my approach to Germany was viewed with suspicion, in some instances even among my personal friends'.[81] And he was dismayed to find that his contacts in high places in the government were uninterested in what he had to report.[82] For days he expected Baldwin to call him. He also tried in vain to obtain an audience with King Edward VIII. The Foreign Office, irritated by 'this eternal butting in of amateurs' who 'render impossible the task of diplomacy', was only too keen to prevent visits such as that of Londonderry finding any response in the government. Only Sir Maurice Hankey, the longstanding Cabinet Secretary, and Sir Edward Ellington, Chief of the Air Staff, showed a flicker of interest.[83] Even so, promoting friendship with Germany – meaning a fundamental change in British policy – now became Londonderry's main purpose. From now on, he would be viewed as one of the leading pro-Nazis in the country.

Still enthused by his visit to Germany, he was persuaded by Ribbentrop to join the recently created Anglo-German Fellowship to 'help things along over there'.[84] We have noted that Londonderry, before becoming Air Minister, had been fleetingly a member of the Anglo-German Association. The successor to this body, which as we saw was wound up in 1935 in the wake of dissension about its remaining Jewish members, and regarded as no longer fitting 'the needs of the time', was quite different in character. It was incorporated in October 1935, aiming, according to its statement of objectives, 'to promote good understanding between England and Germany and thus contribute to the maintenance of peace and the development of prosperity'. It sought to foster contacts with Germans in government, business, and the professions through its sister society, the Deutsch-Englische-Gesellschaft, that had already been established in Berlin. It was purportedly non-political and keen to advertise that 'membership does not imply approval of National Socialism'.[85] In reality, however, the organization served largely as an indirect tool of Nazi propaganda in high places, a vehicle for exerting German influence in Britain. Almost certainly, Ribbentrop was behind the idea.[86] At any rate, one of his leading contacts in Britain, who had served as an important link to influential individuals, the merchant banker Ernest Tennant, had taken the initiative in 1934 which led to the formation of the Anglo-German Fellowship, and had organized its financial backing.[87] The Fellowship was self-consciously elitist. It aimed to recruit the rich and the powerful – those with wealth and influence.

Members of Parliament, generals and admirals, businessmen and bankers were prominently represented.[88] F. C. Tiarks, the Governor of the Bank of England, and Lord Magowan, Chairman of the Midland Bank, were members. Among financial institutions, Schröder, Lazard and the Midland Bank were corporate members. Big industrial firms such as Firth-Vickers Stainless Steels, Unilever and Dunlop also enjoyed corporate membership, while directors of Imperial Chemical Industries, Tate and Lyle and the Distillers Company joined as private individuals. The biggest donations in 1935 came from Unilever and ICI. The interests of the business and financial worlds in economic appeasement with Germany were thereby evident.[89] The Chairman was Lord Mount Temple, a former Conservative minister (as Wilfred Ashley) and father-in-law of Lord Mountbatten (a great-grandson of Queen Victoria). In unguarded comments, Mount Temple made plain his hope that 'in the next war' Germany and Britain would be fighting on the same side.[90] Leading members with strong associations with Nazi Germany included Tennant (the Honorary Secretary) and T. P. Conwell-Evans (whom we have already encountered helping to arrange Lord Lothian's audience with Hitler early in 1935). Another member, whose pro-Nazism would become even more extreme with time, was Admiral Sir Barry Domvile – eccentric, confused and markedly anti-Semitic – who praised the freedom to drive without speed-limits in Germany and admired Himmler as 'a charming person-ality'.[91] Among the aristocracy, Londonderry was in good company. Those with pro-German proclivities included Lords Brocket, Lothian, McGowan, Mottistone, Redesdale (father of the avidly pro-Nazi Diana and Unity Mitford),[92] the Earl of Glasgow, and the Duke of Wellington. Many among the membership of around 250 by early 1936 (increased to 450 by the end of the year)[93] were far from being Nazi sympathizers, simply wanting to promote better Anglo-German relations. But, as has been aptly remarked, 'there were a large number of sharks lurking among the shallows'.[94] There is no indication that Londonderry was a notably active member of the Fellowship.[95] But he was now certainly swimming with the sharks. When Winston Churchill, a few months later, expressed his hope that Londonderry would 'not become too prominently identified with the pro-German view', it was already late in the day.[96]

He and his wife were now also beginning to cultivate their recently made acquaintance with leading Nazis. The effusiveness of their letters went beyond conventional expressions of politeness for the lavish hospitality and courtesy they had received on their German trip. Londonderry, offering Göring 'our deep and sincere gratitude for everything which you were good enough to do to make our stay in Germany thoroughly pleasant and enjoyable', and telling him how he had 'always entertained the friendliest feeling towards your nation' and 'admired the strength and intelligence of your race', twice mentioned how 'deeply touched' he had been by his reception, and his difficulty 'in endeavouring to explain to you our appreciation of the many kindnesses of which we were the fortunate recipients'.[97] In their florid tones, Lady Londonderry's letters surpassed those of her husband. Thanking Hitler for his hospitality, she wrote that 'to say that I was deeply impressed is not adequate. I am amazed. You and Germany remind me of the book of Genesis in the Bible. Nothing else describes the position accurately.'[98] Writing to Göring, she began, with unctuous flattery: 'Dear General der Flieger and Minister President (although I would prefer to call you "Siegfried" as you are my conception of a Siegfried of modern times!)'. She expressed her gratitude for his kindness, saying 'we have never spent such a happy and highly interesting time before'. She sent him a photograph of 'Young Diana' (Lady Mairi) in pilot's garb, a copy of the famous and flattering portrait of herself in uniform, painted by Laszlo during the First World War, and some rose trees for his garden on the Obersalzberg.[99] Göring sent Lady Londonderry his own photograph in return.[100] She wrote back, this time addressing him as 'My dear General der Flieger Siegfried!', to tell him how much his photograph had been admired at a big political reception at Londonderry House.[101] Flattered – and probably amused – he could not resist signing a return letter 'Hermann Göring (Siegfried)'.[102]

However, the letters to the Nazi leaders were not merely reflections of embarrassing aristocratic frippery. They also had a political purpose: to continue to work for the rapprochement which Londonderry thought was so urgently needed. The German responses indicated the continued hopes that the Londonderrys, through their important connections, offered an informal channel to the British government and the possibility of working indirectly for the 'understanding' the Nazi leadership wanted.

Conveying his thanks to Ribbentrop for his courtesy during the Berlin visit, Londonderry took the opportunity to ask about an issue which, he realized, he was still unclear about: 'the actual reasons which control your internal policy in relation to the Jews'. He approached the subject, he said, 'with the greatest diffidence', since it was a matter of domestic policy. On the other hand, it was causing great anxiety in Britain. Besides the dislike of persecution, Londonderry wrote, there was the feeling 'that you are taking on a tremendous force which is capable of having repercussions all over the world' and could only be 'antagonistic to some of your most proper and legitimate aspirations'. Londonderry's evident belief in the international power of Jewry was compounded by what followed: 'As I told you, I have no great affection for the Jews. It is possible to trace their participation in most of those international disturbances which have created so much havoc in different countries,' though he added that it was possible to 'find many Jews strongly ranged on the other side who have done their best with the wealth at their disposal, and also by their influence to counteract those malevolent and mischievous activities of fellow Jews'.[103]

Londonderry was certainly not a racial anti-Semite in the Nazi sense. There is no inkling in his extensive papers and correspondence of obsessive or pervasive hatred of the Jews. Lord and Lady Londonderry had numerous Jewish friends and colleagues, while Lady Londonderry went out of her way to try to help one Jewish refugee, a doctor whose German medical qualification did not entitle him to practise in Britain.[104] Nor was Londonderry associated in any way with the rabidly anti-Semitic British Union of Fascists, Oswald Mosley's Blackshirt thugs.[105] Their politics of violence, targeting Jews and political opponents in London's East End and parts of other big cities and towns, aimed not to uphold, but to challenge the existing social and political establishment of Britain. The Conservative-led National Government, of which until 1935 Londonderry had been a member, was regarded by Mosley's men as a major obstacle to the radical change they sought to bring about. For Mosley, the Conservatives represented the failed past; they were part of Britain's 'old gang' who had to be swept away. This was diametrically opposed to Londonderry's brand of paternalistic Conservatism, which rested upon upholding the old order, and impossible to reconcile with his party loyalties. There were, however, as with the Conservative Right generally, overlaps in ideas on, for example, imperialism and anti-socialism, as well as anti-Semitism.[106] For, though not a racist anti-Semite, there are in the tone of Londonderry's letter to Ribbentrop unmistakable traces of the latent or abstract antipathy to Jews – in the main little more than a vague prejudice against what was seen as an 'alien presence', 'outsiders' in a Christian society, though sometimes linked with resentment at their supposed political influence, presumed financial dominance, or imagined connections with subversive international forces, meaning Bolshevism – which was so common among the British upper classes at the time. Lady Londonderry, who had strongly disapproved of the marriage of her daughter, Helen, to a Jew, Edward (Teddy) Jessel, the previous year,[107] betrayed signs of the same antagonism when she told Göring that the British press was 'controlled to a great extent by Jews'.[108] Stray anti-Semitic remarks, possibly reflecting the underlying attitude of his parents, also occurred in the letters of Londonderry's son, Lord Castlereagh (a Conservative MP), to his father.[109] It all amounted to disdain rooted in well-established stereotypes. Ingrained though the prejudice was, it would not have fostered persecution. So it is easy to see how the viciousness of Nazi persecution was puzzling and alien to Londonderry. It is, however, equally easy to see that it posed in his eyes no barrier to closer relations with Hitler's regime. Writing to his father years later, Castlereagh remarked that 'to robust Conservatives like Mother[,] Nazism makes a certain appeal – [through] its anti-Jew & anti-Russia character & its impatience at the dilatoriness of democracy'.[110] Though he did not say so, the remark applied to Londonderry too.

Nazi anti-Semitism to him was, therefore, an irritant – something which, in its ferocious and pitiless brutality, he did not understand, and which in his eyes posed an unnecessary obstacle to the better relations with Germany that he sought. Compared with the geopolitical implications of German strength and what he assumed to be its certain consequence – expansion, with the great risk of a new European war – Nazi anti-Semitism played only a minor role in his deliberations.

In a long letter to Göring on his return, Londonderry went over some of the ground of their recent talks, agreeing that Britain should join with Germany in opposing Bolshevism, 'a doctrine which, if successful, must bring about a world wide catastrophe of a magnitude which we none of us can envisage'. But he had realized since leaving Germany, he said, that he remained unclear about German intentions in Europe, and exhorted Göring once again to a clear statement of Nazi aims to allay mistrust and anxiety in Britain. He sympathized with 'strong and justifiable' German demands for a reconsideration of the Versailles Treaty, but suggested that the withdrawal from the League of Nations and unwillingness to engage in a multilateral air pact enhanced the misgivings.[111] How far his own naive misreading of Nazi intentions stretched is plain from a comment he made to Ribbentrop. He recalled his own warm support for the 'great conception' underlying the League of Nations, adding that, in the light of distrust created by bilateral negotiations, 'one feels driven back to a common meeting place in Europe for the discussion of great problems'. He concluded: 'I think that is your view also.'[112]

Looking back several years later, Londonderry wrote that he was 'far from satisfied' after his visit to Germany, though confident that there was still time to reach an understanding. If this could not be attained, he continued, he was convinced 'that with France, because we had done our best to alienate Italy [over Abyssinia], we could speak in plain language and even then put a stop to German rearmament'.[113] That is not how it appeared to him at the time. He said a great deal on his return about the need for friendship with Germany, but nothing about stopping German rearmament. His longstanding antipathy to the French had for years persuaded him to place little hope in cooperation, while the French pact with the Soviet Union, signed in May 1935 (but ratified only on 27 February 1936), prompted his fears of British alliance with France bearing the 'danger of our being committed to an alliance with Russia against both Germany and Japan'.[114] Lady Londonderry, echoing her husband's sentiments, saw the Germans wanting a friendly policy towards Britain and also France, 'but if France continues her present policy of trying to encircle them with Russia and they are not given any outlet, and when they have come to the end of their resources in raw material and have no money with which they can buy outside goods, they will be forced to fight or else starve, and they will prefer the former', concluding that 'if this ever happens it will be largely the fault of the French'.[115] Londonderry was critical of the 'drift' of what he saw as an aimless British foreign policy – 'quite absurd', in his wife's words, since 'nobody seems to realise what is happening'. He felt frustrated at his inability to interest the Foreign Secretary, Anthony Eden, or other leading government figures in the cause of the closer relations with Nazi Germany which he was now so enthusiastically advocating. 'Few wished to hear about Germany,' he wrote – meaning his own version of Germany. In some disappointment, he went fishing in the Scottish Highlands.[116] At this point, Hitler remilitarized the Rhineland.

IV

Worries that Hitler might soon move to remilitarize the Rhineland – which had been declared a demilitarized zone in the Treaty of Versailles in 1919 and confirmed by the Treaty of Locarno in 1925 – had, as we noted, been in circulation as early as December of the previous year. In a dispatch on 19 December 1935 the British Ambassador in Berlin, Sir Eric Phipps, had warned the government that Hitler would probably proceed to reoccupy the demilitarized zone 'whenever a favourable opportunity presents itself', prompting Anthony Eden, who had just replaced Sir Samuel Hoare as Foreign Secretary, to compose a memorandum on 'The German Danger' which he circulated to the Cabinet.[117] Eden wanted no concessions to Germany and the most rapid completion possible of British rearmament. However, he was prepared to consider the possibility of reaching an accommodation with Germany, adopting suggestions in the Foreign Office that the demilitarization of the Rhineland could be used as a bargaining counter before, as seemed inevitable, Hitler moved to alter its status. When the German Foreign Minister, Konstantin von Neurath, attended the funeral of King George V in late January, Eden gained assurance that Germany intended to uphold the Treaty of Locarno as long as others did. Eden seems not to have been alerted by von Neurath's added comment that Germany would feel vulnerable from the air in the event of the ratification of the Franco-Soviet Pact.[118]

The French were not reassured by von Neurath's comments. They were convinced that the Germans would soon move on the Rhineland. But Eden gained the impression from the recently appointed French Foreign Minister, Pierre Flandin, that France was unlikely to fight for the Rhineland. This was accurate. Flandin knew that the French military had based its strategy on the defence of France, not of the demilitarized zone. Armed retaliation against a German reoccupation was not contemplated.[119] The position Eden put to the British government was that, to avoid either having to fight for the zone or abandon it in the face of German reoccupation, it was preferable to negotiate, along with the French, for the surrender of the rights of the western powers in the zone 'while such surrender still has bargaining value'. British military chiefs had already told him that they did not consider the Rhineland 'a vital British interest'. By mid-February plans were being drawn up for a 'working agreement' between France, Germany and Britain, involving an air pact, a German obligation not to change the status quo by force, and, in return, a readiness by the western democracies to omit 'certain things to be found in the Treaty of Locarno' – meaning implicitly a renunciation of the demilitarized zone.[120]

The German Foreign Ministry appeared to be interested. But Hitler was not. In the wake of the Abyssinian morass he scented a chance not to be passed over. And his Foreign Minister, von Neurath, was telling him, on the basis of secret intelligence from Paris, that the French were unlikely to take military measures to prevent a German remilitarization of the Rhineland.[121] The divisions between the French and the British on this, as on practically all crucial issues of foreign policy, were all too evident to the Germans. If the French did not move, there was no chance that the British – in any case more open to German revisionist arguments – would intervene by means other than diplomatic protest. After some hesitation, Hitler decided, on 1 March 1936, that the opportunity was too good to miss. 'Fortune favours the brave,' noted his Propaganda Minister, Joseph Goebbels.[122]

Unaware that the die had been cast, but amid growing tension, a nervous Flandin, in line with the rejection of military action by the

French General Staff, refused to assure Britain that France would resist by force. France's immediate reaction, he indicated, would be confined to reporting any breach of the demilitarized zone to the Council of the League of Nations and consulting the other signatories to the Locarno Treaty – Britain, Belgium and Italy – about concerted common action. That any such action would be a belated response to a *fait accompli* was obvious. Moreover, Britain was being asked to fulfil her obligations under Locarno almost certainly alone since Belgium effectively could not and Italy would not try to block or overturn by military means any reoccupation by Germany. The British government recognized public opinion would not be on its side in any attempt to expel Germany from 'its own backyard'.[123] The Cabinet itself, moreover, had some sympathy with Germany on this point. Baldwin concluded that the French ought to be told bluntly what the position was: 'that neither France nor England was really in a position to take effective military action against Germany in the event of a violation of the Treaty of Locarno'.[124] This was 5 March. Two days later, German troops entered the remilitarized zone to a tumultous reception. It was Hitler's greatest triumph to date.

The German Ambassador in London, Leopold von Hoesch, read out to Eden that morning the German memorandum, blaming the Franco-Soviet Treaty for the violation of Locarno, and putting forward Hitler's skilfully devised offer – certain to placate opinion in Britain – to conclude new agreements involving non-aggression pacts for a duration of twenty-five years with his neighbours, a new demilitarized zone now on both sides of the border, a western air pact and German re-entry into the League of Nations.[125] Hitler could easily appear generous. As he was well aware, there was not the slightest chance that his 'offer' would be taken up seriously. The divisions, uncertainties and apprehension among the western powers, fostered by a deep distrust of Hitler, were simply too great for that to be feasible.

For more than two weeks, France and Britain dithered, poring over every possibility of countering the German action, but adopting none themselves which would be remotely effectual. The French, having blocked sanctions on Italy, now decided they wanted them against Germany. Baldwin's government was only too aware of public opinion opposing any risk of war and largely supportive of Germany. It was even more aware of British military weakness. So it left the French in no doubt that it was unwilling to take any steps that would risk military confrontation with Germany. Eventually, Britain put forward – more in hope than expectation – proposals for an international force (largely British, in fact) to police both sides of the frontier on the understanding that Germany would cede its fortifications in the Rhineland. A series of non-aggression pacts, leading towards a permanent settlement, would follow. Eden spoke of negotiations which might form a beginning to 'the appeasement of Europe as a whole'.[126] What prompted the notion that any of this would be of the slightest interest to Hitler is unclear. It amounted to no more than an elegant device to get Britain off the hook of its Locarno commitment without damaging relations with the French – and to concede with minimum loss of face the *fait accompli* of Hitler's act of force. The condemnation of his action by the Council of the League of Nations in mid-March was equally unlikely to shake Hitler. He, too, was well aware that public opinion in Britain, and also parliamentary opinion ranging across the parties from Churchill to the left wing of the Labour Party, would not support any stronger action.

Among those in Britain singled out by the German Ambassador in a report to the Foreign Ministry as one of 'our old friends' who viewed Hitler's 'peace proposals' as the basis of a new, and more promising, future for Europe, was Lord Londonderry.[127]

Londonderry's letter to *The Times* published on 12 March amounted to little more than an apologia for the German action. Using Hitler's own justification for the remilitarization of the Rhineland, Londonderry depicted it as 'a direct and understandable result of the Franco-Soviet Treaty' aimed at the encirclement of Germany. Since Germany had on earlier occasions broken the Treaty of Versailles – 'a document of singular ineptitude' – the move ought to have been expected, and had arisen as a consequence of the French refusal to grant Germany equality of status with other nations. Far from 'a challenge to the world', it was 'a logical sequence to recent events'. Though Hitler indeed now ran the risk that his good faith would in future be questioned, Londonderry attached great weight to his proposals for a settlement and urged the government to 'meet them as they move towards peace in the same manner as they accepted the German naval offer'.[128]

Though Londonderry's public statements were now firmly establishing him as a leading apologist for Nazi Germany, his enthusiasm for Hitler's peace overtures and eagerness for the government to treat them as a serious basis for negotiation was far from an eccentric position in March 1936. Naturally, other advocates of the need for an accommodation with Germany shared his view. Lord Lothian and his supporters, for instance, were equally prepared to minimize Hitler's 'offence' while accepting his declaration 'as made in good faith' with prospects for the future peace of Europe.[129] But the feeling extended beyond outright German sympathizers or major critics of the foreign policy of the government. The British press, even the sections of it which had been consistently anti-German, generally shared the enthusiasm for Hitler's peace proposals.[130] It did not last long. But, curiously, the aftermath of Hitler's strike at the heart of the post-war international order of Versailles and Locarno also represented the high-water mark of pro-German feeling in Britain. An upsurge in anti-French sentiment in the shadow of the Abyssinian crisis and further stirred by France's pact with the Soviet Union was a strong component of the swing to Germany. Certainly, the worry about the spread of Communism in western Europe also played its part. Within weeks, the French general elections, resulting in a Popular Front government of the Left, supported by the Communists – though they declined to participate in the government – would do nothing to assuage such feelings.[131] One shrewd observer of the public mood thought it 'rather fed up with France than actively pro-German, but more pro-German than the Cabinet'.[132] The other side of the coin was the determined German propaganda offensive in 1936, spearheaded by Ribbentrop, and with its high point in the summer Olympics in Berlin, to win over British support.[133] From the German point of view, this meant targeting their established friends and contacts in Britain in the hope of their influence being brought to bear on government leaders.

Londonderry was among those seen by Nazi leaders as a useful – and willing – intermediary. Göring thanked him by telegram 'for all your endeavours for the peace of our countries', expressing his satisfaction that Londonderry had come to know the new Germany 'and understand its sincere desire for peace'.[134] Hoesch, the German Ambassador, wrote to Lady Londonderry, underlining Germany's strong 'desire to come to practical negociations [sic]', and expressing gratitude to Lord Londonderry 'for the way in which he explained the German point of view'.[135] Göring, too, reminded Lady Londonderry 'how much the Leader and all of us desire and love peace', criticized the 'irreconcilable attitude of the French', and expressed gratitude to Lord Londonderry, saying, 'we shall never forget that he has pronounced his point of view so clearly and independently'.[136] Göring's wife, Emmy, and Magda Goebbels, wife of the Propaganda Minister, also wrote to Lady Londonderry in the following weeks, hoping to 'knit the bond of friendship between Great Britain and Germany'.[137]

On 3 April, when presenting to an organization called The All Peoples' Association a gift of around 200 books reflecting 'the life and spirit of Germany today' (including *Mein Kampf* and works by Joseph Goebbels and Alfred Rosenberg), the German Ambassador publicly praised Londonderry, who received the books on behalf of the Association.[138] That same evening, the Londonderrys entertained Ribbentrop to dinner.[139] Germany's roving envoy had been in England a great deal since the middle of March, when he had had to face the Council of the League of Nations, meeting in London, and, as he put it, 'made contact with all our available friends'.[140] There can be no doubt that Ribbentrop once more rehearsed his well-worn themes that evening: the extraordinary personality and achievements of Hitler, the threat of Communism, Germany's need for colonies, and how France and Spain were 'succumbing to the bribery of Moscow'.[141]

Londonderry summarized his own views to Winston Churchill in early May. Taking issue – again – with Churchill's figures on German rearmament in the air, he was adamant that the Germans could not risk war for around four years, and that the British task was to do everything possible in that time to eliminate the prospect of war or, at the very least, ensure it was postponed for some years. He berated the lack of knowledge of Germany and the absence of interest in the information he could have conveyed to the British government. When Churchill replied, forecasting that 'Hitler's government will confront Europe with a series of outrageous events and ever-growing military might', Londonderry demurred. 'Whatever the regime,' he stated, 'if it creates efficient organisation, I feel a certain amount of admiration for it, and that is why I respect Hitler, Mussolini, and Stalin. I should not', he went on,

like to live under these regimes myself because they are the negation of the freedom which we have learnt through the ages to claim and to enjoy, but still they do constitute an organisation and I feel that if the Nazi regime in Germany is destroyed, Germany will go Communist and we shall find a lining up of Communism between France, Germany and Russia.[142]

The last sentiments plainly echoed what he had heard from Ribbentrop, Göring, and Hitler himself.

Lady Londonderry, even more prone than her husband to allowing her new-found enthusiasm for Nazi Germany full expression, published in early May in the *Sunday Sun* an unqualified eulogy of Hitler and the society he ruled. Rhapsodizing about her visit to Germany earlier in the year, she said she had gone there 'full of prejudice, and imbued with antipathy, but that what she had experienced had swept away such feelings. Recounting her meeting with Hitler, she 'beheld a man of arresting personality – a man with wonderful farseeing eyes'. She felt that she 'was in the presence of one truly great. He is simple, dignified, humble. He is a leader of men.' She was, she wrote, 'greatly impressed' by 'this simple man of action, beloved of modern Germany', by his frankness, sincerity, and great desire for friendship with the English. She suggested that the British could take advantage of his Rhineland action 'to try to bring about a change of heart and policy so that we come to know that peace we all so greatly desire'.[143] Evidently pleased with what she had written, she dispatched a copy to Ribbentrop.[144]

A week later, Göring exploited his contact with Lady Londonderry in the mistaken belief that it might serve as a vehicle to exert some leverage on the British government to come to an agreement with Germany. His technique on this occasion was to paint a picture of the looming dangers for Britain in the changing world constellation. The Italian victory in Abyssinia, together with the build-up of the Italian navy and Mussolini's keenness to secure German friendship, posed, he stated, an obvious threat to British interests in the Mediterranean and Middle East and threatened this main artery of the Empire. Beyond that, Britain had to reckon with a severely weakened League of

Nations and increased Bolshevik agitation in western Europe, where Spain was 'almost a Soviet State' and France was 'tending towards the Left under strongly Communistic influences'. Germany, in contrast, stood as a 'bulwark against Bolshevism and for peace and quiet'. The impression Göring successfully created for Lady Londonderry was of the foolishness of British policy, especially in its dependence on France, when such a positive alternative was on offer. She knew, he declared, 'that the Führer has provided for co-operation with England in his political programme'. His hope was 'that the two great Germanic nations, England and Germany, may come together in future to guarantee world peace, or at least peace for our own countries'.[145]

Lady Londonderry duly passed on Göring's letter for the attention of the government. She told him it had been read 'by everybody whom I thought should see it – from the very highest to the most influential'.[146] Sending it to Neville Chamberlain, she remarked that the Germans wanted friendship, but 'a lot besides'. They were 'open to reason and discussion with anyone like yourself, whom they respect. No weakling is any use.' She said she would 'far rather deal with them any day than France. Hitler knows his own mind, respects us, and can reach a decision. Whether you can make this country or cabinet do so is quite another question!!!'[147] Like most unofficial feelers, Göring's letter was politely received by Chamberlain and others to whom Lady Londonderry sent it – and ignored.

It was at this point that the Ribbentrops flew to Northern Ireland for their long weekend with the Londonderrys at Mount Stewart – the weekend of the 'swastika over Ulster'.

V

Ribbentrop's black and silver, three-engined cabin-de-luxe Junkers JU-52 passenger plane, the *Wilhelm Siegert*, named after a First World War flying-ace and bearing a large swastika on its tail-fin, touched down at 6.18 p.m. on Friday, 29 May 1936, at Newtownards airport, some fifteen miles from Belfast, in Northern Ireland.[148] The flight from Croydon airport, outside London, had taken over two and a half hours, a slower trip than normal owing to strong head winds. But the airliner's most eminent passenger had enjoyed the journey, especially the splendid view as the plane had passed over the Isle of Man.

Ribbentrop had travelled to Northern Ireland as part of his continued efforts to bring about the entente between Germany and Great Britain that Hitler so dearly wanted. As Hitler had made plain in *Mein Kampf*, British 'friendship' held for him the key to his expansionist plans, aimed at extending German 'living space' largely at the expense of Russia. As early as 1922, Hitler had begun to turn his back on the traditional enmity towards Britain, and looked to a 'continental policy' which would avoid harm to British interests and enable Germany, with British understanding, to destroy Bolshevik Russia and settle scores with France.[149] Hitler's views remained substantially unchanged over a decade later, when he had attained and consolidated his hold on power. The desired understanding with Britain was still pivotal. And by this time he had come to see Ribbentrop as the man to bring about this understanding.

Joachim Ribbentrop (the 'von' came later) had been born in 1893 at Wesel on the Lower Rhine into a well-to-do officer-class family.[150] Though not intellectually gifted, he was good at riding, excelled at tennis and played the violin very well. He left school at the age of fifteen without formal educational qualifications. But he was proficient in foreign languages, which would later be important to his career advancement. His French was accomplished; his English – acquired during a year in London and several in Canada before the First World War – excellent. He served during the First World War on the eastern and western fronts before being wounded and invalided out of the army in 1917. He seemed to have few obvious career prospects before meeting, then marrying, Annelies Henkell, whose father's firm was the biggest producer of *Sekt* – sparkling white wine – in Germany. The marriage gave him the opening to build up a thriving business importing wines and spirits into Germany. In 1925 he persuaded (with a cash inducement) a distant relative to adopt him formally, so that he could add the aristocratic 'von' to his name – a move that brought him more ridicule than deference. The Nazi Propaganda Minister Joseph Goebbels, never short of a biting phrase, later remarked that Ribbentrop had bought his name and married his money.[151]

By the early 1930s Ribbentrop was a rich man, living in a plush villa in Dahlem, one of the finest residential districts of Berlin. He had had little to do with the Nazis as long as they were an insignificant fringe party. His political leanings, unsurprisingly for someone of his background, were strongly to the Right, but during the 1920s had inclined towards the conservative nationalism of Gustav Stresemann's German People's Party. Ribbentrop was a natural social climber, sensitive to his status, keen to advance through the contacts he was able to establish with the wealthy and influential, often through the cultured receptions and dinner-parties given at his home. Some of his business associates and customers, even his friends, at that time were Jewish. This would soon alter. His sympathies, and those of his wife, were drawn to the Nazis after meeting Hitler and seeing the breakthrough of his party in 1930. In May 1932 Ribbentrop then joined the Nazi Party. This followed a dinner at the Ribbentrops' Dahlem villa attended by Hitler, and a *tête-à-tête* during which, among other things, the Nazi leader had said that he 'was particularly interested in what influential Englishmen thought about National Socialism'. Ribbentrop was completely won over by Hitler's flattering interest in him. From this moment onwards, he was besotted by the Nazi leader. And, as he put it, 'it was the harmony of our views about England which, on this first evening spent together, created the seed of confidence between Hitler and myself'.[152]

The following January, he went on to play a minor, though nonetheless valuable, role in helping to broker the deal by which Hitler was made Reich Chancellor.[153] Thereafter, benefiting from Hitler's distrust for the formal bureaucracy of the German Foreign Office, Ribbentrop gradually began acting as an unofficial emissary, using his personal contacts in France and Britain to gain access to government ministers. It served his careerist purposes and also flattered his already overweening sense of self-importance to think that his personal approach to friends of Germany abroad could succeed where formal diplomatic channels would encounter only obstacles. And in this, he accorded completely with Hitler's own instinctive belief in the virtues of 'private diplomacy'.

Ribbentrop's initial attempt to ingratiate himself, and the Nazi regime, with British political leaders in autumn 1933 had been singularly unsuccessful. But during the summer and autumn of 1934, he was back in England. Lord Rothermere, one of the first members of the British aristocracy to pay a private visit to Hitler, invited him for a weekend stay and introduced him to some prominent businessmen. Then, in the autumn, during a three-week stay, Ribbentrop was drawn into the world of London high society. And one of the first hostesses who showered him with invitations to their fashionable salons was Lady Londonderry.[154] While he was in London, Ribbentrop was also introduced to a number of political figures who were interested in promoting what he wanted. In spring 1935, Ribbentrop went on to win further favour with Hitler by his part in instigating the bilateral talks in Berlin with the British Foreign Secretary, Sir John Simon, and the Lord Privy Seal, Anthony Eden. At the beginning of June 1935, with his credit high in the eyes of his Leader, Ribbentrop was appointed to be Hitler's special envoy to head the German delegation to London to negotiate a naval pact with Great Britain. Despite his overbearing manner, the agreement reached proved a remarkable personal triumph for Ribbentrop. His star continued in the ascendant.

In spring 1936, in the wake of the remilitarization of the Rhineland, Ribbentrop was soon busy once more in London, trying to repair the diplomatic damage that Hitler's move had caused to Anglo-German relations. Though he was icily received by the British Foreign Office, he tried once more through his personal contacts to engineer a breakthrough in British government attitudes towards Germany. It was at this important juncture, at the end of May, that he took up the Londonderrys' invitation to spend the weekend at Mount Stewart. That very weekend, Hitler was indicating in Berlin that Ribbentrop would be his choice as next Ambassador in London, to fill the vacancy left by the previous Ambassador, Leopold von Hoesch, who had died suddenly on 10 April.[155]

Ribbentrop was by this stage forty-three years old. Though his family background was, in fact, far from humble, he always appeared to have the cultivated airs of a *parvenu*. His mannerisms and clothing were selected in a vain attempt to give the impression of being an English gentleman.[156] The Conservative MP Chips Channon, himself a great socialite, who was together with Ribbentrop the night before he flew to Ireland, described him as 'like the captain of someone's yacht . . . not quite without charm, but shakes hands in an overhearty way'.[157] At the talks on the naval pact in 1935, his pomposity had suggested to the recently retired Prime Minister, Ramsay MacDonald, that he had 'stuck a label on his chest: "I am von Germany"'.[158] He was an enormous snob, liking nothing better than to be hob-nobbing with royalty and the English aristocracy. Exceptionally sensitive to any slight, and abnormally status-conscious, to his subordinates he was overbearing and arrogant with more than a touch of the ridiculous about him.[159] He could bore his hosts and fellow guests at dinner-parties to distraction with long-winded disquisitions on the evils of Bolshevism. His vanity and sense of self-importance were matched only by his unsurpassed subservience to Hitler. Among the top leaders of the Third Reich, beneath Hitler, mutual detestation was endemic. But one thing united them: they all despised Ribbentrop.

This was the man who, clothed neatly in a dark overcoat and carrying a homburg hat and gloves, stepped from the Junkers airliner at Newtownards that fine if rather chilly spring evening in May 1936. Accompanying him was his wife, the formidable Annelies, somewhat staid and forbidding in appearance. A strong personality, she was generally reckoned to be the force behind the man, the constant prompt to his pushy careerism. Also in his entourage were the charming Princess Marie Elisabeth zu Wied and her distinctly less charming and more abrasive younger sister, Princess Benigna Victoria. These were the daughters of Prince Viktor zu Wied, a former diplomat and later German envoy in Stockholm (under consideration for a while for the vacant ambassadorship in London, but considered by Goebbels 'too stupid'), and his wife, Princess Gisela (whose lavish Berlin receptions Goebbels had attended, and whom he had admired long before the Nazis took power).[160] The Londonderrys had met the Wieds during their trip to Germany earlier in the year. Two other Germans, his adjutants Heinz Thorner, and Georg von Wussow, also formed part of Ribbentrop's accompaniment. Ribbentrop was, however, somewhat taken aback at the presence of another German guest, Werner von Fries, legation secretary at the German Embassy in London who had arrived several hours earlier. The Embassy had obtained an invitation to the house-party for von Fries so that he could serve as a 'plant' to keep the German Foreign Ministry informed of what their rival, Ribbentrop, was up to at the Whitsuntide weekend party.[161]

Awaiting the visitors, as they descended from the Junkers, were Lady Londonderry, Lady Mairi Stewart, and the Chief of Staff of the Royal Air Force, Air Marshal Sir Edward Ellington, who had arrived the previous day by flying-boat. Fifteen minutes later a plane from London touched down, carrying Ribbentrop's host, Lord Londonderry, and most of the remaining guests for the weekend house-party.[162] These were: Eric Viscount Chaplin (the brother of Lady Londonderry) and his wife, Gwladys; their son, Anthony Chaplin, and his wife, Alvilde; Mrs Laura Corrigan, a rich, generous, somewhat eccentric American heiress, famous in London society for her lavish receptions, and given to amusing malapropisms, who had hosted a lunch attended by the Ribbentrops before she and they left for Ireland;[163] and an old family friend of the Londonderrys (and of the royal family), Sir Hedworth Williamson, an estate owner in the north of England. Also present were George Ward Price, the star foreign correspondent of the *Daily Mail*, described by one contemporary as 'a Nazi heart and soul',[164] certainly strongly pro-German, and one of Hitler's favourite journalists. Ward Price's most recent interview with Hitler had taken place only a few weeks earlier, following the march into the Rhineland.[165] A large and admiring crowd swarmed around Ribbentrop's airliner, the largest plane to land at the small airport. After exchanging pleasantries, the Londonderrys and their guests stepped into the waiting cars to be driven the short distance to Mount Stewart.

VI

Ribbentrop had stepped from his plane announcing that he was 'a great friend of Lord Londonderry, and that is why I am here'.[166] Lord Londonderry had echoed the sentiment, saying that he and Ribbentrop were 'close friends'.[167] This may have been merely for public consumption. Privately, Lord Londonderry is said to have regarded Ribbentrop as 'the rudest man he'd ever met', and Lady Londonderry apparently loathed him.[168] But why, then, invite him to

Mount Stewart? Londonderry portrayed the invitation to Ribbentrop as no more than extending the usual politeness of reciprocation for the hospitality he had received when he, his wife and his daughter had been in Berlin earlier in the year.[169] But this seems to offer only a partial answer. Formal reciprocation would not have demanded that Lady Londonderry, writing in early May, press the Ribbentrops – who had dined with the Londonderrys as recently as 3 April – to stay for as long as a week (enclosing with the invitation a copy of a newspaper article which she had written, praising Hitler).[170] Probably, in fact, the negative sentiments towards Ribbentrop arose subsequently, while he was Ambassador. Correspondence between the Londonderrys and the Ribbentrops around the time of his visit to Mount Stewart certainly *seems* cordial and friendly, even allowing for the conventional dictates of politeness.[171] And Lord Londonderry would himself hint that the dislike of Ribbentrop came later.[172]

His early dealings with Ribbentrop give no hint of tension or animosity. His strong connections with Ribbentrop, which dated back at least to the time when the German envoy was in London in autumn 1934 and had attended Lady Londonderry's reception,[173] had, in fact, by spring 1936, already helped to earn him the reputation, which he would never shake off, as a Nazi sympathizer and admirer of Hitler. Londonderry had indeed done much to invite such an image and readily described himself as 'of course a friend of Germany'.[174] Ribbentrop, for his part, was known in London society, because of the closeness of their relations, as Londonderry's man – as some wits had it, playing on the title of the well-known folk song, 'The Londonderry Herr'.[175]

Officially, Ribbentrop emphasized to reporters on arrival in Northern Ireland that his visit to Mount Stewart was 'a purely private one and had no political significance'. There was 'nothing mysterious about it'; he had simply come for a few days' holiday.[176] Lord Londonderry reacted with greater irritation. The visit, he emphasized, had 'no connection whatever with any public matter. I shall ask whoever I like to spend a holiday with me. That's my private business. It's terrible the way in which suggestions of political significance are published. I am not in the international political business at all.'[177] He was clearly irked by the widespread presumption that a political purpose lay behind the Whitsuntide meeting. One London Sunday newspaper asserted that Londonderry and Ribbentrop had come together to discuss proposals from Berlin 'to make Britain and Germany allies' in a pact of mutual assistance whereby Germany would guarantee British security in western Europe and the Mediterranean in exchange for a free hand for Germany in eastern Europe. Lord Londonderry, the report went on, hoped 'his friends in the Cabinet will force the Government to accept'.[178] Another London newspaper was even more forthright. 'Lord Londonderry', it commented,

may assert to his heart's content that at his weekend party at his mansion in Ulster Herr von Ribbentrop and the chief of our air staff, Sir Edward Ellington, had never any intention of discussing public matters. But who will believe that these two men would come together at such a juncture in Anglo-German relations as the present one and confine themselves to the discussion of the weather . . . ?

The newspaper speculated that the issue of a western European air pact and air limitation was at the centre of the discussions.[179] What, then, did take place during the weekend house-party at Mount Stewart?

On the day after their arrival, a Saturday, the Ribbentrops relaxed with the Londonderrys. There was opportunity to be driven around the neighbouring lovely part of South Down, or to stroll in the gardens of Mount Stewart – at their most resplendent in late spring and described by Ribbentrop himself, in a subsequent letter to Lady Londonderry, as a 'paradise' which 'a fertile ground and the genius of a woman have made . . . of this spot in Ireland'.[180] In the evening, Londonderry and Ribbentrop went off to play a round of golf at the nearby Scrabo Links.[181] Golf was not a usual aristocratic pastime, but apparently Londonderry liked a round.[182] And though golf was not a popular game in Germany at the time, Ribbentrop also seems to have enjoyed the sport, which pandered to his pro-British affectations. How and when he had been introduced to golf is not clear. What is certain is that he was not very good at it. At any rate, despite lessons from a Scottish professional, he lost a round comprehensively two years later to a man who had not played golf for thirty years, ever since his right arm had been mauled by a lion while big-game hunting in Africa.[183] It seems unlikely, therefore, that Ribbentrop won the game against Londonderry, unless diplomacy and hospitality had demanded such a result. A story attributed to the caddy at the round is that Ribbentrop rewarded his services with a tip of half a crown – a generous gratuity in those days – at which Londonderry immediately took the coin out of the man's palm, saying it was far too much, and replaced it with a shilling.[184] The caddy was one of the few people in the universe, therefore, left with a good opinion of Ribbentrop – in his view, a considerate and generous man. Whatever the truth of the story, the tale of Ribbentrop's boating disaster that weekend appears to be apocryphal. Folklore in County Down has it that Ribbentrop had to be fished out of Strangford Lough with a boat hook after Lady Londonderry's boat collided with her husband's during a yacht race, throwing their German visitor overboard.[185] But it is no more than legend. Ribbentrop, it seems, never went sailing at any point during the weekend.[186]

On Whit Sunday, the official high spot of the visit took place when three squadrons of RAF planes – from Glasgow, Edinburgh and Durham – arrived at Newtownards aerodrome, to the delight of the large crowds which had gathered, as they had been doing all weekend, to view Ribbentrop's plane. The thirty-six military aircraft – Hawker Hart two-seater biplanes – landing in perfect formation at the small provincial airport and docking alongside the Junkers airliner that had brought Ribbentrop provided quite a spectacle. The leader of the Glasgow squadron was himself a celebrity – the Marquess of Clydesdale (a great friend of Londonderry's, who had recently made headline news by flying over the peak of Everest in 1933, and would, as the Duke Hamilton, cause an even greater stir some years later when Rudolf Hess flew to Scotland to seek him out).[187] Greatly impressed by the display, Ribbentrop asked whether it was a frequent occurrence. Londonderry lied: 'Yes, they come about once a month.'[188] The fliers were then taken by car to Mount Stewart and lunched in the imposing dining-room, overlooking the beautiful gardens, where, beneath the portrait of King William III at the battle of the Boyne, the chairs of the participants of the Congress of Vienna, presented to Lord Castlereagh, were arrayed. The leading figures sat around the large dining-table in the centre of the room, most of the airmen at little tables around the edges. In the early evening, the squadrons returned to their home bases. The entire show, together with the presence of Sir Edward Ellington, the Chief of the Air Staff, had been devised to impress Ribbentrop with the power of the British air force. Whether that was the impression he took back with him to Germany is unknown.[189]

The Monday, like the preceding Saturday, was uneventful – spent in and around Mount Stewart, leaving plenty of time for Lord Londonderry and his important guest to talk about weighty matters of mutual concern. Early on the Tuesday morning members of the Londonderry family and house guests motored again to Newtownards airport to bid farewell to the Ribbentrops, who arrived back at Croydon shortly after midday.[190]

Ribbentrop stayed a further two days in London, where he met a number of individuals, including Geoffrey Dawson, the influential editor of *The Times*, Thomas Jones, the Welsh former Deputy Secretary to the Cabinet and general busybody, and Lord Lothian, the Liberal peer who had enjoyed a well-publicized audience with Hitler in early 1935 – all of them sympathetic to notions of a rapprochement with Germany. Despite a cooler reception than it seems he had anticipated,[191] he returned to Germany assured that he had courted and won over those who mattered in Britain. He was convinced, as he told Hitler and his entourage shortly afterwards, that pro-German feeling in Britain was growing; that there were greater doubts about France; that Sir Samuel Hoare, the ex-Foreign Secretary, had 'come over to us'; that the critical Anthony Eden, Hoare's successor, had been side-lined; and that the Prime Minister, Stanley Baldwin, was 'completely on the German side'.[192]

How much of this thoroughly mistaken impression had he gleaned through talks with Londonderry? Though he had certainly sounded out further contacts in London, Ribbentrop's report indicated that his trip to Northern Ireland had not, despite the pronounced denial of any political content, been merely an innocent brief holiday among friends. Officials in the German Foreign Ministry apparently believed that Ribbentrop was carrying proposals from Hitler aimed at a pact which would guarantee Britain's security in return for a free hand for

Germany in the east. If so, then they were grossly overestimating Londonderry's influence in government circles, and it seems highly unlikely that tangible proposals were under consideration.[193] That political discussions took place is, however, plain. Many years later, Lord Londonderry's daughter, who had been present throughout the weekend, recalled that her father withdrew on a number of occasions to his study with Ribbentrop, and that there was 'a lot of political talk' in which (as she put it) Londonderry sought 'to find out what he could' about German intentions,[194] while Ribbentrop courted someone whom he regarded as an important intermediary in the German cause with close links to the British government. In a letter he sent to Hermann Göring immediately following Ribbentrop's visit, Lord Londonderry himself confirmed that the German envoy's visit had had a political dimension. 'Herr von Ribbentrop has been staying with me for the Whitsuntide holidays', Londonderry wrote, 'and I have had some very interesting conversations with him.'[195] The content of the 'conversations' is not specified. The main concern, however, both from Londonderry's and from Ribbentrop's point of view, would have been the need to repair relations between Germany and Britain, recently damaged through the remilitarization of the Rhineland, and build the platform for a firm friendship.

Londonderry's letter to Göring goes on to hint that, in the wake of the damage done to Anglo-German relations by Hitler's Rhineland spectacular, he had attempted to persuade Ribbentrop of the need to use his influence to prevent further actions which would undermine the prospect of the desired entente. 'I wish it were possible', Londonderry continued in his letter to Göring, 'to create a fuller understanding between us because it appears to me that so many words and actions of the one are completely misunderstood by the other.'[196] This was evidently a central concern in the Londonderry household at the time, since the same theme was voiced by Lady Londonderry in a letter she drafted to Göring on the very day of the Ribbentrops' arrival at Mount Stewart. She advised Göring, 'if you want an understanding with this country', to 'stick to your word concerning certain undertakings', adding how vital it was 'to remove this mistrust concerning Germany's foreign policy in relation to ours', and that she and her husband 'are both doing all we can to foster friendship and I am sure you will'.[197]

Lord Londonderry's concern, echoed by his wife, about 'misunderstandings' (as he saw them), almost certainly alluded to the bad feeling towards Germany within the British Foreign Office since the German remilitarization of the Rhineland – a sourness attributable, in reality, in no small measure to Ribbentrop's high-handedness and distortions, on top, no doubt, of the realization that British diplomacy had once again been out-smarted by Hitler's boldly unconventional foreign policy. Ribbentrop had made the worst possible impression before the Council of the League of Nations, specially summoned to a meeting in London, in March, to deal with the German breach of the Treaty of Locarno. And in May, he had further angered the Foreign Office by producing a German collection of documents related to the background of the Rhineland issue, purporting to be accurate and complete, and critical of the British 'Blue Book' (which had presented the diplomatic discussions from the British point of view), but amounting to a one-sided and distorted presentation of relevant documents – nothing more than a propaganda exercise. Londonderry, it can be taken for granted, would have said little or nothing at the Whitsuntide weekend which could have been taken as critical of Ribbentrop's part in all this.[198] In any case, Londonderry was already deeply irritated by the Foreign Office and its handling of the German question. As we have seen, his own view, in common with much British opinion, was that the remilitarization of the Rhineland had been both inevitable and justified.[199] So when the Foreign Secretary, Anthony Eden, had responded to Hitler's 'peace plan' at the end of March by drawing up a list of detailed questions seeking clarification of the German proposals (and in the event never to be answered), which, as Londonderry knew, had simply annoyed Hitler, he took it as a further opportunity to try to explore the ground for German friendship, spurned in his view by the Foreign Office.[200] Despite the setbacks, he was, as he told Göring, still hopeful 'that good sense will prevail', adding his further hope 'that you will not consider it right to embark on policies which create anxiety in the minds of those nations whose friendship you are seeking'.[201]

A second issue which Londonderry doubtless discussed with Ribbentrop was the question of arms limitation, particularly in the air. In his letter published in *The Times* of 12 March, defending the remilitarization of the Rhineland, Lord Londonderry had referred to the 'offers . . . of a definite character' that Hitler had made in his speech to the Reichstag five days earlier (and which were to be reformulated and amplified in his 'peace offer' of 31 March). These had been well received in the British media,[202] and Londonderry hoped that the British government would 'meet them in their move towards peace in the same manner as they accepted the German naval offer . . . as a real example of the policy of limitation of armaments'.[203] Among Hitler's offerings, which he had been able to advance in the full certainty that they would not be accepted by Britain and France, paralysed as ever in their foreign policy by their divided attitudes and diplomacy towards Germany, was the suggestion of an air pact to eliminate the dangers of bombing.[204] This was a shrewd adaptation by Hitler of the idea, much discussed (as we noted) – though to little effect – by the British and French in late 1934 and early 1935. The proposition had gone into cold storage following the shock announcement in March 1935 that Germany had already attained air parity with Britain.[205] But we saw that the British Foreign Office was still toying with such a possibility in the weeks before the reoccupation of the Rhineland.

Hitler's 'peace plan' following his coup had resuscitated the idea. Londonderry was anxious not to let the opportunity slip. His reference, in his *Times* letter, to the naval pact of 1935, is an oblique indication that he had not given up hope of something similar with regard to air strength, and his continued interest in the issue of arms limitation would have ensured that this issue, as some newspapers surmised, was discussed during the weekend with Ribbentrop. Since the Chief of the Air Staff, Sir Edward Ellington, was present at the house-party (at which a visit from the three RAF squadrons had been a highlight), it seems certain that the the idea of an air pact, though now (as the Germans wanted) a bilateral agreement between Germany and Britain analagous to the naval pact, was resurrected and that issues of comparable air strength and the possibilities of attaining some limitation were raised with Ribbentrop. And that a further house-guest of the Londonderrys, George Ward Price of the *Daily Mail*, had been granted a two-hour interview with Hitler, centring upon his 'peace proposals', only two days after German troops had marched into the Rhineland,[206] strengthens the suggestion that these issues lay close to the heart of the informal discussions held at Mount Stewart that Whitsuntide.

A third topic of discussion was unquestionably the related issue of British relations with France, which lay at the heart of any mooted alteration in Britain's attitude towards Germany. Londonderry and Ribbentrop would have had no difficulty on agreeing during the weekend on the need to detach British foreign policy from its pro-French stance as a prerequisite to better relations with Germany. The feeling that the French, in their obstinate hostility towards concessions to Germany, were the chief obstacles to continuing European peace on the basis of a fair settlement of Germany's legitimate grievances was a commonplace in Great Britain during the 1930s, and even more so after Hitler's 'peace proposals' following the Rhineland coup.[207]

Ribbentrop must have sensed that the moment was ripe to press upon his contacts in Britain the need to persuade their friends in the government to side with the Germans rather than the French. In the case of Londonderry, he was pushing at an open door. Londonderry's own anti-French prejudice was, as we have already noted, long established. It had been accentuated by the election in April 1936 of a Popular Front government in Paris, headed by a Socialist, Léon Blum. This was anathema to the Londonderrys.

Lady Londonderry fully shared her husband's strong antipathy to the new French regime. In a letter to Göring in early May 1936, she declared: 'As France is at present, there is no use trying to negotiate with her. She is just drifting about helplessly – at the mercy almost of Russia'. In her eyes, France was 'in a very dangerous state', showing 'how necessary it is that our two countries should remain firm friends'.[208] As Londonderry commented to Göring at the beginning of June, just after Ribbentrop's visit, 'I sympathise fully with your apprehensions connected with communism and I look with dismay on the increased number of [Communist] Deputies in the French Parliament and the same conditions existing to a smaller extent in Belgium.'[209]

From such a standpoint, Londonderry would certainly have reinforced the impressions Ribbentrop was to report back to Hitler, that increased doubts about France mirrored the growth in pro-German feeling in Britain. This was scarcely the view in the British Foreign Office. But Ribbentrop was optimistic that his friends in high places would overcome the difficulties experienced in official channels. The chances of the sought-after rapprochement seemed fleetingly rosy.

VII

As the *Wilhelm Siegert* took off from Newtownards airport on the morning of Tuesday, 2 June for the return flight to Croydon, it seems certain, then, that both Ribbentrop and Londonderry were well satisfied with the political as well as the social side of the weekend at Mount Stewart. Londonderry would have been reassured that his own efforts towards a rapprochement with Germany were making progress, despite the coolness of official diplomacy through the Foreign Office. He would have been encouraged that, whatever the blockages in that quarter, private diplomacy through direct talks with those closest to Hitler promised to pay rich dividends. The prospect of lasting European peace through an arrangement with Nazi Germany seemed to him a very real one.[210] Ribbentrop, for his part, took with him the strong impression that he had cemented good relations with an influential friend of Germany. Here was an channel for his country to work through, to build a basis of friendship and cooperation with Great Britain instead of the current antagonism and distrust, and drive an even sharper wedge between British and French interests. Even if Anthony Eden and the Foreign Office remained aloof, Ribbentrop would have calculated, Londonderry and other members of the British aristocracy, with their direct line to Edward VIII, a monarch known to be sympathetic to Germany, and their social and political connections with the most important members of the British government, would have distinct chances of smoothing the path to the entente that Hitler wanted.

So the weekend could be reckoned a success. As a lasting reminder of his memorable visit, Ribbentrop gave Lord Londonderry the remarkable present that we have already noted: the porcelain figurine, always known to the Londonderrys simply as 'the stormtrooper' – a strange relic of Nazi Germany to have found a home in Northern Ireland, a macabre testimonial to the shortlived, but intense, connection of the house and its owner with Hitler's Reich. It was a connection which would utterly destroy Lord Londonderry's reputation.

This was by now firmly established. At home the Londonderrys were now widely seen as the foremost apologists for Hitler's regime. Their public outspoken utterances in favour of Germany, eulogistic speeches and press articles about Hitler and other Nazi leaders, and, especially, their well-advertised close association with Ribbentrop had helped to establish their high profile within the pro-German lobby. And among the Nazi hierarchy they were regarded as champions of the German cause. Though their social status and connections to the highest in the land in Britain were unaffected, their political influence – never as great as they had imagined – was now negligible. Even Londonderry's old friend and Cabinet ally Lord Hailsham now took issue with him. 'As to von Ribbentrop and your Germany friends,' he wrote shortly after the Mount Stewart weekend, 'I am myself quite sure that the Germans won't be satisfied till they have hegemony in the old World and that they are aiming to get it. I dislike them because I honestly believe that peace is the predominant interest of this country and the Germans are the main (though not the only) obstacles to its achievement.'[211] For much of the general public, Londonderry's image now was summed up in a letter from Liverpool, shortly after Ribbentrop had departed, protesting at his 'fraternising with a representative of Nazi Germany' and saying he had 'shocked the people of this country'.[212]

The German courting of Londonderry and the latter's temporary infatuation with Nazi Germany rested upon a double misapprehension. From the German point of view, winning the open advocacy of an ex-Cabinet minister, so recently in office and closely involved in rearmament matters, and belonging to the upper crust of the British aristocracy, was an important diplomatic coup. Ribbentrop plainly believed that such a leading nobleman as Londonderry had more influence than was actually the case. Londonderry, from his angle, was flattered to be apparently so highly regarded by the German leaders. He sought an avenue to the power and influence which in his view had been so unfairly taken away from him by the Prime Minister, Stanley Baldwin. And, absurdly self-confident, he imagined that through old-fashioned personal contacts and private talks he could single-handedly bring about that which the blinkered and obstinate stuffed-shirts of Foreign Office officialdom were unable to achieve: the accord with Germany which, he had convinced himself, was the only way to the future peace of Europe.[213] Psychologically, as we suggested earlier, winning the glory that had accrued to his ancestor, Lord Castlereagh, was almost certainly a strong motive. Not for nothing would Londonderry's book of 1938 carry as its frontispiece a letter of Castlereagh from 1815, at the end of the Napoleonic Wars, to the then British Prime Minister, Lord Liverpool, underlining his aim 'to bring back the world to peaceful habits'.[214]

Londonderry's illusions lasted through the remainder of 1936. But over the subsequent months, they were to fade inexorably. And a position which, in spring 1936, still matched the hopes and beliefs of many in Britain became the increasingly marginalized stance of a politician out of touch with mainstream opinion both in the country and in the corridors of power.

4

Lengthening Shadows

'I feel that we are heading for disaster. The Foreign Office seems quite incapable of doing anything right and goes out of its way to estrange our would-be friends.'

    Lord Londonderry, writing to Lord Halifax, June 1937

'The sands are running out and the situation deteriorating. An understanding between Great Britain and Germany with all its great potentialities seems to me the tonic which the world requires.'

    Lord Londonderry, writing to Lord Halifax, November 1937

The Berlin Olympic Games in the first half of August 1936 marked the high point for the hopes of those, like Lord Londonderry, who wanted to forge closer and more positive links between Great Britain and Germany. No effort was spared by the Nazi leadership to put on a show aimed at presenting the regime's best face to the world – and quite especially to important British guests who might help to engineer the friendship with Germany which remained an integral part of Hitler's vision, aimed at an alliance weaning Britain away from France and providing British support for German eastern expansion and dominance of the Continent. During the fortnight of the Games, the stirring events in the Olympic Stadium were accompanied by extravagant displays of hospitality by leading Nazis, striving to out-do each other in the lavish splendour of their entertainment for hundreds of foreign guests. Grandiose as they were, the huge receptions provided by Ribbentrop and Goebbels were eclipsed by the extraordinary garden party laid on by Göring in the heart of Berlin. Huge spotlights on the tops of neighbouring houses and hundreds of lights placed in trees illuminated the large gardens. Among the 800 or so guests, ministers from the Nazi government mingled with ambassadors and politicians from all over the world. After dining, the guests, seated at tables around the expansive lawn, were treated to a display by a troupe of ballet dancers in eighteenth-century costume, then an air stunt performance by the ace flyer Ernst Udet (who would commit suicide towards the end of 1941 after a major confrontation with Göring about the shortcomings of the Lufwaffe in the war against the Soviet Union). Only the cold and damp weather, which the many electric heaters scattered about the gardens could do little to counter, spoiled the occasion for some; but not for 'Chips' Channon, the socialite, dilettante Conservative MP and highly impressionable, distinctly empty-headed admirer of the new Germany. Relishing every moment, 'Chips' described the Göring party as 'fantastic', with 'roundabouts, cafés with beer and champagne, peasants dancing and "schuplat-tling", vast women carrying brezels and beer, a ship, a beerhouse, crowds of gay, laughing people'. When someone remarked that nothing like it had been seen since the days of Louis XIV, 'Chips' corrected them: 'Not since Nero,' he retorted.[1]

On the fringes of the festivities, serious attempts were made by Nazi grandees to win over the British. Hitler himself entertained representatives of the Anglo-German Fellowship along with Lord Rothermere and Lord Beaverbrook.[2] Ribbentrop attempted the uphill task of converting Sir Robert Vansittart, the leading anti-German at the Foreign Office, to a more amenable stance towards Germany. Vansittart had, it seemed, enjoyed the Ribbentrops' party. As his host noticed, he had danced a lot – taken to be a good sign. In such a congenial atmosphere, Ribbentrop, whose appointment as Ambassador in London had just been announced, thought there was an opening and persuaded him to meet Hitler. It was to no avail. At the audience, Ribbentrop was left to do most of the talking and felt as if were 'addressing a wall'. 'Never was a conversation so barren,' he recalled.[3]

Within weeks, Hitler would be entertaining at the Berghof his most important British visitor to date: the former Prime Minister and war leader David Lloyd George, who would, like so many before him (including Londonderry), return home singing the praises of the new Germany and lauding the 'greatness' of its Leader.[4] But, for Hitler as for Ribbentrop, there was no mistaking the hard fact: none of the British politicians and publicists who had gone away rhapsodizing about the Nazi regime was in power. Vansittart, on the other hand, was at the heart of British deliberations on foreign policy; and his opposition to Germany was implacable. From the outset, Hitlerism had seemed to him the logical culmination of the antagonism and aggression towards Britain which he had already encountered in Germany under the Kaiser. He had never for an instant thought that friendship with Hitler's Germany was an option which would bring peace. He was as insistent as Churchill, and from as early a date, that only maximum deterrence to a grave and inevitable German threat could prevent war. He wrote in 1935: 'My view is a short and simple one. Anything that fails to provide security by 1938 is inadequate and blind.'[5] This view never changed. It made Vansittart a major stumbling-block to the accommodation with Britain that the German leadership sought.

It was not that hope of friendship with Britain was abandoned. Vansittart was, after all, not a government minister and, influential though he was, did not determine policy. But – from the German point of view of relations with Britain – this shadow cast over the glitz and superficial cordiality of the Berlin Olympics denoted the more likely growing estrangement that would take place over the following months. Just before the Olympics had started, the beginning of the Spanish Civil War, in which Hitler had committed Germany to support of Franco's nationalist rebellion, seemed, as the conflict deepened, the harbinger of even worse conflagration to come, and drove a further wedge between Britain and Germany. Flushed with self-confidence following the Rhineland coup, Germany was beginning visibly to flex her muscles. Another sign was the more voluble demand for the restoration of colonies – a demand addressed in the first instance to Britain.[6]

For her part, belatedly, though now, as we have seen, with greater urgency, Britain had adopted extensive measures of rearmament (despite continuing internal difficulties over the cost, speed and economic repercussions of a rearmament programme). By the end of 1936, therefore, and still in the early stages of Ribbentrop's already ill-starred ambassadorship, the prospects of a rapprochement between Germany and Britain were rapidly fading.

From Germany's point of view, despite all the efforts at winning over Britain, including the courting of presumed influential individuals (among them Londonderry), a retrospective of 1936 could offer only a disappointing assessment of achieving the desired basis of friendship. The abdication in December of King Edward VIII, known to the Nazi leadership for his sympathy for Germany, was interpreted by Ribbentrop as a blow to his hopes. Germany had had 'the greatest interest in his remaining King'.[7] His abdication, Ribbentrop told Hitler, had taken place 'because it was not certain whether he would co-operate in an anti-German policy'.[8]

The high hopes, also for British enthusiasts for Germany, had by then all but vanished. Disillusionment was around the corner.

I

Lord Londonderry had been unable to attend the summer Olympics in Berlin, though his son, Lord Castlereagh, had been among the throng of British visitors, and had lunched with Göring (whom he found 'most amiable and pleasant').[9] Shortly before the Games, Göring had sent Lady Londonderry another long letter (which she passed on to some leading politicians) reiterating the case for Anglo-German friendship: the threat of Communism and its advances in France; Germany's interest in upholding the British Empire; but – the veiled threat – Germany's need to look elsewhere for alliances should Britain continue to shun the hand of friendship.[10] The themes would recur in the correspondence which Lord Londonderry carried out in subsequent months with Lord Halifax, a longstanding friend who had succeeded him as Lord Privy Seal. Halifax had been the only government minister, in Londonderry's view, to take an interest in his reports from Germany. Probably, Londonderry was mistaking Halifax's unvaried and unfailing courtesy for serious concern. But the correspondence does indicate Halifax's readiness to engage with

Londonderry's point of view – and hints at the same time at how far the divide had widened between Londonderry's pro-German stance and the negative caution of the government.

Londonderry's class, background, social status and political leanings had made him a lifelong and diehard anti-Socialist, while his fear of Communism can already be glimpsed in the 1920s. He had accused the miners' leaders of having revolutionary leanings and allies in Moscow following the General Strike of 1926, and again towards the end of the 1920s after an unofficial five-week strike at one of his pits in the Durham coal-fields. And in 1931, two years after visiting the Ruhr district, Germany's industrial hub, he had warned of 'grave repercussions on the whole civilized world' if the country should be allowed to collapse and 'be driven into the hands of the Communists'.[11] Revealing the influence of his recent talks with Hitler and Göring, he now, writing to Halifax, deplored 'the apparent indifference with which the Government are treating the menace of Communism', and hinted that the Soviet Embassy in London was a base of subversion and espionage. Ignoring or condoning Communism, he asserted, would undermine hopes of good relations with Germany. He could not understand, he went on, 'why the Government cannot make common ground in some form or another with Germany in their opposition to Communism'. Such an understanding, he thought, would be extremely valuable even without the formal commitments that would arise from an alliance. Refusal, 'under the influence of France and the Foreign Office', to take this route would, he suggested, result in the Germans adopting policies unfavourable to Britain. In such an event, he declared, 'then our blood will be upon our own heads'.[12]

Halifax, who had found Londonderry's notes on his German visit 'most interesting, but also somewhat disturbing'[13] (in ways which he did not define) and saw the gist of his comments reinforced by what Göring had written to Lady Londonderry, politely pointed out how the position of the government differed. This, he noted, was to avoid having to choose between Germany and Russia. 'It would take a great deal of persuasion', he remarked, 'to make our people feel that it is impossible to be good friends with both – indeed good friends all round!'[14] Even as Halifax wrote these words, the intention of continued friendly relations on all sides must have sounded a pious hope more than a realistic proposition. The sentiment was soon enough to ring very hollow indeed.

Feeling irritated, misunderstood and in a 'position of complete isolation', Londonderry returned to the charge. 'The situation to my mind', he wrote, 'is drifting very dangerously, and we are losing the great opportunity we had of being able to influence Germany.' He saw anti-Communism as an issue on which Britain could have wholeheartedly associated with Germany, however much other areas of policy were deprecated or even condemned. He then added a new – rather strained – argument for adopting an overt anti-Communist stance in support of Germany. He thought, built into a basis of friendship with Germany, it would provide 'a get-out for Hitler' who, 'when he finds a policy of his not working out exactly as he desires', would then 'have an excuse of going back on it by saying that he is determined to preserve the good opinion of Great Britain'. Reiterating his annoyance that 'having made the most valuable contacts' in Germany, he had been ignored by every member of the Cabinet, he summed up that, in his judgement, 'the whole of this German matter is being woefully mishandled by the Government'.[15]

Halifax tactfully indicated his agreement, and that of the government, with a policy which would not rule out any possibility of rapprochement with Germany.[16] However, suggesting that Londonderry was unfair in accusing the government of being pro-French, he made plain that any understanding with Germany, from the government's point of view, had to be within the framework of a multilateral agreement which included France. 'Once we can get Germany, France & ourselves round a table', Halifax continued, 'I hope that a good deal will follow', though he immediately added that the Franco-Soviet Pact was bound to be '*the* snag', and that here Britain's interests stood closer to those of Germany than of France. He thought it would be easier to make it plain, especially in the light of events in Spain, that in regard to Communism Britain would regard Germany 'as an ally of ours & of all order-loving folk'. The colonial question posed a problem, though Halifax said he would be willing 'to do a good deal' as part of a general settlement, holding it out as an enticement to German cooperation. He saw no great difficulty, he wrote, in Londonderry talking to the Germans, though gently warned him that they were interested in dividing Britain and France rather than engaging in the inclusive settlement desired by the government, adding that 'the devils of the piece, though, I should be inclined freely to admit – are Russia'.[17]

As Halifax was writing, the Nazi Party Rally was unfolding in Nuremberg. Hitler had dubbed it the Rally 'of Honour' to depict the regaining of independence through the eradication of Germany's subjection to the treaties of Versailles and Locarno. Numerous foreign guests, including many German sympathizers from Britain, heard the relentless attacks on Bolshevism which formed the theme of the Rally and registered, too, the announcement of a new, major economic plan aimed at rendering Germany free from dependence on imports from abroad, along with the renewed demand for colonies.[18] The impressive orchestration of pageantry and power did not fail to leave its mark on most of the British visitors, often already susceptible to the allures of Hitler's Germany. One prominent British journalist, encapsulating the views of many impressionable witnesses of the spectacle, wrote of 'so much in the new Germany that is beautiful, so much that is fine and great. And all the time in this country, we are being trained to believe that the Germans are a nation of wild beasts who vary their time between roasting Jews and teaching babies to present arms. It simply is not true.'[19] Whether reactions would have been so rapturous had those attending known that Hitler's directive for the fundamental restructuring of the economy that he announced at the Rally, soon to be labelled the 'Four-Year Plan', would end by setting the goal of an army and economy ready for war within four years, is doubtful.[20]

Londonderry would certainly have been invited by his friend Ribbentrop, along with so many other influential pro-Germans, to attend the Rally, but was presumably unable to do so. He told Halifax he had been 'frankly disturbed by the speeches at Nuremberg' and had written to Ribbentrop 'exactly how I feel about it', though did not elaborate further. He agreed, he said, with the Germans 'as to the Russian danger', but thought that 'in their desire for hegemony' they were 'merely claiming the Russian obsession so as to be ready to carry out their designs in other directions'. He went on once more to berate the French and, even more strongly than hitherto, the British Foreign Office for the 'disastrous' course of events since the beginning of the Disarmament Conference. He then turned his fire on Sir Eric Phipps, the British Ambassador in Berlin, who, together with the French and American Ambassadors, had (as on earlier occasions) declined invitations to the Party Rally.[21] Phipps, he thought, should have been constantly pressing Hitler 'for an explanation for everything that he did', but 'appeared to be incapable of finding out anything and to be occupying an isolated position'. In contrast, Hitler, Göring and Ribbentrop had apparently been anxious 'to put all their desires before me, who, after all was but an independent stranger not supposed to carry very much weight with the Government'. (This failed, of course, to recognize both that the Nazi leaders had overestimated his influence and that they had been using him as a conduit for their propaganda.) He assured Halifax that he did not want the ambassadorship himself, mainly because 'the position is so subordinate to the Foreign Office in modern days that I feel I should never be able to work harmoniously with my chiefs'.[22] Thus, the tone of Londonderry's letter managed to combine arrogance and naivety in equal measures.

Phipps had been pessimistic from the outset about the prospects of positive relations with Hitler's Germany. By autumn 1936 he had come to view the chances as extremely remote. The new German Ambassador in London, Joachim von Ribbentrop, who took up his appointment in October, gave few grounds for better things to come. The Secretary to the Cabinet, Sir Maurice Hankey, told Phipps early that month that Ribbentrop 'appears to have queer ideas about trying to get the right side of us' when all that was wanted was 'a decent, straightforward man who will really represent his principals and not let us down'. Hankey had 'never despaired of coming to terms with Germany one day' and thought war with Britain would be 'a silly business' and end by exposing both countries to Bolshevism. But he evidently did not think Ribbentrop was likely to improve relations and banish the spectre of war.[23] Phipps himself described the new ambassador as 'a lightweight . . . irritating, ignorant and boundlessly conceited'.[24] This was the man whom Londonderry again invited to be his guest at a weekend house-party, this time at Wynyard, his stately residence in north-eastern England, not far from Stockton-on-Tees, in mid-November 1936.

The second Ribbentrop weekend followed shortly after another visit to Germany by Lord and Lady Londonderry and their daughter

Lady Mairi, in late October. The visit, taking up an invitation by Göring to hunt with him again at Carinhall,[25] was similar to that at the beginning of the year. The Londonderrys were again received by Hitler, who thanked Lord Londonderry for what he had done to foster friendliness between Britain and Germany, and again emphasized the dangers of Bolshevism. Londonderry also had further talks with Göring – in which, no doubt, Germany's need for colonies and expansion figured prominently.[26] He then attended a speech Göring gave on 28 October in the cavernous Sportpalast in Berlin on the Four-Year Plan. The American Ambassador, William Dodd, noted that Göring had 'attacked England shamelessly', despite the presence in the audience of his guest. Londonderry, it was reported, had not understood what was said.[27] Later, Londonderry was to comment of this visit that he had come to place little faith in Göring's remarks about Britain.[28] He gave no indication of this feeling at the time, however, even if his high hopes of the first part of the year had not been realized.

This second visit attracted far less publicity than had been the case the previous February. The flow of British visitors to Germany during 1936 had been so great – Phipps wondered what the object was 'apart of course from the very natural wish of the visitors to see so strange a being as Göring at close quarters'[29] – that the novelty value had diminished. Moreover, Londonderry could add nothing to the impression he had gained on his earlier visit, that Germany's feelings towards Britain were 'very friendly' in character, as his wife echoed in a newspaper interview emphasizing Hitler's friendliness towards Britain while the 'real danger is from Russian Communism'.[30]

Ribbentrop's stay at Wynyard, from 13 to 17 November, was more widely reported, also in some German newspapers, along with photographs of the 'shooting party', which included some longstanding friends of the Londonderrys (such as Sir Hedworth Williamson, a landowner in the area who had met the Ribbentrops at Mount Stewart earlier in the year, Sir Ronald Graham, the former British Ambassador in Rome, and the Duke of Alba, ex-Foreign Minister of monarchist Spain) as well as Viscount and Viscountess Castlereagh, the son and daughter-in-law of the Londonderrys.[31] There was, of course, the opportunity to shoot game-birds. On the first day, the party – thirteen strong, including the Londonderrys themselves and the Castlereaghs – reportedly shot 211 pheasants, a hare, eight rabbits, three woodcock and twenty-eight duck.[32] The high spot of the weekend, however, was the grand ceremony of the Mayoral Service at Durham Cathedral (following Londonderry's reluctant acceptance of office as Mayor of Durham a few days earlier),[33] which Ribbentrop attended. Almost certainly, a unique moment in the long annals of the venerable cathedral was marked when, at the end of the service, the German national anthem, 'Deutschland, Deutschland über alles', was intoned by the great organ, prompting Ribbentrop to jump to his feet, his outstretched arm in the 'Heil Hitler' salute. His arm had to be gently but swiftly lowered by the adjacent Lord Londonderry.[34]

Londonderry continued with his illusory hopes of persuading German leaders to state openly their demands and engage in multilateral talks to secure Europe's peace. He combined them with public advocacy at home of the need to recognize the legitimacy of Germany's claims and to take steps to see that they were met before 'an unsatisfied nation' which was 'arming herself to the teeth' became powerful enough to ignore restraint in righting perceived injustice. He pressed for the greatest possible effort to achieve an understanding with Germany. He held no particular brief for Germany, he stated, and did not sympathize with its system of government, but insisted that it would be impossible to keep 'a population of that sort in subjection'. He couched his rhetoric in terms of action through the League of Nations. But it was plain that what he desired was not a continuation of what he saw as an old, tired and divided body which, dominated by French interests, had failed so dismally to bring about a European settlement. Instead, he wanted a 'proper league of nations' (as he put it) that would 'say where there was injustice' and remedy 'Germany's grievance regarding raw materials' through, it was implied, some colonial readjustment.[35] Though he did not use the word 'appeasement', what he wanted was, in short, exactly that: appeasing Germany through agreed measures to placate German demands before it was too late.

Publicly, Londonderry continued to hold out the prospect of international agreement to secure the peace of Europe. 'If the leaders of the four great nations – Germany, France, Italy and England – could come together and propound to the world that they wanted no more war,' he stated in mid-December 1936 at a grand dinner of the Anglo-German Fellowship, attended by several hundred guests, in honour of Ribbentrop, 'he believed there would be no aggressor in any part of the world who would stand against them.' How vacuous such sentiments were became immediately apparent in Ribbentrop's speech, reflecting the new German assertiveness in its unmistakable tone of impatient demand for the settlement of Germany's territorial needs.[36] Londonderry, to go from his later recollections, was appalled at the lack of diplomacy of the German Ambassador and was now starting to find the Germans 'more and more tiresome' and Ribbentrop 'impossible'.[37] The estrangement from his former house-guest was beginning. He would gradually come to see Ribbentrop in his true colours.

Privately, Londonderry was, in fact, by now growing distinctly pessimistic about the possibility of staving off war in the coming years. 'I am now losing hope myself because I see nothing but a catastrophe,' he wrote to Lord Halifax in December 1936, castigating once more the 'disastrous' and 'hidebound attitude' of the Foreign Office. He suggested as a matter of urgency 'that the real plenipotentiaries should come to some joint agreement', and that if Hitler would not accept this suggestion 'then we must expect the worst'.[38] What Londonderry had in mind became somewhat more apparent in a rather rambling eight-page memorandum which he composed and forwarded to Halifax a few days later.[39]

Criticizing Anthony Eden's lack of initiative, with the Foreign Office 'marking time with a vengeance whilst events are moving very rapidly', Londonderry stated that all his endeavours had been to emphasize the importance of 'a definite policy as regards peace'. This, he adjudged, could not be conducted through 'diplomatic conversations or through the present League of Nations'. His own desire, and what was needed, was 'to pin Hitler down to peace under all circumstances for a period of time if necessary'. If the four great powers of Europe could unreservedly agree to this, then there could be no war. The issue, he thought, was plain: whether, or not, the great powers were determined to keep the peace. Clearly with his eminent nineteenth-century forebear Lord Castlereagh, one of the architects of post-Napoleonic Europe, in mind, Londonderry envisaged a conference of plenipotentiaries with 'a resemblance to [the Congress of]

Vienna' in 1815. If Hitler defaulted, 'then we must proceed along another course and see whether peace cannot be maintained on the contrary theory of the Great Powers armed to the teeth'. His own efforts had been to try to persuade the German leaders to define their political ambitions. He insisted that Great Britain had 'the authority and power to say they [sic] are determined to have answers'. But time was running out, and German military strength was increasing daily.

The problems in what he was proposing seemed apparent to Londonderry even as he composed his memorandum. Why Germany should agree to any four-power agreement, when Hitler had persistently turned his back on multilateral negotiations, was left unclear. Indeed, Londonderry himself doubted, he said, 'whether Hitler now would play up on the lines I have suggested' (claiming Britain had missed a good opportunity some months earlier – following the remilitarization of the Rhineland – to induce him to accept an agreement ensuring peace for the following twenty-five years). Even so, Londonderry thought agreement between the four 'great powers' of Europe was still feasible, and 'could produce remarkable results'. He left open what these might be, though going on to hint that, 'clumsy, ill-mannered, touchy, arrogant and frightened' as the Germans were, concessions had to be made to satisfy their justifiable claims. This could only have meant territorial adjustments in Europe alongside some settlement of Germany's colonial aspirations.

Londonderry's alternative to a four-power conference aimed at the appeasement of Germany almost two years before such a conference did indeed take place (in conditions where the peace of Europe was on a knife-edge) was equally unrealistic. Should international agreement fail, he held out some vague hope that the armed power of other nations might constrain Germany. It was, however, difficult to see how this could be achieved. The suggestion merely, in fact, returned to the heart of the question of how to handle Hitler. Lack of harmony between the two western democracies, Britain and France, was still all too apparent; Mussolini had that very autumn indicated where Italy's interests lay by proclaiming an 'axis' with Hitler's Germany; the Soviet Union, now as before, was beyond the pale of diplomatic rapprochement for the British government. And within the all too obvious crevices in the fabric of European diplomacy, Germany was rearming at a pace which threatened soon to outstrip the strength of any country which might stand in her way. What it amounted to was that individually no country was going to block Germany's mounting aggrandizement, while a workable alliance to pose a serious threat to her increasing might was nowhere on the horizon.

In his memorandum, Londonderry had criticized – almost inevitably, one might say – 'the impasse in which the S[tanley] B[aldwin] sheet anchor has placed us'. Baldwin's policy had, indeed, been largely in stasis throughout the year. He and the Foreign Office uneasily occupied the territory, threatening at any time to turn into quicksands, in the middle of a triangle of those, like Londonderry, at one point, advocating concessions to Germany; Churchill and his followers, at a second point, pressing for maximum rearmament at the greatest speed to prepare for a likely war with Germany; and a still sizeable body of opinion opposed to rearmament at a third. But we have already noted the weak hand in foreign policy which had been delivered to Baldwin by his predecessor, Ramsay MacDonald, arising from Britain's mistakes and slowness to respond to the ominous signs from Germany during the first years of Hitler's regime. The lamentable handling of the Abyssinian crisis had, in the early months of Baldwin's premiership, subsequently exposed Britain to Hitler's move on the Rhineland, making transparent her diminishing power in the new international constellation. The feeble response to Germany's breach of Locarno – epitomized by Anthony Eden's futile 'questionnaire' attempting to elicit German intentions and a clear statement of their claims in early May 1936, which was duly ignored by Hitler (though not without an outburst of rage at its arrogant presumption)[40] – then laid bare Britain's objective weakness, both militarily and diplomatically, which made her unable to act in any way likely to constrain Germany.

Was a chance missed – as Londonderry asserted – in not pursuing Hitler's 'peace offer' following the Rhineland spectacular? Could Hitler have been, if for a time, diplomatically wrong-footed and a precious respite for rearmament bought? It is extremely doubtful that there ever was such an opportunity. Hitler was set on expansion, with or without British support. And during the course of 1936, the introduction of the Four-Year Plan restructuring the German economy and the intervention in the Spanish Civil War at its inception pushed along the momentum for expansion which, short of a change of regime in Germany, was rapidly becoming unstoppable. Though Hitler in 1936 would certainly have been prepared to reach agreement with Britain on a non-aggression pact for the subsequent twenty-five years (or some other lengthy period of time), or a more limited air pact, the price would have been the free hand in eastern Europe which he had always wanted. And though there were those in Britain who argued that this was a price worth paying, since eastern Europe was – they mistakenly claimed – of no strategic concern to the country, others envisaged in the long run a distinct threat to British world power and overseas interests from German hegemony in Europe. The vista unfolded, however dimly, of British interests in the Middle East, the Mediterranean and north Africa fatally undermined by Britain's gradual but inexorable reduction to the status of a junior partner in an alliance with Germany. By that stage, Great Britain's position of strength as a world power at the head of a global empire would have evaporated.

All this was crystal-ball gazing. Irrespective of German intentions, the prospects of Baldwin taking Britain into any wide-ranging accommodation with Hitler's Reich in the summer and autumn of 1936 were as good as non-existent. Baldwin certainly wanted a better understanding with Germany – though not at the expense of relations with France. He had told Eden in May that 'we must get nearer to Germany'. When the Foreign Secretary asked how it was to be done, Baldwin replied: 'I have no idea. That is your job.'[41] It was difficult to conceive how it could be attained without alienating the French. And ultimately, whatever the recurring rifts and disagreements, the Anglo-French alliance was pivotal to the security of both countries. Britain saw in France's huge army a bulwark against any German thoughts of western expansion. France relied on Britain's support, equally, as a deterrent to the threat across the Rhine. So neither Baldwin nor Eden had any interest in jeopardizing the alliance with Britain's closest Continental neighbours. And any move to accommodate Germany would have been deeply contentious within Britain itself. It would, in fact, have split the country. While some strands of opinion would unquestionably have welcomed concessions to Germany; others would have opposed them vociferously and under any circumstances. In government, too, there were natural divisions of opinion on the way forward, but fundamental agreement on the objectives of policy, and on the lack of wisdom in entering into an accommodation with Germany, except as part of a 'general settlement' and not at the cost of an acceptance of any German demands without solid assurances about future conduct. Hitler's determined aggression and relentless drive to war within the next few years were of course less obvious in 1936 than they have become to later generations. And as long as German expansion seemed aimed at the revision of Versailles and bringing 'home into the Reich' ethnic Germans, an apparent legitimacy to Hitler's moves would continue to sow deception and confusion. Yet even at that time it was hard to contest the arguments of Vansittart and others in the Foreign Office that German pressure for expansion would remain insatiable whatever concessions of territory – perhaps a few colonies – were made.

So the prospects of a meeting between Hitler and Baldwin, which the British Prime Minister had been ready to entertain, to explore the possibility of building better relations, were effectively vetoed in June 1936 by Eden, alert especially to the damage that such talks could do to Britain's standing with the French.[42] This inevitably left British policy in a state of passivity, reactive rather than active, with little alternative to that of rearming (though from a low base and at an insufficiently fast rate) and hoping for some tempering of Germany's 'mad-dog' threat to European peace. 'With two lunatics like Mussolini and Hitler you can never be sure of anything. But I am determined to keep the country out of war,' Baldwin had said privately at the end of April 1936.[43] The trouble was that, without any policy of appeasement or any strength in rearmament, he was bereft of real policy options for dealing with the political lunatics at large or, in the directly related issue, for keeping Britain out of war. It amounted, as both Londonderry and Churchill from their differing perspectives put it, to a policy of drift.[44] Vansittart, more elegantly if less straightforwardly, called it a policy of 'cunctation' – meaning, in plain English, inactivity, dilatoriness and delay.[45]

As 1936 drew to a close, Baldwin's attention to foreign affairs was, in any case, distracted by 'the King's matter'. By mid-November the scandal of Edward VIII's relations with an American divorcee, Mrs Wallis Simpson, which had been preoccupying the foreign press for some time, was threatening to break in Britain, where the newspapers had hitherto retained a discreet silence. Only with great difficulty and government pressure on newspaper editors was such restraint sustained for a short while longer. But by early December whether Mrs Simpson could become Queen of England had become the burning question in the press and with the British public. The King had his powerful supporters – among the more influential, Winston Churchill and the press baron Lord Beaverbrook – but majority opinion came to gather behind Stanley Baldwin who, following weeks of highly sensitive negotiation, gained the accolades for insisting upon abdication as the only solution once the King's unwillingness to compromise on Mrs Simpson was evident.

On this, if nothing else, the Londonderrys backed Baldwin. This was, however, only after the King had confirmed his decision, over all else, to stay with Mrs Simpson. Prior to that point, the Londonderrys had sympathized with and supported the King. They had met Mrs Simpson for the first time when the King, somewhat unexpectedly, brought her to a grand reception at Londonderry House at the beginning of November 1936.[46] Her bright red fingernails, 'like talons', left a lasting impression on the young Lady Mairi Stewart, who took an instant dislike to her.[47] Shortly afterwards, Mrs Simpson again met Lady Londonderry, this time at an evening party given by Emerald Cunard in Grosvenor Square. Lady Londonderry warned her about the harm being done by accounts in the American press of her relationship with the King and told her directly that she would not be accepted as queen by the British people. Mrs Simpson acknowledged that no one had been frank with 'a certain person' about popular feeling towards his relationship with her. Replying, Lady Londonderry thought that even now, if the King's 'real friends all help, much can be done to silence all this weird conspiracy'.[48]

When the crisis broke in early December, the Londonderrys cancelled an engagement to host a charity ball at Wynyard, in the northeast of England, and rushed to London where, the irritated organizer of the event commented caustically, it is 'amusing to be listening to all the gossip in London and helping to pull strings'.[49] On 6 December Londonderry travelled to Chartwell to see Winston Churchill, who headed the King's supporters, suggesting that he use his influence, presumably to persuade the King to drop Mrs Simpson. Churchill took the view that the forces against the King were too strong.[50] Churchill had, however, pleaded with Baldwin to work for a delay, and not to force the issue to a head.[51] After meeting Churchill, Londonderry also encouraged Baldwin to contemplate the advantages of some delay, even 'a very short one'.[52] But by this time the die was as good as cast.

And whatever their earlier views about Edward VIII, the Londonderrys, friends of the Duke of York (who, as George VI, would unwillingly inherit the Crown) and his wife (to become Queen Elizabeth), were coming to see him in a more critical light. Londonderry did write, hours after the instrument of abdication had been signed, though still addressing the newly created Duke of Windsor as 'Your Majesty', to offer his 'humble sympathy', and on 19 December, still styling him 'Your Majesty', sent a further unctuously reverential letter, expressing the feeling that 'in losing you we are parting with a great King'.[53] But privately, according to their daughter's later recollection, Lord and Lady Londonderry condemned the dereliction of duty that had prompted the abdication. They had regarded Edward VIII even as Prince of Wales as 'hopeless', she said, and were 'pleased that Mrs Simpson took him away'.[54] Lady Londonderry sent Baldwin a note of thanks, effusive even by her own exacting standards, addressing him by his 'Ark' pet-name 'My dear Bruin', and telling him that he 'must now be known as the "Great Bear"' for his handling of the abdication crisis.[55] Baldwin thanked her for 'one of the kindest letters I have had'.[56]

The abdication of King Edward VIII, whose strong pro-German inclinations and autocratic tendencies would almost certainly have caused difficulties for the government quite beyond the business of Mrs Simpson, proved to be an unalloyed gain for Britain. From the German perspective, the outcome was less satisfactory. Ribbentrop, if not the German Foreign Ministry, had pinned hopes upon Edward VIII to help in bringing about better relations. Never lost for a conspiracy theory, he was now left with an explanation, unconvincing to all but Hitler, that the King had been deposed by a plot of Jews, Freemasons and various plutocrats and reactionaries in the British 'Establishment' opposed to Germany.[57] For Ribbentrop, and for his master in Berlin, the abdication signalled, in effect, the end of the dream of friendship with Britain.[58] 'The German Ambassador's carefully laid English plans and opportunities for intrigue', Sir Eric Phipps put it, 'have, in certain important details, miscarried, and a review of his first official weeks in London can hardly have afforded either himself or Herr Hitler much cause for rejoicing.'[59] The high hopes at the start of the year of a rapprochement, building upon the success of the naval pact of 1935, had been dashed. According to Phipps, 'the reaction of British public opinion to the persecution of the Jews and of the political adversaries of the Nazi regime, to the reoccupation of the Rhineland, and still more to the demand for the return of the colonies, brought about disillusionment'.[60] From now on, a lover spurned, Ribbentrop would become implacably anti-British. For Hitler, the reluctance of the British to be drawn into the basis of friendship he desired was regrettable. But it was no deterrent to expansion and ultimately war. It merely meant that these would now have to be carried out in the face of British opposition rather than with British support.

II

In his speech to the Reichstag on 30 January 1937, styled as a rendering of account to the German people on the fourth anniversary of this takeover of power, Hitler announced that 'the period of so-called surprises' was over.[61] For a little over a year that would indeed prove, as regards Hitler's foreign-policy adventurism, to be the case – compared with the turbulence of 1936 and what was later to follow. Even so, beneath the surface the radicalization of the Nazi regime intensified, while the continued downward drift of relations between Great Britain and Germany was unmistakable. Antagonism towards both the major Christian denominations, the Protestant and Catholic Churches, had been a hallmark of Nazi rule since Hitler had assumed power. Negative attitudes in Britain towards Germany's domestic policy were now sharpened by the continued assault on the Christian Churches, which reached its height during 1937. Externally, Germany's involvement in the Spanish Civil War – emblematically highlighted by the pitiless bombing of the civilian population of the small Basque market town of Guernica on the afternoon of 26 April 1937 – drove another wedge between the two countries. And, not least, the shrill clamour for colonies, which Hitler had voiced in his speech, was a further strand of the growing alienation towards Germany felt in Britain.

It was, in fact, not hard to see that Hitler's speech reflected his growing irritation at Britain's persistent rejection of his overtures towards a basis of friendship between the two countries. A good portion of his speech amounted to a rhetorical reply to a speech made in the House of Commons on 19 January by Anthony Eden, the British Foreign Secretary, who had criticized what he portrayed as Germany's increasing self-isolation in foreign affairs. Hitler had vehemently denied such a suggestion, pointing to Germany's good relations with numerous foreign countries, had reasserted the need for Germany's policy of economic autarky (symbolized in the Four-Year Plan) on account of the weakness and instability of international commerce, had criticized – taking a side-swipe along the way at the impotence of the League of Nations – Britain's failure to recognize the danger of Bolshevism, had repeated Germany's sense of injustice at the loss of her colonies, and had declared that 'the demand for colonies in our densely settled land will always recur as a matter of course'.[62] There was little in the speech to encourage those who, like Lord Londonderry, thought the paths of Britain and Germany should merge together not divide ever further.

In public, nevertheless, Londonderry continued to advocate closer relations with Germany. He urged acceptance of Hitler's repeated offer, dangled once more in his speech, of the possibility of an air pact with Britain and France,[63] and was conciliatory on the colonial question. In a lengthy interview he gave in mid-February in his study at Wynyard 'with a photograph of Göring, wearing a white badge faintly reminiscent of a price ticket in his felt hat, staring out the from the opposite end of the room', he expressed satisfaction at signs that 'we are seeking a real understanding with Germany' since without such a basis of cooperation 'it is impossible to contemplate an era of peace'. Though he cautiously equivocated on the return of colonies to Germany, he implied – and his view was shared by a number of other peers[64] – that her case was 'unanswerable' and that Britain should entertain the prospect of surrendering some of her mandated territories to Germany. He was emphatic that Hitler would not fight for colonies 'or for anything else'. However, he was adamant that, though he wanted nothing to do with Nazism or Fascism at home, 'we have no business to dictate on matters affecting other Powers internally' and since, if Hitler failed, there would be European anarchy and chaos, it was, therefore, 'our duty to do our best to ensure his continuation in power'.[65]

A few weeks later, describing the treatment of Germany since the First World War by the victorious powers as 'a tragic folly', Londonderry returned to the theme. He criticized the lack of statesmanship in Britain that had allowed foreign policy to be controlled by the interests of France. He contrasted this (as he had done in a recent speech) with the stance of those, like his forebear Castlereagh, who had shown great vision in 1815, and regretted the 'stand-offish' attitude to Germany. He urged frank acceptance of Germany's 'rehabilitation as a World Power' and an endeavour to work in harmony with her to preserve peace. He once more advocated a conference of the major European powers to resolve the issue of German demands and, should these prove impossible to accept, a return to old principles of a 'balance of power' to uphold a 'peace ringed with bayonets'.[66] Outside the public arena, Londonderry was, however, becoming increasingly fearful of the future.

The gathering gloom of Londonderry's private thoughts can be gleaned in an exchange of correspondence with Professor Ludwig Noé, a leading figure in the Danzig shipbuilding industry, now in his sixties, with good English, whom he had met on an earlier visit to the Baltic port. Whether on his own accord or on some official prompting, Noé would on a number of occasions over the next two years or so continue to encourage Londonderry's endeavours for better relations with Germany, professing his own lack of Party allegiance while, nonetheless, promoting a strong pro-Nazi line. Noé had sent Londonderry his good wishes for the New Year at a point where 'dark clouds are covering the political sky', praising his recognition of the 'horrible danger menacing the civilisation of western Europe'.[67] Londonderry replied, saying that he did not feel at all hopeful of the future, which looked to him 'very dark and very gloomy'. For the first time, he revealed some disappointment in the German leadership, commenting that his own efforts in persuading 'a large body of opinion in this country to consider the grave difficulties with which Germany is surrounded' had been undermined by 'some rapid and dramatic move' by Hitler 'without taking the necessary steps to acquaint us with his intentions'. He went on to tell Noé that Germany 'would obtain more sympathy from the world if she were to adopt a less challenging and a less uncompromising attitude'.[68] It was as though Londonderry could not see clearly enough to register the fact that this wish was tantamount to wishing that Germany's leader was not Hitler and its government not run by the Nazis.

Londonderry's position at this juncture was most plainly stated in a long and revealing letter he wrote (though apparently then did not send) to Violet Lady Milner, widow of Alfred Viscount Milner, who had been the foremost theorist of Britain's imperial power, as a diversion, he said, from trying to fish in the Brora, on the Sutherland estates in the Highlands of Scotland, 'in a gale of wind and driving snow'. He disarmingly described himself as 'an interested dilettante' and not a politician, though he admitted that, even recognizing that he was 'not clever enough' and 'could not get the following', he would still like to be Prime Minister, 'the only job which would suit me personally'. After this somewhat disingenuous opening, he turned to foreign policy. He voiced once more an underlying and vital misjudgement in his thinking: 'I know Hitler does not want to fight,' he averred; 'in fact, he dreads war.' He thought Hitler did not dare risk another defeat since he knew only too well the consequences of defeat and collapse. For his own part, Londonderry said there were two things he wanted to avert: war and the collapse of Germany, because both would mean 'the establishment of the reign of Communism'. He was not pro-German, he insisted, though he admitted that he preferred the Germans (who were 'stupid') to the French ('a spent force' and 'trying to hang on to the hands of the clock'). He explicitly commended – the triumphant example from the past was ever more present in his mind – 'the policy of my great ancestor Castlereagh', whose vision of Europe's future and cardinal principles of 'stabilisation of the beaten country and making her take her place in the comity of the world' had ensured the preservation of equilibrium on the Continent until 1914. 'That in a nutshell is all I want,' he declared. He contrasted such farsightedness with the 'disastrous' British foreign policy since 1918, which had been conducted in 'a sort of slavish subservience to France and French ideas'. While the French had been 'quite impossible', he remarked, 'we have shilly-shallied in the most lamentable manner'. He berated the way in which Neville Chamberlain had blocked expansion of the air force. (In fact, as we saw, Chamberlain had pushed through modest expansion when Londonderry had seen no need for haste.) This, coupled with the 'foolish' stance of the Foreign Office towards Germany and the unwillingness to undertake 'the revision of the various treaties which have done so much harm', had meant that Britain had missed the opportunity to deal with the Germans 'when they were weak and humble' and had now to try to do so when they were 'strong and truculent'. Britain had not taken the chance when it was on offer to meet Hitler's wishes and 'to show before the world an element of sympathy', and accept the concessions needed to recognize German sovereignty. No alliance had been needed; simply a common basis of understanding rooted in antagonism to Communism. Failure to follow this path had led to Hitler 'reluctantly leaving our friendship because he thinks it is not forthcoming' and finding a substitute in the friendship of Japan and Italy. Londonderry was 'certainly looking gloomily at the future now', he remarked, 'because we are just sliding into the 1914 alignment and calling our side the League of Nations, because the League of Nations consists of G.B., France and Russia'. The prospect of war between Britain and Germany was now looming and, 'if the Germans ever attack us, our Chamberlains, Baldwins and Edens should be hung to [sic] the nearest lampposts', he declared.[69]

As spring approached, the event that was beginning to grip the imagination of the British public was the forthcoming Coronation of King George VI and Queen Elizabeth in May. With opinion in much of the country so hostile to Hitler's regime and with relations between Britain and Germany frostier than they had been for many months, the Coronation posed its own question of diplomatic niceties. Who would represent the German government was a delicate question. The decision was, naturally, Hitler's alone – though even he needed to take sensitivities into account. It was, of course, hardly an issue which Lord Londonderry could seek to influence, let alone determine. Yet he showed little of either political judgement or common sense in writing to Göring in February 1937, inquiring whether he would be attending the Coronation and, if this were the case, inviting him and Frau Göring to stay at Londonderry House.[70] As word of the invitation leaked out, storms of protest arose both in the British press and in Parliament at a possible official visit to Britain by one of Hitler's chief lieutenants. The Labour MP Ellen Wilkinson, speaking in the House of Commons, sought 'some guarantee that this country will not be insulted by the presence of General Goering'.[71] The campaign in the press against a Göring visit intensified. A mass meeting of 3,000 people protested in London at the prospective visit. Göring, furious at his treatment in Britain and specifically referring to Londonderry's invitation at a point before he had even announced his intention of attending, left the British Ambassador in no doubt of his intense displeasure at a social gathering in Berlin on 28 February.[72] Phipps had, in fact, the previous autumn, mentioned his fear that a consequence of Göring's extravagant hospitality, lavished on an array of British visitors, might be an attempt on his part to come to England as Hitler's representative at the Coronation (then envisaged as that of Edward VIII). 'If we resist', Phipps had noted, 'we may incur Göring's undying hostility and if we let him come we run quite a good risk of his being shot in England. Neither of these alternatives', the Ambassador added, drily, 'would be likely permanently to improve Anglo-German relations'.[73] In the event, Phipps was immediately able to relay Göring's anger at the reaction in Britain to the German Foreign Minister, von Neurath, who assured him that the decision had already been taken not to send Göring to the Coronation, and that the likely representative, unless the choice smacked too much of militarism, would be Field Marshal Werner von Blomberg, the War Minister. Phipps told von Neurath that this choice would be seen as admirable, and Blomberg was later confirmed as the German representative at the Coronation.[74]

Göring made little attempt to disguise his pique to Londonderry, saying it was impossible to attend following 'the agitation against my coming to England, which was carried as far as holding meetings and calling me all kinds of names, and sending me many offensive telegrams'. Göring's assessment was 'that relations between Germany and England at the moment are unfortunately much cooler' and 'that the present Government is fanatically against Germany'. He hoped that Lord and Lady Londonderry would soon visit him in Germany again, at the latest in September for the stag hunts.[75] Londonderry told Göring he was 'very grieved' that he could not come to England for the Coronation and explained that, while he condemned the abusive letters and telegrams, criticism in newspapers was something which everyone in public life in Britain had to accept, adding that a free press was a source of great strength to the country. He assured Göring that the government was not against Germany, but did accept some 'lack of understanding', prompting the need for greater contact between 'the responsible people' in both countries.[76]

Göring's remark to Londonderry about the cooling of Anglo-German relations was more forcefully put at his farewell meeting with the outgoing British Ambassador, Sir Eric Phipps, in early April. Göring told Phipps that Britain would come to realize 'that she had "backed the wrong horse"' in not accepting Hitler's offer to work together with Germany. 'Whenever Germany tried to "pick a flower"', he went on, 'the English boot came down upon her, even in regions where Great Britain had no interests at stake.' Consequently, 'Germany was beginning to believe that Great Britain must be numbered amongst her enemies.'[77]

Londonderry's hopes, as these comments of his closest contact in Germany indicated, were now running into the sand. Some encouragement could be gleaned from the replacement as British Ambassador in Berlin of Sir Eric Phipps (now translated to Paris), who in Londonderry's eyes had completely failed to work for better relations with Germany, by Sir Nevile Henderson, who took up his appointment in Berlin at the end of April. Oddly, however, his waning hopes would come in time – though not immediately – to be revitalized by the man who, in Londonderry's view, had earlier stood in the way of his attempts to rebuild the Royal Air Force and who, on 27 May 1937, a fortnight after the Coronation, now succeeded Stanley Baldwin as Prime Minister: Neville Chamberlain.

III

The new Prime Minister was, at the age of sixty-eight, the oldest entrant to 10, Downing Street since 1905.[78] He had indeed been almost fifty when he first entered Parliament, in 1918, after a background, like his father, Joseph Chamberlain, in Birmingham local government, though his rise thereafter had been steep. Within three years he was in the Cabinet as Minister of Health and only a little later, in Stanley Baldwin's first administration of 1923, briefly held office as Chancellor of the Exchequer, one of the highest and most important governmental posts. Chamberlain preferred to return to the Ministry of Health when Baldwin again became Prime Minister in 1924 and made his mark with a significant programme of reform before the Labour victory at the polls in 1929. Following the general election of October 1931, two months after the formation of the National Government, Chamberlain went back to the Treasury. In the subsequent years of world economic depression and dire slump in Britain, the Chancellor of the Exchequer naturally held a dominant position in the Cabinet. And as illness and weariness took their toll of the energies of the Prime Minister, Ramsay MacDonald, Chamberlain's centrality to all avenues of government policy – including foreign affairs – became ever more firmly rooted. 'I am more and more carrying this Government on my back,' he commented in spring 1935, somewhat self-importantly but not totally without justification.[79] Chamberlain remained the key figure when Baldwin took the premiership for a third time, in May 1935, and was the driving-force of the new urgency behind British defence policy. By the time Baldwin gave notice of his intention to retire, as soon as the Coronation was past, Chamberlain was the obvious and only heir-apparent to the power and responsibilities of Prime Minister.

Unlike the bluff and affable Baldwin (whatever astuteness lay behind the avuncular image), who looked like a benevolent country squire, Chamberlain cut an austere and aloof figure.[80] Slight in build, sallow in complexion, his dark hair, bushy eyebrows, and thick moustache now predominantly turned to grey, wearing his invariable starched collar and dark suit, he looked like a provincial bank-manager or chairman of a small-town solicitors' practice. He was not naturally gregarious and kept his sense of humour closely under wraps. He was intensely hard-working. But he could nevertheless relax, and was in good health (apart from occasional gout). He enjoyed weekend parties at grand country houses, and the shoots that invariably accompanied them, relished the solitary pursuit of angling, and was well versed in literary criticism, art and music (in all of which his tastes were predictably opposed to the avant-garde). There was a strong streak of vanity in his make-up, and he courted flattery and praise even more than most politicians. He certainly attracted flattery and praise, even adulation, from his wide band of supporters in the Conservative Party, though, uniquely among British Prime Ministers in the twentieth century, was never to have his wider popularity tested in a general election. In the political arena in Britain he was unmatched in his day – highly intelligent, clear and decisive in judgement (which he imparted in Cabinet and in the House of Commons in clipped, authoritative tones). Whereas Baldwin's last months in office, in which his slow, expansive, undetermining style of leadership were at their most evident, had been characterized by drift and dilatoriness, Chamberlain was sharp, incisive and energetic in the way he ran the government, and could be forbidding in the way he impatiently and imperiously dismissed countervailing arguments in his dry, rasping voice.[81] And where Baldwin had been reluctant to involve himself in foreign affairs, on which he professed lack of knowledge, Chamberlain certainly did not take to heart the humorously chiding remark of his half-brother Austen (who died in March 1937): 'Neville, you must remember you don't know anything about foreign affairs'.[82] On the contrary, he was keen to play an active role in shaping Britain's foreign policy – a feature of his premiership which would eventually lead to a clash with his Foreign Secretary, Anthony Eden.

There was no immediate and perceptible change of course in foreign policy when Chamberlain became Prime Minister. On the surface, continuity rather than change seemed the dominant theme. After all, Chamberlain had helped guide foreign and defence policy under Baldwin, and Eden had remained at the Foreign Office, where Vansittart's influence was as yet undiminished. Nevertheless, a significant shift was beginning – and one which, for a while, would commend itself to Lord Londonderry. If Baldwin's government could be said to have developed any coherent policy towards Germany (apart from rearm as far as possible and hope that the worst did not happen), it amounted to a search for détente within a framework of collective security under the aegis of the League of Nations backed by the deterrent of a strong bomber force.[83] Chamberlain now began to switch the emphasis from deterrence to defence, resting upon a strengthened fighter force at the expense of the bombing arm. This was to have its corollary in a foreign policy based upon a coldly realistic assessment of Britain's international position, stopping the drift and facing the facts as they were, not as they might be desired (as Chamberlain himself put it). This meant shaking off a commitment to collective security, which he saw Britain as largely shouldering alone, based upon pointless lip-service to a moribund and impotent League of Nations. It also entailed diminished dependence upon a dangerously weakened France, where social disaffection, economic weakness and continued governmental instability formed a backcloth to almost total inertia in modernizing the armed forces and lamentable levels of spending on expansion of the air force.[84] The fact had to be faced that Britain had no powerful ally. Consequently, until armaments were completed there was the need to improve relations with Germany. This in turn necessitated taking steps to 'appease' her grievances, and to look for a settlement based not on fear and deterrence but on mutual interest and acceptance of separate spheres of influence. What this implied was a greater readiness by Britain to cooperate in trying to solve the territorial problems of central and eastern Europe: the questions of Austria, Czechoslovakia and Danzig. The underlying aim – that Britain should and could avoid war with Germany – remained unchanged from Baldwin's day. But the method to attain that desirable end was now significantly shifting.[85] It was a shift which seemed belatedly to be moving in the direction that Londonderry had long wanted. But he had urged such a policy from a position of strength. Chamberlain was now adopting it from a position of weakness.

Londonderry's view of Neville Chamberlain at the time he became Prime Minister in May 1937 was largely negative. He had rightly seen Chamberlain as the strong man of the National Government since 1931. He had blamed him for the financial block on the rebuilding of the air force that he, as Air Minister, had striven for and which would 'have had Germany controlled', before, in panic at the inflated figures for German rearmament that Churchill and Lord Rothermere had publicized in 1935, committing the country to 'staggering expenditure'. Though he liked Chamberlain (who was a member of Lady Londonderry's 'Ark') personally, he said, he thought he was a poor politician.[86] He could have placed little confidence, therefore, in the hope he expressed soon after Chamberlain had become Prime Minister that 'the change in leadership may mean that there will be some change in our foreign policy', and certainly was expecting no breakthrough in the policy of friendship with Germany that he had so ardently promoted. His depression at the state of Anglo-German relations was undiminished. 'The Foreign Office seems quite incapable of doing anything right and goes out of its way to estrange our would-be friends,' he lamented. 'I feel that we are heading for disaster.'[87] He was 'truly anxious', he stated, 'lest our friendship with Russia and France will lead us into a position of difficulty vis-à-vis Germany, in which we shall be expected to take some action which will be supported neither by the people of this country nor by the Dominions'.[88] Londonderry was correct to imply that the Dominions preferred a more conciliatory policy towards Germany. The Dominions (apart from New Zealand) had, in fact, at the Imperial Conference held in London in May 1937, just prior to Baldwin's resignation, favoured appeasing the dictators.[89]

Despite such apprehension, Lord and Lady Londonderry were more than ready to accommodate the new Prime Minister's wish to continue the tradition – following the interruption on account of the poor relations with Baldwin – of a grand Londonderry House reception for the government in the forthcoming autumn, on the eve of the opening of Parliament.[90] Londonderry also drew some encouragement from an early speech in Berlin to the German-English Society (corresponding to the Anglo-German Fellowship in Britain) of the new Ambassador, Sir Nevile Henderson, who had referred to previous Anglo-German misunderstandings and prevalent misconception in Britain of the achievements of National Socialism.[91] The speech (heard by such leading figures in the Nazi hierarchy as Heinrich Himmler and Alfred Rosenberg) drew a furious response from some circles in Britain, and Henderson was promptly labelled 'our Nazi British Ambassador at Berlin'.[92] Others, however, and not just the usual pro-Germanists, approved it as 'a real contribution to the cause of peace'.[93] Henderson, aged fifty-five at his appointment, somewhat unprepossessing in appearance, thin, with greying hair and full moustache under a somewhat beaked nose, never without a carnation in the lapel of his dark suit, and with 'a fey streak in his character',[94] had previously been Ambassador in Belgrade and Buenos Aires. He had been appointed to Berlin because Eden and Vansittart could think of no one else 'who was a man and a good shot'.[95] Somewhat bizarrely, it was thought that Henderson's skills in stag-hunting, which his friendship with the autocratic King Alexander in Belgrade had highlighted, would be a diplomatic asset in the new Germany – presumably in finding a point of contact with Göring. Vansittart of all people commended him to Eden, who came bitterly to regret approving the appointment.[96]

Even before taking up his appointment, Henderson had been urged by Chamberlain (still at the time Chancellor of the Exchequer) 'to take the line of co-operation with Germany, if possible'. It was not Britain's business, Chamberlain had said, 'to interfere with forms of Government which other countries chose to have'.[97] Henderson was happy to follow this guideline, which corresponded so directly with his own preferred approach.[98] He had plainly indicated this approach in a memorandum in May in which he had emphatically stated that eastern Europe was not a vital British interest and that 'the German is certainly more civilised than the Slav, and in the end, if properly handled, also less potentially dangerous to British interests'. Accordingly, 'it is not even just to endeavour to prevent Germany from completing her unity or from being prepared for war against the Slav, provided her preparations are such as to reassure the British Empire that they are not simultaneously designed against it'.[99] Though such a line was promptly disavowed by Vansittart as contrary to government policy, Henderson's appointment to the key post of Berlin at a time when a new Prime Minister was proposing a more conciliatory approach to Germany marked an important development. A rift between Chamberlain and the main proponents of an uncompromising position on German demands, Eden and Vansittart, was in the making.

Almost immediately Chamberlain became Prime Minister, Henderson received instructions to make a first overture towards improving Anglo-German relations by extending an invitation to the German Foreign Minister, Konstantin von Neurath, himself a former Ambassador to Britain, to visit London. Eventually, after some hesitation, the invitation was accepted and the visit scheduled for late

June.[100] However, an unsuccessful torpedo attack – one possibly even fabricated by German propaganda[101] – in mid-June on the German cruiser *Leipzig*, carried out by Spanish Republic forces off the north African coast, coming only two weeks or so after the German battleship *Deutschland* had been bombed in the Mediterranean by Spanish government aircraft, prompted a further souring of relations between Berlin and London. The British government, alongside the French, had decided the previous year on a policy of non-interventionism in the Spanish Civil War, in the vain hope that this would discourage other powers from involvement in Spain – a powder-keg, it seemed, likely to explode into general European conflict, unless contained. In 1937 naval patrols of the Spanish coast had been belatedly implemented, supposedly by all the major powers, in an equally futile attempt to prevent repeated breaches of the agreement on non-interventionism (to which Germany, Italy and the Soviet Union, the main culprits in arms deliveries to Spain, had been signatories).[102] The German government now peremptorily demanded far-reaching action by Britain, as a non-interventionist power, to ensure such incidents as that concerning the *Leipzig* would not recur. When Britain, together with France, rejected the demands out of hand, the German press launched biting attacks on Eden, seen as chiefly responsible. The incident was then used by von Neurath as a pretext to call off a visit which, especially given Ribbentrop's baleful presence in London, had never much appealed to him. Chamberlain's first seeds to improve relations with the Germans had fallen on stony ground. The rebuff over von Neurath's visit was also a sign of the changed climate. In the early years of the Nazi regime, Hitler had repeatedly sought to win British friendship, but had met a cool reception. Now Britain was attempting to take the initiative – but finding that Hitler was not easy to please.

By the time Londonderry paid his third visit to Germany within two years, accepting Göring's invitation again to hunt with him at Carinhall, in late September, the outlook was distinctly less rosy than it had been a year earlier. The annual Nazi Party Rally in Nuremberg had only just taken place, its pageantry of power mightily impressing Sir Nevile Henderson as 'a triumph of mass organisation combined with beauty' on the first occasion a British Ambassador had attended, and producing a predictably savage onslaught by Hitler on

Bolshevism, with a side-swipe at the divisions with Britain and France over the Spanish Civil War.[103] And, days later, Mussolini's state visit to the country would underline the closeness of the Axis partners and the combined threat they posed to British interests.[104]

The visit of the 'Duce', Göring told Londonderry when they sat down to talk on 22 September, was 'entirely due to Eden and Vansittart'. Owing to Britain's unwillingness to grasp the still extended German hand of friendship, Germany had been compelled to seek friends elsewhere, and had found them in Italy and Japan. The errors and inconsistencies of British foreign policy had driven together the three countries. Britain, said Göring, had accepted Italian conquest in Abyssinia and Japanese conquest in China, but refused to accept German policy of incorporating in the Reich the German-speaking population of Austria and Czechoslovakia and was, despite claiming global supremacy on the seas, unwilling to grant Germany military superiority on the European Continent. British policy, he declared, 'was to be first everywhere and to claim everything as a right which we [the British] denied to everybody'. The lack of any concession on the colonial question was a further indication of how unwilling Great Britain was 'to assist Germany to obtain her rightful position as a great power'. Definition of spheres of influence could be achieved without any conflict. Instead, there was the prospect of Bolshevik influence in Spain spreading to France and Belgium. Londonderry found Göring 'far less conciliatory' than on earlier occasions, and had the impression of 'a distinct deterioration' in relations with Germany.[105]

Londonderry also detected a note of impatience in Göring that he had not encountered before. Some of this was conceivably personal. Though Londonderry had been courted by leading Nazis on his first visit to Berlin eighteen months earlier, the general cooling of ardour towards Britain can only have prompted a recognition that the aristocratic former Air Minister was a far less weighty and influential personage than had at first been thought. His visits, and those of many other British dignatories who had been wined and dined by the most mighty figures in the Third Reich, had brought no dividend at all. The hunting expedition with Londonderry, though it had followed Göring's invitation, was time the busy German Luftwaffe chief might understandably have thought he could well be spending on other matters. In the event, he told Londonderry that the autumn manoeuvres of the armed forces in Mecklenburg and Pomerania demanded his presence, and fobbed him off with a hunting trip relocated to the state hunting-lodge at Darss on the Baltic coast in Pomerania where he had lined up Franz von Papen, the suave and devious diplomat and ex-Chancellor who had smoothed the path for Hitler's takeover of power, to look after him.[106]

Von Papen, who spoke good English, was a well-chosen host. He was himself of aristocratic descent, and his demeanour and bearing set him apart from the archetypal Nazi leaders Londonderry had mainly encountered. His instincts were deeply reactionary, not radical, and had come close to costing him his life in the 'Night of the Long Knives' purge of June 1934, since when he had served as Hitler's diplomatic representative in Vienna. Having narrowly escaped to tell the tale, he needed no second bidding to swallow all criticism and act as the loyal mouthpiece of the regime. This was the role he now carried out to perfection in persuading Londonderry how desirous Hitler was to bring about a friendly understanding with Great Britain and in eulogizing on the great achievements of the 'Führer' for Germany. He advised Londonderry that outstanding problems would have to be negotiated directly with Hitler, and that solution of these problems would take the wind out of the sails of the Nazi Party's 'exaggerated nationalism'. He suggested, somewhat implausibly, that Hitler's new friendship with Mussolini provided 'a sobering influence', and impressed upon Londonderry his conviction that a generation that had been through the First World War would not permit a second conflagration. 'Lord Londonderry accepted my statements at their face value', he later wrote, 'and I found it an immense pleasure to talk to a man of his honourable and open nature. He was the perfect type of old-world aristocrat.'[107] Londonderry, in other words, had been gullible.

He was, too, left in blissful ignorance of an episode – which caused some amusement to his German hosts – connected with the hunting side of his three-day sojourn at Darss. Göring had at some point, perhaps the previous year, promised Londonderry the chance to shoot a bison on his next hunting expedition in Germany. Londonderry had seized upon the idea with great enthusiasm. As we have noted, Göring had built up a herd of bison at Carinhall. But there were none at Darss – though Londonderry was not told of this. Not to disappoint his guest, Göring arranged for a suitable bull to be transported to Darss from the Carinhall herd. But the head game-keeper at Carinhall was loath to send a prime bull to be shot at by an English lord. Instead, 'a decrepit beast' was shipped off to Darss 'which, as far as he was concerned, might just as well be shot as not'. On arrival, the great beast was released into a part of the forest at Darss that was ringed by beaters and the head keeper there regaled Londonderry with an account of corralling a magnificent animal to provide sport for him on the morrow. Unfortunately, so he told Londonderry next day, a report had come through at four o'clock in the morning that the beast had escaped after attacking one of the beaters. It had been trailed for some hours, but had escaped its track-ers and disappeared. Londonderry was sorely disappointed and had to be placated by shooting a fine stag. In fact, the story of the escap-ing bison was pure invention on the part of the gamekeeper. The truth was that his efforts to keep the bison on its feet throughout the night had failed. It had 'simply keeled over and died from the rigours of the journey'.[108] Londonderry had, it turned out, been as deluded about the hunting side as he had about the political aspect of his trip. And, it seems, he had failed to make much of an impression, even as a sportsman, on his German hosts. When Göring entertained Sir Nevile Henderson to a stag-hunt at the beginning of October, he remarked that Englishmen were no good with a rifle. The week before, he said, he had invited an English sportsman to shoot a stag, and he had missed it three times.[109]

Londonderry returned from Germany this time 'with many misgiv-ings'.[110] He told Ribbentrop that the visit had been 'not altogether very satisfactory' since the military manoeuvres and the visit of Mussolini had limited the opportunities for discussion, except with Göring. He felt unhappy about the future, he wrote, and saw the situation as 'dete-riorating'. He thought there was 'a complete misunderstanding of German ideas and aspirations' in Britain, now also among those 'who, at one time, were most sympathetic and were particularly anxious to fall in with German wishes and ideas'. His own influence, he admitted, was decreasing, and was not helped 'by the speeches reported from

Germany and the actions taken by her statesmen'.[111]

As was the case following earlier visits, Londonderry was disappointed to find that his report of his latest personal discussions with such a prominent figure in the Nazi regime as Göring drew such little interest from the British government. When he arranged to see Chamberlain, he found it 'grimly amusing that I was treated in exactly the same way by Göring and Neville'. Both had been 'petulant and impatient', Göring 'that his and Hitler's good intentions seemed to be ignored by the British Government', Chamberlain that his overtures towards better relations had been ignored (pointedly with the cancellation of von Neurath's visit) and 'that the Germans never carried out any of their undertakings'.[112] Chamberlain did mention his conversation with Londonderry to the Cabinet, but only to repeat the impression he had been given that Göring 'had spoken on his old lines, namely, that it was the British Government that said No to every legitimate German desire'.[113]

Whatever his disappointments, anxieties and misgivings, Londonderry remained undeterred in pressing for an accommodation with Germany. He favoured bringing 'this unfortunate Spanish episode' to an end 'by accepting Franco as the victor and turning our attentions to the claims of Germany in a Conference of the Great Powers'. The alternative, in his view, would be that Germany would become ever stronger and, as a consequence, that Hitler, for prestige reasons, would find it increasingly difficult to modify his claims.[114] He remarked to Churchill that 'our friends here have never known how to control Hitler and Mussolini and they never will' – an added remark that 'Mussolini is the more difficult of the two' offering a further glimpse of his political misjudgement.[115] Churchill, replying, left his second cousin in no doubt about the extent of their disagreement on policy towards Germany:

We certainly do not wish to pursue a policy inimical to the legitimate interests of Germany, but you must surely be aware that when the German Government speaks of friendship with England, what they mean is that we shall give them back their former Colonies, and also agree to their having a free hand so far as we are concerned in Central and Southern Europe. This means that they would devour Austria and Czecho-Slovakia as a preliminary to making a gigantic middle-Europa-block. It would certainly not be in our interests to connive at such policies of aggression. It would be wrong and cynical in the last degree to buy immunity for ourselves at the expense of the smaller countries of Central Europe.[116]

This put the alternatives facing British foreign policy at their starkest (even if Londonderry, extraordinarily, insisted that there was no difference of opinion with Churchill).[117] The government's position hovered somewhere between the two poles. But although Churchill at this time was 'in general agreement with the present Foreign Office policy',[118] Chamberlain was starting to edge towards a position cautiously moving in the direction Londonderry preferred.

Whether or not prompted by his exchange with Churchill, but in any event resentful of the way he was being ignored, sensitive to the criticism repeatedly levelled at him, and anxious about the developing arms race, Londonderry evidently recalled at this juncture his statement (which we noted earlier) on the stance to adopt towards Germany made at a Cabinet Committee in November 1934 and laid out in the letter that he had sent on 22 November 1934 to Lord Hailsham, then War Minister, but 'brushed on one side' at the time.[119] Londonderry had difficulty in tracking down a copy of this statement – no official copy had been kept – which, he claimed, would have had profound consequences for Britain's relations with Germany had his advice been followed.[120] Eventually, Hailsham found one for him. Thereafter, to show where he had stood all along, but more importantly to vindicate (from his point of view) the consistency and correctness of his approach to the problem of Germany, Londonderry – as he would continue to do – liberally sprinkled copies of the letter (and an accompanying missive he had sent to Hailsham) to individuals in positions of importance and influence, including the Prime Minister.[121]

Meanwhile, Londonderry had paid a further short visit to Germany, staying overnight in Berlin on 5 November before returning next morning to London. At Göring's invitation, he had flown with his daughter Lady Mairi (Lady Londonderry, owing to the short notice, was unable to make the trip) to attend a banquet at the opening of the International Hunting Exhibition. He had the chance only of a few words with Göring on this occasion, but stayed at the British

Embassy in Berlin and took the opportunity of a discussion with Sir Nevile Henderson (who impressed him).¹²² In the brief time that he was away, news leaked out to the British press of a significant development which met with his great approval and seemed to offer in his view a first glimmer of hope for a change of direction in government policy: his friend and closest contact in the cabinet, Lord Halifax, was to visit Germany and his stay would include a discussion with Hitler.

IV

Londonderry had, in fact, learnt from Halifax some days earlier of his forthcoming visit to Germany and appeared to claim some credit for the idea which, he said, he had been pondering 'for some considerable time'.¹²³ He later even declared that 'this visit was entirely due to me', since he had 'converted' Halifax over a period of two years 'to the point of view that the Germans had never really had a chance, and that our policy was to try and make friends with them by establishing contacts'.¹²⁴ Halifax certainly consulted Londonderry about the visit, presumably asking about his impressions of Hitler and other Nazi leaders. Londonderry sent Halifax Ward Price's sympathetic depiction of Hitler in his recently published book *I Know These Dictators*,¹²⁵ despite not rating it too highly, to read as preparation, and advised him to 'be as firm as possible and meet truculence with truculence' in attempting to have 'the Germans categorically pinned down to a programme'. Though 'the sands are running out and the situation deteriorating', he wrote, 'an understanding between Great Britain and Germany with all its great potentialities' would be 'the tonic which the world requires'.¹²⁶

Lord Halifax, extremely tall, somewhat lugubrious, with a slightly lisping voice, had succeeded Ramsay MacDonald as Lord President of the Council in Chamberlain's administration, retaining also the leadership of the House of Lords. He admired Chamberlain and was close to him politically, though personally less close than he had been with Stanley Baldwin. He had indicated at the first meeting of Chamberlain's Cabinet his desire to improve contacts with Germany. He was overtly sympathetic to the new Prime Minister's hopes of finding a way to European peace through the appeasement of Germany while at the same time consolidating the entente with France and reintegrating Italy into the sort of positive relationship which had been lost when the Stresa Front had collapsed during the Abyssinian crisis.[127] The Nazi leadership had been wanting Halifax to meet Hitler ever since Baldwin declined to do so in the summer of 1936, and had made suggestions earlier in 1937 that he might pay a visit to Germany.[128] Chamberlain and Eden had not favoured the idea. But in mid-October 1937 a suitable pretext was found when Halifax, in his capacity as Master of the Middleton Hounds (a Yorkshire hunting fraternity) was invited by the German Hunting Association to attend the International Hunting Exhibition, sponsored by Göring, to be held in Berlin, and to shoot foxes in East Prussia, Mecklenburg or Saxony. A new opportunity of diplomatic feelers presented itself under the guise of an informal visit. Chamberlain was keen, even envisaging the visit as the beginning of 'the far reaching plans I have in mind for the appeasement of Europe and Asia and for the ultimate check to the mad armaments race'.[129] Eden was distinctly cooler about the proposition, but went along with it.[130] The episode marked the beginning of the rift between Chamberlain and Eden. When Eden, recovering from 'flu, thought the Prime Minister was undermining his handling of the planned visit, Chamberlain told him he was 'feverish' and advised him to go home and take an aspirin.[131]

Since Hitler, after briefly visiting the Hunting Exhibition (which was not much to his taste) had left Berlin, Halifax had to travel south to Berchtesgaden to meet him, in his alpine eyrie. This, too, did not commend itself to the Foreign Office, anxious to avoid the impression that Britain was 'running after' Hitler.[132] Some of Eden's forebodings about Halifax's audience with Hitler proved well founded. The meeting, on 19 November, was the first between Hitler and a serving British minister since the visit to Berlin by Simon and Eden in March 1935 – an indication of the British government's keenness to avoid being compromised by personal dealings with the German dictator.[133] It did not have an auspicious start when Halifax (to go from his later account) mistook Hitler, as he opened the car door, for a footman. But the potential embarrassment – if the doubtful story can be

believed – passed unnoticed.[134] Hitler, in surly mood, began with a
rant about the difficulty of doing business with democracies. When
the colonial question was raised, Halifax, as the Foreign Office had
stipulated, stated that it could only be solved as part of a general
settlement. It was as the discussion turned to the potential trouble-
spots in central Europe that Halifax came close to straying beyond
his brief. According to the German record of the conversation,
Halifax had spoken of 'possible alterations in the European order'
– including Danzig, Austria and Czechoslovakia – being 'destined to
come about with the passage of time', and of Britain's interest in
seeing such alterations taking place 'through the course of peaceful
evolution' and avoiding any measure 'which might cause far-reaching disturbances'.[135] Halifax's diary entry had him telling Hitler that
'on all these matters we were not necessarily concerned to stand for
the status quo as of today, but we were concerned to avoid such
treatment of them as would be likely to cause trouble'.[136] Though
the British Foreign Office, on Halifax's return, thought he had
acquitted himself well and was less perturbed by such a statement
than Eden later claimed to have been, its significance was not lost
on Hitler. It was tantamount to a signal that Britain would accept a
German incorporation of Austria in the Reich and would not fight for
Czechoslovakia.[137]

Seldom have two less well-suited individuals engaged in talks of
international importance. Halifax himself, like most other British visitors, came away from Berchtesgaden believing that Hitler had been
'very sincere'.[138] He was not the only one to be duped into such a crass
misjudgement.[139] Hitler, for his part, referred dismissively to Halifax,
soon after he had left, as 'the English parson'.[140] Predictably, nothing
tangible had emerged from the talks. 'Chatter and bewilderment' was
all that they had produced, in Churchill's view.[141]

Hitler had not responded to Halifax's suggestion that their discussion might be followed up by formal negotiations. Even so,
Chamberlain thought the meeting had been a success in 'creating an
atmosphere in which it was possible to discuss with Germany the
practical questions involved in a European settlement'.[142] The Foreign
Office more soberly concluded that improved relations would only
follow some satisfaction of Germany's colonial claims, and noted that

Hitler had provided no guarantees on his likely policy in central Europe.[143] The experts on Germany in Whitehall would have been more alarmed had they realized that a mere fortnight before Halifax's visit, on the very day in fact that Londonderry was flying to Germany to attend Göring's banquet, Hitler had been addressing his armed forces' leadership (including, of course, Göring) on the need to solve Germany's problem of 'living space' by force, and that the overthrow of Austria and Czechoslovakia would form the first stage of any war. He had assumed that Britain would not fight for either.[144]

Londonderry had invested high hopes in the Halifax visit. He naturally, therefore, felt deeply disappointed that it had proved so fruitless and saw it as a chance lost to inaugurate better relations with Germany before it was too late.[145] His sense that time was running out was enhanced by Hitler's open attack on 12 December on the League of Nations, the day after Italy had announced its withdrawal, declaring that a return by Germany would never take place.[146] It brought a depressing year for Londonderry to a close. His busy engagements as Mayor of Durham, following in his father's footsteps in holding the office in a Coronation Year, had brought something of a distraction – if not always a welcome one – from the dismal development of international affairs. There had also been the glamour of the Coronation at the beginning of the year and the usual hectic round of receptions and social gatherings. But in the last weeks of the year, Londonderry found himself once again fighting off attacks from Labour on his record as Air Minister and regurgitating for Neville Chamberlain's benefit his old lament of his mistreatment at the hands of Stanley Baldwin.[147] And, as regards Germany, he told Ribbentrop he now felt 'powerless', without influence in bringing about the good relations he had wanted between Britain and Germany, and full of anxiety. He reiterated his futile hopes of a four-power conference to sort out German grievances and achieve a limitation of armaments, but feared that the continued drift would at some point result in German demands that brought Great Britain into outright opposition and 'the catastrophe which we are one and all fearing'. More forthrightly than before, he also clarified for Ribbentrop the limits of his own accommodation of German aims. He could not agree, he said, 'to the absorption of all the German speaking peoples in the Reich', though was sympathetic to 'a much closer association' than the current position, and he rejected the case (other than on grounds of prestige) for colonial expansion. Altogether, he ended, he felt 'very gloomy as to the future'.[148]

V

A copy of one of Londonderry's letters, from December 1937, expressing his growing disillusionment with his earlier hopes of better relations with Germany based upon armaments limitation, and his gathering fears that within two or so years there would be a repeat of 1914, came into the hands of the German Foreign Ministry in Berlin. From there it was forwarded to Hitler himself.[149] Ribbentrop had commented, with reference to the letter, that the attainment of an understanding between Germany and Britain would be 'very difficult, because Germany wants to shape her future in a way which is different from what England is apparently prepared to grant'.[150]

A little earlier, on 28 December 1937, Ribbentrop had finished compiling a 23-page report on Anglo-German relations and how to handle Chamberlain's initiative to improve them. He had worked on the report for nearly a month and intended it to serve as a rendering of account of his ambassadorship in London, leaving Hitler in no doubt as to his diplomatic prowess. The report was marked as to be sent directly to both Hitler and von Neurath. It amounted to a plaintive tale of unrequited love, now turned to bitter hatred for Britain. Here, too, Londonderry was expressly mentioned. He was included, along with the 'Astor group' (otherwise known, if not altogether accurately, as 'the Cliveden set', from the place of weekend gatherings at the home of Lord and Lady Astor of a number of prominent 'appeasers'), *The Times* (whose editor, Geoffrey Dawson, was an 'appeaser' and frequently among the guests at Cliveden), Lord Lothian (the prominent Liberal who had visited Hitler early in 1935 and also a regular guest of the Astors), the left-wing Labour peers and pacifists Lord Allen of Hurtwood, Lord Arnold and Lord Noel-Baker, and city business circles, among the 'conditional friends of Germany'. Though sceptical of German assurances of peace, these individuals and groupings had, wrote Ribbentrop, nonetheless sought ways and means to avoid war and come to an 'arrangement' with Germany, involving some redress of the colonial question and 'understanding' for German needs of 'space in the east', not least with the hope of gaining time until 'events' might hinder Germany's 'expansionist drive' and lead her back to the 'community of nations'. They had tried to impress upon Chamberlain the need for an understanding with Germany. However, they – and at this point Ribbentrop included Edward VIII – had been gradually sidelined by 'the unconditional opponents of Germany', notably the traditionally hostile Foreign Office. Ribbentrop left open the possibility that some in the British government – though he was doubtful whether Chamberlain and Halifax could be counted among their number – existed who still believed in a 'friendly arrangement' with Germany allowing for the return of former German colonies, a 'peaceful Anschluss' to solve the Austrian question, and perhaps cultural autonomy for the Sudeten Germans, in return for a commitment from Germany to tackle all problems by negotiation and to agree to a limitation of air armaments. However, those hostile to Germany – he specifically mentioned Eden, Vansittart, the new First Lord of the Admiralty (and firm anti-appeaser), Duff Cooper, and the new War Minister, Leslie Hore-Belisha (who, as he did not hesitate to point out, was Jewish) – were, he asserted, in the ascendancy.

Distrust of German aims was promoting this strengthening of hostility in the British government, Ribbentrop continued. Halifax had told him of fears that concessions to Germany would not prevent further sudden German action to satisfy national 'honour', while Londonderry, hinting at Austria, had spoken of an unstoppable dynamic once a powerful nation had taken over another country. One purpose of Halifax's visit, according to Ribbentrop, had probably been to try to head off early German moves on Austria and Czechoslovakia to gain time for British rearmament. This, he thought, was behind Chamberlain's initiative. Britain was well schooled in concealing her true intentions, added Ribbentrop, clearly indicating to Hitler that the more conciliatory approach that Chamberlain had prompted was no more than a ruse. In the light of the Anglo-French communiqué that had been issued at the end of November following the visit to London of the French Prime

Minister, Camille Chautemps, and his Foreign Minister, Yvon Delbos, opening up the prospect of concessions of colonies as part of a 'general settlement',[151] Ribbentrop thought it likely that the British and French would arrive at some offer of colonial territory to Germany in return for binding agreements on the territorial status quo in Europe – 'colonies for peace', as he put it. He warned against engaging with such offers, which could prove awkward in tying Germany's hands. On the vital territorial issues which, as he knew, Hitler was increasingly impatient to resolve, he thought Britain and France might accept change in Austria, but was sure that 'territorial revision' in Czechoslovakia could not be achieved by negotiation and would mean war. He concluded by recommending that there should be no illusions about the possibility of a lasting understanding with Britain which would satisfy Germany.[152]

In the accompanying set of 'Personal Conclusions' from his report which he completed a few days later, Ribbentrop ended by acknowledging that his mission to win British friendship had failed. 'I no longer have faith in any understanding,' he told Hitler. 'England does not desire in close proximity a paramount Germany, which would be a constant menace to the British Isles. On this she will fight.'[153] Barely a month later, Ribbentrop replaced von Neurath as Hitler's Foreign Minister.

Unaware that his erstwhile friend was feeding the 'Führer' such negative impressions of Britain's readiness to reach an understanding with Germany, Lord Londonderry and his wife sent Hitler their usual Christmas greetings and good wishes for the New Year (for which he thanked them).[154] But Londonderry admitted in a letter to J. L. Garvin, the influential editor of the important Sunday newspaper the *Observer*, who himself strongly favoured a policy of appeasement, that 'his German stock' was in rapid decline since 'the Germans must see that the advice with which they know I returned here [from his visits to Germany]' had been 'seemingly disregarded by the Government'.[155]

Londonderry had, however, in no way changed his tune. 'Our whole foreign policy towards Germany for the last few years stands condemned', for its 'opportunist hand to mouth' approach 'with no definite plan in mind' other than simply adopting the aim of the French to keep German permanently in subjection, he declared at the beginning of January 1938. Once again he referred to 'the doctrines of Castlereagh and the Duke of Wellington' in 1815 as his guiding light.[156] And, especially for someone as concerned as he was about his reputation, it was a lapse in political judgement which prompted him to give an interview to the *Berliner Tageblatt* for publication on the fifth anniversary of Hitler's takeover of power on 30 January 1938, repeating his belief that Hitler and the German people 'are very desirous to maintain peace' and criticizing the decisions of the League of Nations as 'a threat and a danger'.[157] The interview predictably gave his opponents at home a further stick with which to beat him.[158]

By this time, Londonderry was at work on a short book, aimed at justifying his stance on Germany and publicizing the faults (in his view) of government policy since the start of the Disarmament Conference before Hitler had taken power.[159] While he was writing his tract, news came in from Germany that disquieted him. On 4 February sweeping changes in the Nazi government had been announced in Berlin. The most important were that Hitler himself was personally to take over the command of the armed forces following the resignation (allegedly on health grounds) of the War Minister, von Blomberg, and the Commander in Chief of the army, Werner von Fritsch, while Ribbentrop would replace von Neurath as Foreign Minister. Personal scandals involving von Blomberg and von Fritsch had in fact formed the background, though none of this was made public. Whatever the cause, the consequence was obvious: Hitler's power had been reinforced, and the traditional conservatives in the government had lost ground to radical Nazi influences, most notably at the Foreign Ministry.[160] Londonderry commented the day after the news broke that he did not at all like 'this new aspect of German politics'.[161] He clearly recognized the changes as denoting 'a victory for the more extreme Nazi elements in the German Government', especially in foreign and military affairs. He correctly saw that Germany would now pursue a more radical foreign policy and adjudged that 'with her growing military strength and increasingly efficient organization it looks as if she is prepared to stop at nothing if her demands, particularly in regard to her lost colonial territories, do not meet with some measure of satisfaction in the near future'.[162]

That colonies were not a prime concern of Hitler escaped

Londonderry (as it did many others at the time). But Londonderry's hopes that there might still be time to negotiate 'some measure of satisfaction' for Germany which would head off the increasing likelihood of war at some time in the not too distant future received a boost through developments closer to home. On 20 February Anthony Eden, who in Londonderry's eyes had posed an obstacle to all attempts to reach a rapprochement with Germany, resigned as Foreign Secretary. It had been coming for some time. The rift with Chamberlain had deepened as Eden's resentment grew at what he saw as unhelpful interference by the Prime Minister in foreign affairs, and a readiness to bypass official governmental channels in international relations. Chamberlain's peremptory rejection in January of a proposal by President Roosevelt for a conference of international powers aimed at defusing the dangerous situation in Europe, without consulting Eden (on holiday at the time in the south of France, though not out of touch), rankled greatly. But it was when Chamberlain, briefed by the widow of his half-brother, Austen, who had opened up her own private lines of communication to Mussolini, insisted upon immediate negotiations with the Italians, entailing recognition of their occupation of Abyssinia in return for the withdrawal of some Italian 'volunteers' from Spain and not much else other than promises of goodwill, that Eden drew the line.[163] His resignation marked a clear opening for Chamberlain's policy (backed by the rest of the Cabinet) of the active pursuit of appeasement, initially through looking to closer relations with Mussolini's Italy.[164]

Churchill later wrote, somewhat melodramatically, of Eden's resignation as a defining moment which filled him with 'emotions of sorrow and fear' as the 'waters of despair' overwhelmed him during an insomniac night.[165] Following on the 'promotion' a month earlier of another figure seen by Londonderry as a major hindrance to a more friendly policy towards Germany, Sir Robert Vansittart, who was now given the grandiloquent but empty position of Chief Diplomatic Adviser to the government, Eden's resignation ushered in a perceptible change of course in British foreign policy. From Londonderry's point of view, the change was long overdue. It showed, he said, 'that the negative or static period in the conduct of our relations with foreign powers, notably the two great totalitarian states in Western

Europe, is over – and that we can look forward, by contrast, to a more positive and dynamic trend in our foreign policy'.[166] The fact that Eden's replacement was Lord Halifax, the one person in the Cabinet in whom Londonderry had shown any confidence on foreign affairs, gave him added encouragement.

The shadows over European peace were, however, now starting to lengthen rapidly. Before Eden's resignation, Hitler had subjected the Austrian Chancellor, Kurt Schuschnigg, to a fearful browbeating in an audience at Berchtesgaden which paved the way for Nazi control over the Austrian government.[167] And on the very day of the resignation, 20 February, Hitler had delivered an aggressive speech to the Reichstag, declaring that the separation from the Reich by 10 million fellow Germans on account of borders imposed through peace treaties was 'unbearable'.[168] Both Austria and Czechoslovakia were now plainly in his sights.

During these days, Londonderry finished writing his book. Reflecting towards the end, in the light of the events of February, on the likelihood before long of union between Germany and Austria, he did not think that this 'would unduly disturb the equilibrium of Europe, provided it were accomplished by peaceful means and with the full and unfettered consent of the majority of the Austrian people'. He added: 'Any other solution would be disastrous, and we for one could not subscribe to it.'[169] His words would sooner than he imagined be put to the test: on the early morning of 12 March, Hitler's troops crossed into Austria. Months of tension and drama that would bring Europe to the very brink of war had begun.

5

Hope at Last

*'The fulfilment of all my hopes . . . I can only have the feeling
of great happiness at this moment that all that I have advocated has been brought about in a moment of time.'*
Lord Londonderry, referring to the Munich Agreement,
in the preface to the Second Edition of
Ourselves and Germany, October 1938.

The Anschluss, when it came, was sudden and rapid. Pressure had
been building for months upon Austria to move towards some form
of union with Germany. And after the intense verbal battering that
the Austrian Chancellor, Kurt Schuschnigg, was subjected to by
Hitler in mid-February 1938, on his visit to the Berghof, the dictator's
mountain fastness near Berchtesgaden, such pressure had intensified
drastically. The British government, and the governments of the other
major European powers, were reconciled to some form of Nazi
takeover in Austria within the coming months – and to the likelihood
that this would open the door to action on Czechoslovakia. But not
only foreign governments were taken by surprise by the dramatic
events that unfolded so swiftly between Schuschnigg's wholly unexpected and desperate announcement, on 9 March, of a plebiscite in
Austria, which threatened a result likely to be unpalatable to Hitler,
and the signing, four days later, by the German Leader of a law ending Austrian independence and turning the country into a mere
province of the German Reich. Some leading figures in Hitler's regime
had, in fact, been equally caught unawares by the turn of events.
These included the new Foreign Minister, Joachim von Ribbentrop,

who, to his chagrin, found himself in London, enveloped in the last
obsequies of his ambassadorship and compelled to vacate the field to
his arch-rival in foreign affairs, Hermann Göring.[1] Hitler, furious at
what he saw as Schuschnigg's betrayal of the agreement that had been
wrung out of him at the Berghof, had taken only a brief time to arrive
at the decision that the hour had come to force the issue in Austria.
Unlike his hesitation for weeks in early 1936 about whether to send
troops into the Rhineland, the quick resolve to deal militarily with the
newly arisen problem in Austria was eased by his certainty that
Britain and Italy would do nothing, and that French action was therefore also extremely unlikely.[2]

It was an accurate assessment. Hitler had gleaned a clear insight
into likely British compliance at the audience he had granted, on
3 March, to the British Ambassador, Sir Nevile Henderson, recently
returned from London with instructions that the British government
would be ready, in principle, to discuss all outstanding questions with
a view to a general settlement in Europe. These included, Henderson
told Hitler, 'a peaceful solution of the Czech and Austrian problems,
and the colonial question' (the last of these, as was plain to
Henderson, of little interest to the German dictator).[3] Hitler showed
not the slightest inclination to take up the British offer of a negotiated
general settlement. That did not fit his plans at all. Even so, he sent
Ribbentrop to London, where Neville Chamberlain, at the very
moment that the news of the Anschluss was beginning to unfold,
pressed upon him his 'most sincere wish for an understanding with
Germany'.[4] But the British had little or nothing in tangible terms with
which to tempt Hitler. He could take it anyway.

From the moment German troops entered Austria it became clear
that the British government was not only prepared to contemplate a
peaceful solution to the Austrian problem; it was ready to accept a
forceful solution.[5] As Henderson recognized, it had little choice.
Neither the British government nor British public opinion was ready
to go to war over a country whose population comprised ethnic
Germans, a good proportion of whom enthusiastically favoured
union with Germany. So, as Henderson put it, Britain 'left it to words
to carry conviction'. He conveyed two verbal protests to the German
government, and, when he saw Göring during a huge reception and

ballet performance, while the invasion of Austria was proceeding, objected to German bullying. That amounted, in effect, to the British response. On 13 March, the day the Anschluss was completed, Henderson, travelling as 'a form of demonstration' in his official limousine and sporting a large Union Jack on the bonnet, visited Austria's diplomatic representative in Berlin, and found him in full uniform, ready to leave for a Nazi ceremony, at which, with outstretched arm, he bawled out 'Heil Hitler' with the rest.[6]

Chamberlain did not like the way Hitler had behaved over Austria. But, he told the Cabinet's Foreign Policy Committee, two days after the extinction of Austrian sovereignty by German armed might, that 'he did not think anything that had happened should cause the government to alter their present policy'. In fact, he was all the more convinced that this policy of seeking a general settlement through the appeasement of Germany was correct, and sorry only that it had not been adopted earlier.[7] On the day of the Anschluss itself, he had suggested in a private letter to his sister that 'if we can avoid another violent coup in Czechoslovakia, which ought to be feasible, it may be possible for Europe to settle down again, and some day for us to start peace talks again with the Germans'.[8] For the first time, Hitler had used military might outside German borders to have his way. Austria set in motion the disastrous chain of events which, over subsequent months, took Europe to the brink of war, for a brief period away from the abyss, then, finally, over the edge. The turn of the screws on Czechoslovakia, as widely predicted, was to follow the Austrian triumph within weeks. Hitler was impatient for further success while time appeared to be on Germany's side. In any case, radicalism bred radicalism in the Nazi regime – also with regard to foreign affairs. An unstoppable momentum was rapidly building up. The British government fully recognized that serious trouble was brewing. Though Austria could be viewed as a regrettable use of force resolving, if in highly reproachable fashion, a conflict between two Germanic states, in the case of Czechoslovakia, the risk of general European war was grave: France was obliged by treaty to help the Czechs in the event of a German attack; the Soviet Union, also with treaty obligations to Czechoslovakia, had indicated it would help the French; and Britain, as the closest ally of the French, was almost certain to be drawn in.

1. The 7th Marquess of Londonderry, soon after inheriting the title in 1915, as aide-de-camp to General Sir William Pulteney. The experience of the First World War and its aftermath decisively influenced Londonderry's anxiety to avoid another conflagration and his belief that this could only be achieved by accommodating German demands.

2. Edith Lady Londonderry during the First World War, in the uniform of Commandant of the Women's Legion (from the portrait by Philip de László in the Imperial War Museum).

3. The main entrance to Mount Stewart, County Down, as it is today. The house has been the property of the National Trust since 1976.

4. Lady Londonderry at the head of the grand staircase in Londonderry House in the early 1930s, receiving guests at a reception on the eve of the opening of Parliament. The blurred figure behind her is the Prime Minister, Ramsay MacDonald.

5. The grand staircase at Londonderry House in Park Lane. The mansion was demolished in 1962 to make way for a hotel on the site.

6. Lord Londonderry as Finance Member of the Air Council, leaving the War Office with Winston Churchill, Secretary of State for War and Air, in 1919.

7. The British Prime Minister, Ramsay MacDonald, in earnest discussion during the Disarmament Conference in Geneva, probably in March 1933, when he presented the British 'Draft Convention' on disarmament, known as the 'MacDonald Plan', to the Conference.

8. Stanley Baldwin, Lord President of the Council and one of the most influential members of the British Cabinet, in June 1934, a year before he became Prime Minister for a third time.

9. Lord Londonderry as Secretary of State for Air, launching the new air-mail route from England to Australia, the longest in the world, at Croydon aerodrome, near London, on 19 December 1934.

10. Lord Londonderry, during his time as Air Minister, saying goodbye to his daughters Helen and Margaret as he prepares for take-off in a service aircraft.

11. Anthony Eden, then Lord Privy Seal, and Sir John Simon, the Foreign Secretary, in discussion with Adolf Hitler during their visit to Berlin in March 1935. Hitler's claim that Germany already possessed air parity with Britain stirred great alarm and prompted Londonderry's dismissal from office as Air Minister.

12. Lord Londonderry in the Reich Chancellery, Berlin, with Hitler and Joachim von Ribbentrop on 4 February 1936 during the visit that established his close ties with German leaders and first established his reputation as a leading apologist for Nazi Germany.

13. German troops enter Düsseldorf on 8 March 1936 following Hitler's announcement the previous day of the remilitarization of the Rhineland, in violation of the treaties of Versailles and Locarno.

14. Ribbentrop's plane, a Junkers 52, soon after arrival on 29 May 1936 at Newtownards aerodrome in Northern Ireland, not far from Lord Londonderry's home at Mount Stewart.

15. The Londonderrys and their guests, the Ribbentrops, during the Whitsuntide house party at Mount Stewart in 1936. Left to right: Joachim von Ribbentrop, Lady Londonderry, Anneliese von Ribbentrop, Lord Londonderry.

16. The Mount Stewart house party, 29 May–2 June 1936. Left to right: Alvilde Chaplin, Lady Mairi Stewart, Anneliese von Ribbentrop, Lord Chaplin, Sir Hedworth Williamson, Gwladys Chaplin, Georg von Wussow, Lady Londonderry, Princess Marie Elisabeth zu Wied, Heinz Thorner, Lord Londonderry, George Ward Price, Princess Benigna Victoria zu Wied, Mrs Laura Corrigan, Joachim von Ribbentrop.

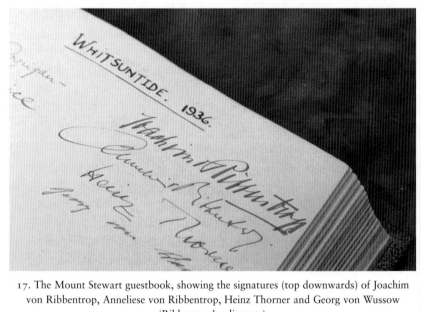

17. The Mount Stewart guestbook, showing the signatures (top downwards) of Joachim von Ribbentrop, Anneliese von Ribbentrop, Heinz Thorner and Georg von Wussow (Ribbentrop's adjutants).

But as Germany had grown more powerful, Britain, in relative terms, had become even more enfeebled, with only a weak hand to play. Writing to his sister on 20 March, Chamberlain bluntly stated Britain's limitations:

You have only to look at the map to see that nothing that France or we could do could possibly save Czechoslovakia from being over-run by the Germans if they wanted to do it . . . Therefore, we could not help Czechoslovakia – she would simply be a pretext for going to war with Germany. That we could not think of, unless we had a reasonable prospect of being able to beat her to her knees in reasonable time and of that I see no sign. I have therefore abandoned any idea of giving guarantees to Czechoslovakia or the French in connection with her obligations to that country.[9]

This dismal acknowledgement of British impotence was a rational, if lamentable, presentation of the position from Britain's point of view as the dust began to settle after the seismic upheaval of the Anschluss.

I

Lord Londonderry had completed the manuscript of his book just a fortnight or so before the momentous events of mid-March 1938. He had already penned his conclusions on Anglo-German relations when 'the news of Herr Hitler's coup in Austria' broke, and, with his text already at the publishers, felt it necessary to add a brief and hurried 'postscript' on the Anschluss.[10] He had, as we have already seen, in late February commented that a peacefully attained union between Germany and Austria, with the full consent of the majority of Austrians, would not disturb 'the equilibrium of Europe'. In other words, it ought, in his view, to meet with international acceptance. Any other solution, however, he immediately added, would be 'disastrous' and 'we' (whether he meant himself or the British government was unclear) 'could not subscribe to it'.[11] What were his views once the Anschluss was a *fait accompli*?

The events had, of course, scarcely unfolded in the 'peaceful manner' that he had endorsed. However much the Nazis tried to obscure the fact, the Anschluss followed an invasion of one sovereign country by another. Nevertheless, in contrast with his stated view of only a week or two earlier, Londonderry no longer saw this as a disaster. To be sure, he did say that any protest – *if* there should be one, he added – ought to be addressed at the 'method of accomplishment' rather than the object achieved.[12] And he thought the British government's show of disapproval was the right one. Hitler's action had been 'dangerous' and – a striking phrase – was 'hardly distinguishable from war itself'. It was cause for even greater apprehension about the future, necessitating 'some procedure, arrived at by international understanding, by which such events cannot possibly take place again'.[13] But, though the means had been regrettable, Londonderry saw the accomplishment of Anschluss as justified. He argued that Austria was a unique case. It had an entirely German-speaking population; Hitler was Austrian; the previous regime had represented only a minority of the people: incorporation in the Reich had therefore been inevitable – merely a matter of time. And Schuschnigg had to be faulted for his 'desperate method' of announcing the plebiscite following the understanding with Hitler, 'intended to safeguard the position in Austria of those who were opposed to the Schuschnigg regime'. Hitler, he implied, was bound to regard this as a betrayal. He cited, without commentary, Hitler's own words that, had he not intervened, Schuschnigg's announced plebiscite would have led to 'bloody revolution', turning Austria into another Spain.[14] Speaking in the House of Lords less than a week after the Anschluss, Londonderry was even more unguarded. The plebiscite, he asserted, 'would have been followed by riots, bloodshed, and revolution'. He then praised Hitler since it was 'by the drastic action of the German Chancellor that bloodshed had been saved'. He repeated his view that the Anschluss had been 'a foregone conclusion'. Accordingly, he deduced that 'the circumstances in which a great nation had passed from a country to a province would, if they had been brought about in another way, have been of the most terrible character'.[15] One informed observer, listening to the speech in the House of Lords, described Londonderry as a 'pure pro-Nazi apologist'.[16] Hitler was, indeed, being effectively exonerated by Londonderry. Responsibility for the way the Anschluss was carried out fell, in this interpretation, as it did in the Nazis' own justification, on the Austrian Chancellor through his precipitate action. It was like blaming the householder for trying to barricade his door against the intruder about to smash his way through it.

Doubtless influenced by the scenes of the joyous crowds welcoming Hitler on his passage to Vienna, and the enormous, delirious gathering in the Austrian capital's Heldenplatz on 15 March to hear him proclaim 'the entry of my homeland into the German Reich',[17] Londonderry unquestioningly accepted that the Anschluss had been favoured by 'the large majority of the Austrian population'.[18] He was neither the first nor the last to make this easy mistake. He was presumably unaware that the vast crowd in the Heldenplatz, for all its genuine enthusiasm, had been carefully orchestrated by the Austrian Nazi Party.[19] But he might have shown greater awareness of the extent of the violence perpetrated by Austrian Nazis favouring Anschluss before it occurred, and, quite especially, of the ferocious repression and intimidation which accompanied it once Himmler's SS had arrived in Vienna on 12 March. In fact, the Anschluss fell upon a deeply divided country. Well under a half of the population, according to the best estimates, welcomed union with Germany.[20]

Londonderry had, in truth, once more shown himself over-ready to accept and explain away Nazi aggression. Privately, his main worry seemed to be its impact in alienating sympathy for Germany in Britain.[21] For all its qualifications, his account amounted to an apologia for Hitler's assault on Austria. He did, however, end by sounding a note of alarm about a repeat of such aggression toward Czechoslovakia – a quite different case. If the incorporation of Austria in the Reich had been 'a legitimate German aspiration', the same, he stated, could not be claimed of Czechoslovakia. 'And', he concluded, 'whereas no international action could with propriety be taken to oppose Herr Hitler in his policy in regard to Austria, a totally different situation arises should the German policy of expansion extend to the incorporation or forcible acquisition of Czechoslovakia.'[22] The issue was to preoccupy him – and the rest of Europe – as the tension mounted during the next six months.

Few people doubted that, should Hitler's expected next move on Czechoslovakia materialize, it would indeed pose 'a totally different situation'. The question was: how should it be handled? Winston Churchill's view was straightforward (though it remained a minority taste). Only a firm show of strength and resolve by Britain, supporting France in the fulfilment of her treaty obligations towards the Czechs, would prevail in the face of German aggression in Czechoslovakia.[23] Londonderry disagreed. For him, the lesson of Austria was that an 'international understanding' on Czechoslovakia had to be reached as a matter of the utmost urgency.[24] Directly contradicting Churchill, he advocated 'conversations with Germany' to 'obtain from her a categorical definition of her policy'. Only if this approach failed should Churchill's 'plan' come into play.[25] Londonderry wrote to Lord Halifax, the new Foreign Secretary, at the end of March, anxious lest 'those very definite conversations' which he had sought should be further postponed by 'some other international event', and a further opportunity for '"getting hold" of the Germans' pass by. He offered to try to make further contact himself with Germany, and recommended that Halifax speak to Ward Price, the *Daily Mail* journalist who had interviewed Hitler in Vienna at the time of the Anschluss.[26]

The British government refrained, of course, from echoing Londonderry's overtly pro-German sentiments, or backing the headlong rush he proposed into talks with Germany (with the obvious implication of making territorial concessions). Even so, the Prime Minister's view was that Czechoslovakia could only be saved by finding a settlement which Germany would accept.[27] This approach would be put into effect during the tension-laden summer as the British government edged closer to Londonderry's position than to that of Churchill.

II

Londonderry's book, which he called *Ourselves and Germany*, was eventually published (after a brief delay caused by the need to add the postscript on the Anschluss) at the beginning of April. A second, paperback, edition published by Penguin later in the year significantly increased its circulation, and the attention paid to it. The book cemented Londonderry's reputation – and greatly expanded

awareness of it – as one of the foremost British advocates of friendship with Germany. But early reviews in major English newspapers
were positive.[28]

Among the first complimentary copies he sent out was one to
Hitler, with inscribed dedication ('To the Führer with my best wishes
and my earnest hopes for a better and lasting understanding between
our two countries'),[29] together with a long letter explaining his
objects in writing the book: 'to put the case for justice to Germany'
and to show his own consistent advocacy for 'a close understanding
between England and Germany as the only method of establishing
peace'. He thought he had succeeded on both counts, though wanted
to warn Hitler that misunderstandings in Germany might conceivably arise because he had been writing for the British public and,
therefore, had felt it necessary to mention 'matters on which I do not
feel myself in full accord with your policy'. A more one-sided 'pro-
German point of view' would have 'carried no weight here at all'. He
pointed out the negative impact in Britain of the reports of repression in Austria, towards Jews and opponents of the Nazis. Still, he
said, he saw events shaping in the way he wanted and hoped the next
few months would bring the two countries closer together. He apologized for the rejection in Britain of Hitler's 'friendly overtures', but
thought he had 'done something to acquaint people here of the
tremendous task which you yourself have performed'. He professed
to recognize all Hitler's 'great difficulties', but was sure that the
'understanding and rapprochement on which so much depends can
be brought about' on the way towards the policy which he himself
believed in: 'that Great Britain and Germany can rule the world and
that there is no necessity whatever for any point of fundamental disagreement to arise between us'.[30]

Hitler thanked Londonderry for the book, saying he shared with
him 'the hope of a better understanding between our two countries
which you have thus expressed'. But he sent his copy on to the
Foreign Ministry, its pages most likely unopened (since he did not
read English and, in any case, had better – at least other – things to
do with his time).[31] Other copies were sent to Göring, Ribbentrop
and von Papen.[32] Göring claimed to have read it 'with great interest', registering his disagreement on the colonial question (where

Londonderry had claimed that Germany's only case rested on the prestige requirements of a great power, with which he sympathized).[33] Doubtless, Göring's remarks were based upon the summary of Londonderry's conclusions, drawn up for him by one of his aides. Like Hitler, Göring was linguistically not up to reading it even in the unlikely event that he had wanted to do so. And in May 1938 he was preoccupied with matters other than the apologia of a British aristocrat, even one sympathetic to Germany. There is no indication of a reply from Ribbentrop (whom Londonderry had thanked on his departure as Ambassador in London 'for the very friendly manner in which you have continually discussed with me those matters affecting the well-being of our two countries').[34] Von Papen, however, plainly read the book and sent Londonderry a lengthy, handwritten, most cordial letter, though taking issue with Londonderry's description of the way Germany had annexed Austria as 'hardly distinguishable from war itself'. Von Papen reiterated that the Austrian issue had been unique and that there had been no other way of settling it after Schuschnigg's 'surprise plebiscite'. The Czech question, he assured Londonderry, would have to be solved quite differently.[35]

At home, Londonderry liberally distributed copies of his book. Lord Halifax, of course, Chamberlain, and other members of the government were among the recipients. Churchill thanked Londonderry in characteristically gracious fashion (despite his profound disagreement with what he had to say) for his copy. 'It is difficult to talk much', wrote Churchill, 'when one feels so strongly about things: but as you know I always wish you well in every way of friendship, and kinship.'[36] And among the leading German sympathizers we have already encountered, the Labour pacifist Lord Allen of Hurtwood (who thought it 'extremely valuable') and the veteran general Sir Ian Hamilton (in full agreement with the sentiments of a 'beautiful book') also received copies.[37] In addition, Londonderry had asked his publishers to send a gratis copy to the former British Ambassador in Berlin, Sir Horace Rumbold, whose views on the German problem, as we have seen, had differed fundamentally from the line taken in *Ourselves and Germany*. In an eight-page letter, Rumbold provided a thoughtful response to the case for German friendship that Londonderry had made out.

Rumbold began by agreeing that Britain's policy towards Germany before 1930 had been deplorable. He blamed primarily the French, but also British subservience to French policy. Relations had improved in the mid-1920s under Gustav Stresemann's stewardship of foreign affairs and, after the death of Germany's Foreign Minister and leading statesman in 1929, continued to be good during the time that Heinrich Brüning was Reich Chancellor from 1930 to 1932. In those years there had been a good deal of sympathy in Britain for Germany's difficulties. 'All this good feeling was scrapped in ten days when the Nazi regime came in,' Rumbold wrote. He saw Hitler as 'an extraordinary product – very cunning, quite far-seeing, a super-demagogue with a strong streak of mysticism'. Von Papen, 'a pleasant but contemptible personality' and 'a light weight if ever there was one', had combined 'treachery and imbecility' with Hindenburg's senility to bring Hitler to power and then, instead of controlling him, had been promptly swallowed by 'that boa-constrictor'. Rumbold disagreed with Londonderry's estimate of Ribbentrop, describing him as 'a good wine merchant' but a 'disaster' in the diplomatic field. He rated Nevile Henderson, the British Ambassador in Berlin, as a failure. (The Ambassador was described by Vansittart, around the same time, as a 'menace' on account of his pro-German sympathies.)[38] Britain had missed the chance, Rumbold suggested, in April 1933 of taking up the German proposal for an army of 300,000 men. This would have breached the military clauses of the Versailles Treaty, certainly, but ought to have been accepted, even in the face of French opposition. It would have been worth at this stage testing Hitler's word. On the colonial question he thought German arguments were 'disingenuous to say the least'. Rumbold then turned to Londonderry's demand in his book – actually, it had been his constant refrain throughout the previous years – that the Germans should be pressed to indicate 'the limit of their ambitions'. Rumbold saw what Londonderry had been incapable of seeing. 'I doubt whether even Hitler could tell you what the limit is,' he remarked. 'Perhaps there isn't one, for Germans are incurable Oliver Twists' – always coming back for more. He pointed to *Mein Kampf*, which had made such an impact on him when he had read it in 1933. It set out, for Rumbold, the programme that 'Hitler is steadily following'. He concluded that Britain should not be chasing friendship with Germany. The methods of the Anschluss spoke against an understanding or agreement with the Germans. 'Let them, therefore, come to us first,' he advised. 'All we want from them is that they should keep the peace and behave decently.'[39]

Londonderry sent a copy of the letter to the Foreign Secretary, saying he agreed with most of the former Ambassador's comments – a somewhat strange claim, since Rumbold's conclusions, though diplomatically couched, ran diametrically counter to his own on how to deal with Germany.[40] Halifax regretted, he wrote in reply, that Rumbold had been removed from Berlin, and saw in his premature departure a contribution to the 'missed opportunities' of British policy towards Germany in previous years.[41]

The publication of Londonderry's book, and the extracts that appeared in the widely read London newspaper the *Evening Standard*, on 6 April spawned a huge correspondence.[42] Most of his postbag was positive, even flattering. But not all comment was favourable, by any means. One anonymous missive accused him of being in the pay of the German government to weaken British defences. 'What about the £125,000 cheque Rippentrop [sic] gave you? You traitor', it thundered.[43] Few, if any, of Londonderry's other letters were as abusive. Some, however, engaged critically with Londonderry's arguments and took issue, not least, with his remarks about the Jews. Londonderry had included in his book a lengthy extract from his letter to Ribbentrop in February 1936, admitting that he had 'no great affection for Jews' and claiming it was 'possible to trace their participation in most of those international disturbances which have created so much havoc in different countries'. He diluted his assertion only by adding that he was aware of other Jews who had done their best 'to counteract those malevolent and mischievous activities'.[44] Towards the end of his book, Londonderry noted that 'we may fail to understand, and many of us undoubtedly condemn, the attitude which the Chancellor adopts towards the Jews and certain religious bodies', and expressed his regret, as one who had 'the cause of Anglo-German friendship at heart', at the 'crude and violent nature' of Nazi anti-Semitic propaganda. But he then immediately qualified these remarks by reminding his readers of 'the German point of view' of excessive Jewish influence in the medical, legal and academic professions and in the fields of commerce, industry and finance.[45] And in his appended postscript on the Anschluss, Londonderry did not refer with a single word to the savage bestiality of the Nazi attacks on Jews – putting in the shade even the brutality of the previous five years of Hitler's rule in Germany – which now pressed itself forcibly upon the conscience of the British public.

Londonderry's comments do not appear to have attracted the attention of the many non-Jews among his correspondents. But one Jewish friend, Anthony Rothschild, of the famous banking family, did take him to task. He asked on what authority Londonderry could make such a sweeping statement which 'savours of the stock in trade of all anti-Semitic writers', and could be used to support the persecution of Jews. Sending Londonderry some notes on the situation in Vienna, he supposed, he wrote, that Londonderry could not realize the gravity of what was taking place there.[46] Londonderry's reply apologized for the personal pain he had caused to a longstanding family friend. He claimed the extract Rothschild had read had not placed his comments in the context of the sustained effort he had made to avoid a war which would mean 'the end of an epoch' that had brought 'a marvellous development of civilisation'. He then went on, in elaborating his attitude towards Jews, to make matters worse. He took a familiar anti-Semitic line of pointing first to his 'many friends amongst the Jews' before turning to 'Jewish influence as a whole', which, he said, had always alarmed him and prompted his 'gravest misgivings'. His anti-Bolshevism, predictably, came into play at this point as he picked up the standard anti-Semitic line that Jews had been behind the 1917 Russian Revolution. This was the 'proof' he offered of his far-reaching assertion. He claimed to have 'condemned the attitude of the Germans towards the Jews in my book' (which, as we have seen, was scarcely a true reflection of his mild and qualified criticism), before compounding still further his damaging remarks. His wife, he said, fearing as he did Jewish influence and believing 'that the Jews in the East End [of London] are a really dangerous element in this country', had suggested that 'those many Jews who exist in all parts of the world and who have made tremendous contributions to progress and the highest form of religious idealism' should seek to control 'the dangerous elements' who were 'so powerful in moulding the destinies of the world'.[47]

Rothschild's remarkably restrained, if understandably cool, response used history and logic to counter Londonderry's 'nebulous accusations', pointing out that

except insofar as in the past those of the Jewish faith living all over the world have attempted to help their persecuted co-religionists elsewhere or in support of Zionism – which was the official, but, as many Jews like myself think, the mistaken policy of the British Government – there is no such thing as Jewish influence as such, and any apprehensions based on the supposition of its existence are entirely imaginary.[48]

Londonderry's final parry in the exchange was to draw Rothschild's attention to 'the tremendous compliment which I am paying to your race' by emphasizing its dominating influence. He repeated his sadness that his words had caused pain, and regretted their inclusion in the book. However, he was adamant that the 'unvarnished words in the book are the feeling in my mind'.[49]

When his secretary replied to another critic – this time of humbler provenance than Anthony Rothschild and not needing his Lordship's personal attention – with a similar remark that Londonderry would have omitted the offending words from his letter to Ribbentrop 'if he had had more time to weigh every sentence', Londonderry was hoist with his own petard. 'Must I then conclude', came the rejoinder, 'that Lord Londonderry has said in his haste things for which he has no foundations? If this is the case then we Jews must expect and must ask Lord Londonderry to retract with all candour statements for which he has no foundation.'[50] Since, as he had told Rothschild, the words did accurately represent his views, naturally, no such retraction was forthcoming.

Londonderry had, as his public and private statements reveal, an ingrained anti-Jewish prejudice – though there was little that was distinctive in a latent antipathy which was common enough on the Conservative Right. Since, as he put it in a later letter, he thought the Jews had 'brought the trouble on themselves to begin with',[51] he was also prepared to go out of his way to try to understand, and to explain away, the Nazi persecution. Even so, he was baffled. Since the centrality of race to the Nazi creed was lost on him, he simply could not comprehend why the German leadership was willing to risk alienating all possible goodwill through brutal treatment of the Jews.[52] Writing to Sir Ian Hamilton, as we have seen, a noted German sympathizer who was not prepared to condemn the attacks on the Jews, Londonderry commented that, though he thought he knew something of the German mentality, 'the continued effort to exterminate the Jews' – the precise words he used – 'is the part of their policy which I cannot understand and this is turning world opinion against them with all its dangerous repercussions'.[53] He told Göring that there was widespread sympathy for Germany in Britain but that the 'propaganda throughout the world' about Germany's 'attitude' towards the Jews was 'doing an incredible amount of harm' to Germany's 'good name'.[54] Regrettable to him though the human suffering undoubtedly was, the harmful impact of the persecution of the Jews on the prospects of friendship between Britain and Germany, and therefore the saving of European peace, was what counted in his eyes.

Alongside the persecution of the Jews, Londonderry had also briefly touched in his book on the Nazi attacks on the Christian Churches, which had reached their height in 1937. As with anti-Jewish policy, he could not understand the assault on Christianity and the neo-pagan ideas that accompanied it. Here, too, however, he consoled himself with the thought that it could be 'no more than a passing phase'.[55] There is little sign that he took much direct interest in it, despite his wife's avid commitment to the Anglican Church. He drafted a letter to Ribbentrop at the behest of Church leaders in England, pointing out the strong feeling in the country at the anti-Church policies.[56] But there is no indication that it was followed up, or that Londonderry took any action when informed by the sister-in-law of the Bishop of Chichester of the poor condition in a German concentration camp of Pastor Martin Niemöller, a leading Protestant clergyman whose outspoken comments had attracted the regime's ire.[57] When another correspondent, who had publicly pleaded for Niemöller's release, sought Londonderry's support, he replied that he was unclear what to do 'in this very difficult matter'. By referring to the 'great deal of political work' that Niemöller allegedly undertook 'in addition to his spiritual duties', Londonderry was nonetheless implicitly suggesting that the Protestant pastor largely had himself to blame for his incarceration.[58] Londonderry's view had been consistently that the persecution of the Christian Churches, like that of the Jews, was, however unpalatable and incomprehensible, an internal matter and no direct concern of Britain (except in that it damaged relations between the two countries).

The principle that persecution was an internal German matter was, however, dropped within the Londonderry household when two Austrian guides well known to Lady Londonderry were arrested following the Anschluss on suspicion of anti-Nazi activities. Even worse, one of the guides had been organizing 'the Londonderry Snow Eagle' ski-race at Obergurgl in the Tyrol at the time. Lady Londonderry had established the race three years earlier after staying in the Tyrol and donated a cup for the winner.[59] She now wrote angrily to Ribbentrop, telling him of the 'storm of indignation in London throughout the sporting world' at the arrests and reminding him of the antagonism they were causing among 'all your erstwhile friends over here'. She felt so strongly about 'these sets of outrage', she wrote, that she was considering going to Vienna herself 'to find out what is really going on'. She added her earnest hope that her cup had not been impounded at the same time. The guides were in the event released, perhaps through the intercession of Göring, who had also been berated by Lady Londonderry. Like her husband, Lady Londonderry was mystified by the ferocity of the repression. She had also asked whether Ribbentrop could do nothing to help in securing the release of Baron Louis Rothschild, whose sister-in-law had contacted her husband to say he had been arrested. She posed the plaintive question: 'Must all these things be?' For all that, she felt that what had taken place in Austria had been 'for the best'.[60]

As the fall-out from the publication of his book began to subside, Londonderry's hopes of a breakthrough in relations with Germany were, like those of his wife, undiminished by recent events in Austria. Though German strength, compared with earlier weakness, was an undeniable fact, he still felt it vital 'to get hold of them, and to seek to find out the scope of their ambitions'. He himself had once had a hold on the Germans, he claimed, though this had now dwindled to vanishing-point and he felt 'quite at a loss now how to proceed'. So he was supporting Neville Chamberlain – 'courageous, approachable and resourceful' – and Lord Halifax because he thought they were 'proposing to call the German bluff'. What would be the consequences of a refusal by Germany to reveal 'exactly what they mean and what they want to do'? Londonderry's answer was that they would be made immediately aware of Britain's hostility and that Britain would 'have to forego progress in the world and try to stabilize the international situation by definitely controlling the power which seeks to achieve the hegemony of the world'.[61] How this would be achieved, he did not say.

III

Wasting no time after his triumph in Austria, Hitler was by now already starting to turn up the heat on Czechoslovakia. Before the end of the summer, the name 'Sudetenland' would be embedded in the consciousness of the British public. Until spring 1938 they had hardly heard of it.

Most people, in Germany as well as in Britain, thought the crisis which brought the spectre of war ever closer was *only* about the Sudetenland – the part of Czechoslovakia abutting the German Reich, where the 3 million or so German speakers constituted the overwhelming majority of the population. The British government laboured throughout the tense months of that summer under the same misapprehension. But for Hitler, the Sudeten Germans were the means, not the end. The aim, for him, was the destruction of Czechoslovakia, not the return of the Sudeten Germans 'home into the Reich'. By the end of May he had stated his goal in the plainest terms to his army leadership. 'It is my unalterable decision to smash Czechoslovakia by military action in the foreseeable future', he declared. Preparations were to be completed by 1 October at the latest.[62] Hitler was intent on war – against Czechoslovakia, certainly, but now, if need be, also against the western powers, France and Britain, whose weakness and divisions had been amply laid bare to him over the previous years, and especially since the débâcle over Abyssinia and their feeble acquiescence in the remilitarization of the Rhineland.[63]

For the Nazi leadership, the destruction of Czechoslovakia was a valuable prize. Allied to Germany's major enemies, France to the west, the Soviet Union to the east, well fortified, with its own sizeable army and a strong industrial base, Czechoslovakia was seen both to pose a strategic threat and to constitute a blockage on pretensions to dominate central and eastern Europe. Beyond that, Czechoslovakia offered rich pickings in its armaments industries and raw materials for an economy which was struggling to combine rapid preparation for expansion with shortages and restrictions at every turn. On top of this came Hitler's heightened self-confidence since his Austrian triumph. Ever more convinced of his own infallibility, his sense was that Germany could not afford to delay. He was determined, therefore, to retain the initiative by striking while the western democracies were still enfeebled and before they could challenge Germany's lead in an arms race. He was, as ever, confident of success. The Wehrmacht would crush the Czech army. The western powers would protest, but do nothing, as usual. And should they, against the odds, decide to fight, they, too, would be defeated.

Not everyone saw it this way. The ebullience was not widely shared. Even in the upper echelons of the Nazi leadership, Ribbentrop's gung-ho approach was countered by Göring's increasing foreboding. Army leaders, too, were divided. They did not object to the destruction of Czechoslovakia. In fact, this prospect was almost universally welcomed. But the fear that an attack on Czechoslovakia would bring intervention by France, which Britain would support, leading to a general European war, which, it was thought, Germany would lose, nagged worryingly at some generals and a number of other prominent individuals in the Foreign Ministry and elsewhere. It was a small minority, to be sure, though an influential one. Hitler, they thought, was courting disaster for the Reich. The only way to avoid it was to remove him. Beneath the surface of the police state, therefore, these few individuals in high places began to contemplate a strike against Hitler should the invasion of Czechoslovakia go ahead.[64]

In all this, the Sudeten Germans were willing pawns.[65] Before Hitler took power, the German minority had no more threatened to undermine the state of Czechoslovakia, which had been founded out of the ruins of the Habsburg empire, than had the other ethnic minorities – Slovaks, Hungarians, Ruthenes and Poles – who lived alongside the majority Czech population. The advent of the Nazis changed this. It gave a new edge to ethnic tensions, already exacerbated by economic depression and poverty in the Sudetenland, the most industrialized region of Czechoslovakia. The Sudeten Germans, under their leader, Konrad Henlein, working to explicit orders by Hitler and egged on by Nazi propaganda at home, started to orchestrate ever more loudly their sense of grievance at discrimination and maltreatment by the Czech government. There was, indeed, discrimination, though it had been on nothing like the scale trumpeted by the Nazis until the antagonism fostered from Berlin began to prompt retaliation. Sometimes vicious, this both spurred further violence and easily fed back into Nazi propaganda about the need to end the oppression of the Sudeten Germans and give them protection – which, it was claimed, could only be safeguarded by the incorporation of the Sudetenland in the German Reich. The plan to destroy Czechoslovakia could be, and was, portrayed, therefore, as another nationalist conflict. And, from a distance, that is what it looked like. If a solution could be found to the plight of the Sudeten Germans by redrawing the borders of Czechoslovakia and handing their territory to Germany, the peace of Europe, it seemed, could be saved. This was ever more the thinking in the western democracies as the long summer months dragged on.

An early scare arose in the middle of May 1938. German troop movements close to the Czech border on 19–20 May – in fact, no more than spring manoeuvres – were mistakenly thought by the Czechoslovakian government to denote imminent invasion. The mobilization of military reserves was ordered. The British Ambassador in Berlin, Nevile Henderson, seeking clarification but exposing himself to an intemperate, warlike tirade from Ribbentrop, then inadvertently alarmed the British government, which presumed that a German invasion was indeed about to happen. Lord Halifax accordingly informed Ribbentrop that, should an attack take place, the French were obliged to intervene and the Germans should not count upon the British standing by.[66] The crisis rapidly blew over when British intelligence indicated that no invasion was underway. But the British government persisted in the false belief that Hitler had backed down under pressure. And, incandescent at this slight on his prestige, Hitler now resolved to destroy Czechoslovakia by the autumn.

For the British government, the destruction of Czechoslovakia was altogether a different proposition from the incorporation of Austria in the German Reich. It would amount to an assault on a country whose population, in the great majority, were not ethnic Germans. If Hitler's army were to be allowed to overrun Czechoslovakia, it would send out clear signals to other countries in central and south-eastern Europe. German domination over much of the European Continent beckoned. Beyond these considerations, Britain's ally, France, was obliged by treaty to support Czechoslovakia against external attack. Britain could find itself under pressure to support France. The prospect of war loomed, therefore, very large. And Neville Chamberlain, like his predecessor as Prime Minister, Stanley Baldwin, saw avoidance of war as the outright and overwhelming priority. Britain's world Empire was at stake. The Japanese advance in China posed an inescapable threat to British interests in the Far East. Fascist Italy spelled potential danger to British strength in the Mediterranean, a prospect not helped by the increasing likelihood of a Franco victory in the Spanish Civil War. And both Japan and Italy were now aligned with Germany. Should Britain become embroiled in a war over Czechoslovakia, there was no telling what the consequences might be. Moreover, the Dominions were anxious that all conceivable steps be taken to avoid conflict and indicated unwillingness to join in a fight over Czechoslovakia. And, at home, rearmament was still far from the level needed to engage in a major war. Still wedded to the generally accepted orthodoxy of balancing the budget through severe financial constraint, the Chancellor of the Exchequer, Sir John Simon, was, in fact, insisting upon cuts in naval expenditure only months before the navy might have been called upon to uphold British power in a war.[67] Not least, French military weakness (especially in the air) was an inescapable fact. And the Minister for the Coordination of Defence, Sir Thomas Inskip (so unfitted for the demands of the post that his appointment in 1936 had been compared by one sarcastic commentator with that of Caligula's appointment of his horse as a consul),[68] had conveyed to the government the military assessment that nothing Britain could do would save Czechoslovakia, which could be overrun by Germany within a week.[69] Moreover, the May Crisis had not done anything to win friends for the Czechs in the British Cabinet; quite the reverse. They were increasingly seen as an obstinate blockage to a peaceable settlement. The May Crisis made Britain, therefore, even more anxious to avoid a recurrence which, this time, might tip Europe over the edge.[70]

It was unsurprising, therefore, that Chamberlain clung to his policy of stretching every sinew to reach agreement with Germany that would avoid war. Equally unsurprising was it that Chamberlain refused to commit Britain to support of French military action in the event of a German attack on Czechoslovakia. He avoided giving such a commitment in a statement to the House of Commons in March;[71] and he expressly rejected it when the new French Prime Minister, Edouard Daladier, and his Foreign Minister, Georges Bonnet, visited London at the end of April and expressed their readiness to fight. To leave Germany guessing about British intentions, the formula (which had been invented by Halifax in March) that, if France intervened, Britain could not guarantee to remain aloof, was as far as Chamberlain would go – together with an insistence that the Czechoslovak government should be pressed hard and urgently, both by Britain and by France, to accommodate the demands of the German minority. Secretly, the French leaders were probably relieved at a policy which, if successful, would let them off the hook.[72] The Soviet Union, bound too by treaty to Czechoslovakia, had also announced its willingness to discuss measures directed at a firm stand to protect peace. Halifax peremptorily rejected the proposal, saying Britain preferred the settlement of 'outstanding problems' to the organization of 'concerted action against aggression'.[73] Chamberlain's view was that a common stand of Britain, France and Russia – redolent of the alliance that had entered the First World War – would only divide Europe into two armed camps and, rather than saving the peace, would inevitably result in war.[74] That left somehow coming to terms with Hitler. In his attempt to bring this about, Chamberlain was far from swimming against the tide of opinion in

Britain. On the contrary, both in Parliament and in the country at large the predominant view was that this must be achieved. 'Appeasement' only became a dirty word after the events of the late summer and early autumn.[75]

Everything revolved, therefore, around negotiations with Hitler – something Lord Londonderry had been urging for years. 'We *must* reach a modus vivendi with Germany,' Sir Alexander Cadogan, Vansittart's replacement as Permanent Under-Secretary at the Foreign Office, summed up, adding, in words which would have met with Lord Londonderry's favour: '*we* should ask Berlin what they want'.[76]

In June, Londonderry, accompanied by his wife and his daughter Lady Mairi, paid his fourth visit to Germany in just over two years, this time for four days, in yet another attempt at personal diplomacy, to see whether *he* could discover what Hitler wanted. Officially, he went as representative of the British Section at the annual conference of the Fédération Aéronautique Internationale, which controlled the sport of flying and was meeting in Berlin for the first time since 1906. The conference, held in the Haus der Flieger, the headquarters of German aviation, was opened on 24 June by General Erhard Milch, Göring's State Secretary in the Air Ministry. Göring himself presided over a festive lunch.[77] Lord Halifax had not wanted Londonderry to go to Germany. Rumours were heard that he would carry some sort of 'appeal' from Chamberlain to Hitler. Halifax asked to see Londonderry 'to stiffen him up a bit' (as Foreign Office officials hoped).[78] Londonderry had told the Foreign Secretary that he did not intend to have any political contacts unless these were suggested to him. But he himself had taken the initiative and had made sure in advance that he would see Göring, at least in a social capacity.[79] His general line, he informed Halifax, would be 'to be rather off-hand with his German friends and tell them that they were behaving in a way that he could not understand and that he could not easily explain to English public opinion'. Halifax was evidently wary that at such a sensitive time, a known German sympathizer might send out the wrong signals. 'The principal thing that we were concerned about was that he should not give any impression to any German whom he might meet that this country was washing its hands of events in Central Europe', Halifax minuted for Sir Robert Vansittart. He wanted Londonderry to make it plain that German professions of seeking a settlement of the Czechoslovak question could not be easily reconciled with recent violent attacks on the Czechs in speeches and radio broadcasts. Londonderry promised to keep this point in mind, and to convey the 'profound anxiety' felt in Britain at 'rumours of the German treatment of distinguished Austrians'. Lady Londonderry, he added, was already intending to speak to Göring and Ribbentrop about one or two such cases, which he thought was a better line of approach.[80]

The redoubtable Lady Londonderry plainly fulfilled her intention. Her anger of the spring at the arrest of the Austrian guides had clearly not altogether subsided. And, obviously, the feared head of the SS held few terrors for Lady Londonderry. Her husband reported to Halifax on his return that she had had 'a "set-to" with Ribbentrop and Himmler in far more outspoken language than I would have had the audacity to make use of in relation to the imprisonment and maltreatment of Austrians'.

Londonderry had a chance himself to speak to Himmler – 'jovially truculent' – and Ribbentrop. Both appeared to him to be 'reciting a well-learnt part'. Londonderry noted the absence of any reference to colonies, and Ribbentrop's comment that once the current territorial problems were solved Germany would be a 'satisfied nation'.

While he was in Germany, Londonderry once more paid a visit to Göring's by now palatially extensive hunting-lodge, Carinhall.[81] He was struck by a change in Göring, whom he found far more anxious and far less confident than he had ever seen him on earlier occasions. His impression seems to have been gleaned, however, from Göring's remark that, once the 'great pre-occupation' with Austria and the Sudetenland was settled, Germany would be able to discuss 'more important matters' with Britain, and most probably arms limitation.[82] It is unlikely that Halifax was as easily taken in by such easy talk as Londonderry evidently had been.[83]

When Londonderry next wrote to Halifax, some three weeks later, it was to express his anxiety about 'this Czechoslovakian matter'. It was plain where his sympathies lay. 'Czechoslovakia', he wrote, 'is one of the unfortunate post-war developments brought about by the diabolical cunning of [Edvard] Beneš and [Thomas] Masaryk' (the current and founding presidents of the country). After studying the problem carefully, he had reached the conclusion that the Czechs were anxious to put the Germans in the wrong. Presumably thinking back to the May Crisis, he said he understood that the Czechs were mobilized and ready for any emergency. 'The Germans, on the other hand,' he added, 'have not moved.' Any frontier incident 'engineered by the Czechs' would result in blame falling upon the Germans, and a predictable anti-German stance by the British government.[84]

Such 'Czechophobia' was far from confined to the extreme Right or established pro-German circles. It was a prominent line, for instance, in the wide-circulation newspapers the *Daily Express* and the *Daily Mail*. Sympathy for the Sudeten Germans mingled with isolationist fears of becoming involved in a war, according to one letter to *The Times*, 'to uphold an artificial State which reproduces in a small area all the mixture of races of the old Austro-Hungarian Empire'.[85]

It was August before the crisis started to become acute. Soothing noises had been heard in July from a German emissary, when Captain Fritz Wiedemann, one of Hitler's adjutants, had come to London with emphatic assurances that the German government 'was planning no resort to force'.[86] On 3 August, Chamberlain then sent his own representative, Lord Runciman, on a protracted exploratory visit to Czechoslovakia with the unpromising remit of trying to persuade the Czechoslovak government to make concessions to the Sudeten Germans. Unsurprisingly, it turned out to be fruitless. And by the time Runciman's report was published, Czechoslovakia had been carved up.[87] Not long after the envoy had departed on his delicate mission, the situation began to deteriorate and ominous signs to accumulate that a German attack on Czechoslovakia in the early autumn was likely. Anxieties in the British population that the crisis would end in war now started to grow sharply. In Germany, a veritable 'war psychosis' was felt over the following weeks as fears of war became acute. The worries were not confined to ordinary people. The German Ambassador in London, Herbert von Dirksen, warned that, while the British government was prepared to go a long way to accommodate the peaceful attainment of German aims, if Germany used force in the Czechoslovakian crisis 'England would without doubt march alongside France to war'.[88] Leading figures in the German army's General Staff greatly feared such an eventuality and thought Germany could not win a war against the western powers which would inevitably ensue from an attack on Czechoslovakia. In mid-August, the Chief of the General Staff, responsible for army strategy, General Ludwig Beck, resigned. Of the top Nazi leadership, Göring more than anyone feared the consequences of general European war, which Germany was not yet ready to face, breaking out over Czechoslovakia.[89]

On 23 August, Göring wrote a long letter to Londonderry, the longest he had sent him. He was, he said, writing 'in confidence as one friend to another', and his words contained 'no deception or falseness'. Göring knew full well, however, that Londonderry was in the habit of passing his letters to important figures in the British government. He had used Londonderry as a conduit before. This was his purpose now. Göring had been behind the sending of Wiedemann to London in July to see Lord Halifax in the hope of heading off war. The letter to Londonderry was, if a less significant and direct approach, nevertheless intended to send a message to the British government. As Chamberlain commented a few weeks later, 'it was interesting because it repeated in almost identical terms what Hitler said to me'.[90]

The letter was ostensibly a reply to a complaint by Londonderry that a publisher in Essen was unwilling to publish a translation of his book.[91] Göring's intervention, so he was now writing to tell Londonderry, had removed any obstacles; the book could be published.[92] He then turned to the main reason why he was writing. After rehearsing the regular complaint of the damage caused by criticism of German internal affairs in the British press, he repeated Hitler's desire for friendship with Britain and the lack of any opposition in Germany to a strong British Empire. He then voiced his concern at the lack of understanding in Britain for the position of the Sudeten Germans, attacking the Czechs – a 'not very highly cultured race' – and suggesting that they wanted a war in order to gain assistance from the western powers in preventing an increase in German strength. And behind Czechoslovakia, he added, was Russia (bound by treaty to lend her support if attacked, and whose troops, he feared, might be

MAKING FRIENDS WITH HITLER

allowed to cross Rumanian soil to attack from the east, should hostilities begin).[93] Germany's sole concern, he continued, was to uphold the interests of the Sudeten Germans. 'Nobody in Germany thinks of attacking Czechoslovakia', he claimed, 'if she is sensible enough in her treatment of the Sudeten Germans and in the restoration of their rights.' Once the Sudeten question was solved, 'Germany would have no further ambitions in Europe'. If Britain could simply accept German rights in this issue, and 'get used to regarding Germany as possessing equal status in all things', there was no reason why friendly relations between the two countries could not be established and the spectre of war banished completely. 'Let us both promise, dear Lord Londonderry,' he concluded, 'to do everything in order to rule out this possibility for ever.'[94]

Londonderry duly passed the letter to Halifax, doubting there was anything in it that he had not heard before. The Foreign Secretary had it translated before sending a copy to Henderson, and another, it appears, to Chamberlain, then politely thanking Londonderry for letting him see it.[95] But Londonderry was right: Halifax had heard it all before. The letter contained nothing new.

IV

By now, the crisis over Czechoslovakia was boiling up. German troop movements in the middle of August were seen as a warning. An offer by the Czech President, Beneš, in early September fleetingly looked to provide a possible way of defusing the situation by granting partial autonomy to the Sudeten Germans. But Hitler remained aggressively unbending. War seemed ever more likely. Halifax, maintaining the strategy of keeping Hitler guessing about British intentions, issued a statement that Britain would stand by France in a general conflict, at the same time as the French were again made aware that they could not rely upon armed British support.[96] Meanwhile, powerful voices supported a political solution – meaning, in effect, pressure to ensure the Czechs gave in to German demands. Most notably, *The Times*, known to have the ear of the British government, recommended in early September that

Czechoslovakia cede the Sudetenland to Germany.[97] A week later, on 14 September, Chamberlain told the Cabinet of his decision, already taken more than a fortnight earlier without consultation, to go to Germany to meet Hitler. No minister objected to the meeting, though the eventual outcome, short of war, could only have been foreseen as an almost inevitable transfer of territory to Germany.[98] By this time, Hitler had violently denounced the Czechs and threatened German intervention in his closing speech at the Reich Party Rally in Nuremberg, martial law had been declared in some parts of the Sudetenland, the British Ambassador in Berlin, Nevile Henderson, was warning of imminent German attack and urging the British government to put pressure on Beneš to stop 'haggling', and it was plain that the French did not want to fight.[99]

On 15 September, Chamberlain flew to Germany for the hastily arranged meeting with Hitler that he had requested (to the German dictator's astonishment), at the Berghof in the mountains above Berchtesgaden. Chamberlain offered, in order to stave off war, to consult his Cabinet colleagues on an agreement providing self-determination for the Sudeten Germans, and, when he had done so, to meet Hitler again. Hitler was pleased at the outcome, feeling he had forced Chamberlain into cession of the Sudetenland. For his part, Chamberlain told the Cabinet on his return that Hitler's objectives were 'strictly limited' to the Sudeten problem and that it would be wrong to go to war to prevent self-determination for the Sudeten Germans. Privately, he told his sister that Hitler 'was a man who could be relied upon when he had given his word'.[100]

He was rapidly disabused of such confidence. The Cabinet had agreed to a transfer of territory, without a plebiscite, though with a guarantee of the new borders of Czechoslovakia. But at the start of their next meeting, on 22 September in the Rhineland resort Bad Godesberg, to Chamberlain's dismay, Hitler increased his demands and threatened immediate occupation of the Sudetenland before eventually backing down at least on the immediacy of action and agreeing on 1 October as the deadline. Yet even now Chamberlain felt able to report back to his Cabinet his belief 'that Herr Hitler was speaking the truth' in claiming he wanted 'racial unity' with the Sudeten Germans, not the domination of Europe. Hitler, the Prime

Minister said, was extremely anxious to secure Great Britain's friendship. He thought 'it would be a great tragedy if we lost this opportunity of reaching an understanding with Germany on all points of difference between the two countries', and that 'a peaceful settlement of Europe depended on an Anglo-German understanding'. Meanwhile, military strength should be built up as a deterrent to German aggression.[101]

In a more hard-headed way, certainly, and clearly without the pro-German intonation, Chamberlain's position had now come close to that so strongly advocated by Londonderry for years, and most directly adumbrated in his statements of November 1934. It was little wonder, then, that in mid-September Londonderry had felt optimistic for the first time in many months at the news that Chamberlain would fly to Germany to meet Hitler. It was, after all, what he had always wanted and, from his point of view, a first, if belated, sign of hope for a new course of British policy towards Germany. 'I have always been anxious, as you know, that this visit should take place, and I feel that nothing but good can come of it,' he told Göring.[102]

Londonderry would have been less sanguine had he witnessed the Cabinet deliberations that followed Chamberlain's account of his second meeting with Hitler, at Bad Godesberg. For the first time, the Prime Minister now encountered opposition, at first tentative than hardening, among his Cabinet colleagues – and articulated, of all people, by the unlikely figure of the Foreign Secretary himself, Lord Halifax, usually the prime seeker of the consensual get-out clause and hitherto Chamberlain's most loyal lieutenant. The Godesberg demands by Hitler had, in Halifax's view, gone too far. They sounded like the diktat of a victorious war leader, and he thought it wrong to put pressure on the Czechs to accept. The French, too, now appeared to prefer the risk of war to concurring in the 'strangulation of a people'. It was eventually agreed that Chamberlain should send his special adviser, Sir Horace Wilson, with a personal appeal of the Prime Minister to Hitler, underpinned by the warning of military action if Czechoslovakia were to be attacked. Hitler was unyielding. Wilson, with Chamberlain's support, recommended nevertheless that the Czechs should be pressurized into allowing German occupation of the areas they were demanding. Halifax said it sounded like complete capitulation to Germany. Chamberlain backed down. War now seemed certain.[103]

It was averted only when Mussolini intervened on 28 September, favouring a four-power conference. Hitler was aware that few, even in the Nazi leadership, thought the risk of war with the western powers was worth taking when so many German demands on the Sudetenland could be satisfied by diplomatic means. Mussolini's intercession, prompted by Göring, allowed him a volte-face. He took the chance to climb down without loss of face and agreed to invite Chamberlain and Daladier, as well as the Italian dictator, to a conference at Munich the following day. Chamberlain was speaking in the House of Commons as the news of Hitler's concession was given to him. He immediately announced it, and the packed House erupted in tumultuous cheering. One MP present, a Chamberlain admirer, wrote that he felt 'sick with enthusiasm, longed to clutch him'. It was 'a scene of riotous delight' as members of the House of Commons 'cheered, bellowed their approval. We stood on our benches, waved our order papers, shouted – until we were hoarse – a scene of indescribable enthusiasm. Peace must now be saved, and with it the world.'[104] Sir John Simon, at the time Chancellor of the Exchequer, later said he had seen nothing like it in over thirty years in the House of Commons.[105] 'Speeches of congratulation came from every side, and when they were finished, members of all parties crowded past the Front Bench to shake Chamberlain's hand. All the party leaders joined in the Te Deum of praise,' was how Sir Samuel Hoare remembered the occasion.[106] Both the Labour leader, Clement Attlee, and the Liberal leader, Sir Archibald Sinclair, gave their support to Chamberlain's mission. Attlee at least declared that peace should be preserved 'without sacrificing principles', and privately informed Chamberlain of Labour's objections to further Czech sacrifices.[107] But both he and Sinclair knew full well what was at stake; that peace would be saved only at the expense of the Czechs.[108]

Two days later, with few alterations – mainly minor German concessions to extend the date of the occupation to spread over ten days, down to 10 October, and internationally supervised plebiscites (never, in the event, held) in some areas – the Godesberg demands were enshrined in the Munich Agreement of the four powers. Chamberlain returned home clutching a worthless piece of paper that, after the formalities of the Agreement, he had presented for Hitler's signature – given without more than the merest glance – expressing the 'desire of our two peoples never to go to war again'. In an unguarded moment, swept away by the enthusiasm of the crowds greeting the hero's return, Chamberlain announced he had secured 'peace for our time'.[109]

It had been bought, however temporarily, at the price of buying off the bully by sacrificing the weakling. The Munich Agreement had been morally repugnant and, in reality, politically humiliating for Britain. It had also left the rest of Czechoslovakia helpless and defenceless, had given Hitler another triumph without bloodshed, and had undermined the nascent internal opposition to the Nazi regime. Two years later, those in the British government who pursued the path of appeasement that led to Munich, Chamberlain in the vanguard, were polemically branded 'guilty men'.[110] Yet at the time that the British Prime Minister had returned from the carve-up of Czechoslovakia, the nation had rejoiced. Little over a week earlier, only 10 per cent of those asked, according to one poll, had favoured peace at any price while 40 per cent had thought Chamberlain's policy was wrong.[111] But now, as he drove back from the airport on his way to meet the King at Buckingham Palace, crowds lined the streets 'with people of every class shouting themselves hoarse, leaping on the running-board, banging on the windows and thrusting their hands into the car to be shaken'.[112] *The Times* trumpeted its view that 'no conqueror returning from a victory on the battlefield had come adorned with nobler laurels'.[113] The Prime Minister received over 40,000 letters of congratulation – among them one from the pacifist former leader of the Labour Party, George Lansbury – and countless gifts from admirers.[114] Only one minister – Duff Cooper, as First Lord of the Admiralty – resigned, though made little stir in doing so.[115] Relief at avoiding what had seemed an inevitable and much dreaded war was the overwhelming sentiment. The shame at how that avoidance had been attained had yet to sink in for most people. It would not take long to do so. Only three days after returning in triumph, Chamberlain faced a House of Commons once more bitterly divided,

and severe criticism also from some on his own side.[116] Even before
the dust had started to settle on the Munich Agreement, the Labour
leader, Clement Attlee, was condemning the betrayal of the Czechs,
while Churchill portrayed Munich as 'the first foretaste of a bitter
cup'.[117]

Neither sentiment, of course, was shared by the pro-German
lobby. Here, relief mingled with the feeling that, at last, a start had
been made towards the understanding with Germany which alone
would secure lasting peace. If German aggression had been regrettable, it had nonetheless been understandable because of the failure
of the western powers, before this point, to right the territorial
wrongs of the post-war settlement. 'The Link', for instance, the outrightly pro-German organization (heavily laced with anti-Semitism
and fervent support for Nazism) founded the previous year 'to work
for friendship and a good understanding with Germany' believed
'that the Munich Agreement was nothing more than a rectification
of one of the most flagrant injustices of the Peace Treaties'.[118]
Londonderry did not associate himself with the overtly pro-Nazi
stance of 'The Link', though he had initially welcomed the foundation of the Ulster branch. Founded by the eccentric former admiral,
Sir Barry Domvile, the membership of 'The Link', in contrast to that
of the Anglo-German Fellowship, was largely middle-class. Retired
military men formed part of its constituency. At least one emeritus
professor of history, Sir Raymond Beazley, was a prominent member. Somewhat later, Lord Redesdale (father of the 'Mitford Girls'),
Lord Sempill, and, just before the war, the Duke of Westminster
became members.[119] But 'The Link' had little of an aristocratic
flavour. Lord Londonderry had been asked early in 1938 to be the
organization's president, but declined to be involved.[120] On Munich,
however, the stance adopted by 'The Link', seeing in the agreement
reached merely the righting of one of the wrongs of Versailles,
matched Londonderry's position. He was consequently prepared to
add his signature to the twenty-five others (including six members
of the council of 'The Link' and various extreme pro-Germanist
individuals) whose letter in this vein to *The Times* was published on
12 October 1938.[121]

Writing to Stanley Baldwin, and unable to resist an allusion to his treatment at the hands of the former Prime Minister, Londonderry commented that he had been disappointed 'to have felt most completely impotent during this crisis, when I know I was right, but was completely powerless, owing to my wrecked political position, to get anything across'.[122] He had been, however, so excited by the news of the four-power conference at Munich that, after joining the crowd of supporters (including the Cabinet) at Heston Airport, not far from London, to wish the Prime Minister well on his momentous mission, he decided to fly himself to the Bavarian capital, accompanied by his friend Ward Price, the *Daily Mail* journalist. He went, he said, in a private capacity 'as a tourist and onlooker' who wanted to experience the atmosphere in Munich on the occasion of the historic meeting, and to meet ordinary people. He also met some less than ordinary people – Göring and Ribbentrop. He met 'his German friends' by accident, he said, since he was staying at the same hotel as the French and German delegations. No discussions had been planned, and only superficial 'conversations' with Göring and Ribbentrop had taken place. A jubilant Göring thought, according to Londonderry's account, that the basis had been laid 'to establish peace for all time'. Ribbentrop, after Hitler the greatest 'hawk' on Czechoslovakia among the Nazi leaders, was, by contrast, in a sour mood. Londonderry parted from his former house-guest on rancorous terms and never saw him again. Even so, his spontaneous visit gave rise to further allegations at home (which he, of course, strenuously denied) that he was pro-German. 'I am astonished to find myself constantly described as a Fascist and a Nazi,' he declared, 'when, as a matter of fact, no one in this country has more consistently expressed himself as opposed to dictatorship in any form and wherever it exists.'[123] Though the vehemence of his denial was understandable – and justified, for Londonderry was indeed no Nazi or Fascist – the assertion of his consistent opposition to dictatorship was overdrawn, or at least in need of qualification. While he had indeed always stated that he preferred democracy as a form of government, especially for Britain, this had not hindered his repeated expressions of glowing admiration for Hitler, and also for Mussolini.[124]

Londonderry was, of course, among those who sent their warm congratulations to Chamberlain on his achievement in Munich. In the second edition of his book, which appeared in autumn 1938, shortly after Munich, with an updated section on the Czech crisis, he described the settlement as 'the fulfilment of all my hopes', and saw 'the international barometer' now as 'Set Fair'. 'I can only have the feeling of great happiness at this moment that all that I have advocated has been brought about in a moment of time,' he wrote. He hoped that the joint declaration of Chamberlain and Hitler that followed the Agreement would form 'a prelude to the greater settlement of all the outstanding international differences in Europe'.[125]

Privately, too, he felt, he wrote on the day after the Agreement had been signed, 'an element of great satisfaction'. Chamberlain had 'averted a terrible catastrophe'. The Prime Minister, he remarked, had returned 'with peace and honour'. His ire at those formerly in charge of the country's foreign affairs was, however, undiminished. 'Baldwin, Simon, and Anthony Eden ought to be hanged,' he declared. The strength of feeling, as always, denoted the resentment at the way his views had been ignored by the Foreign Office, and above all the way he had been put out into the cold by Baldwin. 'If only Baldwin and his friends had taken the advice which I endeavoured to give them four years ago,' he commented (thinking once more of his letters to Hailsham in November 1934 that had been 'brushed aside' by the Cabinet), 'it would not have been necessary for Neville Chamberlain to make the contact I have invariably advocated at the last minute of the eleventh hour.' On account of Baldwin's treatment of him, he wrote, he had been deprived of influence 'because ever since I left the Government, the Foreign Office have cold-shouldered me, and have refused even to consider the policy which I was advocating'. Now, at what he saw as the moment of triumph for the views he had for so long represented, he felt that he, too, deserved some of the credit for the 'right line' that had so belatedly been followed. He referred readers of *The Times* who shared 'the general feeling of thanksgiving' to his book.[126] He was flattered to receive a telegram of congratulations from the Duke of Westminster for his own hand in establishing contact between the leading statesmen of Europe. And he could not desist from noting that the Prime Minister of Northern Ireland, Lord Craigavon, had sent a telegram to Chamberlain but had 'never congratulated me on the very definite line which I have taken about Germany with no encouragement from official sources, and which has proved to be the right line'.[127] He had been decried as a pro-Nazi, he lamented, and his efforts had been 'practically ignored' with 'disastrous results'. At the last moment, his advice had been followed. But it would have been so much better three years earlier when Germany was far less powerful. Instead, 'we find ourselves thoroughly unequipped (and what the administration has been doing all these years I really do not know) and quite incapable of standing up to an aggressive Germany with any hope of immediate success', he complained.[128]

The search for recognition and rescue of his reputation was also unmistakable in a revealing letter which Londonderry sent, soon after Munich as the second edition of his book was under preparation, to H. Montgomery Hyde, his librarian and general factotum. Evidently, Hyde was drafting the additions to the text of the book, based upon 'reflections' sent to him by Londonderry. (Whether this had been the procedure for the first edition is unclear.) 'The fact that my efforts have been completely ineffective', Londonderry began by disingenuously claiming, 'has tickled my sense of humour rather than stimulated any feeling of irritation and annoyance.' Nevertheless, 'human nature being what it is', he promptly added, he wanted included in the new edition a comment to the effect 'that although I had tried very hard to persuade my ex-colleagues and friends, also the general public, as to what the correct policy was, I am quite convinced that my efforts are only known to a very few thousand people of the general public, who simply regard me as one who entertained von Ribbentrop here, and who received lavish entertainment from the Germans when I went to Germany'. The acknowledgement of his public image as a friend of the Nazis had doubtless been reinforced by the hostile comments on the Left about his visit to Germany at the time of the Munich Agreement, and his meetings there with Göring and Ribbentrop. Londonderry wanted the image correcting. 'The fact that I prophesied exactly what has happened, and the fact that I have advocated association of the four great Western Powers, is quite unknown to everybody except my few personal friends,' he reminded Hyde, adding, with reference to yet another perceived personal slight, 'and this is further emphasised by the fact that when I did write a letter to "The Times" [published on 3 October], it is put in a very bad position with my signature appearing on the back page.'[129]

V

For Londonderry, therefore, Munich represented a vindication of what he had been striving for. All too briefly, it appeared to denote the end of 'a terrible story of folly, pusillanimity, disastrous coalition spirit, and lack of conviction' in the National Government's foreign policy.[130] At the same time, the 'happiness' he felt at the gathering of the four powers in Munich that had marked, as he put it, the fulfilment of his hopes, was overladen by his continuing personal quest for belated recognition and the righting of, in his view, a wholly wronged reputation. Later, he was to look back on Munich as a complete failure, a lamentably missed opportunity, for which he blamed Chamberlain's lack of knowledge of 'German character when it came to international affairs'. Chamberlain had failed, he suggested, having managed to assemble in one room 'the representatives of the four great countries on whose word peace or war depended', to make anything of the chance to press them to 'place a veto on war altogether and decide to act in concert for the amelioration of the problems of the world'. Instead, he had been satisfied with Hitler's signature on 'a piece of paper proclaiming eternal friendship between Great Britain and Germany' – 'a veritable anti-climax'.[131]

None of these sentiments is obvious from Londonderry's recorded reactions at the time, or even a few weeks later in the passages on Munich added to the second edition of his book. But even taken at face value, the comments are bizarrely unrealistic. His criticism of Chamberlain's alleged lack of knowledge of German character in international affairs appears, from his less than clear analysis, derived from the 'firm speech' the Prime Minister made in the House of Commons, during the difficult debate immediately after Munich, where he found himself facing heated criticism from the Opposition. According to Londonderry, this speech 'unconsciously played into Hitler's hands' and allowed the German dictator to take advantage of what he claimed to be a repudiation of the agreement signed at Munich. In fact, the German leadership had taken little notice of Chamberlain's speech. He had 'nothing new' to say, Goebbels recorded.[132]

Londonderry also implied that Chamberlain had not taken a firm enough line with Hitler in the negotiations that led up to Munich, and had failed to realize that only demands backed by strength would be effective. This was, however, simply yet another way of saying that his own line of friendly accommodation accompanied by strength in rearmament had been correct all along. In September 1938, he had, as we have seen, welcomed Chamberlain's initiative, even recognizing that Britain was inevitably in a weaker negotiating position than she would have been some years earlier. Moreover, the notion that, having gathered at Munich to provide a diplomatic solution to the Sudeten crisis, the leaders of the four powers ought to have gone on to work out how to place 'a veto on war altogether' and taken a decision to tackle 'the problems of the world' was pure tilting at windmills.

Pointed in Londonderry's comments on Munich, both at the time and later, was the absence of any sense of moral injustice towards Czechoslovakia. Many of those cheering Chamberlain on his return had done so out of immediate and enormous relief that war had been averted coupled with the feeling that at least some time had been bought for Britain to be better prepared for a conflict which had been merely delayed, not prevented. Even these sentiments were almost immediately tempered, also among Chamberlain's admirers, by the uneasy sense that peace had been preserved – but that a grave injustice had been perpetrated which had deeply sullied Britain's name and moral standing. For the many who thought this way, Munich was at best a matter of choosing the lesser evil. There was none of this in Londonderry. Munich was in his eyes not a moral, but purely a political question. For him, appeasing Germany should have come several years earlier, when Britain was strong and Germany weak. A 'sensible' policy in his view would at that time have focused upon framing a four-power agreement of Britain, France, Italy and Germany aimed at rectifying the territorial demands of Germany which had been a product of an unjust post-war peace treaty and ensuring through recognition of rightful

18. Lord Londonderry (second from left) out shooting with Ribbentrop (right) at Wynyard, County Durham, in 1936. The former British Ambassador in Rome Sir Ronald Graham is on the left of the photograph, and behind Ribbentrop is Londonderry's son, Lord Castlereagh.

19. Viscount Rothermere, proprietor of the *Daily Mail*, vehemently anti-communist and a strong advocate of friendship with Germany, though also one of the most forceful proponents of rebuilding Britain's air defences, visiting Hitler at the Berghof, near Berchtesgaden, on 7 January 1937.

20. Sir Nevile Henderson, British Ambassador in Berlin and a keen huntsman, visiting Hermann Göring at the latter's hunting lodge at Rominten, in East Prussia, 3–5 October 1937. Henderson enjoyed his stay 'immensely' and 'had a real personal liking' for Göring.

21. Lord Londonderry leaving Londonderry House with his wife and daughter, Lady Mairi, to attend a ceremony of the Order of the Garter at Windsor Castle in 1937.

22. Hermann Göring, head of the Luftwaffe and second man in the Reich, who combined brutality and ruthlessness with charm and joviality, looking relaxed and contented in summer 1937.

23. Worlds apart: the British aristocrat and the Nazi 'strong man'. Lord Londonderry with Göring, during his visit to the Reich Hunting Master's country estate at Carinhall, north of Berlin, September 1937.

24. Londonderry taking coffee with Göring at Carinhall in September 1937 and listening intently as the head of the Luftwaffe explains some feature of his palatial hunting residence.

25. Cheering crowds greet Hitler (standing, in the front car) as his motorcade drives through Vienna on 15 March 1938, following the German annexation of Austria through the Anschluss.

26. Members of the Reichstag rise to salute Hitler, at the end of his speech on 18 March 1938, and euphorically acclaim his triumph in incorporating Austria into the Reich. Göring, as Reichstag President, is in the centre of the photograph. Rudolf Hess is on Hitler's right. Joseph Goebbels is second from the left on the same row.

27. The British Prime Minister, Neville Chamberlain, with Hitler (and between them the interpreter Paul Schmidt) during the second of their three crisis meetings, leaving the Hotel Dreesen on the banks of the Rhine at Bad Godesberg, near Bonn, on 22 September 1938. Hitler's new demands at the unsuccessful talks left Europe on the brink of war.

28. Ribbentrop speaks to the SS guard at Munich airport on the morning of 29 September 1938, just after the arrival of Neville Chamberlain to attend the Munich Conference, which would temporarily save the peace of Europe by carving up Czechoslovakia in the German interest.

29. Chamberlain waves to crowds in Munich, who warmly applaud him on account of his efforts to preserve peace. Hitler was later heard to remark sourly that the British Prime Minister had spoiled his entry into Prague.

30. The cover of the second edition of Lord Londonderry's book, *Ourselves and Germany*. A first hardback edition published just after the Anschluss had only limited circulation, but the book reached a much wider readership through the Penguin paperback version in autumn 1938, in which Londonderry lauded the Munich settlement as 'the fulfilment of all my hopes'.

31. Troops of the Wehrmacht enter the Sudetenland, the German-speaking part of Czechoslovakia, conceded to Germany by Britain and France at the Munich Conference, in October 1938.

32. German troops entering the gates of Hradcany Castle in March 1939, as Germany occupied the truncated remains of Czechoslovakia. Those, like Lord Londonderry, who had continued to believe in Hitler's good faith now finally had their eyes opened.

33. 'The Stormtrooper': a symbol of Lord
Londonderry's ill-fated links with Nazi leaders.
The porcelain figurine – a present from
Ribbentrop at the Whitsuntide visit in 1936 –
actually represents an SS man and stands on the
mantelpiece of what was Lord Londonderry's
study at Mount Stewart.

German claims and acknowledgement of her equality among the powers that the causes of her grievance were removed, thus enabling a platform for armaments limitation and the construction of European peace. Now, at last, the four-power conference had come about. But the circumstances were so drastically altered, given Germany's newly attained power and dominance, that, as he fully realized, the hopes vested in Munich might well swiftly evaporate. Just how swiftly the fragile expectations built on Munich would disintegrate would already become apparent over the following weeks.

For all that Londonderry criticized Chamberlain's presumed lack of knowledge of German character in international affairs, his own misreading of German intentions had been the underlying flaw in his conception of how British foreign policy should be framed. From the outset he had failed entirely – he was far from alone in this – to understand that, under Hitler, Germany's drive for expansion went far beyond revision of Versailles. The Foreign Office, which he repeatedly maligned, had actually recognized this as early as 1933. We have already noted some of the reasons why, nevertheless, so passive a foreign policy was pursued, culminating in the débâcle of Munich. Under an alternative foreign policy conducted along the lines proposed by Londonderry, a 'Munich' would not have occurred. But this is because Britain would have acquiesced in German territorial demands from the beginning. And along the way, her own power sapped, she would have been drawn gradually but inexorably ever more into the orbit of the most thrusting and dynamic power in Europe, whose thirst for expansion, far from being satiated, would have found an even firmer basis for her aim to dominate the Continent. There were still many, including Londonderry, who were not yet ready to see that Hitler meant unlimited conquest, not nationalist integration. But over the next months, Germany would start to reveal her true colours in ways which even Lord Londonderry would find difficult to justify.

6

End of the Dream

'Your best advocate, which I claim to have been, has been completely destroyed by his [Hitler's] policy having been shown to be quite impossible at the present time and probably for many years to come.'

Londonderry to Franz von Papen, 29 March 1939

'Since the invasion of Czechoslovakia, for which I can find no satisfactory reason, I have found it necessary to remain silent'.

Londonderry to the editor of the *Deutsche Allgemeine Zeitung*, 4 April 1939

For the millions in Great Britain who had rejoiced when Neville Chamberlain returned home from Munich at the beginning of October 1938, thinking peace had been secured – overlooking, ignoring or swallowing the shameful and humiliating price that had been paid – the following six months would shatter the illusions. Thereafter, resignation that war was inevitable generally set in. The widespread rejoicing that followed Munich was understandable, if misplaced. It was largely a spontaneous and shortlived expression of relief that there would be no war. This soon gave way to a myriad of emotions about what had happened at Munich, ranging from shame and moral outrage to praise and admiration for what Chamberlain had achieved. Above all, the sense of relief that war had been averted rapidly evaporated.

For a smaller, but vociferous, sector of opinion, appeasement had not been a policy of desperation – an urgent quest to avoid war at practically any cost (and at the expense of others) arising from a recognition of Britain's weakness – but a desired aim from the beginning. Here, the joy at Munich was not so much from relief as from the feeling that at long last an accommodation of Germany's just claims had been reached. Munich in this view was not a political and moral humiliation for Britain, but the crowning glory of a policy which ought to have been followed much earlier and, even now, held out hope of a future based upon close cooperation between Britain and Germany. This approximated to Lord Londonderry's position. Despite his reputation as Britain's leading apologist for Nazi Germany, Londonderry never belonged to or had any truck with the more outlandish, freakish and eccentric pro-Nazi and racist lobbies, some of them finding voice in the strongly pro-German organization 'The Link'. These continued undeterred in their enthusiasm for Hitler's Reich despite the unmistakable indications of Nazi barbarities and the ominously gathering storm clouds over Europe.[1]

For Londonderry, Munich represented a highly positive and promising step in British foreign policy not just because at the last minute, seemingly, an almost certain war had been averted, but because it offered a new start – along the lines he had been advocating for years – for British foreign policy. However belatedly, it was wholly to be welcomed as a fresh opening for improved Anglo-German relations as the basis of a solid European peace resting upon the international agreement of the major powers. However, just as the spontaneous feelings of relief and unreflected hopes for peace of millions of ordinary citizens would soon be destroyed by further unequivocal signs of Hitler's aggressive intent, Londonderry's more coolly reasoned, ideologically and politically rooted stance was in subsequent months to be entirely undermined. Though, as we shall see, at the eleventh hour, just before war began, he would still hold out a lingering belief that his personal intercession might save peace through, presumably, another 'Munich', his dream of helping to establish the basis for lasting friendship and cooperation between Great Britain and Germany had been effectively ended some months earlier. Already in autumn 1938 the gloom which had only temporarily left him returned as he began to see Munich as a lost opportunity – a real chance of peace which was not being consolidated and built upon. And within weeks the 'Crystal Night' pogrom – the orgy of violence against Germany's Jews on 9–10 November 1938 – and its deeply damaging effect on British public opinion towards Germany provided further disillusionment of the hopes of creating a basis of friendship and understanding with Hitler's regime. But decisive above all else in destroying the dream was Hitler's entry into Prague in March 1939. Not only, as was the case with so many people who had hitherto been prepared to accept Nazi expansionist claims based upon revision of the Versailles Treaty and integration of ethnic Germans in the Reich, did the scales finally fall from his eyes; he now became fully aware that after years of defending German actions, he had no arguments left. Hitler's blatant aggression towards what was left of Czechoslovakia had destroyed them, along with Londonderry's dreams of engineering peace resting upon Anglo-German understanding.

I

A month or so after the Munich Agreement, Londonderry had not given up hope that it might prove the first step in 'a new orientation of our foreign policy' along the lines he had so often advocated. He spoke bitterly of Stanley Baldwin's 'ineptitude during the vital period' and 'criminal neglect of foreign affairs'. He was certain that 'History' would condemn him along with Ramsay MacDonald ('in a very difficult position') and Sir John Simon ('no knowledge whatsoever of foreign affairs'), pointing out again that Baldwin had ignored him when he had gained 'remarkable contacts with German leaders in 1936'.[2] Londonderry felt he understood the German position, and the mentality behind it, much better than those directing foreign policy in the British government. 'I find myself so often in sympathy with Hitler,' he wrote to the European affairs specialist on *The Times*, the veteran journalist A. L. Kennedy, on 29 October 1938. 'I know his history, and the dangers and difficulties through which he has passed and the tremendous successes which he has achieved. He has done this entirely by himself, and with no sympathy, understanding or assistance from this country.' However, Londonderry was aware, he added, that Hitler was now 'gradually getting back to the theories which he evolved in prison', when working on *Mein Kampf*, 'that might is right'.[3]

Based upon an understanding of life as one continual struggle, the logical outcome, Londonderry recognized (as he remarked in another letter written on the same day, 29 October), was war, 'the most powerful illustration of this theory'. In the light of the disasters and humiliation which had befallen their country, Hitler and Göring had felt 'compelled to adopt methods which certainly shock the feelings of civilised nations' in their attempt to regain international standing and self-respect for Germany. He himself, he stated, had been completely misrepresented in Britain – something he deeply resented – and his efforts to improve Anglo-German relations gravely misunderstood. Far from being the ardent pro-Nazi of his public portrayal, he was 'entirely opposed to dictatorship in any form, whether Naziism [sic], Fascism, or Bolshevism' and deplored German methods.[4] But the problem of coming to terms with the Germans had to be faced, however their system of government was viewed. He had, he said, effectively restating his position in the Hailsham letters of November 1934, 'wanted to get hold of the Germans when they were weak[,] in the sense that[,] if they were amenable, we should be able to establish some valuable understanding, and if we realised that they were not amenable, we could have held them in subjection for a generation at least'. But in the meantime 'everything which I feared has come about. The Germans are strong and arrogant, and now we have to come to some arrangement in circumstances in which we have a great deal the worst of the situation.' He acknowledged that there was no limit to the demands of 'an overbearing and arrogant race'.[5]

He concluded that the only way forward was through a

close association of the four great Western Powers, to devise an international policy which will settle all the racial controversies which exist at the present moment and which were aggravated by the unfortunate Treaty of Versailles, and in so doing establish a world-wide order, which, realising the futility of war, will enable us to enter an era of spiritual amelioration and commercial prosperity.[6]

A four-power conference, he suggested, could 'first of all settle the questions of peace and war, the reduction and limitation of armaments, and the whole question of currency and exchange', before turning to working out a solution to the colonial question.[7] It was quite an agenda. Even as he wrote the words, Londonderry sensed how unreal it all sounded. 'I know this must sound like a dream', he wrote, 'but I am quite sure that we should place this ideal in front of us'. What this amounted to in tangible, political terms was to back Chamberlain as 'the man who has averted war, and has established these contacts and brought about a definite association of the four great Western Powers'.[8]

Londonderry's assessment of the dynamic of German expansionism, the pyschological driving-force behind it, and the current weakness of Britain when contemplating how Hitler could be halted, or at least contained, was not unperceptive. But where some, most prominently Winston Churchill (though he still lacked much of a following), concluded that the only hope was to prepare for inevitable war with the utmost speed since there could be no successful bargaining with Hitler, Londonderry persisted in arguing that war was even now not inevitable, and could be averted if the foundations laid at Munich were strengthened. As he himself acknowledged, this was starting to sound ever more 'like a dream', and would appear even more fanciful over the following weeks and months.

The sharp political differences between Londonderry and Churchill found expression in late October at a social gathering at Grillion's, an exclusive London dining-club much favoured by the rich and famous. Summarizing the differences a few months later, Londonderry said Churchill thought war was inevitable, constantly demanded rearmament, and, he believed, 'would have welcomed a preventive war'. His own view was 'that it was best to try first and make friends with Germany, and, in any case, to establish the limitation of armaments'.[9] At Grillion's, Churchill evidently subjected his cousin to a verbal fusillade which left Londonderry 'wounded' and 'unhappy'. Londonderry insisted, perversely, that he and Churchill were 'on the same lines' and differed only as to method. He again claimed that he hated Nazism as he did Bolshevism and Fascism, and 'never liked the Germans as Germans', but wanted to contain them while they were weak as Castlereagh and Wellington had done with the beaten French in 1815. He had foreseen the disasters that had resulted from a gravely mistaken foreign policy. He now found his own policy carried out by Chamberlain at the eleventh hour. There had been no alternative. But the real chance had been missed four years earlier.[10] Churchill replied, expressing his 'deepest anxiety' about the immediate future, saying that Londonderry's policy was 'certainly being tried', and that there was nothing for it but 'to await the results of Chamberlain's hopes and experiment'.[11]

Londonderry persisted in trying to diminish the difference between his view and that of Churchill. 'The only difference that I can see between us', he wrote,

is that I wanted to get hold of the Germans when they were weak and practically defenceless and try to make them good members of the comity of nations as Castlereagh did with France, and you on the other hand never believed that policy could succeed. I do not know who was right but my policy was never tried until it was, I regret to say it, too late. Now I expect our thoughts follow the same line.

He agreed that 'the future is indeed gloomy', but repeated that it was necessary to support Chamberlain.[12] Churchill again replied, and with an indirect criticism of Londonderry's time as Air Minister, no doubt prompted by his cousin's reassertion that he presumed the main difference between them rested on their interpretation of the figures for the German air force in 1935 and that he had been correct all along in his assessment of its strength. Churchill remained adamant: 'I am quite sure that there never was and there never will be any chance of a satisfactory arrangement between the German Nazi party and the British nation, and I am very sorry that we did not begin to arm on a great scale, especially in the air, when the menace of this violent party first appeared.' He feared that Chamberlain's future policy entailed surrendering the colonies and a disarmament convention with Hitler which would 'stereotype our lamentable inferiority in the Air'. He thought Chamberlain was not serious about rearmament.[13]

During this exchange of letters between Londonderry and Churchill – not that a single sentence hinted at it – Nazi hatred of Jews had thrown off all constraints in an explosion of violence on an infamous night of undiluted savagery and devastation: 'Crystal Night' (*Reichskristallnacht*), so called in irony because of the amount of broken glass from Jewish shop-windows littering the streets of Berlin and other cities on the night of 9–10 November 1938. Hundreds of synagogues were burnt down; Jewish shops and other properties were wrecked; close to a hundred Jews were killed, according to official tabulations; many more committed suicide out of terror, and thousands of others were gravely maltreated; some 30,000 male Jews were rounded up in the course of the 'action' and placed in concentration camps as a device to raise foreign funds for their removal from the country. Jewish emigration swelled to a torrent as fearful refugees fled in terror to whichever countries would have them. Those remaining were now reduced to dire penury – pariahs on the fringes of German society, shunned by almost all, their livelihood removed, whatever resources they had still retained robbed by a vengeful state.

The night of horror had been waiting to happen. Ever since the Anschluss had unleashed new extremes of anti-Semitic violence on the streets of Vienna and other Austrian cities, the Nazi persecution of the Jews had entered an even more menacing phase. Pressure to force Jews out of economic life and take over their properties – 'Aryanization' as it was called – formed part of the background. Another strand was the desire of the regime to speed up emigration and force an international readiness to accept more expelled Jews. And behind it all was the ideological drive to make Germany 'Jew-free'. With Jews repeatedly portrayed by Nazi propaganda (and mirroring what Hitler actually thought) as a mighty international, war-mongering threat to Germany – the power behind both Bolshevism in Moscow and capitalism in the City of London and New York's Wall Street – it was little wonder that as tension over the Sudetenland grew during the summer months of 1938 and war seemed ever more imminent, the wave of anti-Semitism intensified. Attacks on Jewish property and anti-Semitic vandalism, directed far more than in earlier years at synagogues and Jewish cemeteries, became commonplace as the summer wore on. Once the Munich Agreement then demonstrated the weakness of the western powers, there was even less need to rein in anti-Jewish outrages on diplomatic grounds. The cauldron of anti-Semitism was simmering close to boiling point when a Legation Secretary in the German Embassy in Paris, Ernst vom Rath, was shot by a young Jew, Herschel Grynspan (whose parents had been brutally deported to Poland by the Nazis a short time earlier) on 7 November, succumbing to his injuries two days later. With Hitler's express approval, the Reich Propaganda Minister Joseph Goebbels then fired up the representatives of the Nazi Party gathered in Munich to celebrate the fifteenth anniversary of Hitler's attempted Putsch of 1923 with a peppery speech inciting Nazi activists to avenge vom Rath's death by turning their fury on to the Jews. The consequence was the 'Night of Crystal' as the synagogues burned the length and breadth of Germany.

Shock waves of horror reverberated around the western world. Was such a thing possible in a modern, economically advanced country steeped in culture? Unfortunately, it was. Culture, as the experience of countries other than Germany has demonstrated, was no barrier to barbarism. 'No foreign propagandist bent upon blaspheming Germany before the world could outdo the tale of burning and beating, of blackguardly assaults upon defenceless and innocent people, which disgraced that country yesterday,' declared *The Times*. 'A pogrom hardly surpassed in fury since the dark ages,' was how the *News Chronicle* put it.[14] The condemnation ran throughout the British press,[15] mirroring attitudes in France and in the USA. 'There is in this country a general desire to be on friendly terms with the German nation,' wrote the Archbishop of Canterbury, Cosmo Gordon Lang, an advocate of friendship with Germany, in a letter to *The Times* on 12 November. 'But there are times when the mere instincts of humanity make silence impossible. Would that the rulers of the Reich could realize that such excesses of hatred and malice put upon the friendship which we are ready to offer them an almost intolerable strain.'[16] Public opinion in Britain was horrified. More than four out of five of those questioned told a Gallup Poll that they thought the persecution of the Jews was 'an obstacle to the good understanding between Britain and Germany'. Government and Opposition supporters did not differ in their views.[17]

The revulsion was also felt in the upper echelons of British government. The Foreign Office was made fully aware of the depths of depravity plumbed in the night of horror. 'I can find no words strong enough in condemnation of the disgusting treatment of so many innocent people,' was the explicit message in one dispatch from

Berlin, from George Ogilvie-Forbes, deputizing for Nevile Henderson while the Ambassador was at home on sick-leave.[18] The Foreign Secretary, Lord Halifax, despite his admission in later life to a friend that he had 'always been rather anti-Semitic', was appalled at the vicious barbarism of the Nazi hordes.[19] He used it to reinforce the view on British foreign policy which he had first taken in September, distancing himself from Chamberlain and reversing his earlier stance on appeasement, that the time had come to correct 'the false impression that we were decadent, spineless and could with impunity be kicked about'.[20] Remarkably, Sir Nevile Henderson, writing from his sick-bed in England, but with no loss of his acquired knack of putting his foot in any foreign policy initiative he recommended, chose precisely this moment, immediately following the 'Crystal Night' outrage, to suggest that the time was now ripe to make a comprehensive offer to return former German colonies.[21] This scarcely fitted Halifax's new determination to avoid further concessions to German expansionism. 'No useful purpose would be served', Halifax told the Foreign Policy Committee on 14 November, 'by a resumption at the present time of the contemplated Anglo-German conversations'.[22]

Chamberlain's reaction to 'Crystal Night' differed in some respects from that of Halifax. He was also repelled by the 'barbarities', as he described them in a letter to his sister Hilda on 13 November.[23] He publicly voiced 'deep and widespread sympathy for those who are being made to suffer' for 'the senseless crime committed in Paris'.[24] And his contribution to easing admission to Britain from Jewish refugees fleeing from Germany was, it appears, greater than was once thought.[25] Clearly, however, as was the case with Halifax, the foreign policy implications rather than the plight of the Jews were his main concern. He chose not to speak in the parliamentary debate on 21 November on the Jewish refugee issue.[26] He agreed to action to help the Jews, but only 'to ease the public conscience', and only if it did not entail economic sanctions against Germany.[27] And, in the aftermath of the pogrom, he was disturbed and depressed at the tirades against Britain in the German press and the absence of the merest gesture of friendship emanating from the Nazi leadership.[28] But whereas Halifax thought that the policy of placating the Nazi leadership had run its course, Chamberlain still thought the 'moderates' in Germany might restrain Hitler, and was unaltered in his commitment to appeasement.[29] For him, the direst consequence of 'Crystal Night' was that 'our policy of appeasement must for the time being be put on the shelf'.[30]

This was the common view among supporters of appeasement (whose numbers had declined fairly sharply since the shortlived exhilaration on Chamberlain's return from Munich).[31] The German Ambassador in London, Herbert von Dirksen, also recognized, as he told the Foreign Ministry in Berlin, that, following the pogrom, support for friendship between Britain and Germany had diminished and Chamberlain's position had become more difficult, so that prospects of a rapprochement had for the time being come to an end.[32] Though depressed, Chamberlain had not given up hope that the Germans would see sense, and that appeasement would lead to a peaceful outcome for Europe. He thought that, as at Munich, the way to German moderation might be through intercession from Mussolini.[33] Unless the Germans could be 'induced, in partnership with others, to improve the general lot', he wrote in December, 'there will be neither peace nor progress in Europe in the things that make life worth living'. But his attitude was hardening. 'It takes two to make an agreement . . . I am still waiting for a sign from those who speak for the German people'.[34]

This corresponded, broadly speaking, to Londonderry's view on relations with Germany following the 'Crystal Night' atrocities. In contrast to the alacrity with which he had rushed to comment publicly, and favourably, on Hitler's major foreign-policy coups – the Rhineland, Austria, the Sudetenland – he reacted with initial silence to the horror of the pogrom. One minor way of publicly indicating his disgust at the Nazi barbarity would have been to resign from the Anglo-German Fellowship, which in the wake of the pogrom was to lose 50 per cent of its membership over the next few weeks. Even the Fellowship's Chairman, Lord Mount Temple, whose first wife had been Jewish, took the step of resigning at least his office – though not his membership – in protest.[35] But there is no indication that Londonderry was among those who resigned.[36] We have already noted his ingrained antipathy towards Jews; but also his dismay at the ferocity of Nazi persecution. He simply could not understand this aspect of Nazism, since it was so evidently damaging to Germany's good name abroad, and to the chances of the friendship with Britain on which Europe's future in his view depended.

It amounted, of course, though Londonderry was far from alone in not recognizing this plainly at the time, to a complete misreading of the essence of Nazism. Londonderry continued, naively, to believe that Hitler wanted peace. In reality, Hitler wanted, with or without British support, an empire based upon racial dominance. It was this crucial misunderstanding of the core doctrine of Nazism, more than any innate prejudice against the Jews, that led Londonderry even now to view the appalling events of 'Crystal Night' more in sorrow than in anger. It would be unjust to suggest that he was left unmoved by the plight of the Jews. He was concerned with what was happening in Germany, he told one correspondent, since he detested any form of persecution.[37] To another, he said (though without explicit reference to the pogrom) that at the present moment, in November 1938, he was 'rather anxious to have no communication whatsoever with the German authorities'.[38] His main response, much like Chamberlain's, was, however, less one of outrage at the inhumanity of the terrible pogrom than depression at its effects on the chances of salvaging the basis of friendship and understanding between Britain and Germany which had fleetingly seemed within grasp after Munich.

In a speech on 13 December 1938, Londonderry did, however, at last make explicit his condemnation of the pogrom, in the context of its consequences for a possible settlement of the 'colonial question'. Londonderry approved, he said, of the government's determination to make no colonial concessions to Germany at the present time, though presumed the matter could be resolved quite easily within the framework of a wider settlement. 'Now, unfortunately,' he went on,

all these matters were complicated in view of the terrible persecution of the Jews which continued in Germany, and at this time we could not in any circumstances hand over any populations which looked to us for protection and guidance to the tender mercies of a country which seemed disposed to exterminate [!] a section of its population, or to allow them to live in conditions of such a barbarous character as to call for the condemnation of every right-minded man or woman throughout the civilized world.

He referred to the 'grievous disappointment' which Hitler's policy had brought to so many people during the past year, and 'had caused us to condemn a persecution which appeared to be so medieval in its ferocity, so unjustified by any information we could obtain, and so antagonistic to that friendly international understanding without which all efforts towards a higher standard of living and cultural and material progress must inevitably come to a standstill'. He made it plain, nevertheless, despite this unequivocal condemnation, that the events of 'Crystal Night' were an unwelcome interruption, but not an end, to efforts at friendship with Germany. 'The peace of the world depended on a real Anglo-German understanding,' he declared, 'and the sooner we could clear away those misunderstandings and establish international confidence, the sooner should we find ourselves on the high road to peace and prosperity.'[39]

Despite implying that he wanted to avoid contact with the German leadership, and only following considerable reflection, he decided, in fact, to write a lengthy letter to Göring, on 24 November 1938, in which he specifically brought up the question of the persecution of the Jews. The letter was couched in tones of regret more than denunciation. It was on the seventh page of the typed ten-page letter, following a protracted recitation of his own efforts to bring about friendship between Britain and Germany and lamentation of the government's failure to exploit the positive personal contacts he had made, that he finally raised Nazi policy towards the Jews. And this was only to remind Göring, as he had warned the previous year during his visit to Carinhall, of its 'unfortunate repercussions' on international opinion. Even the force of this point became diluted as Londonderry moved on to deplore the attacks on Britain in the German press. It was almost at the end of the letter that Londonderry eventually reached the November pogrom. He began the passage again by voicing his lack of comprehension for what had taken place. 'I am completely at a loss to understand your policy towards the Jews,' he wrote. 'While deploring the terrible tragedy on the part of a demented young man which took place at your Embassy in Paris, I cannot feel that it is possible to justify the imposing of penalties on that account on a whole community, but', he added in a remarkable qualification to this somewhat mild stricture, 'I would not venture to argue that particular point with you'. He went on, instead, to disagree that this was a matter of internal politics – something he had in earlier years accepted – since the expulsion of Jews obviously had international implications. He concluded by mentioning the impact on his own position:

I was able for so long to reply to any arguments put forward by those who have never had any belief that Germany had any desire to become a helpful partner in the comity of nations, but in relation to your treatment of the Jews I have no reply whatsoever, and all I can do is to remain silent and take no further part in these matters, in which most people in this country are thinking my opinions have been wrong from the beginning.[40]

Göring by now had little interest in Londonderry, or his views on the persecution of the Jews. When he did reply, in January 1939, it was simply to counter attacks on the persecution of the Jews by claiming hypocrisy on the part of the western democracies that continued to have 'the best and most official relations with the Red Spanish government' which had, he said, presided over the murder and torture of priests in Spain.[41]

The furore in Britain about 'Crystal Night' rapidly subsided.[42] The pogrom had certainly had a negative impact upon relations with Germany. Sir Nevile Henderson, writing in a despondent frame of mind to Londonderry in mid-December 1938 while convalescing at home in Lincolnshire after treatment for cancer, remarked that the peace of Europe could still only be found in an Anglo-German understanding, but 'today with England in the mood it is over the Jews' he did not see how this could be achieved.[43] Had Hitler shown himself more open to the understanding that Henderson (and Londonderry) wanted, there is little doubt that the British government would have pursued it, the pogrom notwithstanding. Serious though the effect had been, the deep pall of gloom which had once again settled over the British government after the fleeting hope presented by Munich was conditioned far more by Hitler's unbending militancy in foreign policy than by his barbaric persecution of the Jews.

II

As the ill-fated year 1938 drew to a close, Londonderry's despondency, momentarily dispelled after Munich, returned with a vengeance. He told the Duke of Windsor (the former King Edward VIII) he was 'looking very gloomily to the future, and hoping that Neville Chamberlain will be able to achieve what looks to be the impossible'.[44] His gloom made him all the more ready to pour out once more his bitter resentment at the way he had been treated in 1935 and at the way the policy he had advocated for four years had been deliberately and catastrophically ignored by those in responsible positions of government. He criticized the former Foreign Secretary, Sir Samuel Hoare, for deliberately ignoring the advice he had given him and his Cabinet colleagues on Germany.[45] But once again it was Stanley Baldwin who felt the full force of Londonderry's 'impotent rage', expounded in a fourteen-page riposte to the ex-Premier's emollient letter at Christmas, which had expressed regret at any unwitting offence he had caused his 'faithful friend'.[46] And as 1938 ended with another refrain of the old story, 1939 began, also in similar vein to previous years – despite all that had happened, with an exchange of Christmas greetings with Hitler and Göring.[47]

Polite niceties apart, this signified that all hope had not been fully extinguished in Londonderry's mind. He continued publicly to defend the policy he had always advocated, of concessions to Germany's just demands, as correct, and to praise Chamberlain for his achievement at Munich, when, said Londonderry, 'my dream came true' – though not early enough to be wholly effective in defusing the threat of war.[48] And at the beginning of February 1939 he was suggesting to Chamberlain that 'it would be worthwhile' to 'get Goering over here'. However, his hopes of resurrecting an active policy of appeasement by this, or any other, route were now no more than residual. His views on the Nazi leaders had also changed significantly since the hey-day of his visits to Germany in 1936. Where he had once lauded Hitler and courted Göring, he now described them to Chamberlain, with the social disparagement of his class, as 'nothing but upstarts' and saw 'something rather pathetic' in their 'rantings and bombast'.[49]

He was also expecting further expansionist moves by Hitler and now starting to face up to the likelihood of armed conflict with the Germany he had wanted to befriend. He was persuaded by a review he read in The Times on 14 February 1939 of Die Revolution des Nihilismus by Hermann Rauschning, the former President of the

Danzig Senate who had broken with Hitler and now provided a former 'insider's' analysis of his regime, that the book showed 'the direction in which Naziism [sic] is moving'.[50] Rauschning had argued, in a tract rich in insight, that the drive for expansion was intrinsic to Nazism, and essentially limitless. Far from being confined to the attainment of German revisionist and nationalist aims, its goal was Continental empire and, ultimately, 'absolute dominion in the world'.[51] Londonderry thought the British government had failed to understand the nature of German policy and was just 'marking time', taking no initiative and simply awaiting some new step by Hitler. He correctly predicted that Memel – the German-speaking enclave in Lithuania, on the Baltic coast – and Danzig would be 'absorbed' by the Reich. 'After that, I am not quite sure in which direction his policy will move,' Londonderry remarked, 'but I am quite convinced that as the two possibilities, first, of making friends with Germany, and[,] second, of controlling her before she became strong, were allowed to slip by, we shall have to take on the new world with an unprecedented determination, or else we shall find ourselves overwhelmed by the strength of this new movement.'[52]

The conclusions on policy Londonderry drew from this assessment were, however, less than clear. In his speech at Belfast the previous month he had spoken of the need 'to adopt a different policy from that followed with such disastrous results during the last twenty years'.[53] The inference was that the country should unite behind Chamberlain's policy of appeasement. But if the speech was long on rhetoric, it was short on constructive ideas and practical steps to head off the looming danger. Londonderry seemed in reality to have little in concrete terms to offer as the world waited for Hitler to make his next move.

Chamberlain had, meanwhile, been far from 'marking time'. The interruption to his aim of appeasement that had followed 'Crystal Night' had indeed been of short duration. By early 1939 he was heading with Lord Halifax to Rome, to try to win Mussolini's favour in the hope, as he had told the Cabinet the previous November, of deterring Hitler from some new 'mad dog' act. Predictably, the meeting brought nothing. But Chamberlain, emerging from the despondency of the autumn and ready to clutch at straws, managed to see positive signs in Mussolini's response to his suggestion that Hitler should be prevailed upon to limit German armaments. Even more remarkably, he thought Hitler's two-and-a-half-hour rant to the Reichstag on 30 January 1939, the sixth anniversary of his takeover of power, relatively constrained, and a positive response to his own avowals of Britain's peaceful aims when he had spoken in Birmingham two days earlier.[54] By mid-February he was again optimistic enough to be telling his sister that the information he was receiving 'seems to point in the direction of peace'. And on 10 March he even predicted the gathering of a disarmament conference at some point in 1939.[55]

On that very day Hitler was telling Nazi leaders that he had decided to smash what remained of the Czech state and occupy Prague. Five days later the Wehrmacht crossed the border and, later on that evening of 15 March, the German dictator himself entered the city.[56] It was to prove the terminal blow for the policy of appeasement, and the breaking point in Lord Londonderry's lingering delusions about building a friendly relationship with Nazi Germany.

III

The government's immediate reaction to Hitler's latest coup was surprisingly tepid. Chamberlain argued at a meeting of the Cabinet soon after the news of the invasion broke that Czechoslovakia had effectively fallen apart and thought 'the military occupation was symbolic'. Halifax – High Anglican, though quite up to the highest Jesuitical standards in his casuistry – persuaded the Cabinet that the guarantee of the Czech borders solemnly provided at Munich and pronounced shortly afterwards to be morally binding had been meant to cover only a short time before the great powers constructed a joint guarantee and, since this had not emerged, had, therefore, lost its validity. Britain, in other words, need feel no moral obligation over Czechoslovakia. The only action taken by the Cabinet to show the government's disapproval of German aggression was the postponement of a planned visit to Berlin by the President of the Board of Trade, Oliver Stanley, the temporary recall for report to the government of the British Ambassador in Berlin, Sir Nevile Henderson, and the cessation of the British financial support for Czechoslovakia that had been provided since Munich.[57] Despite the blow, the government's initial intention was that basic policy towards Germany should proceed unchanged. Chamberlain declared that 'he would go on with his "policy"' of appeasement. The Under-Secretary at the Foreign Office, Sir Alexander Cadogan, noted in his diary on hearing this: 'Fatal!'[58]

Cadogan's reaction was an indication of the continued divergence of views between the Foreign Office and 10, Downing Street on how to handle Hitler. Chamberlain regarded Prague as a disappointment and temporary setback to his great aim of preserving peace – an object, he told the House of Commons on 15 March, 'of too great significance to the happiness of mankind for us lightly to give it up or set it on one side'.[59] Halifax, on the other hand, prodded by the Foreign Office mandarins, did not join in the readiness of most members of the Cabinet to play down the importance of Prague.[60] For him, it marked a turning point. With this latest aggression, Hitler had now extended his domination to non-Germans and the conclusion could reasonably be drawn, as Halifax told the German Ambassador within hours of the invasion, that the German government were 'seeking to establish a position in which they could by force dominate Europe and if possible the world'.[61] The hesitant and stumbling path to a revised foreign policy, followed over the next two weeks, largely sprang from the conflicting positions of a Prime Minister seeking, even now, to avoid war through an accommodation with Germany and a Foreign Secretary wanting to draw a line in the sand, to turn away from attempting to appease a dictator who patently could not be trusted, and to make all preparations for a regrettably necessary war.[62]

This appeared, in fact, to be the position adopted by Chamberlain himself in a powerful speech, bearing signs of Halifax's influence, delivered to a gathering of Conservative Party faithful in his home town of Birmingham on 17 March. To rapturous applause, Chamberlain concluded his peroration with the ringing declaration that 'no greater mistake could be made than to suppose that, because it believes war to be a senseless and cruel thing, this nation has so lost its fibre that it will not take part to the utmost of its power in resisting such a challenge [to dominate the world by force] if it ever were made'.[63] Whatever the rhetoric, however, Chamberlain had far from given up hope that a peaceful arrangement with Germany could still be reached. His speech had been clearly moulded to the needs of public opinion.

Chamberlain had at first been out of touch with the seismic shift in opinion, in Britain and in the Dominions, which had immediately followed the invasion of Czechoslovakia.[64] The British newspapers had in unison been aghast at this latest, and most blatant, demonstration of Hitler's lies, unscrupulousness, untrustworthiness and unquenchable drive for expansion and domination. The wide-circulation liberal newspaper the *News Chronicle* spoke for British public opinion in general in describing the German action as 'an act of naked and unashamed aggression', 'sheer territorial conquest'.[65] The organ of establishment conservativism, *The Times*, used scarcely less forceful language in declaring that 'there is nothing left for moral debate in this crude and brutal act of oppression and suppression'.[66] Across the political spectrum, opinion now hardened that, in attempts to assuage Nazi Germany, enough was enough. 'The country is stirred to its depths, and rage against Germany is rising,' was how one backbench Conservative MP and former German sympathizer put it.[67] Another Chamberlain loyalist also caught the public mood: 'I fear that this will be the death knell of poor Neville's policy of appeasement, and equally of course all his opponents will say "I told you so!" It is also the end, I should imagine, of any further dealing with Hitler – the man henceforward should be treated as outside the pale – and when we are strong enough should be fought.'[68] Indeed, despite the caution of the government, Hitler's entry into Prague marked the definitive shift in British public opinion on appeasement.[69] Denunciation of Hitler was accompanied by widespread recognition, now represented by conservative newspapers as well as the organs of liberal and left-wing opinion (which had been strident since Munich in their criticism of Chamberlain), that the policy of appeasement had failed and should be abandoned.[70] Criticism of Chamberlain and his appeasement policy rose sharply. 'The feeling in the lobbies is that Chamberlain will either have to go or completely reverse his policy,' noted one critic of the Prime Minister. 'Unless in his speech tonight he admits that he was wrong, they feel that resignation is the only alternative.'[71] His Birmingham speech, broadcast to the Empire and to America, belatedly caught the mood and adjusted to it.[72]

Despite his new, defiant tone, Chamberlain had not, unlike most of the country, even at this point given up all hope of appeasement. But he did at least recognize that Prague had altered the situation. Trust in Hitler's word, Chamberlain saw, had been badly misplaced. He had, to put no fine point upon it, been duped.[73] The German dictator had, consequently, to be warned in unequivocal terms that future acts of aggression, most likely to occur in eastern Europe, could result in war with the British Empire.[74] Though no longer trusting Hitler, Chamberlain still entertained the vain hope that Mussolini might 'put the brake' on his Axis partner.[75] But, influenced by Halifax, the Prime Minister now looked to the prospect of a two-front war as a suitable deterrent to new German aggression. This demanded some form of alliance with east European countries. Of these, Rumania, Poland and the Soviet Union were evidently of prime importance. Rumanian oil offered a temptation to Germany in the event of armed conflict, and a temporary – wholly misleading – scare in the jumpy post-Prague atmosphere that Rumania was about to be forced into the German orbit focused minds on the need to deter Hitler from this or similar aggression.[76] The most likely guess, in the light of the increased German pressure on Poland since the beginning of the year to reach agreement (favourable to Germany, of course) on the status of Danzig and on a transit-route through the Polish Corridor that divided East Prussia from the rest of the Reich, was that Poland would be next in line as the target of German expansion. And in any German move eastwards, the stance of the Soviet Union would plainly be pivotal. Its rooted antagonism to Nazi Germany was taken for granted. Since Prague, not just the Labour Party (and, still representing a tiny minority in this regard in Conservative ranks, Winston Churchill) had supported the building of a 'grand alliance' to include the Soviet Union.[77] A wide swathe of public opinion saw this as the necessary and obvious route in redressing the mistakes of appeasement.[78] But this is where the major problems began.

Both Rumania and Poland feared and detested the Soviet Union if anything more than Nazi Germany (with which Poland still had a non-aggression pact dating back to 1934). Neither would therefore entertain the prospect of an alliance involving Stalin's regime.[79] The Soviet leadership, for its part, was still convinced that the western democracies were keen to embroil their country in a bloody conflict with the Nazi ideological arch-enemy which would only benefit capitalists and imperialists.[80] In any case, Chamberlain had a profound distrust of Russia, and Halifax, too, made plain that he would prefer an alliance with Poland if the choice had to be made.[81] Moreover, the advice to the government from the military and the Secret Service was that the Soviets were not capable of effective action.[82] Chamberlain indicated that 'Poland was very likely the key to the situation', and that British overtures should be pressed more firmly than elsewhere. The French, too, favoured Polish over Russian participation. By late March, the Foreign Office had concluded that a diplomatic bloc involving any east European states could only be attained by excluding the Soviet Union.[83] At this point, another scare arose. It seemed for a brief moment that Hitler was about to attack Poland. The prospect of this gave immediate cutting edge to what was already being mooted in the Foreign Office. The government was worried both by the possibility of a German attack, and by the feasibility that Poland might come to terms with Germany, under the pressure of an ultimatum.[84] The result was the guarantee, of which Halifax was the midwife, that Chamberlain, 'looking gaunt and ill', reading his statement 'very slowly with a bent grey head',[85] announced to the House of Commons on the afternoon of 31 March 1939 that 'in the event of any action which clearly threatened Polish independence, and which the Polish Government accordingly considered it vital to resist with their national forces, His Majesty's Government would feel themselves bound at once to lend the Polish Government all support in their power'.[86] As the cheers rang out from all sides of the House of Commons, Members of Parliament were turning their backs on appeasement. 'If Poland is attacked we shall declare war,' was the clear presumption that they were cheering.[87] Chamberlain was determined that it would not come to that.

There was good intent, naivety and cynicism in the guarantee. The good intent was the serious hope that the guarantee would serve to deter Germany, and encourage the saner elements in the Nazi regime to pull Hitler back from dragging Europe into war; that it would pave the way, even at this late hour, for an international agreement to blunt the perilous knife-edge on which peace rested. The naivety was the belief that Hitler could be deterred by such a guarantee. It amounted to an outright misreading of Hitler's character and the manner (already well known from at least the time of the Anschluss and the 'May Crisis' of 1938) in which he reacted with aggression to any provocation or threat. The cynicism was the knowledge that Britain could, in the event of a German attack on Poland, do nothing militarily to uphold the guarantee just given. No discussions with the French were held about an attack on Germany's western borders should Poland be attacked in the east. Military advice was that Poland would be overrun within three months.[88] The guarantee, whatever its appearances, was aimed not at helping Poland fight a war, but in preventing such a war from taking place; or, at least, delaying it until Britain had completed the build-up of its defences – more than a year away at the earliest.[89]

Nor, in Chamberlain's mind at least, did it mean the end of appeasement. He was explicit in stating that Britain was not guaranteeing Poland's existing borders, and indeed saw some merit in those being amended.[90] For Chamberlain, avoiding war, not fighting one, remained the paramount aim. For this, negotiations with Germany were the only possibility. Only through an arrangement to safeguard the British Empire through satisfying Germany's outstanding territorial demands (such as they were imagined to be) could lasting peace be attained. Chamberlain hoped the guarantee would put pressure upon Germany to comply. But Chamberlain now found himself carried by the current on to shores not of his choosing. For others in the government, the main thrust of the guarantee was to restrain Germany by threats. And for the majority of the public, the guarantee was the sign, at last, that Britain was turning its back on appeasement and was ready to stand up and fight Hitler. Though meant essentially as a gesture – a warning to press Germany into negotiations – defiant readiness to fight is, in fact, what the guarantee turned out to represent. It was a decisive moment. If reluctantly, Chamberlain now found himself embarked upon a new course. Further guarantees followed to Rumania and Greece, after Mussolini had invaded Albania on 7 April. But the guarantee to Poland was the crucial one. The guarantee had effectively (if still not altogether in Chamberlain's mind) killed off appeasement. It had cleared the path which, five months later, would end in war. It had in essence left the decision on whether Britain would become involved in war to the outcome of relations between two other countries, Germany and Poland.[91] And, with the Soviet Union left out of the arrangement, it amounted, as David Lloyd George reminded the House of Commons during the debate on the guarantee, on 3 April, to 'a frightful gamble'.[92]

As a deterrent, the guarantee failed at the first hurdle. When the news broke in Hitler's Reich Chancellery in Berlin, Admiral Wilhelm Canaris, head of the German military intelligence service, the Abwehr, expressed his view that any further expansion in the east would mean war. According to Canaris' account, at this Hitler fell into a towering rage. 'With features distorted by fury', Canaris reported, 'he had stormed up and down his room, pounded his fists on the marble table-top, and spewed forth a series of savage imprecations. Then, his eyes flashing with an uncanny light, he had growled the threat: "I'll cook them a stew that they'll choke on."'[93] Hitler had not reckoned with the guarantee. From his perspective, it threw a huge spanner in the works. He had expected the pressure on the Poles to yield fruit in due course, despite the initial obduracy of the Polish government. Danzig and the route through the Corridor would eventually be ceded, he was sure. The western democracies, as usual, would protest, but do nothing. German power politics would, as so often had been the case, once more prevail. Polish hopes placed in the West would evaporate as those of the Czechs had done. Other territorial concessions would follow in due course. Poland would become a German satellite. The way to the big prize of Russia would then lie open. But the British had spoiled the plot. Emboldened, the Poles would now seek to hold out. Well, they would pay the price. If they continued to hold out, he would seize Danzig by force, smash all military resistance and drive the Poles to submission. By mid-April, Hitler had composed a preamble to a military directive for the destruction of Poland. Despite the continuance of the non-aggression pact with Poland, this foresaw the use of military force at any time after 1 September 1939. Hitler still believed that, despite the bravado of a futile guarantee, the western leaders – 'puny worms', he was later to call them[94] – would not fight. They had not done so over Czechoslovakia. Why should they now do so for Danzig, whose population was largely German? He was confident that Poland could be isolated, and destroyed. Britain and France would stand aside and let it happen.[95]

That, broadly speaking, was Hitler's thinking in April 1939, following the British guarantee to Poland. The guarantee rested, therefore, on a double miscalculation. It had come about because the British had calculated, wrongly, that it would deter Hitler from further aggression. And it prompted Hitler to calculate, wrongly, that it was a bluff: that he could destroy Poland, but still avoid conflict with the West. That double miscalculation led over the following months to the beginning of what would turn out to be the Second World War.

IV

Towards the end of February 1939, Lord Londonderry had received a handwritten letter from a clergyman confined to a nursing home in Worcester, who had been reading his book, *Ourselves and Germany*, with interest. The letter was polite, not hostile, but posed a simple question that went to the heart of Londonderry's approach to Germany. 'You seem to believe that Hitler will keep his word,' the clergyman, Canon G. M. Isaac, wrote. But, he went on, Germany had repeatedly broken treaties when it suited. So: 'How can we then believe that what Hitler says is true?'[96] Contrary to his normal courtesy in replying to practically all but the most abusive letters, it does not appear that Londonderry answered the question. And it is unlikely that he thought of Canon Isaac's letter as the dramatic events of mid-March unfolded. But he ought to have done. For this one straightforward question laid bare the naivety of Londonderry, and of many others beside him, including those in high places.[97] The evidence that Hitler could not be trusted had been plain to see long before the spring of 1939.

Together with his wife and daughter Lady Mairi, Lord Londonderry was in Sweden to address a meeting of the Swedish

Aero Club as German troops entered Prague. Just before leaving London, he had written to the German Embassy, deferring a visit to Berlin, arranged for the end of the month, because he had been wanting to see not only Hitler, but Göring, who, he had learned, was currently in Italy.[98] And one of his first social engagements, on arriving in Sweden, was to attend a luncheon on 12 March as the guest of the German Minister in Stockholm, Prince Viktor zu Wied, a longstanding acquaintance whose daughters had been part of Ribbentrop's entourage during the stay at Mount Stewart at the end of May 1936.[99] Nothing up to this point, then, had dented his desire to consolidate friendly relations with Hitler, Göring and other representatives of the Nazi regime. Despite disappointments, he still hoped that the breakthrough reached at Munich could prove a platform on which to build. These hopes were shattered, three days after his luncheon with Prince zu Wied, by the news of the German invasion of what remained of Czechoslovakia.

Immediately on return from Sweden, Londonderry publicly associated himself fully with the stance on Prague taken by Lord Halifax, and by the Prime Minister in his important Birmingham speech. He emphasized the shock at the way Hitler had betrayed the undertakings he had given to Chamberlain at Munich. The whole international situation had, in his view, been completely changed by Hitler's 'wholly unjustifiable move'. Up to this point, he continued, even if the methods were objectionable, Germany had made claims deserving of recognition in the wish to incorporate in the Reich the German-speaking populations of central Europe. But now, Londonderry stated (echoing the sentiments of Halifax), 'Germany appears to have assumed the attitude of world domination', which could not be accepted under any circumstances. His hopes had been that Germany would play its part, with the other Great Powers, in maintaining peace in a new world order. Such hopes had, at least temporarily, to be shelved. He referred approvingly to Chamberlain's speech in Birmingham and the clear demonstration it gave that 'the German policy of aggression' would be resisted by Britain and the British Empire.[100]

Londonderry's dismay at the German occupation of the Czech lands and Hitler's blatant breach of trust was not just for public consumption. One of his first actions was to dispatch an abrupt telegram stating 'Shall not lecture', cancelling an invitation, which he had accepted, to speak in Berlin on civil aviation.[101] And he did not hide his anger at the German action when writing on 20 March to Sven Hedin, the famous Swedish orientalist and explorer (and great admirer of Hitler), now in his seventies, whom Londonderry had met just over a week earlier at Prince zu Wied's luncheon. 'Since I had the pleasure of meeting you in Stockholm', he wrote, 'the German Chancellor has, I regret to say, overstepped all limits and I see no possibility of any confidence ever again being placed in his statements and undertakings.' He regarded the situation as 'very serious' and his only hope was that 'we shall be able to avoid an international catastrophe'.[102]

Still in despondent mood at the end of March, Londonderry, in a lengthy letter, told von Papen, who had entertained him on the hunting expedition at Darss in September 1937, that as 'your best advocate' he had been 'completely destroyed' by Hitler's policy, which had shown the policy of Anglo-German understanding 'to be quite impossible at the present time and probably for many years to come'. He was, Londonderry frankly stated 'at a complete loss to understand the policy which the Chancellor is pursuing at the present moment'. The 'bond of sympathy' between Germany and Britain which he had established, Londonderry continued, and which for a long time developed positively, had been 'entirely swept away'. For this, he had to 'attach the whole blame to the German Chancellor, who, certainly for a generation, has destroyed the possibility of any importance being attached to his words'. He himself had consistently defended German actions, he pointed out. But now he had been rendered completely ineffective and had to remain silent.[103]

The same depressed tone was apparent in two further letters composed for German contacts – though in the event not sent (possibly indicating Londonderry's unwillingness to burn his boats with his German friends by writing so frankly) – a few days later. On 4 April he drafted a letter intended for Erich Gritzbach, head of Göring's personal staff, lamenting that everything he had tried to do during the past three years had been undone by Hitler's action, and that he now felt quite powerless. His high hopes after Munich had been completely dashed.[104] A second letter that day was meant for Dr Silex, the editor of the *Deutsche Allgemeine Zeitung*, who, as we noted, had published a pro-German article by Londonderry the previous autumn after the two had met at the time of the Munich Agreement. Londonderry pointed to the difficulty he had always had – enhanced by Hitler's technique of 'surprises' in foreign affairs – in justifying German policy within Britain. He had publicly supported the German position on all earlier moves, he went on, mentioning the remilitarization of the Rhineland, the Anschluss and the incorporation of the Sudetenland in the Reich, 'but since the invasion of Czechoslovakia, for which I can find no satisfactory reason, I have found it necessary to remain silent'.[105] In other words, Londonderry had run out of arguments. Hitler himself had pulled the rug from beneath the case which he and others had built up patiently, and in the face of much hostility, over years for better relations with Germany.

It was a sobering moment for German sympathizers generally. Many would-be friends of Hitler's Reich now found they could go no further. The Conservative writer and journalist Francis Yeats-Brown, for instance, long an admirer of Italian Fascism who as late as 1938 had written a series of articles in the *Observer* enthusing about Hitler's Germany, saw Prague as the end of the road. 'The law of the jungle prevails,' he wrote. With Hitler's breaking of the pledge he had given at Munich, 'our recent hopes of disarmament and reconciliation lie shattered beyond the possibility of quick repair'.[106] The sentiment was identical with that of Londonderry. Another writer, who had been sympathetic to the sense of German renewal under Nazi rule and supported appeasement, Sir Philip Gibbs, now took the view that Hitler had 'gone beyond the limit of any excuse which could be put up on his behalf by those who, for the sake of avoiding a war which would be the ruin of European civilization, hoped and half believed that, according to his own words many times repeated, Hitler would restrict himself to the rebuilding of his own Germanic Reich'.[107] Again, the words matched Londonderry's naive belief in German promises to this date, and his inner devastation at Hitler's perfidy.

The atmosphere had without question changed dramatically. Another sympathizer with Hitler's Germany, whom we encountered earlier, Sir Ian Hamilton, veteran of the Boer War and First World War, the commander of the British forces at Gallipoli, and subsequently Scottish President of the British Legion, declined an invitation to become a vice-president of 'The Link', commenting that 'the "sane atmosphere in Anglo-German relations" has turned into thunder and lightning'.[108] The idealist core of those who for years had backed Nazi Germany, often with reservations and sometimes with inner anxieties, because they saw making friends with Hitler, whatever the difficulties, as the only way to save European peace, now largely turned away. Londonderry was among their number. And the mainstream centre-ground built, whether out of enthusiasm or resignation, on the belief in the need for appeasement, had collapsed. Those left still supporting Germany were largely the fanatical pro-Nazi and anti-Semitic fringe.[109]

Among those whose attitude towards Nazi Germany had shifted diametrically at the destruction of the remains of Czechoslovakia was George Ward Price, the *Daily Mail* foreign correspondent who had enjoyed close connections to the Nazi leadership and, a longstanding acquaintance of Londonderry, had been present at the Ribbentrop weekend at Mount Stewart in 1936. He had strongly supported the German position on the Sudetenland the previous year, when he was still letting it be known that he was 'Hitler's friend'. That he approved of Munich was a matter of course. After Prague, however, he completely revised his views. 'The possibility of cordial relations has now passed away,' he wrote, and all that remained was 'to consider the factors and forces of the opposing alignment which has taken its place'. He was finally prepared to acknowledge that the Nazis 'had done much evil' within Germany, including the persecution of the Jews, and that their high-handed foreign policy would lead to war.[110] Soon after the German entry into Prague, Ward Price travelled to Berlin, from where he wrote to Lord Londonderry on 25 March 1939. It was plain that his eyes had been opened at last.

He had spoken during his stay in Berlin, Ward Price commented, to Göring, Ribbentrop and several members of Hitler's personal staff. His appraisal of Hitler's foreign policy, in the light of these discussions, was perceptive. Hitler had 'wanted to finish off the whole Czech question last September', Ward Price accurately remarked, and had resented the fact that Chamberlain's intervention had prevented him from doing so. His greatest anxiety just before occupying the rest of the Czech territory, Ward Price was told, had been that '"the old gentleman [Chamberlain] should get into an aeroplane again" and come to try to talk him out of it'.[111] Hitler was determined to bring eastern Europe under German control. Once this control had extended to the Polish Corridor, through 'peaceful negotiation' with the Poles, backed by threats of military action, German aims would be satisfied. (In truth, German aims could never have been satisfied. But before the British Guarantee Hitler indeed reckoned that pressure would over-come Polish intransigency about Danzig and the Corridor.) Ward Price drew realistic conclusions. There was no chance of any disarmament agreement with Germany (a hope that had not been completely aban-doned in the British government); nor was the Nazi regime likely to be deterred by threats of an anti-German coalition of forces. Even so, the German leadership was still prepared to reach an agreement with Britain, but only 'on the basis of full British acknowledgement of Germany's dominant position on the Continent'.[112]

The last point was one that Londonderry directly addressed in his reply (which was not, however, sent, probably since Ward Price was about to leave Berlin for further destinations and it was uncertain whether the letter would reach him). He was prepared without reser-vation to accept German dominance on the Continent as a basis of any future negotiation, and did not favour the attempts currently mooted by the British government to form alliances in eastern Europe, which – agreeing with Nazi propaganda on this point – would amount to 'some policy of encirclement of the Reich'. Predictably, he looked upon the prospect of an alliance with Stalinist Russia 'with the gravest suspicion'. 'World revolution' remained the bogey in his mind. He was sure that Stalin was hoping to profit from a war among the western powers, and that world revolution would follow a major war. He was aware that Hitler's 'first major mistake' – breaking his word on Czechoslovakia – meant that there was no current possibility of any accommodation with Germany. But he was, he indicated, 'not unwilling to try to treat with the Germans again', on the basis of a readiness to accept their position of strength in cen-tral Europe 'and not to pay too much attention to their "Drang nach [Osten]"' – their 'Drive to the East'. He was surprisingly confident – it must have been one of his less gloomy days – that the Nazi regime would not come to dominate 'a great portion of the world', and that through the stimulation of international trade and good statesmanship the existing tensions could be relieved.[113]

The phraseology is opaque in places. But the drift of the letter seems clear enough. Londonderry was plainly, even now, not prepared to close the door to further negotiations with Germany. The current moment, following Prague, was however scarcely propitious, and time would have to be allowed for the dust to settle. Whatever negotiations proved possible would then have to be on the basis which the Nazi leadership had always wanted: recognition of German pre-eminence on the Continent and a free hand for Germany in the east in exchange for what he took to be the unthreatened co-existence of the British Empire. Londonderry's instinct was, it appears, to concede the new balance of power in Europe rather than entertain the alternative of war.

Londonderry exempted Chamberlain from blame (a view he would later amend), but otherwise attributed the disastrous course of events to the 'terrible mistakes' of successive governments.[114] He remained anxious, as ever, to prove that he had been right all along. 'It will not take 50 years to discover whether I was right or wrong' about policy towards Germany, he told Baldwin (in yet a further lament about his dismissal from the Cabinet in 1935). 'I was obviously right, and the Government obviously wrong.'[115] Dogmatic and stubborn persistence in the attempt to vindicate his actions, also against the continued Labour attacks on him for his defence of bombing,[116] was a characteristic feature of Londonderry's personality, and a remnant of the psychological bruising he had suffered at the time of his dismissals from government office in 1935. On foreign policy, he was convinced that the entire course of events would have been different had the government followed the line he had advocated as early as 1934. 'I have to remain comparatively silent at this time,' he told one correspondent, 'but no one can say with greater truth than myself to many of those who have criticised me: "I told you so".'[117]

Unsurprisingly, therefore, around this time he dispatched to numerous individuals further copies of his letters to Lord Hailsham from November 1934 – now of emblematic status in his own mind. Viscount Sankey, a Labour 'renegade' in 1931 who had been an undistinguished

Lord Chancellor in Ramsay MacDonald's government,[118] and had favoured the search for an understanding with Germany, told Londonderry, on reading the Hailsham letters, that his treatment by the government had been 'a grave injustice'. He thought it 'little short of a calamity that your advice was not followed. Had it been[,] we should now have had a peaceful Europe & a friendly Germany, and not an England with diminished prestige.' He ended in a manner which would have pleased Londonderry: 'Forgive my saying what a pity we didn't trust to a Statesman who had the same blood as Castlereagh in his veins, rather than to small[-]minded & vacillating politicians.'[119] Another recipient of the Hailsham letters, Lady Violet Bonham Carter – daughter of Herbert Asquith, a Liberal of strong opinion, and often at political loggerheads with Londonderry – also wrote, saying the 'letters *must* be preserved as a record of a tragically missed opportunity'. If Londonderry's advice had been taken at the time, she suggested, 'we should have had *either* reconciliation or parity [in armaments]'.[120]

Perhaps she was simply being polite (though Sankey was surely sincere in his comment). For the notion that Londonderry's letters had constituted a serious alternative policy in 1934, which could have brought peace to Europe, was an illusion. It had been a well-meaning but ill-thought-out expression of desire, rather than a genuine policy option. Londonderry did, even so, have a point. The equivocal stance adopted towards Germany ever since Hitler's takeover of power married to the long delay in facing the obvious need to rearm with all speed formed an umbilical cord that led inexorably to Chamberlain's appeasement policy in 1938–9 from a position of weakness.

The Polish Guarantee now tried to remedy that weakness by building alliances in eastern Europe, though without Russian involvement Britain's position amounted to little more than a mirage of strength. Londonderry, like the vast majority of his fellow-countrymen, welcomed the guarantee, commenting that 'the time has come when we have got to make a stand'.[121] But he was keen that Germany should not feel encircled and for this reason (quite apart from his ingrained anti-Bolshevism) was keen 'that Russian help should not be invited'. His reaction showed how little he understood the workings of Hitler's mind and the thrust of Nazi foreign policy. 'I am sure your strong guarantee to Poland[,] and I should extend it[,] is all that is required

now,' he told Neville Chamberlain. For all his alleged knowledge of
the mentality of the German leadership, he misjudged the impact
of the guarantee on Hitler, and was as a result unduly sanguine about
avoiding the dangers of war. 'It is later that I think the real war danger arises,' he suggested to the Prime Minister. He had revised his earlier view that this would not occur before 1942, but 'still if you get
the support you deserve I have no fear of war'.[122]

Londonderry's own support for Chamberlain was, however, more
muted than his letter suggested. Though he avoided public attacks,
behind the scenes he was becoming increasingly critical of the government, and of the Prime Minister personally. As had so often been
the case with Londonderry – a man of some vanity and self-
importance, whose pleasant and charming demeanour and fine manners concealed an inner touchiness and sensitivity when he felt his
status was not given due recognition – a keen sense of rejection
played a central part. 'Although I suppose I know more about
Germany and the German leaders than anyone else,' he informed Sir
Kingsley Wood, who had taken over as Air Minister in May, 1938,
'Neville Chamberlain never had one single conversation with me on
the subject.' He also found Lord Halifax wanting. The result was
'that during all this time when my advice might have been helpful, I
have been left out in the cold. I have never received an invitation to
the Reception and Banquets which have taken place at the Foreign
Office, but people like Winston [Churchill] and George Lloyd [an
ennobled Tory grandee, who had been Governor of Bombay and
High Commissioner in Egypt] are invited.' As far as foreign policy
was concerned, he said, 'I have had to give up the Prime Minister and
Halifax – they are both very nice and very charming – but neither of
them is going to listen to me.'[123]

He poured out the same complaint to Chamberlain himself at the
beginning of May 1939, in a letter distinctly cooler than that of a
month earlier. He claimed he had at one time had influence with the
German leadership which could have been used to advantage. But
'after being ignored by the great majority of my colleagues, it was
very obvious that I could get nothing across in this country, with the
result that my policy of contacts was left until last September, when
it really was too late to do anything'.[124] Chamberlain, an attached

note from his Private Secretary points out, decided not to reply.[125] Londonderry's laments were evidently becoming tedious. And he had little that was constructive to suggest.

His connections with German leaders, on which he had placed such great store, had by now also fallen away drastically. The days of the search for British friendship during 1935 and 1936 had long since vanished. An interest in coming to some arrangement with Britain remained – but now only on German terms, meaning a free hand for Germany's expansionist aims in the east, backed by British support or at least neutrality. Londonderry, it was plain, lacked influence. For the German leadership, therefore, as he himself recognized, he was now an irrelevance.[126] Even so, contact did not yet quite cease. Von Papen, replying to Londonderry's letter sent at the end of March, offered an outright apologia for German aggression – 'a piece of special pleading devoid of any principle' by a 'failure' and a 'lightweight' who 'should have stuck to his vocation as a gentleman rider', in the withering judgement of Sir Horace Rumbold, the former British Ambassador in Berlin.[127]

As usual, Londonderry could not leave a letter unanswered. In this case, his 'last word' was literally that; he did not hear from von Papen again. His riposte to von Papen's apologia was as strongly worded a letter as ever he sent to a prominent German. Hitler, he wrote, had not deviated 'by one hair's breadth' from the policy aims he had laid down in *Mein Kampf*. He himself had now reached the point where he hoped 'that Great Britain will take a much stronger line and say that until there is some sign of a desire for accom[m]odation on the part of the Germans, we shall go on arming and looking upon Germany as a potential enemy'. He could not now see 'in which direction we can move so as to induce Germany to collaborate in a policy of conciliation'. He rejected claims of encirclement. Whatever international collaboration there was to maintain the peace had been wholly induced by German aggression. He had changed his own mind, he continued, when Germany overran Czechoslovakia and showed clearly 'that an undertaking made by Germany has no real basis'. There ought to be no illusions about British readiness to comply with German aggression. On the contrary: 'We are really becoming deeply incensed at the manner in which Germany appears to be seeking to establish her domination throughout the world and are determined to resist that claim no matter what that resistance may entail.' There was now no point in his travelling to Berlin for further talks with Hitler and Göring. 'The conversations which we had before have proved to be completely ineffective and the policy which I sought to establish here, which in time might have been successful, has been rendered abortive by all that has been done by the Chancellor.'[128]

Londonderry was firm about the futility of further discussions in a last – unanswered – letter to Göring towards the end of May expressing the feeling that his 'efforts are at an end'. Were there the possibility of achieving anything, he wrote, he 'would come to Germany to have further discussions with you, even though I am certain that on my return I would find it extremely difficult to gain a sympathetic hearing, since all my suggestions and pleas in the interests of English-German relations are regarded as completely wrong'.[129] He was not quite closing the door. Though acknowledging his political isolation and his image in public opinion, he still deluded himself that in certain circumstances he might even now serve a useful purpose as a liaison between Göring and the British government. But as the crisis deepened over the summer months, Göring would turn to others to try to exert some influence on British policy.[130] Londonderry recognized that his endeavours to avoid war and build peace on friendship between Britain and Nazi Germany were at an end. He was to have no further communication with the German leaders he had at one time so assiduously courted.

V

The upper-class social rituals of an English summer – garden parties and receptions on the terraces of fine houses, sporting events at Ascot, Wimbledon and the Eton versus Harrow cricket match at Lord's – continued as usual in 1939, as the storm clouds gathered ever more menacingly over Europe. The feeling that this might be the last such summer for a long time, and that things would never be the same again after the new war that was threatening, inspired a carefree, live-for-now, *carpe diem* spirit to life in high society. Could this be the last fling before 'the end of civilization' that everyone was predicting would follow another war?

'Chips' Channon, the socialite Conservative MP who revelled in a life consisting of one long round of parties, receptions and banquets, thought it might. His diary entries caught the atmosphere. On 7 July he went to a 'stupendous' ball at Blenheim Palace, near Oxford, the magnificent stately home that Queen Anne had given to the Duke of Marlborough to show the nation's gratitude for his epic victory over the French in 1704. 'The palace was floodlit, and its grand baroque beauty could be seen for miles. The lakes were floodlit too and, better still, the famous terraces. They were blue and green and Tyroleans' – presumably performers in Alpine costumes – 'walked about singing; and although there were seven hundred people or even more, it was not in the least crowded.' As usual, 'Chips' was reluctant to leave such gatherings while 'literally rivers of champagne' were flowing. He eventually did so at 4.30 a.m. 'and took one last look at the baroque terraces with the lake below, and the golden statues and the great palace. Shall we ever see the like again?' he asked. 'Is such a function not out of date? Yet it was all of the England that is supposed to be dead and is not.'[131]

A month later, 'Chips' was at his country home, Kelvedon Hall, in Essex, enjoying the summer relaxation. His nostalgic, romanticized vision hinted at a world about to pass. On a long walk through the woods he saw 'yokels working, clearing out the debris, and the Essex sun shone through the tree'. Back home, 'we lazed all day, lay about in the gardens which are looking a dream of vernal lush beauty'. But the threat of war penetrated even this arcadia. 'The political atmosphere or rather the international one is worsening, and I am genuinely apprehensive,' he added. Later in the month, under the shock of the news that Germany and the Soviet Union, ideological arch-enemies, were about to sign a pact, he realized that war was imminent. 'I cannot bear to think that our world is crumbling to ruins,' he commented. 'I refuse to admit it.'[132]

Though his lifestyle was less exotic than that of 'Chips' Channon, Lord Londonderry, too, was as usual also heavily committed with social engagements in that last summer of peace in 1939. Listed among his numerous engagements in June and early July 1939 were: luncheon in the royal stand at Ascot (13 June); dinner with the Duchess of Westminster (14 June); Handley Page banquet at Grosvenor House (19 June); Dinner and dance for Lady Mairi, attended by 445 guests, at Londonderry House (20 June); luncheon at which the ex-Queen of Spain was present (21 June); annual dinner of the 1900 Club of Conservative MPs, at which he presided, with Lord Halifax as guest of honour and Winston Churchill to deliver the address of welcome (21 June); dinner at Holland House to meet the King and Queen (6 July).[133] It was by any stretch of the imagination 'the high life'. Londonderry was, like his forebears, close to the very pinnacle of society, part of the very centre of the social Establishment. Politically, it was another matter. And Londonderry was nothing if not a political animal. He smarted intensely under the realization that he was no longer, as he had once been, on the inside of the *political* Establishment. For all his social grandeur, his titles, his money, his connections, his aristocratic status which had opened so many doors, and despite the many lavish receptions he and Lady Londonderry had hosted on behalf of the Conservative Party, there was no denying that he stood outside the handful of politicians and civil servants at the head of the government and in the Foreign Office who were determining the fate of the country as the crisis over Poland worsened. Unable even now to accept his dismissals from office in 1935 which, he claimed, had left him 'under a stigma' and caused him 'untold harm', he lamented pitifully: 'I sometimes feel rather shamefaced vis-à-vis my ancestors. I feel that they are murmuring, "Well, he might have done better than that".'[134] Naturally, it was as ever Lord Castlereagh, the architect of European peace in 1815, whom he had chiefly in mind.

For someone so steeped in politics, and who prided himself on his diplomatic skills, Londonderry was remarkably prone to gaffes. There was certainly more than a touch of the nineteenth century about his approach to politics and, possibly, his failing antennae when it came to political self-preservation owed much to his belief that as an aristocrat of high standing, who had gained his power and position through birthright and patronage, he had no need to obey the rules of modern politics in trimming to suit the whims of public opinion.[135] But other high aristocrats of his generation were better at adjusting. Probably the main reason was, in fact, simply a matter of temperament – a feature of his personality. We have noticed that as long ago as the First World War he had thought of himself as a leader. His was an instinctive, paternalistic authoritarianism, far removed from the Fascist variety. But he presumed that members of the social and political oligarchy that had traditionally been formed from the British nobility had a born right to rule. Though he usually concealed it, he had an inbuilt arrogance and disdain for 'the bourgeoisie' – meaning, particularly, Neville Chamberlain ('a second-class parochially-minded tradesman', as he described him)[136] – now governing Britain in place of the aristocracy. 'I never think that, as yet, the bourgeoisie have a correct view of international affairs,' he wrote, dismissively to Prince Paul of Yugoslavia in July 1939. 'They have a knowledge of trade and finance, but the flair for handling people is something which they have not yet acquired.'[137] He had a high opinion of his own abilities in this regard and did not doubt his own gifts of intelligence. However inwardly diffident, he did not suffer fools gladly (especially when they belonged to the 'Socialist' opposition). He had the political self-righteousness of the dogmatist. And he could never beat a tactical retreat from an argument, even if failing to do so could only tempt political disadvantage and disfavour. His outspokenness and lack of a sense of political self-preservation reflected these characteristics. He was an early example of the complete inability to follow the classic political advice: 'when in a hole, stop digging'.

He had demonstrated his self-destructive streak in paradigm fashion in 1935 with the infamous reference to retention of bombing in the outbacks of the Empire that had caused him such trouble with the Left and made him such an electoral liability for his own side, thus dooming his political career. His outspoken defence of Hitler's actions on so many occasions in subsequent years, when the most obvious course of action would have been at least to keep quiet, had then spawned the reputation, which he had actively earned, as the greatest exponent of friendship with Nazi Germany. That he had strong sympathies for the ideology of Nazism was an inaccurate, though scarcely surprising, allegation, which, however vehemently he denied it, stuck. This remained the case in the summer of 1939. Though he had repeatedly stated, in the wake of the German aggression against the Czechs, that he would keep silent, his instinct for political self-destruction prevailed yet again when he found himself provoked into writing a letter to *The Times*, which the newspaper published on 22 June 1939. The letter said nothing that was new but lambasted once again the failings of British foreign policy to come to an accord with Germany. The only suggestion that Londonderry could come up with for preserving peace and improving international relations was agreement by the Great Powers 'either at a conference or through diplomatic agencies', with a commitment 'to abide by the decisions which might be arrived at by those methods of discussion'. In the prevailing climate, engendered by Hitler tearing up an agreement which itself had been seen as shameful, Londonderry's letter showed a marked lack of political *savoir faire* and a readiness to highlight once more, in such a tense atmosphere, his reputation as a German sympathizer. The heading given to the letter in *The Times*, 'Germany's Point of View', could not have helped his cause.[138]

By now, Londonderry was being consumed by recrimination. He constantly berated the failures of those in charge of British politics over previous years. If Baldwin had for long remained top of the opprobrium league, Chamberlain was now overhauling him, and even Halifax did not escape. 'I am very anxious lest the policy you are pursuing meets with some disaster which will destroy all confidence in this country', Londonderry wrote to the Foreign Secretary, adding that he had decided to leave politics and belong to no party – a threat he did not follow up.[139] 'It has been so clearly borne in on me that although I have been right and most other people have been wrong, still none of you has any desire to have my counsel in any shape or form,' he complained to Halifax a little while later.[140] This did not deter him from sending the Foreign Secretary copies of correspondence which he thought relevant to relations with Germany, including some letters from an English contact in Essen (whom he called his 'Intelligence Department') giving impressions of popular support for Hitler and anti-war feeling in Germany.[141] Quite what the Foreign Secretary was meant to do with such letters in unclear. But Halifax remained, even in the mounting crisis, courteous as ever.

Londonderry, in any case, was far from the most outrightly pro-German fellow-aristocrat the Foreign Secretary had to contend with at the time. Halifax felt it necessary, for instance, to warn Lord Brocket, a Conservative peer of no real standing but a nuisance on account of his forthright pro-Nazi views, about the harmful effect of his German contacts at such a critical juncture.¹⁴² Londonderry was anxious to distinguish himself from any such intimations and to reaffirm his credentials as a British patriot. He told Halifax that he had refused an invitation to become president of 'The Link' because he preferred to work alone and had 'no sympathy with the friends of Germany' – a somewhat disingenuous claim, since he had at one time openly admitted being 'a friend of Germany'. He had, he avowed (and here his words can be accepted at face value), 'no sentiments in this at all except for my own country'.¹⁴³

Recrimination was now more than simply railing at the way Londonderry felt he had been mistreated and ignored. It covered the recognition that, politically, he was finished. He had admitted, in the wake of Prague, that he had run out of arguments to defend Hitler. Though he could continue to bemoan the mistakes of the past, he had nothing now to offer as a way out of the current crisis. Even he realized that an appeal to an international conference no longer had any currency. His suggestion that Britain might still find common ground with Germany by giving Hitler the free hand he wanted in the east was equally certain to fall upon deaf ears. But on the one hand he supported Britain's firm stand that had to be taken after Prague, while on the other he still did not want to close the door on negotiations. He told Churchill he was in full accord with him 'that there is no accommodation now, and that any suggestion of appeasement is quite out of the question. We must arm to our full strength, and we must hope by so doing we shall convince Germany that we are determined to resist aggression policy to the fullest extent.'¹⁴⁴ But at the same time he was anxious to go to Germany himself, even at this late stage, to intercede with Nazi leaders. And he envisaged the possibility of a future where British acceptance of German military power would allow for 'a sphere of influence which in no way conflicted with the British Empire'.¹⁴⁵ He had defended Chamberlain's guarantee to Poland. Yet he now found Chamberlain wanting at every turn. Even more than Ramsay MacDonald and Baldwin, he now saw Chamberlain as 'the real villain of the piece'. Partly, this was because he felt Chamberlain had not seized the initiative after Munich to pave the way for a general settlement of Europe's problems. 'He undid all the good he had done by letting the whole thing flop when he really had a chance of keeping close contacts,' was how he put it to Halifax.[146] It was an unfair allegation; but it was how Londonderry saw it. The main reason, however, was connected with Londonderry's *bête noire*: the accusation, still rankling, that he had badly misjudged the extent of rearmament of the German air force in 1935. Chamberlain, whom he described as 'the dictator of the Administration from 1931 until the present day', had preferred Churchill's exaggerations to his own correct assessment of German rearmament, lost confidence in him, and 'refused to allow the Government to obtain any sympathetic understanding with the Germans'. Only later, when it was too late, had Chamberlain realized the need for this. Hence, Londonderry reached the conclusion that 'whatever may be the outcome of this present very difficult situation, the responsibility for it . . . is entirely due to Neville Chamberlain'.[147]

As the crisis over Poland dragged on, Londonderry, prompted it seems by some parliamentary colleagues, held out some last hope that another visit by him to Berlin might have some effect. This of course contradicted what he had been saying only weeks earlier, that there was no longer any point in trying to talk to his ex-friends among the Nazi leaders. But by this time Londonderry was full of contradictions. What good he thought another visit in August 1939 might serve is unclear. He later claimed he had not wanted to go and 'that it was most unlikely that I, or anyone else, could do anything useful or effective'.[148] This is not quite how it looked to him at the time. He thought somehow that because of his 'very close connections with Hitler himself and also with Göring' he 'might be able to put the whole case before them in a manner which I am inclined to think has not been done before'.[149] The meaning of this was, admittedly, left completely in the air. In another communication with Halifax, he stated that he wanted to stress to the German leadership, representing 'the spirit of the British Government and people', the determination 'to resist any further act of aggression' – hardly an original notion.[150] Londonderry's idea of a visit plainly followed on that by the press baron Lord Kemsley, proprietor of the *Sunday Times*, to the Wagner festival at Bayreuth in late July, where, at a meeting with Hitler, the German dictator had implied that discussions between

Germany and Britain were still possible, noting that he would want Germany's colonies returned and the cancellation – largely for prestige purposes, it is clear – of the by now almost redundant Treaty of Versailles.[151]

Londonderry's fear of war remained his overriding aim. The earnestness of his motive in seeking peace at such a desperate moment is not in doubt. But it is hard to avoid the sense that the sniff of a moment of glory, in achieving at the eleventh hour the breakthrough which the professionals could not attain, and proving worthy of his great ancestor, Castlereagh, also figured as a motive. Whatever the reason, Londonderry's intention of travelling to Germany at such a sensitive moment set alarm bells ringing as soon as he mentioned it to Halifax. The last thing British diplomats wanted, with war and peace in the balance, was an amateur diplomat, and a German sympathizer at that, sending the wrong signals to Hitler. Halifax made his worries plain. He feared that, even were Londonderry to stick to his intention of simply conveying the British determination to resist further aggression, Hitler might sense anxiety in the visit.[152] This was merely a polite way of saying that Halifax did not want the visit to take place. With some reluctance, Londonderry agreed not to go, though postponed rather than cancelled the trip.[153] He was sure – on what grounds is not plain – that he 'could have done some good', and some weeks afterwards was still hoping to go.[154] Halifax later graciously replied that, had he not dissuaded Londonderry from going his 'intervention might have thrown some weight on the right side'.[155] But this was no more than characteristic Halifax politeness.

The only conceivably viable policy in summer 1939 which offered any alternative to increasingly certain war was to forge a military alliance with the Soviet Union. An opinion survey carried out in April 1939 found 87 per cent of respondents in Britain in favour.[156] But this did not include the two individuals effectively determining British foreign policy at this stage: Chamberlain and Halifax. Londonderry had for his part set his face against such an alliance even before it was seriously mooted. When the idea – backed most prominently by Churchill, as well as by the Labour Party – became taken up as a policy option, he dubbed it 'disastrous'.[157]

He had no need to worry. Chamberlain retained his distrust of the

Soviets (to match Soviet distrust of British motives). He was in no hurry to act, despite worrying rumours of a sharp improvement in relations between Nazi Germany and Stalinist Russia. Eventually, but only on 5 August, delegations headed by the French General Joseph Doumenc and the unlikely named British admiral Reginald Aylmer Ranfury Plunkett-Ernle-Erle-Drax set sail for the Baltic on the *City of Exeter* for further travel by train to Moscow. Sluggish talks began only on 12 August.[158] They were overtaken on 23 August by the stunning news that Ribbentrop was on his way to Moscow for talks with the Soviet leadership. Hours later, the pact was signed that meant there was soon going to be war.[159]

Hitler was anxious to have his war to destroy Poland. But he still hoped that he could keep Britain and France out of the conflict. He was puzzled and irritated by the British resolve, even after the announcement of the German-Soviet Pact, to stand by its obligation to Poland. The diplomatic manoeuvres on Berlin's part during the next few days – when Hitler actually called off the invasion of Poland, planned for 26 August, after mobilization had begun – were an attempt to wean Britain at the last minute from the commitment to war. Hitler, though misjudging how British attitudes had changed since Prague, was aware that there were those in Britain who even now favoured peace over war at the price of concessions to German demands in Poland. The British Ambassador in Berlin, Sir Nevile Henderson, was one of those. Another was R. A. Butler, who in the post-war era would become a leading force in the Conservative Party and at this time was Under-Secretary at the Foreign Office and chief spokesman on foreign affairs in the House of Commons. Butler, once memorably described by Lloyd George as 'playing the part of the imperturbable dunce who says nothing with an air of conviction',[160] favoured putting pressure on the Poles, even at this juncture, to come to terms with Germany. He saw 'a German-British agreement including Colonies AND a reasonable Polish settlement' as the only alternative to war. But the Foreign Office mandarins were having none of these suggestions of a 'Polish Munich'.[161] The last attempts to save an unsaveable peace expired on 30 August. Early the next morning, Hitler gave the order for the attack on Poland to begin at dawn on 1 September.[162]

As Europe teetered on the brink, Londonderry was still engaged in correspondence with his friend Lord Hailsham about the circumstances in which his now fabled letters of November 1934 had been 'brushed aside'.[163] Vindication (of which recrimination was a key part) of his own efforts to advance a policy which could have prevented the disaster of war was what now mattered most to him. The time of admiration of the Londonderrys for Hitler and his achievements was over. Lady Londonderry, who had once published eulogies of Hitler's 'greatness', now, with the German invasion of Poland underway, remarked to her husband: 'I think Hitler is going out like the Gotterdamerung [sic]!! I hope so anyhow.'[164]

On the morning of 3 September Neville Chamberlain broadcast to the British people that Britain was at war with Germany. For Londonderry, what he had in his own way striven so long and hard to prevent had come to pass. His dream of playing a major role in creating a new European order to safeguard a peace resting upon a division of powers and friendly relations between Britain and Germany was over.

7

Out in the Cold

'I should not be human if I did not regret having to remain aloof from all the great work which is going on at the present moment. The point is that I backed the wrong horse.'

Lord Londonderry, July 1940

'I have no doubt that I shall receive the full vindication to which I am entitled, but it is also quite possible that I shall not receive it during my lifetime.'

Lord Londonderry, July 1940

Sunday, 3 September 1939 was a beautiful late summer's morning in southern England. The day which turned out to be so momentous had dawned bright and sunny after heavy thunderstorms the previous evening. Beneath the brilliant sunshine, the streets of central London looked ready for war. Sandbags were being placed against buildings to protect against bomb-blast. The guards outside Buckingham Palace were dressed in khaki, not their normal ceremonial uniforms. Most of the children had already been evacuated. So had the animals from London Zoo. The newspapers were full of news of the fighting in Poland, and of advice on gas-masks and rationing. Only the last obsequies of peace remained. The British Ambassador in Berlin, Sir Nevile Henderson, in full ambassadorial insignia, had solemnly presented to the German Foreign Minister, Joachim von Ribbentrop, at 9 a.m. that morning the British ultimatum that, if Germany had not suspended aggression against Poland and indicated its readiness promptly to withdraw forces from Polish territory, the United

Kingdom would fulfil its obligations to Poland. At 11 a.m., British summer time, the ultimatum expired. Minutes later, Chamberlain's sad and weary voice came over the air waves. No assurance of willingness to comply with the terms of the ultimatum had been received. 'Consequently, this country is now at war with Germany.'[1]

As the national anthem intoned, following Chamberlain's broadcast, the air-raid sirens started wailing. Fears of an air attack on London had been widespread. It seemed as if Hitler was losing no time in launching one. It was rapidly established that it was a false alarm. In fact, there were to be no air-raids on London until the following summer. And not until the German western offensive in May 1940 did the British army engage in military action. Its expeditionary force did not even arrive on the Continent until 30 September.[2] Only at sea, in these early months of hostilities, did the sinking by a U-Boat in the Atlantic of the passenger liner *Athenia*, en route to Canada, already on 3 September, bringing the first civilian casualties of the conflict; the loss of the aircraft carrier *Courageous* on 19 September with half its crew; and the bold entry of a German submarine into Scapa Flow on 14 October to torpedo the *Royal Oak*, with over 800 lives lost, drive home grim reality.[3] Some called this strange period 'the twilight war'.[4] For the French it was the 'drôle de guerre'. The Germans came to refer to it as the 'Sitzkrieg' (or 'sitting war'). The Americans dubbed it 'the phoney war'. In Britain, too, this appellation stuck.

From the point of view of the Poles there was nothing at all 'phoney' about the war. After not much more than three weeks of savage fighting, the Polish army was utterly destroyed by the might of the Wehrmacht, and Warsaw, its population of more than a million bombed and shelled mercilessly, had surrendered. The eastern part of the country had by this time been ceded by the Germans to the tender mercies of the Soviet Union, under the most cynical part of the cynical Hitler–Stalin Pact. The declaration of war by Britain and France had not helped the Poles militarily in the slightest. As had been foreseen from the outset, the western allies were powerless to intervene in eastern Europe. And no diversionary attack, which would have given the German army something to ponder, had been envisaged on Germany's western frontier.[5] There was little doubt that, if the war could not be ended by some form of negotiated settlement, that frontier would see military action before too long. In the event, Hitler's next move was some months in coming – though this was not of his own volition; he would have attacked the West without delay, had not his generals persuaded him that the risks of an immediate assault would be too great. Meanwhile, with the Poles now under the Nazi yoke, the rest of Europe waited in an uneasy calm for what that move might be.

In Britain, the declaration of war enjoyed massive popular support. The bitter divisions of the past months and years were, at least temporarily, papered over. Voices favouring peace would rapidly be heard again. But those opposing the war were confined to small minorities without influence. Pacifism on the Left had lost its force.[6] Hitler had seen to that. On the extreme Right, Mosleyite Fascists, already fallen substantially in numbers since their heyday in the mid-1930s, were torn between avowed patriotism and identification with a regime and ideology with which Britain was at war. Opposition to the war from this quarter could cut little ice. Though not much effort was put into curtailing their activities during the first months of the war, their support was miniscule and their influence in high quarters non-existent.[7] Finally, there were those politicians and peers – individuals rather than organized groups – mainly, though not invariably, attached to the Conservative Party who had been strongly pro-German during the 1930s. Lord Londonderry was one of these. Their hopes of saving European peace had ended on 3 September 1939. They were left now with the desire to end the conflict as soon as possible through a negotiated peace. But, though they had the best of political and social connections, they also lacked power and influence. They were out in the political cold.

I

It was unclear in the earliest phase of hostilities precisely what British war aims amounted to. At any rate, Sir Alexander Cadogan, Under-Secretary at the Foreign Office, had difficulty in defining them. 'Must try and think this out,' he noted in his diary in late September. Two weeks later he had thought it out. He decided that the war aim was to 'get rid of Hitler'. Beyond that, 'war aims' and 'peace aims' were such loose terms, he considered, that they were not strictly definable.[8] Lord Halifax, the Foreign Secretary, also thought that the 'real object was to destroy Hitler'.[9] Chamberlain, too, saw no end to the struggle as long as Hitler remained in power.[10] He spoke rather vaguely of the need to defeat the German force and the German spirit.[11] He envisaged 'the liberation of Europe' once Hitler had been eliminated.[12] He was prepared to come to terms with Germany once the Nazi regime had been changed (or at least modified), frontiers had been restored, and disarmament had taken place. In return, and on the basis of safeguards for Jews and the Austrians, Germany could expect economic assistance, discussions on colonies and no demand for reparations.[13] The government and armed forces leadership reckoned with a war lasting three years. There was a wholly misplaced optimism that the German economy, already presumed to be under enormous strain, would collapse as supplies of essential raw materials ran out under the throttling constrictions of a blockade. Time, it was felt, was on Britain's side.[14]

This was as yet no world war. Italy and Spain were neutral. So, despite its non-aggression pact with Hitler, and its land-grabbing in Poland and the Baltic, was the Soviet Union. Japan, in evident dislike for the Soviet-German rapprochement, had become less cool towards Britain. The United States remained unwilling to become involved – which, in fact, accorded with Chamberlain's wishes. The Prime Minister, though his moods fluctuated, retained an underlying optimism that the German dictator would not succeed in the war. But he did not think outright military victory was possible. He hoped, rather, for a collapse of the German home front as the German people realized that Hitler could not win. 'The way to win the war is to convince the Germans that they cannot win,' was how he put it.[15] He did not expect the conflict would be over soon.

Some, however, thought that effort should be put into ensuring that it would be. This meant negotiations. Paradoxically, Chamberlain, who had been prepared to negotiate to the very eve of declaring war, now feared a reasonable peace offer from Hitler which would tempt the many who favoured a negotiated and rapid end to the struggle.[16] When Hitler did make an offer – in his speech to the Reichstag on 6 October 1939 – to settle Europe's problems of peace and security, on his own terms of course, it was half-hearted, and was outrightly rejected by the British government.[17] But Chamberlain was well aware even so of a growing swell of feeling at home, even if it was a minority strain of public opinion, advocating a move to end the war. Close to a fifth of his postbag in mid-September had been on the theme of 'stop the war'. In early October, he received 2,450 letters in the space of three days, 1,860 of which had wanted to 'stop the war'.[18] Around 14,000 letters of support for the apparent readiness of the monarchs of the Netherlands and Belgium to seek peace were received by the pacifist former Labour leader, George Lansbury, in November.[19] Some prominent figures thought negotiation was inevitable. Lloyd George thought Britain could not win the war, and envisaged overtures for peace, perhaps with President Roosevelt's support.[20] Lord Rothermere still ranked Hitler and Germany highly, and thought Britain was 'finished'.[21] Soon after war began, he put the arguments for peace in a draft letter to Chamberlain which, in the event, he decided not to send.[22] Lord Beaverbrook, too, at this stage favoured a negotiated peace.[23] Other figures in public life and business also made plain their wish for an early negotiated settlement.[24]

In the main, the pressure for peace in the early months of the war came from a number of individuals on the pacifist wing of the Labour movement (including Lansbury, and Lord Noel-Buxton, whose search for peaceful relations with Germany had at times come close to turning him into an apologist), the Fascists (headed by Oswald Mosley), and a group of Conservative MPs and peers. The latter included not a few of those who had stood out for their pro-German views. Lord Brocket, a wealthy brewer and former Conservative MP, still only in his mid-thirties, was a Hitler-admirer whom we have already encountered, making a nuisance of himself to the Foreign Secretary shortly before war began. Suspicions about his motives could be heard voiced by his fellow peers.[25] The Duke of Buccleuch, in his mid-forties, an officer in the King's Household, whose sister had married the King's brother, also admired Hitler whom, like Brocket, he had met in more promising times. His enthusiasm had led him to fly to Berlin in April 1939 to join in the celebrations of the Führer's

fiftieth birthday.[26] He took the view that peace would have to be negotiated before long with the same German leaders, so it made sense to
undertake the negotiations before much damage had been caused by
the war and while economic ruin could be averted.[27] The Duke of
Westminster, aged sixty, one of the richest men in England, with a
propensity to share some of the Nazis' delusions about Jews and
Freemasons, had joined 'The Link' in 1939 at precisely the time that
others were losing their ardour for Hitler's Germany. He was said to
have been keen on avoiding bombs dropping on central London since
he owned so much of it. Westminster, Brocket and Buccleuch were
supported by a number of other peers, including those with such
good pro-German credentials as Lords Mottistone, Arnold, Sempill,
Mount Temple and Tavistock. At least two meetings of pro-peace
peers and MPs were held in September 1939 at the home of the Duke
of Westminster. Lord Halifax was told that the atmosphere was 'of a
very defeatist character'.[28] The individuals who took part, however,
carried little weight. They amounted to rank political outsiders. The
government had no need for concern.[29]

Lord Londonderry had before the war shared many of the sympathies for Germany that characterized the peace lobby. In the eyes of
the public, he was probably the most notorious German sympathizer
of all. But he does not appear to have taken any part in the meetings
of those pressing for a negotiated peace in the autumn of 1939. A letter from an agent to the German Foreign Ministry in January 1940
did name Londonderry as one of three peers favourable towards
peace who would agree to any conditions if they had the power they
desired. (The other two were Lord Lymington, for whose weird and
mystical social and political views, linked to pro-German sentiment,
'eccentric' would be the most generous description imaginable,[30] and
the outspokenly pro-German Lord Brocket.)[31] But the information
was worthless. It had, in fact, been planted by MI5 and passed on by
a double-agent.[32] All three of those mentioned had been well known
before the war for their strong sympathies for Germany. So there
was no surprise that their names had surfaced in this context. But none
had the remotest proximity to positions of power in the autumn
of 1939.

Londonderry's own position, once the war he had so dreaded had come about, was an unenviable one. His earlier defence of German interests and association with leading Nazis left him exposed to public ignominy and without political friends, other than the few, like him out in the cold, who shared his views. He retreated now in the main to his Northern Irish home at Mount Stewart. There he carried out his normal civic duties in County Down (as he continued to do in County Durham, in northern England). His offer to assist in military recruitment was accepted by the government of Northern Ireland.[33] He helped in attempts in increase aircraft production, and offered his aerodrome at Newtownards in Northern Ireland.[34] And he was to find some fulfilment in the role of Northern Ireland Regional Commandant of the Air Training Corps.[35] But his involvement with the centre of political life of Great Britain – other than a momentary flicker in the dying embers in spring and summer 1940 – had come to an end. So had the grand social occasions that kept him in touch with the great and the good of the land. Lavish receptions at his London mansion scarcely accorded with wartime austerity. And Londonderry House was expensive to run. When it closed its portals in autumn 1939, 'Chips' Channon, who had practically made an unrepentent career of flitting from one extravagant party to another, remarked with sadness 'that the houses of the great will never again open their hospitable doors'. He likened it to the 'Twilight of the Gods'.[36] Londonderry himself sensed an age was passing. 'He has nothing to do now and, like me, feels that the world is crumbling before his eyes,' noted Sir Cuthbert Headlam, a leading Conservative in the north-east and longstanding political associate of Londonderry.[37] 'Nothing to do' meant to Londonderry not a life of idleness or leisure, but that he was out in the cold, without any political role, purpose, power or influence. In his enforced retreat, there was much time to mull over the mistakes of the past as the anger, bitterness and resentment that had possessed him for so long gnawed away inside him. He felt 'a broken reed';[38] for all the trappings of wealth and status, isolated and deeply unhappy, driven on by a thirst for vindication.

First he had to defend himself against a wave of rumours sweeping Northern Ireland, and spreading elsewhere, in September 1939 that he had been interned as a spy and a traitor.[39] The rumours reached Parliament. When Lord Zetland saw Londonderry in the House of

Lords, he remarked: 'Dear old chap, I'm glad to see you haven't been interned.' His surprise at seeing Londonderry was not unfounded, since 'a very substantial rumour' about his internment coursed through the House. Londonderry retorted furiously: 'Not one of my old colleagues, and not a single newspaper, has one good word to say for me.'[40] He told one old family friend that the 'cruel accusations' had 'come from Ireland from a section of the population who have [sic] always traduced my family and to this day heaped every obloquy on the head of my great ancestor, Castlereagh'. He found the rumours 'very wounding and quite impossible to refute, because people read these stories but they never read the answers'.[41] Perhaps, in fact, they did take notice of the denials after these appeared in the *Daily Mail* and elsewhere, in mid-September.[42] The *Sunday Sun* dubbed the story the 'silliest rumour of the war'.[43] Even Harold Nicolson, the National Labour MP and political columnist, whose views on foreign policy had differed markedly from Londonderry's, defended him vehemently in the important weekly *The Spectator*. He had been driven 'to the pitch of fury', Nicolson wrote, by the attack on Lord Londonderry. 'I have known that great gentleman for many years,' he added, generously. 'Only a maniac could conceive that his former endeavours to get to know and understand the Nazi leaders were anything but honourable attempts to prevent a disaster which he was one of the first to foresee'.[44] Perhaps the press refutation worked. At any rate, the rumours died away as quickly as they had surfaced.

However, Londonderry's pre-war entertainment of Ribbentrop came back to haunt him. Both privately and publicly he vehemently rejected allegations that he had been pro-Nazi. He told a Rumanian representative in London in October 1939 that he had been forced to endure criticism since he had been unable to explain to the public what he had been trying to do. 'The result is that I am supposed merely to have entertained Ribbentrop because of my personal affection for him and the doctrines which he and his colleagues propound.'[45] Unsurprisingly, Londonderry reacted more strongly to a letter suggesting that the war was 'due to a noble lord who told the racketeer von Ribbentrop that England would not fight, in fact was unprepared'.[46] He had come into contact with Ribbentrop, Londonderry rejoined angrily, 'in exactly the same way as His Majesty the King, Mr Neville Chamberlain the Prime Minister, Lord Derby and a great many other people in that we entertained him in our houses. This is an ordinary hospitality which has always been extended to Ambassadors and other important foreign personages.'[47] He made the same point publicly in a full-page spread in the *Sunday Sun* in early October, explaining 'Why I Entertained Ribbentrop',[48] and felt compelled to repeat the exercise with a big article, 'I Answer My Critics', in the *Sunday Dispatch* in mid-January 1940.[49] This article was in response to the newspaper's questioning of the appointment as War Minister of Oliver Stanley, 'son-in-law of Lord Londonderry, who before the war was host to Ribbentrop and who is associated in the public mind with peace-time friendship for the Nazi regime'. Writing to the owner of the newspaper, Esmond Harmsworth, son of Lord Rothermere, Londonderry protested at the unfairness of the article, claimed that he had 'always condemned Nazism', and demanded a published correction.[50] Despite Londonderry's justified irritation and spirited self-defence, the damage had long since been done. It was difficult now to repair his sullied reputation.

That he was feeling deeply wounded by the attacks when, in his view, he had been right all along made him both all the more bitter towards those he blamed for his situation – Britain's leaders since Hitler had come to power – and all the more anxious to vindicate his own stance. The Hailsham letters of November 1934 had, as we have seen, long acquired in his own mind the status of 'crown evidence' of his own correct approach. He had wanted them publishing in *Ourselves and Germany* in spring 1938, but had been refused permission by Neville Chamberlain. With the onset of war, he began again to contemplate publication of the documents which, he felt, would clear his name once and for all. Conceivably, this was the germ of the idea for his second book, *Wings of Destiny*, which would see the light of day only in 1943 – a treatise attempting to justify his demands for a level of rearmament in the air that the government of the day would not entertain and his claim of a far-sighted policy towards Germany when all around him were blinkered.[51] Once again, however, he was to be disappointed. Cabinet officials deliberated further on the 'long and melancholy story of the two Londonderry letters'. A cutting note prepared for the Cabinet Secretary, Sir Edward Bridges, remarked 'with astonishment that Lord Londonderry should think that their publication now would redound to his credit, or increase his reputation for political sagacity'.[52] Eventually, Chamberlain told Londonderry he could not alter the decision arrived at the previous year, and recommended that he simply précis the documents, as indeed he had done in his book *Ourselves and Germany*.[53] Londonderry was forced to leave the matter there – but only for the time being; and not without another bitter rehearsal for Chamberlain (who had heard it so many times) of how he had been mistreated and misunderstood by those in government. 'That I personally should have been destroyed and that my reputation for all time must suffer is only a matter of importance to myself and my family,' Londonderry lamented. On the publication of the documents, he added – quite disingenuously – that 'it does not matter one way or the other as far as I am concerned'.[54]

Chamberlain, evidently taken aback by the tone of the letter, took the trouble to jot a handwritten note to Lady Londonderry: 'Charley writes to his friends so bitterly that I thought you must have given me up as a bad job though I am totally unaware of having ever done him an injury'.[55] Lady Londonderry's reply hinted at her husband's vanity as the source of his resentfulness. 'It would have been so easy for you and would have appealed to him,' she admonished the Prime Minister, 'had you ever asked him to go and see you', to discuss relations with Germany. 'I shall always believe that in those days' (referring to the years 1936 to 1938), she continued, 'much might have been done, but he has always been studiously ignored and he could have given you very useful help. This at least is what we both feel.'[56]

Londonderry remained indefatigable in writing an unending flow of letters to a wide array of correspondents lambasting government ministers responsible for Britain's foreign affairs in the 1930s, defending his record as Air Minister and repeating the justification of his attempts to build friendly relations with Germany. He also voiced publicly and privately his reflections on Britain's war aims and the likely outcome of the conflict.

In public, Londonderry stood staunchly and uncritically behind the war effort. He portrayed it as a fight for freedom and legality against thraldom and dictatorship under the Nazi doctrine.[57] 'We are witnessing at the present time the downfall of Hitler,' he declared, denouncing the German leader he had once admired as 'devoid of any plan for the well-being of his own people' and 'merely an egotist seeking his own personal aggrandisement at the cost of the lives of numbers of young men, the spreading of havoc and devastation on a large scale and also the destruction of the German nation'. Though predicting a hard struggle, he depicted Britain's position as favourable and its strength, backed by the Dominions, as greater than Germany's. He was explicit about peace proposals. No compromise was possible with Britain's ideals and aims, he stated. 'Until Germany has either been rendered innocuous or has shown a national character very different from the one which Hitler has sought to develop, we shall refuse to lay down our arms or even enter into negotiations which would prove ineffective and abortive.'[58]

Privately, the tone was different. He told Lord Halifax in November he was 'trying to establish faith in the Government, which is very far indeed from my true feelings'.[59] Writing to Churchill on the same day, he said he was 'beginning to doubt whether we are following the right lines to win the war'.[60] He was also uncertain 'whether our attempt to separate the German people from Hitler is a sound policy'.[61] He complained that he had difficulty in understanding what the war aims were.[62] He thought Germany was becoming stronger, not weaker, and worried whether enough was being done to gain support in neutral countries, particularly America.[63] And, still wedded to his fear of Communism, he added Bolshevism to Nazism as the tyranny that Britain had to remove.[64] 'There is a great deal of force', he wrote towards the end of the year, 'in the contention that the danger from Russia is far greater than the danger from Germany'.[65] He thought the war was 'directly playing up to Russian policy', and that 'the continuance of this struggle must result in the Bolshevising of Central Europe and that terrible influence extending throughout the world'.[66] He linked the thought with considerations about possible peace negotiations.

Writing to Lord Halifax in December 1939, he appeared to be of two minds about the desirability of seeking a negotiated settlement. He rejected the view (which the Duke of Buccleuch, among others, had articulated) that a better peace could be negotiated before the 'chaos and destruction' which would inevitably ensue if the war continued. In his view, Londonderry remarked, 'it is quite impossible to talk peace when there is the remotest possibility of Germany being strong enough to carry on the aggressive policy which she was allowed to develop, and which has been the direct reason for the present hostilities'.[67] This seemed explicit enough. But only a few days later, in a further letter to the Foreign Secretary, he was more equivocal. He was in sympathy, he wrote, with the suggestion that 'every avenue which points to the possibility of negotiation' should be explored. He would be glad to see something come of it, he added, 'because I have always felt that by far the greater danger to all our ideals and ideas is the Russian menace'. The monarchs of Belgium and the Netherlands had recently made overtures towards a peace settlement, and he understood their offer was still open. Once the current 'pause' and the opportunities of contact and inquiry through neutral channels came to an end, however, the opportunity would be gone. He realized, of course, the difficulties of any move towards a negotiated settlement. This 'would be construed as a desire on our part to withdraw from the very definite attitude which we have adopted of destroying Naziism [sic] and restoring Poland and Czecho-Slovakia'. He differed slightly from the government on these war aims, he commented. The implication was that he was less ready to restore the pre-war Polish and Czech borders. He hoped that every channel of information was being explored. However, he supported the government's firm stance in the absence of 'some complete change in the German attitude as I see it now'.[68]

In the first months of 1940, Londonderry was in touch with a number of peers who were prominent in the peace-lobby, though he continued to retain his distance from them. The Duke of Buccleuch congratulated him on his article in the *Sunday Dispatch*, defending himself against his critics, and took the opportunity to advocate the search for a peace settlement, perhaps brokered by Mussolini, the Pope and the Dutch. He thought Hitler and Ribbentrop could be removed from power and replaced by Göring and army chiefs. Though the prospects were less favourable than they had been in October, the outlook would be 'disastrous' for Britain and other European nations if war continued, leading to the ruin and bolshevization of Germany.[69]

Londonderry's reply does not seem to have survived. His views at this juncture can, however, be ascertained from an exchange he had with another leading proponent of peace, Lord Brocket. Londonderry said he favoured a move for peace, as long as this came from outside the government (avoiding, therefore, the impression of weakness). He mentioned Roosevelt and Mussolini as possible intermediaries. But his own remarkable suggestion was to try to persuade Stanley Baldwin to intervene. He had already written to him to this effect. He envisaged even the possibility of Baldwin travelling to Berlin to state his case.[70] It was remarkable since Londonderry had for years done little but spew out bile over Baldwin's maltreatment of him and his ineffectual leadership. It was also remarkable since Baldwin, during his premiership, had both avoided all attempts to persuade him to meet Hitler and had left international affairs almost entirely in the hands of his Foreign Secretaries.

Writing to the former Prime Minister in the most emollient terms he had used for almost five years, Londonderry described him as 'an independent person possessing a world-wide reputation'. He pointed out 'the disaster which must follow the prolongation of the present hostilities', and wondered whether Baldwin might 'take up this independent position and call upon the belligerents to realise the reponsibilities to the world which rest upon their shoulders'. Unless the menace of German aggression could be completely eliminated, he said, it was better to continue the conflict until total defeat had been inflicted upon Germany. But he was sure Hitler was 'in a very difficult position' and had been informed by those apprised of neutral opinion 'that he would gladly come to some terms which would bring to an end the possibility of the disaster which must overwhelm Germany in the end'. He saw it as a duty to future generations to avoid 'senseless slaughter' if at all possible. Londonderry had spoken about the matter to Lord Arnold (a former Council Member of the Anglo-German Fellowship, and strong lobbyist for a peace settlement). Arnold's line, similar to that of Buccleuch, was that the time for peace terms was more propitious than it was ever likely to be in the future. He thought Germany would be prepared to give guarantees for the future. Londonderry was not so sure. And unless it was certain that Germany no longer posed a threat to the world, 'it appears hopeless to talk about peace'. Even so, he thought 'some move should be made'.[71] Baldwin did not reply. But when he saw Londonderry, a short time afterwards, he let it be known that 'he was not proposing to touch the matter' and was convinced that he could achieve nothing.[72]

Brocket's own suggestion as a basis for peace negotiations did not endear itself to Londonderry. An Italian source had told him, Brocket said, that Göring might replace Hitler in an army *coup d'état* if agreement could be reached allowing for Austria, the Sudetenland, Danzig, the Corridor and Silesia to remain part of Germany. Colonial demands would be dropped, and a disarmament conference would be proposed. 'Surely', wrote Brocket, 'the two sides could get together on that basis.'[73] But Londonderry was unconvinced. He was sceptical about the proposals of 'the Goering Party'. The concessions did not amount to much, he thought, and were 'very little different to Hitler's original suggestion' – presumably meaning in his 'peace speech' of 6 October 1939 – 'that he should keep what he has taken and start a peace on that basis', something wholly in conflict, as he said, with British war aims.[74]

Whatever his stance had been in the autumn, Londonderry was by now, then, in correspondence with those most directly involved in the peace-lobby. These were in the main, as we have seen, Conservative peers and MPs. But some from the pacifist wing of the Labour Party also pressed for peace moves. Among them were the former Minister of Agriculture in Labour administrations, Lord Noel-Buxton, and his brother Charles Roden Buxton, a Quaker and pacifist who had formerly been Chairman of the Labour Party's Advisory Committee on International Questions. Both had belonged to the Anglo-German Group, a predominantly leftish organization set up under the influence of Dr Margarete Gärtner (whom we have encountered as the most prominent liaison figure between Britain and Germany in the inter-war years) and chaired by the pacifist Labour peer Lord Allen of Hurtwood, which had idealistic aims for improving international relations between the two countries and maintaining world peace.[75] Charles Roden Buxton, among a tiny minority within his own party, had wanted to go far beyond Chamberlain's concessions in 1938 in redistributing territory to Germany. The thought was that removal of economic grievances would eliminate the imperialist urge to war, while international cooperation would eradicate capitalist competition.[76] His brother had favoured, against the views of the majority in the party which supported a British guarantee for Czechoslovakia, backing a settlement based upon autonomy for ethnic groups; that is, a break-up of the existing state.[77] Once hostilities broke out in September 1939, both brothers became active in the pursuit of a peace settlement. And both were in touch with Lord Londonderry about this.

Charles Roden Buxton sent Londonderry a pamphlet in January 1940 (which he in turn passed on to Baldwin), evidently in connection with peace suggestions.[78] At the beginning of the following month his brother, Lord Noel-Buxton, invited Londonderry to a small gathering of those who had already met on a number of occasions to discuss war aims. Lord Brocket, who had coordinated the earlier meetings, was too ill to attend, but it had been suggested that Londonderry and one or two others should discuss the matter confidentially.[79] Londonderry said he would have gladly attended, but would not be in London at the time. Lord Arnold would be able to tell the meeting of their own deliberations. Londonderry also mentioned the approach to Baldwin, on which he had heard nothing. He then, however, gently but specifically distanced himself from the peace-lobby. 'I am regretfully coming to the conclusion', he wrote,

that our well-meaning efforts to bring about a cessation of hostilities must come to nought. The whole attitude of the German Government is so contemptible and so outrageous that I see no alternative but to work for the courses which we were seeking to avoid, and that a peace will have to be established in which the German force for evil will be once and for all destroyed.[80]

For all his earlier enthusiasm for friendship with Germany, Londonderry's position equated with that of the appeasers who had courted Hitler but then, seeing their trust in him totally destroyed, felt that they had to see the struggle through to the bitter end. He had, in other words, recognized that treating with Hitler had no prospect. In this he differed both from Conservatives such as Brocket, Buccleuch and Westminster, who had shared Londonderry's desire for friendship with Germany but continued to press for a negotiated settlement which would have seen Hitler retain most of his ill-gotten gains; and from the pacifist lobby centred on the Buxtons, which wanted peace both out of a general detestation of war and because they feared certain carnage and destruction, should war continue, more than they feared a settlement with the Nazi leadership.

Lord Noel-Buxton wrote to Londonderry again on 27 February 1940, this time enclosing an 'absolutely private and confidential' memorandum prepared by 'a small group of peers and M.P.'s'. He wanted to add Londonderry's name to the signatories of those in general agreement with it (if not necessarily with every point) before sending it on to the Prime Minister. The memorandum was headed 'Policy in Relation to the War', and was marked 'Confidential'.[81] It pressed the urgency of negotiation, prepared by private inquiry and contact, through neutral channels or otherwise. It wanted to set no preconditions for talks. It did not take Hitler's proven lack of trustworthiness as a central obstacle. It looked instead to the creation of a new European order based upon negotiation and content, created with the participation of smaller and neutral states. It would take account 'of the natural and legitimate aspirations, and of the actual balance of interests and power' of the Great Powers. And it would afford a secure economic basis for all states, including Germany, and provide for a collective guarantee of all participating in the proposed conference, 'subject, of course, to revision by peaceful methods of change'. In this context, 'it is easy to see that the trustworthiness or otherwise of Herr Hitler is far from being the only question'. Possibly, negotiations would in any case be carried on with some other person or group, perhaps Göring or the army leadership. Even if Hitler still retained authority, 'his power to upset Europe, by breaking treaties, would be limited by the opposition of Russian, Italian, and other interests, which would find their place in the ultimate treaty, as well as by the opposition of Britain and France, whose determination to resist has been conclusively proved by their entry into war'. Under these conditions, the memorandum concluded, 'any future act of aggression would be a defiance of all the signatories to the treaty, and its real nature would be so obvious that it could not be disputed'.

Londonderry was sceptical. He placed a large question-mark in the margin against a passage which read:

The best possible guarantee of future stability must be secured. There is, however, much evidence, coming from different sources, which, while not conclusive, strongly suggests that terms could be secured in an eventual conference, which would realise our essential aim – the setting up of genuine Polish and Czech States, and the entrance of Germany into a definite system of European order, based on consent, combined with disarmament, and guaranteed by all the Powers participating in the conference.

Londonderry must have felt he had been through all this – or at least much of it – before. The next sentence also caused him to ponder. 'Such a settlement as this, contrasted with the colossal sacrifices of the war, would represent a failure, evident enough to German eyes, of the policy of aggression; and would lead to an overwhelming popular feeling against any such policy in future.' 'I wonder,' Londonderry jotted in the margin. He thought, as again he remarked in an annotation, that British demands for any end to the conflict 'admitted of very little modification'. He did, however, see substance in the view that the expressed intention to wage a prolonged war and ostentatiously to refuse all discussion of terms was not likely 'to bring the enemy to reason' and more likely to stiffen resistance and backing for Hitler.[82]

It was an extraordinarily idealistic tract – reminiscent in some regards of the idealism that had initially underpinned the establishment of the League of Nations. It was little wonder that Londonderry demurred. Replying to Noel-Buxton, he commented that, though sympathetic, he could not add his signature to those supporting the memorandum. His letter provides a good insight into his thinking at this juncture. He would have signed the memorandum, he said, had the war situation been more favourable for Britain. As it was, he saw great dangers in the proposals. The only overtures for peace, therefore, had to come, in Londonderry's view, via friendly neutrals. The British government's position had been clearly laid out. Britain's war aims – as we have seen, they included the removal of Hitler and the withdrawal of German troops from conquered territory – could not be fulfilled, he suggested, without the destruction of German armed strength. The Germans were unlikely to consider any limitation of this armed strength, on which they believed their security to depend. Consequently, there was no basis for negotiations. Londonderry then came to the nub of his own view. Before war, every attempt had to be made to reach terms that would prevent ruinous hostilities. But once war had broken out, the time for negotiations had passed. 'As soon as we revert to barbarism by declaring war', he remarked, 'then the remedies for bringing that war to an end must be akin to the character of the disease. In this case, it means the victory of one side over the other.'[83]

Londonderry elaborated on his assessment of the war at this stage in two long letters he sent to his old friend George Ward Price, the *Daily Mail* correspondent, who had expressed his views on Mussolini's uncertainty and apprehension and the likelihood of the Germans completing their war aims through acquiring economic hegemony in the Balkans then proposing a peace settlement.[84] Londonderry's replies combined both perception and delusion.

As in his reply to Noel-Buxton, he saw no alternative, once in war, 'but a fight to a finish'. Britain's war aims were correct, he thought. There could be no cooperation with Germany. At the end of this war she would have to be kept 'in bondage and subjection'. Progress on a comprehensive international settlement would be 'relegated to the far distant future'. He had been 'terribly mortified' by the actions of his earlier political contacts, of Hitler and quite especially of Göring. (He was 'not really fond of foreigners', he commented, and had looked after them in Britain 'as a duty and as a civility' and abroad because they were 'useful'. The gulf in language and 'outlook' had presented a barrier in relations with Göring. He had liked Ribbentrop less, while Goebbels, Hess and Himmler were merely 'unpleasant subordinates'.)[85] His understanding of the balance of forces led him to optimistic conclusions. He thought the current 'phoney war' could continue for a year or so. He did not believe the Germans had the power to invade either through Holland and Belgium or in the Balkans. There were many indications, he thought, that the Germans were not very powerful. 'Their army is untrained and the young men are undernourished and they are also uneducated.' The air force, too, 'in training, personnel and machines, is decidely inferior to ours', and was 'overloaded with junk' – out-of-date Dorniers, Heinkels and Messerschmit 109s. He was 'sure the Germans cannot take on an offensive of any magnitude as they cannot carry the casualties'. A defensive stalemate could continue for a long time, he imagined, 'but if we can apply two squeezes then the strain would be too great for Germany'.[86]

A few weeks later, he seemed more persuaded that some form of negotiated settlement, with Germany still in a strong position, would be the outcome. This could not embrace a restoration of the 'artificial existence' of Poland and Czechoslovakia. Rather, it would imply 'spheres of influence'. He still envisaged something along the lines of what Göring had wanted: confining British interests to the Empire and naval supremacy, leaving Germany a free hand in central and eastern Europe. A German offer of peace from a position of strength, perhaps backed by Russia, and with support from other neutral countries, would, he thought, leave Britain high and dry in pursuit of a war in which (as Ward Price had suggested to him) she would increasingly appear to be the aggressor. Militarily, he thought there could be a stalemate for some time. He discounted 'the idea of a German push in the Spring'. He still thought a British military offensive would 'probably have decisive results'.[87] However, he had no confidence in Britain's political leaders. 'I feel there is a lack of real strategic planning and of leadership,' he wrote, 'but I see no one qualified for this. I do not think any of them see one month ahead'.[88] Naturally, the Prime Minister was his main target. Chamberlain was 'quite ignorant about the duty which he has in hand,' Londonderry told Halifax (about whom he was privately also critical). He believed he was 'conscientiously sustaining this stalemate position' and doing nothing towards winning the war. He was sure 'we want someone with much more drive and with much more knowledge to lead us at this juncture'.[89]

Londonderry's own antipathy towards Chamberlain, in particular, was, of course, long established and had personal as well as directly political roots. But by spring 1940 there were many others, within the Prime Minister's own party (despite the superficial loyalty) as well as among the Opposition, who shared Londonderry's dissatisfaction with his war leadership. Chamberlain was well aware of the discontent fermenting just below the surface. It had been present since the beginning of the war. But despite some calls for Churchill to take over, no alternative figure had been able to command remotely enough support to pose a serious challenge to the Prime Minister. And conditions of war imposed their own demands on loyalty. As late as April 1940, Chamberlain could still feel secure. Even so, there were those behind the scenes preparing the ground for a change of leadership should the Prime Minister falter. Londonderry's last, brief involvement in actions close to the heart of government would see him join the machinations.

II

On 1 April 1940 Londonderry received a letter from Lord Salisbury, the head of the redoubtable house of Cecil, one of England's most influential aristocratic families since the era of Elizabeth I. He had written asking Londonderry to join a body he and a number of like-minded political associates were establishing 'to watch the conduct of the War'.[90] The intention was to bring together a group of twenty or more members of both Houses of Parliament 'who should consider any difficulties arising out of the conduct of the War by the Government and make the necessary representations'.[91] Salisbury, together with the other family members who joined the Committee – his son, Viscount Cranborne, brother, Viscount Cecil of Chelwood, and nephew, Viscount Wolmer – had been strong critics of Chamberlain's appeasement policy and had been appalled by Munich. Their confidence in Chamberlain fell still further at Hitler's destruction of the remains of the Czech state. It was only momentarily stilled at the outbreak of war. Most of the other leading lights in the Committee had also been strong opponents of appeasement – among them, from the House of Commons, Leo Amery, Harold Nicolson and the former Cabinet Minister Duff Cooper, who had resigned over Munich. These were not usual political bedfellows for Londonderry. Those who had favoured the policy of appeasement – let alone, like Londonderry, had supported an even more positively pro-German policy – were in a small minority on the Committee. But Londonderry did not owe his place to his earlier views on Germany or his backing for Chamberlain at Munich. His critical stance towards Chamberlain's war leadership must have been known to Salisbury and presumably played its part. But more important was his knowledge of the air force. Londonderry's membership had been proposed by his immediate successor as Secretary of State for Air, Lord Swinton.[92] And his old ally Lord Trenchard, former Marshal of the Royal Air Force, was asked to join at the same time.[93] Salisbury was anxious to encourage a more dynamic approach to the war and wanted to promote the potential of the air force to launch an assault on Germany. When, within a brief time, Trenchard had devised a strategic plan for a bombing campaign, Londonderry hailed it as 'unanswerable', telling Salisbury it was 'valuable and impressive', and fully in line with his own opinions.[94]

Plans to establish a committee to serve as a 'watchdog' on the conduct of the war had been formed several months earlier. The initial aim was to serve as a loyal 'ginger group' which would 'harass ministers when they ought to be harassed'.[95] There was lingering suspicion that there might even now be some in the Cabinet wanting a negotiated peace and concessions. There was suspicion above all about Chamberlain. And he appeared to lack a clear view to prosecute the war. The differing opinions coagulated in the expressed wish for a reconstruction of the government around a small executive War Cabinet. However, Chamberlain dismissed the idea out of hand when Salisbury presented it to him on 10 April. There was as yet no concerted thought within the Committee about replacing Chamberlain. Even so, Salisbury's brother, Lord Cecil, had convinced Londonderry 'that the structure of the War Cabinet is by no means the most important thing, because the main object is to obtain the proper driving force at the top'.[96] Londonderry picked up the point. He was not sure, he told Salisbury, that Chamberlain possessed either the 'driving power' or the knowledge for effective war leadership. He had no alternative to suggest. But he added, presciently, that 'if some disaster should occur which was obviously the result of lack of knowledge and lack of preparation on the part of the Government, the effect of this lack of confidence on the country would be very serious indeed'.[97]

The disaster was not long in coming. On 4 April, Chamberlain had confidently proclaimed that, by not attacking Britain and France by this time, Hitler had 'missed the bus'.[98] The boast promptly backfired. Five days later, German troops invaded Denmark and Norway. Britain, with Churchill (recalled to the government the previous

September as First Lord of the Admiralty) as the main driving-force, had for months been mulling over plans to lay mines in Norwegian waters to cut supplies of Swedish iron-ore reaching Germany. But precisely as the decision was being taken to implement the plan, Hitler, alert to the looming threat of British intervention in Scandinavia, had acted. The British government were caught unawares. Hastily assembled and ill-prepared troops were rushed to Norway. But landings on 14 and 17 April at the small fishing ports of Namsos and Aandalsnes could not be secured. During the first days of May the troops had to be evacuated. It would take until the end of the month before the larger force sent to Narvik was able to take the port – then holding it only briefly before evacuating it on 8 June. By this time, the Scandinavian disaster had brought the downfall of Neville Chamberlain and his replacement, ironically, by the minister who bore greatest reponsibility for the débâcle: Winston Churchill.

Lord Salisbury had told Chamberlain at their meeting on 10 April that 'a failure in Norway would be fatal to the Government'. Chamberlain had retorted that 'if people did not like the administration of the present Government they could change it'.[99] By the beginning of the following month, the feeling was mounting within Chamberlain's own party as well as among the Opposition that this would have to be done. The Watching Committee was prominent behind the scenes in orchestrating the criticism of the Prime Minister. Londonderry was part of a delegation to meet the Foreign Secretary, Lord Halifax, on 29 April. It was to no avail.[100] It was a 'distinctly disappointing' meeting, though Londonderry hoped it had conveyed to Halifax the anxieties about the conduct of the war.[101] The Committee had, in fact, subtly altered its position over the course of a month. From a body wanting a reconstruction of the War Cabinet and a more dynamic prosecution of the conflict, it was turning into a pressure-group aiming to replace the Prime Minister. And it was now voicing a sentiment that could be commonly heard in the corridors of Westminster, as well as in the country at large. Confidence in Chamberlain was rapidly haemorrhaging. During the debate on Norway on 7–8 May, the Watching Committee liaised with the Labour Party. Once satisfied that the Conservative rebellion would be substantial, the Labour leader, Clement Attlee, decided to force a vote of confidence. The Committee favoured a change of Prime Minister. When the vote was taken in the House of Commons at the end of the debate, on the evening of 8 May, the representatives of the Watching Committee voted against the government. Chamberlain won the division, though with a majority reduced catastrophically from over 200 to a mere 81, and with 33 Conservatives voting against him and a further 65 abstaining. The core of the opposition within his own party came from the Watching Committee and its allies.[102]

The next day, Lord Salisbury met Halifax to demand Chamberlain's resignation and a government representing all parties. Halifax excluded himself as a possible successor. On 10 May, Chamberlain, still hoping to cling on to power, learnt that the Labour Party had refused to join the government under his leadership. Resignation was now the only option. The news had come in that morning of the German invasion of Belgium and Holland. Lord Salisbury informed the Private Secretary of the King that the Watching Committee was insistent on Chamberlain's departure. He had already expressed his view privately that Churchill should become Prime Minister during the course of the day.[103] That afternoon, Chamberlain resigned. A little later, Churchill was called to Buckingham Palace and charged with forming a new administration.

Londonderry had taken no direct part in the dramatic events at Westminster. His active participation in the meetings of the Watching Committee had been limited by a bout of illness and, especially, by the fact that he was now mainly based in Northern Ireland and absent from the intrigues in central London. Nonetheless, he had been part of a body which had played a significant part in Chamberlain's downfall. His participation had been in a minor key. But he was doubtless immensely satisfied to have played even a limited role in helping to unseat the man he regarded as responsible above all others for Britain's disastrous foreign policy and now equally damaging conduct of the war. And he felt that Britain's war leadership had been placed in the hands of the only man fitted for the task at that moment. The change of Prime Minister, he remarked, had given him 'great satisfaction'.[104] His kinsman, Winston Churchill, could not be blamed for the abysmal failures of the government except, in Londonderry's eyes, for causing panic on rearmament in the air force through propagating false information on the strength of the Luftwaffe in the mid-1930s.[105] Despite their political differences over policy towards Germany and the rearming of the air force, he had high respect for Churchill's drive and energy. He would now bring, Londonderry correctly imagined, the dynamism in war leadership that had been so lacking in Chamberlain. He even fleetingly, it seems, entertained the vain hope that his cousin, who had provided him with political patronage some twenty or so years earlier, might even now find a place for him in his War Cabinet.[106] It indicated Londonderry's continued belief in the power of patronage. But it was, of course, anything but a realistic hope. Churchill never gave the matter even the most cursory thought.

Churchill had scant regard for Londonderry's political judgement. They had fallen out over the menace posed by the German air force, over Londonderry's preference for friendship with Germany rather than France, over Italy (when he had argued that it was foolish to alienate Mussolini), and over the Spanish Civil War (when Churchill had not shared his cousin's enthusiasm for a pro-Franco policy, advocating 'the strictest neutrality').[107] Their personal relations had suffered as a consequence – to Londonderry's regret, though less so to Churchill's. 'I used to know him intimately', Londonderry commented, just after Churchill's elevation to the office of Prime Minister, 'and I owe him more than I can ever repay in support and friendship, but we gradually got further and further apart.'[108] His true feelings were somewhat less complimentary. 'I have fallen out several times with our friend,' he told his longstanding confidante, Lady Desborough.

I remember having a difference of opinion over the abdication. He was then very insulting to me at Grillions Club [the London dining-club frequented by the well-to-do] on his general condemnation of my trying to see whether it was practicable to get hold of both the dictators whilst they were developing their strength, and we had practically a stand-up row at Lady Cunard's [a renowned hostess] when he attempted to browbeat me across the table, and I was not standing for it, nor was I ready to kowtow.[109]

Londonderry had told his cousin 'that the French were no use and would certainly let us down and that the Jewish influence was much too strong in this country, France, and America'. It was at this point that

Churchill lost his temper and, with around thirty guests enjoying the spectacle, the fur began to fly.[110] Reminiscing, years later, Londonderry returned to the argument with his cousin at Lady Cunard's. 'Chips' Channon recalled Londonderry telling over lunch

how his political prospects were blighted by an unfortunate dinner party at Emerald's [Lady Cunard] before the war, when he argued with Winston, and said that France was unreliable and rotten and could not be depended upon. Winston lost his temper, being a fanatical Francophil; and could not forgive Londonderry then, and certainly not later, for being proved right.[111]

The alienation was real enough. But the 'blighted prospects' of a political resurrection were a figment of Londonderry's imagination. The bleak reality for him was that he remained, under Churchill as under Chamberlain, out in the cold.

Londonderry's connections nevertheless left him with a toe-hold on the outer edge of politics during the course of events which were determining Britain's future. His good personal contacts, particularly with Lord Halifax, enabled him even now to attempt to intervene and to seek to use influence in high quarters. An opportunity rapidly presented itself.

Churchill's first weeks in office saw him confronted with the greatest threat there had ever been to the country's independence – greater even than the time of the Spanish Armada in the sixteenth century. The speed of the German advance into northern France had all but destroyed French military resistance and ruthlessly cut off the British Expeditionary Force. By the 24 May most of it – over 300,000 men – was stranded at Dunkirk, the last remaining port in Allied hands. The danger was grave in the extreme. Some intelligence estimates indicated that a German attack on the British Isles was imminent, even before a French capitulation.[112] The optimism of the 'phoney war', when eventual victory was largely presumed, had given way to deep anxiety, and a good deal of pessimism about Britain's hopes of escaping defeat.

A few days earlier, Londonderry had received a letter reflecting this mood. It had been sent by Kenneth de Courcy, a colourful acquaintance, well connected to the British Secret Service, confidant of

Cabinet ministers, former dining companion of the Duke of Windsor, and many years later a guest in Her Majesty's Prison at Wormwood Scrubs after being found guilty of forgery, fraud and perjury. Writing on 21 May, Courcy, acting as secretary of the strongly pro-appeasement Imperial Policy Group, of which he was the mainstay, had spoken of a 'rapidly deteriorating' situation in Europe, verging on the 'disastrous'. It was clear that Britain had underrated the enemy. He thought 'the sands are running out', but added, cryptically: 'I am sure there is a clear course to follow if only we had the intelligence to see it'.[113] Plainly, Londonderry grasped what Courcy meant. Without doubt they had already discussed the matter verbally. Next day he sent a carefully couched letter to his friend Lord Halifax, the Foreign Secretary. He advised him to do all he could to keep Mussolini out of the war. He thought this is what Mussolini himself would want, and that 'he would bring pressure to bear on Hitler to arrive at some modus vivendi'. He professed, disin-genuously, to know nothing of the military situation. But if this were giving rise to anxiety, the diplomatic move, he suggested, would be 'the card to play'.[114] Halifax replied on 24 May, stating that every-thing was being done to keep Mussolini out of the war, and that the government 'had already moved in the sense of some of the sugges-tions you make'. They were also trying to pull strings through the French and the USA.[115] Londonderry had told Halifax that he had not spoken one word of the matter to anyone. But he promptly now relayed the gist of Halifax's letter to Courcy, who in return indicated his satisfaction that the representations had been made and that 'moves have already been taken in the right direction'. He hoped that Britain would 'take the right course while the going is good', and added: 'Another friend of mine has seen the Italian Ambassador since I saw you and he made exactly the same points again'.[116] Londonderry and Courcy had evidently met at some point to discuss Italy's position – and, it would appear, the possibility that Mussolini might act as an intermediary with Hitler.[117] This, it seems certain, was the implication of Londonderry's delphic letter to Halifax.

The Italian Ambassador in London was Giuseppe Bastiniani. He had already let it be known that he enthusiastically favoured a British approach to Germany through Italian channels.[118] On 25 May, with the prospect looming of total military collapse on the Continent, Halifax met Bastiniani. In diplomatic language, Halifax suggested that Mussolini might serve as an honest broker at a conference aimed at a general European settlement. As an incentive, he indicated the possibility of unspecified territorial concessions to Italy. German demands, it was obvious, would also have to be met. With German forces on the verge of victory in France, it was obvious who would hold the whip hand.[119] When Halifax reported to the Cabinet, the military situation could scarcely have looked bleaker. Halifax argued that there could be no harm in approaching Mussolini; if he posed unreasonable terms, they could be rejected. The French leaders, clutching at straws, also favoured an approach. Churchill himself did not outrightly reject the idea. He voiced the opinion that 'if we could get out of this jam by giving up Malta and Gibraltar and some African colonies he would jump at it'. But he remained sceptical, pointing out that 'the only safe way was to convince Hitler he couldn't beat us'.[120] Any terms, he thought, would limit Britain's armaments, forcing cessions of naval bases, and thus expose her to the danger of further German threats whenever Hitler wanted to turn the screw. Moreover, news of the approach to Mussolini would leak out, damaging morale in Britain and indicating weakness to Hitler. Halifax was asked to submit a paper to the Cabinet. Entitled 'Suggested Approach to Mussolini', it indicated a wish to satisfy Mussolini's territorial demands in return for cooperation in securing a settlement – meaning peace with Germany.[121] But by then the Cabinet had slept on the matter. Critically, Chamberlain – still leader of the Conservative Party and a member of the War Cabinet – was cool towards the idea. The other members of the Cabinet also showed no liking for Halifax's initiative. Churchill intervened decisively to state that 'the approach would ruin the integrity of our fighting position in this country'. It was 'not only futile, but involved us in a deadly danger'.[122] The key moment had passed. The suggestion of an approach to Mussolini was finally discarded at a meeting of the full Cabinet on 28 May when Churchill stated that 'it was idle to think that, if we tried to make peace now, we should get better terms from Germany than if we went on and fought it out. The Germans would demand our fleet – that would be called "disarmament" – our naval bases, and much else. We should become a slave state.'¹²³

It was a critical episode in Britain's war. With the fall of France which followed within weeks, Britain was left facing a mighty enemy now little more than twenty miles away across the English Channel. Determination to fight on had emerged almost by default.¹²⁴ Churchill had been sure only that an attempt to explore a negotiated settlement was a dangerous mistake. How the war would now develop was a further, unanswered question. The hopes pinned on the United States had up to then produced nothing of tangible benefit. Material assistance was still some months away. Goodwill from across the Atlantic was welcome but, in the long run, insufficient. However, the skies brightened within days as news of the successful relief – far beyond anyone's initial expectations – of the hundreds of thousands of troops trapped at Dunkirk came through. Churchill could make a triumph out of a military disaster to lift the spirits of the British people. The perils of a long summer were only just beginning. But as long as Churchill remained at the helm, there would be no more government initiatives to seek peace with Hitler.

Londonderry had been as much in the dark about the crucial deliberations in the Cabinet as the rest of the country. But his minimal role in the events preceding them, encouraging the Foreign Secretary in the thoughts he was in any case entertaining, is sufficient to indicate where he would have stood on the issue of an approach to Mussolini had he still been a member of the government. His own position had evidently wavered, in the wake of the calamitous military collapse in May 1940, from the resolution he had shown in the spring to acceptance of the need to seek negotiable terms. In this, he was reverting, like Halifax, to the hopes he had seen raised by Mussolini on an earlier occasion – when the Italian dictator had intervened to influence German policy by initiating the Munich Conference of September 1938.

Londonderry expressed tentative views on peace negotiations with Hitler on one further occasion. This was shortly after Hitler had made his final 'offer' to Britain, following the fall of France. This amounted to no more than a brief 'appeal to reason' tagged on to his triumphant Reichstag address on 19 July.¹²⁵ The British government peremptorily rejected it. As Churchill later remarked, 'it was in fact an offer not of peace but of readiness to accept the surrender by Britain of all she had entered the war to maintain'.[126] Lord Halifax dismissed the 'offer' in a broadcast on 22 July as Hitler's 'summons to capitulate to his will'.[127] There were, however, even now those who thought possible terms ought at least to have been explored. German diplomatic representations had been made through a number of neutral countries in the days after Hitler's speech. One feeler, through the United States, reached Lord Lothian, who in the mid-1930s had preceded Londonderry in trying to engineer friendship with Nazi Germany and was by this point British Ambassador in Washington. Lothian, on his own authority, had sought through an intermediary to explore what German peace terms might be.[128] Londonderry had, of course, no government position and was not able to intervene as Lothian had done. But there is a hint in a tactfully phrased letter to Halifax shortly after his broadcast speech that Londonderry, too, would at least have preferred to take soundings on possible peace terms. 'I presume that if Hitler gave up all his ill-gotten gains and retired into Germany as it was before the invasion of Czechoslovakia, that we would be prepared to consider negotiating a peace,' he wrote to Halifax, adding that 'many other details' would also have to be included. 'I am wondering whether it is proposed to state in very definite terms our conditions for the cessation of hostilities,' he mused, thinking this 'would be of great value now and certainly in the future'.[129] Of course, Londonderry was well aware that, just after conquering France and with much of Europe at his feet, Hitler would hardly have contemplated a withdrawal to the boundaries of 1938. But it is hard to see the letter as other than a suggestion that the door should not be closed on negotiation. Halifax replied blandly, saying 'that it would be unwise to endeavour to be more precise at this moment about exactly what we want'.[130] Londonderry pressed Halifax on one further occasion, in August 1940 with the threat of invasion looming, 'for a statement of detailed peace aims'.[131] Halifax's reply this time was even more nondescript.[132]

It was effectively Londonderry's last attempted sally into the arena of central government policy-making. Because of his social status, he could not be entirely ignored. But, plainly, despite his own refusal to accept the fact, he had long been politically a spent force. Churchill had little reason to pay attention to his cousin. Halifax replied courteously to his friend, but that was all. Londonderry had pinned his colours to the mast years earlier as an arch-appeaser. With Britain, in a war which he had striven hard to avoid, now faced with the possibility of invasion, and led by the man who had directly crossed swords with him on pre-war policy towards Germany, Londonderry's time was well and truly past. He acknowledged Churchill's standing and his achievements as a war leader. He described him as 'the only man who can lead the country and the Empire at this particular moment in history'.[133] But on a personal level he regretted that the Prime Minister had overlooked him for office. At the end of July 1940 he commented: 'I should not be human if I did not regret having to remain aloof from all the great work which is going on at the present moment. The point is', he added (straining a sporting metaphor from his beloved horse-racing), 'that I backed the wrong horse and although my horse, which was to get hold of the Germans and keep them weak, was quite good enough to win, the National Government proved to be a very bad jockey.'[134]

For an individual for whom political involvement and activity had always been so central, being confined to the fringes, powerless and without influence, was hard to take. 'I do not like being the silent observer of all these happenings,' he told Halifax. 'It is very sad to feel that I can give no assistance to the only contemporary politicians, Winston and yourself, for whom I have ever felt any affection or regard.'[135] He remarked at one point, somewhat theatrically, of his 'anguish of soul'.[136] Lady Londonderry, following a family altercation that had left her deeply unhappy, saw what was wrong. 'What you want is a real job that interests you,' she told her husband. 'The only times you are really happy are when you are working at something definite. Anything else drives you frantic. I know this is the correct diagnosis.'[137] Not only was Londonderry politically out in the cold and deprived, in his own mind, of a genuine sense of purpose, a real sphere of activity. His own reputation had been ruined. He was forced 'to remain under a cloud', as he put it.[138] He still faced repeated attacks for his dealings with Ribbentrop and other Nazi leaders in the 1930s. And as the threat from the Luftwaffe loomed ever larger, his failure as Air Minister was also a recurrent theme of criticism.

Londonderry's inner malaise drove him to almost fixated lengths in self-defence, both of his record as Air Minister and of his stance towards Germany. He responded allergically to every criticism. He insisted that his own policy had been right all along. His castigation of the catastrophic errors made by Chamberlain, Baldwin, Ramsay MacDonald and successive Foreign Secretaries had become a ritual incantation. The events which had brought his own political downfall in 1935 had never ceased to preoccupy him. By now they had become an obsession. Here, too, he never deviated in the slightest from the belief that he had been right in his assessment of German air strength. What rankled deeply with him was that Churchill's alternative figures had proved persuasive with Baldwin and his Cabinet colleagues, and had contributed to his own dismissal. The unfairness ate into him. He had been right all along, he claimed, and Churchill wrong. But Churchill was now the Prime Minister and popular symbol of Britain's defiance, whereas he was in the political wilderness, his reputation destroyed for ever. The need to vindicate his own actions for posterity was all that was left to him. 'I have no doubt that I shall receive the full vindication to which I am entitled, but it is also quite possible that I shall not receive it during my lifetime,' he remarked.[139] Working for this vindication was from now on his main task. 'I am writing a narrative of 1933 to 1940 with every single thing I can remember in that narrative,' he told Halifax at Christmas 1940 (referring to what would develop into his book *Wings of Destiny*). 'It may in years to come be a very useful corrective to what people are trying to establish now, that this war was inevitable.'[140]

In the summer of 1940 the war finally came home to Britain with a vengeance. Churchill's rhetoric matched the defiant mood. But the threat of invasion hung over the country like a pall. In August the Battle of Britain began. Londonderry was proud of the role of the Royal Air Force in Britain's defences and – unlike most people – was not inclined to ignore or underrate his own contribution to the growth of the all-important air arm. But, curiously, he did not emphasize his part in the development of the Hurricanes and Spitfires that were to repel the German raiders during those epic weeks. It was left to Churchill, who by then could afford to be magnanimous, to point out after the war that Londonderry's great achievement as Air Minister was the designing and promotion of the famous fighters. 'Londonderry does not mention this in his defence,' wrote Churchill, 'but he might well have done so, since he took the blame for so much that he had not done.'[141]

That same month, August 1940, the first bombs rained down on London in what came to be known as 'the Blitz'. In the middle of September, at the height of the Battle of Britain, the raids, which had continued for several nights in the docklands of east London, culminated in a heavy daylight attack on the centre of the city. On 13 September the King and Queen narrowly escaped injury when Buckingham Palace was hit by two bombs.[142] It was probably during the same raid that Londonderry House, in Park Lane, not far from the Palace, also suffered damage. George Ward Price, the *Daily Mail* correspondent, described the scene. The splendid mansion of the would-be friend of Germany had been reduced to 'a pitiful sight', like 'a face of which the eyes had been gouged out, for every window facing Park Lane was gone', so that 'the torn curtains streamed out of the windows'. As he stood on the step, 'littered with broken glass and pieces of wrought-iron grille with your monogram in the middle', Ward Price was reminded of Göring declining the invitation to stay at Londonderry House for the Coronation in 1937 since he had not wanted to expose Londonderry to the risk of having his windows broken. 'He has certainly made up for his scruples on that occasion,' he commented wryly.[143]

The damaged Londonderry House presaged the fall of the house of Londonderry. It appeared to symbolize the ruin of Lord Londonderry's own career, and of the aristocratic world of old-style diplomacy. This had brought glory to his ancestor, Lord Castlereagh, but for Londonderry himself, in an era of ruthless modern-day dictators, nothing but ignominy.

Epilogue: Mount Stewart, September 1947

'We needed never have had the war with its ghastly results as the price for Winston [Churchill] gaining an everlasting historical name as a war-leader.'

Lord Londonderry, September 1947

I

The war so dreaded by Lord Londonderry had been over for two years. Like so many others, he had feared it would usher in the end of civilization. Perhaps, for him, it had done so. Great Britain, as he had always prophesied, had proved victorious. But the price of victory had been colossal.

Britain was a bankrupt country. Its coffers were empty, its war debts huge – especially those owed to the USA. The Socialists (as he always called them), so repellent to Londonderry, had been in government since the general election of July 1945, when, amazingly as it seemed to international observers, Winston Churchill, the very symbol of Britain's war triumph, had been dispatched from office in a Labour landslide. In fact, the Labour victory was no surprise. Churchill's personal popularity as a war leader had not eclipsed the widespread distrust of the Conservatives on the vital and urgently needed programme of reform and reconstruction.[1] Memories of the hardships of the Depression – and of the failures of appeasement – were still too vivid. With the war over, most people were concerned less with foreign affairs, the future of the Empire or the treatment of Germany than they were with their own circumstances – with jobs, housing and social security. Conservatives symbolized the grim years of the 1930s. Labour seemed the face of the future. When the votes were counted, Labour had won an overwhelming electoral victory. Clement Attlee, who had led the assault on Londonderry for his defence of bombing during the 1935 election campaign, had become Prime Minister. Two of Londonderry's other arch-adversaries in the Labour Party, Herbert Morrison and Hugh Dalton, were leading figures in the Labour Cabinet. What they were soon presiding over was a regime of austerity as the worst winter of the century in 1946–7 led to a fuel crisis, falling industrial output and a run on the pound.[2] The pomp and circumstance of the extravagant, glamorous and grandiose pre-war Londonderry receptions, when so much of upper-class London society had mounted the grand staircase of Londonderry House to be greeted by Lord and Lady Londonderry and the Prime Minister of the day, were a distant memory. That world had vanished.

So had a world in which Britannia 'ruled the waves'. A continued presence among the Great Powers could not conceal the true diminution of Britain's international standing. The Empire had in his younger years seemed to Londonderry the great and lasting manifestation of British world power and civilization. But the edifice of the Empire, shaken by the first world conflagration, its widening cracks patched up during the second, was now visibly tottering. Londonderry had at one time hoped to become Viceroy in India. In August 1947 he had to accept what no one in his youth could have imagined: the end of British imperial rule in India. There could be no doubt that the loss of other possessions would follow. The Empire as he had known it was no more. Neither politically nor economically was it any longer a viable concern. The future dominant forces in the world, it was already clear, would be the two emergent superpowers: the USA (which Londonderry and so many among the British upper class had tended earlier to look down their noses at) and the Soviet Union that he had feared and hated so intensely. Communist dominance now extended over the eastern half of Europe, with baleful consequences for the peoples of the countries under the sway of Moscow. It threatened, he and many others thought, to engulf the rest of the Continent. Germany, a country he had so admired, was in ruins, divided and occupied by the victorious Allies, its eastern regions now ruled by the Communists he so detested. Nazism had been defeated, Hitler and his regime vanquished. For Londonderry, these had been a positive and necessary outcome of an unnecessary war. Once the war he had tried to avert had come, he had conducted himself with impeccable patriotism. He shed no tears for the Germany he had once courted. But whether, in his view, its destruction, at such great cost, had been worthwhile when this paved the way for the advance of Communism (as he had predicted it would) is uncertain. He had by the outbreak of the war modified his earlier clear preference for Nazism over Communism, and had come to regard them as equal scourges. But there is no indication that by the end of the war he had gone still further and, in the light of revelations of the crimes of Hitler's regime, come to see Nazism as the greater evil.

How he reacted to the gross crimes against humanity perpetrated in the name of Germany is not recorded. There is little doubt that it was with the shock and revulsion common to the civilized world. But, unlike most people, he had personally known some of those most responsible. Hitler, Himmler and Goebbels had all committed suicide. The two he had known best, Göring and Ribbentrop, had been arraigned at Nuremberg by the International Military Tribunal and condemned to death. Göring had cheated the hangman by killing himself on the eve of his execution. Ribbentrop had wanted to call numerous persons in high places – including the Duke of Windsor, Winston Churchill, the Duke of Buccleuch, the Earl of Derby, Lord Vansittart, the press barons Lord Beaverbrook and Lord Kemsley and Lord Londonderry himself – to testify to his 'desire for Anglo-German co-operation' and 'hopes for peace' before the war. The Tribunal agreed that those who held no public positions might provide written submissions in response to defence questions though would not be required to appear in court. Londonderry duly sent in his deposition – accompanied by a bill from a notary who had had to go to his home to acquire his signature, on the grounds that his Lordship was too ill to attend the solicitor's office. Reluctantly, and keen to establish that it should not set a precedent, the Foreign Office paid.[3]

The submission did the Third Reich's Foreign Minister no good. Londonderry's lapidary answers to the six questions put to him accepted the undeniable: that Ribbentrop had expressed the desire for friendly German-English relations and had tried to convince him of this. But he claimed – somewhat dubiously – that he had not been persuaded of Ribbentrop's sincerity. This allowed him, asked whether he agreed with Ribbentrop's views, to say: 'had I been convinced of their sincerity I would have agreed with them'. He then acknowledged that Ribbentrop had sought an understanding of Germany's interests from influential British politicians and statesmen, but did not concur with the suggestion that he had found a predominantly negative attitude. The final question was clumsily worded: 'Are you of the opinion that von Ribbentrop worked many years for the establishment of German-English friendship and, according to his repeated declarations, saw in the attaining of this goal his life-mission?' Londonderry felt able to give a negative answer when, had only the first part been presented, he would arguably have been compelled in honesty to reply in the affirmative.[4] Probably it made no difference. But Londonderry, whose disdain for Ribbentrop had sharpened markedly in the later 1930s, once the initial good relations had soured, evidently lacked all inclination to provide evidence in favour of a man he had come to despise, now indicted with complicity in some of the worst crimes of humanity in history. On 16 October 1946, along with nine other convicted major war criminals, Ribbentrop, detested even by those about to be executed alongside him, was hanged.

Lord Londonderry, meanwhile, had all but disappeared from the public eye. Until a serious glider accident towards the end of 1945, he had remained a notable figure in Northern Ireland, if not in England. But the months of convalescence at Mount Stewart following the accident, then a series of minor strokes that affected his speech, increased his sense of solitude and isolation.[5] In so far as he was remembered at all by the general public – certainly those outside Northern Ireland – it was for the two lasting blights on his political career: his defence of the bomber and, especially, his friendship with the arch-Nazis who had just been hanged. Victory in a war against the enemies whom Londonderry had wanted to befriend was no basis for any rehabilitation of his reputation. However unfair it had all been, in his view, the obloquy into which he had fallen remained with him.

It was all the more galling for him since his cousin, Winston Churchill, with whom he had quarrelled seriously just before the war, was now, despite his election defeat, the national hero, widely regarded as Britain's saviour. From Londonderry's lonely perspective, Churchill certainly deserved credit for his war leadership. But the war should never have been fought. *He*, Londonderry, had been right, and Churchill wrong about German air strength in 1935. *He* had been right, and Churchill wrong, in the need to offer concessions to the Germans to deflect the sense of humiliation that was feeding their aggression, at the same time controlling them while they were weak. Churchill, instead, had continually favoured the French over the Germans. The perils of this stance had been graphically demonstrated by the French military débâcle in 1940. And, thought Londonderry, the results of even a victorious war had predictably proved catastrophic for Britain. How ironic it seemed to him that Churchill was now the hero, for fighting a war which had destroyed Britain's wealth and Empire, while he had attracted nothing but ignominy for wanting to prevent the war which, as he had foreseen, had ended Britain's greatness.[6] He now felt helpless in the face of the way history would be written. His own constant search for vindication, and the feeling that 'history' *would* vindicate him, had given way to greater pessimism in the light of the victorious war. Appeasement now seemed not an honest search to prevent a second Armageddon and avoid the collapse of Britain's power and prosperity as a nation but simply the purblind feebleness of politicians unwilling to stand up to an evil dictator, a badge of shame in the nation's history; while attempts to befriend that dictator were viewed as the actions of 'guilty men'. And many of those who had so vehemently condemned any and all steps towards rearmament in the 1930s now criticized the politicians then in power for not rearming sufficiently or fast enough. Londonderry, caught in the crossfire of post-war denunciations of the politics of the 1930s, had lost not only the arguments, but his place in history as well.

II

A sense of depression, as well as bitterness, runs through the last of countless letters that Londonderry had written to his friend and confidante Lady Desborough, sent from Mount Stewart on

21 September 1947. Describing a recent minor stroke, suffered during a flight back from London and affecting the clarity of his speech and use of his right hand, as 'a light warning', he recognized that his 'active life' was 'really over'. He mentioned his 'endless worries and sorrows' during the 1940s, 'with you and Edie [Lady Londonderry] as my only real friends and supports'. He thought the worries had weighed on him more than he had realized. He admitted that he had plunged himself into an array of minor duties as compensation for the major duties that no longer came his way. 'One's regrets have just got to be forgotten,' he commented, looking forward to leading 'a much easier life'. He could, however, in reality no more forget the past now than in the years when he had repeatedly berated Baldwin, then Chamberlain, about the injustices done to him.[7] He went on, disingenuously and with all the cynicism that stemmed from deep disappointment and bitterness, to claim he was no longer 'bothering about these politics' and to decry politicians as 'quite useless'. He had been reading histories of the previous century and concluded that 'all the politicians were actually the most terrible liars, foreign affairs was a game and no one ever wrote a letter or a dispatch without his tongue in his cheek'. Doubtless he tacitly excluded his hero, Lord Castlereagh, from such general condemnation. He saw himself, too, as standing above the mediocrities, though not comprehending them. This was, as he perceived it, the cause of his downfall. 'I now see why I failed to understand the very second-class people I had to deal with and how glad they must have been to get me out of the way,' he wrote. Implicitly, it seems, he was lamenting the passing of the age in which men of his status and background had run Britain's affairs, and the way the democratization of politics had seen control of the country pass into the hands of the commercial classes, the manufacturers and traders, the Baldwins and Chamberlains. He came, finally, to Churchill. Retaining his longstanding illusion that he and Churchill had been essentially in agreement on Germany, he regretted his failure 'to handle Winston because he really could have saved the war instead of gaining the credit which he fully deserves of winning it, and we are now paying the price'. He concluded with an unlikely piece of counterfactual imagery: 'If only someone had been powerful enough to combine Chamberlain with his passion for peace with Winston even as late as 1937,' he suggested,

'we needed never have had the war with its ghastly results as the price for Winston gaining an everlasting historical name as a war-leader.' 'That is all that has been achieved on our account,' he adjudged in his somewhat jaundiced verdict on the war, 'and I do not believe the price has been anything like paid yet, if it ever will be.'[8]

Within a month of writing this letter, Lord Londonderry suffered another stroke – this time a more severe one, seriously affecting his speech and movement. His condition declined. Communication became largely impossible. The doctors told his family that he would 'never be able to speak again or think consecutively'.[9] Nor could the avid letter-writer any longer write.[10] In one of the last letters before silence descended, Londonderry, commenting that he had been 'very ill for some time' and was doing little work, advocated the writing of a book 'about the failure of the National Government'. He would be writing 'some things about it' himself, he said: 'the failure of the Foreign Office should really be written down'.[11] Plainly, Londonderry's own thirst for vindication, the leitmotiv of his existence since his down-fall in 1935, was still not quenched as his life drew to a close. Despite his strivings, in books, newspapers articles, speeches and countless let-ters, he had failed to achieve it. The war and its aftermath had made his goal an ever more vain one. In the silence which now cocooned him, he must have continued to dwell upon the events which had blighted his life and career, preoccupied as ever by the sense of injustice at what had befallen him.

The war years, as he remarked to Lady Desborough, had been unhappy ones for him. Cut off from the centres of power, influence or information, after his last attempted but ineffective interventions in the summer of 1940 he had endeavoured for a time to keep abreast of 'insider' knowledge of the progress of the war through unofficial intelligence reports provided by his contact Kenneth de Courcy, of the self-styled Imperial Policy Group, who had increasingly close ties with British intelligence agencies.[12] Londonderry's connections with leading figures in government naturally faded, however, as the war progressed. Churchill had other things on his mind than continuing the fruitless debate with his querulous kinsman about German air strength in 1935. Halifax, his closest link with the Cabinet for some years, had crossed the Atlantic in December 1940 to become

Ambassador in Washington and was now effectively out of touch. Other Conservatives in the War Cabinet – including Anthony Eden (Foreign Secretary after Halifax's departure for Washington), Sir Kingsley Wood (Chancellor of the Exchequer), and Lord Beaverbrook (Ministry of Supply, then of War Production) – had been on reasonably cordial terms with Londonderry before the war, but were not close personal or political friends. Labour members of the War Cabinet – Clement Attlee (Lord Privy Seal, then Deputy Prime Minister and Secretary of State for Dominion Affairs), Ernest Bevin (Minister of Labour), Arthur Greenwood (Minister without Portfolio) and Sir Stafford Cripps (Attlee's successor as Lord Privy Seal in February 1942) – had long ranked among his political enemies and regarded him with disdain. If they continued at all to register Londonderry's existence, it was in a purely negative way, and as the remnant of an age that they were glad to see passing.

Though his political role was by now irredeemably over, Londonderry continued untiringly to take up the cudgels in his own defence. He dispatched innumerable letters replying to slurs on his name for his relations with the Nazi leaders and his alleged failings as Air Minister in the early 1930s or indicting the record of leaders of the National Government.[13] His chief obsession was proving that he had been right (and Churchill wrong) in his assessments of German air strength in 1935, relentlessly collecting statistical data from the supportive Sir Edward Ellington, former Chief of the Air Staff, in the vain attempt to back his own position in fighting anew the battles of bygone years.[14] Though his efforts in November 1940 to persuade the government to grant permission to write an article on German air strength before the war predictably ran up against obstacles resting on the need to protect official secrets,[15] Londonderry was determined to put his own side of the story, to vindicate his actions at the critical juncture in 1935, in an account of the difficulties he had faced as Air Minister and his own endeavours, against the odds, to develop the necessary air defences. By autumn 1941 he had made headway on the composition of the book which would eventually be published in spring 1943 as *Wings of Destiny*. Work on the book (on which he had assistance in research and writing) was, he commented in October that year, 'at a standstill'. But having recorded his own stance he felt satisfied. 'It is a full answer to my critics,' he wrote. 'Whether it is worth while to give it to the public is another matter. If [I] am free to do so, I shall do it, but I doubt if I shall be able to.'[16]

His doubts about the way officialdom would view his book were justified. He had learnt from the difficulties he had encountered in 1938 and again in 1939 over his wish to publish the 1934 Hailsham letters, how obstructive the Cabinet Office could be in any matter touching upon government confidentiality. Despite receiving permission to consult Cabinet papers related to his research in the summer of 1941, when he had – with more optimism than realism – told Lord Beaverbrook that the Hailsham letters would soon be made public,[17] he soon ran into difficulties about publication. For over six months in 1942, with Britain engaged in a world war, its population trying to cope with the austerities of the wartime economy, and its military leaders preparing a major onslaught on German forces in North Africa at El Alamein, the Cabinet Office and other government officials wrestled with the issue of Lord Londonderry's book.

Churchill himself was drawn directly into the affair on one occasion; so were the Foreign Office and the Ministry of Information. Some documents were sent for vetting to the King. Londonderry had explained to the Cabinet Secretary, Sir Edward Bridges, in May that the book, by now in page-proof, 'had been written as a necessary personal justification, since he was regarded on all hands as pro-German'.[18] Bridges' own view, on a first reading, was that it was 'of third-rate quality and of no importance whatsoever, except as regards its author'. Far from restoring Londonderry's reputation, he felt, it 'would do him damage'. However, he felt that on account of its handling of information to which Londonderry had been privy as a Cabinet Mininster, the book should not be published.[19] Londonderry was plainly regarded as a nuisance, bombarding officials with 'a barrage of letters and telephone calls' about his book.[20] Thanking one official for noting the contents of a twenty-minute telephone complaint by Londonderry, the Cabinet Secretary, Sir Edward Bridges, laconically added: 'I'm sure this was a liberal education.'[21] Brendan Bracken, Minister of Information, told Londonderry that his book had been written 'in a very bad temper' and would not do him any good.[22] The head of the Privy Council Office, Sir Rupert Howorth, said the book 'simply astounds and horrifies me', was certain 'to give deep offence in many quarters', and would 'provoke endless controversy and recrimination'. He felt strongly that the book should not be published.[23]

Eventually, after an endless flow of letters, memoranda, minuted notes, vettings of the typescript and reluctant acceptance by Londonderry of a large number of excisions and amendments,[24] it was agreed to allow an expurgated version to appear. Months after the initial publication date, the book was finally released in March 1943. Far from stirring the 'endless controversy' that Sir Rupert Howorth had feared, the book, appearing in the middle of a world war, concerning itself with what Churchill described as 'ancient history' and 'a period which has ceased to count',[25] and transparently aimed at restoring the reputation of a long-discredited former Cabinet Minister, attracted far less attention than Londonderry's earlier publication, *Ourselves and Germany*, had done. If it did not do further damage to his reputation, as Bridges had surmised it would, it certainly did little or nothing to repair it.[26]

Londonderry's reputation by now, however, mattered little outside his family and circle of close friends. Few people remembered the circumstances that had led up to his dismissal from office in 1935. And if they did remember, surrounded by their daily worries in the middle of a world war, they did not much care. As Churchill had remarked, it seemed 'ancient history'. Even Londonderry's dealings with Nazi leaders had by this time little lasting resonance in public memory. The main problem was not public, but private. Londonderry's own preoccupation with the reasons for his fall from the heights of government office to little more than a political outcast, for what he saw as his own failure – human, political and as the head of his illustrious house – had become an outright obsession. This, in his last years more than ever, was eating into his psyche. Despite all his advantages, he told his friend Lady Desborough, he had been 'a miserable failure'. Inevitably, he went back to his 'bitter exchanges with Baldwin and Chamberlain, whom I knew were wrong', and to his quarrel with Churchill 'because I wanted to achieve by what I thought was statesmanship what he wanted to achieve by war'. He was, he added, 'bitterly disappointed'. He had had 'great chances', but 'missed them by not being good enough'. He was no longer wanted for the 'big things' and the 'smaller things' and 'figurehead duties' were 'uninteresting by themselves'. And 'so the war, the crisis of our lives, finds me completely isolated and under a sort of shadow which I cannot get away from'.[27]

The shadow was to remain with him to the end. He had continued in the later years of the war and its immediate aftermath, before his glider accident, to speak in the House of Lords from time to time, and give a number of other public speeches, mainly on civil aviation or policy on coal mining.[28] He had taken up his duties as Northern Ireland Regional Commandant of the Air Training Corps.[29] He had also accepted honorific offices such as the Vice-Presidency of the Royal Aero Club.[30] But none of it had provided much compensation. The obsession would not leave him. It seldom showed in public. But he stirred great anger on the benches of the House of Lords in January 1945 with a remarkable outburst, asserting that 'in the years before the war there was no foreign policy in this country at all', and blaming the Foreign Office for the war. Lord Cranborne, the Leader of the House of Lords, 'could hardly believe his ears'. An outraged Lord Vansittart described it as a 'gratuitous and mendacious attack' on the Foreign Office, an 'utter falsehood', and 'a mean and unfounded charge'. He threatened, if Londonderry did not withdraw his allegations, to bring in public an 'annihilating' case against him, contrasting his record on pre-war relations with Germany with his own repeated warnings about the dangers of Nazism. 'The killing', he wrote, 'which will be all too easy – will be extremely painful to Londonderry.'[31] Within a few days Vansittart had calmed down, after receiving appropriate and soothing assurances from Londonderry that it had all been a misunderstanding.

In fact, Londonderry's own apologia for what he had said amounted to little more than yet another lengthy account of his travails in the 1930s and the injustice he had suffered.[32] He would simply not let the past drop. Over and again he returned in his voluminous correspondence to the issues of German air strength in 1935, his dealings with Ribbentrop, and, above all, how he had been unfairly maligned and cast out into the political wilderness.[33] He had now reached the point of claiming that 'I was the only person who was right' during the 1930s.[34] Such obtuse self-certainty made him insensitive to the reasons for his fall from grace to be sought in his own actions, and produced an inevitable urge to attribute blame to others. 'Winston's determined attitude towards me is all the more incomprehensible and I doubt if I shall ever know why he went out of his way to destroy me, which he certainly did,' he wrote to Lady Desborough.[35] He accused Churchill – though not to his face – of doing him 'irreparable injury over these last few years' (notably in connection with the saga of *Wings of Destiny*), and bemoaned the fact that he had 'spent these six war years practically ostracised' and had 'never been called upon by anyone in an official position to do anything whatsoever for the war'.[36] He tried to refight old (and lost) battles with the Cabinet Office again in 1946.[37] And in 1947 he was still vainly seeking access to confidential material on German air strength, now as preparation for publication in a new account he was aiming to write, proving that he had been correct in his assessment of the German air force and in his determination to 'save the bomber'.[38] Londonderry was by this time already in failing health. Within months, his serious stroke put paid to any last attempts to rescue his damaged reputation.

Immobilized and unable to speak, Lord Londonderry lived for almost another year and a half. His estrangement from his son and heir, Lord Castlereagh, which had depressed him over a number of years, compounding the blow suffered by the premature death of his eldest daughter Maureen in 1942 from tuberculosis, must have added to his misery, and to that of his wife and their other daughters, as they watched his decline. Despite their troubled relationship, Castlereagh wrote to console his mother on the occasion of his father's seventieth birthday in May 1948 with the thought that 'he is at least free from all the disappointments and bitterness which have made him so unhappy for so many years'.[39] Lord Londonderry died at Mount Stewart during the night of 10–11 February 1949. 'Worry killed him,' recalled his youngest daughter, Lady Mairi.[40] He was buried three days later in the grounds of his home.[41]

The obituaries were kind to him. The *Daily Telegraph* pointed out his role in the development of the Hurricane and the Spitfire – the fighters that had assured victory in the Battle of Britain – and referred to the glitter of Londonderry House receptions in describing him as 'the last figure of a bygone political age'. The *Belfast Telegraph* thought he had been 'a victim of misunderstanding', highlighting 'the sincerity of his convictions and actions and the spirit in which he faced disappointment at the hands of his friends'. *The Times* applied the necessary qualifications. 'Excellent no doubt though his intentions were in constituting himself an amateur ambassador of good will, it is not surprising that, as the intentions of the Nazis became increasingly revealed, he should have fallen heavily in the popular esteem' – adding, fairly, that once the war had come 'he affirmed that there were no terms to be made'.[42] 'Chips' Channon, the socialite Conservative MP, jotted in his diary his own brief but warm obituary. 'In the long run he will be proved right politically,' he concluded. 'He always maintained that there were only two possible courses for us: either to make friends with Germany, or, if this was impossible, to re-arm. We did neither, and war was the result. But he was unpopular and much criticised at the time for his views.'[43] Coming out of the memorial service to Lord Londonderry in Westminster Abbey three days later, Channon heard Arthur Henderson, Air Minister in the Labour government, remark: 'Possibly Londonderry was right all the time.' 'Of course he was,' retorted Channon.[44]

III

Was he? Could either of his main propositions – making friends with Hitler and intensive rearmament – have prevented war? Here we enter the realms of conjecture and counterfactual scenarios. But unless history is presumed to be a one-way street, these have to be faced. Was the six-year conflict with Nazi Germany 'the unnecessary war'? Londonderry, of course, had thought it was. But so, from an entirely different perspective, did Winston Churchill, who coined the phrase.[45]

Londonderry's position, as 'Chips' Channon had summarized it, sounded straightforward and persuasive. Moreover, Londonderry had not seen friendship with Germany and rearmament as alternatives, as Channon had suggested, but as complementary strands of the same policy. As we have seen, for all his sympathies for Germany, Londonderry was no crypto-Nazi or Mosleyite Fascist. He was a serious-minded, if gullible, Conservative politician and his views were shared, at least in part, by other equally serious-minded and often respected political figures, such as Lord Lothian and David Lloyd George. Could making friends with Hitler, coupled with more energetic rearmament, have provided an alternative foreign policy which might have saved the peace of Europe and prevented Britain's involvement in a second world conflagration? Even to pose the question of whether seeking friendship with Hitler ought to have been adopted as British policy seems now distasteful. Yet that is not how it appeared to all observers of the political scene at the time.

Once the war had been won, at great sacrifice and huge cost, and especially once Winston Churchill's war memoirs had defined the historical record for public memory, the notion that a deal might have been contemplated with Hitler's horrific Nazi regime seemed anathema. The very word 'appeasement' had come to epitomize the pusillanimous policy of the 1930s, the opposite of everything that Churchill had stood for. Of course, Churchill's far-sightedness and prophetic warnings need no emphasis. They were remarkable in their time. And they received their vindication by the course of events. But it is worth recalling that Churchill was out in the political cold without much of a following before 1939 (and even then neither backed nor trusted by the majority of his own party). The Conservative Party had, at least until Munich in the autumn of 1938, strongly supported appeasement. So even had many Liberals. And the Labour Party, despite its dwindling pacifist wing, had nonetheless clung to principles of disarmament and opposed government rearmament policies well into the later 1930s.

Londonderry, as we have repeatedly seen, castigated the failures in foreign policy of the National Government and did not describe himself as an appeaser. Nevertheless, that is what he was – if in differing fashion from Neville Chamberlain, Lord Halifax, and others chiefly associated with the term – through his desire for 'pro-active' appeasement from a position of strength and pro-German sentiment rather than 'reactive' and reluctant appeasement out of weakness and aversion to Nazi Germany (as was eventually attempted).

He took the view, as he expressed it looking back in April 1940, that Britain had had three inter-linked duties since the advent of Hitler: to arm, to seek friendship with Germany and to stop Germany becoming strong.[46] This was essentially the position he had outlined in his fabled letters to Lord Hailsham in November 1934. At that time, however, the three strands of his proposed policy on Germany were not concurrent but had by implication to follow on each other. Only if the Germans could not be made 'helpful partners' would Britain 'immobilise their hostile activities', and only if they proved 'wholly aggressive and unwilling to join in a peaceful comity of nations' would they be 'arraigned in their true colours before the world'.[47]

We have already encountered some of the problems with this thinking. At what point was it to be concluded that the Germans could not be turned into 'helpful partners'? Londonderry, as we have seen, was enthusiastic – along with many others – about a pact with Germany as late as 1936, when he welcomed the remilitarization of the Rhineland and Hitler's overtures towards a German-British rapprochement that accompanied it. Only the following year did he start to have doubts about the German readiness to become a 'helpful partner', and had not altogether given up hope even at the time of the Munich Conference. But if the decision could only be taken so late that Germany was not willing to act as a 'helpful partner' to Britain, where did that leave his accompanying recommendations to stop her becoming strong by 'immobilising' German 'hostile activities', rearming, and revealing her aggressive intent in its 'true colours'?

He had repeatedly urged 'getting hold of' Germany while she was weak. But he himself had on every occasion been prepared to defend German breaches of international treaties, and had only reluctantly abandoned hope of her becoming Britain's partner at a time when she had already built up her armed strength. He had, it is true, been a strong advocate of British rearmament, especially in the air force, while this was still politically unfashionable and under attack from practically all sides. In a difficult climate, he had achieved only the beginnings of the build-up of a strong air force. In the main, the shortcomings in British policy to rearm in the air before the mid-1930s had not been his fault. But the vehemence with which he asserted, time and again, the weakness of the Luftwaffe compared with the Royal Air Force for years to come and predicted that Germany would not be ready for war before 1942 – showing, as Sir Robert Vansittart put it, an optimism 'shared by no one else in Europe'[48] – suggests that he placed less weight upon the deterrent of rearmament than he did upon the attractions of friendship with Germany. His enthusiastic dealings with Nazi leaders during the mid-1930s lend support to this suggestion.

So by the time that overtures of German friendship towards Britain had been replaced by signs of mounting enmity, it is difficult to see how the level of rearmament which would have satisfied Londonderry could have halted Hitler's aggressive foreign policy. Halting it could, in any case, only have been attempted either through direct military action or on a basis of international cooperation. Direct action could have been undertaken only in collaboration with the French – and in the teeth of British public opinion. There was no prospect of it taking place before the Sudeten crisis (by which time German armed might was well established). And with the United States in isolation and Europe as divided and incapable of action as the Abyssinian crisis of 1935–6 revealed it to be, the notion that there could have been any agreed international action to remove Hitler, even in his first years in power while Germany was still weak, was merely a figment of the imagination.

The two occasions when, it is commonly thought, international armed intervention could and should have been taken against Hitler related to later circumstances: the remilitarization of the Rhineland in March 1936 and the German threat to Czechoslovakia in autumn 1938. Londonderry, of course, as we have seen, supported and defended the German action on both occasions and would not have entertained the idea of British military intervention. That apart, it is hard to see its feasibility on either occasion. As regards the Rhineland, voices raised in Britain, before or after, in favour of armed intervention were few indeed. There was no appetite for the risk of war over entry by Hitler 'into his own back-garden'.[49] And without a British commitment to military action – which could, indeed, have halted Hitler in his tracks – the French were unprepared to move. In 1938, the military arguments for engaging in armed conflict with Germany over Czechoslovakia were weak. Chamberlain, following military advice, thought the odds on a British victory were not high. Britain might well be defeated. The shameful sacrifice of Czech sovereignty to German bullying was the logical political consequence of such a pessimistic military calculation.

The only prospect of deterring Germany through a policy of

rearmament would have been for Britain to rearm, especially in the air, at a rate which few beyond Winston Churchill and Lord Rothermere were at the time prepared to tolerate. The economic repercussions of the Depression and the established priorities of balancing the budget, the defence needs of a world-wide empire, and public opinion at home, all militated against a policy of rapid rearmament until the later 1930s. If Germany could not be deterred, could war have been averted by responding to the blandishments of friendship, as Londonderry had so ardently desired? Certainly, Britain could have avoided involvement in general European war by the end of the 1930s by such a policy. But the cost would have been high in the short to medium term, and exorbitant in the long run. Securing the British friendship he (and Ribbentrop) had so much wanted to attain would have presented Hitler with a major propaganda coup. His domination within Germany would have been still more firmly cemented. But his thirst for war and expansion would not in the slightest have been quenched. To imagine that it would have been (as Londonderry and others did) was to misinterpret fundamentally the essence of Nazism. Hitler's regime was incapable of drawing a line under its territorial possessions and standing still. The difference is that its limitless expansion would, had Londonderry's policy been followed, have been carried out with British backing.

Britain would, however, have been progressively weakened in its course. The British alliance with France would, axiomatically, have been fatally undermined through friendship with Germany. Wedged between Germany and Britain, France's military weakness would have been apparent long before 1940. Probably, France would have had to reach some sort of terms with Germany even without war and defeat. Britain would most likely have installed a government increasingly dependent upon Berlin's goodwill, coming increasingly to resemble the later Vichy regime in France. Anxious about the menace of Japan in the Far East, and beset by problems in holding the Empire together, Britain's position would not have been a strong one. The German navy had by the later 1930s worked out a strategy to take over the dominance of the seas. Pressure would have mounted on Britain to cede some colonies, and, more importantly, positions in the Mediterranean and in the oil-rich areas of the Middle East. With naval strength in decline and air strength, under such a policy, almost inevitably inferior to Germany's, Britain would have waned over the medium term into the status of a German satellite power. There is little doubt that German race policies would have been introduced in Britain, or that willing hands would have been found to enforce them. Eventually, when Germany came to take on the United States, Britain would have been under pressure to join in on the German side. Meanwhile, war against the Soviet Union would have been launched by Hitler – but with British backing. Conceivably, over time British troops would have been sucked into the fighting on Germany's side in the maelstrom of the eastern front.

As with all counterfactual speculation, much could have turned out differently and other scenarios are certainly possible. But in none is it likely that Britain would have emerged strengthened, its Empire intact, its society untouched and unsullied by association with the brutal inhumanity of Nazi Germany. Far from being avoidable, it was absolutely necessary for Britain, whatever the cost, to fight the war to defeat Nazism.

Londonderry's own formula for handling Germany was, therefore, far less self-evidently correct than Channon presumed. In fact, it was misconceived, misguided and mistaken on practically all counts. Londonderry, as we followed the development of his attitude towards Nazi Germany, was certainly well intentioned and sincere. But it is impossible to avoid the conclusion that he was extremely naive in his political views and gullible in his readiness (shared by many others) for so long to place his trust in Hitler and in presumed German peaceful objectives. Though he constantly railed at their inadequacies and failure, the mandarins of the Foreign Office – most notably Sir Robert Vansittart, before he was sidelined in 1938 – had a far shrewder view of the dangers posed by Hitler's Germany than did Londonderry, and were correctly dismissive of his attempts to make friends of the Nazi leaders.

The case of Lord Londonderry, even if his views found mercifully little resonance among British policy-makers, nevertheless casts light on the mentalities and political structures that shaped appeasement. A focus on Londonderry's keenness for friendship with Germany highlights what was *not* possible for the British government; or at least what would have been an exceedingly dangerous line of policy. Emphasis on the second strand of his preferred strategy, rearmament, indicates why – leaving aside his own limitations as a minister – the government only turned to it so late, even when the Foreign Office recognized the danger that Hitler posed. The very rejection of Londonderry's approach to relations with Nazi Germany shows, in other words, just how narrow the line was that was trodden by the British government, and how inevitable it was that the policy choices since 1933 would end in outright appeasement, leading to the shame of Munich.

Put in simplified terms, the choices facing the British government once Hitler had come to power were stark.

For all the prevailing misapprehensions – illusions and delusions – about Hitler, the government, fed reports from the Foreign Office taken from perceptive information from its Ambassadors in Berlin, was well aware of the looming dangers. The option of befriending Hitler was ruled out. In immediate terms of international relations this would have demanded a breach with France, Britain's main ally, itself with strong diplomatic ties in central and eastern Europe. It would, in other words, have thrown the post-war international order into disarray. Moreover, the threat such an option posed in the long term for British interests was well understood. Given the level of apprehension in the Foreign Office of a resurgence in Germany of the military power responsible, in most British eyes, for the world war fought so recently, and with an insatiable thirst for domination, befriending Hitler – seen initially as the front for such forces – could be ruled out.

The option of forcibly removing Hitler – 'regime change' – was never even seriously considered before the war. Initially, it was expected that Hitler's rule would prove shortlived. The fear was that what succeeded him – either dangerous military dictatorship on the one hand, or Communist revolution on the other – would be worse. Once he had settled in power, with the evident backing of a large proportion of the population, the possibility of a pre-emptive strike to remove him had disappeared. In reality, it had never existed. Quite apart from its implications in international law, public opinion in Britain would have been aghast at the risks such a move would have entailed. So would the military strategists. It would have been viewed as an absurd proposal. The dangers were too palpable. And there was a good deal of support for what Hitler was trying to do, if not for the methods he used to bring about the country's revitalization. A move would have had to be coordinated with the French, whose own experience of their intervention in 1923 would not have been encouraging. However, such ruminations have little point. For this option was no option at all. It was not rejected; it was not even contemplated.

If Hitler could not have been befriended or removed, could he have been contained, or deterred? Containment would have demanded a level of international agreement and cooperation which – as Abyssinia most classically demonstrated – was simply not existent. Imposition, let alone prosecution, even of economic sanctions on Germany would never have been agreed. The League of Nations was toothless and divided. Britain and her most important ally, France, could concur on little in the handling of Hitler's Germany. Exploiting the cracks of such disunity, Hitler was able to tear up the post-war settlement and forge the 'axis' with Italy. The United States, meanwhile, stood on the sidelines. And the Soviet Union, both disdained and feared in Britain, was not considered as a possibly eastern ally before it was too late – and then only half-heartedly.

This left deterrence. This could only have been achieved through a major and accelerated programme of rearmament as soon as Hitler came to power. That, too, was not feasible. Britain, deep into the 1930s, was the one major country still wedded to disarmament. The moral reasons were impeccable. Economic priorities lent them support. The politics, however, were distinctly shaky. As we have seen, Londonderry had to strive hard to prevent further reductions to the strength of the Royal Air Force, and was only, towards the end of his tenure of office, able to make the modest beginnings of a rearmament programme in the air. Even the Conservative Party was in the main still resistant to rearmament at this stage. The Labour Party remained wedded to disarmament and intensely hostile to any moves to rearm. The Liberals also opposed rearmament. Churchill began from 1934 onwards to utter what were seen to be Cassandra-like warnings about German rearmament, and the dangers it posed for Britain. Seen by the Opposition and by much of his own party as a reactionary die-hard, out of touch with mainstream opinion, lacking sound judgement, and disgruntled at his own exclusion from office, he found little support for his views. Only the revelations of the scale of German rearmament (misleading though the figures may have been) following the visit by Simon and Eden to Berlin in March 1935 brought a change in the climate with regard to rearmament. But by then it was too late to serve as a deterrent. Even when a government programme for more extensive and accelerated rearmament was approved in early 1936, the reluctance to transfer skilled workers from civilian to military production meant that it could not be completed within five years.[50]

Without policies of befriending, removing, containing or deterring Hitler, Britain was left with hope, drift and forced concessions in turn as its approaches to avoiding another war. The hope, rapidly shown to be vain, was that Hitler would either disappear from the scene or turn into a 'normal' politician under the constraints of office. The drift was the inaction that followed, in the absence of a strategy of any sort, from the realization that, far from becoming a 'normal' politician, Hitler was a 'mad dog' let loose in the international arena. The forced concessions were Chamberlain's response, once he had succeeded Baldwin, supported by much of his own party and by the British Dominions, in the realization that war was inevitable if Hitler's 'revisionist' aims (as they were presumed to be) were not met, but that Britain was in no military state to confront Germany.

For all his limitations, Londonderry had recognized at an early stage the fundamental absence of any clear strategy in Whitehall for dealing with Hitler. One part of his own approach – accelerated rearmament – would have been the only way, short of the path that led to appeasement, of dealing with Hitler. This far, he was right. But there was a good chance that a major and rapid rearmament programme would have led to direct and early confrontation with Germany, and to the war that he was anxious to do everything to avoid. This was the point of his fundamental disagreement with Churchill. While his cousin increasingly thought that war against Hitler's Germany was inevitable, and there would be no peace in Europe until Nazism was destroyed, Londonderry pressed all the more strongly the second, and dominant, element in his approach: befriending Hitler. The fact that, after the double removal from office in 1935 had left him so embittered, Londonderry threw his energies not, like Churchill, into support for a massive rearmament programme, but into an increasingly

counter-productive advocacy of friendship with an ever more menacing Nazi Germany, destroyed his political standing and determined
the isolation and personal misery of his last years.

IV

Londonderry's failings were, of course, personal – a reflection of his
temperament, intelligence, understanding and aptitudes. He was at so
many junctures, as we have witnessed, his own worst enemy – unable
to let sleeping dogs lie, unable to avoid an ill-judged rejoinder to a
perceived slight, unable to realize when it was better to keep quiet
than to speak out, unable to acknowledge his own past mistakes,
unable to recognize that continued fighting of old battles was unlikely
to bring the vindication he so desperately desired, unable above all to
see that sustained defence of his association with Nazi Germany
rather than acceptance of an earlier flawed judgement shared with
others was damaging to his cause. In all these ways, Londonderry
sounded the death-knell of his own reputation – the reputation he
was so desperate to uphold.

In other ways, Londonderry's failings reflected those of his social
class. That so many notables in Britain flirted with (or wholeheartedly
backed) the extreme Right, finding appeal in Fascism and sympathizing with so much in Nazism, was not simply a reflection of personal
taste or an historical accident. Londonderry, as we have seen, never
associated himself with British Fascism. His conservatism, socially and
ideologically ingrained as well as party-political, was far too deeply
instilled in his character for that. But his sympathy with many of the
values of the Fascist as well as Conservative Right was nevertheless
instinctive and a product of his social background. He had grown up
in the Victorian era, and was already in his early twenties when
Edward VII came to the throne at the end of his mother's long reign in
1901. His entire formative years fell into an era when the British
Empire was at its height, and when the aristocracy took its place in the
government of country and Empire as a birthright. Londonderry's
autocratic and dogmatic disposition fitted this world of traditional
authority and patronage, of paternalism and deference, of ostentatious

hospitality matched to an undiluted sense of patriotic duty, of the upholding of family status and honour. Londonderry had a pronounced feeling for his own status, but equally for his public duties. Most acutely, he felt the legacy of family honour, the need to meet the expectations of a lineage which included his hero, the great Lord Castlereagh of Napoleon's era. A number of contemporaries, as we have seen, portrayed Londonderry as a figure reflecting the appearance, bearing, demeanour and attitudes of a past era. These did not best acclimatize him to the changes in society and politics already underway before the First World War and greatly accelerated after it.

In some ways, Londonderry saw clearly the need to adapt to the visible and unstoppable changes. His enthusiasm for flying and promotion of aviation were an obvious manifestation of his adoption of modern technology. He admired Mussolini and (in his early years in power) Hitler for their dynamism, and as reflecting a new order in which men could rise from the lower classes of society to regenerate their nations. But he also envied the authority they wielded. Though he repeatedly defended the virtues of British democracy to his new-found German friends, he lamented inwardly the passing of the traditional authority which he associated with the patrician class. He owed his own political career, until its sudden halt in 1935, largely to patronage. And it was the natural assumption of his own authority that made him unable to adjust easily to the requirements of democractic politics – perhaps one reason why he was so insensitive towards public opinion.[51]

The story of Lord Londonderry's rise to political prominence, then his slide into disrepute, the descent from hosting the glittering Londonderry House receptions to the sad isolation of the last years in Mount Stewart, symbolizes in some ways, therefore, the fading power and position of the British aristocracy.

It certainly mirrored the decline of the Londonderrys. The social splendour rapidly tarnished once war started. Londonderry House lost its forty-four servants. Lord Londonderry, on his increasingly rare visits there, was reduced to opening the door to visitors himself.[52] The grand Park Lane mansion, damaged though not devastated in the 1940 bombing, had been requisitioned by the army during the war. Notions of the National Trust taking over its upkeep once war was

over fell through.[53] In 1946 much of it was given over to the Royal
Aero Club as a national centre for aviation.[54] In urgent need of great
expenditure on its restoration and maintainance, the great house was
demolished in 1962, three years after the death of Lady Londonderry.
A hotel replaced it on the site. Greatly occupied during the last war
years with drawing up his will, making settlement, and attempting to
avoid death duties, Lord Londonderry disposed of some of his other
properties soon after the conflict was over. He donated his Welsh
mansion, Plâs Machynlleth, to the local community and handed over
Dene House, at Seaham Harbour in County Durham, for use as a
miners' clinic.[55] Wynyard, near Stockton-on-Tees in the north-east of
England, which he had contemplated demolishing in 1940, was
turned mainly into a teacher training college with a wing kept for the
family of his son, Lord Castlereagh, and was eventually sold off completely in 1987.[56] The coal mines of the north-east, source of much of
the Londonderrys' wealth, had meanwhile passed into state ownership under the nationalization programme of the post-war Labour
government. Lord Londonderry nevertheless died a millionaire, leaving – to the disappointment of his son, Lord Castlereagh – his Irish
property to his widow and, on her death, to his youngest daughter,
Lady Mairi Bury. Castlereagh, now the 8th Marquess of
Londonderry, was given a life tenancy at Wynyard, which on his
death in 1955 was inherited by his son (the 9th Marquess).[57]

Only Mount Stewart, the last of the Londonderry homes, its spectacular gardens laid out by Lady Londonderry and sheltered from the
winds that blow across Strangford Lough, remained. Lady
Londonderry herself donated the gardens to the National Trust in
1955. The forty-room mansion was handed to the Trust in 1976 by
Lady Mairi.[58]

What remains to this day as a reminder of the house's brief but
fateful connection with Hitler's Germany is the porcelain statue of the
Nazi stormtrooper still standing on the mantelpiece of what had been
Lord Londonderry's study – his present from Ribbentrop at their
weekend house party at Mount Stewart in the spring of 1936.

Abbreviations

DBFP	*Documents on British Foreign Policy, 1919–1939; 2nd Series, 1929–1938; 3rd Series, 1938–1939*, London, 1947–61
DGFP	*Documents on German Foreign Policy, 1918–1945; Series C (1933–1937), The Third Reich: First Phase; Series D (1937–1945)*, London, 1957–66
DRO	Durham County Record Office
Ourselves	The Marquess of Londonderry, *Ourselves and Germany*, London, 1938
Ourselves II	The Marquess of Londonderry, *Ourselves and Germany*, 'Penguin Special', 2nd edition, Harmondsworth, 1938
PRO	Public Record Office, London
PRONI	Public Record Office of Northern Ireland, Belfast
UL	University Library
Wings	The Marquess of Londonderry, *Wings of Destiny*, London, 1943
WSC, V/2	*Winston S. Churchill, Vol. V, Companion, Part 2, Documents. The Wilderness Years, 1929–1935*, ed. Martin Gilbert, London, 1981
WSC, V/3	*Winston S. Churchill, Vol. V, Companion, Part 3, Documents. The Coming of War, 1936–1939*, ed. Martin Gilbert, London, 1982

Notes

Preface

1. I am indebted to Mr Colin M. Ross for information on the origins of the figurine. It was a special presentation piece, known as 'The Standard Bearer' ('Der Fahenträger'), produced in the Allach porcelain factory in Bavaria, owned and managed by the SS, and reserved for those upon whom the Nazi hierarchy wished to bestow honour. In 1937 Allach production was moved into the complex of Dachau concentration camp, not far away, and around fifty camp internees worked in the factory from 1941 onwards. Production ceased at the liberation of the camp in 1945.

2. Lord Londonderry described the gardens in a letter to Ramsay MacDonald, then Prime Minister, as 'the outward and visible sign of Circe's [his wife's] creative genius as she has done the whole thing herself with her mind and even with her hands' (PRO 30/69/678/2, fol. 420, L to MacDonald, 31.7.32). Lady Londonderry's own description of the gardens is provided in her pamphlet, The Marchioness of Londonderry, *Mount Stewart*, n.d. (1956).

3. 'The past is a foreign country, they do things differently there', is the first line of L. P. Hartley's novel, *The Go-Between*, London, 1953.

4. For the family background and setting, see H. Montgomery Hyde, *The Londonderrys: a Family Portrait*, London, 1979, a book written by Lord Londonderry's former librarian, secretary and general factotum, at the behest of and with the imprimatur of Lady Mairi Bury, his youngest daughter. Insights into his family life are also provided in the biography of Lady Londonderry by Anne de Courcy, *Circe. The Life of Edith, Marchioness of Londonderry*, London, 1992, though the chief interest appears to be Lord Londonderry's love affairs and the social life and ambience of the book's heroine. Lady Londonderry's own book, *Retrospect*, London, 1938, gives a taste of her lifestyle, if only by way of aristocratic gossip and tittle-tattle.

5. Paul Schwarz, *This Man Ribbentrop. His Life and Times*, New York,

1943, p. 164, attributing the designation to the American Ambassador, William E. Dodd.

6. See Simon Haxey, *Tory M.P.*, London, 1939, ch. 8, esp. pp. 208–9; and Richard Griffiths, *Fellow Travellers of the Right. British Enthusiasts for Nazi Germany 1933–39*, London, 1980, p. 185.

7. Among a library of works, old and new, the following have proved particularly useful: Martin Gilbert and Richard Gott, *The Appeasers*, London, 1963; Martin Gilbert, *The Roots of Appeasement*, London, 1966; Keith Middlemas, *The Diplomacy of Illusion. The British Government and Germany 1937–39*, London, 1972; Maurice Cowling, *The Impact of Hitler*, Cambridge, 1975; John Charmley, *Neville Chamberlain and the Lost Peace*, London, 1989; Andrew Roberts, *'The Holy Fox': the Life of Lord Halifax*, London, 1991; paperback edn, 1997; R. A. C. Parker, *Chamberlain and Appeasement*, London, 1993; R. A. C. Parker, *Churchill and Appeasement*, London, 2000; and David Dutton, *Neville Chamberlain*, London, 2001.

8. The book by Richard Griffiths, *Fellow Travellers of the Right* (see note 6 above).

9. He said 'appeasement' was a term he did not care about, 'but which to a large extent expresses the object we have in view' (*DGFP*, D/I, doc. 104, p. 183).

10. Neil Fleming, *The Seventh Marquess of Londonderry: a Political Life*, Ph.D. thesis, Queen's University Belfast, 2002. I was well embarked upon the research and writing of this book when I learnt that Neil Fleming was preparing a doctoral thesis on Londonderry. We met on a couple of occasions to exchange views. It was plain that he was attempting a full political biography of Londonderry, from beginning to end of his career, whereas my own interest was confined to his involvement with Nazi Germany – something which formed only one aspect of the thesis. I read his thesis, with admiration, only when my book was almost complete, adding a belated reference here and there in the footnotes where I thought it added to (or differed from) my own findings.

11. Cited sympathetically in the post-war memoirs of a Conservative Member of Parliament, whose political stance differed sharply from Londonderry's: Robert Boothby, *I Fight to Live*, London, 1947, p. 140.

Prologue: A Patrician's Progress

1. See, above all, on the changing position of the aristocracy in the late nineteenth and early twentieth century in Britain, the magisterial study by David Cannadine, *The Decline and Fall of the British Aristocracy*, New Haven/London, 1990, chs. 9–12.

2. David Cannadine, *Class in Britain*, London, 2000, pp. 111, 115, 132.

3. Cited in Cannadine, *Class in Britain*, p. 107.

4. A. J. P. Taylor, *English History 1914–1945*, Harmondsworth, 1970, p. 226.

5. Charles Loch Mowat, *Britain Between the Wars 1918–1940*, London, 1956, pp. 134, 204.

6. Mowat, p. 666.

7. Mowat, p. 145; Peter Clarke, *Hope and Glory. Britain 1900–1990*, London, 1996, p. 119.

8. Cannadine, *Class in Britain*, p. 132.

9. The content and limited influence of radical anti-Semitic propaganda in Britain in the 1920s (most of it drawing on the crude Russian forgery *The Protocols of the Elders of Zion*, widely taken as genuine on the racist Right at the time, purporting to describe a Jewish plot to attain world domination) is assessed by Richard Thurlow, *Fascism in Britain. A History, 1918–1985*, Oxford, 1987, ch. 4.

10. G. C. Webber, *The Ideology of the British Right 1918–1939*, London, 1986, p. 19.

11. For admiration of Mussolini in Britain, see Richard Griffiths, *Fellow Travellers of the Right. British Enthusiasts for Nazi Germany 1933–39*, Oxford, 1983, pp. 13–25.

12. On the changing nature of the Conservative Party after the First World War, see David Dilks, 'The Rise of Baldwin', in Norman Gash, Donald Southgate, David Dilks and John Ramsden, *The Conservatives. A History from Their Origins to 1965*, London, 1977, pp. 273ff; and John Ramsden, *An Appetite for Power. A History of the Conservative Party since 1830*, London, 1998, chs. 9–10.

13. Neil Fleming, *The Seventh Marquess of Londonderry: a Political Life*, Ph.D. thesis, Queen's University Belfast, 2002, pp. 108–9. Londonderry agreed with a correspondent, Major Stanley Appleby, a local Conservative in County Durham, who attributed Bolshevism in England to the influx of 'alien blood'.

14. The following from H. Montgomery Hyde, *The Londonderrys. A Family Portrait*, London, 1979, chs. 1–3.

15. Lord Londonderry used the quotation as the preface to his book, *Ourselves and Germany*, London, 1938, p. 6.

16. Hyde, *The Londonderrys*, p. xix. In terms of gross income, Lord Londonderry was, around 1880, the fourteenth most prosperous landowner in Britain, with estates totalling 50,323 acres (Cannadine, *The Decline and Fall of the British Aristocracy*, p. 710).

17. The houses were Wynyard Hall and Seaham Hall (both in County Durham),

Mount Stewart (in Ulster), Plâs Machynlleth (Wales), Garron Tower (on the Antrim coast in Ireland, and no longer in the family's possession by the time of the 7th Marquess). There was also a hunting-lodge at Ranksborough, near Oakham, in Rutland. Almost quarter of a million pounds was spent on the purchase (in 1822) and renovation of Londonderry House (known until 1872 as Holdernesse House) (Hyde, *The Londonderrys*, pp. xix–xx, 30, 186).

18. Earl of Halifax, *Fulness of Days*, London, 1957, p. 50; and Andrew Roberts, 'The Holy Fox': the Life of Lord Halifax, London, 1991, paperback edn, 1997, p. 152.

19. Anne de Courcy, *Circe. The Life of Edith, Marchioness of Londonderry*, London, 1992, p. 1. This biography, and the Marchioness of Londonderry's own gossipy memoirs, *Retrospect*, London, 1938, provide details of her family background and upbringing.

20. Hertfordshire Record Office, D/ERV/C2482/88, L to Lady Desborough, 21.9.47; extract printed in Hyde, *The Londonderrys*, p. 262.

21. Lord Londonderry's affairs and Lady Londonderry's reactions are dealt with at length in Courcy, pp. 54ff, 68ff, 73ff, 92ff, 136ff, 148ff.

22. Cited Hyde, *The Londonderrys*, p. 116.

23. Cited Hyde, *The Londonderrys*, p. 127.

24. Hyde, *The Londonderrys*, pp. 128–9.

25. Cited Hyde, *The Londonderrys*, pp. 132–3.

26. Hyde, *The Londonderrys*, pp. 133–5.

27. Hyde, *The Londonderrys*, p. 136.

28. Hyde, *The Londonderrys*, pp. 139–49.

29. Andrew Boyle, *Trenchard: Man of Vision*, London, 1962, p. 396. Lord Londonderry dedicated his book *Wings of Destiny*, London, 1943, to Trenchard, whom he described (p. 8) as 'one of the most remarkable men I have ever met'. On Londonderry's time as Under-Secretary of State for Air, see H. Montgomery Hyde, *British Air Policy Between the Wars*, London, 1976, pp. 70–72.

30. Churchill's satisfaction can be read into his regret at Londonderry's resignation in May 1921 (Hyde, *The Londonderrys*, p. 143). Lady Londonderry later exaggerated her husband's role (*Retrospect*, p. 170) when she said he 'practically controlled the Air Ministry' at this time.

31. See Hyde, *The Londonderrys*, pp. 102–4, and Courcy, pp. 62–3, for the visit to India, embellished with lavish hospitality at every turn by imperial grandees and loyalist Maharajahs, and including horse-racing at the Viceroy's Cup, polo, pig-sticking and tiger- and crocodile-shooting.

32. Hyde, *The Londonderrys*, pp. 141–2, 165.

33. PRONI, D/3099/2/17/37A, L to Baldwin, 29.12.38; D/3099/2/17,

51A, L to Baldwin, 20.5.39; PRO, PRO 30/69, fol. 167, Lady L to MacDonald, 8.1.36. Londonderry's name was even briefly considered as a possible Viceroy as late as 1941 (*The Empire at Bay. The Leo Amery Diaries 1929–1945*, ed. John Barnes and David Nicholson, London, 1988, p. 713 (5.9.41)).

34. PRONI, D/3099/2/4/80, 82, Lord Stamfordham (Private Secretary to the King) to L, 21.1.31; King George VI to L, 25.1.31; Hertfordshire Record Office, D/ERV C2482/71, L to Lady Desborough, 25.1.31.

35. Hyde, *The Londonderrys*, p. 143.

36. Hyde, *The Londonderrys*, p. 153, citing Londonderry's letter to Lady Desborough of 25.10.22.

37. This is Fleming's speculation in *The Seventh Marquess of Londonderry*, p. 146. For Londonderry's association with the Conservative 'Diehards', see Webber, pp. 19–23.

38. This summary of Londonderry's involvement in Irish politics in the early 1920s draws upon the full account in Fleming, chs. 2 and 4; see also Hyde, *The Londonderrys*, pp. 154–5.

39. Hyde, *The Londonderrys*, p. 167; and H. Montgomery Hyde, *Baldwin: the Unexpected Prime Minister*, London, 1973, p. 260, note.

40. This aspiration was one shared by his wife until the mid-1930s. Even then, Londonderry did not give up hope (however unrealistic it might have seemed to others) that he might be called back to high office, possibly as Foreign Secretary, by Winston Churchill (Interview with Lady Mairi Bury, Mount Stewart, 22.10.02).

41. Obituary of Lord Londonderry, *The Times*, 12.2.49. Some had momentarily and illusorily seen him as heading a coal owners' delegation to negotiate with the miners – by making minor concessions, not discussing 'fundamentals' – in the hope of heading off a general strike. Londonderry refused to be involved in any 'intrigue' (*The Crawford Papers. The Journals of David Lindsay, 27th Earl of Crawford and 10th Earl of Balcarres 1871 to 1940 During the Years 1892 to 1940*, ed. John Vincent, Manchester, 1984, p. 515 (10.5.26)).

42. J. C. C. Davidson, Chairman of the Conservative Party at the time, who had in general no high opinion of Londonderry, later noted that 'as a mine-owner in Durham he had quite a good reputation', adding, however, that 'the people who were his agents were regarded as a pretty hard lot' (Robert Rhodes James, *Memoirs of a Conservative. J. C. C. Davidson's Memoirs and Papers 1910–37*, London, 1969, p. 405).

43. Fleming, pp. 182–92.

44. Fleming, p. 185; Hyde, *The Londonderrys*, p. 171.

45. Hyde, *The Londonderrys*, p. 172. In a letter written during the General

Strike to Ramsay MacDonald, then leader of the Labour Party in Opposition, Londonderry spoke of 'selfish agitators', though described himself as 'an apostle of peace in the industry' (John Rylands UL, Manchester, RMD/1/14/74, L to MacDonald, n.d. (1926)).

46. Fleming, pp. 192–3.

47. Mowat, p. 336.

48. Fleming, pp. 201–2.

49. A term coined by Ramsay MacDonald, the Prime Minister (Clarke, p. 151).

50. See Hyde, *The Londonderrys*, pp. 192–3; Courcy, p. 220; Cannadine, *Decline and Fall*, p. 344.

51. *Lloyd George. A Diary by Frances Stevenson*, ed. A. J. P. Taylor, London, 1971, pp. 254, 302. The correspondent of *The Times*, A. L. Kennedy, noted in his diary that 'Lord L[ondonderry] has an undue amount of influence over MacDonald through Lady L[ondonderry]' (*The Times and Appeasement. The Journals of A. L. Kennedy, 1932–1939*, ed. Gordon Martel, Camden Society Fifth Series, vol. 16, Cambridge, 2000, p. 47, and see also p. 79).

52. Hyde, *Baldwin*, p. 235. The quoted criticism was voiced by Beatrice Webb.

53. John Rylands UL, Manchester, RMD/1/14/68, Lady L to MacDonald, 13.1.26. Later, by which time MacDonald was again Prime Minister, she was never too busy to alter her arrangements to suit him (*The Diaries of Sir Robert Bruce Lockhart, Vol. 1, 1915–1938*, ed. Kenneth Young, London, 1973, p. 250).

54. Hyde, *The Londonderrys*, pp. 197, 199.

55. This added to the distrust of MacDonald in the Labour Party before his 'defection' and the formation of the National Government (Malcolm Muggeridge, *The Thirties: 1930–1940 in Great Britain*, London, 1940, p. 49). Thereafter, his socializing with 'the class enemy' simply confirmed to Labour Party supporters that they had been right all along in their distrust.

56. *The Diaries and Letters of Robert Bernays, 1932–1939. An Insider's Account of the House of Commons*, ed. Nick Smart, Studies in British History, vol. 30, Lewiston/Queenston/Lampeter, 1996, p. 18 (22.11.32).

57. PRO, PRO 30/69/760, fols. 72–3, Lady L to MacDonald, 9.7.33; also cited in Hyde, *The Londonderrys*, p. 203; and David Marquand, *Ramsay MacDonald*, London, 1977, p. 689.

58. Marquand, p. 689.

59. *The Political Diary of Hugh Dalton 1918–40, 1945–60*, ed. Ben Pimlott, London, 1986, pp. 116–17 (9.7.30).

60. *The Diaries of Sir Robert Bruce Lockhart*, p. 280 (22.11.33).

61. PRO, PRO 30/69/755, fol. 572, Lady L to MacDonald, 8.8.33.

62. Oswald Mosley, *My Life*, London, 1968, pp. 241–2.

63. Interview with Lady Mairi Bury, Mount Stewart, 23.5.02. For the MacDonald relationship, see Hyde, *The Londonderrys*, ch. 5 and Courcy, pp. 189–230; also Marquand, pp. 687–92. The MacDonald letters to Lady Londonderry are in PRONI, D/3099/3/20–1–423, with a selection made for Hyde's book in D/3084/C/D/4/1–72. Some of Lady Londonderry's to MacDonald are in John Rylands UL, Manchester, RMD/1/13; others are scattered through the extensive Ramsay MacDonald Papers (PRO 30/69) in the Public Record Office in London.

64. Obituary in the *Newcastle Journal*, 12.2.49, in PRONI, D/3099/10/55; Margot, Countess of Oxford and Asquith, *More Memories*, London, 1933, p. 78 (where Lord Londonderry was among those described as having 'the finest manners of any men that I have ever known').

65. Rhodes James, p. 405, citing J. C. C. Davidson's recollection.

66. Harold Nicolson, *Diaries and Letters 1930–1964*, ed. Stanley Olson, New York, 1980, p. 93.

67. *Chips. The Diaries of Sir Henry Channon*, ed. Robert Rhodes James, London, 1967, p. 434.

68. Courcy, p. 245.

69. *Chips*, p. 434; interview with Lady Mairi Bury, Mount Stewart, 22.10.02.

70. *The Times and Appeasement*, pp. 281, 285.

71. *Parliament and Politics in the Age of Churchill and Attlee. The Headlam Diaries 1935–1951*, ed. Stuart Ball, Camden Society Fifth Series, vol. 14, Cambridge, 1999, p. 120.

72. *Parliament and Politics in the Age of Churchill and Attlee*, pp. 145, 346, 386–7, 572–3, where Londonderry is described as 'a weak, rather vain, man – but when you get to know him [he] has a heart of gold'.

73. Harold Macmillan, *Winds of Change 1914–1939*, London, 1966, pp. 196–7.

74. Thomas Jones, *A Diary with Letters, 1931–1950*, London, 1954, p. 100.

75. *Chips*, pp. 28, 190, 264, 424, 430.

76. *Parliament and Politics in the Age of Baldwin and MacDonald. The Headlam Diaries 1923–1935*, ed. Stuart Ball, London, 1992, p. 183 (17.12.30) – and pp. 103, 110, 279 for further unflattering remarks about Lord and Lady Londonderry.

77. PRONI, D/3099/13/2/1372, Lady L to L, 11.10.38.

78. Marchioness of Londonderry, *Retrospect*, pp. 19–20; Courcy, pp. 20, 63, 77–87.

79. PRONI, D/3099/3/12/3, 5–6, 37 ('Ark Biographies').

80. See Marchioness of Londonderry, *Retrospect*, pp. 236ff; Hyde, *The Londonderrys*,
p. 132; Courcy, pp. 115ff; *The Times and Appeasement*, p. 79 and n. 189.
81. The description of a reception in Londonderry House in 1933 by Robert Bruce Lockhart, *Retreat from Glory*, London, 1934, p. 11.
82. The liaison between Ramsay MacDonald and Lady Londonderry, it has been noted, turned Londonderry House into 'a social centre' for the National Government, and – bizarrely in this mansion epitomizing high Conservatism – the National Labour Party held a major reception there in 1932 (*The Times and Appeasement*, p. 79 n. 189). In 1935, just after Londonderry had been dropped from the Conservative Cabinet, the traditional reception at Londonderry House did not take place. Lady Londonderry denied that this was on account of a rift between Lord Londonderry and the Prime Minister, Stanley Baldwin (*News Chronicle*, 25.11.35, in PRONI, D/3099/10/47). This was, nonetheless, the reason.
83. *Parliament and Politics in the Age of Baldwin and MacDonald*, p. 155 (17.10.28). When Londonderry was appointed First Commissioner of Works at the formation of the National Government in August 1931, Headlam noted: 'Circe has played her cards well' (p. 214 (26.8.31)).
84. Keith Middlemas and John Barnes, *Baldwin: a Biography*, London, 1969, p. 806; also cited in Hyde, *Baldwin*, p. 295, drawing on a memorandum by Londonderry's son, Lord Castlereagh, dating from March 1936.

1 Illusions and Delusions about Hitler

1. See Ian Kershaw, *The 'Hitler Myth'. Image and Reality in the Third Reich*, 2nd edn, Oxford, 2001; and Philipp W. Fabry, *Mutmaßungen über Hitler. Urteile von Zeitgenossen*, Düsseldorf, 1969.
2. An extensive survey of the gamut of attitudes towards Nazi Germany is provided by Dietrich Aigner, *Das Ringen um England*, Munich/Esslingen, 1969, part 2, pp. 105–268. For briefer overviews of British images of Germany, see Reinhard Meyers, 'Das Dritte Reich in britischer Sicht. Grundzüge und Determinanten britischer Deutschlandbilder in den dreißiger Jahren', in Bernd-Jürgen Wendt (ed.), *Das britische Deutschlandbild im Wandel des 19. und 20. Jahrhundert*, Bochum, 1984, pp. 127–44; Martin Gilbert and Richard Gott, *The Appeasers*, London, 1963, paperback edn, 1967, ch. 1; and, an excellent short summary, D. C. Watt, *Britain Looks to Germany*, London, 1965, pp. 20–27.
3. Detlev Clemens, *Herr Hitler in Germany. Wahrnehmung und Deutungen des Nationalsozialismus in Großbritannien 1920 bis 1939*, Göttingen/Zurich,

1995, provides the fullest assessment of the knowledge of Hitler and the Nazi movement accumulated in the British Foreign Office since the beginning of Hitler's political 'career'. Also valuable in this regard is F. L. Carsten, *Britain and the Weimar Republic: the British Documents*, London, 1984.

4. Brigitte Granzow, *A Mirror of Nazism. British Opinion and the Emergence of Hitler, 1929–1933*, London, 1964, pp. 34–5.

5. Ian Kershaw, *Hitler, 1889–1936: Hubris*, London, 1998, pp. 333ff.

6. *The Diaries of Sir Robert Bruce Lockhart, Vol. 1, 1915–1938*, ed. Kenneth Young, London, 1973, p. 125 (entry for 15.9.30).

7. Granzow, pp. 127, 132.

8. F. R. Gannon, *The British Press and Germany, 1936–1939*, Oxford, 1971, p. 75.

9. Malcolm Muggeridge, *The Thirties: 1930–40 in Great Britain*, London, 1940, p. 9.

10. Granzow, pp. 41, 81, 131, 133ff.

11. Granzow, p. 139.

12. Granzow, pp. 106, 127; Clemens, p. 164.

13. Granzow, pp. 101–2.

14. *Hitler. Reden, Schriften, Anordnungen: Februar 1925 bis Januar 1933*, ed. Institut für Zeitgeschichte, 5 vols. in 12 parts, Munich 1992–8, vol. 3, part 3, p. 452, n. 2, citing the *Daily Mail*, 27 September 1930 (interview of Rothay Reynolds with Hitler).

15. Granzow, p. 143.

16. Granzow, p. 174.

17. Granzow, p. 171.

18. Granzow, pp. 182–5.

19. Granzow, pp. 180–81.

20. *The Times*, 30.1.33, p. 10.

21. *The Times*, 31.3.33, p. 10. The commercial councillor at the Berlin Embassy, Frank Thelwall, indicated in a memorandum to the Foreign Office on 15 February 1933 that as long as von Neurath and von Krosigk 'remain at their posts there is a guarantee that the worst follies will not be committed or, if committed, will be remedied' (Carsten, pp. 275–6; Clemens, p. 262 and n. 41).

22. *News Chronicle*, 31.1.33, p. 6. The Berlin correspondent of the newspaper, writing on the same page, nevertheless prophetically warned that Hitler would 'never of his own will relax his grip upon power' and, should he fail, would 'like another Sampson, involve others, perhaps Germany herself, in his own doom'.

23. See Kershaw, *Hitler, 1889–1936: Hubris*, p. 421.

24. *The Times*, 31.1.33, p. 11.

25. Granzow, p. 217.

26. *Daily Herald* 31.1.33, p. 8: 'Hitler – the Clown who wants to Play Statesman'.

27. *Daily Worker*, 31.1.33, p. 1; 1.2.33, p. 1; 3.2.33, p. 2; 4.2.33, p. 5. According to one assessment by a sympathizer, 'Hitler's victory [on 30 January 1933] was the last thing expected by anyone in the world Communist movement' (Noreen Branson, *History of the Communist Party of Great Britain, 1927–1941*, London, 1985, p. 110). Another analysis indicates that the response of the British Communist Party to the appointment of Hitler as German Chancellor on 30 January 1933 was, like that of the Communist International and the world Communist movement, 'indecisive', 'confused', and 'reluctant to commit itself ahead of the C[ommunist] I[nternational]', whose officials were hesitant and divided in opinion. (Andrew Thorpe, *The British Communist Party and Moscow, 1920–1943*, Manchester, 2000, p. 201). The membership of the Communist Party of Great Britain was only in the region of 3,000 at the beginning of the 1930s. A mere 51,042 voters had supported the Party in the general election of 1929 (L. J. MacFarlane, *The British Communist Party. Its Origin and Development until 1929*, London, 1966, pp. 297–302; James Eaden and David Renton, *The Communist Party of Great Britain since 1920*, London, 2002, p. 31).

28. Granzow, pp. 220–21.

29. Carsten, p. 280.

30. *Manchester Guardian*, 8.4.33, p. 13: 'More Facts About The Nazi Terror'; also cited in Martin Gilbert, *Britain and Germany between the Wars*, London, 1964, p. 74.

31. A number of reports from the *Manchester Guardian* were included in a compilation put together by the Comité des Délégations Juives and published in Paris in 1934, *Die Lage der Juden in Deutschland 1933. Das Schwarzbuch: Tatsachen und Dokumente*, repr. Frankfurt am Main, 1983, pp. 496ff.

32. A brief summary of press reports is provided by Carsten, pp. 285–7.

33. For the events and significance of the episode, see Kershaw, *Hitler, 1889–1936: Hubris*, ch. 12.

34. *The Times*, 3.7.34.

35. *Manchester Guardian*, 8.4.33.

36. See Clemens, p. 263.

37. *Lloyd George. A Diary by Frances Stevenson*, ed. A. J. P. Taylor, London, 1971, p. 287 (6.11.34).

38. *The Times*, 30.5.34, p. 13. And see the entry in the diary of A. L.

Kennedy, who had written the leading article, for that date in *The Times and Appeasement. The Journals of A. L. Kennedy, 1932–1939*, ed. Gordon Martel, Camden Fifth Series, vol. 16, Cambridge, 2000, p. 140.

39. W. P. Crozier, *Off the Record. Political Interviews 1933–1943*, ed. A. J. P. Taylor, London, 1973, pp. 3–4.

40. Crozier, pp. 5–6 (4.11.33).

41. Gannon, pp. 7–8.

42. PRO, FO 371/16744, fols. 69–86, 'Notes by Sir Maurice Hankey on Hitler's External Policy in Theory and Practice', 24.10.33; quotation fols. 69, 79. And see Stephen Roskill, *Hankey: Man of Secrets, Vol. 3, 1931–1963*, London, 1974, pp. 84–5, pointing out that 'though Hankey made no attempt to solve the riddle himself the whole tenor of this remarkable paper suggests that his answer was that the Hitler of *Mein Kampf* had not fundamentally altered'.

43. For Rumbold's period as Ambassador in Berlin, see Martin Gilbert, *Sir Horace Rumbold. Portrait of a Diplomat, 1869–1941*, London, 1973, pp. 318–86.

44. PRO, FO 371/9828, Annual Report, Bavaria during 1923, pp. 6–7.

45. See Clemens, pp. 45–94 and Carsten, pp. 108–22.

46. Cited Carsten, p. 109; and Clemens, p. 47.

47. Carsten, p. 110.

48. Clemens, p. 73.

49. Clemens, pp. 80–81.

50. Carsten, p. 113.

51. Clemens, p. 89.

52. Clemens, p. 143; Carsten, p. 214.

53. Carsten, p. 264.

54. Clemens, pp. 162–3.

55. See Clemens, pp. 171–3, 208.

56. Clemens, pp. 237, 242, 245.

57. Clemens, p. 193.

58. Clemens, pp. 213, 215–16. The report was compiled in December 1931 by Group-Captain Malcolm Christie, who had been born in Germany, had studied there, had served from 1927 to 1930 as Air Attaché in the British Embassy in Berlin, and was a friend of Hermann Göring. Christie stood in the early 1930s in close contact with Sir Robert Vansittart, the leading civil servant in the Foreign Office. See Clemens, p. 224 for Christie's view in spring 1932 that Hitler might go down in history as 'the consummate drummer or the supreme pied-piper, but never as a great statesman'. Christie's perceptive reports formed the basis of the

post-war book, acknowledging his own pre-war failure to understand the real nature of Nazism, by T. P. Conwell-Evans, *None So Blind*, London, 1947.

59. Granzow, p. 188.

60. *DBFP*, 2/IV, no. 232, pp. 400–401. Von Neurath's own first impressions of Hitler, so he told Rumbold, were not unfavourable, not least since the new Chancellor had spontaneously sought his advice on a number of occasions (no. 235, pp. 406–8).

61. *DBFP*, 2/IV, no. 243, p. 426; Carsten, p. 274.

62. *DBFP*, 2/IV, no. 243, p. 424: Clemens, p. 257.

63. Cited Clemens, p. 259.

64. Cited Clemens, pp. 259–60.

65. Cited Clemens, p. 267.

66. Quotations from *DBFP*, 2/V, no. 139, p. 235, and no. 30, p. 42; also cited in Clemens, pp. 279–80.

67. *DBFP*, 2/V, no. 36, pp. 47–55 (for subsequent quotations); and see Gilbert, *Rumbold*, pp. 377–9; and Clemens, pp. 281–9.

68. *DBFP*, 2/V, p. 55, n.5.

69. *DBFP*, 2/5, no. 127, pp. 213–17, quotation p. 216.

70. Clemens, p. 287. Vansittart fully approved of Temperley's memorandum and suggested it be circulated to the Cabinet, which was done on 16 May (*DBFP*, 2/V, p. 213, n.1).

71. PRO, FO 371/16723, fols. 9–15. Vansittart commented (fol. 8) that the optimism in Wigram's memorandum conflicted with Rumbold's *Mein Kampf* dispatch, indicating 'that the present régime in Germany will, *on past and present form*, loose off another European war just so soon as it feels strong enough', and with his own knowledge of Germany. See also Ian Colvin, *Vansittart in Office. The Origins of World War II*, London, 1965, p. 23; and Clemens, p. 286. On the hopes behind the Pact, see Arnold J. Toynbee, *Survey of International Affairs 1933*, London, 1934, pp. 209ff.

72. Kershaw, *Hitler, 1889–1936: Hubris*, p. 492.

73. PRO, Cab. 24/241, fols. 48–51v, 'The Foreign Policy of the Present German Government', C.P. 129 (33), 16.5.33, with Enclosure, 'Germany and Disarmament', 7.5.33.

74. PRO, Cab. 23/76, fols. 88–9, minutes of Cabinet 35/33, 17.5.33.

75. Clemens, p. 289.

76. *DBFP*, 2/V, no. 229, pp. 384–90, quotation p. 390; Clemens, pp. 293–4, 301.

77. Colvin, *Vansittart in Office*, p. 24. Vansittart's memorandum had been written on 10 May 1933.

78. PRO, Cab. 24/241, fol. 48–48v, Sir John Simon's memorandum: 'The Foreign Policy of the Present German Government'.

79. Clemens, pp. 312–14. Vansittart later recalled that Rumbold's last dispatch had also been weakened in its impact by his comment that the German regime was not hostile to Britain (Robert Vansittart, *The Mist Procession*, London, 1958, p. 478).

80. Clemens, pp. 303ff, 342, 373–5. Writing to the British Ambassador, Sir Eric Phipps, on 10 July 1934, the Consul-General in Munich D. St Clair Gainer, noted: 'The feeling amongst the Reichswehr officers is that Hitler has given the army back its self-respect, and the army are therefore prepared to co-operate with him provided he will to some extent modify his Socialist programme and keep his followers and minor chieftains in proper subjection.' Here, too, therefore, the impression that Hitler was dependent upon army cooperation could easily be understood to mean that he was now subjected to their dominance (PRO, FO 371/17708, fol. 73).

81. On Phipps, see the short but valuable study by Johann Ott, *Botschafter Sir Eric Phipps und die deutsch-englischen Beziehungen. Studien zur britischen Außenpolitik gegenüber dem Dritten Reich*, Ph.D. thesis, Erlangen/Nuremberg, 1968.

82. Churchill Archives Centre, Churchill College, Cambridge, Phipps 10/1, Berlin Diary, vol. 1, p. 10 (24.10.33). Hitler took an instant dislike to Phipps (Ott, p. 17; and, for his lasting detestation of the British Ambassador (and his wife), Paul Schwarz, *This Man Ribbentrop. His Life and Times*, New York, 1943, pp. 188–9). Phipps was not short of detractors in Britain (including Lord Londonderry) – see Gilbert and Gott, pp. 36–8.

83. *DBFP*, 2/V, no. 492, pp. 715–20, quotations p. 720.

84. *DBFP*, 2/VI, no. 60, pp. 81–91, quotation pp. 90–91; Churchill Archives Centre, Churchill College, Cambridge, Phipps 10/1, Berlin Diary, pp. 16–17 (21.11.33). Phipps continued with a cautious belief in Hitler's sincerity about wanting peace (Phipps 10/1, p. 78 (8.8.34); Phipps 10/2, Berlin Diary, vol. 2, p. 169 (10.12.35)).

85. Writing to Phipps in late November 1933, Sir Maurice Hankey stated: 'I think Ministers are beginning to see that the re-armament of Germany is not likely to be stopped except by the most drastic measures, – for which I do not believe public opinion either here or in France would stand' (Churchill Archives Centre, Churchill College, Cambridge, Phipps 3/3, Hankey to Phipps, 24.11.33).

86. Clemens, pp. 351–2.

87. The Earl of Avon, *The Eden Memoirs. Facing the Dictators*, London, 1962, p. 44.

88. *DBFP*, 2/VI, no. 195, pp. 299–300, quotations p. 300; Churchill Archives Centre, Churchill College, Cambridge, Phipps 10/1, Berlin Diary, p. 28 (22.1.34).

89. A point correctly emphasized by A. J. P. Taylor, *The Origins of the Second World War*, Harmondsworth, 1964, p. 88.

90. Clemens, p. 353.

91. Clemens, pp. 318–19. The diplomatic framework of the intended agreement of the four powers had been described at length by Sir Ronald Graham, the British Ambassador to Rome, in a dispatch to the Foreign Minister, Sir John Simon, on 19 June 1934 (*DBFP*, 2/V, no. 216, pp. 358–73).

92. Keith Middlemas, *The Diplomacy of Illusion. The British Government and Germany 1937–39*, London, 1972, p. 33.

93. Clemens, pp. 367–8. Eden describes his meeting with Hitler in Avon, ch. 4.

94. Phipps noted in his diary on 8 August 1934: 'German rearmament proceeds apace and my French colleague [M. François-Poncet, the French Ambassador in Berlin] affirms that the triple expansion of the Army will be completed by October'. On 27 October, Phipps added: 'Germany is steadily rearming and means to be in a very strong position indeed in three or four years' time' (Churchill Archives Centre, Churchill College, Cambridge, Phipps 10/1, pp. 78, 82).

95. Middlemas, pp. 33–4; and at length in Keith Middlemas and John Barnes, *Baldwin: a Biography*, London, 1969, chs. 27–8.

96. Clemens, pp. 380–81. Phipps had noted in his diary the previous August that it was 'highly desirable' to 'bind Germany and her rulers by an Eastern pact of mutual assistance' (Churchill Archives Centre, Churchill College, Cambridge, Phipps 10/1, p. 79 (8.8.34)).

97. Kershaw, *Hitler, 1889–1936: Hubris*, pp. 549ff.

98. From Hitler's point of view, the naval treaty represented the first fruits of the bilateral arms agreement with Great Britain that he had sought from the outset. Britain had until this point insisted on a general agreement to prevent the division of Europe into two armed camps, as had been the position before 1914 (Churchill Archives Centre, Churchill College, Cambridge, Phipps 10/1, p. 86 (27.11.34)).

99. Gannon, p. 32.

100. Richard Thurlow, *Fascism in Britain. A History, 1918–1985*, Oxford, 1987, p. 124.

101. Richard Griffiths, *Fellow Travellers of the Right. British Enthusiasts for Nazi Germany 1933–39*, Oxford, 1983, pp. 38ff.

102. See Griffiths, pp. 127ff.

103. Margarete Gärtner, *Botschafterin des guten Willens*, Bonn, 1955,

pp. 18ff; D. C. Watt, *Personalities and Policies. Studies in the Formulation of British Foreign Policy in the Twentieth Century*, London, 1965, pp. 120-21. Watt dates the foundation of the Anglo-German Association to 1929. This applied to the German wing of the Association. The British wing had been founded the previous summer. On the foundation, see Gärtner, pp. 163-4.

104. Hamilton Papers 14/2/1, King's College London, Liddell Hart Centre for Military Archives. Minutes of a meeting of the Anglo-German Association, 3.12.29, and attached list of members. A membership list of the Association from 11 June 1934 does not, however, include Londonderry's name. When his membership lapsed is unclear, though it may conceivably have been when he became a member of the Cabinet in 1931. The first indication of a specific interest in Germany on Londonderry's part was the visit, arranged by Margarete Gärtner, which he made, as part of a small 'study-group', in April 1929. Part of the visit concerned the German coal-producing district in the Ruhr (Gärtner, pp. 162-3). By late 1931, now as Minister for Air, Londonderry was prepared to introduce Dr Gärtner to other influential members of the House of Lords (Gärtner, pp. 217-18).

105. Hamilton Papers, 14/2/1: 'Report of the Dinner given by the Committee of the Anglo-German Association to Herr von Lineiner-Wildau, M.d.R. . . .'

106. Hamilton Papers, 14/2/4 (Hamilton to Garvin, 18.11.31 and 24.11.31; Garvin to Hamilton, 23.11.31; Hamilton to Sir Robert Hutchison, 24.11.31). Extensive rumours continued into December that Hitler was about to make a visit to London (*The Diaries of Sir Robert Bruce Lockhart, Vol. 1*, pp. 193-4 (2.12.31)).

107. Hamilton Papers, 14/2/3 (Hamilton to Rebecca West, 15.3.33, and to Colonel Ernst Heyne, 25.4.33; Cicely Andrews, alias Rebecca West, to Hamilton, 13.3.33).

108. Hamilton Papers, 14/2/4 (Hamilton to Evan Bernard Morgan, Association Secretary, 12.5.33).

109. Hamilton Papers, 14/2/4 (Hamilton to Morgan, 20.6.33).

110. Hamilton Papers, 14/2/3 (Hamilton to Frau von Flesch-Brunningen, Munich, 30.11.33, and to Ch. T. J. Schwartz, The Hague, 24.7.34).

111. His views on distinctive Jewish appearance and character traits are clear in a letter to the editor of the *Evening Standard* of 27 January 1939 (Hamilton Papers, 14/2/12). He appears to have been implicitly anti-Jewish, like many officers from the landed classes, at the time of his distinguished service as Lord Kitchener's Chief of Staff in the Boer War. In 1902 he wrote to Winston Churchill, suggesting that the incorporation of the Boers into the

MAKING FRIENDS WITH HITLER

Empire would do far more 'for the future of our race and language, than by assimilating a million Johannesburg Jews'. (Johannesburg was commonly referred to at the time as 'Jewburg' or 'Jewhannesburg', and Hamilton told one Jewish correspondent in 1938 who had objected to some remarks he had made at a speech 'that we did capture Johannesburg and especially the area round Doorn Kop mainly for the Jews' (Denis Judd and Keith Surridge, *The Boer War*, London, 2002, pp. 243–4; Hamilton Papers, 14/2/12, Hamilton to Sidney Salomon, 7.11.38.)

112. Hamilton Papers, 14/2/9, Hamilton to Mrs H. Thomson, 28.5.36.

113. According to a letter from the British Consulate-General, Hamburg, of 14 March 1935, to Basil C. Newton at the British Embassy in Berlin, the dissolution of the German branch had the previous July been prompted by Ribbentrop, by now Hitler's most trusted adviser on foreign policy, who objected to 'non-Aryans' among its members. The decision to replace the old organization by a new one was, it was said, taken after consultation with Hitler himself (PRO, KV 5/3, MI5 file (unfoliated)).

114. Meinertzhagen's name appears, alongside that of Lord Londonderry, as 'accepted' for membership of the Anglo-German Association in the minutes of its meeting on 3 December 1929 (Hamilton Papers, 14/2/1).

115. Hamilton Papers, 14/2/4 (Morgan to Hamilton, 14.11.34; Hamilton to Thorne, 4.3.35; Thorne to Hamilton, 7.3.35; Hamilton to Vance, 6.3.35, 12.3.35, 21.3.35; Vance to Hamilton, 8.3.35, 14.3.35, 21.3.35; Meinertzhagen to Hamilton, 19.3.35). Hamilton refused to join the Anglo-German Fellowship because, he said, he would not 'touch any association with purely business connections' (Hamilton Papers, 14/2/8, Hamilton to C. E. Carroll, 3.2.36, and see also his letter to Lady Down, 20.3.36).

116. For example: Hamilton Papers, 14/4/4, Hamilton to Dr Arnold Köster, 29.1.35; and Hamilton Papers, 13/4/3, Hamilton to Rebecca West, 15.3.33.

117. Graham Wootton, *The Official History of the British Legion*, London, 1956, p. 305. The listed membership was 451,413 in 1935, and rising. Since some members were exempt from paying fees, the actual total was, in fact, somewhat higher.

118. Griffiths, pp. 130–31.

119. Hamilton Papers, 14/2/5–6.

120. Hamilton Papers, 14/2/7–13.

121. For a description of Rothermere, see *Fleet Street, Press Barons and Politics. The Journals of Collin Brooks 1932–1940*, ed. N. J. Crowson, Camden Society Fifth Series, vol. 11, London, 1998, p. 72.

122. *Fleet Street*, p. 23 n. 15.

123. Maurice Cowling, *The Impact of Hitler. British Politics and British Policy, 1933–1940*, Cambridge, 1975, pp. 46–7.

124. Gannon, pp. 25–6, 34.

125. Viscount Rothermere, *My Fight to Rearm Britain*, London, 1939, pp. 3–18 (p. 18 for the phrase 'salvation of Britain').

126. *Daily Mail*, 10.7.33.

127. *Daily Mail*, 28.11.33 ('Why not a Franco-British Alliance?')

128. Rothermere, pp. 25, 28–9, 107.

129. *Adolf Hitler: Monologe im Führerhauptquartier 1941–1944. Die Aufzeichnungen Heinrich Heims*, ed. Werner Jochmann, Hamburg, 1980, p. 384.

130. *Adolf Hitler: Monologe*, p. 384.

131. For Tennant, see Griffiths, pp. 116–18.

132. E. W. D. Tennant, *True Account*, London, 1957, p. 187. Tennant's description of the dinner-party (pp. 185–7) is similar to that of George Ward Price, *I Know These Dictators*, London, 1937, pp. 29–32.

133. *Daily Mail*, 28.12.34 ('Germany On Her Feet Again') 'What magic has restored hope to German hearts,' he asked, 'given to German eyes the flash of courage and self-confidence, and magnetised this mighty nation until one feels in its midst as if one were in a gigantic power-house? Hitler. That is the whole answer.' Rothermere went on to describe British news reports on Nazi Germany – singling out reports of the persecution of Jews – as 'pure moonshine'.

134. Rothermere, pp. 80–82; *Fleet Street*, pp. 283–4. The eight-page German text is in PRO, FO 800/290, fols. 241–8 (3.5.35).

135. Griffiths, pp. 164–5.

136. See Griffiths, pp. 152–5; and Martin Gilbert, *The Roots of Appeasement*, London, 1966, pp. 144–7.

137. Thomas Jones, *A Diary with Letters, 1931–1950*, London, 1954, pp. 514–15.

138. Sir Robert Vansittart, on 4 February 1935, shortly after Lothian's return from his visit to Hitler. Cited in G. T. Waddington, '"An Idyllic and Unruffled Atmosphere of Complete Anglo-German Misunderstanding": Aspects of the Operations of the Dienststelle Ribbentrop in Great Britain, 1934–1938', *History*, 82 (1997), pp. 44–72, here p. 54.

139. J. R. M. Butler, *Lord Lothian (Philip Kerr) 1882–1940*, London, 1960, p. 45.

140. Cowling, pp. 133–4.

141. Butler, p. 190.

142. Politisches Archiv des Auswärtigen Amtes, Berlin, R27692, fols.

D525492–525511 (reports of a visit by the 'Deutsche Gruppe (Anglo-German Discussion Group)' to Blickling, 22–25.7.38, and note of a private discussion involving Lothian and Dr Karl Megerle of the Reich Propaganda Ministry, together with former Deputy Secretary to the Cabinet, and friend of Lloyd George and Baldwin, Dr Thomas Jones, who suggested British acceptance of German predominance in south-eastern Europe and British pressure on Prague in return for withdrawal of German involvement in Spain; also an unfoliated attached twelve-page 'Protokoll' summarizing the general discussion).

143. Jones, p. 44 (3.7.32).

144. Butler, p. 197. See also Lothian's remarks, in a private letter in February 1935: 'In some degree the brutality of National Socialism is the reaction to the treatment given to Germany herself since the war. I believe the best way of restoring reasonable rights to the Jews in Germany is not to counter hate by hate but to undermine the source of the evil aspects of National Socialism by giving to Germany her rightful place in Europe . . .' (Martin Gilbert, *Britain and Germany between the Wars*, pp. 78–9). Lothian's self-perception was not necessarily how others saw him. After talking to him in May 1937, the American Ambassador in Berlin thought him 'more a Fascist than any other Englishman I have met' (*Ambassador Dodd's Diary 1933–1938*, ed. William E. Dodd and Martha Dodd, London, 1941, p. 411 (6.5.37)).

145. Butler, pp. 199–202.

146. Butler, pp. 202–3. For Conwell-Evans, see Griffiths, pp. 146–8. Conwell-Evans, assisted by Margarete Gärtner, prepared the text of Lothian's statement to Hitler (Gärtner, p. 309).

147. Butler, pp. 203, 330–37. No German transcript of the discussion appears to have been retained (*DGFP*, C/III, p. 838 n. 7). The German Ambassador's recommendation that Lothian be granted an audience with Hitler is no. 445, pp. 837–8, and the notes of Lothian's conversation with Blomberg, Hess, and Ribbentrop is no. 468, pp. 885–7. Lothian was apparently disappointed at the audience (Gärtner, p. 309). See also Gilbert and Gott, pp. 38–41.

148. Butler, pp. 203–6.

149. PRONI, D/3099/2/16/56, Lothian to L, 7.2.35 (misplaced in file D/3099/2/17).

150. Watt, *Personalities and Policies*, p. 124.

151. For Lord Allen's audience with Hitler, see Martin Gilbert, *Plough My Own Furrow: the Life of Lord Allen of Hurtwood*, London, 1965, pp. 160–64; and Arthur Marwick, *Clifford Allen, the Open Conspirator*, Edinburgh/London, 1964, pp. 358–9, where his letter to the German dictator of 4.2.35, after his return from Berlin, is quoted (p. 359): 'Every word

that passed between us filled me with hope that it might now be possible to bring about a final understanding between our two nations.'

2 Downfall of the Air Minister

1. There were certainly family hopes that Londonderry would eventually become Foreign Secretary. In July 1932 his son, Lord Castlereagh, wrote to him, saying: 'I hope you will keep Londonderry House intact, because when you become the Foreign Secretary you will need such a place for the shows that you alone can give' (PRONI, D/3099/2/13/45, Castlereagh to L., 11.7.32).

2. PRONI, D/3099/2/9/1–82 contains the congratulatory messages. Churchill's is D/3099/2/9/16.

3. H. Montgomery Hyde, *The Londonderrys: a Family Portrait*, London, 1979, pp. 191–2. For Lady Londonderry's determining influence in her husband's appointment, see also H. Montgomery Hyde, *British Air Policy Between the Wars*, London, 1976, p. 275.

4. Londonderry deals extensively with the Geneva episode in *Ourselves*, chs. 3–4, and *Wings*, chs. 3–5. See also Hyde, *British Air Policy*, ch. 6.

5. B. H. Liddell Hart, *Memoirs*, vol. 1, London, 1965, pp. 205–6.

6. PRONI, D/3099/2/16/2B, L to Hailsham, 22.2.32; and *Wings*, p. 54.

7. PRONI, D/3099/2/16/22, Notes for a lecture at the Northern Counties Area Political School, Keswick, 4.5.32, but not delivered.

8. See Ian Kershaw, *Hitler, 1889–1936: Hubris*, London, 1998, pp. 490–94.

9. Gerhard L. Weinberg, *The Foreign Policy of Hitler's Germany. Diplomatic Revolution in Europe, 1933–36*, Chicago/London, 1970, pp. 161–95.

10. PRONI, D/3099/2/16/31, L to Col. Sir Maurice Hankey (Secretary to the Cabinet), 24.7.32.

11. G. M. Young, *Stanley Baldwin*, London, 1952, p. 174.

12. Keith Middlemas and John Barnes, *Baldwin: a Biography*, London, 1969, pp. 731–3; Cambridge UL, Baldwin Papers, Baldwin 129, Fols. 90–96 (Simon to Baldwin, 5.4.34, enclosing the Foreign Office's memorandum 'Immediate Problem of the Attitude to be taken by His Majesty's Government in regard to the question of Bombing from the Air', agreeing with Baldwin's position, and criticizing the stance of the Air Ministry). See also Uri Bialer, *The Shadow of the Bomber. The Fear of Air Attack and British Politics 1932–1939*, London, 1980, p. 29.

13. PRO, PRO 30/69/678/2, fol. 414, L to MacDonald, 30.5.32.

14. *Wings*, pp. 54–5.

15. Middlemas and Barnes, p. 732, and note.

16. Middlemas and Barnes, p. 733.

17. PRONI, D/3099/2/12/13–14, L to MacDonald, 9.6.32, 10.6.32; and PRO, PRO 30.69/678/2, fol. 415.

18. Middlemas and Barnes, p. 733; *Wings*, pp. 58–9.

19. PRO, FO 800/291, fols. 35–7: L to Sir John Simon (Foreign Secretary) and Sir Herbert Samuel (Home Secretary and leader of the Liberal Party), 22.6.32. See also Malcolm Smith, *British Air Strategy between the Wars*, Oxford, 1984, p. 118, for Londonderry's defence of the Air Ministry's position against the abolitionists.

20. *Series of League of Nations Publications*, IX. *Disarmament*, Gereva, 1932, IX.51 (in PRONI, D/3099/2/16/30C).

21. PRONI, D/3099/2/12/16, L to Ramsay MacDonald, 19.7.32; D/3099/2/16/29A–30A, L to Sir Clive Wigram, 21–22.7.32; *Wings*, p. 59.

22. PRO, PRO 30/69/678/2, fol. 422, L to MacDonald, 31.7.32.

23. PRONI, D/3099/2/12/18, MacDonald to L, 28.7.32.

24. PRONI, D/3099/2/12/21, L to MacDonald, 9.1.33.

25. Middlemas and Barnes, p. 739.

26. PRONI, D/3099/2/12/23, L to MacDonald, 20.1.33. (reporting from Baghdad, and later continuations of his report from Athens and Rome); *Wings*, pp. 68–9. For the positive image of Mussolini's Italy on the Conservative Right, see Richard Griffiths, *Fellow Travellers of the Right. British Enthusiasts for Nazi Germany, 1933–39*, Oxford, 1983, pp. 13–25. A. J. P. Taylor, *English History 1914–1945*, Harmondsworth, 1970, p. 397, points out the friendly attitude towards Mussolini of Ramsay MacDonald and Austen Chamberlain, half-brother of Neville. Churchill's essentially positive stance towards Mussolini during the 1920s and early 1930s is examined by Hans Woller, 'Churchill und Mussolini', *Vierteljahrshefte für Zeitgeschichte*, 49 (2001), pp. 563–94, here pp. 566–72.

27. In a speech to the Air Commission on 20 February 1933, for example, Londonderry gave assurances that the government was 'prepared to subscribe to universal acceptance of the abolition of naval and military aircraft and of air bombing, except for police purposes', but then immediately added the qualification that this was dependent upon 'an effective scheme for the international control of civil aviation which will prevent all possibility of the misuse of civil aircraft for military purposes' (Cambridge UL, Baldwin Papers, Baldwin 129, fols. 116–23).

28. PRO, PRO 30/69/679, fol. 522 (copy in PRONI, D/3099/2/12/24), L to MacDonald, 24.2.33; see also L's letters to Sir John Simon on 14–15 February 1933 in PRO, FO 800/291, fols. 213–22; *Ourselves*, pp. 55–6; *Wings*, pp. 69–72. The Foreign Office's irritation at Londonderry and the

'difficult position created by the Air Ministry' was mentioned by Anthony Eden to the senior foreign correspondent of *The Times* A. L. Kennedy in February 1933 (*The Times and Appeasement. The Journals of A. L. Kennedy, 1932–1939*, ed. Gordon Martel, Camden Society Fifth Series, vol. 16, Cambridge, 2000, p. 74 (18.2.33)).

29. PRONI, D/3099/15/11 (guest list); *Wings*, p. 72.

30. *Wings*, p. 73; H. Montgomery Hyde, *British Air Policy Between the Wars*, p. 291.

31. Cited in Martin Gilbert, *Winston S. Churchill, Vol. V, 1922–1939*, London, 1976, p. 455.

32. Gilbert, *Churchill*, pp. 457–8.

33. Gilbert, *Churchill*, pp. 459–62.

34. See *Wings*, pp. 76–7.

35. The title of chapter 4 of *Wings* and a phrase used in a letter of 24 June 1933 to Sir Austen Chamberlain, half-brother of Neville and a former Foreign Secretary (PRONI, D/3099/2/16/44).

36. *DBFP*, 2/V, no. 191, pp. 303–5; PRONI, D/3099/2/16/44–5, L's exchange with Sir Austen Chamberlain, 24 and 26.6.33; D/3099/2/12/26, L to MacDonald, 14.7.33; PRO, PRO 30/69/679, fols. 533–7, L to MacDonald, 11.7.33; L to Eden, 11.7.33; *Wings*, pp. 79–81. Ramsay MacDonald told Londonderry that he was 'disturbed about this continued friction' between him and the Foreign Office over the police bombing issue (PRO, PRO 30/69/679, fol. 538, MacDonald to L, 13.7.33).

37. *Wings*, p. 83 (citing a speech L made at Liverpool on 7.7.33).

38. See *Wings*, pp. 78–9.

39. *DBFP*, 2/V, nos. 200–201, pp. 315–22. Nadolny's conversation with Londonderry took place in Geneva on 2 June 1933, and was accompanied by a written 'Statement of the German Point of View in the Disarmament Question', which the German delegate handed over. Londonderry was due to be in Paris with days for talks with Norman Davies, American Ambassador-at-large in Paris, and Edouard Daladier, the French President of the Council of Ministers, in an attempt to persuade the French to adopt a more accommodating line on disarmament (*DBFP*, 2/V, no. 202, pp. 322–3; Institut für Zeitgeschichte, Munich, MA 804/1/D676446 (Aufzeichnung, Auswärtiges Amt, 3.6.33, of Göring's telephone inquiry about the meeting in Paris)).

40. Weinberg, *Foreign Policy*, pp. 47–52.

41. *Wings*, p. 85; Ivone Kirkpatrick, *The Inner Circle*, London, 1959, p. 49.

42. *Wings*, pp. 87–9.

43. Gilbert, *Churchill*, p. 488.

44. *Wings*, p. 108.

45. Gilbert, *Churchill*, p. 495.

46. Gilbert, *Churchill*, pp. 505–6 (and n. 1).

47. PRONI, D/3099/2/12/32, MacDonald to L, 7.2.34.

48. Gilbert, *Churchill*, pp. 506–7.

49. *Wings*, p. 105.

50. Middlemas and Barnes, pp. 744–7. John F. Naylor, *Labour's International Policy. The Labour Party in the 1930s*, London, 1969, pp. 62–4, qualifies the pacifism of the Labour candidate, John Wilmot, though accepts that he 'professed pacifist tenets' and stood on a platform which 'was no model of clarity'. Naturally, domestic issues also influenced the notable success of the Labour Party. But the exploitation of the fear of another war – not pacifism as such, but one of its roots – certainly played a significant part.

51. Cited Middlemas and Barnes, p. 745. Pacifist opinion in Britain is thoroughly analysed by Martin Ceadel, *Pacifism in Britain 1914–1945: the Defining of a Faith*, Oxford, 1980. For pacifism in the Labour Party, a strong force in the 1920s but increasingly merged in the 1930s into the wider pressure for disarmament, see Naylor, pp. 9–15, 61ff.

52. Gilbert, *Churchill*, p. 507; Middlemas and Barnes, p. 754. Even King George V – certainly no pacifist left-winger – told David Lloyd George in an 'extraordinary outburst' in May 1935 that he would 'go to Trafalgar Square and wave a red flag' rather than allow Britain to be drawn into another war (*Lloyd George. A Diary by Frances Stevenson*, ed. A. J. P. Taylor, London, 1971, p. 309 (10.5.35)).

53. See *Wings*, pp. 94–6, where Londonderry stated: 'I should always have felt unwilling to resign no matter what the provocation, because I had the feeling that he [Ramsay MacDonald] required so much assistance and that it was the duty of every one of us to give him the fullest measure of service we were capable of', adding 'I had no intention in my heart of resigning, however much I might be thwarted from time to time'.

54. *Ourselves*, pp. 62–4.

55. *Wings*, p. 107.

56. *Ourselves*, pp. 59–62; *Wings*, p. 109. The Foreign Office was initially taken with the idea of preparing a new British disarmament plan in response to Hitler's 'proposals', but the Cabinet rejected the suggestion (PRONI, D/3099/2/4/89, Hailsham to L, 28.12.33).

57. Middlemas and Barnes, pp. 747–8.

58. Londonderry himself was insistent on conceding no more than 500 aeroplanes to Germany and thought that any larger claims should be refuted (PRO, Cab. 27/506, fols. 143–5, 26.2.34).

59. The Earl of Avon, *The Eden Memoirs. Facing the Dictators*, London, 1962, pp. 79–83; Middlemas and Barnes, pp. 751–2.

60. PRO, Cab. 27/506, fols. 159–64, 174 (6.3.34). He told Lord Arnold that Germany had 'at least 250 camouflaged military aircraft of modern design and is steadily adding to her resources', but was 'certainly "committed" to the abolition of air armaments' – the inverted commas implying that a deal could still be struck on armaments reduction and limitation 'at the lowest possible figures', if the French could be pressed into agreement (Cambridge UL, Baldwin Papers, Baldwin 129, Fols. 128–33, L to Lord Arnold, 1.3.34).

61. It was the last time the German budget figures would be published (Erich Kordt, *Wahn und Wirklichkeit. Die Außenpolitik des Dritten Reiches. Versuch einer Darstellung*, Stuttgart, 1948, p. 61 n. 1).

62. Avon, pp. 42, 44.

63. Avon, pp. 79–82.

64. PRO, Cab. 27/506, fols. 255–60, 271 (9.4.34).

65. PRO, Cab. 16/109, fols. 391–418, quotation fol. 393v (repeated with minor variations, fol. 407); also cited in Keith Middlemas, *The Diplomacy of Illusion. The British Government and Germany 1937–39*, London, 1972, p. 33.

66. PRO, Cab. 16/109, fols. 395v, 403–407v; Cab. 16/111, fols. 138–43, 164–6, 169; Gilbert, *Churchill*, p. 506. Two members of the Committee, Sir Robert Vansittart and – remarkably – Sir Warren Fisher, Permanent Secretary to the Treasury, had pressed for greater and more rapid expansion of the air force, but had not prevailed against the majority, comprising Sir Maurice Hankey, Secretary to the Cabinet, and the three Chiefs of Staff. (For Vansittart's objections, see PRO, Cab. 16/111, fols. 81–7, 182–3.) The Chief of the Air Staff, the conservative and compliant Sir Edward Ellington (whom Londonderry had nominated for the post), suppressed his own disquiet and went along with the main recommendations of the Committee (Stephen Roskill, *Hankey: Man of Secrets, Vol. 3, 1931–1963*, London, 1974, pp. 103–4; Lord Vansittart, *The Mist Procession*, London, 1958, pp. 443–4; G. C. Peden, *British Rearmament and the Treasury 1932–1939*, Edinburgh, 1979, pp. 118–19; Andrew Boyle, *Trenchard: Man of Vision*, London, 1962, pp. 679–81; Hyde, *British Air Policy*, p. 298).

67. Middlemas and Barnes, pp. 753–4.

68. PRO, Cab. 16/110, fols. 102, 177 (Disarmament Conference 1932. Ministerial Committee, 4.5.34, 15.5.34).

69. PRO, Cab. 16/110, fols. 100, 105 (4.5.34). A lengthy memorandum by Sir Edward Ellington, Chief of the Air Staff, passed to the Ministerial Committee on 29 May 1934, began by stating: 'I do not see any reason to

suppose that a German Air Force in 5 years time will be more formidable, aircraft for aircraft, than the French were in 1923' (PRO, Cab. 16/111, fol. 139).

70. PRO, Cab. 16/111, fol. 193 (20.6.34); Hyde, *British Air Policy*, p. 304. Chamberlain referred to his intervention in a letter he wrote on 17 October 1940, less than a month before his death, to Stanley Baldwin: 'You remember how I, as Chancellor of the Exchequer, asked leave of the Cabinet to review the programmes put up by the Service Ministers, & submitted a programme which was accepted by you & the others which provided for a larger Air Force than Charley Londonderry had ventured to propose' (cited in Keith Feiling, *The Life of Neville Chamberlain*, London, 1946, p. 456).

71. PRO, Cab. 16/110, fols. 312–13 (26.6.34). It has been fairly pointed out that, had Londonderry advocated six months earlier such expenditure as was now envisaged, 'the Treasury would have been after his head' (Robert Paul Shay, Jr, *British Rearmament in the Thirties: Politics and Profits*, Princeton, 1977, p. 38).

72. PRO, PRO 30/69/1753/2, fol. 28, Ramsay MacDonald Diary, entry for 16.5.35. Londonderry later berated MacDonald for not supporting him in Cabinet when he had informed him that there were 'intrigues' against him (PRO, PRO 30/69/683, fol. 172, L to MacDonald, 13.11.36).

73. *Wings*, p. 115 (and n. 1).

74. PRO, Cab. 27/506, fols. 289–90, 297 (20.4.34).

75. Information from Lady Mairi Bury, interview at Mount Stewart, 22.10.02.

76. Anne de Courcy, *Circe. The Life of Edith, Marchioness of Londonderry*, London, 1992, pp. 250–53.

77. Neil Fleming, *The Seventh Marquess of Londonderry: a Political Life*, Ph.D. thesis, Queen's University Belfast, 2002, p. 248, implies that personal contact dated back to early 1934 in citing a telegram from Frau Göring to Londonderry of 2 March 1934. This is, however, an error. The telegram, in German, is from Hermann Göring himself to Londonderry and the context, in which he speaks of his pleasure that the Marquess 'has come to know the new Germany', indicates that it post-dates his visit to Germany in early 1936. Although the date stamp is partially obscured, the telegram is in fact not from 1934, but from 19 March 1936 (PRONI, D/3099/2/19/2).

78. Londonderry had been one of those sought out in early July 1934 by Kapitänleutnant a.D. Obermüller, head of the 'England Section' of Alfred Rosenberg's *Außenpolitisches Amt. Das politische Tagebuch Alfred Rosenbergs 1934/35 und 1939/40*, ed. Hans-Günther Seraphim, Munich, 1964, p. 49.

79. *The Times and Appeasement*, p. 74 (18.2.33).

80. PRONI D/3099/2/19/3, 'Record of an Interview granted by General Göring to Lady Maureen Stanley and Lady Margaret Stewart'.

81. PRONI D/3099/17/33. L's speech at the Lord Mayor's Banquet, 9.11.34 (wrongly filed in D/3099/3/15).

82. PRO, Prem. 1/155, fols. 70–74, 77.

83. PRO, Cab. 21/2676, L to Hailsham 'Secret and Personal', 22.11.34. Londonderry followed up this letter with a further one to Hailsham the next day, adding that the principle of equality had been conceded to Germany on 11 December 1932, blaming French objections for the fact that this had not been put into effect and had been allowed to remain in abeyance, and drawing attention to what he saw as reasonable German proposals on the strength of their air force (not to exceed 30 per cent of the combined air forces of Germany's neighbours or 50 per cent of the military aircraft possessed by France, whichever figure was less). Londonderry's comment about his letter being 'brushed on one side' came to be frequently made, but is cited here from his letter, also in the file, to Sir Maurice Hankey, 18.11.37. Because the letters later seemed so prescient, Londonderry (who surprisingly had kept no copies) had Hailsham make copies for him in December 1937 (PRONI, D/3099/2/17/25) and, eventually, return the originals to him in November 1938 (D/3099/2/17/1A–2A, 31–2). He then liberally distributed copies to his friends and former political colleagues, including Neville Chamberlain (Birmingham UL, Chamberlain Papers, NC7/11/30/96). His attempts to persuade Chamberlain, then later Churchill, to allow the papers to be cited *verbatim* in his publications were unsuccessful. Londonderry was, accordingly, forced to summarize the content in *Ourselves*, pp. 63–4 and *Wings*, pp. 118–20.

84. See Ritchie Ovendale, 'Britain, the Dominions and the Coming of the Second World War, 1933–9', in Wolfgang J. Mommsen and Lothar Kettenacker (eds.), *The Fascist Challenge and the Policy of Appeasement*, London, 1983, pp. 323–38, here esp. p. 328.

85. WSC, V/3, pp. 1452–3, L to Churchill, 14.4.39; and similar sentiments in PRONI, D/3099/4/51, L to Churchill, 3.8.39.

86. Gilbert, *Churchill*, pp. 551–2.

87. Gilbert, *Churchill*, p. 553; Hyde, *British Air Policy*, pp. 318–22; J. A. Cross, *Lord Swinton*, Oxford, 1982, p. 136.

88. Gilbert, *Churchill*, pp. 553–4.

89. Gilbert, *Churchill*, pp. 554–6.

90. Gilbert, *Churchill*, pp. 559, 568–9.

91. Gilbert, *Churchill*, p. 559 has Hankey stipulating 'much more than 5 years'; Roskill, p. 122, has 'much more than 2 years to develop'.

92. Gilbert, *Churchill*, p. 568; Middlemas and Barnes, p. 787.

93. Hyde, *British Air Policy*, p. 327.

94. PRO, FO 800/291, fol. 407, L to Baldwin, 29.11.34, and fol. 406, L to Simon, 30.11.34; Cab. 23/80, fol. 246. At the meeting of the Cabinet, Simon 'raised as a matter of urgency the question whether, in the Debate that afternoon, the Government should state that we believed that the total number of aircraft of service types possessed by Germany was about 1,000'. A telegram from the Air Attaché in Berlin the previous day had, in fact, suggested that Germany had no more than 600 service aircraft. A French source indicated a figure of 1,100 military aircraft. The Cabinet agreed, however, with Londonderry's suggestion 'that it would be unwise to state any figure in the House of Commons which could be successfully challenged by Germany'.

95. Middlemas and Barnes, p. 787; Hyde, *British Air Policy*, p. 327.

96. *Wings*, pp. 126, 128.

97. Gilbert, *Churchill*, pp. 576–7.

98. *WSC*, V/2, p. 933 (from the diary of Frances Stevenson, 22.11.34). Londonderry played down almost to the point of disappearance the very real differences which existed on the rearmament issue and on foreign politics between himself and Churchill. See pp. 974–5, L to Churchill, 30.12.34.

99. Middlemas and Barnes, p. 787.

100. PRO, Cab 23/80, fols. 237–40 (meeting of 26.11.34); Gilbert, *Churchill*, p. 572.

101. PRO, Prem. 1/155, fols. 67–9 (partial draft PRONI, D3099/2/12/38), L to MacDonald, 26.11.34; printed in *WSC*, V/2, pp. 942–3.

102. Gilbert, *Churchill*, pp. 572–6.

103. Maurice Cowling, *The Impact of Hitler. British Politics and British Policy, 1933–1940*, Cambridge, 1975, p. 72.

104. *Parliamentary Debates, House of Commons*, vol. 295 (1935), cols. 878–83; Middlemas and Barnes, pp. 787–9; Gilbert, *Churchill*, p. 578.

105. PRO, FO 800/291, fols. 409–10 and (draft) PRONI, D/3099/2/16/52.

106. Middlemas and Barnes, pp. 790–95.

107. PRONI, D/3099/2/16/57, four-page unsigned draft memorandum entitled 'The German Reply', dated (apparently in Londonderry's hand) '18.2.35', and certainly composed by him. It is unclear for whom precisely the memorandum was intended – possibly the Prime Minister – and whether it was ever sent.

108. PRO, Cab. 27/508, fols. 108–17 (19.2.35). Londonderry's cited comment (fol. 116) is in the context of the discussion on whether the talks should take place in London or Berlin and does not reflect his stance on the substantive issues of the Air Convention and Eastern Pact which were to be raised in the talks.

109. Weinberg, pp. 204–5; Kershaw, pp. 549–53; Kordt, *Wahn und Wirklichkeit*, pp. 70–71.

110. *DGFP*, CIII, no. 555, pp. 1043–80 (p. 1073 for Hitler's remark that parity in military air strength had been reached with Britain); Paul Schmidt, *Statist auf diplomatischer Bühne. Erlebnisse des Chefdolmetschers im Auswärtigen Amt mit den Staatsmännern Europas*, Bonn, 1953, p. 306; Avon, pp. 133ff for the visit, p. 141 for Hitler's claim of air parity; Viscount Simon, *Retrospect*, London, 1952, p. 202 for a cursory mention of the claim.

111. Avon, p. 141.

112. *Das Deutsche Reich und der Zweite Weltkrieg*, ed. Militärgeschichtliches Forschungsamt, vol. 1, Stuttgart, 1979, p. 484.

113. *WSC*, V/2, p. 1143, n. 1.

114. PRO, FO 800/290, fol. 200, copy, dated 2.4.35, of a memorandum prepared by Group Captain Don, Air Attaché at the Embassy in Berlin, on the basis of a conversation on 30 March 1935 with Colonel Wenninger, German Attaché in London; also *Wings*, p. 127.

115. Middlemas and Barnes, p. 799.

116. Taylor, *English History*, p. 471.

117. Gilbert, *Churchill*, pp. 627–9.

118. PRO, FO 800/290, fols. 123–4, L to Simon, 21.2.35. The latent tension between Londonderry and Simon was perceptible in the Foreign Secretary's proposed amendment to the wording of the prepared memorandum on 'General Policy' (regarding the Air). Londonderry had included the phrase 'In the light of the great and growing importance of the air arm . . .', which Simon wanted replacing by 'In the light of the sudden dangers which might arise from misuse of the air arm'. Londonderry somewhat petulantly reacted by stating that 'even the most carping of pacifists' could scarcely take exception to his 'mere statement of fact', but that rather than accept Simon's amendment, he would omit the phrase altogether (fols. 124, 130–31).

119. Gilbert, *Churchill*, p. 631. By the time of the Munich Conference at the end of September 1938, when Londonderry's plan was due for completion, the minimum German first-line strength was 3,200 planes, the British maxium first-line strength 1,606 planes (Gilbert, *Churchill*, p. 635, n. 1). And as Churchill and his informants continued to argue, in the arcane (and often speculative) debate over figures, front-line strength (which the Air Ministry invariably took as its criterion) had also to be linked to numbers of trained pilots, the number of aerodromes and the capacity for both rapid production of planes and the potential for the conversion of civilian to military aviation. When these factors were included in the equation, the German advantage was even greater.

120. *WSC*, V/2, pp. 1131–3.

121. PRONI, D/3099/4/56, L to Simon, 22.1.40.

122. PRONI, D/3099/2/12/41, MacDonald to L, 10.4.35. Londonderry's propensity for verbal infelicities did little to instil confidence. In a letter to *The Times*, 12.4.35, he felt it necessary to correct the impression he had given in a recent speech that the Air Ministry had been 'a somnolent institution in which no one ever did very much'. Wholly misjudging the popular mood, he had meant this to be a 'jocular expression'.

123. PRO, FO 800/290, fols. 198–200.

124. *WSC*, V/2, p. 1138.

125. PRONI, D/3099/2/5/26, Churchill to L, n.d., but from the context mid-April 1935. Churchill had been angered (and later, graciously but probably unnecessarily, apologized for the high level of his indignation) when he thought he understood Londonderry to claim that Britain had parity with Germany, though it seems he had been meaning to say that air parity was promised. It had apparently been a misunderstanding. 'Pray therefore let my indignant words including "scandalous" – pass from yr mind', wrote Churchill.

126. Born in 1877, Ellington (knighted in 1920) had long experience in the army, then the Royal Air Force, serving for much of the 1920s in positions of command in the Middle East, India and Iraq, before Londonderry appointed him as Chief of the Air Staff in 1933 (a position he held until 1937). The first Chief of Air Staff, Sir Hugh (later Lord) Trenchard, was critical, and later dismissive, of Ellington's inadequate response to the rapidly changing needs of expanding the air arm. See Boyle, pp. 687–9, 701–2. Ellington retired as Inspector General of the Royal Air Force in 1940, and continued after the war to correspond with Londonderry (supporting his disputed figures on the strength of the Luftwaffe in 1935). He died in 1967.

127. Gilbert, *Churchill*, pp. 636–7.

128. PRONI, D/3099/13/2/1335, Lady L to L, 17.4.35.

129. *WSC*, V/2, p. 1143, L to Churchill, 17.4.35.

130. *WSC*, V/2, pp. 1155–61. Churchill told Baldwin (p. 1153) that the memorandum would form the basis of the case he would outline in the debate on the Air Estimates scheduled for May.

131. *WSC*, V/2, p. 1162, L to Churchill, 30.4.35.

132. PRONI, D/3099/2/12/42, L to MacDonald, 17.4.35.

133. PRONI, D/3099/2/12/44, L to MacDonald, 17.4.35.

134. Vansittart, in his memorandum of 23 April, had castigated the readiness to accept inferiority in the air for at least five years under the Air Ministry's plan, and pointed out the damaging effect of weakness in the air on British foreign policy (Gilbert, *Churchill*, pp. 636–7). Londonderry commented to

Simon: 'I was rather sorry about Vansittart's memorandum which you sent to the Cabinet, because that has had the unfortunate effect of scaring our colleagues and making them think that you and I are not agreed on this very serious matter' (PRO, FO 800/290, fol. 219, L to Simon, 7.5.35).

135. Neville Chamberlain to his sister, Hilda, 12.5.35, cited in David Dilks, '"The Unnecessary War"? Military Advice and Foreign Policy in Great Britain, 1931–1939', in Adrian Preston (ed.), *General Staffs and Diplomacy before the Second World War*, London, 1978, pp. 93–132, here p. 110.

136. The above discussion in PRO, Cab. 27/508, fols. 120–35 (30.4.35).

137. *Wings*, p. 133; *Daily Express*, 16.5.35, p. 1. Londonderry was furious at the article, but the Prime Minister thought him 'much to blame' (PRO, PRO 30/69/1753/2, fol. 28, Ramsay MacDonald Diary, entry for 16.5.35).

138. *Wings*, p. 130. Rumours had reached the Ministry early in May that Londonderry 'has not got sufficient drive', and that the department was viewed as 'lacking in imagination' (letter from Charles Evans, a senior civil servant at the Air Ministry, to former Chief of the Air Staff, Sir Hugh Trenchard, cited in Boyle, p. 689).

139. *Wings*, p. 134. Churchill later remembered his warning (*WSC*, V/3, p. 243, Churchill to Sir Henry Page Croft, 14.7.36; PRONI, D/3099/2/5/41A, Churchill to L, 15.4.39).

140. Cited Hyde, *The Londonderrys*, p. 212. In a letter to the Prime Minister on 6 May, Londonderry denied 'that the Air Min[istry] is in an awkward position at all if the case can be stated . . . [I] will vindicate everything I have said and done . . .' (John Rylands UL, Manchester, RMD/1/13/5). He had written in similar vein to MacDonald on 24 April (PRO, PRO 30/69/1180, fol. 205).

141. PRONI, D/3099/13/2/1336, Lady L to L, 2.5.35.

142. See *Wings*, p. 129, for Rothermere's claim in a letter to Londonderry that the German air force had 11,000 planes according to the figure Hitler had given him, and Londonderry's reply that this figure must have included gliders. Londonderry's described Rothermere's claims as 'a fantastic over-statement' (*Wings*, p. 131). In early May, Rothermere had widely circulated an eight-page letter that Hitler had sent him on the 3rd of the month, pressing the case for a German-British 'understanding' (PRO, FO 800/290, fols. 241–8).

143. PRO, FO 800/290, fols. 265–70 (Eden's note for Simon, L to Eden, Eden's reply, all 16.5.35); PRONI, D/3099/2/16/69 (partial copy of L to Eden); *Wings*, p. 132. A week before writing to Eden, Londonderry had persuaded Simon to dictate a telegram to Sir Eric Phipps, Ambassador in Berlin, requesting precise information from the Luftwaffe on the numbers of planes they possessed. Simon then had second thoughts since any figures provided by the Germans, even though unlikely to be accurate, would force the

government to disclose British figures – something which the Cabinet had decided not to do because of its difficulties over Baldwin's pledge the previous November (PRO, FO 800/290, fols. 252–4, Simon to L, 9.5.35).

144. Birmingham UL, Chamberlain Papers, NC7/11/28/34, L to Chamberlain, 4.5.35.

145. Birmingham UL, Chamberlain Papers, NC7/11/28/35, L to Chamberlain, 20.5.35.

146. Birmingham UL, Chamberlain Papers, NC7/11/28/34 (Lady L to Chamberlain, 2.5.35), NC7/11/28/31 (Lady L to Chamberlain, 18.5.35), NC7/11/28/32 (Chamberlain to Lady L, 21.5.35), NC7/11/28/33 (Lady L to Chamberlain, 21.5.35).

147. PRONI, D/3099/2/12/46, MacDonald to L, n.d., written on 'Sunday morning', probably from its content 12 May, possibly 19 May, 1935.

148. PRO, PRO 30/69, 1753/2, fols. 25–6, Ramsay MacDonald Diaries, entry for 10.5.35. Londonderry was evidently aware that the Prime Minister had thought he had been 'caught napping' and defended himself vigorously: 'I have known and I have kept the Government informed as to the growing German air plans and mentality,' he told MacDonald. 'The only thing that has surprised me is Hitler *claiming* a first line parity with us which he has not got. It is the lurking idea in the minds of so many influential people which is doing the mischief. This must be stopped and should have been stopped a long time ago' (John Rylands UL, Manchester, RMD/1/14/75, L to MacDonald (incomplete and date missing, but evidently May 1935)).

149. Gilbert, *Churchill*, p. 650; Hyde, *British Air Policy*, p. 342.

150. Middlemas and Barnes, pp. 814–15. The uneasy relations between Londonderry and Cunliffe-Lister were palpable. See PRO, Cab. 27/508, fols. 142–4, 169–70 (Defence Requirements Committee meetings, 10.5.35, 20.5.35). And see Cross, p. 135 for Baldwin's increasing reliance on Cunliffe-Lister rather than the 'lightweight' Londonderry.

151. Weinberg, p. 208.

152. *Hitler. Reden und Prokamationen 1932–1945*, ed. Max Domarus, Wiesbaden, 1973, pp. 505–14; and see Kershaw, pp. 556–7.

153. Lady Londonderry seems at this point to have been more hesitant about Germany than her husband. Her reaction to the speech was that it 'makes one feel rather sceptical of the intentions behind Hitler's system except in so far as to quieten the good hearted Britisher's suspicions' (DRO, D/Lo/C251 (23), Lady L to Mrs Cory, 23.5.35). The impact of Hitler's speech was not confined to Conservatives and sympathizers with Germany. There was also momentary optimism about the prospects of peace in the light of the speech

among Labour MPs (Hugh Dalton, *The Fateful Years. Memoirs 1931–1945*, London, 1957, p. 64).

154. *Parliamentary Debates, House of Lords*, vol. 96 (1935), cols. 1002–19 (col. 1017 for the notorious passage on retention of bombers for policing purposes); *Wings*, pp. 136–41 (where (p. 136) the debate is mistakenly dated to 21 May 1935).

155. Lord Londonderry, 'Bombing from the Air', *The Nineteenth Century*, March 1939, p. 11 (a defence of his stance on bombing), in PRONI, D/3084/C/C/4/1.

156. On the fear of bombing, and its implications for policy-making, see Bialer.

157. *Wings*, p. 143.

158. PRONI, D/3099/2/12/46, MacDonald to L, n.d., 'Sunday', probably 26 May 1935. For some time there had been talk that when poor health forced MacDonald to resign as Prime Minister, the 'dead wood' associated with him (including Londonderry) would have to be cut away (Nick Smart, *The National Government, 1931–40*, Basingstoke, 1999, p. 91).

159. See Middlemas and Barnes, pp. 806–7.

160. Cited Middlemas and Barnes, p. 806; and H. Montgomery Hyde, *Baldwin: the Unexpected Prime Minister*, London, 1973, pp. 381–2, from a memorandum by Lord Castlereagh, March 1936. Given the warnings Londonderry had received about the danger to his position, it was disingenuous of him, in a letter written shortly after his dismissal, to claim 'ignorance of what was going to happen' in Baldwin's reshuffle (PRONI, D/3099/2/17/5, L to Sir Alec Cadogan, 18.6.35).

161. Winston S. Churchill, *The Second World War, Vol. 1: The Gathering Storm*, London, 1948, p. 115. Already in May 1935, the Air Parity Sub-Committee saw the 'Hawker' (which became the 'Hurricane') and the 'Supermarine' (to emerge as the 'Spitfire') as holding great promise for the future (Cross, p. 140).

162. Middlemas and Barnes, pp. 1085–91. A document in the Londonderry Papers (PRONI, D/3099/4/80) without author or provenance (perhaps a copy of a government minute most likely prompted by a communication from Lord Londonderry), dated 23 November 1945 and headed 'Radar', comments: 'The President of the Board of Trade's attention has been called to an inaccuracy in his statement made at a Press Conference on August 14, in which he said that Lord Swinton was Secretary of State for Air when the original Committee of Scientists was appointed to work with the Air Staff in finding means for detecting the approach of Aircraft at a distance. Actually it was Lord Londonderry who was Secretary of State for Air when this first

Committee was appointed.' The sequence of events leading to the establishment of the original Committee and its later replacement under Swinton by the Sub-Committee on Air Defence Research, responsible directly to the Cabinet rather than to the Air Ministry, is then described.

163. Charles Loch Mowat, *Britain between the Wars 1918–1940*, London, 1955, p. 626.

164. Middlemas and Barnes, pp. 804–5.

165. Londonderry spoke on leaving the Air Ministry of his time there as 'singularly happy years'. Sir Christopher Bullock, Permanent Secretary at the Air Ministry, formally expressed on behalf of his colleagues 'our regret at losing a Secretary of State who has so whole-heartedly identified himself with the well-being of the Ministry and the Force' (PRO, Air/2/2234, L's farewell letter, 8.6.35; Bullock to L, 15.6.35). The letter gave Londonderry much satisfaction (*Wings*, p. 146). Sir John Salmond, former Chief of Staff, thanked Londonderry for 'the great fight you have, and are, putting up for the Department and more so for the future of the Country' (PRONI, D/30992/16/68, Salmond to L, 12.7.[?35]).

166. *Flight*, 13.6.35, pp. 625–6. The other main aeronautical magazine, *The Aeroplane*, edited by the pro-German and anti-Semitic C. G. Grey, had a less critical evaluation, commenting that 'Lord Londonderry's many friends will be glad that he remains in the Cabinet, where his personal devotion to aviation may still carry great weight', adding that 'British aviation owes a great deal more to Lord Londonderry than most people know' (*The Aeroplane*, 12.6.35, pp. 672–3). An informed retrospective assessment was that 'Londonderry's influence with the Prime Minister enabled him to be more helpful to the R.A.F. than expected, and he served it well in many ways, but it was not in him to take a strong lead in urging radical changes, particularly the redistribution of the defence budget that was needed to meet changed conditions and future emergencies' (Liddell Hart, p. 158).

167. Churchill, *The Gathering Storm*, p. 114.

168. Middlemas and Barnes, p. 805.

169. Churchill, *The Gathering Storm*, p. 114. This was also Trenchard's view. He thought the Air Ministry had made a mistake in becoming drawn into a battle over which figures were correct, instead of pressing for immediate and major expansion (Boyle, p. 690).

170. Middlemas and Barnes, pp. 821–4. The main changes, other than Londonderry's removal (to be replaced by Cunliffe-Lister), were that Simon went to the Home Office and Sir Samuel Hoare took over at the Foreign Office.

171. Lady Londonderry had mentioned in her letter to Neville Chamberlain

on 2 May that she had been told that the post of Air Minister 'should be held by someone other than a peer [and based] in the House of Commons' (Birmingham UL, Chamberlain Papers, NL7/11/28/30).

172. Middlemas and Barnes, p. 807.

173. It had been rumoured in the press that Londonderry would be dropped altogether. This was what Chamberlain favoured. But following intercession on Londonderry's behalf by Lord Hailsham, the War Minister, Baldwin decided to retain the former Air Minister in the government, but in a different – more harmless – capacity, and without a governmental department to run (Hyde, *The Londonderrys*, pp. 218–19).

174. Cambridge UL, Baldwin Papers, vol. 171, fols. 152–5, L to Baldwin, 6.6.35 (drafts in PRONI, D/3099/2/17/3A–C). Baldwin replied the same day: 'Of course, you continue in the Cabinet: it was, as I told you, my desire and that of our colleagues that you should remain with us' (also cited in Hyde, *The Londonderrys*, p. 219).

175. Middlemas and Barnes, p. 805.

176. Though Ribbentrop, as we have noted, had been entertained by the Londonderrys (and other British hosts) in autumn 1934, it was only after the Anglo-German Naval Agreement in June 1935, and after Londonderry's dismissal as Air Minister, that the Dienststelle Ribbentrop began a concerted attempt to cultivate significant contacts in Britain, including Lord Londonderry (G. T. Waddington, '"An Idyllic and Unruffled Atmosphere of Complete Anglo-German Misunderstanding": Aspects of the Operations of the Dienststelle Ribbentrop in Great Britain, 1934–1938', *History*, 82 (1977), pp. 44–72, here pp. 51, 55–6).

177. Margarete Gärtner, *Botschafterin des guten Willens*, Bonn, 1955, pp. 162–3.

178. Gärtner, pp. 217–18.

179. Griffiths, pp. 69–79, 137–40.

3 Nazi Friends

1. *Daily Express*, 22.5.36, referring to the forthcoming Whitsun Party at Mount Stewart.

2. Thomas Jones, *A Diary with Letters, 1931–1950*, London, 1954, p. 191.

3. A. J. P. Taylor, *English History, 1914–1945*, Harmondsworth, 1970, pp. 467–8; Keith Middlemas and John Barnes, *Baldwin: a Biography*, London, 1969, pp. 835–6; Charles Loch Mowat, *Britain between the Wars 1918–1940*, London, 1955, pp. 541–2; John F. Naylor, *Labour's International Policy. The Labour Party in the 1930s*, London, 1969, pp. 65–7.

4. Viscount Templewood, *Nine Troubled Years*, London, 1954, ch. 11; The Earl of Avon, *The Eden Memoirs. Facing the Dictators*, London, 1962, pp. 220–25, 230–34; Middlemas and Barnes, pp. 834–5; A. J. P. Taylor, *The Origins of the Second World War*, Harmondsworth, 1964, p. 119.

5. Templewood, ch. 12, here p. 170; also cited in Middlemas and Barnes, pp. 856–7.

6. The election results are analysed by Tom Stannage, *Baldwin Thwarts the Opposition. The British General Election of 1935*, London, 1980, pp. 226–39. See also Taylor, *English History*, pp. 405–6, 472–3; Middlemas and Barnes, p. 869; Peter Clarke, *Hope and Glory. Britain 1900–1990*, London, 1996, pp. 174–5, 179, 407–8; and Michael Bentley, 'Power without Office. The National Government and the Churchill Coalition', in Anthony Seldon (ed.), *How Tory Governments Fall. The Tory Party in Power since 1783*, London, 1996, pp. 285–312, here pp. 290–91.

7. 'The myth that rearmament was not a major issue at the 1935 election' is disposed of by David Dilks, 'Baldwin and Chamberlain', in Norman Gash, Donald Southgate, David Dilks and John Ramsden, *The Conservatives*, London, 1977, pp. 364–9.

8. *Wings*, p. 144.

9. PRONI, D/3099/2/12/49B, MacDonald to L, 23.11.36.

10. W. P. Crozier, *Off the Record. Political Interviews 1933–1943*, ed. A. J. P. Taylor, London, 1973, p. 48 (12.6.35).

11. *Wings*, p. 147.

12. DRO, D/LO/C251 (25), Mrs Eva Bell-Irving to Lady L, 20.10.35, with attached memorandum of 23.10.35 for Lord L and note of 14.11.35 that 'His Lordship made no comment'. Perhaps Lady Londonderry was more impressed by the criticism of the League rather than the support for Italy in the letter she received, since she had commented to her husband immediately following the invasion of Abyssinia that 'I believe Mussolini has gone mad' (PRONI, D/3099/13/2/1344, Lady L to L, 4.10.35).

13. In a speech at Southampton on 7.11.35, reported in the *Southern Daily Echo*, 8.11.35 (PRONI, D/3099/10/47/37). Some pencilled jottings by Londonderry, attached to his description of his visit to Germany in late January and early February 1936 but apparently unrelated to this visit, indicate his view that the League of Nations, as the 'sheet anchor of British Foreign Policy . . . means very little unless we are prepared first with economic sanctions and no exceptions and followed by war sanctions to bring the aggressor to book' (D/3099/2/19/9B).

14. The last point emerges from draft notes for a letter (which appears not to have been sent) to Baldwin just prior to the November election (PRONI,

D/3099/2/17/3C (handwritten notes attached to a letter of L's to Baldwin of 6.6.35, without date but from the context early November 1935)).

15. PRO, PRO 30/69/1180, fols. 208–9, L to MacDonald, 21.9.35.

16. PRONI, D/3099/2/17/7A, Lord Hailsham (Douglas Hogg) to L, 17.9.35.

17. Cambridge UL, Baldwin Papers, vol. 171, pp. 157–8, L to Baldwin, 17.10.35; copy in PRONI, D/3099/2/17/10B; another copy, sent to Lord Halifax, in Borthwick Institute, York, Halifax Papers, A4.410.28.1. Londonderry had written to Baldwin on 16.10.35 seeking an interview with him 'on a personal matter' (Cambridge UL, Baldwin Papers, vol. 171, p. 156, L to Baldwin, 16.10.35). According to his daughter, Lady Mairi Bury (interview at Mount Stewart, 22.10.02), Lord Londonderry announced one morning, to the delight of his wife, that he was going to see Stanley Baldwin to resign. On the way to 10, Downing Street, he bumped into Lord Hailsham who, as we noted, had already written to Londonderry in September discouraging him from contemplating resignation, and now dissuaded him by saying 'You can't let Stanley down'. Londonderry accordingly changed his mind, incurring the wrath of his wife on his return home. Assuming the recollection is accurate, it cannot refer to the period preceding his first dismissal, from the Air Ministry, when Londonderry was determined to hold on to his office, and presumably refers to this audience with Baldwin, the first Londonderry had had for a long time.

18. *Wings*, pp. 147–50; PRONI, D/3099/2/16/58, memorandum to L, 29.10.35 with illegible initials, suggesting that Attlee's allegations amounted to 'a serious libel'.

19. *Northern Whig*, 6.11.35; *The Times*, 8.11.35; *Birmingham Post*, 8.11.35; *Southern Daily Echo*, 8.11.35; *The Times*, 30.12.35: 'The Abolition of Bombing. Lord Londonderry's View. Reply to Labour Accusation'; *The Times*, 31.12.35, Attlee's reply, repeating that 'the failure of the Disarmament Conference was due . . . to the presence of men like Lord Londonderry' (Press cuttings in PRONI, D/3099/10/47; H. Montgomery Hyde, *The Londonderrys: a Family Portrait*, London, 1979, p. 224.

20. *Newcastle Journal*, 7.11.35; *Yorkshire Post*, 8.11.35 (in PRONI, D/3099/10/47). Lady Londonderry had defended her husband's record as Air Minister in a private letter to J. L. Garvin, editor of the *Observer*, on 28.7.35 (DRO, D/Lo/C251 (25)), and wrote to Londonderry supportively of his performance on 4.10.35 and 19.10.35 (PRONI, D/3099/13/2/1344 and 1346).

21. PRONI, D/3099/13/2/1348, Lady L to L, 21.11.35.

22. Birmingham UL, NC2/23A, Chamberlain Diaries 1933–36, p. 214 (21.11.35); Hyde, *The Londonderrys*, p. 236.

23. For Halifax's career, see Andrew Roberts, *'The Holy Fox'. The Life of*

Lord Halifax, London, 1991, paperback edn, 1997, (which supersedes the earlier study by The Earl of Birkenhead, *Halifax. The Life of Lord Halifax*, London, 1965) and the pallid autobiography, *Fulness of Days*, London, 1957.

24. Londonderry repeatedly harked back to his second sacking, and that no plausible public statement by Baldwin explaining it had ever been given, in subsequent letters to Baldwin, which went unanswered (Cambridge UL, Baldwin Papers, vol. 171, pp. 163–5, 192–4 (18.5.36), pp. 166–71 (19.5.36), pp. 172–3 (21.5.36), pp. 175–7 (1.12.36), copies in PRONI, D/3099/2/17/14A, 15, 16. Londonderry sent a copy of his letter of 18.5.36 to Chamberlain (Birmingham UL, NC7/11/29/37). Baldwin's only reply was a bland one, saying he needed more time to digest Londonderry's letter, and that he was 'more than usually busy' (Birmingham UL, NC7/11/29/38, Baldwin to L, 21.5.36).

25. PRONI, D/3099/2/17/11, Baldwin to L, 21.11.35; Cambridge UL, Baldwin Papers, vol. 151, pp. 159–61, drafts of Baldwin to L, 21.11.35, Baldwin to Lady L, n.d. (but almost certainly 21.11.35).

26. Cambridge UL, Baldwin Papers, vol. 151, p. 162, L to Baldwin, 22.11.35 (copy in PRONI, D/3099/2/17/12).

27. Hyde, *The Londonderrys*, p. 227.

28. Interview with Lady Mairi Bury, Mount Stewart, 22.10.02.

29. Hyde, *The Londonderrys*, p. 226; and see H. Montgomery Hyde, *Baldwin: the Unexpected Prime Minister*, London, 1973, pp. 400–403.

30. PRONI, D/3099/13/2/1348, Lady L to L, 21.11.35, makes plain that the decision not to hold the usual reception was Londonderry's. Press reports and statements (*Daily Dispatch*, 22.11.35, *News Chronicle*, 25.11.35) are in D/3099/10/47. Londonderry's suggestion to Baldwin and press statement in Cambridge UL, Baldwin Papers, vol. 170, pp. 136, 173.

31. Cambridge UL, Baldwin Papers, vol. 143, pp. 100–101, Lady L ('Circe') to Baldwin ('My dear Bruin'), 12.12.36.

32. Cited Hyde, *The Londonderrys*, pp. 231–2.

33. Cambridge UL, Baldwin Papers, vol. 171, pp. 178–91 (copy in PRONI, D/3099/2/17/37A), L to Baldwin, 29.12.38.

34. Hyde, *The Londonderrys*, p. 236; Middlemas and Barnes, pp. 806–7. In a letter to Lady Londonderry of 28.10.47 (when Lord Londonderry was incapacitated following a stroke), her son, Robin (Lord Castlereagh), remarked that he had had a long talk with Baldwin who 'was always very fond of Father' (PRONI, D/3099/13/11/30).

35. PRONI, D/3099/2/4/105 and 119 (L. G. S. Reynolds to L, 24.11.35; Rudyard Kipling to L, 30.11.35); D/3099/2/18/3 (Halifax to L, 24.11.35).

36. Baldwin had, in fact, evidently contemplated putting Londonderry on the

important Defence Requirements Committee, which dealt with rearmament needs, and on the powerful Committee of Imperial Defence, which framed defence policy. He was dissuaded from this course of action by Londonderry's friend Ramsay MacDonald, who told Baldwin: 'I think it would be a mistake to put Londonderry on the Defence Requirements Committee. He would naturally tend to show his feelings; but even if that were not so, if you put him on, you could not very well refuse others who I know would like to be there. To summon him to the Committee of Imperial Defence might also be awkward; it could not be done solely because he is Leader in the House of Lords' (PRO, PRO 30/69/1180, fol. 1, MacDonald to Baldwin, 19.7.35).

37. Borthwick Institute, York, Halifax Papers, A4.410.28.1, L to Halifax, 28.11.35. The rancour was undiminished almost a year later, when Londonderry refused an invitation to the dinner at the Opening of Parliament, repeating much of the sentiment of the above letter in his outpouring of bitterness towards Baldwin (PRONI, D/3099/2/18/14, L to Halifax, 8.10.36).

38. Hertfordshire Record Office, D/ERV C2482/89, L to Lady Desborough, n.d., probably 1943; copy in PRONI, T/3201/54; lengthy extract printed in Hyde, *The Londonderrys*, pp. 259–60.

39. PRONI, D/3099/13/2/1351–1352, Lady L to L, 8.12.35, 12.12.35; Anne de Courcy, *Circe. The Life of Edith, Marchioness of Londonderry*, London, 1992, pp. 262–3.

40. Cambridge UL, Baldwin Papers, pp. 172–3, L to Baldwin, 21.5.36 (copy in PRONI, D/3099/2/17/16).

41. Hertfordshire Record Office, D/ERV C2482/89, L to Lady Desborough, n.d., probably 1943; copy in PRONI, T/3201/54; a lengthy extract in Hyde, *The Londonderrys*, pp. 259–60.

42. PRO, PRO 30/69/1180, fol. 212, L to MacDonald, 21.9.35.

43. Quotations from a letter Londonderry had sent to Sir Alexander Cadogan, later to become Permanent Under-Secretary at the Foreign Office, on 18.6.35 (PRONI, D/3099/2/17/5).

44. The above draws on points made by Lady Mairi Bury in an interview at Mount Stewart, 22.10.02.

45. *Wings*, p. 154.

46. *Ourselves*, p. 79; *Wings*, p. 158. Londonderry had told Göring this in a letter of 25 February 1936, shortly after returning from Germany (PRONI, D/3099/2/19/19A).

47. *Wings*, pp. 159–60, quoting a letter Londonderry sent to Lady Oxford and Asquith on 26.2.36.

48. PRONI, D/3099/2/19/19A, L to Göring, 25.2.36.

49. *Wings*, pp. 154–5.

50. G. T. Waddington, '"An Idyllic and Unruffled Atmosphere of Complete Anglo-German Misunderstanding": Aspects of the Operations of the Dienststelle Ribbentrop in Great Britain, 1934–1938', *History*, 82 (1997), pp. 44–72, here pp. 55–6.

51. Hertfordshire Record Office, D/ERV C2482/89, L to Lady Desborough, n.d., probably 1943; copy in PRONI, T/3201/54; Hyde, *The Londonderrys*, p. 260.

52. Zachary Shore, *What Hitler Knew. The Battle for Information in Nazi Foreign Policy*, Oxford, 2003, pp. 72–4.

53. Hoare's own account of the crisis and his resignation is offered in Templewood, chs. 13–14.

54. Churchill College, Cambridge, Churchill Archives Centre, Phipps 10/2, Berlin Diary, vol. 2, September 1935–April 1937, pp. 163 (10.12.35), 172 (13.12.35), 180 (14.12.35), 192 (22.1.36).

55. The main escort and interpreter on visits and inspections was Regierungsrat Dr Böttger, from Göring's office (PRONI, D/3099/2/19/16A, 18A); *Ourselves*, pp. 92–3.

56. *Ourselves*, pp. 80–82. In *Wings* (p. 155), written more than four years after his first book, Londonderry curiously misdated the start of his German visit to 1 February. Londonderry's handwritten notes, in the form of a diary of his visit, and typescript drawn up from them, which formed the basis of his published account (*Ourselves*, pp. 80ff), are in PRONI, D/3099/2/19/9A–9B.

57. Lady Londonderry, 'Hitler – Man of Simplicity and Action', *Sunday Sun*, 3.5.36 (PRONI, D/3099/10/47). It was the Londonderrys' first glimpse of Hitler, who arrived to take the salute. Some 30,000 stormtroopers had been brought to Germany to attend an open-air address by Hitler at lunchtime on 30 January (*Hitler. Reden und Proklamationen 1932–1945*, ed. Max Domarus, Wiesbaden, 1973, p. 569). The procession took place, as usual, that evening. The Londonderrys must have watched it before they dined with Göring since they did not return to their hotel until 2 a.m. (*Ourselves*, p. 82).

58. Interviews with Lady Mairi Bury, Mount Stewart, 23.5.02, 22.10.02.

59. For a full description of the house and estate, see Volker Knopf and Stefan Martens, *Görings Reich. Selbstinszenierungen in Carinhall*, Berlin, 1999.

60. Göring had created a new bison enclosure at Carinhall in the spring of 1934: see Churchill College, Cambridge, Churchill Archives Centre, Phipps 10/1, p. 55 (entry for 11.6.34). Phipps' critical report – known in the Foreign Office as the 'Bison Dispatch' – on the festive viewing, together with around

forty other guests, of Carinhall and the bison enclosure came to Göring's attention and led to a distinct cooling of relations with the British Ambassador (Knopf and Martens, pp. 37–8).

61. PRONI, D/3099/2/19/19A, L to Göring, 25.2.36.

62. See *Ourselves*, pp. 86–7; James T. Emmerson, *The Rhineland Crisis, 7 March 1936*, London, 1977, p. 93; Rainer F. Schmidt, *Die Aussenpolitik des Dritten Reiches 1933–1939*, Stuttgart, 2002, p. 196.

63. *Ourselves*, pp. 84–8; PRONI, D/3099/2/19/9B; Paul Schmidt, *Statist auf diplomatischer Bühne. Erlebnisse des Chefdolmetschers im Auswärtigen Amt mit den Staatsmännern Europas*, Bonn, 1953, pp. 338–41; interview with Lady Mairi Bury, Mount Stewart, 22.10.02.

64. *Morning Post*, 6.2.36 (PRONI, D/3099/10/47). The Berlin correspondent of the *Morning Post* had reported the previous day that Londonderry and Göring had had an important meeting lasting two hours in the Adlon Hotel on the evening of Saturday, 1 February (D/3099/10/47).

65. For the background to the naval pact, its nature, and its consequences, see Gerhard L. Weinberg, *The Foreign Policy of Hitler's Germany. Diplomatic Revolution in Europe, 1933–36*, Chicago/London, 1970, pp. 210–16; and Ian Kershaw, *Hitler, 1889–1936: Hubris*, London, 1998, pp. 556–8.

66. Middlemas and Barnes, pp. 826–8; Avon, p. 231.

67. The quotation is from PRONI, D/3099/2/19/9B, on p. 5 of a seven-page transcript describing the visit to Germany. *Ourselves*, pp. 88–91 picks up the quotation which, as the diary entry shows, was contemporary, not retrospective.

68. *Wings*, pp. 156–7.

69. For what follows, see *Ourselves*, pp. 94–107; and also p. Schmidt's briefer account (*Statist auf diplomatischer Bühne*, pp. 341–2). Londonderry's handwritten notes (PRONI, D/3099/2/19/9A) on his visit to Germany (and the typescript of these notes, D/3099/2/19/9B) are incomplete on Londonderry's audience with Hitler, while the brief typescript summary of their meeting (D/3099/2/19/8) provides only a digest of Londonderry's own comments, as they are reproduced in *Ourselves*. The meeting between Hitler and Londonderry took place on the day of the murder of the leading Nazi functionary in Switzerland, Wilhelm Gustloff, by a young Jew, David Frankfurter. Hitler was probably still unaware of the incident when he met Londonderry. He was anxious, given the imminent Winter Olympics in Garmisch-Partenkirchen, to avoid anti-Semitic violence in Germany, and – in contrast to the pogroms unleashed in November 1938 when a German official was shot dead by a young Jew in Paris – the country remained quiet.

70. Reproduced opposite the title page of *Ourselves*. The photograph appeared in some British and German newspapers (PRONI, D/3099/10/47, *Manchester Guardian*, 7.2.36; Bundesarchiv Berlin-Lichterfelde, R/901/58084, cuttings from various German newspapers, mainly 6.2.36). It was probably among the photographs which Ribbentrop sent to Londonderry (PRONI, D/3099/2/19/10A). The original is catalogued by the Public Record of Northern Ireland as held in D/3084/C/G/1–43, wrongly dated to 1937, but appears to be missing.

71. Interview with Lady Mairi Bury, Mount Stewart, 22.10.02. *The Ghost Goes West* had proved highly popular in the late autumn of 1935. Neville Chamberlain was among those who 'laughed consumedly' at the light comedy (R. A. C. Parker, *Chamberlain and Appeasement. British Policy and the Coming of the Second World War*, London, 1993, p. 8 and n. 12 on p. 349).

72. *Ourselves*, pp. 107–9

73. Interview with Lord Londonderry in the *Belfast News-Letter*, 21.2.36 (PRONI, D/3099/10/47), typescript (20.2.36) in D/3099/2/19/11A.

74. Churchill Archives Centre, Churchill College, Cambridge, Phipps 3/4, L to Phipps, 21.2.36.

75. Politisches Archiv, Auswärtiges Amt, R76990, Blatt 052, Deutsche Botschaft (signed Hoesch) to Auswärtiges Amt, 22.2.36.

76. See, for instance, the fairly brief reports in *The Times* and the *Morning Post*, 22.2.36. These contrast with the lengthy reports in Germany carried on 23 February, for example, in the main Nazi newspaper, the *Völkischer Beobachter*, and in the *Frankfurter Zeitung* (which was among the most influential newspapers in the country).

77. Politisches Archiv, Auswärtiges Amt, R76990, Bla. 052–7, accompanying Hoesch's report to the Foreign Ministry of 22.2.36. A copy was sent to the Reich Chancellery: Bundesarchiv Berlin/Lichterfelde, R43II/1435, fols. 61–3v, 80v–2.

78. *The Times*, 24.2.36; *Daily Telegraph*, 24.2.36; *Durham Chronicle*, 28.2.36, in PRONI, D/3099/10/47.

79. *Manchester Guardian*, 24.2.36.

80. The *Frankfurter Zeitung*, 25.2.36 prominently reported the speech (via the German News Agency, the *Deutsches Nachrichtenbüro*), under the heading 'Germany wants Friendship with England'.

81. *Wings*, p. 157.

82. *Wings*, p. 160; interview with Lady Mairi Bury, Mount Stewart, 22.10.02.

83. PRONI, D/3099/2/21/A/103 and 137A, L to W. S. Martin, 21.10.38; L to the Duke of Windsor, 26.11.38; Waddington, p. 59.

84. PRONI, D/3099/2/19/10A, Ribbentrop to L, 18.2.36. For the Anglo-German Fellowship, see Simon Haxey, *Tory M.P.*, London, 1939, ch.8, esp. pp. 198–203, 207–9, 230–32.

85. Cited in Ernest W. D. Tennant, *True Account*, London, 1957, pp. 193–4.

86. Richard Griffiths, *Fellow Travellers of the Right. British Enthusiasts for Nazi Germany 1933–39*, Oxford, 1983, p. 183. Ribbentrop had forced the dissolution of the German branch of the earlier Anglo-German Association (PRO, KV5/3 (MI5 dossier on the Anglo-German Fellowship), letter from Basil C. Newton at the British Embassy, Berlin, to Rex Leeper at the Foreign Office, 18.3.35).

87. Tennant, p. 179. Tennant was described as involved in the initiation in a letter by Colonel R. Meinertzhagen to Sir Ian Hamilton, asking him to join (King's College, London, Hamilton Papers, 14/2/4, Meinertzhagen to Hamilton, 19.3.35).

88. Tennant, p. 194; Waddington, p. 62.

89. PRO, KV5/3 (MI5 dossier on the Anglo-German Fellowship), 'Annual Report 1935–36'. 'Document No. 5' in the file, undated but certainly from 1935, naming eight major companies and noted that they had recommended 'to their respective Boards of Directors that they should give a minimum donation of £50 towards the foundation expenses of the Anglo-German Fellowship'. See also Haxey, pp. 230–32; Scott Newton, 'The Economic Background to Appeasement and the Search for Anglo-German Détente before and during World War 2', *Lobster*, 20 (1990), pp. 25–33, here pp. 26–7; and Griffiths, p. 185. For concern in the City of London for improved Anglo-German relations, see the thorough analysis by Bernd-Jürgen Wendt, *Economic Appeasement. Handel und Finanz in der britischen Deutschland-Politik 1933–1939*, Düsseldorf, 1971, here esp. pp. 342–3; and also the study by Scott Newton, *Profits of Peace: the Political Economy of Anglo-German Appeasement*, Oxford, 1996, which, however, is too inclined to indulge in conspiracy theories about government and big business based upon a 'hegemonic group' dominated by the Treasury, the Bank of England and the City of London.

90. *The Diaries of Sir Robert Bruce Lockhart, Vol. 1, 1915–1938*, ed. Kenneth Young, London, 1973, pp. 333–4 (5.12.35); also, see Haxey, p. 236; and Griffiths, pp. 185–6.

91. For Domvile, see Griffiths, pp. 177–82.

92. On the 'Mitford girls', see Mary S. Lovell, *The Sisters. The Saga of the Mitford Girls*, New York/London, 2002; David Pryce-Jones, *Unity Mitford: a Quest*, London, 1976; and (for the most accurate survey of the dealings of Diana and Unity with the Nazis) Anton Joachimsthaler, *Hitlers Liste. Ein*

Dokument persönlicher Beziehungen, Munich, 2003, pp. 517–40.

93. According to Tennant, in an address to the first Monthly Social Gathering of the Fellowship, on 11 March 1936 (PRONI, D/3099/2/19/22). An undated membership list in the Londonderry papers contains the names of 217 individuals and 26 companies (D/3099/2/19/344). The 'Annual Report 1935–36' listed a total membership of 450, including 41 corporate members, on 1 December 1936 (PRO, KV5/3 (MI5 dossier on the Anglo-German Fellowship)).

94. Griffiths, pp. 185–6.

95. Records of some meetings of the Fellowship are contained in Londonderry's papers (e.g. PRONI, D/3099/2/19/22–3, 26–7, though he does not appear to have attended them, and held no office in the organization. Lady Mairi Bury confirmed (interview at Mount Stewart, 22.10.02) that her father had not been an active member.

96. *WSC*, V/3, p. 143, Churchill to L, 6.5.36.

97. PRONI, D/3099/2/19/19A, L to Göring, 25.2.36.

98. PRONI, D/3099/3/35/2A, Lady L to Hitler, 21.2.36; 2C is a (mediocre) translation into German. The Chancellery of the Führer (which dealt with personal correspondence to Hitler) sent an acknowledgement on 29.2.36 (D/3099/3/35/6), apologizing for the demands on Hitler's time that prevented him responding in person.

99. PRONI, D/3099/3/35/4, Lady L to Göring, 21.2.36.

100. PRONI, D/3099/3/35/10B, Göring to Lady L, 2.4.36.

101. PRONI, D/3099/3/35/13A, Lady L to Göring, 4.5.36.

102. PRONI, D/3099/3/35/24A, Göring to Lady L (in German; translations 24B, 35), 3.7.36.

103. PRONI, D/3099/2/19/17A, L to Ribbentrop, 21.2.36; printed with minor omissions in *Ourselves*, pp. 110–13.

104. Her apparently unsuccessful intercession with the Home Office in July 1934 is in DRO, D/Lo/C251/19.

105. A number of diatribes against the Jews by the 'Blackshirts' are contained in the files (e.g. PRONI, D/3099/2/19/12–15), though they appear to have been sent unsolicited and there is no indication of a response by Londonderry, who showed no sympathy at all for the Mosleyites.

106. On relations between the Conservative and Fascist Right in Britain, see J. R. Jones, 'England', in Hans Rogger and Eugen Weber, *The European Right. A Historical Profile*, London, 1965, pp. 29–70, here pp. 64–7; and G. C. Webber, *The Ideology of the British Right 1918–1939*, London, 1986. Oswald Mosley's second wife, Diana, née Mitford, was the daughter of Lord Redesdale. Despite sharing Londonderry's pro-German sympathies, and of course being acquainted with him socially and through their membership of

the House of Lords, Redesdale and the Mitfords had little or nothing to do with the Londonderrys. Unity Mitford, the most fanatical pro-Nazi of the Mitford daughters and for a time welcome in Hitler's circle, was said to have described Lord Londonderry in the summer of 1937 at a lunch with the dictator's entourage as 'a joke' (Pryce-Jones, p. 160).

107. See her letters in DRO, D/Lo/C251/21. Lady Londonderry, a staunch Anglican, appears to have disapproved primarily on religious grounds of her daughter's wedding to a Jew. In a letter in March 1936, she commented casually of her elder daughters that she had 'hoped they would marry some nice hunting men instead of the two Jews they have selected', referring here also to Alan Muntz, the husband of Lady Margaret (D/Lo/C251/26, Lady L to Sir Herbert Maxwell, 5.3.36). See also Anne de Courcy, Circe. *The Life of Edith, Marchioness of Londonderry*, London, 1992, pp. 253, 272–3, who also recounts Teddy Jessel's comments that, once the marriage had taken place, the Londonderrys showed him no animosity and much kindness.

108. PRONI, D/3099/3/35/4, Lady L to Göring, 21.2.36.

109. Examples in PRONI, D/3099/2/13/3/49, 52, 55; D/3099/2/13/11 (unnumbered, to Lady L, 31.7.41).

110. PRONI, D/3099/2/13/3/65, Castlereagh to L, 31.10.44.

111. PRONI, D/3099/2/19/19A, L to Göring, 25.2.36.

112. PRONI, D/3099/2/19/17A, L to Ribbentrop, 21.2.36; *Ourselves*, pp. 112–13.

113. *Wings*, p. 164.

114. PRONI, D/3099/2/19/21, L to L. S. Amery, 26.2.36. Amery was a heavyweight Conservative critic of the National Government and protagonist of British imperialism, who had written to Londonderry the previous day (D/3099/2/19/20) fearing an alliance with Russia and suggesting that, since Hitler wanted expansion of German power at the expense of the Soviet Union, 'common sense would suggest that we should leave him to it'. On Amery, see Maurice Cowling, *The Impact of Hitler. British Politics and British Policy, 1933–1940*, Cambridge, 1975, pp. 120–22.

115. DRO, D/Lo/C251 (26), Lady L to Sir Herbert Maxwell, 5.3.36.

116. PRONI, D/3099/19/21, L to L. S. Amery, 27.2.36; DRO, D/Lo/C251 (26); *Wings*, p. 164. He stayed with his wife at Sutherland Castle, fishing in the Brora.

117. *DBFP*, 2/XV, nos. 404, 460; Middlemas and Barnes, p. 906; Johann Ott, *Botschafter Sir Eric Phipps und die deutsch-englischen Beziehungen. Studien zur britischen Außenpolitik gegenüber dem Dritten Reich*, Ph.D. thesis, Erlangen/Nuremberg, 1968, pp. 63–4.

118. Middlemas and Barnes, p. 906.

119. Emmerson, pp. 49–51.

120. Middlemas and Barnes, pp. 906–8.

121. Zachary Shore, 'Hitler, Intelligence, and the Decision to Remilitarize the Rhine', *Journal of Contemporary History*, 34 (1999), pp. 5–18; and *What Hitler Knew*, ch. 3; also Ian Kershaw, *Hitler, 1936–1945: Nemesis*, London, 2000, pp. 863–4, n. 346.

122. *Die Tagebücher von Joseph Goebbels. Sämtliche Fragmente, Teil 1, Aufzeichnungen 1924–1941*, ed. Elke Fröhlich, 4 vols., Munich, 1987, vol. 2, p. 577 (2.3.36).

123. Lord Lothian would suggest that Hitler was merely entering 'his own back garden' in excusing the remilitarization of the Rhineland and the breach of the Treaty of Locarno (cited in L. S. Amery, *My Political Life, Vol. 3: The Unforgiving Years 1929–1940*, London, 1955, p. 188).

124. Middlemas and Barnes, pp. 913–14.

125. The last point was seen as decisive by Hitler, who put it to Ribbentrop as the means by which 'we can occupy the Rhineland without friction'. Since the idea had also occurred to him, Ribbentrop saw this as telepathy between himself and the Führer (*The Ribbentrop Memoirs*, London, 1954, p. 53).

126. Cited in R. A. C. Parker, *Churchill and Appeasement*, London, 2000, p. 89.

127. Middlemas and Barnes, pp. 915–23.

128. *The Times*, 12.3.36.

129. Jones, pp. 179–81.

130. F. R. Gannon, *The British Press and Germany, 1936–1939*, Oxford, 1971, pp. 93–8; Griffiths, p. 201.

131. Griffiths, pp. 209–11.

132. Jones, p. 185.

133. See Griffiths, pp. 213ff. Shortly before his death on 10 April 1936, Leopold von Hoesch, the German Ambassador in London, expressed his scepticism to his government, in a report which allegedly angered Hitler, that Germany would succeed in gaining British friendship (Churchill College, Cambridge, Churchill Archives Centre, Phipps 10/2, pp. 205–6 (19.4.36)).

134. PRONI, D/3099/2/19/2, 2, 25A–C, Göring to L, 19.3.36. This was in the immediate aftermath of the condemnation of Germany's Rhineland action by the Council of the League of Nations.

135. PRONI, D/3099/3/35/8, Hoesch to Lady L, 24.3.36.

136. PRONI, D/3099/3/35/10B, Göring to Lady L, 2.4.36.

137. PRONI, D/3099/3/35/1A, Emmy Göring to Lady L, 20.3.36; D/3099/3/35/12, Magda Goebbels to Lady L, 24.4.36 (quotation from the latter).

138. *The Times*, 4.4.36 (PRONI, D/3099/10/47).

139. DRO, D/Lo/C251 (26), Lady L to 'Braddle', 4.4.36.

140. *The Ribbentrop Memoirs*, p. 56; Michael Bloch, *Ribbentrop*, London, 1994, pp. 85–8.

141. These were the topics of his conversation with Tom Jones on 8 April and were Ribbentrop's stock-in-trade of his talks with his British contacts in this period (Jones, p. 186).

142. *WSC*, V/3, pp. 129–31, 142–3, 145–6, L to Churchill, 4.5.36, 9.5.36; Churchill to L, 6.5.36 (= PRONI, D/3099/2/5/27–9).

143. Lady Londonderry, 'Hitler – Man of Simplicity and Action', *Sunday Sun*, 3.5.36 (PRONI, D/3099/1047).

144. PRONI, D/3099/3/35/15, Lady L to Ribbentrop, 9.5.36.

145. PRONI, D/3099/3/35/16, Göring to Lady L, 16.5.36.

146. PRONI, D/3099/3/35/37, Lady L to Göring, 29.5.36 (a handwritten draft. An earlier, partial draft written in pencil is attached). DRO, D/Lo/C251 (27), is a letter from Sir Maurice Hankey, Secretary to the Cabinet, thanking Lady L for the extract from Göring's letter that she had sent him.

147. Birmingham UL, Chamberlain Papers, NC7/11/29/36, Lady L to Chamberlain, 14.6.36. She explicitly mentions the extract from Göring's letter that she was sending him.

148. Based on the accounts in: the *Newtownards Chronicle*, 6.6.36, p. 6; the *Northern Whig and Belfast Post*, 30.5.36, p. 7, 1.6.36, p. 7, and 2.6.36, p. 6; the *Belfast News-Letter*, 29.5.36, p. 9, 30.5.36, pp. 8–9; and 3.6.36, p. 7; and the *Belfast Telegraph*, 1.6.36 and 2.6.36.

149. See Kershaw, *Hitler 1889–1936: Hubris*, p. 247.

150. The following is based upon Bloch, chs. 1–6; and Wolfgang Michalka, *Ribbentrop und die deutsche Weltpolitik 1933–1940*, Munich, 1980, chs. 1–2.

151. Rudolf Semmler, *Goebbels – The Man Next to Hitler*, London, 1947, pp. 18–19; Bloch, p. 18.

152. *The Ribbentrop Memoirs*, pp. 27–8.

153. *The Ribbentrop Memoirs*, pp. 22–6.

154. Erich Kordt, *Nicht aus den Akten . . .*, Stuttgart, 1951, p. 82; also Bloch, p. 62.

155. *Die Tagebücher von Joseph Goebbels*, vol. 2, p. 619 (31.5.36).

156. See Bloch, p. 15.

157. *Chips. The Diaries of Sir Henry Channon*, ed. Robert Rhodes James, London, 1967, p. 62.

158. PRO, PRO 30/69/753/2, Ramsay MacDonald Diary, fol. 34, entry for

20.6.35; and see Kershaw, *Hitler, 1889–1936: Hubris*, p. 557.

159. See Reinhard Spitzy, *So haben wir das Reich verspielt*, 4th edn, Munich, 1994, pp. 83ff, for an account of his style as Ambassador in London from his former secretary in the Embassy at that time.

160. *Die Tagebücher von Joseph Goebbels*, vol. 2, p. 619 (31.5.36) and vol. 1, p. 497 (8.2.30).

161. Paul Schwarz, *This Man Ribbentrop. His Life and Times*, New York, 1943, p. 165. Schwarz, who had quit his service in the Foreign Ministry in April 1933 and emigrated to the USA, was in general well informed about Ribbentrop's activities, though not in his comment that the emissary was accompanied on his trip to Mount Stewart by 'a noisy gang of SS men', some in uniform. No uniforms were worn during the weekend; and Ribbentrop's accompaniment, other than his wife and acquaintances, was confined to his two adjutants (information from Lady Mairi Bury, 9.10.03).

162. Two further guests, C. W. James, and Sir William Milner, joined the house party later in the weekend (information from Lady Mairi Bury, 4.12.02, and the Mount Stewart Guest Book). Lord Lothian, who had visited Hitler in 1935 and subsequently become a leading supporter of friendship with Germany, had been invited but was evidently unable to be present (DRO, D/Lo/C251 (26), Lady L to Lothian, 13.5.36).

163. For Mrs Corrigan, see Courcy, *Circe*, p. 198. The Ribbentrops and their accompaniment had gone to a performance of 'Tosca' at Covent Garden the previous evening, then stayed the night at Londonderry House (*Belfast News-Letter*, 29.5.36, p. 9).

164. *The Times and Appeasement. The Journals of A. L. Kennedy, 1932–1939*, ed. Gordon Martel, Camden Society Fifth Series, vol. 16, Cambridge, 2000, p. 265. For an assessment of Ward Price, see Griffiths, pp. 165–8, who is duly critical of the comment by Gannon, p. 34, that Price was 'almost totally unideological'.

165. The following year, G. Ward Price's book, *I Knew These Dictators*, London, 1937, was published. Ward Price was a frequent correspondent of Lord Londonderry until 1940, and their acquaintance was picked up again after the war.

166. *Newtownards Chronicle*, 6.6.36, p. 6.

167. *Belfast News-Letter*, 30.5.36, p. 7.

168. Interviews with Lady Mairi Bury, Mount Stewart, 23.5.02, 22.10.02. Londonderry himself later claimed that he 'had never had any illusions about him. He was shallow, loquacious and self-opinionated' (*Wings*, p. 171).

169. *Sunday Dispatch*, 14.1.40; also *Sunday Sun*, 8.10.39, 'Why I Entertained Ribbentrop', in PRONI, D/3099/2/10/51. The invitation to visit

Mount Stewart had, indeed, been extended to the Ribbentrops during the Londonderrys' stay in Germany (*Belfast Telegraph*, 1.6.36; *Newtownards Chronicle*, 6.6.36, p. 6; *Morning Post*, 2.6.36; *Wings*, p. 171; interview with Lady Mairi Bury, Mount Stewart, 22.10.02).

170. PRONI, D/3099/3/35/15. The article, 'Hitler – Man of Simplicity and Action', appeared in the *Sunday Sun*, 3.5.36. A letter of Lady Londonderry to 'Braddle', dated 4 April 1936, mentions that 'last night Herr v. Ribbentrop' came to dine (DRO, D/Lo/C251 (26)).

171. PRONI, D/3099/3/35/14, Ribbentrop to Lady L, 7.5.36; D/3099/3/35/15, Lady L to Ribbentrop, 9.5.36; D/3099/3/35/20, Ribbentrop to Lady L, 5.6.36; D/3099/3/35/23, Lady L to Frau von Ribbentrop, 23.6.36; D/3099/3/35/25, Ribbentrop to Lady L, 9.7.36. It has been claimed that Londonderry and Ribbentrop were on first-name terms (Martin Gilbert and Richard Gott, *The Appeasers*, 1963, paperback edn, London, 1967, p. 28). There was no sign of this in spring 1936, when the mode of address was still formal (though the tone was cordial).

172. *Sunday Dispatch*, 14.1.40, 'I Answer My Critics', in PRONI, D/3099/10/51. See also Bloch, pp. 116–17.

173. Bloch, p. 62. Londonderry commented, somewhat vaguely, that it had been 'several years after the Great War at the house of one of my friends' (*Sunday Dispatch*, 14.1.40, 'I Answer My Critics', in PRONI, D/3099/10/51).

174. *Belfast Telegraph*, 1.6.36.

175. *Chips*, p. 62.

176. *Northern Whig*, 30.5.36, p. 7; 1.6.36, p. 7.

177. *Belfast Telegraph*, 1.6.36; *Morning Post*, 2.6.36, in PRONI, D/3099/2/10/47.

178. Cited in the *Northern Whig*, 1.6.36, p. 7.

179. *The Star*, 2.6.36, cited in the *Belfast News-Letter*, 3.6.36, p. 7.

180. PRONI, D/3099/3/35/20, Ribbentrop to Lady Londonderry, 5.6.36; interview with Lady Mairi Bury, Mount Stewart, 22.10.02.

181. *Newtownards Chronicle*, 6.6.36, p. 6.

182. Interview with Lady Mairi Bury, Mount Stewart, 22.10.02. Lady Londonderry, too, played golf. In a letter to Ramsay MacDonald on 1 April 1932 she remarked: 'I do wish you were here. I would have taken you on at golf . . .' (PRO, PRO 30/69/754, fol. 640).

183. Tennant, *True Account*, p. 206 (and p. 39 for the lion incident, in September 1910); also Bloch, p. 61. On Tennant, see Griffiths, pp. 116–18, 182–3.

184. Information from Professor David Sturdy, University of Ulster.

185. Courcy, p. 276; Bloch, p. 94.

186. Interview with Lady Mairi Bury, Mount Stewart, 22.10.02.

187. For Clydesdale's spectacular flight over the Himalayas, see the account by his son: James Douglas-Hamilton, *Roof of the World. Man's First Flight Over Everest*, Edinburgh, 1983; and for Hess's flight in 1941 to Scotland to see the Duke of Hamilton, James Douglas-Hamilton, *Motive for a Mission*, Edinburgh, 1979.

188. Interview with Lady Mairi Bury, 22.10.02.

189. Based upon: *Newtownards Chronicle*, 6.6.36, p. 6; *Belfast Telegraph*, 1.6.36; *Northern Whig*, 1.6.36, p. 7; interview with Lady Mairi Bury, 22.10.02.

190. *Newtownards Chronicle*, 6.6.36, p. 6; *Belfast Telegraph*, 2.6.36. The Princesses zu Wied stayed on for a few days (information from Lady Mairi Bury, 20.11.02).

191. Schwarz, pp. 164, 189.

192. *Die Tagebücher von Joseph Goebbels*, vol. 2, p. 622; Bloch, pp. 94–5. For Baldwin's lack of enthusiasm – encouraged by the Foreign Office – to comply with the suggestion that he meet Hitler, see Middlemas and Barnes, pp. 954–8.

193. Schwarz, p. 164.

194. Interview with Lady Mairi Bury, 22.10.02.

195. PRONI, D/3099/2/19/28A, L to Göring, 3.6.36. From the copy of a letter which Lady Londonderry sent towards the end of that month, without date or addressee but probably to Göring, it seems clear that she, too, discussed political matters with Ribbentrop (D/3099/3/38).

196. PRONI, D/3099/2/19/28A, L to Göring, 3.6.36.

197. PRONI, D/3099/3/35/37, Lady L to Göring, handwritten draft, 29.5.36.

198. Even so, Londonderry did write, in a letter to Lord Monsell, First Lord of the Admiralty, on 31 May 1936, composed even while Ribbentrop was staying at Mount Stewart, that he had emphasized 'with as much truculence as a host can use to his guest . . . that we [Britain and Germany] are in exactly the same position, and that it is quite impossible for us to remain on terms of close friendship, when no assurance given can be said to have any binding influence on Germany' (cited *Wings*, pp. 171–2).

199. The report to the German Foreign Ministry (which Hitler's attention was drawn to) by the German Ambassador in London, Leopold von Hoesch, on 10 March 1936 pointed out that public opinion in Britain was broadly sympathetic to the German action in remilitarizing the Rhineland, and singled out Lord Londonderry, who, noted Hoesch, had 'written to me privately to say that he will do his share towards ensuring an enlightened attitude as

regards policy towards Germany' (*DGFP*, C/V, no. 66, pp. 92–5).

200. For the proposal and the British response, see *DGFP*, C/V, nos. 242, 313, pp. 355–63, 513–17; *Hitler. Reden und Proklamationen*, pp. 618, 622; Kershaw, *Hitler, 1936–1945: Nemesis*, pp. 3–4; Cowling, pp. 144–6; Bloch, p. 92; Middlemas and Barnes, pp. 948–53.

201. PRONI, D/3099/2/19/28A, L to Göring, 3.6.36. For Foreign Office reaction to Ribbentrop's presentation of the German case after the remilitarization of the Rhineland, see Bloch, pp. 86–8. The draft of a Foreign Office memorandum, criticizing Ribbentrop's distortions in his documentary collection, is in D3099/3/35/22. Leopold von Hoesch, the German Ambassador in London, whose position was increasingly usurped by Ribbentrop, took a more conciliatory line and was far better received in Whitehall. His hesitancy and cold feet at the prospect of military conflict arising from the march into the Rhineland, even to the extent of suggesting that the German troops be withdrawn, went down less well in Berlin. Ribbentrop, on the other hand, had egged on Hitler in his planned aggression, and was as a result selected as the German delegate who would put the case to the Council of the League of Nations (see Bloch, pp. 84–5).

202. Griffiths, p. 201; and Gannon, pp. 93–8.

203. *The Times*, 12.3.36; cited *Ourselves*, p. 122 (where the date given, 10 March, is that on which Londonderry sent the letter), and *Wings*, pp. 166–7.

204. *Hitler. Reden und Proklamationen*, p. 595. The extended proposal for an air pact, as part of the 'Peace Plan' of 31 March 1936, is in *DGFP*, C/V, pp. 362–3.

205. See Middlemas and Barnes, pp. 792–5; and *Wings*, pp. 119–26 for Londonderry's enthusiasm for the idea.

206. *Hitler. Reden und Proklamationen*, pp. 598–601.

207. See Middlemas and Barnes, p. 792: 'public opinion was not only overwhelmingly pacific, it was also extraordinarily sympathetic to Germany and hostile to France'; and also Griffiths, pp. 201–5.

208. PRONI D/3099/3/35/13A, Lady L to Göring, 4.5.36.

209. PRONI D/3099/2/19/28A, L to Göring, 3.6.36.

210. Lady Londonderry, according to her daughter, Lady Mairi Bury, was already far more dubious about the prospects of avoiding war (interview on 22.10.02). If this was so, however, it was not reflected in the tone of her correspondence with Nazi leaders at the time.

211. PRONI, D/3099/2/17/75B, Hailsham to L, 8.3.[36]. Though the year is not given on the letter, the context indicates that it is 1936.

212. PRONI, D/3099/4/35, M. Allenson to L, 2.6.36 (and L's reply two days later stating that he was merely repaying the hospitality Ribbentrop had

showed to him during his visit to Germany earlier in the year).

213. Certain that he was right and official British foreign policy hopelessly misguided, Londonderry described the Prime Minister, Stanley Baldwin, and his Foreign Secretary, Anthony Eden, as 'demented' in a letter to Ramsay MacDonald on 19 June 1936, in which he claimed that 'it is indeed difficult to defend our foreign policy during the last six months' (PRO, PRO 30/69/683, fol. 169).

214. *Ourselves*, facing p. 7.

4 Lengthening Shadows

1. *Chips. The Diaries of Sir Henry Channon*, ed. Robert Rhodes James, London, 1967, p. 111 (13.8.36). The earlier part of the description of Göring's party is based upon *Ambassador Dodd's Diary 1933–1938*, ed. William E. Dodd and Martha Dodd, London, 1941, p. 346 (14.8.36). Dodd, the American Ambassador, thought the party 'the greatest display I have ever seen'. See also Richard D. Mandell, *The Nazi Olympics*, London, 1971, pp. 156–8.

2. Richard Lamb, *The Ghosts of Peace, 1935–1945*, Salisbury, 1987, p. 46 (without source reference).

3. *The Ribbentrop Memoirs*, London, 1954, pp. 64–5. Vansittart's discussion with Hitler proceeded in affable fashion. Vansittart noted: 'Of his [Hitler's] talk nothing could have been more friendly, but nothing could have been more general'. Ribbentrop had, at lunch preceding the audience with Hitler, given Vansittart a clear warning of what lay in store if British accommodation of German aims was not established: 'If England did not give Germany the possibility to live, there would eventually be war between them and one of them will be annihilated' (Ian Colvin, *Vansittart in Office. The Origins of World War II*, London, 1965, pp. 108–9).

4. Thomas Jones, *A Diary with Letters, 1931–1950*, London, 1954, pp. 241–50; Martin Gilbert, *The Roots of Appeasement*, London, 1966, pp. 197–211; Richard Griffiths, *Fellow Travellers of the Right. British Enthusiasts for Nazi Germany 1933–39*, Oxford, 1983, pp. 223–4. Lloyd George was still speaking, over a year later, of Hitler's 'fundamental greatness' (Martin Gilbert, *Britain and Germany between the Wars*, London, 1964, p. 102).

5. Cited in Colvin, p. 131. Vansittart later publicized his strong feelings about Germany in a number of wartime broadcasts which, despite their propaganda purpose, were a fair reflection of his stance (Robert Vansittart, *Black Record. Germans Past and Present*, London, 1941).

6. The major study of colonial policy in the Third Reich is that of Klaus Hildebrand, *Vom Reich zum Weltreich. Hitler, NSDAP und koloniale Frage 1919–1945*, Munich, 1969. British responses to German colonial claims are examined by Andrew J. Crozier, *Appeasement and Germany's Last Bid for Colonies*, London, 1988.

7. *The Ribbentrop Memoirs*, p. 70.

8. *The Ribbentrop Memoirs*, p. 208.

9. PRONI, D/3099/2/13/3/49, Castlereagh to L, 6.8.36. Londonderry had written to Göring on 30 July hoping that he would be able to receive his son and daughter-in-law (D/3099/2/19/31B).

10. PRONI, D/3099/3/35/24A, Göring to Lady L, 3.7.36. Sir Samuel Hoare, in a letter of 22 July, thanked Lady Londonderry for the copy of Göring's letter, which he had read 'with great interest' (D/3099/3/15/75). Lord Londonderry saw that Lord Halifax also saw a copy (D/3099/2/18/10, Halifax to L, 16.7.36).

11. *The Times*, 20.7.31, from a speech by Londonderry at St Helens two days earlier; and see Neil Fleming, *The Seventh Marquess of Londonderry: a Political Life*, Ph.D. thesis, Queen's University Belfast, 2002, pp. 192, 204, 278.

12. PRONI, D/3099/2/18/8, L to Halifax, 4.7.36.

13. PRONI, D/3099/2/18/9, Halifax to L, 6.7.36 (and also D/3099/2/18/7, Halifax to L, 1.7.36).

14. PRONI, D/3099/2/18/10, Halifax to L, 16.7.36.

15. PRONI, D/3099/2/18/11, L to Halifax, 17.7.36.

16. PRONI, D/3099/2/18/12, Halifax to L, 25.8.36.

17. PRONI, D/3099/2/18/56, Halifax to L, 12.9.36. The year is not given on this handwritten letter (misdated in the PRONI catalogue), but is plainly 1936.

18. *Hitler. Reden und Proklamationen 1932–1945*, ed. Max Domarus, Wiesbaden, 1973, p. 637.

19. Beverley Nichols, in the *Sunday Chronicle*, cited in Griffiths, p. 227 (and pp. 224–8 for other reactions).

20. Wilhelm Treue (ed.), 'Hitlers Denkschrift zum Vierjahresplan 1936', *Vierteljahrshefte für Zeitgeschichte*, 3 (1955), pp. 184–210.

21. Churchill College, Cambridge, Churchill Archives Centre, Phipps 10/2, p. 219. Against the advice he had received from within the Embassy, Phipps had found an excuse not to attend the Party Rally in 1933, and continued to avoid the occasion in subsequent years. See Johann Ott, *Botschafter Sir Eric Phipps und die deutsch-englischen Beziehungen. Studien zur britischen Außenpolitik gegenüber dem Dritten Reich*, Ph.D. thesis, Erlangen/Nuremberg, 1968, pp. 163–7.

22. PRONI, D/3099/2/18/13, L to Halifax, 16.9.36. The letter to Ribbentrop does not appear to have survived.

23. Churchill College, Cambridge, Churchill Archives Centre, Phipps 3/3, fols. 61–2, Hankey to Phipps, 9.10.36.

24. Churchill College, Cambridge, Churchill Archives Centre, Phipps 10/2, p. 222 (21.10.36).

25. PRONI, D/3099/2/19/31A–32A, Oberjägermeister Menthe to L, 5.9.36, L to Göring, 20.9.36. The pictures published in the German press of Londonderry shooting with Göring were meant to suggest, so it has been claimed, 'a reassuring symmetry in British and German national lives' (Gerwin Strobl, *The Germanic Isle. Nazi Perceptions of Britain*, Cambridge, 2000, p. 32).

26. The British Ambassador in Berlin, Sir Eric Phipps, hinted that Göring had spoken frankly to Londonderry's daughter, Lady Maureen Stanley, about Germany's expansionist aims (*DBFP*, 2/XVII, no. 365, p. 531, Phipps to Eden, 10.11.36: 'You will probably have heard at first hand the impressions of Lord and Lady Londonderry, Lady Maureen (to whom Goering appears to have made an 'expansionist' confession), and Castlereagh'). See also David Irving, *Göring. A Biography*, London, 1989, p. 174, who refers (without source reference, but probably based upon Phipps' comment) to Göring 'laying bare' his expansionist strategies of overrunning Czechoslovakia, then Danzig, in conversation with Londonderry and his daughter, Lady Maureen Stanley, in October 1936. Phipps (and Irving) appear to have been mistaken. Lady Mairi Stewart, then aged fifteen, accompanied her parents to Berlin on this occasion (*The Times*, 2.11.36 and *Daily Telegraph*, 2.11.36, in PRONI, D/3099/2/10/50), though there is no evidence – nor does Lady Mairi recall – that her eldest sister, Lady Maureen Stanley, was present.

27. *Ambassador Dodd's Diary*, p. 365 (9.11.36).

28. *Wings*, p. 179.

29. Churchill College, Cambridge, Churchill Archives Centre, Phipps 10/2, p. 231 (10.11.36).

30. Extracts from reports in the *Morning Post*, 31.10.36, the *Daily Telegraph*, 2.11.36, and the *Yorkshire Post*, 2.11.36, in PRONI, D/3099/10/50, which also contains the extract from Lady Londonderry's interview in the *Sunday Sun*, 15.11.36, relating to her recent visit to Germany. Lady Londonderry also defended Fascism and Nazism as 'the only alternative to Communism' in a speech asserting that Russia was trying to dominate the Balkans and was 'behind the Spanish revolution' (*Northern Echo*, 11.11.36 (D/3099/10/50)).

31. Extracts (with photos) from some English newspapers in PRONI, D/3099/10/50 and from a greater number of English and some German newspapers in Bundesarchiv Berlin/Lichterfelde, R901/58084, 58093, 58624 and 59264.

32. Anne de Courcy, *Circe. The Life of Edith, Marchioness of Londonderry*, London, 1992, p. 278.

33. Lady Londonderry, writing on 20 September 1936, told her friend Ramsay MacDonald: 'We become Mayor and Mayoress of Durham on 9th Nov. We have withstood the dignity for years – but no further excuse . . .' (PRO, PRO 30/69/759, fol. 626; printed in H. Montgomery Hyde, *The Londonderrys: a Family Portrait*, London, 1979, p. 237).

34. The *Daily Telegraph*, 16.11.36, *The Times*, 16.11.36, and the *North Mail and Newcastle Chronicle*, 16.11.36, all mention the playing of the German national anthem (PRONI, D/3099/10/50), as does the weekly *Durham Advertiser* of 20.11.36 (information from Mr Brian Crosby). Lord Londonderry himself (according to his daughter) placed the incident at the opening of the hymn song to the tune of 'Austria', composed by Haudyn, which Ribbentrop alllegedly mistook for the German national anthem, since the melody is identical. Though an enticing version of events, the evidence does not support this interpretation.

35. Londonderry's speech at Sunderland on 18 November 1936 (*Sunderland Daily Echo*, 19.11.36 (PRONI, D/3099/2/50)), Speaking later in the month at the Oxford Union, Londonderry advocated the reform of the League, though in unspecific terms. *The Church of England Newspaper*, 27.11.36 (in the same file).

36. *The Times*, 16.12.36. The press comment in Britain was generally most unfavourable towards Ribbentrop's claims. See Michael Bloch, *Ribbentrop*, London, 1994, p. 124. Paul Schwarz, *This Man Ribbentrop. His Life and Times*, New York, 1943, pp. 208–10, describes the speech and also indicated (p. 210) that 'it did not make a strong impression'. Ribbentrop nevertheless went away convinced from his audience of German sympathizers, noted Schwarz, 'that England would not fight under any circumstances' (p. 209).

37. *Wings*, p. 181. Londonderry claimed to have had a heated conversation with Ribbentrop about Germany's reassertion, in mid-November 1936, of sovereignty over four rivers which had hitherto been controlled by an International Commission, telling the German Ambassador that 'these high-handed actions were destroying whatever sympathy there might be for Germany in this country' (*Wings*, p. 179).

38. PRONI, D/3099/2/18/17, L to Halifax, 19.12.36.

39. What follows is based on PRONI, D/3099/2/18/18A, a memorandum by

Londonderry intended for Lord Halifax (though no addressee is named), 24.12.36 (date in pencil). This is a draft, with some omissions (scored through in pencil). A second copy, without any indication of the deletions in the draft, is D/3099/2/18/18B. Extracts were published in *Ourselves*, pp. 130–34.

40. The British government asked Hitler, for example, what view Germany took of the continued maintenance in force of the still operative clauses of the Treaty of Versailles, or any agreement arising from it; and whether Germany recognized and respected the existing territorial and political status of Europe, leaving aside any possible modifications through free negotiation and agreement. See Keith Middlemas and John Barnes, *Baldwin: a Biography*, London, 1969, pp. 952–3; and Jones, p. 195, n. 1; *DBFP*, 2/XVI, ch. 4, and no. 301, for Hitler's irritation at the questionnaire.

41. The Earl of Avon, *The Eden Memoirs. Facing the Dictators*, London, 1962, p. 374.

42. Jones, pp. 201, 205, 208, 214–15, 218–19, 224; Middlemas and Barnes, pp. 955–8.

43. Jones, p. 191 (30.4.36). Just over a year later, Baldwin would refer to Hitler and Mussolini in similar terms as 'two madmen loose in Europe', warning that 'anything may befall' (Middlemas and Barnes, p. 1033).

44. In a powerful speech to the House of Commons on 12 November 1936, Churchill criticized the government's policy as 'decided only to be undecided, resolved to be irresolute, adamant for drift, solid for fluidity, all powerful to be impotent . . . preparing more months and years – precious, perhaps vital, to the greatness of Britain – for the locusts to eat' (cited Middlemas and Barnes, pp. 969–70; *WSC*, V/3, p. 406, n. 1).

45. Keith Middlemas, *The Diplomacy of Illusion. The British Government and Germany 1937–39*, London, 1972, p. 41.

46. PRONI, D/3099/3/604B/5, copy of an article by H. Montgomery Hyde in *Harpers & Queen* magazine, July 1980.

47. Interview with Lady Mairi Bury, Mount Stewart, 22.10.02.

48. PRONI, D/3099/3/2/604B/1, Wallis Simpson to Lady L, 7.11.36, and the reply of the following day.

49. *Parliament and Politics in the Age of Churchill and Attlee. The Headlam Diaries 1935–1951*, ed. Stuart Ball, Camden Fifth Series, vol. 14, Cambridge, 1999, pp. 101–2, entries for 5.12.36, 7.12.36.

50. *Wings*, p. 180.

51. Susan Williams, *The People's King. The True Story of the Abdication*, London, 2003, pp. 175–7.

52. H. Montgomery Hyde, *Baldwin: the Unexpected Prime Minister*, London, 1973, p. 496.

53. PRONI, D/3099/3/2/604B/3–4, L to the Duke of Windsor, 11 and 19.12.36.

54. Interview with Lady Mairi Bury, Mount Stewart, 23.5.02. And see Hyde, *The Londonderrys*, p. 238 (and pp. 206–7 for Londonderry's resentment at the Prince of Wales' disparaging comments in 1929 about conditions in the north-eastern coal-fields which he owned).

55. Cambridge UL, Baldwin Papers 143, fols. 100–101, Lady L to Baldwin, 12.12.36.

56. PRONI, D/3099/3/15/22, Baldwin to Lady L, 19.12.36; Hyde, *The Londonderrys*, p. 238.

57. Erich Kordt, *Nicht aus den Akten . . .*, Stuttgart, 1951, pp. 159–61; Bloch, p. 123.

58. See Reinhard Spitzy, *So haben wir das Reich verspielt*, 4th edn, Munich, 1994, pp. 98–100 (where the role of Frau Ribbentrop in bolstering the resentment towards Britain is stressed).

59. Churchill College, Cambridge, Churchill Archives Centre, Phipps 10/2, p. 235 (23.12.36).

60. Churchill College, Cambridge, Churchill Archives Centre, Phipps 10/2, p. 240 (12.1.37).

61. *Hitler. Reden and Proklamationen*, p. 668.

62. *Hitler. Reden and Proklamationen*, pp. 668–73, quotation p. 673.

63. *The Times*, 1.2.37, and *Northern Whig*, 1.2.37, in PRONI, D/3099/10/50.

64. Crozier, p. 158, points out that the German colonial claim found backing from Lords Lothian, Rennell, Mount Temple and Noel-Buxton, among others.

65. 'Lord Londonderry on Herr Hitler's Colonial Demands', *Newcastle Journal*, 11.2.37, in PRONI, D/3099/10/50.

66. 'Shake! – Hitler', *The Leader*, 20.3.37, in PRONI, D/3099/10/50. Londonderry had spoken in a speech at the end of January of the need to save Europe as 'the wisdom of Castlereagh and Wellington' had saved France and Europe from disaster in 1815 (*Northern Whig*, 1.2.37, in PRONI, D/3099/10/50).

67. PRONI, D/3099/2/18/19, Noé, to L, 1.1.37.

68. PRONI, D/3099/2/18/20, L to Noé, 12.1.37. Noé replied on 23 January, encouraging Londonderry to transcend his sense of disappointment in the cause of European peace and wrote again on 9 February extolling Hitler's speech of 30 January and expressing his regrets that the speech had made no positive echo in Britain (D/3099/2/18/21–2).

Londonderry sent copies of Noé's correspondence to Lord Halifax (D/3099/2/18/23 (L to Halifax, 13.2.37)). Noé, staying at the Carlton Hotel in London for a few days, was among the guests at a luncheon party at Londonderry House on 24 February (D/3099/15/11 (Londonderry House Parties, 1937–1939)).

69. DRO, D/Lo/C237, L to Lady Milner, 11.3.37 (with attached note from L's secretary stating that he did not think the letter was ever sent). Further typescript copies are contained in PRONI, D/3099/2/17/19B – 19A is a handwritten draft – and Hoover Institution, Stanford, California, Kenneth de Courcy Papers, box 2 folder 2.

70. PRONI, D/3099/2/17/33A, L to Göring, 22.2.37; and see *Ourselves*, p. 139. Stefan Martens, *Hermann Göring. 'Erster Paladin des Führers' und 'Zweiter Mann im Reich'*, Paderborn, 1985, suggests that Londonderry had the intention of formally inviting Göring should he not be the official German representative at the ceremony, though this is not borne out by Londonderry's letter or Göring's reply.

71. PRO, FO 372/3273, fol. 257 (22.2.37). The Speaker refused to allow her question.

72. PRO, FO 372/3273, fol. 286 (Phipps' dispatch to the Foreign Office, 28.2.37).

73. Churchill College, Cambridge, Churchill Archives Centre, Phipps 10/2, p. 231 (10.11.36); *DBFP*, 2/XVII, no. 365.

74. PRO, FO 372/3273, fols. 285–7 (Phipps' dispatch to the Foreign Office, 28.2.37 and Foreign Office cover note).

75. PRONI, D/3099/2/19/34A, Göring to L, 24.3.37, printed in *Ourselves*, pp. 139–40.

76. PRONI, D/3099/2/19/35B, L to Göring, 5.4.37.

77. Churchill College, Cambridge, Churchill Archives Centre, Phipps 10/2, pp. 248–9 (9.4.37).

78. See David Dutton, *Neville Chamberlain*, London, 2001, pp. 8–26 for a brief summary of Chamberlain's career; Keith Feiling, *The Life of Neville Chamberlain*, London, 1946, remains, despite many advances in scholarship, an impressive biography.

79. Cited in Dutton, p. 18.

80. A good pen-picture of Chamberlain's character can be found in R. A. C. Parker, *Chamberlain and Appeasement. British Policy and the Coming of the Second World War*, London, 1993, pp. 1–11.

81. Feiling, pp. 303–6; Middlemas, pp. 59–61; C. L. Mowat, *Britain between the Wars 1918–1940*, London, 1956, p. 592.

82. Avon, p. 445.

83. Middlemas, p. 1.

84. Eugen Weber, *The Hollow Years. France in the 1930s*, New York, 1994, pp. 163–74, 244–56; also Middlemas, pp. 24–5.

85. Middlemas, pp. 2–3; Feiling, pp. 323–5; Parker, pp. 95–6.

86. PRONI, D/3099/2/17/19B, L to Lady Milner, 11.3.37. A retrospective judgement on Chamberlain from a Conservative MP who had been hostile to his appeasement policy essentially concurred, seeing him as 'affectionate and sensitive' in private life, but 'aloof, arrogant, obstinate and limited' in his public persona (Lord Boothby, *My Yesterday, Your Tomorrow*, London, 1962, p. 124).

87. PRONI, D/3099/2/18/24, L to Halifax, 10.6.37.

88. PRONI, D/3099/2/18/26, L to Halifax, 12.6.37.

89. Middlemas and Barnes, p. 1033.

90. Chamberlain expressed his appreciation to Lady Londonderry that the reception would take place, 'in spite of anything that happened in the past', in a letter to her on 28 July 1937 (PRONI, D/3099/3/15/46).

91. *Ourselves*, p. 136.

92. Nevile Henderson, *Failure of a Mission. Berlin 1937–1939*, London, 1940, pp. 19–20; and see Peter Neville, *Appeasing Hitler. The Diplomacy of Sir Nevile Henderson 1937–39*, London, 2000, p. 31.

93. Griffiths, p. 282.

94. Ivone Kirkpatrick, *The Inner Circle*, London, 1959, p. 91.

95. Jones, p. 314 (15.2.37).

96. Robert Vansittart, *The Mist Procession*, London, 1958, p. 360; Avon, pp. 503–4. The background to the appointment is explored by Neville, pp. 20–24.

97. Cited in Middlemas, p. 53.

98. Henderson, p. 17.

99. Cited in Middlemas, pp. 73–4.

100. Henderson, p. 67.

101. Gerhard L. Weinberg, *The Foreign Policy of Hitler's Germany. Starting World War II, 1937–1939*, Chicago/London, 1980, pp. 100–101.

102. Avon, pp. 402–18, 434–9, 446–7.

103. Henderson, pp. 70–71; *Hitler. Reden and Proklamationen*, p. 730.

104. See Ian Kershaw, *Hitler, 1936–1945: Nemesis*, London, 2000, pp. 44–5.

105. PRONI, D/3099/2/19/36, three-page memorandum by Londonderry on his conversation with Göring on 22.9.37, summarized in *Ourselves*, pp. 146–9. Three photographs of Londonderry during his visit to Carinhall are in D/3099/17/36.

106. *Ourselves*, pp. 144–5; Franz von Papen, *Memoirs*, London, 1952, p. 399.

107. *Ourselves*, pp. 150–53; von Papen, pp. 399–400.

108. Von Papen, p. 400.

109. Henderson, p. 89.

110. DRO, D/Lo/C237, L to Sir Nevile Henderson, 7.10.37; *Wings*, p. 184.

111. PRONI, D/3099/4/44, L to Ribbentrop, 26.10.37.

112. PRONI, D/3099/2/18/27, L to Halifax, 7.10.37.

113. PRO, Cab. 23/89, Cabinet 35 (37), 29.9.37.

114. DRO, D/Lo/C237, L to Leo Amery, 8.10.37.

115. *WSC*, V/3, pp. 781–2, L to Churchill, 7.10.37.

116. PRONI, D/3099/2/5/32, Churchill to L, 23.10.37, printed in *WSC*, V/3, pp. 812–13 and *Wings*, pp. 187–8.

117. PRONI, D/3099/2/5/33A, L to Churchill, 26.10.37, printed in *WSC*, V/3, pp. 815–16.

118. *WSC*, V/3, p. 815 (and p. 782, n.1).

119. An expression he used repeatedly of the letters, cited here from Londonderry's letter to Sir Maurice Hankey of 18 November 1937 (PRONI, D/3099/4/44 and PRO, Cab. 21/2676).

120. PRONI, D/3099/4/44, L to Sir Donald Banks, Air Ministry, 4.11.37.

121. Birmingham UL, Chamberlain Papers, NC7/11/30/95–7, L to Chamberlain, 14.12.37; and see also PRONI, D/3099/4/44, L to Hailsham, 2.11.37, and 11.11.37; L to Sir Donald Banks, Air Ministry, 4.11.37; Banks to L, 11.11.37; L to Hankey, 18.11.37 (also in PRO, Cab. 21/2676); L to Lord Kemsley, 22.11.37; Oliver Stanley to L, n.d., *c*.7–8.11.37; L to Stanley, 9.11.37; L to Eden, 24.11.37 (also PRO, FO 954/7, fols. 491–4); PRONI, D/3099/2/17/25, L to Hailsham, 3.12.37; D/3099/2/18/28, L to Halifax, 2.11.37; D/3099/2/18/34, L to Halifax, 29.11.37; PRO, Cab. 21/2676, Hankey to L, 19.11.37.

122. PRONI, D/3099/4/44, L to the Prince of Hesse, German Embassy, 3.11.37; Norman J. Hulbert, MP, to L, 8.11.37; D/3099/10/49, press reports of the visit, *Evening Standard*, 5.11.37 and *The Times*, 6.11.34. Stanley Baldwin, curiously, expressed an interest in Londonderry's visit and wanted to hear his impressions (D/3099/2/19/39).

123. PRONI, D/3099/2/18/28, L to Halifax, 2.11.37; D/3099/4/44, L to Norman J. Hulbert, MP, 8.11.37; D/3099/2/19/41A, L to Ribbentrop, 8.12.37 (also in *Ourselves*, p. 156).

124. PRONI, D/3099/2/21/A/217, L to a Mr Glasgow, 5.5.39.

125. G. Ward Price, *I Know These Dictators*, London, 1937. Ward Price's newspaper, the *Daily Mail*, had, under the ownership of Lord Rothermere,

not essentially changed its stance on Germany since 1933. Little actual news from Germany was reported. The newspaper's position was mainly reflected in feature articles and Ward Price's interviews with Hitler. The motto which Ward Price himself coined in June 1936 for Anglo-German relations, 'Negotiate – but arm', reflected Rothermere's own position, admiring of Hitler but advocating massive rearmament, especially in the air (Franklin Reid Gannon, *The British Press and Germany 1936–1939*, Oxford, 1971, pp. 9–10, 34).

126. PRONI, D/3099/2/18/31, L to Halifax, 13.11.37.

127. Andrew Roberts, *'The Holy Fox'. The Life of Lord Halifax*, London, 1991, paperback edn, 1997, p. 62.

128. Jones, p. 215; Roberts, p. 64; Avon, p. 508.

129. Cited in Roberts, p. 63.

130. Avon, p. 509. Halifax's own recollection differs. He recalled the suggestion that some advantage might come of going to Germany under the cover of an informal visit to the Hunting Exhibition actually coming from Eden himself, who stuck to the idea despite Halifax's own doubts (The Earl of Halifax, *Fulness of Days*, London, 1957, p. 184); and see Roberts, p. 65. Eden's account corresponds with Churchill's version (Winston S. Churchill, *The Second World War. Volume 1: The Gathering Storm*, London, 1948, p. 224). The dislike of the visit in the Foreign Office is described by Roberts, pp. 64–7.

131. Avon, pp. 511–12.

132. Avon, p. 510.

133. For descriptions, see Halifax, pp. 184–91; Avon, pp. 513–16; Paul Schmidt, *Statist auf diplomatischer Bühne. Erlebnisse des Chefdolmetschers im Auswärtigen Amt mit den Staatsmännern Europas*, Bonn, 1953, pp. 384–6; Kirkpatrick, pp. 94–8; The Earl of Birkenhead, *Halifax. The Life of Lord Halifax*, London, 1965, pp. 368–74; and Roberts, pp. 70–73.

134. It was most likely a later embellishment by Halifax. Ivone Kirkpatrick, who accompanied Halifax, recalled Hitler meeting them at the top of the steps leading up to the house (Kirkpatrick, p. 94). This is far more probable than Hitler opening the car door himself, which would have been most unusual.

135. *DGFP*, 4/I, no. 31, pp. 54–67, quotation pp. 62–3; also cited in Avon, p. 515.

136. Borthwick Institute, York, Halifax Papers, 410.3.3 (vi), fol.9; Halifax, p. 187.

137. Weinberg, p. 122 and n. 90; Avon, p. 515.

138. Borthwick Institute, York, Halifax Papers, 410.3.3., fol. 12.

139. A point made by Roberts, p. 69; and see Kirkpatrick, pp. 90–91.

140. P. Schmidt, p. 386 ('diesen englischen "Pfarrer"'); Roberts, p. 73.

141. Churchill, p. 224.

142. Cited, from Chamberlain's diary, by Feiling, pp. 332–3.

143. Avon, p. 516.

144. See Kershaw, pp. 48–9.

145. In a letter to the editor of the *Belfast News-Letter*, Londonderry commented that 'the Halifax visit with which I was not altogether unassociated has not fulfilled my expectations' (PRONI, D/3099/2/21/A/46, L to W. H. McKee, 10.1.38). In a letter written a few days earlier to the same editor, Londonderry had pessimistically stated of Halifax's visit that 'when so much could have been done for good, nothing but harm will now result' (D/3099/2/21/A/4, L to the Editor, *Belfast News-Letter*, 5.1.38). Writing to the editor of the *Observer*, J. L. Garvin, himself strongly supportive of an appeasement policy, Londonderry remarked that he 'had hoped that something important would come out of Halifax's visit . . . but calling on Hitler as if it were an after-thought seemed to me an unfortunate attitude to adopt' (D/3099/2/21/A/16, L to Garvin, 20.1.38). He repeated the criticism in a later letter, commenting that Halifax should have made the trip to Germany 'as a Minister of the Crown', which would have been 'by far the most dignified attitude to take up' (D/3099/2/21/A/217, L to Mr Glasgow, 5.5.39).

146. *Hitler. Reden und Proklamationen*, pp. 766–7; *Ourselves*, pp. 157–8.

147. DRO, D/Lo/C237, L's exchange of letters (17.11.37, 25.11.37 and 29.11.37) with Herbert Morrison, one of the leading figures in the Labour Party; PRONI, D/3099/12/21, L's statement for the Press Association, 8.12.37, on his record in office; D/3099/2/17/28, L to Lord Strabolgi, a Labour peer, 12.12.37 (bewailing the fact that he had to defend himself, without the assistance of his 'colleagues and so-called friends' who had 'never raised a finger to help me through my difficulties'), and the previous exchange of letters with Strabolgi (nos. 21, unnumbered, and 22), of 19, 22, 23 November 1937. Londonderry's long and bitter recitation of his grievance against Baldwin (D/3099/2/17/29), an eight-page handwritten draft letter which is not to be found in Chamberlain's papers and may not have been sent, was prompted by a letter of his wife to Chamberlain (following a defence by the Prime Minister of Londonderry's successor, Lord Swinton, in the press), enclosing a copy of Londonderry's letter to Baldwin of 18 May 1936 saying it was 'a little hard on C[harley] that nothing has ever been said of the wonderful efforts he made to keep the Air Force – shorn to its barest necessities as it was – a perfect fighting unit, capable of expansion the moment the word was given that it should be increased' (Birmingham UL,

Chamberlain Papers, NC7/11/30/98 (and NC7/11/29/37, the copy of the letter to Baldwin)).

148. PRONI, D/3099/2/19/41A, L to Ribbentrop, 8.12.37; *Ourselves*, pp. 155–7.

149. The letter was included along with a summary of Ribbentrop's 'Conclusions' on Anglo-German relations (*DGFP*, D/I, no. 93, pp. 162–8). Londonderry's letter is *DGFP*, D/I, no. 104, pp. 183–5. It had been sent on 6 December to a Major Lionel Gall, an active member of the Anglo-German Fellowship. A copy came by some means, presumably from Gall, into the hands of the Lord Mayor of Frankfurt, who passed it on to the German Foreign Ministry. From there it was sent to the Reich Chancellery and returned on 5 February 1938 with an attached note stating that Hitler had read a translation (see p. 183, no. 46.) Gall had been in touch with Londonderry on a number of occasions in November, seeking his help in furthering Anglo-German relations (PRONI, D/3099/4/44, Gall to L, 4, 10, 11 and 16.11.37). No copy of the letter appears to have been kept in Londonderry's papers.

150. *DGFP*, D/I, no. 93, p. 166. See also *The Ribbentrop Memoirs*, pp. 205–6. This document gave Hitler 'Strictly Confidential and Personal Conclusions concerning the report "German Embassy London A5522" on the future of Anglo-German Relations'.

151. Avon, pp. 516–19.

152. Politisches Archiv des Auswärtigen Amtes, Berlin, R28895a, 'A5522, Das deutsch-englische Verhältnis und die Weiterbehandlung der Initiative Chamberlains', 28.12.1937, signed by Ribbentrop and marked 'dem Führer und Reichskanzler (bezw. dem Reichsaussenminister direkt zugestellt)'. The document, evidently the copy originally retained by the German Embassy itself, found its way after the war into the records of the British Foreign Office and was only returned to the German Foreign Ministry in 1994, when it first came to light. It was, therefore, not available to be included in the printed series of records of German foreign policy from the period. The 'Conclusions' (see note 150 above) were based upon it. Ribbentrop's staff at the Embassy had avoided collaboration on the report and 'Conclusions'. The main assistance in the laborious process of compliation had come from his wife (Spitzy, pp. 190, 193–6; Erich Kordt, *Wahn and Wirklichkeit. Die Außenpolitik des Dritten Reiches. Versuch einer Darstellung*, p. 175; Bloch, pp. 146–8).

153. *DGFP*, D/I, no. 93, p. 168; see also *The Ribbentrop Memoirs*, pp. 207–8.

154. PRONI, D/3099/3/35/32, Hitler to Lord and Lady L, 10.1.38. Lady Londonderry had also been thanked by Hitler for her good wishes on his birthday the previous April (D/3099/3/35/31, Hitler to Lady L, 23.4.37).

155. PRONI, D/3099/2/21/A/16, L to J. L. Garvin, 20.1.38. In a letter of 7 January 1938 to Lord Phillimore, a strong supporter of Franco, Londonderry wrote of his political isolation and of being ignored by Chamberlain (D/3099/2/19/46).

156. PRONI, D/3099/2/21/A/4, L to the Editor, *Belfast News-Letter*, 5.1.38.

157. PRONI, D/3099/12/23, letters to L of 13.1.38 and 22.1.38 from E. Gerwin, Financial Correspondent of the *Berliner Tageblatt*, and three-page draft of the interview.

158. Londonderry's interview was reported in the British press, and he was castigated for it by the liberal newspaper the *News Chronicle* (PRONI, D/3099/10/49 (extracts from the *Yorkshire Post*, 1.2.38, and the *News Chronicle*, 1.2.38)). Next day, the *News Chronicle* 'revisited' in its leading article Londonderry's 'infamous record' on allegedly preventing the abolition of bombing while he had been Air Minister (D/3084/C/C/7/5, copy of a leader in the *News Chronicle*, 3.2.38).

159. PRO, Cab. 21/2676, L to Hankey, 5.2.38. Londonderry's attempt to include in his book transcripts of his talismanic letters of November 1934 to Lord Hailsham spawned a considerable correspondence (most of it in this file) between Londonderry and the Prime Minister's office in what proved a vain attempt to gain official permission for the publication of documents regarded as pertaining to government business by a serving Cabinet minister. Londonderry wrote personally to Neville Chamberlain to seek permission. However, Chamberlain declined to allow publication, consoling Londonderry with the thought that although he could not do all that he would wish to do to vindicate his own position, 'your name will in the end not suffer when history comes to be written' (Birmingham UL, Chamberlain Papers, NC7/11/31/-183-4, and PRONI, D/3099/2/17/30; exchange of 19 and 24 November 1938). Londonderry had to content himself with a summary of the views he had expressed in his letters to Hailsham, in *Ourselves*, pp. 63-4. He later, in fact, claimed that the two Hailsham letters had given him the idea of writing his book (PRO, Cab. 21/2676, L to Sir Edward Bridges, Secretary to the Cabinet, 3.2.39).

160. On the crisis which had prompted the government reshuffle, and its implications, see Karl-Heinz Janßen and Fritz Tobias, *Der Sturz der Generäle. Hitler und die Blomberg-Fritsch-Krise 1938*, Munich, 1994; and Kershaw, *Hitler, 1936–1945: Nemesis*, pp. 51–60.

161. PRONI, D/3099/2/21/A/19, L to J. L. Garvin, 5.2.38.

162. *Ourselves*, pp. 159–60.

163. See Avon, chs. 12, 14; Halifax, pp. 193–5; Feiling, pp. 336–9; Maurice Cowling *The Impact of Hitler. British Politics and British Policy,*

1933–1940, Cambridge, 1975, pp. 166–76; Parker, pp. 114–23; Dutton, pp. 45–7; Roberts, pp. 82–5; Mowat, pp. 594–9; A. J. P. Taylor, *English History, 1914–1945*, Harmondsworth, 1970, pp. 517–19.

164. Even the War Minister, Duff Cooper, normally a supporter of Eden and regretful about his resignation, approved the move towards better relations with Italy (Duff Cooper, *Old Men Forget*, London, 1953, pp. 211–14).

165. Churchill, p. 231.

166. PRONI, D/3099/12/23, draft of L's speech in the Foreign Affairs Debate in the House of Lords on 24 February 1938.

167. See Kershaw, *Hitler 1936–1945: Nemesis*, pp. 69–72.

168. *Hitler. Reden und Proklamationen*, p. 801.

169. *Ourselves*, p. 162.

5 Hope at Last

1. Ribbentrop gave every appearance of being taken aback when the news of the Anschluss was broken to him while he was attending his farewell lunch as Ambassador in London. Lord Halifax was convinced that he was in the dark about the events, or was 'a most successful and barefaced liar in concealing his knowledge of it' (Viscount Templewood, *Nine Troubled Years*, London, 1954, p. 282).

2. Ian Kershaw, *Hitler, 1936–1945: Nemesis*, London, 2000, p. 74 (and pp. 65–86 for the events leading up to and accompanying the Anschluss).

3. Nevile Henderson, *Failure of a Mission. Berlin 1937–1939*, London, 1940, pp. 114–15; DBFP, 2/XIX, nos. 512, 514, 609–12, 614–15; DGFP, D/I, no. 138, pp. 240–49. On the colonial question (p. 247), Hitler told Henderson that Germany was primarily interested in the disposition of her former colonies, but he realized that the problem was not yet ripe for a settlement, which could be deferred for as long as ten years. See also Peter Neville, *Appeasing Hitler. The Diplomacy of Sir Nevile Henderson, 1937–39*, London, 2000, pp. 51–3.

4. *DGFP*, D/I, nos. 150–51, pp. 273–5, quotation, p. 273. Speaking privately with Ribbentrop after lunch on 11 March, Chamberlain expressly asked the German Foreign Minister (p. 276) to tell Hitler that 'it had always been his desire to clear up German-British relations' and that 'he had now made up his mind to realize this aim'. Ribbentrop was convinced of his sincerity in this. See also Michael Bloch, *Ribbentrop*, London, 1994, p. 172.

5. On the Cabinet's deliberations immediately following the German entry into Austria, see Ian Colvin, *The Chamberlain Cabinet*, London, 1971, pp. 104ff.

6. Henderson, pp. 123–7.

7. Cited in R. A. C. Parker, *Chamberlain and Appeasement. British Policy and the Coming of the Second World War*, London, 1993, p. 133.

8. Cited in Parker, p. 134.

9. Cited in Keith Middlemas, *The Diplomacy of Illusion. The British Government and Germany, 1937–39*, London, 1972, p. 188; also in Keith Feiling, *The Life of Neville Chamberlain*, London, 1946, pp. 347–8, and Margaret George, *The Warped Vision. British Foreign Policy 1933–1939*, Pittsburgh, 1965, p. 184. Whereas Feiling, sympathetic to Chamberlain, sweeps rapidly past the reactions to the Anschluss, George, scathingly critical of the Prime Minister's appeasement policy, emphasizes that the lesson he took from Austria was the need to reinforce his reliance on appeasement (p. 183).

10. *Ourselves*, pp. 178–84, quotation p. 178.

11. *Ourselves*, p. 162.

12. *Ourselves*, p. 180.

13. *Ourselves*, p. 182.

14. *Ourselves*, pp. 180–81.

15. *The Times*, 17.3.38.

16. *The Diplomatic Diaries of Oliver Harvey, 1937–1940*, ed. John Harvey, London, 1970, p. 118 (16.3.38). Oliver Harvey was Principal Private Secretary to the Foreign Secretary, since 20 February 1938 Lord Halifax, and politically close to the former Foreign Secretary, Anthony Eden.

17. *Hitler. Reden und Proklamationen 1932–1945*, ed. Max Domarus, Wiesbaden, 1973, p. 824.

18. *Ourselves*, pp. 181–2 (and pp. 179–80: 'a large proportion of the Austrian population').

19. See Kershaw, pp. 81–2. Perceptive contemporaries realized what had happened. A British observer wrote to Churchill on 18 March, telling him that 'many hundreds of lorry-loads of NS supporters from Graz and Linz were brought into Vienna, to make it a hell hot enough to hold the Führer' (Martin Gilbert, *Winston S. Churchill, Vol. V, 1922–1939*, London, 1976, p. 924, and n. 2).

20. Kershaw, p. 868, n. 95, provides the estimates of Nazi support, which some experts put as low as 25 per cent.

21. See, for example, PRONI, D/3099/2/19/70, L to Comtess de la Feld, 23.3.38: 'The people of this country certainly have been thoroughly shocked, and the growing sympathy with Germany has received a check.'

22. *Ourselves*, p. 184.

23. See Gilbert, p. 921.

24. *Ourselves*, p. 184.

25. Draft comment on Churchill's article in the *Evening Standard* of 18.3.38 in PRONI, D/3099/12/23.

26. PRO, FO 800/313, fols. 52–3, L to Halifax, 30.3.38; also D/3099/2/18/35.

27. R. A. C. Parker, *Churchill and Appeasement*, London, 2000, p. 152, citing Chamberlain's comments to the Foreign Policy Committee on 18 March 1938.

28. PRONI, D/3084/C/C/6/15 contains copies of largely positive reviews in the *Observer, The Sunday Times*, the *Daily Mail* and the *Daily Telegraph*.

29. Politisches Archiv des Auswärtigen Amtes, Berlin, R102777, fol. 040905, Otto Meissner, Chef des Präsidialkanzlei des Führers und Reichskanzlers, to the Auswärtiges Amt, 11.4.38.

30. PRONI, D/3099/2/16/19, L to Hitler, 5.4.38. Londonderry's letter was forwarded by the Foreign Ministry to the Reich Chancellery on 21 April, together with a translation. Hitler stated his intention to answer it personally (Bundesarchiv Berlin/Lichterfelde, R43II/1436, fols. 154–66). Hitler's brief letter of 30 April thanked Londonderry for the understanding he had always shown for 'his work' and expressed his conviction that an understanding between Germany and Britain would provide the most secure basis for a lasting peace. This letter (of which apparently no copy exists among Londonderry's papers) was far shorter than the three-page draft, itself amended from an earlier draft, probably prepared by Fritz Wiedemann in Hitler's adjutancy, criticizing the British press and casting doubt on whether a further visit by Londonderry to Germany in the immediate future would contribute anything substantial to an Anglo-German understanding (Bundesarchiv Berlin/Lichterfelde, NS/10/362, fols. 109–122).

31. Politisches Archiv des Auswärtigen Amtes, Berlin, R102777, fol. 040906, Hitler to L, 10.4.38 (PRONI, D/3084/C/C/6/36, has a photocopied translation) and note that his copy is being sent to the Foreign Ministry. Mussolini, on the other hand, so the Italian Ambassador in London, Count Grandi, said, had 'read the volume with great interest, and has warmly appreciated your kind thought and cordial expressions' (D/3099/2/21/A/30, Grandi to L, 14.4.38).

32. PRONI, D/3084/C/C/6/13, L to Dr Ernst Woermann, German Embassy, 31.3.38, sends copies of his book to be forwarded 'by the first available bag, for presentation to The Führer, Herr von Ribbentrop, Field-Marshal Göring and Herr von Papen respectively'. They were sent on that same day to Berlin (Politisches Archiv des Auswärtigen Amtes, Berlin, R102777, fol. 040893, Woermann to Legationsrat von Bieberstein at the Auswärtiges Amt, 31.3.38).

33. PRONI, D/3084/C/C/6/36, translation of Göring to L, 30.5.38; *Ourselves*, p. 174.

34. PRONI, D/3099/2/19/56, L to Ribbentrop, 17.2.38.

35. PRONI, D/3099/2/19/80, von Papen to L, 17.4.38.

36. *WSC*, V/3, pp. 1035–6, Churchill to L, 21.5.38.

37. PRONI, D/3099/2/21/A/43, Allen to L, 10.5.38; King's College, London, Liddell Hart Centre for Military Archives, Hamilton Papers, 14/2/10, L to Hamilton, 9.8.38 and Hamilton to L, 17.8.38.

38. *The Diaries of Sir Robert Bruce Lockhart, Vol. 1, 1915–1938*, ed. Kenneth Young, London, 1973, p. 390 (5.4.38).

39. PRONI, D/3099/2/21/A/27A (also PRO, FO 800/313, fols. 110–17), Rumbold to L, 12.4.38.

40. PRO, FO 800/313, fol. 109 (and PRONI, D/3099/2/18/36), L to Halifax, 26.4.38.

41. PRONI, D/3099/2/18/37, Halifax to L, 2.5.38 (and Halifax's draft reply in PRO, FO 800/313, fol. 109).

42. The files PRONI, D/3099/2/21A and D/3084/C/C/6 contain several hundred letters, a good number of them relating to Londonderry's book. A selection of responses, including the letters from Hitler, Göring and von Papen, was included as an appendix to the second (Penguin) edition of *Ourselves*, Harmondsworth, 1938 (henceforth *Ourselves* II), pp. 166–83.

43. PRONI, D/3084/C/C/6, 17, Anon. to L, n.d., probably April 1938.

44. *Ourselves*, pp. 111–12.

45. *Ourselves*, pp. 169–71. This commonplace of Nazi propaganda was widely used by anti-Semites and German sympathizers in Britain and elsewhere to justify the persecution of the Jews by Hitler's regime. For instance, one of a number of letters sent to the German Foreign Ministry by Sir Raymond Beazley, the former Professor of Modern History at Birmingham University, and prominent member of the pro-German 'Link' organization, quoted figures of 85 per cent of lawyers, 80 per cent of newspapers, and 75 per cent of banks as Jewish, to demonstrate how Jews try 'to get everything into their hands' (Politisches Archiv des Auswärtigen Amtes, Berlin, R102778, fol. 38275). In fact, 17 per cent of lawyers, 11 per cent of doctors and 5 per cent of editors and writers were Jewish in 1933, according to official statistics (*Nazism, 1919–1945, a Documentary Reader*, eds. Jeremy Noakes and Geoffrey Pridham, vol. 2, Exeter, 1984, p. 522). The figures, of course, only in any case had relevance to those with an existing prejudice.

46. PRONI, D/3099/2/21/A/22A, Anthony Rothschild to L, 8.4.38.

47. PRONI, D/3099/2/21/A/24A, L to Anthony Rothschild, 11.4.38. Similar

views to those which he expressed privately to Rothschild were publicly presented in the Marquess of Londonderry, 'My Attitude towards the Jews', *Query, Book No. 2, 'The Jews'*, London, 1938, p. 61.

48. PRONI, D/3099/2/21/A/25A, Anthony Rothschild to L, 12.4.38.

49. PRONI, D/3099/2/21/A/28A, L to Anthony Rothschild, 13.4.38.

50. PRONI, D/3099/2/21/A/29 and 32, exchange between Lord Londonderry's secretary and Mrs Gladys M. Hirsch, 14.4.38 and 18.4.38. Mrs Hirsch had initially queried Londonderry's published remarks in a letter of 6 April 1938 (D/3099/2/21/A/1).

51. PRONI, D/3099/4/56, L to Herbert Hensley Henson, who had been Bishop of Durham between 1920 and 1939, 6.1.40.

52. The sentiment was expressed in a number of letters, such as that of 3 May to his Danzig contact, Professor Noé (PRONI, D/3099/2/21/A/42).

53. King's College London, Liddell Hart Centre for Military Archives, Hamilton Papers, Hamilton 14/2/10, L to Hamilton, 9.8.38.

54. PRONI, D/3099/2/19/108A, L to Göring, 9.7.38; *Wings*, p. 200. Londonderry said he had so far been able to answer his critics, who thought him wrong in his assertions of Germany's desire for peace and cooperation, 'with assurance and conviction on all points which they have raised, but when I am asked now as to the meaning of German policy in relation to the Jews, I can find no answer whatever that satisfies me.' He remarked that he had read speeches by Julius Streicher, the Jew-baiting Gauleiter of Franconia, 'with amazement' and wondered 'whether he speaks with full authority when he gives vent to such surprising doctrines'. See also Londonderry's letter of 25.8.38 to F. W. Pick (a German living in Britain who prepared the German translation of *Ourselves*) that he was now having difficulties in explaining German policy on the Jews (PRONI, D/3099/2/21/A/73).

55. *Ourselves*, pp. 171–2.

56. PRONI, D/3099/2/19/53, L to Ribbentrop, 20.1.38.

57. PRONI, D/3099/2/19/111, note of telephone call from Miss Livingstone, 15.7.38.

58. PRONI, D/3099/2/21/A/70, L to Sir James Marchant, 17.8.38.

59. Information from Lady Mairi Bury, 9.10.03. Lady Londonderry had referred to her stay in the Tyrol with Lady Mairi, mentioning one of the guides who was to be arrested three years later, in letters to her husband on 5.2.35 and 4.4.35 (PRONI, D/3099/13/2/1330, 1332).

60. PRONI, D/3099/3/35/33, Lady L to Ribbentrop, 19.3.38 (handwritten draft). Lady Londonderry showed a profound ignorance of recent German history in expressing the vain hope 'that Austria will not be treated in the

very harsh manner that was necessary in Germany, where there had been a Communist revolution'. Lady Londonderry had written to Göring on 15 March to protest about the arrest of the guides. In an otherwise uncompromising reply (D/30999/3/35/34A), Göring had nevertheless agreed to look into the matter. The *Evening Standard*, 1.4.38 (in D/3099/10/49) recorded the release of the guides. And see Anne de Courcy, *Circe. The Life of Edith, Marchioness of Londonderry*, London, 1992, p. 286.

61. PRONI, D/3099/2/4/125, L to Viscount Cecil of Chelwood (founder of the League of Nations Union), 2.5.38.

62. *DGFP*, D/II, no. 221, p. 358. And see no. 282 for Hitler's 'General Strategic Directive' for an attack on Czechoslovakia, dated 18 June 1938.

63. For a fuller description of German policy towards Czechoslovakia in summer 1938, see Kershaw, pp. 87ff.

64. See Peter Hoffmann, *Widerstand, Staatsstreich, Attentat. Der Kampf der Opposition gegen Hitler*, 4th edn, Munich, 1985, ch. 4; and Terry Parssinen, *The Oster Conspiracy of 1938*, New York, 2003.

65. See Ronald Smelser, *The Sudeten Problem, 1933–1938. Volkstumspolitik and the Formulation of Nazi Foreign Policy*, Folkestone, 1975.

66. *DBFP*, 3/1, nos. 250, 264, pp. 332–3, 341. And, for the May Crisis, see Gerhard L. Weinberg, *The Foreign Policy of Hitler's Germany. Starting World War II, 1937–1939*, Chicago/London, 1980, pp. 366–70; Gerhard L. Weinberg, 'The May Crisis, 1938', *Journal of Modern History*, 29 (1957), pp. 213–25; and Donald Cameron Watt, 'Hitler's Visit to Rome and the May Weekend Crisis: A Study in Hitler's Response to External Stimuli', *Journal of Contemporary History*, 9 (1974), pp. 23–32. The British government's reactions are summarized in Colvin, pp. 127–34.

67. Duff Cooper, *Old Men Forget*, London, 1953, pp. 215–17.

68. Cited in Gilbert, p. 716. The remark was later made famous in 'Cato', *Guilty Men*, London, 1940, as the title of chapter 12 ('Caligula's Horse').

69. Cited in Andrew Roberts, *'The Holy Fox'. The Life of Lord Halifax*, paperback edn, London, 1997, p. 93.

70. Middlemas, pp. 242–3.

71. C. L. Mowat, *Britain between the Wars 1918–1940*, London, 1956, p. 604.

72. Parker, *Chamberlain and Appeasement*, p. 145.

73. Cited in Parker, *Chamberlain and Appeasement*, p. 140.

74. Chamberlain's comment in the House of Commons on 4 April 1938, cited in Mowat, p. 604. Chamberlain was reacting to a call from the Labour movement for a common stand against aggression by Britain, France, and

the Soviet Union. Among the governing Conservatives, even among critics of the government, there was no pressure for overtures to the Soviet Union before Munich (Neville Thompson, *The Anti-Appeasers. Conservative Opposition to Appeasement in the 1930s*, Oxford, 1971, p. 49). On the contrary, antipathy to the Soviet regime, not just on the extreme Right, underpinned aversion to any suggestion of a pact with the USSR. See, for such a view, Richard Griffiths, *Fellow Travellers of the Right. British Enthusiasts for Nazi Germany 1933–39*, Oxford, 1983, pp. 298–9. In practice, the Soviet Union took no steps to prepare for military action in the event of war over Czechoslovakia. Soviet forces could, in any case, only have reached Czechoslovakia by passage through Poland or Rumania, neither of which countries would have been happy to grant such passage.

75. See Thompson, p. 43, referring to the Conservative Party: 'With only slight exaggeration it might be said that there were no anti-appeasers before Munich.' Beyond the political interest in avoiding conflict with Germany lay also significant economic concerns over growing German dominance in south-eastern Europe and the need to reach an economic arrangement which would help to remove obstacles to foreign trade and reintegrate Germany in the international economy. For an emphasis on this aspect of appeasement, see Bernd-Jürgen Wendt, *Economic Appeasement. Handel und Finanz in der britischen Deutschland-Politik 1933–1939*, Düsseldorf, 1971, here esp. pp. 418ff, and Bernd-Jürgen Wendt, *Appeasement 1938. Wirtschaftliche Rezession und Mitteleuropa*, Frankfurt am Main, 1966.

76. *The Diaries of Sir Alexander Cadogan, 1938–1945*, ed. David Dilks, London, 1971, p. 71 (25.4.38), where Cadogan commented that the 'parrot-cry of "Rearmament" is mere confession of failure of foreign policy', and p. 73 (29.4.38).

77. *The Aeroplane*, 29.6.38, extract in PRONI, D/3099/10/49.

78. *The Diplomatic Diaries of Oliver Harvey, 1937–1940*, p. 153 (14.6.38).

79. PRONI, D/3099/2/19/96: Oberführer Görnnert, Göring's adjutant, writing on 15 June 1938, thanked Londonderry for his letter and stated that the Generalfeldmarschall would be glad to see him, his wife, and daughter, at the conference. (D/3099/2/19/95 is a translation.)

80. PRO, FO 371/21657, fols. 208–9, Halifax's minute for Vansittart, 20.6.38.

81. PRONI, D/3099/2/19/108A, L to Göring, 9.7.38; *Wings*, pp. 199–200.

82. PRO, FO 800/313, fols. 149–51, L to Halifax, 28.6.38.

83. Lord Hailsham, the Lord President of the Council, reported to the Cabinet that Londonderry 'had found Field-Marshal Goering somewhat worried about the position in Germany, as well as about the Austrian

situation, and did not want the inclusion of a Czechoslovak population in the German Reich' (PRO, Cab. 23/93, fol. 64). The claim that Germany had no interest in the incorporation of non-ethnic Germans in the Reich was part of the propaganda depiction of German demands as purely nationalist in nature and confined to the 'protection' of the Sudeten Germans. Hitler was to make the same claim in his major speech in Berlin just prior to the Munich Conference (Kershaw, p. 117).

84. PRONI, D/3099/2/18/39, L to Halifax, 20.7.38.

85. Cited in Griffiths, pp. 298–9.

86. Cited in Parker, *Chamberlain and Appeasement*, p. 150.

87. Henderson, p. 143.

88. Bundesarchiv Berlin/Lichterfelde, R43II/1436, fols. 210–15v, German Embassy to the Foreign Ministry, 'Der gegenwärtige Stand der deutsch-englischen Beziehungen', 18.7.38. A copy was sent some weeks later direct to Hitler. Another, slightly different, copy of the memorandum, bearing the wrong date of 10 July 1938, found its way from the Foreign Ministry archives into Soviet hands and was published after the war in English translation in the collection *Documents and Materials Relating to the Eve of the Second World War, Vol. 1, November 1937–1938*, Moscow, 1948, pp. 122–33.

89. See Kershaw, pp. 103–7; and Stefan Martens, *Hermann Göring. 'Erster Paladin des Führers' und 'Zweiter Mann im Reich'*, Paderborn, 1985, pp. 140–42.

90. PRONI, D/3099/3/15/40, Chamberlain to Lady L, 20.9.38. Chamberlain had been handed a copy of Göring's letter on 9 September (Martens, p. 319, n. 343, though there is no record of Londonderry sending the letter direct to Chamberlain, as Martens presumes; it was probably passed to the Prime Minister by Lord Halifax). Londonderry was thus mistaken in later claiming (*Wings*, p. 204, n. 1) that the letter had presumably been 'pigeon-holed' by the Foreign Office, suggesting he knew 'for a fact that Chamberlain never saw it until I sent Sir Horace Wilson a copy just before he went to Munich'.

91. PRONI, D/3099/2/19/115, L to Göring, 17.7.38. The German version was published as *England blickt auf Deutschland*, Essen, 1938. The translator, F. W. Pick, a German living in England, told Londonderry on 22 August, before the receipt of Göring's letter, that there were no longer any difficulties about the German version (D/3099/2/21/A/72, Pick to L, 22.8.38; also D/3099/2/21/A/76–7, exchange Pick and L, 10. and 15.9.38).

92. When it appeared, the dustjacket warned German readers that some of Londonderry's assessments were necessarily to be rejected, but recommended nevertheless 'such words as have hitherto never been spoken

about the new Germany by a truly prominent Englishman' (PRONI, D/3099/2/21/A/278).

93. Martens, p. 140.

94. PRONI, D/3099/2/19/118B, Göring to L (transl.), 23.8.38. Part of the original German letter is (apparently misfiled) in D/3099/2/16/60. Londonderry later remarked that the letter represented a full description of Göring's point of view, and that he had no thoughts of challenging Great Britain or of seeking to acquire 'world domination' (*Wings*, pp. 189–90, and pp. 200–204 for extracts from the letter).

95. PRONI, D/3099/2/18/40, Halifax to L, 6.9.38; PRO, FO 800/314, fols. 100–102v, L to Halifax, 1.9.38 (with Halifax's cover note of 6.9.38); FO 371/21736, fols. 29–38, Foreign Office memoranda and copy of Göring's letter to Henderson.

96. Mowat, p. 607; Middlemas, p. 323.

97. *The Times*, 7.9.38; and see *The Times and Appeasement. The Journals of A.L. Kennedy, 1932–1939*, ed. Gordon Martel, Camden Society Fifth Series, vol. 16, Cambridge, 2000, pp. 276–8. Other British newspapers, however, indicated a readiness to fight for Czechoslovakia – see Middlemas, pp. 323–4.

98. Parker, *Chamberlain and Appeasement*, pp. 154–61. Of the innumerable, often excellent, accounts of the events leading up to Munich, the following draws mainly on the particularly lucid description of policy decisions in the British Cabinet by Parker, *Chamberlain and Appeasement*, chs. 7–8 and the more detailed examination by Middlemas, chs. 12–13.

99. Parker, *Chamberlain and Appeasement*, p. 160; *Hitler. Reden und Proklamationen*, pp. 900–905 (for Hitler's speech); Henderson, p. 147 (for the impact of Hitler's speech).

100. Feiling, pp. 365–8; Parker, *Chamberlain and Appeasement*, pp. 163–4; Kershaw, pp. 110–12.

101. Parker, *Chamberlain and Appeasement*, pp. 169–70.

102. PRONI, D/3099/2/19/123A, L to Göring, 17.9.38.

103. Parker, *Chamberlain and Appeasement*, pp. 170–78; Middlemas, pp. 370ff; Roberts, pp. 114ff; Colvin, pp. 163–4; John Charmley, *Neville Chamberlain and the Lost Peace*, (1989) paperback edn, London, 1991, pp. 123–5.

104. *Chips. The Diaries of Sir Henry Channon*, ed. Robert Rhodes James, London, 1967, p. 171 (28.9.38).

105. Viscount Simon, *Retrospect*, London, 1952, p. 247.

106. Templewood, p. 319.

107. John F. Naylor, *Labour's International Policy. The Labour Party in the 1930s*, London, 1969, pp. 247–9.

108. Feiling, p. 374.

109. Parker, *Chamberlain and Appeasement*, pp. 178–81; Charmley, pp. 136–41. Chamberlain, to the astonishment of many who heard him, admitted in his speech to the House of Commons on 6 October that his famous phrase had been uttered 'in a moment of some emotion, after a long and exhausting day' (Parker, *Chamberlain and Appeasement*, p. 184; Harold Nicolson, *Diaries and Letters 1930–1964*, edited and condensed by Stanley Olson, New York, 1980, p. 140 (6.10.38)).

110. 'Cato', *Guilty Men*. For the lasting impact of the polemic on Chamberlain's reputation, see David Dutton, *Neville Chamberlain*, London, 2001, ch. 3.

111. Middlemas, p. 370.

112. Chamberlain's description in a letter to his sister, cited in Middlemas, p. 404.

113. Cited in Mowat, p. 619.

114. Feiling, pp. 378–82; Parker, *Chamberlain and Appeasement*, p. 182 (who has 20,000 letters and telegrams).

115. Middlemas, p. 416; see Cooper, ch. 14, for his own account of his resignation, and its background.

116. See Charmley, p. 145. Based upon an examination of grass-roots Conservatives, it has been suggested that unease at appeasement policy was more widespread than once thought following Munich. On the other hand, less than a tenth of the Parliamentary Conservative Party was estimated to be opposed to Chamberlain (N. J. Crowson, *Facing Fascism: the Conservative Party and the European Dictators 1935–40*, London, 1997, pp. 119–20).

117. Cited in Mowat, p. 620.

118. King's College London, Liddell Hart Centre for Military Archives, Hamilton Papers, 14/2/12, 'The Link' flyer (first quotation) and C. E. Carroll to Hamilton, 4.10.38 (second quotation) seeking – in vain – his signature for 'The Link' letter to be sent to *The Times* (and published on 12.10.38). See also Griffiths, pp. 304–5 and, for 'The Link' more generally, which greatly expanded its membership in 1938, pp. 307–17, together with Simon Haxey, *Tory M.P.*, London, 1939, pp. 203–6. The files kept by MI5 on 'The Link', and its founder Sir Barry Domvile, are available as PRO, KV5/2 and KV2/834. 'The Link' was not regarded by the Nazi regime with anything like the interest which had initially been bestowed upon the Anglo-German Fellowship. By early 1939, the more extreme members of the Anglo-German Fellowship, which had disappointed its Nazi sponsors, were said to have transferred to 'The Link' (PRO, KV 5/3, MI5 agent's report on the 'Anglo-German Fellowship and the Link', 17.2.39).

119. Griffiths, p. 308.

120. PRONI, D/3084/C/C/6/4, C. E. Carroll to L, 26.2.38.

121. *The Times*, 12.10.38; Griffiths, pp. 329–30.

122. PRONI, D/3099/2/17/33A, L to Baldwin, 19.12.38.

123. PRONI, D/3099/10/49, extracts from *Belfast News-Letter*, 1.10.38; *Newcastle Journal*, 11.10.38; *Sunderland Echo*, 11.10.38; D/3099/10/51, *Sunday Dispatch*, 14.1.40, 'I Answer My Critics'; *Wings*, pp. 208–9.

124. In a private letter in mid-October, Londonderry claimed he was the reverse of pro-Nazi – presumably, then, anti-Nazi – and that he objected to dictatorship in all its forms. However, he went on to voice his recognition 'that the Dictatorship in Germany has achieved remarkable results in the last five years' (PRONI, D/3099/2/21/A/100, L to Leslie Gardner, 17.10.38).

125. *Ourselves* II, pp. xi, xiii, 164.

126. PRONI, D/3099/2/21/A/80, L to Editor of *The Times*, 2.10.38; *The Times*, 3.10.38.

127. PRONI, D/3099/2/19/133, L to James Andrews, Lord Chief Justice of Northern Ireland, 1.10.38; D/3099/2/19/138, L to the Duke of Westminster, 4.10.38; D/3099/2/21/A/83A, L to Karl Silex, Chefredakteur of the *Deutsche Allgemeine Zeitung* (whom he had met in Munich), 4.10.38.

128. PRONI, D/3099/2/21/A/97, L to Robert V. Harcourt (a former MP who had been in the House of Commons together with Londonderry before the First World War), 14.10.38.

129. PRONI, D/3099/2/21/A/85, L to H. Montgomery Hyde, 9.10.38. Londonderry's repetition of his 'prophetic' perception was linked in his own mind, as always, to his letters to Lord Hailsham in November 1934. When sending a copy of the first edition of his book to one correspondent, three days after he had written to Hyde, Londonderry drew his attention in particular to the paraphrasing of his 1934 letters (D/3099/2/21/A/89, L to Sir Frederick Hamilton, 12.10.38).

130. PRONI, D3099/2/18/54, L to Halifax, 25.12.39.

131. *Wings*, pp. 209–11.

132. *Die Tagebücher von Joseph Goebbels. Teil I, Aufzeichnungen 1923–1941*, ed. Elke Fröhlich, 9 vols., Munich, 1993 – (new edition), part 1, vol. 6, p. 129 (5.10.38).

6 End of the Dream

1. See for such opinion Richard Griffiths, *Fellow Travellers of the Right. British Enthusiasts for Nazi Germany 1933–39*, Oxford, 1983, chs. 10–12 and, specifically for 'The Link', pp. 307–17.

2. PRONI, D/3099/2/21/A/114, L to W. A. Chaplin, 29.10.38.

3. PRONI, D/3099/2/21/A/113, L to A. L. Kennedy, 29.10.38. Londonderry's characteristic sense of an affront to his standing recurs in his complaints to Kennedy that he was being ignored by *The Times* or even 'insulted' since a letter of his had been placed in the newspaper only after two letters of 'comparatively newly-made Peers' even though he himself had at one time been Leader of the House of Lords (D/3099/2/21/A/121, L to Kennedy, 5.11.38). Kennedy shared many of Londonderry's views on relations with Germany at this time (see D/3099/2/21/A, A. L. Kennedy to L, 30.10.38, and *The Times and Appeasement. The Journals of A. L. Kennedy, 1932–1939*, ed. Gordon Martel, Camden Society Fifth Series, vol. 16, Cambridge, 2000, pp. 279–80).

4. PRONI, D/3099/2/21/A/114, L to W. A. Chaplin, 29.10.38.

5. PRONI, D/3099/2/21/A/123, L to A. L. Kennedy, 9.11.38; the last phrase is taken from D/3099/2/19/156, L to Bishop of London, 29.10.38.

6. PRONI, D/3099/2/21/A/114, L to W. A. Chaplin, 29.10.38.

7. PRONI, D/3099/2/21/A/122, L to Rev. Philip Houghton, 9.11.38.

8. PRONI, D/3099/2/21/A/114, L to W. A. Chaplin, 29.10.38.

9. PRONI, D/3099/2/18/54, L to Halifax, 25.12.39.

10. WSC, V/3, pp. 1250–51, L to Churchill, 31.10.38

11. PRONI, D/3099/2/5/33B–33C, Churchill to L, 5.11.38; printed in *WSC*, V/3, p. 1256.

12. PRONI, D/3099/2/19/167 (and D/3099/2/5/34), L to Churchill, 10.11.38. The quoted passage is also printed in *WSC*, V/3, p. 1272, n. 1.

13. PRONI, D/3099/2/5/35A–B, Churchill to L, 12.11.38, printed in *WSC*, V/3, p. 1272. Londonderry's last letter in this exchange contained nothing new, other than his – somewhat belated – expression of regret that Churchill had not been made Minister of Defence at the time that Sir Thomas Inskip had been appointed in 1936 (D/3099/2/5/37A–B, L to Churchill, 14.11.38, printed in *WSC*, V/3, p. 1275). Churchill's last letter in the sequence was a mere few lines of politeness, saying he was glad to learn that they were after all in 'full accord' on several points on which he had thought they were at variance (D/3099/2/5/38A–B, Churchill to L, 18.11.38).

14. Cited in Lionel Kochan, *Pogrom. 10 November 1938*, London, 1957, p. 125.

15. F. R. Gannon, *The British Press and Germany, 1936–1939*, Oxford, 1971, p. 226.

16. Cited in Rita Thalmann and Emmanuel Feinermann, *Crystal Night. 9–10 November 1938*, London, 1974, p. 147.

17. Cited in Kochan, p. 141.

18. PRO, FO 371/21637, Ref. C13733/1667/62, Ogilvie-Forbes to Halifax, 13.11.38; also cited in Peter Neville, *Appeasing Hitler. The Diplomacy of Sir Nevile Henderson 1937-39*, London, 2000, p. 126. As Neville points out (p. 127), the most powerful civil servant at the Foreign Office, the Under-Secretary of State, Sir Alexander Cadogan, was apparently so little moved by such reports that he did not refer to the pogroms at all in his diary entries for November 1938.

19. Andrew Roberts, '*The Holy Fox*'. *The Life of Lord Halifax*, London, 1991, paperback edn, 1997, pp. 128-9. Halifax did not refer to 'Crystal Night' in his bland memoirs, *Fulness of Days*, London, 1957.

20. Cited in Roberts, p. 129. And see Donald Cameron Watt, *How War Came. The Immediate Origins of the Second World War, 1938-1939*, paperback edn, London, 1991, p. 89.

21. Neville, p. 126. The point, made by Neville, p. 127, that Henderson was away from Berlin and therefore may not have realized the full magnitude of what had taken place, seems weak, given the extensive press coverage and condemnation. However, he correctly draws attention to Henderson's own outright denunciation of the Nazi action in his memoirs (Sir Nevile Henderson, *Failure of a Mission. Berlin 1937-1939*, London, 1940, pp. 172-3, 181).

22. Cited in John Charmley, *Neville Chamberlain and the Lost Peace*, paperback edn., London, 1991, p. 148; and see Watt p. 90.

23. Watt, p. 89; Keith Feiling, *The Life of Neville Chamberlain*, London, 1946, p. 390. Chamberlain's reaction to the pogroms of November 1938 merits only the briefest mention in Feiling's lengthy biography. But Feiling does mention Chamberlain refusing an intivation to accept the honorary presidency of the Deutsche-Shakespeare-Genossenschaft on the grounds, it seems, that the learned society had expelled its Jewish members.

24. Cited in Kochan, p. 140.

25. Louise London, *Whitehall and the Jews, 1933-1948*, Cambridge, 2000, p. 107. For the British government's reaction to the refugee crisis following the pogrom, see also Andrew Sharf, *The British Press and Jews under Nazi Rule*, Oxford, 1964, pp. 171ff.

26. Kochan, pp. 140, 142.

27. Roberts, p. 129; London, p. 99.

28. Feiling, p. 392.

29. Watt, p. 91; Feiling, p. 390.

30. Cited in Charmley, p. 148.

31. Eight Parliamentary by-elections in the autumn of 1938, with recriminations over Munich at their height, showed a fall in support for the

government. Two of the by-elections were lost by the government, the remainder held with an average swing of almost 6 per cent against the government (Keith Middlemas, *The Diplomacy of Illusion. The British Government and Germany 1937–39*, London, 1972, pp. 417; R. A. C. Parker, *Chamberlain and Appeasement. British Policy and the Coming of the Second World War*, London, 1993, pp. 189–90).

32. *DGFP*, D/IV, no. 269, pp. 333–4, Dirksen to German Foreign Ministry, 17.11.38; Kochan, p. 143; Watt, p. 89.

33. *The Diaries of Sir Alexander Cadogan, 1938–1945*, ed. David Dilks, London, 1971, p. 125.

34. Cited in Feiling, p. 392.

35. *Daily Telegraph*, 19.11.38; Simon Haxey, *Tory M.P.*, London, 1939, p. 198, no. 2; Robert Benewick, *The Fascist Movement in Britain*, London, 1972, p. 290.

36. PRO, KV5/3, MI5 Agent's report, 23.11.38, indicating the disastrous effect of 'Crystal Night' on the Anglo-German Fellowship. Griffiths, pp. 339–40, relying upon Haxey, p. 198, no. 2, has only twenty out of 900 members resigning. There was no protest statement. From the MI5 reports, the number of resignations seems too low, and the size of the membership too high. Internal records indicated around 600 members towards the end of 1937. It seems unlikely that there had been such a large influx during 1938.

37. PRONI, D/3099/2/21/A, 136, L to Arnold Thompson Esq., 25.11.38.

38. PRONI, D/3099/192/19/176, L to Douglas Veale, University Registry, Oxford, 17.11.38.

39. *The Times*, 14.12.38, also in PRONI, D/3099/10/49 (together with other newspaper extracts of the same speech). The speech, to the Overseas League, was also reported abroad. See extracts from the *Natal Mercury*, Durban, and the *Cape Times*, Cape Town, both of 14.12.38, in D/3099/10/51.

40. PRONI, D/3099/2/19/184A, L to Göring, 24.11.38.

41. PRONI, D/3099/192/217A, Göring to L, 9.1.39 (in German). A translation was provided by the Privy Council Office, which added its own gloss (D/3099/2/19/222). Londonderry wrote again to Göring a few days later, acceding to a request from Oxford University's registry to intervene on behalf of a German national who had been taken into custody, but received, several months later, a lapidary note from Göring's office that he was unable to comply with the request (D/3099/2/19/244, 294, L to Göring, 13.1.39; Ministerialdirektor Dr Erich Gritzbach to L, 17.5.39).

42. See Griffiths p. 343.

43. DRO, D/LO/C237, Henderson to L, 12.12.38 (wrongly catalogued as 12.12.37). 'Had y[ou]r views held the field two or three years ago',

Henderson had remarked, 'it w[ou]ld have been all so much easier. It makes one weep to see all the good cards we have thrown away & how badly we have played our hand.'

44. PRONI, D/3099/2/21/A/137A, L to Duke of Windsor, 26.11.38. The letter, written in an ingratiating tone, accompanied the copy of the second edition of *Ourselves* which he was sending to the Duke.

45. PRONI, D/3099/2/21/A/140, L to Hoare, 29.11.38.

46. Cambridge UL, Baldwin Papers, Baldwin 171, fols. 178–91, L to Baldwin, 29.12.38 (copy PRONI, D/3099/2/17/37A); D/3099/2/17/36A–B, Baldwin to L, 24.12.38. Writing to Baldwin, Londonderry claimed once again that he had been right all along in the foreign policy he had advocated, referring to the position he had adumbrated in 1934. This obliquely denoted the letters to Hailsham, written in November that year, which had by now acquired near legendary status in his mind. It was no coincidence that, with these evidently fresh in his thoughts, Londonderry had, four years later almost to the day since writing them, regained the originals from Hailsham (D/3099/2/17/31–2, L to Hailsham, 22.11.38; Hailsham to L, returning the letters, 24.11.38).

47. PRONI, D/3099/2/19/212, 248, Göring to L, 31.12.38; German Embassy to L, 20.2.39, thanking him for the New Year's greetings sent to Hitler.

48. *Belfast Telegraph*, 20.1.39; *The Times*, 21.1.39; extracts from both in PRONI, D/3099/10/51. Londonderry's speech in Belfast on 20 January 1939 gave rise to a further flurry of attacks on his stance on bombing in the early 1930s, entailing another round of his usual defence. See e.g. D/3084/C/C/7/15; D/3084/C/E/6/109.

49. Birmingham UL, Chamberlain Papers, NC/11/32/156, L to Chamberlain, 1.2.39.

50. PRO, Cab. 21/2676, L to E. E. Bridges, Secretary to the Cabinet, 14.2.39; *The Times*, 14.2.39.

51. The German version of Rauschning's book was published in Zurich in 1938. It appeared in English, under the title *Germany's Revolution of Destruction* in June 1939 (quotation from this version, p. 239).

52. PRO, Cab. 21/2676, L to E. E. Bridges, Secretary to the Cabinet, 14.2.39. This letter forms part of a further protracted correspondence with the Cabinet Office about the two letters, to which he attached such importance, that Londonderry had sent to Lord Hailsham in November 1934. We have already noted the failure of Londonderry's attempts in spring 1938 to gain permission for his letters to be printed in *Ourselves*. He now sent Bridges the originals, which Hailsham had recently returned to him, along with a copy

of *Ourselves*. The Cabinet Office, having received the letters, was then keen to retain them as government property. On Londonderry's dogged insistence that they were his private possession, and in a matter of evident irritation to the Cabinet Office, they were eventually returned to him. The business of the Hailsham letters was even now not at an end. It would recur during the war when Londonderry was preparing the publication of *Wings*.

53. *Belfast Telegraph*, 20.1.39, in PRONI, D/3099/10/51.

54. Parker, p. 195. The response of the British press to Hitler's speech was one of cautious optimism (Gannon, pp. 232–3). Hitler's notorious threat, made in this speech, that the Jews of Europe would be destroyed in the event of another war, went unnoticed in the attention given to its significance for the prospects of war or peace. For the passage, and the question of its interpretation in the light of the subsequent genocidal policy of the Nazi regime, see *Hitler. Reden und Proklamationen 1932–1945*, ed. Max Domarus, Wiesbaden, 1973, p. 1058 (translated in *Nazism 1919–1945, a Documentary Reader*, eds. Jeremy Noakes and Geoffrey Pridham, vol. 3, Exeter, 1988, p. 1049); Hans Mommsen, 'Hitler's Reichstag Speech of 30 January 1939', *History and Memory*, 9 (1977), pp. 147–61, here pp. 150–51; and Ian Kershaw, 'Hitler's "Prophecy" and the Final Solution', *Occasional Paper No. 8, The Center for Holocaust Studies at the University of Vermont*, Burlington, Vermont, 2002.

55. Parker, pp. 192–7; see also Charmley, ch. 15.

56. See Ian Kershaw, *Hitler: 1936–1945: Nemesis*, London, 2000, pp. 169–72.

57. Parker, pp. 200–201; Middlemas, p. 439; Roberts, p. 142; A. J. P. Taylor, *English History, 1914–1945*, Harmondsworth, 1970, pp. 538–9; Christopher Hill, *Cabinet Decisions on Foreign Policy. The British Experience October 1938–June 1941*, Cambridge, 1991, p. 20.

58. *The Diaries of Sir Alexander Cadogan*, p. 157 (15.3.39).

59. Cited Charmley, p. 166.

60. Parker, pp. 200–201; Middlemas, p. 439.

61. Cited in *The Diaries of Sir Alexander Cadogan*, p. 157 (editorial note); and see Roberts, p. 142.

62. See Charmley, pp. 167–75.

63. Cited Feiling, p. 400; Parker, p. 202; and Maurice Cowling, *The Impact of Hitler. British Politics and British Policy, 1933–1940*, Cambridge, 1975, pp. 295–6.

64. See Watt, pp. 166–7.

65. *News Chronicle*, 16.3.39, cited in Barbara Benge Kehoe, *The British Press and Nazi Germany*, Ph.D. thesis, University of Illinois at Chicago

Circle, 1980, University Microfilms International, Ann Arbor, 1989, p. 263.

66. *The Times*, 16.3.39.

67. *Chips. The Diaries of Sir Henry Channon*, ed. Robert Rhodes James, London, 1967, p. 186 (15.3.39).

68. *Parliament and Politics in the Age of Churchill and Attlee. The Headlam Diaries 1935–1951*, ed. Stuart Ball, Camden Society Fifth Series, vol. 14, Cambridge, 1999, p. 151 (15.3.39).

69. The gulf between the government's reaction and that of public opinion is emphasized by C. L. Mowat, *Britain between the Wars, 1918–1940*, London, 1955, p. 637.

70. For summaries of the reactions in the British press, see Kehoe, pp. 260ff; and Gannon, pp. 233ff.

71. Harold Nicolson, *Diaries and Letters 1930–1964*, ed. Stanley Olson, New York, 1980, p. 146 (17.3.39).

72. Simon Newman, *March 1939: the British Guarantee to Poland*, Oxford, 1976, pp. 103–4. Newman's book is the most thorough analysis of the background to the guarantee.

73. This has been seen, indeed, as the simplest but most persuasive reason for Chamberlain's change of tone between his weak condemnation of the German aggression on 15 March and his firm defiance on 17 March, in his Birmingham speech (P. M. H. Bell, *The Origins of the Second World War in Europe*, London, 1986, p. 253).

74. Parker, p. 205.

75. Charmley, p. 171.

76. Watt, pp. 169ff; Newman, pp. 107ff. Ian Colvin, *The Chamberlain Cabinet*, London, 1971, pp. 187–98, explores the Cabinet's deliberations in the aftermath of the German takeover in Prague.

77. An indication of Churchill's isolation within his own party is that four out of five backbench Conservative MPs still did not want Churchill in the Cabinet in July 1939 (N. J. Crowson, *Facing Fascism: the Conservative Party and the European Dictators 1935–40*, London, 1997, p. 185).

78. See Kehoe, pp. 263–7.

79. Newman, pp. 142–3.

80. The Soviet perspective on the events following Germany takeover in Prague, and the strong distrust of Chamberlain's motives and policy choices, is provided by the former Ambassador in London, Ivan Maisky, *Who Helped Hitler?*, London, 1964, pp. 102ff. See also, for Soviet foreign policy and the failure of negotiations towards an alliance with Britain, Michael Jabara Carley, *1939: the Alliance that Never Was and the Coming of World War II*, Chicago, 1999.

81. Feiling, p. 403; Parker, p. 210; Roberts, pp. 144–5; Charmley, p. 171;

Hill, pp. 51–6; and see Colvin, pp. 199–216 for the varying views expressed in the Cabinet about a possible alliance with the Soviet Union.

82. Watt, p. 180.

83. Roberts, pp. 144–5; Charmley, pp. 171–5.

84. Parker, p. 213; Watt, pp. 182ff; Newman, pp. 182ff.

85. Nicolson, p. 147.

86. Cited Parker, p. 215; and Newman, p. 203. For Halifax's role, see Roberts, pp. 146–7. And for the Foreign Office perspective, see *The Diaries of Sir Alexander Cadogan*, pp. 165–7.

87. Nicolson, p. 147.

88. Parker, p. 215.

89. Cowling, p. 297. Though Britain was by now rearming fast, it was not until 1940 that aircraft production, which had the highest priority, overtook Germany's (Parker, p. 272).

90. Parker, pp. 216–17; Watt, p. 186; Charmley, p. 189. Chamberlain thought the leading article of *The Times* on 1 April 1939, pointing out that 'the new obligation which this country yesterday assumed does not bind Great Britain to defend every inch of the present frontiers of Poland', and the comment that the Prime Minister 'thinks that there are problems in which adjustments are still necessary' was 'just what I meant'. Halifax was also in full agreement with the article (*The Times and Appeasement*, pp. 286–7). See also Cowling, p. 298.

91. See Watt, pp. 185–6, and the somewhat overdrawn comment of Richard Lamb, *The Ghosts of Peace, 1935–1945*, Salisbury, 1987, p. 103: 'Chamberlain, in temporary outrage at Hitler breaking his word, had given a blank cheque to the Poles'.

92. Cited in R. A. C. Parker, *Churchill and Appeasement*, London, 2000, p. 218; and see Taylor, p. 544, quoting Lloyd George as remarking that, without the help of Russia, Britain was 'walking into a trap'.

93. Hans Bernd Gisevius, *To the Bitter End*, Boston, 1947, p. 363.

94. See Kershaw, *Hitler, 1936–1945: Nemesis*, p. 208.

95. For Hitler's reaction to the British guarantee, Kershaw, *Hitler, 1936–1945: Nemesis*, pp. 177–80; Watt, ch. 11; Gerhard L. Weinberg, *The Foreign Policy of Hitler's Germany. Starting World War II, 1937–1939*, Chicago/London, 1980, pp. 559ff.

96. PRONI, D/3099/2/21/A/182, Canon G. M. Isaac to L, 22.2.39.

97. It was disingenuous of Londonderry to claim, once war had begun, that he had 'never intended to trust Hitler' (PRONI, D/3099/4/56, L to Ralph Pride, 15.1.40). It is true that, along similar lines to those proposed by Lord Rothermere, Londonderry had advocated rearmament at the same time as

friendly overtures to Germany, implying trust from a position of armed strength. In reality, however, he had been prepared, down to March 1939, to trust Hitler even without strength in rearmament. (See also Londonderry's letter cited in note 105 below.)

98. PRONI, D/3099/2/19/256, L to General Wenninger, Air Attaché at the German Embassy, 10.3.39.

99. *Sunderland Echo*, 11.3.39; *The Times*, 13.3.39; extracts in PRONI, D/3099/10/51.

100. *Belfast Telegraph*, 20.3.39, in PRONI, D/3099/10/51.

101. PRONI, D/3099/2/19/255, 261.

102. PRONI, D/3099/2/21/A/191, L to Sven Hedin, 20.3.39. Hedin had four days earlier sent Londonderry a handwritten card (together with a photograph) thanking him for his book, *Ourselves*, which he was reading 'with the greatest interest and sympathy'. He replied to Londonderry's angry letter of 20 March, saying 'I quite understand your feelings towards the latest events. However a world war would be worse'. He hoped future events would allow Londonderry to 'return to the opinion you so well explain in your valuable book'. Hedin referred to this exchange of letters in the book he wrote after the war, commenting that the world would have been different had Londonderry's cause of creating a basis of understanding between Britain and Germany been taken up in London and Berlin (Sven Hedin, *Ohne Auftrag in Berlin*, Tübingen/Stuttgart, 1950, pp. 36–9). For Hedin's outspokenly pro-Nazi views in the 1930s, see John Toland, *Adolf Hitler*, London, 1977, p. 409.

103. PRONI, D/3099/2/19/272, L to von Papen, 29.3.39.

104. PRONI, D/3099/2/19/278A, L to Gritzbach, 4.4.39.

105. PRONI, D/3099/2/19/279, L to Dr Silex, 4.4.39. He expressed the same point, if anything still more forcefully, in a letter written a few weeks later to a retired German diplomat, whom he had known years earlier at the German Embassy in London: 'Whereas I have always said in conversations, speeches and articles that Hitler could be trusted, this absolute volte face on his part has destroyed any arguments that I can put forward . . . I have no defence for the manner and the methods which Hitler is employing at the present time' (D/3099/2/19/326, L to Botschaftsrat Constantin Graf Deym, 13.7.39 (another copy in D/3099/4/51)).

106. Cited in Griffiths, p. 347.

107. Cited in Griffiths, p. 349.

108. King's College, London, Liddell Hart Centre for Military Archives, Hamilton Papers, Hamilton 14/2/12, Hamilton to C. E. Carroll, 25.3.39. Carroll, former editor of the British Legion paper and now Secretary of 'The Link' and editor of the anti-Semitic and avidly pro-German *Anglo-German*

Review, later to be interned for his pro-German proclivities, had written to Hamilton on 21 March. The British Legion abandoned its pro-German stance in the light of the events of March 1939 (Griffiths, p. 350 (and p. 239 and n. 2 for Carroll)).

109. Griffiths, pp. 349–50. C. E. Carroll, writing to Sir Ian Hamilton on 21 March 1939, did, however, remark that 'a great many distinguished people have joined The Link in the past fortnight (including, for instance, the Duke of Westminster, who joined today)' (King's College, London, Liddell Hart Centre for Military Archives, Hamilton Papers, Hamilton 14/2/12). Even before the German march into Prague, British intelligence had recorded a move of 'the more extreme members' of the Anglo-German Fellowship to 'The Link' (PRO, KV5/3, MI5 note of 17.2.39 (also indicating the Nazis' loss of confidence in the Fellowship, which they now regarded as 'useless')).

110. Griffiths, pp. 348–9.

111. The comment attributed to Hitler, though it cannot be verified, sounds plausible since it accords with what he was to say, in the build-up to the attack on Poland, when he feared, alluding to Munich, 'that at the last moment some swine or other will yet submit to me a plan for mediation' (Kershaw, *Hitler, 1936–1945: Nemesis*, p. 208).

112. PRONI, D/3099/2/19/268, Ward Price to L, 25.3.39.

113. PRONI, D/3099/2/19/271, L to Ward Price, 28.3.39.

114. PRONI, D/3099/2/21/A/198, L to Rev. N. G. Davies, Dorking, 29.3.39.

115. PRONI, D/3099/2/17/51A, L to Baldwin, 20.5.39. He continued the repetitive lament in July: D/3099/4/51, L to Baldwin, 20.7.39 and (with slightly different wording suggesting one of the two drafts was sent) 24.7.39.

116. See on around this date his letters to the Labour peer Lord Strabolgi (PRONI, D/3099/2/17/44A) on 21 March and to Sir Douglas Hacking, the Conservative Party Chairman (D/3099/2/17/48B) six days later.

117. PRONI, D/3099/2/21/A/197, L to John Moffett, Literary Editor, *Otago Daily Times*, Dunedin, New Zealand, 28.3.39.

118. For Sankey, see Cowling, pp. 61–2.

119. PRONI, D/3099/2/17/47, Sankey to L, 25.3.39; L to Sankey, D/3099/2/17/45, 21.3.39.

120. PRONI, D/3099/2/17/50, Violet Bonham Carter to L, 15.5.39; L's letter to her is D/3099/2/17/49.

121. PRONI, D/3099/2/21/A/201, L to Professor Gilbert Waterhouse, Belfast, 1.4.39.

122. Birmingham UL, Chamberlain Papers, NC7/11/32/158, L to Chamberlain, 2.4.39.

123. PRO, Air 19/27, L to Kingsley Wood, 18.4.39.

124. Birmingham UL, Chamberlain Papers, NC7/11/32/160, L to Chamberlain, 4.5.39 (copy in PRONI, D/3099/4/51).

125. Londonderry's letter accompanied the copy of an eight-page letter, reasserting the correctness of his own approach and assailing 'the ineptitude of our foreign policy which refused to understand the German point of view', that he had sent to the editor of The Times, Geoffrey Dawson, taking issue with an editorial which had castigated the deceit, bullying, and disingenuous claims of Hitler in conducting his foreign policy (The Times, 29.4.39; Birmingham UL, Chamberlain Papers, NC7/11/32/161, L to Geoffrey Dawson, 2.5.39 (copy in PRONI, D/3099/4/51)).

126. See PRONI, D/3099/2/19/277, L to W. H. Troughton, 4.4.39, which states as much.

127. PRONI, D/3099/2/19/292, von Papen to L, 14.5.39; D/3099/2/19/314, Rumbold to L, 21.6.39 (after Londonderry had forwarded him a copy of the letter).

128. PRONI, D/3099/2/19/306B, L to von Papen, 8.6.39.

129. PRONI, D/3099/2/19/297A, L to Göring (a translation into German of an English original which no longer exists). In a reply to a letter in late June recommending that, since he had 'the ear of Germany', it would crown his 'splendid efforts' were he to make an appeal to Hitler which Mussolini would doubtless follow, Londonderry wrote: 'I have a great difficulty in doing what you suggest because my efforts as regards the general public have merely gained for me the character of being an admirer of the Nazi system in general and of dictators in particular [sic], so it is quite impossible for me at this moment to go to Germany, which I should like to do very much' (D/3099/2/21/A/230, L to Sir James Marchant, 26.6.39; no. 226 is Marchant's letter to L of 22.6.39).

130. The most thorough account of Göring's feelers towards an accommodation between Britain and Germany in summer 1939, using intermediaries who he thought might influence those at the centre of British decision-making, is that of Stefan Martens, Hermann Göring. 'Erster Paladin des Führers' und 'Zweiter Mann im Reich', Paderborn, 1985, ch. 8. See also Charmley, pp. 192–3, 202–5; and Watt, pp. 394–404.

131. Chips, pp. 204–5 (entry for 7.7.39).

132. Chips, pp. 208–9 (entries for 8.8.39, 22.8.39).

133. PRONI, D/3084/C/E/6/17, Lord Londonderry's Engagements, 1938–39; D/3099/15/11, Guest List to Lady Mairi's dance (listing 445 names); WSC, V/3, pp. 1527–31 for Churchill's speech at the 1900 Dinner.

134. PRONI, D/3099/2/17/51A, L to Baldwin, 20.5.39.

135. A point made by Neil Fleming, *The Seventh Marquess of Londonderry: a Political Life*, Ph.D. thesis, Queen's University, Belfast, 2002, pp. 1, 3–4, 338–9.

136. PRONI, D/3099/4/56, L to Bishop Herbert Hensley Henson, 6.1.40.

137. PRONI, D/3099/4/51, L to Prince Paul of Yugoslavia, 27.7.39.

138. *The Times*, 22.6.39.

139. PRONI, D/3099/2/18/41A, L to Halifax, 12.6.39.

140. PRONI, D/3099/2/18/42, L to Halifax, 4.7.39. The tone of his letter lends little support to the presumption of one of his fellow peers that Londonderry must have been contrite on account of his his attempts to win German friendship (*The Crawford Papers. The Journals of David Lindsay, 27th Earl of Crawford and 10th Earl of Balcarres 1871 to 1940 during the Years 1892 to 1940*, ed. John Vincent, Manchester, 1984, p. 602 (30.8.39)).

141. PRO, FO 800/316, fols. 5–16, L to Halifax, 6.7.39. The contact was Robert Jamieson, who spent several months in Essen during the spring and summer of 1939, partly financed by Londonderry. How Londonderry came to know him is unclear, but evidently in return for subsidies he provided reports on the situation in Germany, as he saw it. He worked, at least for part of his stay, at the Berlitz Language School in Essen, presumably as an English teacher, though he had journalistic friends (and, perhaps, pretensions, since he was the author of a couple of pamphlets on Germany). He was plainly a staunch Conservative and pro-German – at least in some respects pro-Nazi – and was somewhat gullible and uncritical about the opinions registered through conversations with ordinary Germans. (See, apart from the correspondence passed to Halifax, PRONI, D/3099/2/19/330, 336.) Since his own German was limited, such conversations were in any case mainly with those who spoke good English. In his letter to Londonderry of 19 June, passed on to Halifax (PRO, FO 800/316, fol. 7), he mentioned rumours (already reaching the Foreign Office through more reliable sources) that relations between Germany and Russia were becoming more friendly.

142. PRO, FO 800/316, fols. 62–3, 67, 71, 116. Arthur Ronald Nall-Cain, 2nd Baron Brocket, who was in his mid-thirties, had been a Conservative MP in the early 1930s before inheriting his title. He was not held in much esteem by either Chamberlain or Halifax (Cowling, p. 358. For Brocket's pro-German attitude, see Griffiths, p. 304 and n. 1).

143. PRONI, D/3099/2/18/50, L to Halifax, 12.8.39.

144. PRONI, D/3099/4/51, L to Churchill, 3.8.39.

145. PRONI, D/3099/4/51, L to Prince Paul of Yugoslavia, 27.7.39.

146. PRONI, D/3099/2/18/50, L to Halifax, 12.8.39.

147. PRONI, D/3099/4/51, L to Churchill, 3.8.39. Similar sentiments, in part in near-identical wording, were expressed to Halifax (D/3099/2/18/41A, L to Halifax, 12.6.39).

148. *Wings*, p. 224.

149. PRONI, D/3099/2/18/45, L to Halifax, 2.8.39.

150. PRO, FO 800/316, fols. 175-6v, L to Halifax, 2.8.39. The flurry of exchanges that day comprised two letters from Londonderry to Halifax (with a further letter drafted but not sent) and two from Halifax to Londonderry (following his initial letter of 1 August) (D/3099/2/18/45-6, 49; PRO, FO 800/316, fols. 174-9).

151. Charmley, pp. 193-4.

152. PRO, FO 800/316, fol. 174v, Halifax to L, 2.8.39.

153. PRONI, D/3099/2/18/48, L to Halifax, 2.8.39 (and in the differently drafted letter, not sent, D/3099/2/18/45). In his letter to the German Ambassador, Herbert von Dirksen, on 2 August, Londonderry remarked that he was postponing – that is, not cancelling – his visit (D/3099/4/51).

154. PRONI, D/3099/2/18/50, L to Halifax, 12.8.39. His English contact in Germany, Robert Jamieson (now moved from Essen to Berlin), still thought Londonderry might be coming to Germany as late as 23 August 1939 (D/3099/2/19/336, Jamieson to L, 23.8.39).

155. PRONI, D/3099/2/18/51, Halifax to L, 21.8.39.

156. Parker, *Churchill and Appeasement*, p. 223.

157. PRONI, D/3099/2/18/41A, L to Halifax, 12.6.39.

158. For the background, see especially Parker, *Chamberlain and Appeasement*, ch. 11.

159. See Kershaw, *Hitler, 1936–1945: Nemesis*, pp. 209-11.

160. Cowling, p. 403.

161. Charmley, pp. 201-2.

162. Kershaw, *Hitler, 1936–1945: Nemesis*, pp. 212-20 describes the last-minute diplomatic activity; and for the unfolding drama in the British Cabinet, see Colvin, *The Chamberlain Cabinet*, pp. 234-59.

163. PRONI, D/3099/2/17/52A, Hailsham to L, 29.8.39 (replying to a letter by Londonderry seeking Hailsham's recollection of the matter surrounding the reception of the two letters).

164. PRONI, D/3099/13/2/1407, Lady L to L, 1.9.39.

7 Out in the Cold

1. Donald Cameron Watt, *How War Came. The Immediate Origins of the Second World War, 1938–1939*, paperback edn, London, 1991, pp. 590ff,

captures the drama of the last hours of peace. The terms of the ultimatum are laid out in *Documents Concerning German-Polish Relations and the Outbreak of Hostilities between Great Britain and Germany on September 3, 1939*, London, 1939, p. 175, Doc. no. 118.

2. Andrew Roberts, *'The Holy Fox'. The Life of Lord Halifax*, paperback edn, London, 1997, p. 177.

3. C. L. Mowat, *Britain between the Wars 1918–1940*, London, 1956, p. 650.

4. Chamberlain referred to the 'war twilight' on 23 September 1939 (Keith Feiling, *The Life of Neville Chamberlain*, London, 1946, p. 424).

5. The French crossed the German border in one place, but withdrew as soon as they were fired upon (A. J. P. Taylor, *English History 1914–1945*, Harmondsworth, 1970, p. 561).

6. Taylor, p. 558.

7. See Richard Thurlow, *Fascism in Britain. A History, 1918–1985*, Oxford, 1987, pp. 178ff; Colin Cross, *The Fascists in Britain*, London, 1961, pp. 190–91.

8. *The Diaries of Sir Alexander Cadogan, 1938–1945*, ed. David Dilks, London, 1971, p. 219 (23.9.39); p. 221(7.10.39); and see pp. 221–2 (early October).

9. Cited in Roberts, p. 177.

10. Feiling, p. 419.

11. Feiling, p. 425.

12. Maurice Cowling, *The Impact of Hitler. British Politics and British Policy, 1933–1940*, Cambridge, 1975, p. 357.

13. John Colville, *The Fringes of Power. Downing Street Diaries 1939–1955*, London, 1985, p. 45 (29.10.39).

14. Taylor, pp. 561–2.

15. Cited in Cowling, p. 355; and Roberts, p. 179.

16. Feiling, p. 424; Cowling, pp. 355, 357–8.

17. *The Diaries of Sir Alexander Cadogan*, pp. 221–4. Though a positive response to Hitler's speech was ruled out straight away, the drafting of Chamberlain's speech, following consultation with the Dominions and France, took six days (Christopher Hill, *Cabinet Decisions on Foreign Policy. The British Experience October 1938 – June 1941*, Cambridge, 1991, pp. 115–26, 144). Chamberlain held out no hope of negotiation, but made plain that he was ready to accord a 'proper place in Europe' to a non-Nazi Germany 'able to dwell in friendship with others'. Feelers for peace continued to come from an array of unofficial German sources for many months, though few were believed to be serious. See, especially, Ulrich Schlie, *Kein Friede mit Deutschland. Die Geheimen Gespräche im Zweiten Weltkrieg*

1939–1941, Munich/Berlin, 1994. The text of Hitler's speech on 6 October 1939 is in *Hitler. Reden und Proklamationen 1932–1945*, ed. Max Domarus, Wiesbaden, 1973, pp. 1377–93; and see Ian Kershaw, *Hitler, 1936–1945: Nemesis*, London, 2000, p. 265.

18. Feiling, p. 424.

19. Roberts, p. 180.

20. Harold Nicolson, *Diaries and Letters 1930–1964*, ed. Stanley Olson, London, 1980, p. 166 (20.9.39).

21. *Fleet Street, Press Barons and Politics. The Journals of Collin Brooks 1932–1940*, ed. N. J. Crowson, Camden Fifth Series, vol. 11, Cambridge, 1998, pp. 256–7 (15.10.39).

22. N. J. Crowson, *Facing Fascism: the Conservative Party and the European Dictators 1935–40*, London, 1997, p. 175.

23. Cowling, p. 358; John Charmley, *Churchill: The End of Glory. A Political Biography*, London, 1993, p. 399.

24. Roberts, p. 180; Charmley, p. 399.

25. *The Crawford Papers. The Journals of David Lindsay, 27th Earl of Crawford and 10th Earl of Balcarres 1871 to 1940 during the Years 1892 to 1940*, ed. John Vincent, Manchester, 1984, p. 608 (15.11.39).

26. Roberts, p. 151.

27. Colville, p. 83 (9.2.40).

28. Stephen Roskill, *Hankey. Man of Secrets, Vol. 3, 1931–1963*, London, 1974, p. 431; Cowling, pp. 358, 526 (nn. 30–33); Roberts, p. 179; Crowson, p. 175; Charmley, p. 399; Richard Griffiths, *Fellow Travellers of the Right. British Enthusiasts for Nazi Germany 1933–39*, Oxford, 1983, p. 363; *The Crawford Papers*, pp. 607–8 (15.11.39).

29. Cowling, p. 358.

30. See Griffiths, pp. 317ff.

31. Peter Padfield, *Hess. The Führer's Disciple*, paperback edn, London, 1995, p. 150.

32. Padfield, pp. 148–50.

33. Neil Fleming, *The Seventh Marquess of Londonderry: a Political Life*, Ph.D. thesis, Queen's University Belfast, 2002, pp. 323–4.

34. *Evening News*, 19.9.39, in PRONI, D/3099/10/51.

35. H. Montgomery Hyde, *The Londonderrys: a Family Portrait*, London, 1979, p. 255.

36. *Chips. The Diaries of Sir Henry Channon*, London, 1967, p. 224 (2.11.39).

37. *Parliament and Politics in the Age of Churchill and Attlee. The Headlam Diaries 1935–1951*, ed. Stuart Ball, Camden Society Fifth Series, vol. 14, Cambridge, 1999, p. 182 (19.2.40). Londonderry told Headlam in February

1940 that he was closing down Londonderry House and removing the furniture to save paying rates of £4,000 a year. According to 'Chips' Channon (see previous note), Londonderry House was already closed at the beginning of November 1939. It was offered to Sir John Anderson, the Home Secretary, for use in connection with the war effort. In fact, the house was requisitioned by the army for the duration of the war. Wynyard in County Durham was used for the housing of sixty-five evacuated children (*Evening News*, 19.9.39, in PRONI, D/3099/10/51; Hyde, *The Londonderrys*, p. 258). Lady Londonderry wrote to her husband in January 1940, suggesting that Wynyard be closed, though the house in fact remained in use throughout the war (D/3099/13/2/1424, Lady L to L, 14.1.40).

38. PRONI, D/3099/4/56, L to J. L. Garvin, 25.3.40.

39. PRONI, D/3099/4/52, Mrs M. E. Templer to L, 15.9.39 (and L's reply of 19.9.39); Donald Banks to L, 20.9.39 (writing from Darlington, in northern England); A. Bradfield-England to L, 21.9.39 (writing from Dublin; L's reply of 23.9.39, referring to the allegations as 'wounding' though of no importance); P. Calvin to L, 26.9.39; L to A. H. Coulter, 26.9.39 (referring to 'these foolish rumours').

40. *The Crawford Papers*, pp. 604–5 (21.9.39).

41. PRONI, D/3099/4/52, L to Sir Abe Bailey, Cape Town, 7.10.39.

42. *Daily Mail*, 19.9.39; *Evening News*, 19.9.39, in PRONI, D/3099/10/51. Londonderry sent a copy of the *Daily Mail* article to Neville Chamberlain (Birmingham UL, Chamberlain Papers, NC7/11/32/162, attached to a letter of L to Chamberlain of 19.9.39).

43. *Sunday Sun*, 24.9.39, in PRONI, D/3099/10/51.

44. *The Spectator*, 6.10.39, in PRONI, D/3099/10/51.

45. PRONI, D/3099/4/52, L to the Rumanian Minister, London, 9.10.39.

46. PRONI, D/3099/2/21/A/235, Philip Tengely, Richmond, to L, 23.9.39.

47. PRONI, D/3099/2/21/A/236, L to Tengely, 26.9.39. Londonderry felt so strongly about it that he invited Tengely by telephone and telegram to visit him 'to discuss the subject in which you take so much interest'.

48. *Sunday Sun*, 8.10.39, in PRONI, D/3099/10/51.

49. *Sunday Dispatch*, 14.1.40 (and *Durham Chronicle*, 26.1.40), in PRONI, D/3099/10/51.

50. PRONI, D/3099/4/56, L to Esmond Harmsworth, 8.1.40. He remarked to Ward Price that the newspaper had 'behaved infamously to Oliver [Stanley] especially and to me in a secondary degree, and when I made an offensive démarche, as I seldom let anything go by default, the S[unday]D[ispatch] responded very well and gave a lot of help' (D/3099/4/56, L to Ward Price, 5.2.40).

51. He referred more than once to preparation of an article (presumably for the press). But commiserating with Sir Kingsley Wood, who at the beginning of April 1940 had followed in his footsteps by losing his place as Air Minister and being made Lord Privy Seal, Londonderry returned to the saga of his own downfall five years earlier, saying: 'this is old history, but as I have a certain amount of time I am writing all this down very carefully' (PRONI, D/3099/4/56, L to Sir Kingsley Wood, 4.4.40). Shortly afterwards, writing to the MP and political journalist Beverley Baxter, he stated: 'I am quite sure that it is very important that a very careful survey of the last nine years should be undertaken. My capacity to write a book, I feel, is very limited, but as at my age I have not so much work to do as most of you, I am proposing to collect some material. I would naturally want to make it as objective as possible, although I feel intensely indignant at the sheer incompetence of our rulers' (D/3099/4/56, L to Beverley Baxter, 1.5.40). By August 1940 he had drafted 'a narrative', as he put it, relating to the matter of air power in 1935 'perhaps for later publication' (D/3099/4/57, L to Churchill, 16.8.40). This must have gestated into the basis of his eventual vindicatory book, *Wings of Destiny*.

52. PRO, Cab. 21/2676, unauthored memorandum to Sir Edward Bridges, headed 'Secretary', 22.9.39.

53. PRO, Cab. 21/2676, L to Chamberlain, 19.9.39; Chamberlain to L, 27.9.39 (and first draft of the letter). The file also contains related correspondence, drafts, and memoranda within the Cabinet Office, as well as copies of the Hailsham letters. Copies of the correspondence are also contained in Birmingham UL, Chamberlain Papers, NC7/11/32/162–70, and PRONI, D/3099/2/17/53, 54, 54A.

54. PRONI, D/3099/4/52, L to Chamberlain, 1.10.39.

55. PRONI, D/3099/3/15/47, Chamberlain to Lady L, 22.12.39.

56. PRONI, D/3099/3/15/47, Lady L to Chamberlain, 7.1.40.

57. *Belfast News-Letter*, 1.11.39, 23.12.39, in PRONI, D/3099/10/51.

58. *Belfast News-Letter*, 3.1.40; *Northern Whig*, 3.1.40; *Newtownards Chronicle*, 3.1.40, in PRONI, D/3099/10/51.

59. PRONI, D/3099/4/52, L to Halifax, 17.11.39.

60. PRONI, D/3099/4/52, L to Churchill, 17.11.39. Londonderry could not resist adding: 'I have not been to see you because I hate to call on the powers that be, and it is not likely that your colleagues will send for me because I have been right and they have been invariably wrong.' Londonderry also expressed to Lord Halifax his 'grave misgivings' as to whether Chamberlain's 'conception of winning the war is altogether the correct one' (D/3099/2/18/53, L to Halifax, 2.12.39).

61. PRONI, D/3099/4/52, L to Sir Campbell Stuart, 19.10.39; D/3099/2/18/53, L to Halifax, 2.12.39.

62. PRONI, D/3099/2/18/53, L to Halifax, 2.12.39.

63. PRONI, D/3099/2/18/54, L to Halifax, 25.12.39 (a sixteen-page account of his views on the past failings of government and current policy in the war).

64. PRONI, D/3099/4/52, L to Editor, *Iron and Coal Trades Review*, 10.10.39.

65. PRONI, D/3099/4/57, L to Halifax, 17.12.39.

66. PRONI, D/3099/2/18/54, L to Halifax, 25.12.39.

67. PRONI, D/3099/4/57, L to Halifax, 17.12.39.

68. PRONI, D/3099/2/18/54, L to Halifax, 25.12.39.

69. PRONI, D/3099/4/56, Duke of Buccleuch to L, 15.1.40.

70. PRONI, D/3099/4/56, L to Brocket, 27.1.40.

71. PRONI, D/3099/4/56, L to Baldwin, 26.1.40.

72. PRONI, D/3099/4/56, L to Noel-Buxton, 28.2.40. In an earlier letter to Noel-Buxton, Londonderry had stated: 'I did put a point of view before Lord Baldwin, but, needless to say, I have received no answer from him' (D/3099/4/56, L to Noel-Buxton, 6.2.40).

73. PRONI, D/3099/4/56, Brocket to L, 30.1.40.

74. PRONI, D/3099/4/56, L to Brocket, 31.1.40.

75. Griffiths, p. 111.

76. John F. Naylor, *Labour's International Policy. The Labour Party in the 1930s*, London, 1969, p. 217.

77. Naylor, p. 238.

78. PRONI, D/3099/4/56, L to Baldwin, 26.1.40. The pamphlet is mentioned in the postscript to the letter. Baldwin did not approve of its contents (D/3099/4/56, L to Noel-Buxton, 28.2.40).

79. PRONI, D/3099/4/56, Noel-Buxton to L, 2.2.40.

80. PRONI, D/3099/4/56, L to Noel-Buxton, 6.2.40.

81. The text, dated 23.2.40, is contained in PRONI, D/3099/12/22, which otherwise has notes and drafts relating to Londonderry's articles and speeches. There is no signatory, but the proximity of the date to Noel-Buxton's letter suggests that this is the memorandum in question. Another memorandum in the file, with neither date nor signatory, possibly pre-dates it but may well emanate from the same source. A third memorandum, on which Londonderry himself has written 'From Lord Noel-Buxton', is attached to the correspondence between Noel-Buxton and Londonderry in D/3099/4/56. But although the adjacent letter from Noel-Buxton, dated 27.2.40, mentions 'the enclosed memorandum', this cannot possibly be the one to which he refers, since its internal content dates it after 22 July 1940.

82. Quotations from 'Policy in Relation to the War', in PRONI, D/3099/12/22.

83. PRONI, D/3099/4/56, L to Noel-Buxton, 28.2.40.

84. PRONI, D/3099/4/56, Ward Price to L, 24.1.40, 25.3.40.

85. In a letter to Sir John Simon, Londonderry commented 'that Goering is a business man and that he detests Goebbels, Himmler, Hess and Ribbentrop, so if and when they are prepared to come to terms, it is not altogether unnecessary to make Goering think that we might be able to do business with him' (PRONI, D/3099/4/56, L to Simon, 27.1.40). He anticipated 'if and when we can score a success and Hitler fails to deliver the goods, to see Goering and the Reichswehr associated in controlling German destinies to the exclusion of Goebbels and Himmler and the rest of the Nazi crowd' (D/3099/4/56, L to General Sir Hugh Elles, 15.3.40).

86. PRONI, D/3099/4/56, L to Ward Price, 5.2.40.

87. PRONI, D/3099/4/56, L to Ward Price, 28.3.40. Writing to the editor of the *Observer*, J. L. Garvin around the same time, Londonderry remarked that in his view 'the Germans have not really got "a punch" unless they turn their forces on to a Czecho-Slovakia or a Poland or perhaps Roumania' (D/3099/4/56, L to Garvin, 25.3.40).

88. PRONI, D/3099/4/56, L to Ward Price, 5.2.40.

89. PRONI, D/3099/4/56, L to Halifax, 14.3.40. Privately, he criticized Halifax, too, as diffident, uncertain, doubtful, lacking knowledge, and 'absolutely out of touch' (D/3099/4/56, L to Garvin, 25.3.40).

90. PRONI, D/3099/4/56, Salisbury to L, 1.4.40.

91. Cited in Larry L. Witherell, 'Lord Salisbury's "Watching Committee" and the Fall of Neville Chamberlain', *English Historical Review*, 116 (2001), pp. 1134–66, here p. 1146. The Committee settled around an initial membership of twenty-eight (Witherell, pp. 1165–6). On the Watching Committee, see also Crowson, pp. 173–4 and Cowling, pp. 377–8.

92. This is clear from Salisbury's letter to Londonderry of 1 April 1940 in PRONI, D/3099/4/56.

93. Witherell, pp. 1143, 1166.

94. PRONI, D/3099/4/56, L to Trenchard, 22.4.40; L to Salisbury, 22.4.40 (also cited in Witherell, p. 1151).

95. Cited in Witherell, p. 1146. The following is based upon this article, pp. 1146ff.

96. PRONI, D/3099/4/56, L to Salisbury, 11.4.40. Londonderry did not know at this point of the outcome of the meeting between Salisbury and Chamberlain.

97. PRONI, D/3099/4/56, L to Salisbury, 13.4.40. See also Witherell, p. 1152 for citation of part of Londonderry's letter.

98. Cited in Winston S. Churchill, *The Second World War. Vol. 1: The Gathering Storm*, London, 1948, p. 526.

99. Cited Witherell, pp. 1150–51.

100. Witherell, p. 1153.

101. PRONI, D/3099/4/57, L to Halifax, 30.4.40.

102. Witherell, pp. 1159–61.

103. Witherell, p. 1163.

104. PRONI, D/3099/4/57, L to Beverley Baxter, 14.5.40; and, in the same file, to his longstanding confidante, Lady Desborough: 'The political changes are all to the good and the administration looks to me efficient. I cannot feel sorry for Neville as P.M. although fully sympathetic as regards wounded feelings' (L to Lady Desborough, 16.5.40).

105. Londonderry wrote, a few days before Churchill became Prime Minister: 'I cannot help blaming Winston a good deal for this delusion [about the strength of the German air force in 1935]. After all, he was a professional and he knew that it was quite impossible to improvise an air force in two years, but when public opinion became uneasy because Germany was rearming [,] the opportunity of attacking the Government on their delinquencies in that respect was too strong for him, and I am quite sure that he began to believe his own stories about the development of German rearmament' (PRONI, D/3099/4/56, L to Beverley Baxter, 1.5.40).

106. Interviews with Lady Mairi Bury, Mount Stewart, 23.5.02, 22.10.02.

107. See PRONI, D/3099/4/57, L to Beverley Baxter, 14.5.40, where he outlines these differences. For Churchill's advocacy of neutrality in the Spanish Civil War, see Martin Gilbert, *Winston S. Churchill, Vol. 5, 1922–1939*, London, 1976, p. 782.

108. PRONI, D/3099/4/57, L to Beverley Baxter, 15.4.40. Writing to Churchill himself some weeks earlier, Londonderry commented that 'it has been a great sorrow to me that our old alliance, which was so valuable to me in years gone by, suddenly came to an end by reason of my being quite unable to explain to you what I was at, or rather you never would listen because you had made up your mind that war with Germany was a certainty' (D/3099/4/56, L to Churchill, 12.3.40).

109. PRONI, D/3099/4/57, L to Lady Desborough, 26.8.40.

110. PRONI, D/3099/4/58, L to Halifax, 23.12.40.

111. *Chips*, p.381 (4.12.43).

112. David Reynolds, 'Churchill and the British "Decision" to Fight On in 1940: Right Policy, Wrong Reasons', in Richard Langhorne (ed.), *Diplomacy and Intelligence during the Second World War*, Cambridge, 1985, p. 150; Roberts, p. 211.

113. PRONI, D/3099/4/57, Courcy to L, 21.5.40. A copy of the letter does not appear to have been kept along with other correspondence with Lord Londonderry in the Kenneth de Courcy's Papers (box 2 folder 2) in the Hoover Institution, Stanford, California.

114. PRONI, D/3099/4/57, L to Halifax, 22.5.40. Londonderry's emphasis on the role of Mussolini possibly owed something to a letter he had recently received from his friend Ward Price, who thought the Italian dictator would look to a favourable moment 'to commit his country to the fortunes of his fellow-Dictator', and thought he held the key to the situation in the Balkans, where Hitler would not intervene if he did not do so (PRONI, D/3099/4/57, Ward Price to L, 11.5.40).

115. PRONI, D/3099/4/57, Halifax to L, 24.5.40. The Foreign Office wanted Roosevelt to let Mussolini know that the Allies were prepared to 'consider his Mediterranean grievances and negotiate a settlement of them' if he stayed out of the war, and would also offer him a seat at an ensuing peace conference as if he had been a belligerent (*The Diplomatic Diaries of Oliver Harvey, 1937–1940*, ed. John Harvey, London, 1970, pp. 367–8 (entries for 25 and 26.5.40). In the event the appeal to Roosevelt was not sent (Roberts, pp. 211–12).

116. Hoover Institution, Stanford, California, Kenneth de Courcy Papers, box 2 folder 2, L to Courcy, 27.5.40; Courcy to L, 29.5.40 (copies in PRONI, D/3099/4/57).

117. Within a few days, Courcy had given up any such hopes. On 4 June 1940 he wrote to Londonderry: 'I think there is very little, if any, chance of a conference on the lines I envisaged when we last talked and when I thought there might be some chance through astute diplomacy of averting Italian intervention and by using the help of the United States bringing them a step nearer our side. The situation is now somewhat different and I suspect the hour is too late for that policy' (Hoover Institution, Stanford, California, Kenneth de Courcy Papers, box 2 folder 2).

118. Roberts, p. 212.

119. Roberts, pp. 212–14; John Lukacs, *Five Days in London: May 1940*, paperback edn, New Haven/London, 2001, pp. 91–4.

120. Cited in Roberts, p. 217.

121. Roberts, p. 218; Lukacs, pp. 146ff.

122. Cited in Lukacs, pp. 148–9; and see Roberts, p. 220.

123. Cited in Lukacs, p. 183.

124. See Reynolds, p. 166; and also Hill, pp. 152–63.

125. Kershaw, *Hitler 1936–1945: Nemesis*, pp. 303–4; *Hitler. Reden und Proklamationen*, pp. 1540–59 for the text of the speech.

126. Winston S. Churchill, *The Second World War. Vol. 2: Their Finest Hour*, London, 1949, p. 229.

127. Cited in Churchill, *Their Finest Hour*, p. 230; and see Roberts, pp. 249–50.

128. Roberts, p. 250; Schlie, pp. 220–21. Churchill forbade any communication with the German Chargé d'Affaires (Churchill, *Their Finest Hour*, p. 229).

129. PRONI, D/3099/4/57, L to Halifax, 25.7.40.

130. PRONI, D/3099/4/57, Halifax to L, 26.7.40.

131. Borthwick Institute, York, Halifax Papers, A4.410.28.2, L to Halifax, 17.8.40 (copy in PRONI, D/3099/4/57).

132. PRONI, D/3099/4/57, Halifax to L, 19.8.40.

133. PRONI, D/3099/4/58, L to Halifax, 23.12.40.

134. PRONI, D/3099/4/57, L to Beverley Baxter, 30.7.40.

135. PRONI, D/3099/4/58, L to Halifax, 10.10.40.

136. PRONI, D/3099/4/57, L to Lady Desborough, 16.5.40.

137. PRONI, D/3099/13/2/1450, Lady L to L, 5.10.40.

138. PRONI, D/3099/4/58, L to Churchill, in a long handwritten letter of 24.12.40, marked 'not sent'.

139. PRONI, D/3099/4/57, L to R. M. Sayors, *Belfast Telegraph*, 6.7.40.

140. PRONI, D/3099/4/58, L to Halifax, 23.12.40.

141. Churchill, *The Gathering Storm*, p. 115.

142. Churchill, *Their Finest Hour*, p. 334.

143. PRONI, D/3099/4/58, Ward Price to L, 18.9.40.

Epilogue: Mount Stewart, September 1947

1. The shift to the Left in British opinion during the war years is well explored by Paul Addison, *The Road to 1945. British Politics and the Second World War*, London, 1975.

2. Peter Clarke, *Hope and Glory. Britain 1900–1990*, London, 1996, pp. 215–16, 224–31; A. J. P. Taylor, *English History 1914–1945*, Harmondsworth, 1970, pp. 721–4.

3. PRO, FO 371/57544, Ref. U3350/120/73, Receipted account in regard to the Notary Public's charges (Lord Londonderry; letter from R. A. Beaumont, Foreign Office, to A. J. Riley Esq., British War Crimes Executive, 1.4.46; Riley's reply, 5.4.46; *The Times*, 23.11.45, 29.11.45, 28.2.46; and see Ann Tusa and John Tusa, *The Nuremberg Trial*, London, 1983, pp. 253–4).

4. PRO, FO 371/575/540, Ref. U2358/120/73, Interrogatories by Ribbentrop: Lord Londonderry, and covering minute of 26.2.46.

5. For the accident and the minor strokes, see H. Montgomery Hyde, *The Londonderrys: a Family Portrait*, London, 1979, pp. 261–2; *Belfast Telegraph*, 8.12.45 and *Northern Echo*, 4.10.47 (extracts from both in PRONI, D/3099/10/54); Hertfordshire County Record Office, Desborough Papers, D/ERV C2482/85, L to Lady Desborough, 16.11.45.

6. Londonderry's detachment from the admiration, even adulation, for Churchill was noted as early as 1943, when he 'held forth about his cousin Winston' at a lunch gathering (*Chips. The Diaries of Sir Henry Channon*, ed. Robert Rhodes James, London, 1967, p. 381 (4.12.43)).

7. Stanley Baldwin, whose intrinsic kindness has been a rarity among British Prime Ministers, ignored Londonderry's repeated castigation and paid him a visit in a London hospital, following his glider accident in 1945 (A. W. Baldwin, *My Father: the True Story*, London, 1955, p. 324).

8. Hertfordshire County Record Office, Desborough Papers, D/ERV C2482/88, L to Lady Desborough, 21.9.47; copy in PRONI, T3201/55.

9. According to his son, Lord Castlereagh, as reported by Sir Cuthbert Headlam, a longstanding political associate of Lord Londonderry as Chairman of the Northern Counties Area of the Conservative Party (*Parliament and Politics in the Age of Churchill and Attlee. The Headlam Diaries 1935–1951*, ed. Stuart Ball, Camden Society Fifth Series, Vol. 14, Cambridge, 1999, p. 554 (entry for 18.4.48)). Information from Londonderry's daughter, Lady Mairi Bury, 9.10.03, confirmed that he could not speak following his major stroke.

10. Hyde, *The Londonderrys*, p. 262; letters from Lord Castlereagh, to Lady Londonderry in October express concern over his father's health (PRONI, D/3099/13/11/29, Castlereagh to Lady L, 4, 15, 28.10.47).

11. PRONI, D/3099/12/24, L to Sir Walford Selby, 29.9.47.

12. Hoover Institution, Stanford, California, De Courcy Papers, box 2 folder 2, contains thirty-five letters exchanged between Lord and Lady Londonderry and Courcy between 27 May 1940 and 19 December 1941. It is clear from the correspondence that, in addition, Londonderry and Courcy met on a number of occasions, usually in London, to talk about the progress of the war.

13. A good number of such letters are contained in PRONI, D/3099/4/57 and D/3099/4/58 (including, in the latter file, an exchange with the young John F. Kennedy on 28.10.40 and 6.12.40, following published claims by Kennedy that British calculations of German air strength in the 1930s had been 'startlingly wrong').

14. A protracted correspondence, with a bewildering exchange of rival statistics, ensued in autumn 1940 over claims by Peter Masefield, Air

Correspondent of the *Sunday Times*, that German air strength in 1935 had been equivalent to Britain's (PRONI, D/3099/2/17/63A–70A). Ellington provided detailed statistical information in support of Londonderry's assessment (D/3099/2/21/68A, 70A). He nevertheless realistically concluded that he would never succeed in having Baldwin's official statements of German air strength in 1935 corrected (D/3099/2/17/72, Ellington to L, 19.1.41).

15. PRO, Cab. 21/2676, exchange of correspondence between Sir Edward Bridges and Sir Rupert Howorth, 7.1.40.

16. Hoover Institution, Stanford, California, De Courcy Papers, box 2 folder 2, L to Kenneth de Courcy, 15.10.41. An undated memorandum, almost certainly from 1941 or 1942, in the Londonderry papers indicates plainly that Londonderry was receiving assistance in the research, planning, and writing of his book (PRONI, D/3099/2/21/A/277). It is tempting to presume, as does Neil Fleming, *The Seventh Marquess of Londonderry: a Political Life*, Ph.D. thesis, Queen's University Belfast, 2002, p. 327, that the collaborator was H. Montgomery Hyde, Londonderry's sometime librarian, secretary and general factotum, who had certainly assisted him (as we have noted) in 1938 in the writing of at least the revised and extended second edition of *Ourselves and Germany* (see D/3099/2/21/A/85, L to Hyde, 9.10.38). But the style of the memorandum does not ring true as that of Hyde. Sir Edward Bridges, the Secretary to the Cabinet, remarked that he thought, from a casual comment dropped by Londonderry, 'that the book is written by a Fleet Street "ghost"' (PRO, Cab. 21/2677, Minute by Bridges, 15.5.42).

17. Fleming, p. 327.

18. PRO, Cab. 21/2677, 'Note for Record', by Sir Edward Bridges, Cabinet Secretary, 14.5.42.

19. PRO, Cab. 21/2677, Minute by Bridges, 15.5.42.

20. PRO, Cab. 21/2677, Minute by Bridges for Major Desmond Morton, 11.8.42.

21. PRO, Cab. 21/2677, Bridges' note appended to memorandum to him by Captain J. N. O. Curle, 22.7.42.

22. PRO, Cab. 21/2677, Bracken to Bridges, 22.6.42.

23. PRO, Cab. 21/2677, Howorth to Bridges, 27.5.42.

24. PRO, Cab. 21/2677, an undated memorandum (from August 1942) by Bridges listed 119 objectionable passages in the book; eventually, as lists in PRO, Cab. 21/2678 make clear, fifty-six passages were noted as 'to be deleted unless otherwise stated', and another lengthy list outlined action needed by Londonderry to paraphrase or alter passages to accommodate the demands for alteration.

25. PRO, Cab. 21/2677, Prime Minister's Personal Minute, 7.6.42. Partly, as

the minute indicates, with a view to the post-war publication of his own writings, Churchill was anxious to avoid over-restrictive rules on the usage of official documents. A marginal annotation by a civil servant added to the minute: 'Riposte from Churchill the author!'. But his key concern was 'that we must not be hampered in the conduct of the war until it is won'. He favoured, therefore, exclusion or excision of quotations from official documents in Londonderry's book in the 'public interest'.

26. 'It is not very exciting and mainly a defence of his conduct as Air Minister', Sir Cuthbert Headlam noted in his diary on reading it. 'Personally I should not have written it had I been in his place, but as he chose to write it he might have done it infinitely worse. What he naturally does not appreciate is that he is not, and has never been, a big enough man to be a Cabinet Minister – but, considering his limitations, he did well enough and in the main, I imagine, he took good advice and in very difficult times did all in his power to promote the efficiency of the Air Service' (*Parliament and Politics in the Age of Churchill and Attlee*, p. 361 (19.3.43)).

27. Hertfordshire County Record Office, D/ERV C/2482–89, L to Lady Desborough, n.d., apparently 1943; copy in PRONI, T3201/54; lengthy extract in Hyde, *The Londonderrys*, pp. 259–61.

28. Extracts from various newspaper reports in PRONI, D/3099/10/53; and *The Times*, 27.2.42; 5.6.42; 12.6.42; 11.2.43; 12.3.43; 13.5.43; 14.7.43; 23.7.43; 20.1.44; 28.1.44; 13.10.44; 17.1.45; 16.3.45.

29. *The Times*, 29.4.42; 23.7.42.

30. *The Times*, 29.3.43.

31. *The Times*, 26.1.45; PRONI, D/3099/4/78, Vansittart to Cranborne, 27.1.45. Vansittart had sent a copy of his letter to Londonderry.

32. PRONI, D/3099/4/78, a draft four-page 'commentary on the incident in the House of Lords', written 'for my own satisfaction', n.d. [late January 1945]; and Vansittart's remarkably gracious reply to Londonderry's second letter (copies of neither of Londonderry's two letters appear to have been kept), 8.2.45.

33. Examples in PRONI, D/3099/4/78, correspondence in May–July 1945 with Sir Edward Ellington, Winston Churchill, Godfrey Thomas, Max Beaverbrook, P. Bonsford, George Ward Price, Air Commodore L. L. Maclean, Viscount Trenchard, Ralph Assheton, and Kingsley Martin.

34. PRONI, D/3099/4/78, L to P. Bonsford, 6.6.45.

35. Hertfordshire County Record Office, D/ERV C2482/74, L to Lady Desborough, 16.7.45.

36. PRONI, D/3099/4/78, L to Beaverbrook, 1.6.45; L to Churchill, 7.5.45 (not sent). See also the undated post-war reflections on their past differences in D/3099/2/17/77–8.

37. PRO, Cab. 21/2678, L to Sir Edward Bridges, 11.3.46; Bridges to L, 29.4.46; L to Bridges, 14.5.46.

38. PRO, Cab. 21/2678, Secretary of State for Air (P. J. Noel-Baker) to L, 28.2.47; Memorandum by the Chairman of the Committee on the Use of Official Information in Private Publications: Application of Lord Londonderry, initialled by Sir Edward Bridges, April 1947; PRONI, D/3099/2/21/A/261, L to P. J. Noel-Baker, 7.3.47.

39. PRONI, D/3099/13/11/32, Castlereagh to Lady L, 11.5.48.

40. Information from Lady Mairi Bury, 9.10.03.

41. Hyde, *The Londonderrys*, p. 263.

42. Extracts, 11–12.2.49, in PRONI, D/3099/10/55.

43. *Chips*, p. 343 (entry for 11.2.49).

44. *Chips*, p. 343 (entry for 17.2.43); also cited in Hyde, *The Londonderrys*, pp. 263–4.

45. In a speech in November 1945, cited by Patricia Meehan, *The Unnecessary War. Whitehall and the German Resistance to Hitler*, London, 1992, p. 2.

46. PRONI, D/3099/4/56, L to Beverley Baxter, 24.4.40.

47. PRONI, D/3099/2/17/1A, L to Hailsham, 22.11.34.

48. Ian Colvin, *Vansittart in Office. The Origins of World War II*, London, 1965, p. 128.

49. A phrase attributed to Lord Lothian. Cited in Martin Gilbert and Richard Gott, *The Appeasers*, paperback edn, London, 1967, p. 41.

50. R. A. C. Parker, *Chamberlain and Appeasement. British Policy and the Coming of the Second World War*, London, 1993, pp. 273–5.

51. Fleming, pp. 338–41.

52. Hyde, *The Londonderrys*, p. 258. A letter to Montgomery Hyde long after the war from a former maid in the Londonderry household waxed lyrical about 'the days when manners *were* manners, and we had much respect for the gentry and upper staff'. She recalled: 'Things were not quite the same when War came, all the footmen left, and my health let me down, but until then from 1934 I loved the pomp of Londonderry House . . .' (PRONI, D/3084/C/f/6/262, Mrs A. Muir to Hyde, n.d. [?September 1979]).

53. Hyde, *The Londonderrys*, p. 258.

54. *The Times*, 22.6.46; Hyde, *The Londonderrys*, p. 261.

55. *The Times*, 25.5.46; Hyde, *The Londonderrys*, p. 261.

56. Hyde, *The Londonderrys*, pp. 258–9; PRONI, D/3099/13/2/1424, Lady L to L, 14.1.40. Wynyard had been closed for a time during the Slump. Lord Castlereagh accused his parents of disliking and running down the house

(D/3099/2/13/3/45, Castlereagh to L, 11.7.32; D/3099/13/11/32, Castlereagh to Lady L, 11.5.48).

57. *The Times*, 20.6.49; Hyde, *The Londonderrys*, p. 258; *Parliament and Politics in the Age of Churchill and Attlee*, pp. 585–6 (1.5.49). Information from Lady Mairi Bury.

58. PRONI, D/3084/C/F/6/22, cutting from the *Daily Telegraph*, 9.4.76. Lady Mairi retained a suite of rooms for her own use and continues to live at Mount Stewart.

Archival Sources

Birmingham University Library
Neville Chamberlain Papers, NC2/23A, NC7/11

Borthwick Institute, York
Papers of the Earl of Halifax, A4.410.28,1–3

Bundesarchiv, Berlin/Lichterfelde
Adjutantur des Führers und Reichskanzlers, NS10/362
Auswärtiges Amt, R901/58084, 58093, 58624, 58634, 58918, 59624
Reichskanzlei, R43/II/135, 1435–6

Cambridge University Library
The Baldwin Papers, vols. 129, 143, 170, 171

The Churchill Archives Centre, Churchill College, Cambridge
Papers of Sir Eric Phipps, 3/3, 3/4, 10/1, 10/2

Durham County Record Office
Papers of Lord and Lady Londonderry, D/Lo/C/237 (1–13), 251 (18–27)

Hertfordshire County Record Office
Papers of Lady Desborough, D/ERV/C2482/71–91

Hoover Institution, Stanford, California
De Courcy Papers, box 2 folder 2

Institut für Zeitgeschichte, Munich
Fb2, MA 804/1

ARCHIVAL SOURCES

John Rylands University Library, Manchester
Papers of James Ramsay MacDonald, RMD/1/13–14, 3/2

Liddell Hart Centre for Military Archives, King's College, London
Papers of Sir Ian Hamilton, 14/2/1–13

Politisches Archiv des Auswärtigen Amtes, Berlin
Büro des Staatssekretärs, R29570–71, 29575, 29689–90
Büro Reichsaußenminister, R27090, 28895a
Politische Abteilung II, R102778–80
Politische Abteilung III, R76990
Dienststelle Ribbentrop, R27090
Handakten Hewel 22, R27477
Handakte Megerle 3/6, R27692

Public Record Office, London
AIR2/2234, 19/27–8
Cab. 16/109–11, 21/2676–8, 23/89–94, 24/239, 248, 27/506–8, 35/33
FO371/16719, 16723, 20748–9, 21637, 21652, 21657, 21736, 57540–41, 57542, 57544
FO372/3233
FO800/13, 290–91, 313–20
FO954/7B
PREM1/155
Ramsay MacDonald Papers, PRO30/69/678–83, 754–60, 1180, 1446, 1753

Public Record Office of Northern Ireland, Belfast
The Londonderry Papers, D/3099/2/4/1–154, 5/1–51, 9/1–69, 12/1–20, 16/1–71, 17/1–38, 18/1–56, 19/1–352, 21/A/1–279, 21/B/1–6; D/3099/3/15/1–253, 20/1–423, 35/1–42; D/3099/4/21, 35, 39, 44, 51, 52, 54, 56, 57, 58, 78, 80; D/3099/10/47–51; D/3099/12/21–4; D/3099/13/2/1328–1529; D/3099/13/3/1–71; D/3099/13/11/1–32; D/3099/15/10–11; D/3099/17/33, 36, 38
The Montgomery Hyde Papers, D/3084/C/C/3/1–12, 4/1, 6/1–90; 7/1–15; C/D/4/1–72; C/E/6/1–122; C/F/6/1–291; C/G/1/1–43; C/G/2/1–27
The Desborough Papers (copies), T/3201/1–55

List of Newspapers and Magazines Cited

The Londonderry Papers in the Public Record Office of Northern Ireland include several files (D/3099/10/47–51) containing cuttings taken from numerous newspapers which were relevant to the Londonderry family in the period from August 1935 to December 1940. Cuttings from various German and British newspapers in connection with Lord Londonderry's visit to Germany in February 1936 and Ribbentrop's stay at Wynyard in November of the same year are held in the Bundesarchiv, Berlin/Lichterfelde (R/901/58084, 58093, 58624 and 59624). References to those newspapers in the following list which are kept in these files are given in the appropriate place in the notes. Otherwise the list refers to newspapers consulted mainly in the British Library at Colindale.

The Aeroplane
Anglo-German Review
Belfast News-Letter
Belfast Telegraph
Berliner Tageblatt
Birmingham Post
Cape Times
The Church of England Newspaper
Daily Dispatch

Daily Express
Daily Herald
Daily Mail
Daily Telegraph
Daily Worker
Deutsche Allgemeine Zeitung
Deutsches Nachrichtenbüro
Durham Chronicle
Evening News

LIST OF NEWSPAPERS AND MAGAZINES CITED

Evening Standard
Flight
Frankfurter Zeitung
Harpers & Queen
Iron and Coal Trades Review
The Leader
Manchester Guardian
Morning Post
Natal Mercury
Newcastle Journal
News Chronicle
Newtownards Chronicle
Northern Echo
Northern Whig and Belfast Post
North Mail and Newcastle

Chronicle
Observer
Otago Daily Times
Southampon Daily Echo
Southern Daily Echo
The Spectator
Star
Sunday Chronicle
Sunday Dispatch
Sunday Sun
The Sunday Times
Sunderland Echo
The Times
Völkischer Beobachter
Yorkshire Post

List of Works Cited

Addison, Paul, *The Road to 1945. British Politics and the Second World War*, London, 1975.

Adolf Hitler: Monologe im Führerhauptquartier 1941–1944. Die Aufzeichnungen Heinrich Heims, ed. Werner Jochmann, Hamburg, 1980.

Aigner, Dietrich, *Das Ringen um England*, Munich/Esslingen, 1969.

Ambassador Dodd's Diary 1933–1938, ed. William E. Dodd and Martha Dodd, London, 1941.

Amery, L. S., *My Political Life, Vol. 3: The Unforgiving Years 1929–1940*, London, 1955.

Außenpolitisches Amt. – Das politische Tagebuch Alfred Rosenbergs 1934/35 und 1939/40, ed. Hans-Günther Seraphim, Munich, 1964.

Avon, The Earl of (Sir Anthony Eden), *The Eden Memoirs. Facing the Dictators*, London, 1962.

Baldwin, A. W., *My Father: the True Story*, London, 1955.

Bell, P. M. H., *The Origins of the Second World War in Europe*, London, 1986.

Benewick, Robert, *The Fascist Movement in Britain*, London, 1972.

Bentley, Michael, 'Power without Office. The National Government and the Churchill Coalition', in Anthony Seldon (ed.), *How Tory Governments Fall. The Tory Party in Power since 1783*, London 1996, pp. 285–312.

Bialer, Uri, *The Shadow of the Bomber. The Fear of Air Attack and British Politics 1932–1939*, London, 1980.

Birkenhead, The Earl of, *Halifax. The Life of Lord Halifax*, London, 1965.

Bloch, Michael, *Ribbentrop*, London, 1994.

Boothby, Robert (Lord), *I Fight to Live*, London, 1947.

— *My Yesterday, Your Tomorrow*, London, 1962.

Boyle, Andrew, *Trenchard: Man of Vision*, London, 1962.

Branson, Noreen, *History of the Communist Party of Great Britain, 1927–1941*, London, 1985.

Butler, J. R. M., *Lord Lothian (Philip Kerr) 1882–1940*, London, 1960.

Cannadine, David, *The Decline and Fall of the British Aristocracy*, New Haven/London, 1990.

— *Class in Britain*, London, 2000.

Carley, Michael Jabara, *1939: the Alliance that Never Was and the Coming of World War II*, Chicago, 1999.

Carsten, Francis L., *Britain and the Weimar Republic: the British Documents*, London, 1984.

'Cato', *Guilty Men*, London, 1940.

Ceadel, Martin, *Pacifism in Britain 1914–1945: the Defining of a Faith*, Oxford, 1980.

Charmley, John, *Neville Chamberlain and the Lost Peace*, London, 1989, paperback edn London, 1991.

— *Churchill: the End of Glory. A Political Biography*, London, 1993.

Chips. The Diaries of Sir Henry Channon, ed. Robert Rhodes James, London, 1967.

Churchill, Winston S., *The Second World War. Vol. 1: The Gathering Storm*, London, 1948.

— *The Second World War. Vol. 2: Their Finest Hour*, London, 1949.

Clarke, Peter, *Hope and Glory. Britain 1900–1990*, London, 1996.

Clemens, Detlev, *Herr Hitler in Germany. Wahrnehmung und Deutungen des Nationalsozialismus in Großbritannien 1920 bis 1939*, Göttingen/Zurich, 1995.

Colville, John, *The Fringes of Power. Downing Street Diaries 1939–1955*, London, 1985.

Colvin, Ian, *Vansittart in Office. The Origins of World War II*, London, 1965.

— *The Chamberlain Cabinet*, London, 1971.

Comité des Délégations Juives, *Die Lage der Juden in Deutschland 1933. Das Schwarzbuch: Tatsachen und Dokumente*, Paris, 1934, repr. Frankfurt am Main, 1983.

Conwell-Evans, T. P., *None So Blind*, London, 1947.

Cooper, Duff, *Old Men Forget*, London, 1953.

de Courcy, Anne, *Circe. The Life of Edith, Marchioness of Londonderry*, London, 1992.

Cowling, Maurice, *The Impact of Hitler. British Politics and British Policy, 1933–1940*, Cambridge, 1975.

The Crawford Papers. The Journals of David Lindsay, 27th Earl of Crawford and 10th Earl of Balcarres 1871 to 1940 during the Years 1892 to 1940, ed. John Vincent, Manchester, 1984.

Cross, Colin, *The Fascists in Britain*, London, 1961.

Cross, J. A., *Lord Swinton*, Oxford, 1982.

Crowson, N. J., *Facing Fascism: the Conservative Party and the European Dictators 1935–40*, London, 1997.

Crozier, Andrew J., *Appeasement and Germany's Last Bid for Colonies*, London, 1988.

Crozier, W. P., *Off the Record. Political Interviews 1933–1943*, ed. A. J. P. Taylor, London, 1973.

Dalton, Hugh, *The Fateful Years. Memoirs 1931–1945*, London, 1957.

Das Deutsche Reich und der Zweite Weltkrieg, ed. Militärgeschichtliches Forschungsamt, vol. 1, Stuttgart, 1979.

The Diaries and Letters of Robert Bernays, 1932–1939. An Insider's Account of the House of Commons, ed. Nick Smart, Studies in British History, vol. 30, Lewiston/Queenston/Lampeter, 1996.

The Diaries of Sir Alexander Cadogan, 1938–1945, ed. David Dilks, London, 1971.

The Diaries of Sir Robert Bruce Lockart, Vol. 1, 1915–1938, ed. Kenneth Young, London, 1973.

Dilks, David, 'Baldwin and Chamberlain', in Norman Gash, Donald Southgate, David Dilks and John Ramsden, *The Conservatives. A History from Their Origins to 1965*, London, 1977, pp. 364–69.

— 'The Rise of Baldwin' in Norman Gash Donald Southgale, David Dilks and John Ramsden, *The Conservatives. A History from Their Origins to 1965*, London, 1977, pp. 273–94.

— '"The Unnecessary War"? Military Advice and Foreign Policy in Great Britain, 1931–1939', in Adrian Preston (ed.), *General Staffs and Diplomacy before the Second World War*, London, 1978, pp. 93–132.

The Diplomatic Diaries of Oliver Harvey, 1937–1940, ed. John Harvey, London, 1970.

Documents and Materials Relating to the Eve of the Second World War, Vol. 1, November 1937–1938, Moscow, 1948.

Documents Concerning German-Polish Relations and the Outbreak of Hostilities between Great Britain and Germany on September 3, 1939, London, 1939.

Documents on British Foreign Policy, 1919–1939; 2nd Series, 1929–1938; 3rd Series, 1938–1939, London, 1947–61.

Documents on German Foreign Policy, 1918–1945; Series C (1933–1937), The Third Reich: First Phase; Series D (1937–1945), London, 1957–66.

Douglas-Hamilton, James, *Motive for a Mission*, Edinburgh, 1979.

— *Roof of the World. Man's First Flight Over Everest*, Edinburgh, 1983.

Dutton, David, *Neville Chamberlain*, London, 2001.

Eaden, James, and Renton, David, *The Communist Party of Great Britain since 1920*, London, 2002.

Emmerson, James T., *The Rhineland Crisis, 7 March 1936*, London, 1977.

The Empire at Bay. The Leo Amery Diaries 1929–1945, eds. John Barnes and David Nicholson, London, 1988.

Fabry, Philipp W., *Mutmaßungen über Hitler. Urteile von Zeitgenossen*, Düsseldorf, 1969.

Feiling, Keith, *The Life of Neville Chamberlain*, London, 1946.

Fleet Street, Press Barons and Politics. The Journals of Collin Brooks 1932–1940, ed. N. J. Crowson, Camden Society Fifth Series, vol. 11, London, 1998.

Fleming, Neil, *The Seventh Marquess of Londonderry: a Political Life*, Ph.D. thesis, Queen's University Belfast, 2002.

Gannon, Franklin R., *The British Press and Germany, 1936–1939*, Oxford, 1971.

Gärtner, Margarete, *Botschafterin des guten Willens*, Bonn, 1955.

George, Margaret, *The Warped Vision. British Foreign Policey 1933–1939*, Pittsburgh, 1965.

Gilbert, Martin, *Britain and Germany between the Wars*, London, 1964.

— *Plough My Own Furrow: the Life of Lord Allen of Hurtwood*, London, 1965.

— *The Roots of Appeasement*, London, 1966.

— *Sir Horace Rumbold. Portrait of a Diplomat, 1869–1941*, London, 1973.

— *Winston S. Churchill, Vol. V, 1922–1939*, London, 1976.

Gilbert, Martin, and Gott, Richard, *The Appeasers*, London, 1963, paperback edn, London, 1967.

Gisevius, Hans Bernd, *To the Bitter End*, Boston, 1947.

Granzow, Brigitte, *A Mirror of Nazism. British Opinion and the Emergence of Hitler, 1929–1933*, London, 1964.

Griffiths, Richard. *Fellow Travellers of the Right. British Enthusiasts for Nazi Germany 1933–39*, London, 1980, paperback edn, Oxford, 1983.

Halifax, Earl of, *Fulness of Days*, London, 1957.

Hartley, L. P., *The Go-Between*, London, 1953.

Haxey, Simon, *Tory M.P.*, London, 1939.

Hedin, Sven, *Ohne Auftrag in Berlin*, Tübingen/Stuttgart, 1950.

Henderson, Nevile, *Failure of a Mission. Berlin 1937–1939*, London, 1940.

Hildebrand, Klaus, *Vom Reich zum Weltreich. Hitler, NSDAP und koloniale Frage 1919–1945*, Munich, 1969.

Hill, Christopher, *Cabinet Decisions on Foreign Policy. The British Experience October 1938–June 1941*, Cambridge, 1991.

Hitler, Reden, Schriften, Anordnungen: Februar 1925 bis Januar 1933, ed. Institut für Zeitgeschichte, 5 vols. in 12 parts, Munich, 1992–8.

Hitler. Reden und Proklamationen 1932–1945, ed. Max Domarus, Wiesbaden, 1973.

Hoffmann, Peter, *Widerstand, Staatsstreich, Attentat. Der Kampf der Opposition gegen Hitler*, 4th edn, Munich 1985.

Hyde, H. Montgomery, *Baldwin: the Unexpected Prime Minister*, London, 1973.

— *British Air Policy between the Wars*, London, 1976.

— *The Londonderrys: a Family Portrait*, London, 1979.

Irving, David, *Göring. A Biography*, London, 1989.

Janßen, Karl-Heinz, and Tobias, Fritz, *Der Sturz der Generäle. Hitler und die Blomberg-Fritsch-Krise 1938*, Munich, 1994.

Joachimsthaler, Anton, *Hitlers Liste. Ein Dokument persönlicher Beziehungen*, Munich, 2003.

Jones, Thomas, *A Diary with Letters, 1931–1950*, London, 1954.

Judd, Denis and Surridge, Keith, *The Boer War*, London 2002.

Kehoe, Barbara Benge, *The British Press and Nazi Germany*, Ph.D. thesis, University of Illinois at Chicago Circle, 1980, University Microfilms International, Ann Arbor, 1989.

Kershaw, Ian, *Hitler, 1889–1936: Hubris*, London, 1998.

— *Hitler, 1936–1945: Nemesis*, London, 2000.

— *The 'Hitler Myth'. Image and Reality in the Third Reich*, 2nd edn, Oxford, 2001.

— 'Hitler's "Prophecy" and the Final Solution', *Occasional Paper No. 8, The Center for Holocaust Studies at the University of Vermont*, Burlington, Vermont, 2002.

Kirkpatrick, Ivone, *The Inner Circle*, London, 1959.

Knopf, Volker, and Martens, Stefan, *Görings Reich. Selbstinszenierungen in Carinhall*, Berlin, 1999.

Kochan, Lionel, *Pogrom. 10 November 1938*, London, 1957.

Kordt, Erich, *Wahn und Wirklichkeit. Die Außenpolitik des Dritten Reiches. Versuch einer Darstellung*, Stuttgart, 1948.

— *Nicht aus den Akten . . .*, Stuttgart, 1951.

Lamb, Richard, *The Ghosts of Peace, 1935–1945*, Salisbury, 1987.

Liddell Hart, B. H., *Memoirs*, vol. 1, London, 1965.

Lloyd George. A Diary by Frances Stevenson, ed. A. J. P. Taylor, London, 1971.

Lockhart, Robert Bruce, *Retreat from Glory*, London, 1934.

London, Louise, *Whitehall and the Jews, 1933–1948*, Cambridge, 2000.

Londonderry, The Marchioness of, *Retrospect*, London, 1938.

— *Mount Stewart*, n.d. (1956).

Londonderry, The Marquess of, *Ourselves and Germany*, London, 1938.

— *Ourselves and Germany*, 2nd edn, Harmondsworth, 1938.

— [the Marquess of Londonderry], 'My Attitude towards the Jews', *Query, Book No. 2, 'The Jews'*, London, 1938.

— 'Bombing from the Air', *The Nineteenth Century* (March 1939).

— *Wings of Destiny*, London, 1943.

Lovell, Mary S., *The Sisters. The Saga of the Mitford Girls*, New York/London, 2002.

Lukacs, John, *Five Days in London: May 1940*, paperback edn, New Haven/London, 2001.

MacFarlane, L. J., *The British Communist Party. Its Origin and Development until 1929*, London, 1966.

Macmillan, Harold, *Winds of Change 1914–1939*, London, 1966.

Maisky, Ivan, *Who Helped Hitler?*, London, 1964.

Mandell, Richard D., *The Nazi Olympics*, London, 1971.

Marquand, David, *Ramsay MacDonald*, London 1977.

Martens, Stefan, *Hermann Göring. 'Erster Paladin des Führers' und 'Zweiter Mann im Reich'*, Paderborn, 1985.

Marwick, Arthur, *Clifford Allen, the Open Conspirator*, Edinburgh/London, 1964.

Meehan, Patricia, *The Unnecessary War. Whitehall and the German Resistance to Hitler*, London, 1992.

Meyers, Reinhard, 'Das Dritte Reich in britischer Sicht. Grundzüge und Determinanten britischer Deutschlandbilder in den dreißiger Jahren', in Bernd-Jürgen Wendt (ed.), *Das britische Deutschlandbild im Wandel des 19. und 20. Jahrhundert*, Bochum, 1984, pp. 127–44.

Michalka, Wolfgang, *Ribbentrop und die deutsche Weltpolitik 1933–1940*, Munich, 1980.

Middlemas, Keith, *The Diplomacy of Illusion. The British Government and Germany, 1937–39*, London, 1972.

Middlemas, Keith, and Barnes, John, *Baldwin: a Biography*, London, 1969.

Mommsen, Hans, 'Hitler's Reichstag Speech of 30 January 1939', *History and Memory*, 9 (1977), pp. 147–61.

Mosley, Oswald, *My Life*, London, 1968.

Mowat, Charles Loch, *Britain between the Wars 1918–1940*, London, 1955, 1956.

Muggeridge, Malcolm, *The Thirties: 1930–1940 in Great Britain*, London, 1940.

Naylor, John F., *Labour's International Policy. The Labour Party in the 1930s*, London, 1969.

Nazism, 1919–1945, a Documentary Reader, eds. Jeremy Noakes and Geoffrey Pridham vol. 2, Exeter, 1984.

Nazism, 1919–1945, a Documentary Reader, eds. Jeremy Noakes and Geoffrey Pridham, vol. 3, Exeter 1988.

Neville, Peter, *Appeasing Hitler. The Diplomacy of Sir Nevile Henderson 1937–39*, London, 2000.

Newman, Simon, *March 1939: the British Guarantee to Poland*, Oxford, 1976.

Newton, Scott, 'The Economic Background to Appeasement and the Search for Anglo-German Détente before and during World War 2', *Lobster*, 20 (1990), pp. 25–33.

— *Profits of Peace: the Political Economy of Anglo-German Appeasement*, Oxford, 1996.

Nicolson, Harold, *Diaries and Letters 1930–1964*, ed. Stanley Olson, New York, 1980.

Ott, Johann, *Botschafter Sir Eric Phipps und die deutsch-englischen Beziehungen. Studien zur britischen Außenpolitik gegenüber dem Dritten Reich*, Ph.D. thesis, Erlangen/Nuremberg, 1968.

Ovendale, Ritchie, 'Britain, the Dominions and the Coming of the Second World War, 1933–9', in Wolfgang J. Mommsen and Lothar Kettenacker (eds.), *The Fascist Challenge and the Policy of Appeasement*, London, 1983, pp. 323–38.

Oxford, Margot, Countess of, *More Memories*, London, 1933.

Padfield, Peter, *Hess. The Führer's Disciple*, paperback edn, London, 1995.

von Papen, Franz, *Memoirs*, London, 1952.

Parker, R. A. C., *Chamberlain and Appeasement. British Policy and the Coming of the Second World War*, London, 1993.

— *Churchill and Appeasement*, London, 2000.

Parliament and Politics in the Age of Baldwin and MacDonald. The Headlam Diaries 1923–1935, ed. Stuart Ball, London, 1992.

Parliament and Politics in the Age of Churchill and Attlee. The Headlam Diaries 1935–1951, ed. Stuart Ball, Camden Society Fifth Series, vol. 14, Cambridge, 1999.

Parliamentary Debates, House of Commons, vol. 295 (1935).

Parliamentary Debates, House of Lords, vol. 96 (1935).

Parssinen, Terry, *The Oster Conspiracy of 1938*, New York, 2003.

Peden, G. C., *British Rearmament and the Treasury 1932–1939*, Edinburgh, 1979.

The Political Diary of Hugh Dalton 1918–40, 1945–60, ed. Ben Pimlott, London, 1986.

Preston, Adrian, ed., *General Staffs and Diplomacy before the Second World War*, London, 1978.

Pryce-Jones, David, *Unity Mitford: a Quest*, London, 1976.

Ramsden, John, *An Appetite for Power. A History of the Conservative Party since 1830*, London, 1998.

Rauschning, Hermann, *Germany's Revolution of Destruction*, London, 1939.

Reynolds, David, 'Churchill and the British "Decision" to Fight On in 1940: Right Policy, Wrong Reasons', in Richard Langhorne (ed.), *Diplomacy and Intelligence during the Second World War*, Cambridge, 1985, pp. 147–67, 297–303.

Rhodes James, Robert, *Memoirs of a Conservative. J. C. C. Davidson's Memoirs and Papers 1910–37*, London, 1969.

The Ribbentrop Memoirs, London, 1954.

Roberts, Andrew, *'The Holy Fox'. The Life of Lord Halifax*, London, 1991, paperback edn, 1997.

Rogger, Hans, and Weber, Eugen (eds.), *The European Right. A Historical Profile*, London, 1965.

Roskill, Stephen, *Hankey: Man of Secrets, Vol. 3, 1931–1963*, London, 1974.

Rothermere, Viscount, *My Fight to Rearm Britain*, London, 1939.

Schlie, Ulrich, *Kein Friede mit Deutschland. Die Geheimen Gespräche im Zweiten Weltkrieg, 1939–1941*, Munich/Berlin, 1994.

Schmidt, Paul, *Statist auf diplomatischer Bühne. Erlebnisse des Chefdolmetschers im Auswärtigen Amt mit den Staatsmännern Europas*, Bonn, 1953.

Schmidt, Rainer F., *Die Aussenpolitik des Dritten Reiches 1933–1939*, Stuttgart, 2002.

Schwarz, Paul, *This Man Ribbentrop. His Life and Times*, New York, 1943.

Semmler, *Goebbels – The Man Next to Hitler*, London, 1947.

Series of League of Nations Publications, IX. Disarmament, Geneva, 1932.

Sharf, Andrew, *The British Press and Jews under Nazi Rule*, Oxford, 1964.

Shay, Jr, Robert Paul, *British Rearmament in the Thirties: Politics and Profits*, Princeton, 1977.

Shore, Zachary, 'Hitler, Intelligence, and the Decision to Remilitarize the Rhine', *Journal of Contemporary History*, 34 (1999), pp. 5–18.

— *What Hitler Knew. The Battle for Information in Nazi Foreign Policy*, Oxford, 2003.

Simon, Viscount, *Retrospect*, London, 1952.

Smart, Nick, *The National Government, 1931–40*, Basingstoke, 1999.

Smelser, Ronald, *The Sudeten Problem, 1933–1938. Volkstumspolitik and the Formulation of Nazi Foreign Policy*, Folkestone, 1975.

Smith, Malcolm, *British Air Strategy between the Wars*, Oxford, 1984.

Spitzy, Reinhard, *So haben wir das Reich verspielt*, 4th edn, Munich, 1994.

Stannage, Tom, *Baldwin Thwarts the Opposition. The British General Election of 1935*, London, 1980.

Strobl, Gerwin, *The Germanic Isle. Nazi Perceptions of Britain*, Cambridge, 2000.

Die Tagebücher von Joseph Goebbels, Sämtliche Fragmente, Teil I, Aufzeichnungen 1924–1941, ed. Elke Fröhlich, 4 vols., Munich, 1987.

Die Tagebücher von Joseph Goebbels. Teil I, Aufzeichnungen 1923–1941, ed. Elke Fröhlich, 9 vols., Munich, 1993– (new edn).

Taylor, A. J. P., *The Origins of the Second World War*, Harmondsworth, 1964.

— *English History 1914–1945*, Harmondsworth, 1970.

Templewood, Viscount, *Nine Troubled Years*, London, 1954.

Tennant, E. W. D., *True Account*, London, 1957.

Thalmann, Rita, and Feinermann, Emmanuel, *Crystal Night, 9–10 November 1938*, London, 1974.

Thompson, Neville, *The Anti-Appeasers. Conservative Opposition to Appeasement in the 1930s*, Oxford, 1971.

Thorpe, Andrew, *The British Communist Party and Moscow, 1920–1943*, Manchester, 2000.

Thurlow, Richard, *Fascism in Britain. A History, 1918–1985*, Oxford, 1987.

The Times and Appeasement. The Journals of A. L. Kennedy, 1932–1939, ed. Gordon Martel, Camden Society Fifth Series, vol. 16, Cambridge, 2000.

Toland, John, *Adolf Hitler*, London, 1977.

Toynbee, Arnold J., *Survey of International Affairs 1933*, London, 1934.

Treue, Wilhelm, ed., 'Hitlers Denkschrift zum Vierjahresplan 1936', *Vierteljahrshefte für Zeitgeschichte*, 3 (1955), pp. 184–210.

Tusa, Ann, and Tusa, John, *The Nuremberg Trial*, London 1983.

Vansittart, Robert (Lord), *Black Record. Germans Past and Present*, London, 1941.

— *The Mist Procession*, London, 1958.

Waddington, G. T., '"An Idyllic and Unruffled Atmosphere of Complete Anglo-German Misunderstanding": Aspects of the Operations of the Dienststelle Ribbentrop in Great Britain, 1934–1938', *History*, 82 (1997), pp. 44–72.

Ward Price, George, *I Know These Dictators*, London, 1937.

Watt, Donald Cameron, *Britain Looks to Germany*, London, 1965.

— *Personalities and Policies. Studies in the Formulation of British Foreign Policy in the Twentieth Century*, London, 1965.

— 'Hitler's Visit to Rome and the May Weekend Crisis: A Study in Hitler's Response to External Stimuli', *Journal of Contemporary History*, 9 (1974), pp. 23–32.

— *How War Came. The Immediate Origins of the Second World War, 1938–1939*, paperback edn, London, 1991.

Webber, G. C., *The Ideology of the British Right 1918–1939*, London, 1986.

Weber, Eugen, *The Hollow Years. France in the 1930s*, New York, 1994.

Weinberg, Gerhard L., 'The May Crisis, 1938', *Journal of Modern History*, 29 (1957), pp. 213–25.

— *The Foreign Policy of Hitler's Germany. Diplomatic Revolution in Europe, 1933–36*, Chicago/London, 1970.

— *The Foreign Policy of Hitler's Germany. Starting World War II, 1937–1939*, Chicago/London, 1980.

Wendt, Bernd-Jürgen, *Appeasement 1938. Wirtschaftliche Rezession und Mitteleuropa*, Frankfurt am Main, 1966.

— *Economic Appeasement. Handel und Finanz in der britischen Deutschland-Politik 1933–1939*, Düsseldorf, 1971.

Williams, Susan, *The People's King. The True Story of the Abdication*, London, 2003.

Winston S. Churchill, Vol. V, Companion, Part 2, Documents. The Wilderness Years, 1929–1935, ed. Martin Gilbert, London, 1981.

Winston S. Churchill. Vol. V, Companion, Part 3, Documents. The Coming of War, 1936–1939, ed. Martin Gilbert, London, 1982.

Witherell, Larry L., 'Lord Salisbury's "Watching Committee" and the Fall of Neville Chamberlain', *English Historical Review*, 116 (2001), pp. 1134–66.

Woller, Hans, 'Churchill und Mussolini', *Vierteljahrshefte für Zeitgeschichte*, 49 (2001), pp. 563–94.

Wootton, Graham, *The Official History of the British Legion*, London, 1956.

Young, G. M., *Stanley Baldwin*, London, 1952.

Index

'L' indicates Lord Londonderry; 'Lady L' indicates Lady Londonderry.